£11.70

Computer-Communication
Networks

Prentice-Hall Computer Applications in Electrical Engineering Series
FRANKLIN F. KUO, *Editor*

Computer-Communication Networks

edited by

NORMAN ABRAMSON

FRANKLIN F. KUO

University of Hawaii

PRENTICE-HALL, INC., Englewood Cliffs, N.J.

Library of Congress Cataloging in Publication Data

ABRAMSON, NORMAN.
    Computer-communication networks.

    (Computer applications in electrical engineering
series)
    1. Data transmission systems. I. Kuo, Franklin F.,
joint author. II. Title.
TK5102.5.A283   001.6′44′04   73-945
ISBN 0-13-165431-4

Printed in the United States of America

10 9 8 7 6 5 4 3 2 1

PRENTICE-HALL INTERNATIONAL, INC., *London*
PRENTICE-HALL OF AUSTRALIA, PTY. LTD., *Sydney*
PRENTICE-HALL OF CANADA, LTD., *Toronto*
PRENTICE-HALL OF INDIA PRIVATE LIMITED, *New Delhi*
PRENTICE-HALL OF JAPAN, INC., *Tokyo*

Contents

5. Common-Carrier Data Communication   *142*

ROBERT W. LUCKY

8. Multiple-Access Communications for Computer Nets   *269*

JAY W. SCHWARTZ AND MICHAEL MUNTNER

9. Regulatory Policy and Future Date-Transmission Services   *295*

PHILIP M. WALKER AND STUART L. MATHISON

10. Economic Considerations in Computer-Communication Systems

D. A. DUNN AND A. J. LIPINSKI

11. The Dartmouth Time Sharing Network

ROBERT F. HARGRAVES AND THOMAS E. KURTZ

12. Exploratory Research on Netting at IBM   *457*

DOUGLAS B. MCKAY, DONALD P. KARP, JAMES W. MEYER,
AND ROBERT S. NACHBAR

13. The ARPA Network   *485*

LAWRENCE G. ROBERTS AND BARRY D. WESSLER

14. The Aloha System

NORMAN ABRAMSON

Index

Preface

In his recent book *System Analysis for Data Transmission*, (Prentice-Hall, 1972) James Martin wrote: "The most rapidly growing use of the world's telecommunications links is for data transmission. The most rapidly growing area in the exploding data processing industry is teleprocessing. The reason is the power and versatility that the interlinking of computers can bring, plus the potential benefits to the individual of having this power at his fingertips. In all walks of life and in all areas of industry, the devices connected to distant computers will change the realms of what is possible for man to do." Many books and papers have been written on data communications for computers with emphasis on time-sharing systems between collections of terminals and a single central computer. One of the most successful aspects of the experiments in the use of time-shared computer systems conducted during the past decade was the ability to share computing resources among the users of the systems.

As the time-sharing industry matured, it became apparent that the main rationale for time sharing is not just the sharing of CPU *time*, but sharing of all the *resources* of the computation center including peripheral devices, memory, and software.

In 1970 the ARPA Network came into existence as a communications network for the sharing of resources among a large number of computer centers. The ARPANET and its resource sharing capabilities became feasible because of the use of a new method of communication system organization—called packet switching. A packet switched system, in contrast to the circuit switched system designed for use with voice signals in the worldwide telephone network, is a communication system designed for use by computers and for efficient transmission of the peculiar kind of signals generated by digital information processing systems.

With the success of the ARPA Network, other computer-to-computer communications networks are being planned, both in the United States and in the rest of the world. A large body of knowledge and techniques has been developed over the past two or three years on computer-communication networks. There is no book at present that deals with computer-communication networks in reasonable depth for professionals in the field. In this book our objective is to present a broad, comprehensive, high level, detailed coverage concerning all aspects of computer-communication networks. There are chapters concerning planning, system design, scheduling, queueing, and file allocation. Other chapters deal with common carrier data communications, interfacing and data concentration, and asynchronous time division multiplexing. There are chapters that deal with regulatory policies as well as economic issues in computer networks. Finally, several specific networks are described including the ARPA, ALOHA, Dartmouth, and several experimental IBM networks.

The book is intended primarily as a reference volume for computer and communications specialists, to familiarize them with the topics covered. In addition, the book could be used for self study by the serious student in electrical engineering or computer science; it could also be used as a text in various courses and seminars dealing with computer communications. The background required for the book is the maturity of an advanced undergraduate or graduate student in engineering, the physical sciences, or computer science.

Let us now examine the contents of the book. In Chapter 1 Howard Frank and Ivan Frisch discuss planning of computer-communication networks using techniques to optimize network costs, layout, routing, throughput, delays, and reliability. Chapter 2, by Peter Neumann, is concerned with system design concepts including dynamic resource allocation, protection and sharing, large on-line information storage capacities, and synchronization of processes. The concepts in this chapter are of sufficient generality to be relevant to the design of time-sharing systems as well as to inter-computer communications nets. In Chapter 3 Wesley Chu formulates an integer programming solution to an important problem in computer networks—that of shared usage of files and data bases via interconnected computers.

Chapter 4, by Leonard Kleinrock, deals with the problems of scheduling and delays in computer networks and time-shared systems, by means of an analytic approach based upon queueing theory. Robert Lucky, in Chapter 5, discusses common carrier data transmission facilities, and how to use these facilities in setting up a computer network. Chapter 6, by David Pehrson, attacks a basic problem in setting up a computer network—that of designing interfaces and concentrators between transmission facilities and computers. This chapter is perhaps the most hardware-oriented chapter in the book and provides specific design information for engineers working in computer systems design. In Chapter 7 Wesley Chu describes the principles of asynchronous time division multiplexing systems in which message switching rather than channel switching forms the basis of communications. Chapter 8, by Jay Schwartz and Michael Muntner, deals with multiple access techniques including satellite and line-of-sight channels for computer nets.

The next two chapters deal with regulatory policies and economic considerations for computer communications. Stuart Mathison and Philip Walker, the authors of the well-received book, *Computers and Telecommunications: Issues in Public Policy*, (Prentice-Hall, 1970), describe in Chapter 9 the present and planned data transmission services provided by today's common carriers, the emergence of new data-oriented carriers, the various policy considerations, and the likely effects of the new entries from the viewpoint of the user and designer of computer-communication systems. In Chapter 10 Donald Dunn and A. J. Lipinski go through a cost-performance analysis of computer-communications systems treated on the basis of a decision problem. Projections are made concerning future demands for computer communications services and the costs of providing these services.

The next four chapters deal with specific computer communications networks. In Chapter 11 Robert Hargraves and Thomas Kurtz discuss the Dartmouth time-sharing network, which is one of the largest time-sharing systems in operation today, with the capability of serving up to 160 simultaneous users at Dartmouth and around New England. In Chapter 12 Douglas McKay, Donald Karp, James Meyer, and Robert Nachbar discuss two experimental computer networks projects of IBM. The first project, the *TSS* network, is a homogenous net with IBM 360/67 computers at every node. The second project, *Network 440*, is an inhomogeneous net with disparate machines running under different operating systems at every node. The interesting point to note here is that the various processors in the network are viewed as actually comprising one large multiprocessor, so that different steps of a single job can be executed on different participating systems.

Perhaps the best known and certainly the largest computer-communication network is the ARPANET. In Chapter 13 Lawrence Roberts and Barry Wessler describe the design criteria and the implementation of the ARPANET, which by early 1973 has more than thirty nodes, including a 50 kilobit satellite node, THE ALOHA SYSTEM in Hawaii. Chapter 14, by Norman Abramson, describes the experimental UHF-radio computer-communication network, THE ALOHA SYSTEM. THE ALOHA SYSTEM seeks to provide an alternative to present day common carrier communications for the system designer of a computer-communication network and to determine those situtations in radio which communications for computers are preferable to conventional wire communications.

This preface is meant to describe and explain the contents of the fourteen chapters that follow. Through these chapters we hope to indicate the scope and the speed of the development of computer-communication networks since 1968. In another sense, however, this book is but a preface to a sequence of vast changes in the nature of such computer-communication networks. In Chapters 11 to 14 we provide descriptions of some computer networks in operation by 1972 and of some of the technological forces that have led to their formation and to their present form. But to better emphasize today's dynamic nature of these technological forces we should describe what appears to be the next major change in the sequence of changes we have mentioned.

In April 1965 the scope and nature of human communication was irreversibly altered by the successful launch of INTELSAT I, the first geosynchronous communication satellite. Since that time the cost of information transmission over long distances has decreased at a rate that makes even the present decrease in information processing costs seem mild by comparison. The cost per year of a single voice grade channel in INTELSAT I was about \$20,000 per year; that satellite had a capacity of 240 such channels. The corresponding cost on INTELSAT IV, launched in January 1971 was about \$2,000 per year, and each INTELSAT IV has about 5,000 channels. The regulation necessary in the communications industry has masked the effects of these economic changes upon the consumer of satellite communications, but they will be felt.

The reflection of these economic changes in the area of computer-communication networks can already be seen as this preface is being written. A communication satellite is not just a big cable in the sky. Communication satellites possess certain properties that make them particularly well suited as a communications medium for computer-communication networks. Among these properties are the high volume, low cost capabilities of these communication channels, their broadcast nature (as opposed to conventional point-to-point channels), and their information feedback nature (the ability of a transmitter to listen to his signal as repeated by the satellite). The effective utilization of these special properties is slowed, but not halted, by the conservative principles required in operating the regulated public communication utilities.

By the beginning of 1973 the lower cost, higher channel capacity, higher power, and smaller ground stations required by new communication satellites had suggested the magnitude of the impact these developments would make in computer-communication networks of the future. By the beginning of 1973 two separate satellite links, one using a commercial INTELSAT IV channel and one using an experimental ATS-1 channel, had been incorporated into THE ALOHA SYSTEM and (by a 50 kilobit/second satellite link) into the ARPANET. Thus the pace of the technological developments discussed above is changing the work reported in the last two chapters of this book even as we write the book's preface.

We have mentioned that the regulated nature of the communications industry slows the rate at which technological changes appear in commercial telecommunication systems. With the advent of less expensive, higher capacity satellites and much smaller (and therefore more numerous) ground stations, however, regulation will be a less effective brake on the pace of technological change. By the end of 1972 the worldwide satellite comunication net of INTELSAT had been completed, two domestic communication satellite systems were in operation (the USSR and Canada) and two more domestic communication satellite systems had been announced (the United States and Japan). In addition several military satellite communication systems and NASA experimental satellite communication programs were in operation. With this sort of proliferation of systems accelerating, the designer of a computer-communication network can look forward to an economical commercial satellite system for computer communications based upon packet switching and employing some of the special properties of communication satellites we have mentioned. In the United States such a development can be anticipated in the middle of this decade as the U.S. domestic satellite system goes into operation.

We express our gratitude to the many people whose criticisms and co-operation made this volume possible. Particularly we thank all of the contributors whose interest and enthusiasm for this project made the undertaking most enjoyable.

Honolulu, Hawaii

NORMAN ABRAMSON
FRANKLIN F. KUO

1

Planning Computer-Communication Networks

H. FRANK

I. T. FRISCH

Network Analysis Corporation

INTRODUCTION

The planning of modern large-scale networks has stimulated the growth of a new discipline called network analysis [1]. This discipline encompasses problems arising in traffic systems, power systems, and communications systems—in short, almost every kind of network-like structure. The most recent of these to become a technical reality—computer-communication networks—has provided some of the most intricate challenges to network analysis and, in turn, has become one of its major beneficiaries.

Our purpose in this chapter is to present some of the fundamental techniques of network analysis, and show how they have been applied to the study of computer-communication networks. The techniques are used to optimize network cost, layout, routing, throughputs, delays, and reliability.

1

1.1 FLOWS IN NETWORKS

In considering the performance of a network (Fig. 1.1) it is often necessary to maximize the flow between a source and a terminal. This calculation is sometimes called the one-commodity flow problem, because the flows in the network correspond to a single commodity, such as electric power, water, information, or air traffic. Flows of a single commodity behave in certain

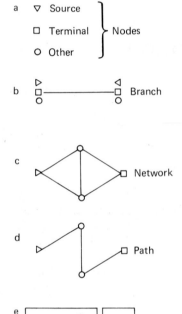

FIGURE 1.1   Glossary of network analysis terms listing five basic concepts: node, link, network, path, and cut. A node (a) may be the source where flow originates, a terminal where it ends, or a point through which it passes. A link (b) conducts flow between nodes. A network (c) consists of nodes connected to one another by links. A path (d) is a sequence of nodes and links that conducts flow between source and terminal. There are node disjoint paths and link disjoint paths. Node disjoint paths are paths that share no nodes with one another. Link disjoint paths are paths that share no links with one another. A cut (e) consists of the links that connect a set of nodes with the remaining nodes.

predictable ways. For all nodes other than the source and the terminal, the total flow into the node equals the total flow out of that node. This property is called *conservation of flow*. Each link can accommodate a maximum amount of flow, called the *capacity* of the link. It follows that the total flow out of any node is limited by the capacity of the links that must handle this flow.

The maximum flow is determined by a fundamental structural property of the network called a *cut*. A cut consists of a set of links that connect one group of nodes to all remaining nodes (Fig. 1.1). The capacity of a cut, that is, its ability to handle flow, is defined as the sum of the capacities of its links. If a cut consists of two links, each with a capacity of two units of flow, the cut's capacity is four units.

An important conclusion can be drawn from this set of facts. If the source and the terminal are in different groups of nodes, all flow from one to the other must pass through the cut that connects them. Therefore, the maximum flow from source to terminal cannot exceed the capacity of the cut; in particular, it cannot exceed the capacity of the minimum cut, that is, the cut of smallest capacity (Fig. 1.2). One of the most important results in the theory of flows, the max-flow min-cut theorem [1, 2] can now be stated: *The maximum flow from source to terminal is equal to the capacity of the minimum cut between them.* Furthermore, if certain nodes between the source and the terminal also have limited capacity, then the maximum flow is limited by the capacities of these nodes. The max-cut min-flow theorem can relate flows to capacities of nodes as well as to capacities of links.

We shall see that solution of the one-commodity flow problem yields the answer to a number of questions arising in the study of the reliability of computer networks. However, for the study of routing problems, a more general

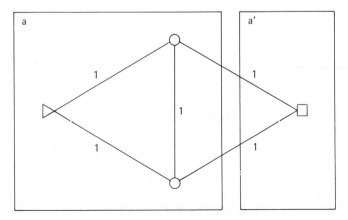

FIGURE 1.2   Max-flow min-cut theorem. Capacity of minimum cut shown is 2. Maximum flow is 2.

formulation involving more than one type of flow must be considered. One would expect that variations of the max-flow min-cut theorem would hold in more general situations. In particular, let us consider the multicommodity flow problem in which there are two or more different commodities being sent through a network. In this problem each commodity has a single source and a single terminal. A given node may, however, be a source or a terminal for more than one commodity. The flow of each commodity is conserved at each node except for its own source or terminal. The sum of the magnitudes of the flows of the various commodities in a link must not exceed the capacity of that link. We then want to find the maximum of the sum of the flows of the various commodities from their sources.

The max-flow min-cut theorem tells us that for one commodity the minimum cut will determine the maximum flow. The proposition can be stated in more familiar terms. A flow follows a path from a source to a terminal. This path is an alternating sequence of nodes and links, beginning with the source and ending with the terminal, such that no nodes or links are repeated and each link is connected to the nodes immediately preceding and following it in the sequence. All paths from the source to the corresponding terminal can be broken by the removal of one or more links. In the one-commodity case, it is clear that the flow cannot exceed the minimum capacity among such sets of links.

For a time it was thought that maximum flow equaled capacity for all flows of more than one commodity. This conjecture, however, does not hold true in all cases. To indicate the elusiveness of the problem, let us describe three situations, two in which flow equals capacity and one in which flow is less than capacity.

We have already seen that flow equals capacity for the one-commodity case. It has been shown [3, 4] that the maximum flow equals capacity when there are only two commodities in the network. In the case of three commodities, if every node is the source or terminal for exactly one commodity and each commodity has only a single source, flow will equal capacity [5].

It is possible, however, to construct a network with three commodities for which maximum flow is always less than capacity (Fig. 1.3). Each link in this network has a capacity of 2. There are three sources and three terminals—one source and one terminal for each of three commodities. The minimum number of links that must be removed to separate the sources from the corresponding terminals (the equivalent of the minimum cut) is 4. Since the capacity of each link is 2, we know that the capacity (C) of this set of links is 8. We might therefore expect the maximum flow to be equal to 8.

It is, however, less than 8. This conclusion is easily shown by using the interesting fact that in this network every path between a source and its terminal consists of at least three links. Thus every unit of flow of any commodity between its source and its terminal must occupy at least three units

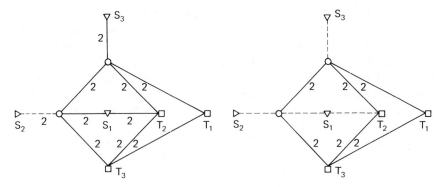

FIGURE 1.3   Three-commodity flows.

of link capacity. Three times the quantity of flow, V, of a commodity cannot exceed 20 units of capacity, the total of all the link capacities. Stated algebraically, $3V \leq 20$ or $V \leq \frac{20}{3}$. But $C = 8$, and hence V is less than C.

In spite of rather serious limitations in the present understanding of the multicommodity flow problem, efficient computational methods are available. The problem can clearly be stated as a linear program. In fact, it can be shown [6] that the problem can be formulated as

$$\max \sum_j x_j$$

subject to

$$a_{i,j}x_j + s_i = b_i \qquad (i = 1, \ldots, M; j = 1, \ldots, M)$$

$$x_j \geq 0, \qquad s_i \geq 0$$

where M is the number of links in the network, and the other variables are appropriately defined.

1.2 RELIABILITY ANALYSIS

The max-flow min-cut theorem and related rules enable network analysts to understand and solve many important problems. One is the problem of reliability. The larger and more complex a network is, the less likely it is that all its components will operate perfectly at all times. Accordingly, one of the most important objectives in designing a large network is to guarantee that it will function effectively even after some of its elements fail. The study of the possible failure of network elements and the subsequent overall degradation of network performance is called *vulnerability* or *reliability analysis*.

The first step in studying the reliability of a system is to formulate precise criteria for its failure. The choice of criteria depends on the type of network being considered and its purpose. A computer-communication network might be said to fail if (1) a message from a sender to a receiver must be re-layed through a large number of intermediate nodes to reach its destination, (2) a specified set of senders cannot communicate with a specified set of receivers, or (3) at least one sender cannot communicate with at least one receiver. To understand some of the aspects of the reliability problem, sup-pose that a network fails if at least one sender and one receiver are discon-nected. It will be said that a network is *connected* if there is at least one path between each pair of nodes; otherwise, it will be said to be *disconnected*.

A fundamental problem is to find the minimum number of nodes or links that must fail in order to disconnect a given network. It may be very dif-ficult to answer this question. Yet it is essential to be able to identify such nodes and links efficiently for two reasons. First, it may be necessary to determine the reliability of an existing network. Second, it may often be necessary to analyze and modify a proposed network repeatedly before a reliable design is achieved.

Here the max-flow min-cut theorem can be used to find the minimum number of nodes and links that must be removed in order to disconnect a network. Let us illustrate this point in more detail by indicating how one can find the minimum number of links. If each link is assigned a capacity of one unit, the maximum flow between any two nodes is equal to the minimum number of links that must be removed to break all paths from one of the nodes to another node. It can also be shown that this flow is equal to the maximum number of paths between the nodes that have no links in common. Such paths are called *link disjoint paths*. We can now repeat this calculation to find the maximum flow between all pairs of nodes in the network. The number of links is then given by the smallest of these maximum flows. Similarly, to find the minimum number of nodes that must be removed to break all paths, we can assign capacities equal to 1 to all nodes other than the source and the terminal. These capacities represent the upper bounds on the flows into the nodes. We can then find the maximum flow from the source to the terminal by a standard algorithm [7]. This number is equal to the maximum number of paths that have no nodes in common except the source and terminal. These paths are called *node disjoint paths*. The calculation is repeated for all pairs of nodes. The number of nodes that must be discon-nected is then revealed by the smallest of the maximum flows.

Significant simplifications can be made in this kind of calculation. A typical problem is to determine whether or not a network of 1000 nodes will be disconnected if as many as four arbitrarily chosen nodes fail. To solve the problem, the number of node disjoint paths connecting each pair of nodes could be counted. Such a procedure might involve almost 500,000 sets of flow maximizations, because each node would have to be examined in conjunction with every other node. It would also involve far more work than is actually necessary. The answer can be derived by performing the following calculations [8].

Choose any node and verify that there are at least four node disjoint paths from this node to every other node. Remove the node and all the links connected to it. From the resulting network choose another node and verify that there are at least three node disjoint paths connecting this node to every other node. Remove this node and its links, choose another, and then verify that there are at least two node disjoint paths from it to every other node. These are the only calculations that are required. If the number of disjoint paths between each pair of nodes had been only three, then at the last stage of repetition it would have been impossible to verify that the required number of paths existed (Fig. 1.4).

The solution of the above problem of finding the number of nodes involves 3999 flow maximizations for a network of 1000 nodes, a number smaller by a factor of more than 100 than the total number of maximizations that must be made in a straightforward counting procedure. Given any number of nodes and any number of required node disjoint paths, this method

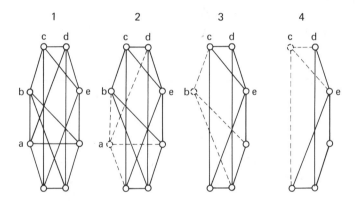

FIGURE 1.4   Verification that minimum node cut is at least four. The problem is to find out if the removal of fewer than four nodes will disconnect the network shown in (a). According to our algorithm, the number of nodes that must be removed can be determined in the following way. In 1 select any node, such as node a, and verify that there are at least four node disjoint paths from it to every other node. Remove this node and its links. The result of this operation is the network in 2. (White indicates nodes and branches removed.) The operation is repeated on this network and then on the resulting networks in 3 and 4. Each time the required number of node disjoint paths is one fewer than it was before. In 4, after node c has been removed, at least one path connects the nodes. It can therefore be concluded that to disconnect the network at least four nodes must fail.

makes it unnecessary to examine all possible combinations of nodes in the network. It is also more efficient, because with each repetition one node and its associated links are removed, so that the difficulty of executing the next step is reduced.

A measure of performance for a network affected by random factors, such as aging and equipment failure, is the probability that it is connected. Such networks have peculiar properties that are not easily deduced by studying the analogous properties in networks not subject to random disturbances. We have already discussed the problem of finding the minimum number of nodes that must be removed from a connected network in order to disconnect it. If nodes fail randomly, the corresponding problem is to compute the probability of the network remaining connected.

Both networks shown in Fig. 1.5 have eight nodes and twelve links. Suppose that we attempt to disconnect both by removing the smallest possible number of nodes. We can disconnect the first network by removing nodes 1 and 2. In fact, after these nodes are removed, along with the links connected to them, there are no links left in the network, and so all the other nodes are isolated from one another. The minimum number of nodes that must be removed from the second network, however, is three. For example, the removal of nodes 6, 8, and 3 will separate node 7 from the rest of the network.

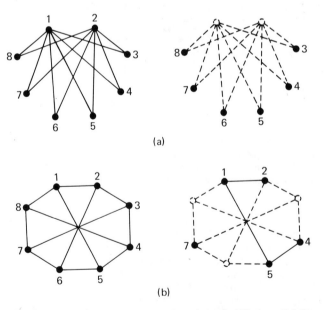

FIGURE 1.5   Networks for study of probabilistic reliability concepts.

Now, suppose that the nodes fail randomly, so that the failure of one does not affect the operation of any other. The measure of the reliability of the network will be the probability that at least two nodes do not fail and that the network consisting of the operating nodes remains connected. In general it is extremely difficult to compute this probability for a network with many nodes and links. Because these two networks are simple, however, the calculations are easily done. The first network will be connected unless nodes 1 and 2 fail simultaneously or nodes 3, 4, 5, 6, 7, and 8 fail simultaneously. In the second network there are eight combinations of three nodes whose failure will disconnect the network.

Because the first network can be disconnected by removing two nodes and the second cannot be disconnected by removing any pair of nodes, it might be expected that the first is less reliable than the second. Actually, it is by no means clear which network is "better." If nodes 1 and 2 in the first network do not fail, all six remaining nodes must fail before it is disconnected. On the other hand, the second network has eight distinct combinations of three nodes whose removal will disconnect it.

A number of general results about networks with randomly failing elements are available. It is possible to use some of these results to show [9] that if the probability that any node is functioning properly is small enough, the probability that the first network is connected is always greater than the probability that the second is connected. If, however, the probability of correct functioning is large, the second network is more reliable. This relation means that it is not always possible to find a "best" network. A situation may arise in which a network is attacked. The nodes may operate 99 per cent of the time if there is no attack, whereas each node may have only an 80 per cent chance of survival when the network is attacked. In this situation the first network will be less vulnerable, but also less reliable, than the second one.

1.3 CENTRALIZED COMPUTER NETWORKS

Thus far we have considered examples in which we were examining only structural properties of networks. Network analysis also provides methods for solving complex design problems involving many different considerations, such as choosing the most economical plan for the layout of computer-communication networks.

Many computer networks consist of a set of remote sites connected to a central node. For example, most time-sharing systems, computer reservation systems, and accounting systems are of this type. Major problems that arise in designing such systems are the layout and sizing of the connections between nodes. These problems are difficult because of the enormous number of possible link locations and because one must usually choose link capacities from a finite set of available options. Consequently, the network designer is faced with a discrete design problem, which is intractable using existing integer programming methods for problems of practical size.

A common objective is to select link locations and capacities so that the average time delay required to transmit a standard-sized message from any node to the central node does not exceed a specified number. This maximum allowable average delay time may, in some cases, vary from node to node. The design problem is then to find the least-cost system that satisfies the time-delay constraints for specified levels of traffic between nodes.

A strong case can be made for designing treelike centralized computer networks. That is, the nodes are connected by the minimum number of possible links, and there is exactly one transmission path between any pair of nodes. Although it is possible to construct situations in which trees are not optimal, they represent a reasonable class of networks for the layout problem. However, even if one reduces his range of designs to trees, the globally optimal network is usually impossible to find.

Let us consider the optimal design of centralized computer networks. We describe a method to select *globally least-cost* link capacities for a specified tree structure when maximum average delay times are specified for each node. We also give a heuristic method for finding *low-cost* tree structures. The methods, which grew out of design studies for natural-gas and irrigation systems, have been programmed and are capable of handling networks with thousands of nodes. In addition, they allow an arbitrary set of link capacities and cost structure and do not depend on the mathematical model used to calculate average time delay [10, 11].

1.3.1 Network Model

Computer networks may be ranked quantitatively by the speed with which they service their users and the cost per transmitted bit. In many systems response time is the most crucial performance criterion. Time-sharing systems often succeed or fail depending upon how long a user must wait for his message to be acted upon. For example, the ARPA Computer Network (Chapter 13) has as its major performance constraint the requirement that the average time delay to transmit any short message from source to destination cannot exceed 0.2 s. On-line reservation systems and the like have similar constraints.

In this section we consider the following network model:

1. The network topology is a tree. The network contains N nodes numbered from 1 to N. A link between nodes i and j is denoted by the unordered pair (i, j). Node 1 is the central computer.

2. Each link may be assigned one of a finite number of capacities, C_1, $C_2, \ldots,$ C_K. The capacity of link (j, k) is denoted by $c(j, k)$, and although not necessary, for simplicity we assume each link is fully duplex (Chapter 5).

3. The cost of assigning capacity C_i to link (j, k) is an arbitrary function of various parameters, such as distance, capacity, error rate, data set, and so on. For example, the cost of a typical American Telephone & Telegraph (AT&T) option may be the sum of a *fixed* charge for data sets and a linear cost per mile.

4. The average time delay $\tilde{t}(j, k)$ required to transmit b_i bits per second from node j to node k over link (j, k) can be expressed as $t(j, k) = T(c(j, k), b_i, \ldots) = T(c(j, k), \alpha)$, where α represents all parameters other than $c(j, k)$. The only property that we impose upon the function $T(\cdot)$ is the physically motivated one that $T(C_i, \alpha) < T(C_j, \alpha)$ if $C_j < C_i$.

5. Nodal time delays are insignificant. (This restriction can be removed; but a complete treatment is lengthy.)

6. A traffic matrix $\mathbf{R} = [r_{i,j}]$ is specified, where $r_{i, j}$ is the number of bits per second from node i to node j. All traffic from node i to node j $(i \neq 1, j \neq 1)$ must be routed through node 1. Thus the network traffic can be described by two vectors:

$$\mathbf{R}_1 = (\tilde{r}_{1,2}, \tilde{r}_{1,3}, \ldots, \tilde{r}_{1,N})$$

and

$$\mathbf{R}_2 = (\tilde{r}_{2,1}, \tilde{r}_{3,1}, \ldots, \tilde{r}_{N,1})$$

where

$$\tilde{r}_{1,i} = r_{1,i} + \sum_{\substack{j=2 \\ j \neq i}}^{N} r_{j,i}$$

$$\tilde{r}_{i,1} = r_{i,1} + \sum_{\substack{j=2 \\ j \neq i}}^{N} r_{i,j}$$

In a time-sharing system with only one main computer, $r_{i,j}$ may equal zero when neither i nor j represents the central node 1. On the other hand, all the off-diagonal entries in R may be nonzero for a computer-communication network.

1.3.2 Link Capacity Optimization

Consider a fixed topological structure G, such as the one shown in Fig. 1.6. Capacities are to be assigned with minimal cost to this tree so that the maximum average time delay for transmission from any node to node 1 does not exceed $t_{\max}$. A tree has the property that there is exactly one path between each pair of nodes. Consequently, given G, $\mathbf{R}_1$, and $\mathbf{R}_2$, the flows in each

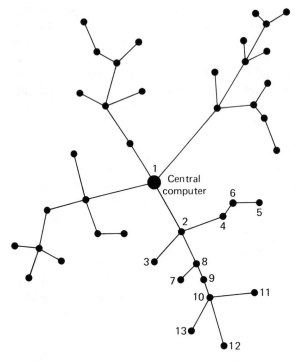

FIGURE 1.6   Centralized computer network.

network link are uniquely determined. Let d_i, the *degree* of node i, be the number of links incident at i. A node j is said to be *pendant* if $d_j = 1$. Let $\bar{t}_i$ be the average time required to send a message from node i to node 1. With these definitions it is easy to see that $\max \bar{t}_i \leq t_{max}$ if and only if $\max_{i:d_i=1} \bar{t}_i \leq t_{max}$. That is, to guarantee that t_{max} is not exceeded for transmission from any node in the network, we need only guarantee that this is true for pendant nodes. This property is used in the algorithm to follow, since limitations on network performance can be determined by considering only pendant nodes.

Given R_1 and R_2, the first problem to be considered is to find the least-cost set of link capacities so that the maximum time delay required to transmit a message from any node to node 1 does not exceed a specified constant t_{max}. Choosing capacities for some of the links and leaving the remaining capacities unspecified will be called a *partial assignment*. Methods will now be given to recognize partial assignments that cannot be in the optimal assignment. These partial assignments are discarded without discarding any partial assignment that might be in an optimal assignment.

Associate with each link two lists, called COST and DELAY. The ith component of COST is the cost associated with the ith smallest capacity choice. The ith component of DELAY is the time delay for that link arising from a choice of the ith smallest capacity. The values of the elements of COST are in increasing order and those of DELAY in decreasing order. The two lists taken together will be called a *link array*. Two techniques will now be given that, when used together on a given tree, can efficiently process these lists to obtain the optimal capacity assignment. These techniques were first applied to the design of offshore natural-gas pipeline networks [10].

The first technique is called the *parallel merge*. The procedure can be used on any set of links that directly connect pendant nodes to a common node. We shall use links (11, 10), (12, 10), and (13, 10) from the tree of Fig. 1.6 to illustrate the procedure.

Suppose that there are seven possible capacities for each link and that the arrays for these links are as follows:

(11, 10) array:	DELAY:	(120, 111, 92, 66, 54, 40, 31)
	COST:	(13, 17, 23, 29, 36, 45, 58)
(12, 10) array:	DELAY:	(150, 139, 118, 87, 75, 70, 67)
	COST:	(6, 9, 14, 21, 30, 40, 56)
(13, 10) array:	DELAY:	(94, 86, 80, 61, 55, 48, 32)
	COST:	(8, 12, 18, 26, 34, 43, 57)

where the delays are in milliseconds and costs in hundreds of dollars. A *testing block* is set up at follosw:

	(11, 10)	(12, 10)	(13, 10)
DELAY	120	(150)	94
COST	13	6	8
INDEX	1	1	1

Each link is assigned a column in the testing block as indicated. If the index in a column is set to i, the DELAY and COST entries in that column will be the ith components of the list. Initially, the indices are set to 1 and the testing block is as shown.

The procedure locates the largest entry in the DELAY row of the testing block. In our example, this occurs in column 2 and the entry is shown circled. If the smallest capacity is chosen for (12, 10), the delays at nodes 11 and 13 can never exceed t_{max}. Thus, choosing other than the minimum capacities for these links when (12, 10) has the minimum capacity will increase the total cost of the links, but cannot reduce the maximum time delay.

We now enter the circled DELAY entry and the sum of the COST entries of the testing block in a new array. This entry in the new array corresponds to the partial assignment of minimum capacities to (11, 10), (12, 10), and (13, 10) and is

DELAY: (150)
COST: (27)

Since no better choice of capacities for (11, 10) and (13, 10) is possible with (12, 10) at this capacity, we increase the index in the second column of the testing block, which yields

	(11, 10)	(12, 10)	(13, 10)
DELAY	120	(139)	94
COST	13	9	8
INDEX	1	2	1

In the updated testing block, the new maximum DELAY entry is still in the second column. This means that if (12, 10) has the second-smallest capacity, it still will not pay to have (11, 10) or (13, 10) at any capacities other than the smallest. We make a second entry in the new list as before to give

DELAY: (150, 139)
COST: (27, 30)

This new entry represents a partial assignment of the second-smallest capacity to (12, 10) and the smallest capacity to (11, 10) and (13, 10).

The process terminates when the largest entry of the DELAY row of the testing block occurs in a column whose index has been promoted to its maximum value, 7. Further promotion of the other indices would correspond to partial assignments of greater cost and no possible savings in maximum time delay.

Each entry in the final new array (shown next) represents an assignment of capacities to the links (11, 10), (12, 10), and (13, 10). Furthermore, no other partial assignments for these links need be considered. Note that the number of possible partial assignments for these three links is $7^3 = 343$. However, the parallel-merge techniques will produce an array with at most 19 columns, one from the original testing block and one each from the testing blocks resulting from a maximum of 18 index promotions. The minimum number of columns in a new list is 7.

DELAY: (150, 139, 120, 118, 111, 94, 92, 87, 86, 80, 75, 70, 67)
COST: (27, 30, 35, 39, 46, 52, 56, 62, 71, 77, 85, 95, 111)

The parallel merge produces an array whose entries correspond to partial assignments that are candidates for inclusion in the optimal assignment. The new array can be viewed as the DELAY and COST lists of an equivalent link which replaces those links whose arrays were merged. This equivalent link can be thought of as a link connected between node 10 and a node consisting of a combination of nodes 11, 12, and 13. (Hence, the name parallel merge.) Note that the components of the equivalent COST and DELAY lists are respectively in increasing and decreasing order so that no reordering is required.

It now becomes desirable to combine the array of the equivalent link with the array of (10, 9) to create a new equivalent array for (11, 10), (12, 10), (13, 10), and (10, 9). Again we wish to retain as few partial assignments as possible without eliminating any partial assignments that can possibly be in the optimal assignment. A technique for accomplishing this, called the *serial merge*, is available for this purpose [10, 11].

1.3.3 Layout Optimization

In the last section we gave a globally optimal method to efficiently select link capacities for a specified tree. We now give a heuristic method for finding low-cost configurations. Other heuristic methods for finding low-cost trees have been given in the past [12, 13]. However, these methods do not seem nearly as powerful as the one presented here. In combination with the capacity-assignment algorithm, this method appears to produce optimal or near-optimal results in all cases.

The design problem is similar to other network design problems for which computationally practical solutions have recently been obtained. These include the classical "traveling-salesman problem" [14], the design of survivable networks [15], the interconnection of Telpaks in telephone networks [16], the design of offshore natural-gas pipeline networks [10], and the design of the ARPA Computer Network [17]. Problems of this type have long resisted exact solution; however, recent developments have led to efficient methods of finding low-cost solutions in practical computation times.

A *feasible* network is one that satisfies all the network constraints. An *optimal* network is a feasible network with the least possible cost. The design method consists of a *starting* routine to generate a feasible starting network, and an *optimizing* routine, which examines networks derived from the starting network by means of a "local" change in network topology. If a feasible network with lower cost is found, it is adopted as a new starting network and the process repeated. A feasible network is eventually reached whose cost

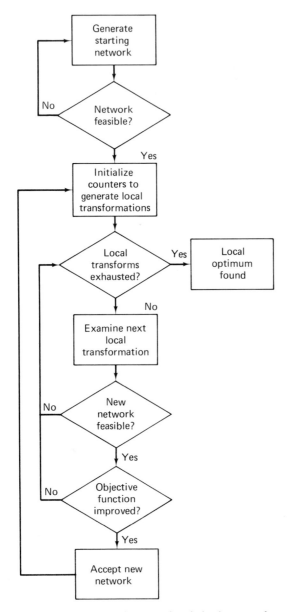

FIGURE 1.7   Block diagram of optimization procedure.

cannot be reduced by applying additional transformations of the type being considered. Such a network is called a *locally optimum network*. After a locally optimum network is found, the entire procedure is repeated with a different starting network.

The efficiency of the approach depends crucially on the particular transformation used in the optimizing routine. Local transformations are generated by identifying a set of links, removing these links, and adding a new set to the network. For example, in the problem of designing offshore natural-gas pipeline networks, dramatic cost reductions were achieved by removing and adding one link at a time [10]. In the design of survivable networks, a link exchange consisted of removing and adding two links at a time. In general, it is not necessary that the same number of links be added and removed during each application of the transformation. A block diagram of the optimization procedure is shown in Fig. 1.7.

For the centralized network design problem, an effective local transformation is a special kind of elementary tree transformation [11]. It can be shown that any tree can be obtained from any other tree by a sequence of elementary tree transformations. The elementary transformation used is as follows: For a given tree, choose a node i and find the node i_1 closest to i but not already connected to i. Add link (i_1, i) to the tree and identify the circuit formed. Suppose that this circuit consists of links $(i_1, i), (i, i_2), (i_2, i_3)$, ..., (i_j, i_1). New trees are formed by deleting in turn links $(i, i_2), (i_2, i_3), \ldots$ and finally (i_j, i_1). Each time a link is deleted, the capacity-assignment algorithm is applied to determine optimal link capacities and network cost. As each node i is scanned in turn, link additions from i to its d nearest neighbors are considered. Whenever L lower-cost trees have been generated, the node scan is begun again. This procedure has proved to be extremely powerful in finding low-cost trees. In nearly every case, whenever the problem has been small enough to exhaustively find optimal trees, the method has converged to the optimum solution.

1.4 THE ARPA COMPUTER NETWORK

In this section we discuss the application of the above principles to the design of the ARPA Computer Network. The ARPA Network, discussed in detail in Chapter 13, provides store-and-forward communication paths between more than 40 computers distributed across the United States. In contrast to the centralized networks discussed earlier, the ARPA Network has multiple communication paths between each pair of nodes. Important design considerations for the ARPA Network include line layout, routing, time delay, and reliability.

1.4.1 Network Model

The message-handling tasks at each node in the network are performed by a special-purpose Interface Message Processor (IMP) located at each computer center. The centers are interconnected through the IMPs by fully duplex 50-kbaud lines. When a message is ready for transmission, it is broken into a set of packets, each with appropriate header information. Each packet independently makes its way through the network to its destination. When a packet is transmitted between any pair of nodes, the transmitting IMP must receive a positive acknowledgment from the receiving IMP within a given interval of time. If this acknowledgment is not received, the packet will be retransmitted, either over the same or a different channel, depending on the network routing doctrine employed.

   A design goal of the system is to achieve a response time of less than 0.2s for short messages. The final network must also be reliable, and it must be able to accommodate variations in traffic flow without significant degradation in performance. To achieve a reasonable level of reliability, the network must be designed so that at least two nodes and/or links must fail before it becomes disconnected. Consequently, it cannot be a tree, since a tree has exactly one path between any pair of nodes.

1.4.2 Time-Delay Analysis

The heart of the network model is the time-delay analysis. Response time T is defined as the average time a message takes to make its way from its origin to its destination. Short messages are considered to correspond to a single packet, which may be as long as 1008 bits or as short as a few bits plus the header. If T_i is the mean delay time for a packet passing through the ith link, then

$$T = \frac{1}{r} \sum_{i=1}^{M} f_i T_i$$

where r is the total traffic rate input to the network from all IMPs (in bits per second), f_i is the average flow rate in the ith link (in bits per second), and M is the total number of links. T can be approximated as [18, 19]

$$\frac{1}{r} \sum_{i=1}^{M} \left(\frac{1/\mu}{C_i - f_i} - \frac{1}{C_i \mu} + \frac{1}{C_i \mu'} + d_i \right) f_i \qquad (1.1)$$

where C_i = capacity of link i
   $1/\mu'$ = average information packet length
   $1/\mu$ = average packet length in the system, including requests for next messages, header, acknowledgments, and parity check
   d_i = propagation delay of link i in seconds
Here the expression

$$\frac{1/\mu}{C_i - f_i} - \frac{1}{C_i \mu} + \frac{1}{C_i \mu'} + d_i$$

represents the average time delay experienced on link i by an information packet. The expression

$$\frac{1/\mu}{C_i - f_i} - \frac{1}{C_i \mu}$$

is the average time an information packet spends waiting at the IMP for link i to become available. Since the information packet must compete with acknowledgments and other overhead traffic, the overall average message length $1/\mu$ appears in the expression. The term $\frac{1}{C_i \mu'}$ is the time required to transmit an information packet of average length $1/\mu'$. Finally, d_i is the actual time required for a bit to propagate through link i.

Basic network optimization problems are to specify network structure, line capacities, and routing strategy.

Network structure can be derived by using procedures similar to the one illustrated by Fig. 1.7. However, to use such a procedure we must analyze each network generated during the optimization process. This means we must specify the line capacities and routing strategy to be used. We first consider the routing problem when each line and its capacity are already specified.

1.4.3 Routing

The object of route selection is to find routes that can accommodate a specified traffic with minimum average time delay. The method of route selection depends on the amount of information available about flow requirements throughout the network. The smallest average time delay is achieved if complete (i.e., global) information is available. In this case, the routing problem can be formulated as a multicommodity flow problem.

In standard multicommodity problems, commodities originate at sources and are destined for terminals. The flow problem consists of finding a flow that either maximizes the amount of commodities delivered to the terminals or delivers a specified amount of commodities at least cost. For the computer network the commodities are packets of data to be transmitted through the network. Each node is a terminal as well as a source. Element $r_{k,i}$ in the traffic-requirement matrix can be viewed as the amount of commodity i supplied from node k and destined for node i. All traffic destined for node i can be viewed as commodity i. If the network contains N nodes, there are then N commodities. Each node demands exactly one distinct commodity and supplies $N - 1$ others. The problem is to route the specified flows to minimize (1.1). This problem can then be formulated as the following mathematical programming problem: Minimize

$$\frac{1}{r} \sum_{i=1}^{M} \left(\frac{1/\mu}{C_i - f_i} - \frac{1}{C_i \mu} + \frac{1}{C_i} + d_i \right) f_i \qquad (1.1)$$

subject to

$$A\mathbf{f}_i = \mathbf{r}_i \qquad \text{for } i = 1, 2, \ldots, N \tag{1.2}$$

$$\sum_{i=1}^{N} f_{i,j} - f_j = 0 \qquad \text{for } j = 1, 2, \ldots, N \tag{1.3}$$

$$\mathbf{f} \leq C \tag{1.4}$$

Expression (1.1) represents the average time delay experienced when flows $f_1, f_2, \ldots, f_M$ are established in links $1, 2, \ldots, M$. Constraints (1.2), (1.3), and (1.4) ensure that the solution to the minimization problem corresponds to a physically realizable set of flows which satisfies all flow requirements. These constraints are *linear* equations with the following interpretations:

Constraint (1.2) is called the *conservation constraint*. This constraint requires that the flow into any node be equal to the flow out of that node. In this equation, $\mathbf{f}_i$ is a vector whose jth component, $f_{i,j}$, is the flow on the jth link destined for node i; $\mathbf{r}_i$ is a vector whose jth entry, $r_{i,j}$, equals flow rate required from node j to node i for $i \neq j$ and equals the negative of the total flow required at node i for $i = j$. The matrix A is the nodal *incidence matrix* of the network. That is, $a_{i,j} = 1$ if link j is directed out of node i, $a_{i,j} = -1$ if link j is directed into node i, and $a_{i,j} = 0$ if link j is not incident at node i. Thus a typical member of the set of equations (1.2) is

$$\sum_{j=1}^{N} a_{k,j} f_{i,j} = r_{i,k}$$

This equation states that the flow requirement $r_{i,k}$ from node k to node i must be equal to the difference of the total flow destined for node i that arrives at node i and the total flow destined for node i that leaves node i.

Constraint (1.3) indicates that the flow in any link is equal to the sum of flows at all commodities in that link. The vector $\mathbf{C}$ in (1.4) is the capacity vector whose jth component is equal to the capacity C_j of the jth link. Constraint (1.4) requires that the total flow in any link be no greater than the capacity of the link. This constraint is known as the *capacity constraint*.

The expression to be minimized is the sum of a set of convex functions. Each term in the sum can be approximated by straight line segments. If this is done, the problem can be solved by standard linear programming algorithms. If P linear segments are used in the approximation, the program has $N^2 + 3M$ constraints and $(N + P + 1)M$ variables. Hence, with N approximately equal to 20 and M approximately equal to 25, this approach provides a tractable means to optimize routing for a specified network. In fact, even if line capacities are not specified, the same approach can be used. In this case, line capacities become variables and we must solve a mixed integer–continuous linear program. Since the number of integer variables is equal to the number of lines, this problem can be solved using existing programming packages.

Unfortunately, the layout procedure involves the repeated analysis and modification of network structure, and so the above approach is not fast enough. Instead, we must use a *suboptimum* procedure. To be effective, the procedure must be very much faster and use local rather than global information.

The total traffic within the network depends on three factors: the total traffic input to the network; overhead, such as headers, acknowledgments, parity checks, etc.; and the numbers of links in the paths chosen for routing. This last factor can be extremely critical.

Suppose that we wish to send 10,000 bits from node i to node j. If there is a direct link from i to j, we can transmit the flow over the link, and the contribution of this requirement to the total traffic flow is 10,000 bits. On the other hand, suppose that we must transmit the 10,000 bits over a path which contains two intermediate nodes, k and l. We must first transmit the 10,000 bits from i to k, then the 10,000 bits from k to l, and finally the 10,000 bits from l to j. We have thus effectively added 30,000 bits to the total flow within the network. This example indicates that, wherever possible, we should route flow over paths with as few intermediate nodes as possible.

We now give a routing procedure based on the assumption that for each message a path which contains the fewest number of relay nodes from origin to destination must be used. Intuitively, such a procedure should yield small time delays.

For a given topology and traffic matrix, routes are determined as follows:

1. With node i as an initial node, generate all paths containing the fewest number of intermediate nodes to all nodes with nonzero traffic from node i. Such paths are called *feasible paths*.
2. If node i has nonzero traffic to node $j(j = 1, 2, \ldots, N, j \neq i)$ and the feasible paths from i to j contain more than Q intermediate nodes, the topology is considered infeasible.
3. Nodes are grouped as follows, and considered in the following order:
   (0)　All nodes connected to node i.
   (1)　All nodes connected to node i by a feasible path with one intermediate node.
   .
   .
   .
   (k)　All nodes connected to node i by a feasible path with k intermediate nodes.
   .
   .
   .
   (Q)　All nodes connected to node i by a feasible path with Q intermediate nodes.

Traffic is first routed from node i to any node j, which is directly connected to i, over link (i, j). Consequently, after this stage some flows have been assigned to the network. Each node in each group is then considered. For any node j in this group, all feasible paths from i to j are examined, and *functions* of the flow thus far assigned to each link and the required capacity for this flow are evaluated. If $\pi_1, \pi_2, \ldots, \pi_k$ are all paths containing a minimum number of nodes from node i to node j, the evaluation functions for each path may have one of the following forms:

1. The maximum *path flow*, i.e., the maximum flow in any link in the path.
2. The minimum *residual capacity*, i.e., the minimum difference between the least-cost capacity required to accommodate the existing flow and the value of that flow for any link in the path.
3. The maximum *link utilization*, i.e., the maximum ratio of the existing flow and the least-cost capacity required to accommodate that flow for any link in the path.

With the above factors we select paths that have minimum "resistance" to additional flow. Consequently, we could select paths whose maximum path flow is minimum. Alternatively, we could select a path with the largest minimum residual capacity or one with the smallest maximum link utilization. From the subset of paths thus selected, the path whose total physical length is minimum is then chosen, and all traffic originating at i and destined for j is routed over this path. Note that with this routing procedure the final capacity of each line is the least-cost capacity which can accommodate the total flow in that line.

The suboptimum routing procedure has the advantage of yielding near-optimal routes in a fraction of the time required to compute optimal routes (a few hundred milliseconds compared to several minutes). For example, Fig. 1.8 shows the ARPA Network design as of April 1970 [20]. This design was obtained by means of the optimization procedures discussed in this chapter. Figure 1.9 shows the average time delay as a function of the average

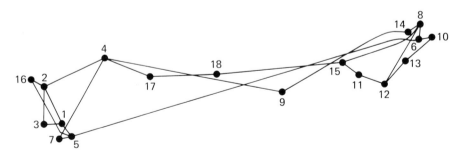

FIGURE 1.8a   Layout of the 18-node ARPA network.

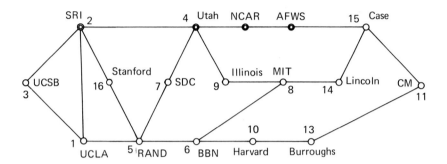

ARPA network
June 1971
All lines 50 Kilobaud

FIGURE 1.8b Topological structure of the 18-node ARPA network.

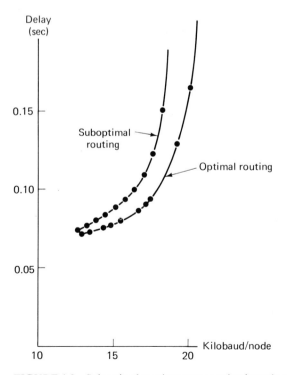

FIGURE 1.9 Suboptimal routing versus optimal routing.

23

number of bits per second per node. In this case, equal traffic between all node pairs is assumed, and both the optimal and suboptimal time-delay characteristics are shown. At saturation (i.e., average delay $= 0.2$ s), the average traffic per node for the suboptimum routing is within 10 per cent of the traffic for the optimum routing.

In addition to providing near-optimal traffic levels at specified time delays, the suboptimum routing procedure produces high throughputs under substantial variations in traffic requirements. Figure 1.10 shows the results of a simulation in which 100 randomly generated traffic patterns were routed through the network shown in Fig. 1.8. The suboptimum routing procedure was applied to derive the average output per node at saturation. The simulation was performed by selecting the output $TR(i)$ for node i uniformly at random between 2000 and 38,000 bps for $i = 1, \ldots, N$. For each i, $N - 1$ additional uniform random numbers were then generated to allocate flow from each node to the other nodes.

As we can see, even though there are significant variations in the flow

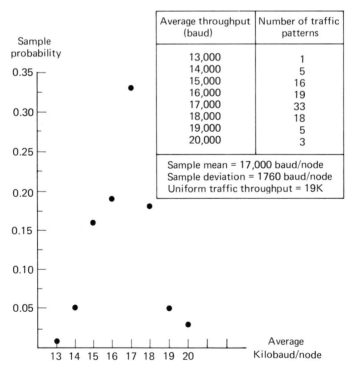

Average throughput (baud)	Number of traffic patterns
13,000	1
14,000	5
15,000	16
16,000	19
17,000	33
18,000	18
19,000	5
20,000	3

Sample mean = 17,000 baud/node
Sample deviation = 1760 baud/node
Uniform traffic throughput = 19K

FIGURE 1.10   Empirical probability distribution for 18-node network.

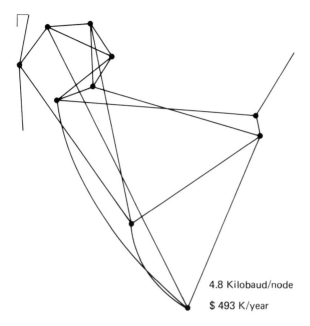

4.8 Kilobaud/node

$ 493 K/year

FIGURE 1.11a

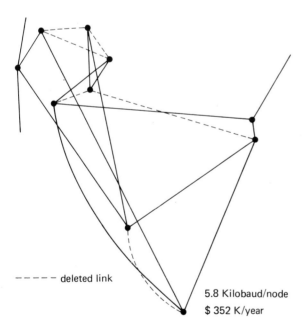

- - - - - deleted link

5.8 Kilobaud/node

$ 352 K/year

FIGURE 1.11b

FIGURE 1.11 Example of layout optimization for distributed
network.

25

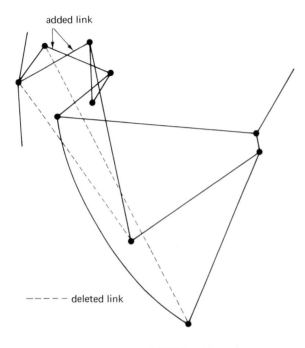

added link

----- deleted link

6.7 kilobaud/node

FIGURE 1.11c

requirements, the routing procedure is able to accommodate these variations with little degradation in performance.

The significance of these results is that we can use the fast and near-
optimal routing algorithm as a subroutine for the layout optimization problem. The routing and time-delay analyses are incorporated in the tests
indicated in Fig. 1.7 for network feasibility and improvement in the objective
function. Link additions and deletions similar to those discussed in Section
1.3.3 can be applied. Figures 1.11a, b, and c give an example of such an
optimization. The system shown in Fig. 1.11a is the starting network. The
network has an average throughput at 0.5-s time delay of 4800 bps/node and
a yearly cost of $493,000. For this network, the computer's optimization
operates by first deleting links and reassigning capacity more efficiently, and
then simultaneously adding and removing links. Figure 1.11b indicates the
state of the network after six links have been deleted; Fig. 1.11c shows the
final design after two more links have been deleted and two added. The optimization has resulted in a network with approximately 40 per cent higher
throughput at 30 per cent lower cost. The time required for this optimization
was less than 5s on the CDC 6600 computer.

REFERENCES

[1] H. FRANK and I. T. FRISCH, *Communication, Transmission and Transportation Networks*, Addison-Wesley, Reading, Mass., 1971.

[2] L. R. FORD, JR., and D. R. FULKERSON, Maximal Flow Through a Network, *Can. J. Math.*, **8** (1956), 399–404.

[3] T. C. HU, Multicommodity Flows, *Operations Res.*, **11** (1963), 344–360.

[4] S. L. HAKIMI, Simultaneous Flows Through Communication Networks, *IRE Trans. Circuit Theory*, **CT-9** (1962), 169–175.

[5] B. ROTHFARB and I. T. FRISCH, On the 3-Commodity Flow Problem, *SIAM J. Appl. Math.* **17** (1969) 46–58.

[6] T. C. HU, *Network Flows and Integer Programming*, Addison-Wesley, Reading, Mass., 1970.

[7] I. T. FRISCH, An Algorithm for Vertex Pair Connectivity, *Intern. J. Contr.*, **6** (1967), 579–593.

[8] D. J. KLEITMAN, Methods for Investigating Connectivity for Large Graphs, *IEEE Trans. Circuit Theory*, **CT-16** (1969), 232–233.

[9] H. FRANK, Maximally Reliable Vertex Weighted Graphs, *Proc. Third Princeton Conf. Inform. Sci. Syst.*, 1969.

[10] B. ROTHFARB, H. FRANK, K. STEIGLITZ, D. J. KLEITMAN, and D. ROSENBAUM, Optimal Design of Offshore Natural Gas Pipeline Systems, *Operations Res.*, **18**(6) (1970), 992–1020.

[11] H. FRANK, I. T. FRISCH, W. CHOU, and R. VAN SLYKE, Optimal Design of Centralized Computer Networks, *Proc. Intern. Conf. Commun.*, June 1969, 21.1–21.8, *Networks* (Sept. 1971), 43–57.

[12] D. R. DOLL, The Efficient Allocation of Resources in Centralized Computer-Communication Network Design, Ph.D. dissertation, University of Michigan, 1969.

[13] L. R. ESAU and K. C. WILLIAMS, On Teleprocessing System Design: Part 2, A Method for Approximating the Optimal Network, *IBM Syst. J.*, **5**(3) (1966).

[14] S. LIN, Computer Solutions of the Traveling Salesman Problem, *Bell Syst. Tech. J.*, **44**(10) (1965), 2245–2269.

[15] K. STEIGLITZ, P. WEINER, and D. J. KLEITMAN, Design of Minimum Cost Survivable Networks, *IEEE Trans. Circuit Theory*, **CT-16** (1961), 455–460.

[16] B. ROTHFARB and M. GOLDSTEIN, The One Terminal Telpak Problem, *Operations Res.*, **19**(1) (1971), 156–169.

[17] H. FRANK, I. T. FRISCH, and W. CHOU, Topological Considerations in the Design of the ARPA Computer Network, *AFIPS Conf. Proc.*, **36** (May 1970), 543–549.

[18] L. KLEINROCK, Analytic and Simulation Methods in Computer Network Design, *AFIPS Conf. Proc.*, **36** (May 1970), 569–579.

[19] L. KLEINROCK, Models for Computer Networks, *Proc. Intern. Conf. Commun.*, (June 1969), 21.9–21.16.

[20] L. G. ROBERTS and B. D. WESSLER, Computer Network Development to Achieve Resource Sharing, *AFIPS Conf. Proc.*, **36** (May 1970), 543–549.

2

System Design
for Computer Networks

PETER G. NEUMANN

Stanford Research Institute
Menlo Park, California

INTRODUCTION

This chapter is concerned with computer systems used in computer networks. Of particular interest here are multiprocessor computer systems and multisystem computer networks. The multiplicity is desirable for various reasons, e.g., increasing capability, reliability, and cost effectiveness. The main purpose of this chapter is to provide a conceptual framework for understanding computer systems and computer networks, more or less independent of hardware and software implementation details. As such, the chapter is structured according to various fundamental capabilities of systems and networks. These capabilities tend to be conceptually invariant from one system to the next, although this invariance is often masked by curiosities of the implementations involved. Each capability also tends to be found at various levels within systems and networks, with considerable functional similarity from one level to the next. For example, concepts of communications, storage management, and resource allocation are found in one form or another at essentially all levels.

It is relatively unimportant conceptually whether a particular capability is found in hardware, in microprogram, or in software. Although such issues are of course critical to the overall cost effectiveness of the entire system or network, they do not basically alter the understandability of the particular capability. However, all the capabilities discussed here require adequate hardware support to be realistically implementable. (Some of the issues of cost effectiveness are considered in Chapter 9.) What is important here is the range of capability and the basic concepts involved. Thus this chapter presents no particular system design in detail, although it bears strong conceptual similarities with the Multics environment [1–7], from which many examples are cited. Various specific environments are given in the last four chapters of the book.

This chapter does not attempt to be complete, an impossibility in any event, but especially so in the limited space available. However, it does attempt to cite enough relevant literature and to provide enough insight into systems and networks that the interested reader can easily delve further. Several basic references may be particularly useful. Rosen [8] provides a summary of the historical evolution of computer hardware; Bell and Newell [9] present a superb compendium of hardware (although ignoring software). Hellerman [10] discusses various principles of system design. Rosin [11] gives a summary of the historical evolution of computer operating systems, and Rosen [12] provides a useful collection of basic software articles. Wilkes [13] and Watson [14] present concepts of time-sharing design. A survey of some recent conventional commercial operating systems is found in [15]. Other useful relevant references are found in [16, 17]. It is hoped that the reader will pursue these references, as well as others cited here.

The range of capability of computer systems and networks is quite wide, reflecting a wide range of goals and designs. This range includes capabilities of handling large numerical calculations, symbol manipulation and language processing (whether computer languages or natural languages), communications, and control applications. It includes systems devoted to one or a few special-purpose applications, as well as systems able to handle a wide general-purpose range of applications. It includes systems that permit interactive use with very fast response to requests from terminal users, and/or noninteractive use (e.g., traditional batch processing and remote batch processing) with results typically available via a deferred high-speed printout. It also includes systems with large on-line storage capabilities and systems with none. The ability to link diverse systems into a network can greatly increase the usefulness of such systems.

In selecting material for inclusion in this chapter, emphasis has been placed on the relevance and importance of concepts in computer-communication networks and in network-like systems. As examples, concepts such as large on-line information-storage capacities, protection and sharing, dynamic resource management, and synchronization of processes are very significant and hence are included. It is not necessary, however, that each system in a network have all the capabilities included here. In fact, it is quite meaningful for a network to include exceedingly special-purpose systems such as a mammoth numerical processor (a "number cruncher") with no long-term information-storage capacity. The systems view presented here is therefore a general-purpose one from the viewpoint of potential capabilities, and includes those capabilities which seem useful to networks and large network-like systems. Although for any particular system some of the concepts presented here may not be applicable, this chapter may be useful as a framework for comparison. By pursuing the references, the reader may also find the chapter useful as a guide to deeper study.

It has been difficult to write a totally self-contained chapter defining all basic concepts used. A rudimentary level of sophistication with computers has therefore been assumed. Some sense of the structure within the chapter may be gleaned from scanning the section titles for this chapter. (The casual reader may wish to omit Section 2.2. He should also not be distressed at finding a term for which he is not yet prepared. It is difficult to write a chapter of this scope which can be read in a linear order and understood on the first pass.)

2.1 PRELIMINARIES—BASIC CONCEPTS OF SYSTEMS AND NETWORKS

This section provides an overview of various concepts relevant to computer systems and networks of systems. Various types of structure are indentified within which these concepts are more or less invariant from one level to the next.

2.1.1 Hardware and Software—Levels of Dependence

There is a basic distinction in most computer systems between hardware and software. Traditionally, *hardware* generically refers to that portion of a system which is implemented in terms of physical components, and which is supposedly hard to change; *software* refers to that portion which is implemented in terms of programs, and which is supposedly relatively much easier to change. The term *microware* (often called *firmware*) is used to refer to that portion implemented through microprograms (see below), which are interpreted by the hardware by means of special control circuits central to the hardware. A distinction may readily be made among various levels of closeness to the hardware. These levels also may be interpreted as layers of successive dependence, with each layer being built on the capabilities of preceding layers. The levels of dependence may be designated as follows.

HARDWARE.   The basic level on which a system is built is of course the hardware. Hardware includes various kinds of processors (e.g., central, peripheral, micro- and miniprocessors), memories, and input–output devices (terminals, tapes, etc.). A surprisingly wide variety of different hardware system organizations is found in past, present, and future systems, as seen in [9, 18]. This variety includes traditional serial designs (the *mainline* approach), as well as highly overlapped serial-parallel designs (the *pipeline* approach, such as in the IBM 360/195, CDC 7600, and CDC STAR computers) and highly parallel designs (the *wideline* approach, as in the ILLIAC IV), as well as independent-task systems with many loosely coupled processors (the *multiline* approach, often with *sideline* subsystems as well).

MICROWARE (FIRMWARE).   Each instruction of a computer is composed of a sequence of microoperations interpreted by the hardware. In microprogrammed systems such a sequence is explicitly definable as a programmable sequence of microoperations, rather than built into the circuitry. This permits the instruction set to be changed, or at least specified independently of the hardware [19]. Some microprograms are extremely difficult to change (e.g., factory made); others may be easily changed under program control, being stored in a writeable control memory. Alterable microprograms provide some of the flexibility of software (see below), while permitting the potential speeds of hardware (sometimes). More significantly, they permit widely different instruction sets to exist compatibly (although not necessarily at the same time on the same processor) within the same basic hardware configuration. Thus one hardware system may be able to simulate in microware (*emulate*) a wide class of different machines. Microprogrammed processors may be very effective in performing various functions too costly to be implemented in software. Some microprograms may also be alterable under user-program control [20].

OPERATING SOFTWARE.   Operating software consists of a collection of programs using the hardware and microware capabilities (low-level capabilities) to provide a higher-level set of capabilities more directly usable from a programming point of view. Operating software of present vintage generally includes facilities for storage management and basic input–output, resource allocation and job scheduling, and usually some sort of accounting. Some of these functions are heavily used by most users, and thus it is desirable that the programs be shareable among the users of the system. Some of these functions also need to be isolated from the users to prevent misuse.

COMMAND SOFTWARE.   The command software of a computer system comprises the interface to the users of the system and includes commands for the use of various language translators (e.g., assemblers and compilers), editors, debuggers, storage and input–output capabilities, and special-purpose subsystems, such as data-management systems and "turn-key" inquiry systems. The set of command software available to users may differ from one user to the next, as may some of the operating system software in some cases.

USERWARE.   The users of some systems are only permitted to use the command software directly, as in the case of transaction-oriented and query systems (e.g., reservations, bank information, and credit-inquiry systems). In general-purpose systems users often write their own programs as well. Such programs may be called *userware* and include programs useful to many other users (e.g., a "supersystem" built on top of the command software), as well as programs useful only to a particular user. In some systems there is a clear distinction between software and userware. In principle (and in this chapter) there need be no such distinction, apart from levels of protectability.

Historically, the succession of levels of dependence described above has usually corresponded to the increasing ease of changes being made without adversely affecting the entire system; the closer to the hardware, the harder it has been to affect change. This motivates the use of the terms hardware, firmware, and software. However, in light of program-alterable microcode and the use of various system structures described here, this succession of levels no longer necessarily corresponds to increasing ease of change. (Thus the term *firmware* is eschewed here.)

At each successive level of dependence there are interface languages which permit the use of the facilities at that and at lower levels, and which should increase the usability of the system. (In most systems the potential capability actually decreases as the level increases.) The levels of language are summarized in Table 2.1, along with simple examples at each level. It is often possible to intermix language statements from different levels, particularly command level. In addition, there is often no functional distinction between external system calls and system commands, although the latter normally imply a greater orientation toward ease of human use.

A program consists of executable procedures and various associated data. To be precise about the activity within a computer system, it is desirable to distinguish among several stages in the life of a program:

1. *Specification time*, when a problem is formulated.
2. *Implementation time*, when a program is written, in one or more human-oriented source languages.

3. *System entry time*, when a source program is read into the system.
4. *Compilation* (or *assembly*) *time*, when a source-language program is converted to a machine-oriented language (object language).
5. *Static linking time*, when separately compiled programs are bound together to form one large object program.
6. *Static loading time*, when an object program is loaded into memory preparatory to its execution.
7. *Execution time* (*run time*), when a program is actually in execution.
8. *Dynamic linking time*, when access is required to procedures and/or data not linked at static link time.
9. *Dynamic loading time*, when parts of linked procedures and/or data are loaded (e.g., because execution cannot otherwise proceed) that were not loaded at static loading time.

These are the basic recognizable stages (although debugging environments may provide several forms of run time). The last two stages are invoked by various actions during run time. Each of the above stages adds machine-dependent information to the program or collection of programs in execution. For example, arguments to a particular macroinstruction could be evaluated ("bound") at compile time, link time, load time, or run time, providing successively greater potential flexibility. In general, program usage iterates repetitively through these stages. Linking, loading, and execution may be done without continued recompilation if the object programs are retained.

In the levels of language of Table 2.1 it is clear that each level draws on the facilities of the preceding levels. In the narrow sense the term *operating system* is used to include just the operating software. In a broader sense it is sometimes used to include command software as well. Throughout this chapter it is the totality of hardware, microware, operating software, and command software that is of interest. The intent of a computer system is to provide its user community with a set of useful and usable functional capabilities, with ease of use appropriate to the level of language. (For example, some users may use only elementary commands, such as BASIC and APL, whereas others may write their own microprograms.)

The total systems view of computer systems taken here is functionally invariant to hardware–microware–software tradeoffs. In fact, the whereabouts of the various dividing lines are sometimes fuzzy within a given system; they may vary in time both within a given system and from one system to its successor. Such dividing lines also have radically different appearances from one manufacturer's system to another's. Generally, software tools established as useful at some point in time frequently emerge in microware or in hardware in subsequent systems, as suggested in Table 2.2. Hardware technology also progresses independently of software advances. For example, fast execution buffers, fast read-only memories and fast once-

TABLE 2.1   *Levels of Language*

Level of Dependence	*Level of Language*	*Examples (circa 1972)*
(Low)	Circuit diagrams	Interconnect one gate's output to another's input.
Hardware		
	Microoperations	Move contents of one register to another. Increase or decrease the contents of a register.
	Macros of microoperations	"Mini-instructions."
	Microprograms	Microassembly language programs.
Microware		
	Instructions	Load a word from memory into a register and add. Transfer control conditionally.
	Macroinstructions	Call a subroutine, first arranging to save the process state and to set up a return.
	Programs	Assembly language (instruction oriented). Higher-level language (statement oriented).
Operating software		
	Interrupts	Respond to the detection of a missing resource. Respond to the arrival of a resource.
	Internal system calls (subroutines, co-routines)	Dynamically allocate system resources, e.g., processors, memory, input–output channels.
	External system calls	Manipulate logical units of storage and of input–output. Evaluate a standard numerical function. (*Note:* Most of the capability at this level is usually available at command level, through a more human-interfaced form.)
Command software		
	Commands and command environments (including interactive and noninteractive requests within commands)	Create, delete, protect units of on-line storage. Perform input–output at the file level, e.g., print. Perform text and program manipulations, e.g., editing, microassembling, assembling, compiling, debugging, program execution, microprogram simulation, command preparation. Perform network operations, e.g., remote data access, remote execution.
	Macrocommands	Command-interpreting commands. Compiler generation using editing with audit trails and autodocumenting capabilities. Elaborate noninteractive sequences of commands.
(High)		

TABLE 2.2   *Influence of Software on Hardware and Microware*

Hardware Features Once Found in Software

Multiplication
Division
Indexing
Indirect addressing
Floating-point operations
Multiple precision
Clocks, relative and absolute
Character-oriented and data-structure-oriented instructions
Interrupt handling, including hierarchies of interrupts
Protection
Call linkage mechanisms
List, queue, and stack manipulation
Input–output processors
Peripheral processors and microprocessors for various dedicated tasks
Relocation via base registers
Relocation via page tables
Segmentation and two-dimensional virtual addressing
Metering, recording, tracing, and debugging mechanisms
Emulation (simulation)

Anticipated Hardware Features Now in Software

Advanced versions of some of the above (e.g., direct hardware implementation of virtual memories, more sophisticated protection, interrupt-handling, and interface mechanisms)
Tree structures, directory hierarchies
Variable-length allocation and manipulation (e.g., to effectively implement varying strings)
System module and network interface mechanisms, and automatic aids to dynamic reconfigurability

writable (disposable) memories are expected to have an enormous effect on system designs. In general, software overhead is to be avoided. Thus the most frequently used system features should appear in hardware or microware, possibly in special-purpose micro- or miniprocessors.

2.1.2   Organization and Disorganization— Levels of Structure

The stages in the life of a program mentioned in Section 2.1.1 generalize into a sequence of stages in the development of a system or network. Briefly, these stages include goal setting, design formulation, detailed design specification, implementation, debugging to remove logical errors in the implementation, testing to remove logical errors in the design, verification of the validity of algorithms, interfacing pieces of the system together, integrating these pieces into a working system, maintaining a continually working system, evaluating the performance of the system, improving the performance, and generally evolving the system to satisfy changing user needs. Each of these stages of development also implicitly involves a managerial function.

In dealing with computer systems involving various levels of hardware and software (and possibly including various levels of system-wide and per-user microware), as well as many stages of development, the potential complexity of such systems [21] presents many serious problems throughout each stage of system evolution. Control of the potential complexity dictates that a system must have some basic underlying structure, rather than just reflect haphazard evolution, in order to combat Parkinson's third law (expansion begets complexity, and complexity begets decay). The organization of a system into modules that carefully reflect such a functional division is the concept of *modularity*. A well-modularized system reflects a fundamental understanding of the flow of information and control within the system. Modularity is also of value throughout the stages of system development, although excessive modularity or poorly chosen modules and interfaces can result in enormous inefficiency.

To be useful, modularity must reflect a meaningful organization. To this end it is often desirable that modules or collections of modules have some well-defined structure or hierarchy. Examples include orderings based on levels of sensitivity to misuse and the need for protection, on levels of successive dependence, and in some cases on levels of relative interdependence. In rare cases it is possible to linearly order all modules according to some such basis (e.g., a *metric*). More commonly it is possible to group modules into collections of modules with (roughly) comparable characteristics such that between any two collections there is a well-defined ordering with respect to a particular metric. That is, there is a linear ordering among collections, but perhaps only a partial ordering (e.g., a *lattice* ordering) among modules. Another common ordering is a tree-structured ordering among modules or among collections; that is, there is an ordering only along the paths of a tree. In other cases there may be no consistent orderings with respect to a given metric.

Several structures of ordering are represented in Fig. 2.1. The structures of Figs. 2.1b and d can be mapped onto the linear ordering of Fig. 2.1a if all nodes at a given level are grouped into a collection (even if they are incomparable). The situation in Fig. 2.1c is more complicated, requiring that nodes at different levels be grouped in order to obtain a linear ordering of the collections. In Fig. 2.1e such a grouping into more than one level is impossible. In general, grouping modules into collections may be undesirable

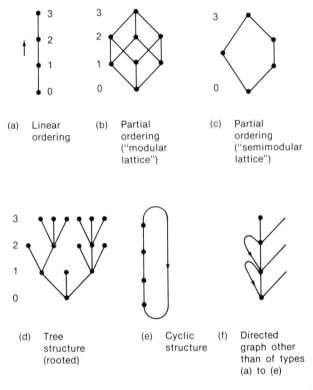

(a) Linear
     ordering

(b) Partial
     ordering
     ("modular
     lattice")

(c) Partial
     ordering
     ("semimodular
     lattice")

(d) Tree
     structure
     (rooted)

(e) Cyclic
     structure

(f) Directed
     graph other
     than of types
     (a) to (e)

FIGURE 2.1   Structures of order. All branches leaving a node upward imply the same relative ordering with respect to the given metric.

or unmeaningful, and the mapping onto a linear structure may in fact be unnecessary. In other cases, even approximate groupings may be very useful as long as there are no uncontrollable side-effects, e.g., a violation of the system protection scheme. The orderings discussed here are relevant in this chapter to various types of collections, including not just modules but data structures and other entities, as well as to the flow of control within modules and collections of modules, subroutines, and co-routines (e.g., routines which may call each other without regard to strict stacking of returns).

Despite the fact that linearly ordered structures are highly restrictive, they arise in various ways. They provide an extraordinarily powerful structural tool. An example is given by the levels of dependence of Section 2.1.1. Other example are found below. The one-dimensional concept of a linear ordering (e.g., *string* structure) is often represented as a two-dimensional concept (e.g., *ring* structure), as in Fig. 2.2; here levels 0, 1, 2, . . . correspond

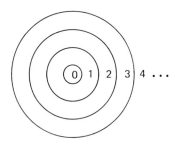

FIGURE 2.2   Ring structure.

to successive linear levels. (There is a choice between using the rings or the annuli as levels; the latter choice seems more natural here.) The one-dimensional linear ordering is also found disguised as a three-dimensional concept (*onion* structure). In some cases the multi-dimensional view is meaningful, e.g., when peeling a portion of one layer exposes only a portion of the next inner layer. (Here a tree structure may be a better representation.) Note that the term *layer* is often used as equivalent to *level*.

It should be noted that if a linear ordering exists for one metric, the ordering may be different—or may not exist at all—for another metric. For example, the levels of language in Table 2.1 do not correspond uniquely to levels of capability; a particular macroinstruction could be more or less powerful than an internal system procedure, or may be incomparable.

The linear structure is the basis for the THE system of Dijkstra [22], in which each successive higher level conceals details meaningful only to lower levels. In that environment the levels are called *levels of invisibility* or *levels of abstraction*. The precise function of each level is particularized to that system. A more generally relevant example is given in Section 2.1.4.

The linear structure arises in Multics in several ways. It is found as levels of dependence in the system design, and as levels of invisibility in the virtual memory and the virtual input–output (see Section 2.1.4). It also arises as the basis for the protection mechanism [23], where each higher level corresponds to a collection of weaker protection. (Traditional computer systems have generally provided only two levels.) Lampson's generalized protection structures [24] offer potentially greater flexibility by handling generalized objects and by relaxing the linear restriction. (See Section 2.2.1.1.) In general, protection can only be guaranteed where there is some form of partial well-ordering, e.g., a tree structure, to avoid violations resulting from transitivity of authority.

Tree structures are seen to be useful in Sections 2.2.2 and 2.2.3, whereas directed graphs and undirected graphs are useful in network configurations and in analysis of flow of control.

2.1.3 Systems and Networks—Levels of Communication

A multicomputer complex may be classified according to how communication is handled, both inside and outside the complex. Within such a complex there is a wide spectrum of possible means of communication. If the complex is geographically distributed, communication is necessarily relatively restricted and control is relatively distributed. If the complex is geographically centralized, control may still be distributed, or else it too may be centralized. If the complex is strongly coupled by its intercommunications, it is here called a *system;* if it is loosely coupled, it is called a *network*. This distinction is is never completely precise, but is formalized in what follows.

The intercommunications within a computer structure generally involve sharing of common memory, or sharing of control signals and communication paths, or both. In the shared-memory case, the relative speeds of memory play a vital role in determining what capabilities the structure can provide. There are often many levels of memory in a computer system. These include not only primary memories (fast, random, directly addressable) and secondary memories (slower, often sequential, often not directly addressable), but also very fast invisible buffer memories (e.g., associative, and *scratch-pad* or *cache* memories), as well as very slow off-line extensions of secondary memories.

There is obviously no fine line between systems and networks. The degree of coupling runs a very wide spectrum similar to the spectrum of memory. For present purposes, a system is a complex of one or more processors held together by heavily used common memory and/or common control signals. A network is a complex of interconnected systems of networks. (By combining communications across the spectrum of memories and the spectrum of communication links, it is meaningful to speak of networks of networks, etc.) In fact, a complex may be viewed as both a network and a system at the same time. For example, an on-line interactive computer complex with multiple processors and remote communication links may be viewed as a system from the viewpoint of the computer structure and as a network from the viewpoint of the communications.

2.1.3.1. Computers and Communications. In discussing computer-communications networks, it is desirable to specify the relative roles of computers and communications. For example, it is meaningful to consider communications among different computer systems, which link these systems into a *computing network* more powerful than any one of the systems. It is also possible to consider computers used as part of a *communications network*, as for example in store-and-forward communication. In general, a single network may take on both views simultaneously, serving as a computing and communications network. For present purposes, therefore, neither one of these two views is adopted as the dominant view.

2.1.3.2. Levels of Communication. Within systems and networks, communication exists at many levels. Since some functions and capabilities are found at many levels, it is worthwhile to outline these levels briefly along with various functions common to several levels. These levels are (as usual) not always totally distinguishable.

Intraprocessor and processor-memory communication includes communication within a single-processor system via control signals, programs, and data.

Intramemory communication includes various forms of communication of programs and data among various levels of memory upward and downward in a hierarchy, including a potentially wide range of speeds, accessing modes, and availability. (This may or may not require a processor for communication, utilizing the above level if it does.)

Input-output communication includes communication of the system with local and remote devices via dedicated or switched lines. Devices typically include unit-record equipment (printers, card readers, card punches, paper-tape devices), typewriters, graphic terminals, private tapes, and system tapes.

Interprocessor communication within a multiprocessor system includes control signaling among the processors. It may also involve coordination of the use of programs and data through shared common memory. The processors may be physically identical, in which case the system may treat them as either functionally interchangeable (the symmetric case) or functionally noninterchangeable (the asymmetric case). The processors may be physically nonidentical, as in the case of systems with particular processors (e.g., peripheral processors) dedicated to specific functions, as in direct-coupled systems [9, 18].

Intersystem communication involves the exchanging of data, procedures, and control signals among different systems. Media include high-speed and low-speed communication lines, hard-wired (dedicated) private lines, and switched telephone lines. Since communication paths may be switched dynamically, the network configuration may vary from time to time. The systems in the network may be essentially identical (except for minor differences such as configuration) or may be quite different, with diverse command structures, diverse conventions and types of use, and even totally different hardware. These are again symmetric and asymmetric cases, respectively. The symmetric case is reasonably tractable without too many elaborate mechanisms required to interface the systems into the network. The asymmetric case in its full generality is quite complicated (see Section 2.3 and Chapter 13).

Internetwork communication is also possible among distinguishable networks, presumably with a level of communication different from intersystem communication in terms of capability, flexibility, capacity (bandwidth), or ease of use. At this level the hierarchy of networks of networks begins to be less clearly identifiable.

Associated with each level of communication is a language for communication, as in the levels of dependence above. These levels demonstrate the variability of the needs for communication in computer complexes. Concepts such as storage management, command or instruction sets, input–output capabilities, scheduling, accounting, and performance analysis arise at essentially all levels in ways that are very similar from one level to the next. Thus the approach taken in this chapter is to try to identify many of the functions invariant from one level to the next.

2.1.4 Virtual Systems and Virtual Networks— Levels of Invisibility

This section presents a generalized illustration of the concept of levels of invisibility. Consider a multiprocessor system with a hierarchy of storage devices and an assortment of input–output devices. At the zeroeth level, nothing is invisible; this corresponds to the raw hardware, with no support of any kind. At the first level are such issues as powering on and off, startup and initialization, establishing hardware configurations, and handling certain emergency interrupts. The abstraction of removing such issues from concern results in *virtual hardware*.

At the second level are microcode issues, such as what microcode instruction set is in system-wide use for each processor at each moment, and how and when this microinstruction set is changed (e.g., under system control while in execution, or only at startup). The abstraction of removing these issues from visibility results in *virtual micromachines*.

The next level involves issues of multiprocessing, resulting from the multiplexing of multiple processors. For the purposes of this chapter, an *execution process* is defined as that which is in execution on a given processor during some continuous time period on behalf of some recognizable user or system function. An execution process involves a collection of programs and data that are used during the period of execution. (The portion of this collection which is more or less in use at a given moment is called the *working set* of the execution process [25].) An execution process is thus the unit of processor allocation; it is that to which a processor is allocated and is relevant only when in execution. *Multiprocessing* is then the simultaneous execution of multiple execution processes on the multiple processors of the system. Issues considered at this level involve, e.g., interprocessor interference, the handling of processor interrupts, processor allocation, and the problems involved in switching from one execution process to another. The abstraction of removing these multiprocessing issues from visibility produces an environment in which a collection of logically independent processors (called *virtual processors*) is visible as a pool of easily allocatable resources.

The next level of invisibility involves issues of multiprogramming, resulting from the multiplexing of programs simultaneously competing for execution on a virtual processor, irrespective of whether there is more than one processor actually available. (In the case of a single physical processor, only a single execution process can exist at one time, even though many programs may be competing for execution.) A *virtual execution process* (as distinct from an execution process) is a sequence of execution processes that would correspond to a single execution process had there been no interruptions; it performs some logically continuous chain of activity identifiable as a functional unit, e.g., a user job, or the activity of keeping high-speed printers running. For simplicity, the virtual execution process is called a *process*. A process thus survives (as a unit of virtual execution) despite periods of nonexecution. The totality of all procedures and data accessible to a process constitutes the process address space and includes the working set at any moment. *Multiprogramming* is then the interleaved execution of multiple processes on a processor or virtual processor. (If only a single processor exists, there is of course no simultaneous execution; the competing processes are then broken up into execution processes.) Issues of process interference, process protection, and process priorities occur at this level, along with process creation, termination, and scheduling. Interrupts appear at this level as symbolic or *virtual interrupts*. Microcode particular to an individual user [20] (as in the Gemini system [26]) also arises here. The abstraction at this level, the *virtual process*, corresponds to one or more processes for each logical user, possibly allowing for parallelism within the virtual process. Processes are discussed in Section 2.2.1.

The next level concerns issues of storage management, such as physical memory addresses within the multilevel hierarchy of on-line and off-line storage media managed by the system, and the organization of information within this hierarchy (data and procedures) into a directory structure (itself possibly multilevel). Problems arise in moving this information around in the hierarchy, into and out of working memories, in protecting information from misuse and from system malfunction, and in providing recovery mechanisms in case of malfunction. The abstraction at this level results in all memory appearing to be on line at the same level (*single-level store*) [27], addressable as if it were immediately available. This logical storage medium is called a *virtual memory*, and is discussed in Section 2.2.2.

The next level concerns input–output management, such as buffering strategies, device multiplexing, external communications disciplines, timing and synchronization, device formats, and character code interpretation. The abstraction of removing these issues from visibility (except where required) is called *virtual input–output*, and is discussed in Section 2.2.3.

There are still two more levels of invisibility to be considered. The next level concerns issues in the implementation of the command software. It is at this level that most of the typical inconveniences of system use should be masked from the users, so that the command structure can be uniform, simple, and easy to use. The resulting abstraction is a *virtual system*, which may differ widely from one user to the next. (There are many language levels here; see Table 2.1.) This level is discussed in Section 2.2.4.

The final level considered here involves network aspects. For example, it is sometimes meaningful for a user of one system to be able to execute programs on other systems without having to worry too much about the idiosyncracies of the other systems, or indeed in some cases without even having to know on what system his programs are running. The abstraction of making such concepts invisible results in a *virtual network*.

The levels of invisibility identified above are summarized in Table 2.3.

TABLE 2.3 *Levels of Invisibility*

Level	*Concepts Made Invisible* (Levels of Multiplexing)
Virtual hardware	Configurations
Virtual micromachines	System-wide microcode (microcode)
Virtual processor	Multiprocessing (processor)
Virtual process	Multiprogramming and user-dependent microcode (process)
Virtual memory	Memory allocation (storage)
Virtual input–output	Device dependence, synchrony (I–O)
Virtual system	System idiosyncracies (user)
Virtual network	Multisysteming (system)

Not all these levels are relevant in all existing systems. When relevant, they may or may not be explicitly recognizable, often not. They seem to be more visible in recent systems than in earlier ones. The relative order of the levels may also vary from one system to the next. Note that the levels of invisibility do not imply that a function be implemented totally at one level. Many of the functions may in fact be distributed over corresponding inner levels of implementation, in addition to having sublevels. Input–output provides a good example, for which there are usually implications on the hardware and on memory management. Virtual input–output contains aspects of low levels (e.g., invisible asynchrony of buffer usage) and high levels (e.g., virtual printing at command level). The existence of various kinds of associative memory common to all processors is another example with similar implications. Thus levels of invisibility do not necessarily correspond via an order-preserving mapping with the levels of dependence, with the levels of communication, or indeed with the levels of protection (although local ordering is often preserved, as in a tree structure).

The preceding discussion is intended to display the spectrum of levels often implicit in the design of a system or network. The structuring of such a complex according to the levels of structure in this and the foregoing sections is of enormous aid in the design of the complex, including the verification of the correctness of the design. It is also valuable in studying systems, for it provides a canonical framework frequently useful in making comparisons. If judiciously applied, this formulation can also be exceedingly valuable in the implementation, debugging, maintenance, modification, and use of the complex. There are, however, several disclaimers that need to be made. First, the structure implied should never be used blindly as a panacea. The physical interposition of six layers of overhead resulting from six explicit layers of implementation could be an enormous obstacle to achieving adequate efficiency. (This is in fact not necessary.) Also, capability at inner levels may be needed directly at outer levels, and must not be sealed off in cases where it is essential. In general, the levels of structure discussed here are extremely powerful as conceptual design tools. Their use in implementation is potentially very valuable, but full of possibilities for misuse or overzealous use. With adequate hardware and microware support, however, these potential difficulties can normally be overcome. (A simplified implementation of the Graham ring mechanism, for example, is found in hardware in the Hitachi system [28]. See also [29].)

In Section 2.1.3 various levels of intrasystem communication are identified. Consideration of the above levels of invisibility implies commmunication at each level. Additional levels of communication worthy of mention are the following.

1. *Intraprocess communication* within a process includes the passing of pointers and symbolic names, data, calling sequences, and arguments;
2. *Interprocess communication* among competing independent processes and among cooperating parallel processes includes event signaling and interlock mechanisms;
3. *Interuser communication* within a system includes transmitting and receiving postal-like messages.

(Interuser communication and intrauser communication—courtesy of seaofthepants hyphenless editing—outside of a system but within a network include the transmitting and receiving of procedures and data, as well as executing remotely. A user may in fact have coordinating processes executing on his behalf on several systems in a network. These are forms of intersystem communication mentioned above.)

Many of the functional capabilities described in Section 2.2 are found at many different levels of invisibility. One such example involves the notion of synchronizing parallel operation, which exists at levels of multiprocessing, multiprogramming, input–output multiplexing, multitasking at the compiler-language level (e.g., tasking within PL/I), and parallel computation at the command-language level by explicitly or implicitly creating parallel processes on either the same system or on another system within a network. Another such example involves the notion of dynamic storage allocation, which exists at various levels as dynamic loading of part or all of a virtual process, dynamic allocation of input–output buffers, register allocation within a compiler (invisible to a compiler user), and explicitly by a user at the compiler-language level (e.g., "allocate" and "free" within PL/I). A more general view looks upon processors (central, micro, peripheral, etc.), memories and memory locations, and input–output devices and media as a collection of resources available to the system as needed, or even as a collection of systems available to a network. Resource allocation, whether static or dynamic, may be found at most levels of Table 2.3. Examples include the allocation of channels to interfaces, the allocation of processors, memory and input–output capabilities to processes (or families of processes), and the allocation of processes to users. A still more general view, e.g., that of Holt and Warshall [30], looks on a computer system as a loosely coordinated collection of resources all of which may be instantaneously allocated and deallocated. This view may consider resources down to the level of arithmetic units, shift registers, special memories, control units, etc.; alternatively it may consider a vast collection of small processors. In such a view the concept of a process may be meaningful, but the concept of an execution process may be distributed into small fragments.

2.1.5 Basic Goals and Principles

There are many problems in the design and implementation of a large computer operating system [31–36]. Some of these are technical, but many are problems involving people, either individually or in group interactions. Education of such people is complicated, since first-hand experience in the development of a particular system is often more valuable than any formal education. However, what has been learned in the development of one system often seems irrelevant to other systems because of the context in which it was learned. Thus it is essential to attempt to focus on fundamental principles, and to try to select those aspects which are reasonably invariant from one system to the next. This section provides a common set of guidelines by which to evaluate a particular system. These guidelines are discussed in the framework of a general-purpose system, although most of them are relevant to special-purpose systems as well.

From the point of view of the user community, the basic goals of a general-purpose computing facility include the following.

1. *Capability.* The system should be able to fulfill the current needs of its user community, providing adequate performance (throughput, response time, etc.), computing and storage capacity, availability, and generality.

2. *Evolvability.* The system should be able to continue to fill the changing needs of its user community by graceful evolution. There should be long-term continuity of the user interface, including continuity of system commands, conventions, and standards. This does not necessarily imply total compatibility, as is seen in Section 2.2.4. From the view of Fig. 2.2 in terms of levels of invisibility, this can be achieved if the interface to the user level does not change, almost irrespective of the interfaces to the inner layers.

3. *Convenience of use.* A system should be easy to learn and easy to use. It should be well documented. It should provide a simple user interface, with ease of program and data handling, and should be tolerant of user shortcomings. There should be no fundamental incompatibilities between interactive and noninteractive use, especially with respect to storage usage.

4. *Reliability.* If the system attempts to maintain information on line in a system-managed storage hierarchy, the continued availability of this information should be guaranteed. The hardware and software should operate with little or no malfunction. In case of any malfunctions, ill effects should be made invisible to the users whenever possible.

5. *Efficiency*, or more properly, *cost effectiveness.* The efficiency of hardware utilization or of software is only a partial contributor to the overall cost effectiveness of a system. Many other factors must be considered, weighting the relative importance of hardware, software, and userware economies. Optimization must be considered over the entire user community, examining the cost effectiveness of the system with respect to planning, designing, implementing, debugging, integrating, maintaining, managing, using, and evolving the system. Such global optimization is of course extremely difficult to evaluate. Furthermore, cost must be measured in various units, only some of which are monetary; the intangible costs of system unavailability, bad documentation, security violations, and system misuse are also relevant (although exceedingly difficult to evaluate).

There are many tradeoffs implicit among these goals, as seen throughout the chapter. Care and judgment and, above all, common sense must be exerted at all stages of design, implementation, integration, and evolution of the system. As a specific example, the use of various mechanisms for dynamic symbolic accessing (of storage or of input–output) enormously simplifies the implementation and use of the system. However, the use of these mechanisms on all occasions can be extremely costly. Thus there is a tradeoff between effective initial symbolic accessing for simplicity and cost-effective faster accessing for normal usage, for example, by using an associative or content-addressed access. Similar remarks apply to many of the mechanisms discussed in this chapter. Good design permits such a mechanism to be used whenever it is valuable, and also provides shortcuts when its use is disproportionally costly. Various examples of such mechanisms are given in this chapter. In general, these mechanisms contribute greatly to otherwise difficult problems as far as the user and the system programmer are concerned. For cost-effective implementations, however, it is often desirable to provide hardware or microware support. Hardware implementation may also be required to guarantee the integrity of the system, e.g., to enforce a protection mechanism or to enforce a locking strategy to avoid interprocessor and interprocess interference.

The above goals may be called *motivational goals*, as opposed to the structural or *functional goals* related to specific requirements. From the point of view of system programmers, the motivational goals of system development are surprisingly similar to the motivational goals of the user community listed previously. They include the following.

1. *Capability* of the system adequate to support each stage of the development as needed. It is highly advantageous to use a system as a development tool for its own development as soon as possible. In this way the use of the system is shaken down as a by-product of the development, and considerable experience can be gained. Difficulties tend to become visible sooner, and thus to be correctable sooner.

2. *Evolvability* of a system is at least as critical to system programmers as it is to users. No one is omniscient. A system should be designed in such a way that even the most catastrophic design and implementation errors can be gracefully corrected.

3. *Convenience* of program development, program debugging, program interfacing, documenting, and maintaining is essential. An apparent detour in building a development tool, a debugging environment, or an interfacing mechanism can often be significantly rewarding in later stages of development. Convenience is enhanced by rigorously enforced standards and conventions and by automated design aids, such as languages suited to defining operating system functions.

4. *Reliability* is critical to system programmers if the system is to provide a useful self-contained development environment. Its achievement depends on the entire development process, including the correctness of the original specifications of system goals.

5. *Flexibility*, especially dynamic flexibility, is particularly important. A system should be able to be highly reconfigurable, both at system startup and while in execution, operating with a wide variety of configurations as needed, and able to operate in spite of various component outages. The system should be able to enter into networking configurations without major redesign.

There are numerous motivational goals implicit in the above summary, many of which interact with one another. Table 2.4 provides an ungraded alphabetical list of some relatively self-explanatory good words, each of which provides a guideline by which to evaluate a given operating system [34]. The weights of importance that must be assigned to each of these good words are of course different from one system to the next, as well as from one user or system programmer to the next on the same system. Nevertheless, these words provide useful comparative guidelines.

TABLE 2.4   *A Collection of Motivational Goals*

automatedness	generality
availability	interfaceability
capability	maintainability
convenience	modularity
debuggability	monitorability
documentedness	portability
effectiveness	reliability
efficiency	simplicity
evolvability	uniformity
flexibility	usefulness
forgivingness	verifiability

In the wake of rapidly advancing technology and rapidly expanding desires for increased capability and capacity, we find a corresponding increase both in the cost of developing complex systems and in the time to completion. The ultimate goal of system development and operation is therefore an evolutionary one. *It must become possible to develop an evolvable operating system environment that can remain stable and relatively compatible with itself over long periods of time.* The environment must be able to withstand major changes in hardware, microware, and software and to enter into effective network operations, reflecting a continual increase in capacity and capability. At the same time it should resists expansion for the sake of expansion, heeding Parkinson's first law. The use of the levels of structure explicitly in implementation helps to provide such evolvability, along with the use of other techniques described in the next section.

2.1.6 Basic Operating System Development Tools

The motivational goals of the preceding section are useful measures of
system evaluation, but they are unattainable without a workable set of
functional goals. Even with realistic functional goals, the motivational goals
are hard to achieve without a sensible system design. This section considers
several design approaches that facilitate the achievement of many of the
motivational goals. These approaches contribute in varying degrees to all
the development stages, as aids to goal setting, design, implementation,
debugging, testing, verifying, interfacing, integrating, performance evaluation, management, and ultimately toward evolving the system or network.
They also affect the use of the system, although in less obvious ways.

MODULARITY AND DESIGN STRUCTURE.   The structures of Fig. 2.1 reap-
pear in many guises throughout the operating system design concepts presented here. As mentioned above, these structures provide fundamental
conceptual tools in all stages of system development, but as a means to some
particular end rather than as an end in themselves. Modularity has also
emerged as a fundamental hardware concept, with systems capable of being
configured over wide ranges simply by plugging subsystem components
together, e.g., processors (micro, mini, or otherwise), memories (with upper
limits to both physical and virtual memory sizes becoming very large), and
input–output devices. Some of the hardware interfaces might even be called
virtual interfaces.

STANDARD INTERFACE MECHANISMS AND TABLE-DRIVING TECHNIQUES.
There are numerous interfaces within a system, between users, between
processors, between modules, between languages, between subsystems, etc.
A major simplification in both design and implementation results if standard
interface mechanisms and/or table-driving mechanisms can be used in such
cases. An example is in the procedure call linkage mechanism (subroutine
linkage, e.g., "call," "save," and "return" [37], which permits different procedures to call one another freely as subroutines or as co-routines, with stack
disciplines and possible returns standarized. Another example is the symbolic
linkage mechanism that associates a symbolic name (or names) with procedure or data. In such cases the comments in Section 2.1.5 on tradeoffs
are particularly relevant. Some of these mechanisms may be tremendously
beneficial for the initial implementations, but too costly for permanent use.
In such cases back doors or trap doors may be needed under specially controlled circumstances to bypass the otherwise standard mechanisms. On the
other hand, if the system is evolvable and coded in a reasonable higher-level
language, it is often possible and useful to change such a standard mechanism
when significant improvements can result, assuming suitable attention has

been paid to the levels of invisibility and their interrelationship with the various dynamic mechanisms.

Other examples of the use of such standard mechanisms involve self-identifying data structures and decision tables and table-driving techniques in general, e.g., in memory accessing and in input–output, as seen in Sections 2.2.2 and 2.2.3. The use of indirection through tables combined with the isolation of interface-dependent information into a directly accessible form provides a very powerful approach to the structuring of a system in order to help achieve the above goals. Another example involves the use of standard mechanisms to assure cooperative execution of parallel processes.

HIGHER-LEVEL LANGUAGES. Higher-level languages are widely used for userware and are particularly useful when incorporated with higher-level debugging capabilities. The use of higher-level languages for system implementation is rapidly gaining acceptance [38–40]. Such use can greatly simplify and speed up the overall development of an operating system, and can enormously increase the understandability, documentability, and maintainability of the system. It can also provide greater evolvability. These benefits are based on the choice of and consistent use of a suitable higher-level language, however. A poorly chosen language (especially if poorly embodied in a compiler) can cause problems to be created throughout the operating system, which are not intrinsic problems of the operating system but rather are due to the unfortunate properties of the language, e.g., in its handling of data structures, its interface conventions, or its basic lack of needed capability. Multics PL/I [40], Burroughs ALGOL, and Lawrence Radiation Laboratory's LRLTRAN are examples of higher-level languages found useful in system or subsystem implementation. Efficiency of system code execution need not be a problem (see optimization, below), although the increased size of the resulting code may be a severe problem unless the storage-management problems are well handled. A potential impact of software needs (reflecting system needs) on future hardware organization is provided by this example, for the availability of large, cheap, fast read-only memories, and once-writeable memories may largely remove this difficulty in the use of higher-level languages for system implementation. Another direction is provided by the SYMBOL system, in which the higher-level language is integrated effectively into the hardware [41].

PERFORMANCE MEASUREMENT, EVALUATION, AND OPTIMIZATION. In designing an operating system, it is unrealistic to assume that the design will be perfect, or even adequate. Furthermore, it is generally not clear in advance what detailed optimization techniques will be valid. Therefore, it is wise to allow for imperfect design and to permit the system to evolve easily despite needs for major redesign or major reoptimization. In general, optimization in the large is difficult, with local optima much easier to find than global optima. Optimization in the small runs a serious risk of being irrelevant. In general, it is difficult to know in advance exactly where the most serious bottlenecks will be. Experience seems to show (e.g., [34, 42],) especially in the early stages of development, that a large percentage of the overhead of a system is often due to a very small percentage of the system (whether hardware, microware, and/or software), and that enormous performance improvement can be obtained in such cases with rather little effort. This depends critically, however, on being able to determine how the overhead is distributed. Thus in system design it is essential to provide for good performance measurement tools, carefully integrated into the system to minimize the effects on the system resulting from measuring it (Heisenberg uncertainty). If overhead is concentrated in a few places, there is a clear indication of where to optimize; in other cases, considerable understanding of the environment may be required. (Hardening functions from software to microware to hardware may in some cases be desirable.) Functional modularity contributes greatly, both to the ability to measure the system and to the ability to modify it.

In general, for a module carefully coded in a suitable higher-level language, only a relatively small improvement (a factor of 2 or 3) in the execution time of that module can be expected from carefully recoding the module by hand in a machine-oriented assembly language. Note that it clearly does not usually pay in terms of execution efficiency to recode 90 per cent of the system which is in execution only 10 per cent of the time, with accompanying greater effort in time, manpower, and debugging resources. (Note also that improvements in the object code generated by a compiler are reflected across all system code written in that compiler language, by recompilation.) Besides, substantially greater improvements are often available by other means. Examples include avoidance of unwieldy compiler features, careful choice of algorithms, modification or redesign of existing algorithms and of modules based on performance evaluation, and intelligent management, including the careful selection of programmers. A study by Sackman et al. shows that the last of these factors can be extraordinarily large [43], e.g., including a human performance ratio of 28 to 1 among experienced programmers.

An example of an algorithm-level optimization of an ALGOL compiler [42] implemented in FORTRAN is instructive. This led to a tenfold increase in the speed of the entire compiler as a result of four relatively simple stages of local optimization. About 5 per cent of the code was rewritten in assembly code to achieve this result. This example is interesting even though the scope of compiler optimization is much simpler than that of system optimization.

Performance measurement tools fall roughly into four categories, depending upon whether the real system or a model of it is used, and upon whether the measurements are internal (at hardware, microware, or even software levels) or external (at software or userware levels). These four categories are summarized in Table 2.5.

TABLE 2.5   *Performance Measurement and Evaluation Techniques*

Level \\ Model	External	Internal
Live model (the real system)	Gedanken experiments on the command behavior of a real system, e.g., measuring response time, turnaround, throughput, availability, reliability, effectiveness; using benchmark tests and driven experiments as well as a real user community; comparison with alternatives.	Probes on internal mechanisms, e.g., measuring resource allocation algorithms, schedulers, interrupt mechanisms, input–output buffering strategies; comparison with alternative strategies.
Abstract model	Gedanken experiments on the external behavior of models, using simulation and prediction. Theoretical analysis. Comparison of the model behavior with real behavior to improve the model.	Simulations of internal mechanisms. Algorithm design, using theoretical analysis and simulations.

A significant bibliography of about 200 papers on performance evaluation is found in [44] and reflects a rapidly growing interest in this area. Particularly relevant references include [45–48].

2.2   SYSTEM DESIGN FUNDAMENTALS

The main portions of the design of a computer operating system involve process management, storage management, input–output management, and command management. These are outlined in Sections 2.2.1–2.2.4, respectively. Subjects outside these areas are treated summarily (if at all), e.g., implementation, languages and compilers, graphics, and command environments. This chapter attempts to provide a basic familiarity with the concepts and structures of operating systems. Many of these concepts are relevant throughout computer systems and networks at many levels. As examples, process and/or buffer synchronization, dynamic storage allocation, dynamic name association, and protection arise in varying degrees in hardware, microware, operating software, and command software (particularly in higher-level languages).

2.2.1 Process Management

The innermost layers of software introduced in Section 2.1.4 are concerned with concepts of static and dynamic sharing of processors, memories, and input–output equipment arising in multiprocessing, multiprogramming, and multimicroprogramming (whenever microprograms can be changed under program control). Problems arise in various forms due to the nonindependence of serial and parallel processes, e.g., to critical timing interactions or to conflicts in concurrent demands. A process as defined in Section 2.1.4 is roughly a sequence of virtual execution corresponding to some recognizable function being performed. It involves a collection of procedures and data available for use by the process, but not necessarily all available to other processes. The totality of information known to a process forms its address space. The address space of each process may grow and shrink as time progresses, and is essentially independent of the address space of any other process (although there may be information commonly available to several processes). The scope and duration of a process may vary widely. For example, a process may correspond to the activity of a single user, or may act on behalf of all users (e.g., a process dedicated to running high-speed printers). A process may create coordinated subprocesses, and may be joined together with other processes to form some sort of superprocess. The system may be split up into separate processes and/or may be distributed throughout each (user) process as shareable procedure. In general, the hardware and software designs will interact with decisions as to the use of processes, dictating how often processes may be created and terminated and how easily they may be coordinated. For example, this greatly influences the decomposition of activities into processes, such as whether each command is treated with a separate subprocess or whether the entire activity from "login" to "logout" of a user corresponds to a single process. Relevant references on process management are provided by [49–52].

A process may serve a variety of purposes, e.g., to define the scope of execution control. It provides a compartmentalization for (semi-)independent functions in time (possibly in parallel), with independent protectability and independent naming spaces.

2.2.1.1 Intraprocess and Interprocess Isolation—Protection. The concept of isolating two system objects or collections of objects arises at many (virtual) levels. A process should be protectable from other processes, but also from itself. In particular, some parts of a process (e.g., those devoted to system management, security, and reliability) may have a greater degree of criticality and may need isolation from other parts. Protection of files from users and from errant processes is also desired. Such protection mechanisms require great care in design and implementation, and good support in hardware to

be effective. There are many potential pitfalls, including transitivity of authority, handling of abnormal situations, and aborts.

The Multics "ring" mechanism [23, 29] (viz. Fig. 2.2) is such a mechanism
devoted to inter- and intraprocess protection. It provides a number of different layers (rings) of successively weaker protection within each process,
and gives users and subsystems the ability to create additional layers. It also
permits different versions of all but the (critical) inner ring procedures to
exist in different processes. It further provides strict interprocess isolation,
with communication permitted among processes only via the mechanism
described in 2.2.1.2 below.

The Lampson dynamic protection structures [24] have similar goals, and
provide protection of generalized objects, including processes, files, access
keys, and collections of other objects (whence the concept of *Russelling
catalogs*). The unified consideration of all objects is of significant value.

These two approaches are examples of mechanisms of great promise for
enforcing system protection. Such a mechanism is of course reflected at
higher levels (e.g., see the discussion of access control in Section 2.2.2.1).

2.2.1.2 Interprocess Communication. Another very basic problem in
process management involves the need for flexible interprocess communication among competing as well as cooperating processes. Various basic facilities are required. Two main mechanisms controlling the flow of cooperating
processes in time involve a *wait* signal and a *notify* signal. Suppose that two
different processes are sharing a common first-in first-out buffer, or *queue*,
with process A appending data to the end of the queue and process B removing data from the beginning of the queue (*preremoving*, or *premoving*).
Difficulties may arise when A fills the queue (A is too far ahead of B) or when
B empties the queue (B is too far ahead of A). Assuming nothing about
the relative capabilities of A and B (e.g., whether B can keep up with A), a
simple way of coordinating the two processes is as follows.

WAIT AND NOTIFY.   Two signals are available for use by processes A and
B, the *queue-not-full* event (qnf) and the *queue-not-empty* event (qne). If A
(or B) cannot proceed because the queue is full (empty), it waits until signaled
by B (A) that the queue is no longer full (empty). The waiting process may
then continue. In this case the *notify* signal need be only "qne" or "qnf."
A block diagram is given in Fig. 2.3. Note that by adhering to this communication discipline, A and B may operate asynchronously (whether multiprogramming or multiprocessing, serial or parallel, is not important). A general
implementation of *wait* and *notify* is given in [49].

Figure 2.3 implicitly assumes that process A always has something to
append to the queue. Minor modifications permit the capability of the figure
to be used only when called upon (that is, subroutinely). Figure 2.3 does not
assume, however, any particular strategy to determine how often to actually

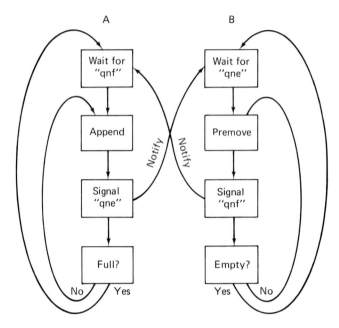

FIGURE 2.3   Block diagram of *wait* and *notify* used for queue synchronization.

use the *notify* mechanism. For example, it could be used (perhaps inefficiently) after every append or premove operation, at some cost in overhead. It seems more realistic to use it just when A appends to an empty queue ("qne") or when B premoves from a full queue ("qnf"). Care must be exerted in this case to assure that a one signal cannot get lost, in which cases process may wait forever. The careful reader will find that this entails using interlocks at certain critical moments (see *lock*, below), or else periodic *notifies* in the absence of signals (see *wakeup*, below).

Incidentally, this example is intended to be illustrative of the use of *wait* and *notify*. The reader should not try to conclude that *wait* and *notify* are the only way to achieve the necessary cooperation between two (or more) processes. Various alternative approaches are possible in any particular case. However, *wait* and *notify* provide a very powerful general capability.

BLOCK AND WAKEUP.   For efficiency reasons, waiting normally involves relinquishing execution rather than looping in continuous execution (unless the wait is exceedingly short). Thus the implementation of *wait* and *notify* involves the ability to discontinue execution of a process and to resume it subsequently, logically as if no discontinuity had occurred. This is achieved by the *block* and *wakeup* mechanisms. A process is able to block itself (to discontinue execution temporarily), pending the arrival of some specified event (e.g., the arrival of some specified signal or one of a set of signals). When the event occurs, the process undergoes a change in status that makes it eligible for execution (see scheduling, below). It goes from *blocked* status to *ready* status (virtual execution), and then eventually to *running* status (as an execution process). The process may revert to blocked status (e.g., waiting for input–output or secondary storage) or to ready status, or may be terminated (another meaning of "executed"!).

Implicit in these mechanisms is the establishment of the communication path via which events may be signaled. Such paths are called *event channels*. Some event channels may be preestablished at process creation time. Others may need to be established dynamically. This requires naming conventions if more than one channel can exist, and queueing or storing of events if multiple processes or multiple events are involved. Such queueing mechanisms are called *mailboxes*, and may contain a queue of events, appended to by the signaling process and premoved from by the signaled process. Thus the queue discipline itself resembles that of Fig. 2.3.

LOCK AND UNLOCK.   To coordinate the shared data (events) in the event queue, various access control mechanisms are needed (see Section 2.2.2). In addition to access control required on the mailboxes, two other mechanisms are required in the implementation of *wait* and *notify*. These guarantee that only one process can access a particular data base (e.g., mailbox) at a time during modification of the data base, while permitting shared access from one stable moment to the next. Numerous schemes exist to do this [22, 49–51], but they are all roughly equivalent.* A conceptually instructive scheme is that used on the GE 645. The instruction STAC Y stores the contents of the accumulator into location Y conditionally, if and only if the contents of Y are zero at the start of the instruction; otherwise the instruction does nothing. The instruction operates in a special indivisible mode that does not permit any interfering accesses to Y during the instruction execution (e.g., an interrupt or access to Y by another processor). The locking scheme then consists of two primitives, *lock* and *unlock*. The *lock* attempts to store a unique identifier associated with the process in a lock location Y via the STAC Y instruction, and then reads Y to see if it has succeeded in setting the lock on behalf of the process. If it fails, it may be tried again, immediately, if the lock can reasonably be expected to be of short duration. The *unlock* merely stores zero in Y, whenever the process has the right identifier. This

---

*Design and use of such mechanisms is rather tricky, requiring careful validation. Dijkstra's *P* and *V* operators for locking and unlocking [22] are fairly popular. However Patil exhibits an example with three processors for which the operators are not adequate [53] under a simplified interpretation of *P* and *V*. Patil, Parnas, and Habermann [53] have shown that this problem can be avoided, in at least two ways.

guards nicely against interference between multiple processes competing for the use of a changing data base.

There are various levels of interprocess communication possible. The most basic assumes a known mailbox and a fixed collection of known events. More general levels (see [49]) permit symbolic naming and dynamic creation of event channels, mailboxes, events, and event classes. They also permit uniform treatment of hardware and software interrupts.

DEADLY EMBRACE PROBLEMS. A fundamental problem that arises in dynamic resource allocation involves conflicts in availability. The generic example is as follows. Suppose that process A is using resource R and needs in addition resource S to which process B currently has exclusive access. The *lock* and *unlock* mechanisms help in guaranteeing the integrity of each resource. As long as B eventually relinquishes resource S, there is no inherent problem other than that A may be tying up resource R while waiting for resource S. A fundamental conflict does arise, however, when process B then decides it needs resource R before it can relinquish S, as suggested by Fig. 2.4. In the figure a solid line indicates current usage and a dotted line indicates concurrent additional needs. This conflict is essentially unresolvable except by backtracking or preplanning, and is called a *deadly embrace* [50].

A conceptually simple but nondynamic solution to this problem is to require all resources that may possibly be needed to be preallocated, anticipating the total needs of each process at the outset. This is unrealistic in many environments. It requires inordinate preplanning. It may produce enormous blockades when individual resources are actually only used for a short time. Furthermore, total resource needs may be in excess of instantaneous capability (e.g., if the total number of shareable tapes needed exceeds the number of tape drives).

A compromise between total preallocation and dynamic backtracking involves the "banker's algorithm." All resources held by a process requiring additional resources must first be released before attempting to allocate all needed resources simultaneously. This is also rather unwieldy.

Several partial solutions to this problem exist [54–56], although none provides a practical solution to the general dynamic problem. In each case significant preplanning is required, and recognition and explicit prevention

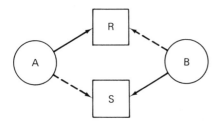

FIGURE 2.4 Deadly embrace.

of potential deadly embraces in the critical portions of the system are essential. Special care must also be taken to assure that such prevention strategies are able to survive the sudden termination or sidetracking of a process (either accidentally or intentionally) in the midst of a potential deadly embrace. Termination without removing temporary locks can have catastrophic side effects. Incautious removal of such locks may also be catastrophic, e.g., if critical data bases are in a transient state at the time. These termination problems may often be solved by requiring return to some minimum (safe) level before doing anything else. The explicit use of various levels of structure may contribute to the control of such problems (see [22]). Conflict resolution may also be aided by incorporating precedences (priorities) among the various resources.

2.2.1.3 Resource Allocation. A computing system consists of diverse physical resources, typically processors, memories and, input–output resources. Given a system or network, one of the most fundamental problems in using this complex is in effectively distributing the available resources among the various processes competing for these resources. Unfortunately, this is an ill-defined multidimensional problem, with strong coupling among the resources. Conflicts and tradeoffs exist at several levels, from advance reservations and static (predetermined) allocation of high-level resources (e.g., tapes and removable disks) to dynamically controlled allocation at much lower levels (e.g., allocation of resources on a millisecond basis, such as temporary memory space or interactive processor capability). Such a conflict arises, for example, when a process requires large primary memory allocations and large amounts of processor time in a heavily loaded interactive environment.

In general, it is not possible to anticipate all resource requirements as a function of (virtual or real) time within a system, or even within a process. What is possible is to decouple in part the allocation mechanisms for processes, storage, and input–output into at least three different parts. The residual coupling required among these three parts is then treated separately. Storage and input–output allocations are discussed in Sections 2.2.2 and 2.2.3. Processor allocation and process scheduling are discussed next. Interactions between the three allocation mechanisms are indicated when relevant.

PROCESS SCHEDULING. Process scheduling is the activity of maintaining a list of the ready processes (eligible to run) in some order reflecting priorities. *Dispatching* is the activity of selecting the most eligible process on this ready list, at which point the process is ready for processor allocation. When dispatched (to running status) from ready status, the process must be loaded and provided with whatever resources it may need initially to run.

Much concern has been devoted to the selection of appropriate scheduling algorithms (see Chapter 4 and [57–58]) with great variety available. Round-robin algorithms are popular pedagogically, but may fail in any but the simplest environments. Multiqueue multipriority algorithms are becoming widely used and provide different classes of service for different types of users at different stages of use. The best algorithm for a particular environment depends critically on the environment and should be highly flexible to accommodate dynamically changing system usage and system loading. Conservative algorithms (e.g., square-robin) do not seem to fly as well as dynamically alterable ones in unpredictable environments.

There is clearly interaction among dispatching, scheduling, and the availability of storage and input–output resources. It makes little sense to dispatch a process with large memory requirements unless adequate memory is available. Great care must be taken to avoid thrashing [59], which results from an imbalance of resource needs with resource availabilities.

There are other levels of process allocation farther removed from dispatching and scheduling. These might be called second- and third-order scheduling. First, some information data base must be maintained about the relative system costs associated with the various resources and about inherent priorities assigned to various processes. This information is used by the scheduler and may change dynamically.

Another level involves provision for advance resource reservations, such as "I (a user) want to use two processors heavily along with 60 per cent of available primary memory for 4 minutes around 2 P.M. this afternoon, and I have appropriate administrative authorization," or "this process has high priority, and will need four more tape drives simultaneously in about 5 minutes." Some mechanism is also required for observing incompatible priorities for a given set of processes or even a single process among different resources. Finally, especially when real-time requirements are important, there must be some evaluation of how effectively the various scheduling levels are living up to the demand, with corrective feedback to the scheduler as needed. (Some of this may not be needed in special-purpose environments.) This entire allocation process (including some storage and input–output allocation information) should be observable in real time, e.g., via a graphics console, and dynamically alterable on line. Detailed performance information is required not just for performance evaluation, but also for accounting purposes. Accounting techniques should permit charging of users for resource utilization, e.g., on the basis of processor usage, storage occupancy at various levels, and input–output usage.

2.2.2 Storage Management

Storage management has two basic functional goals:

1. To provide a uniform, reliable, and simple means of accessing all procedures and data maintained by the system on behalf of its users.

2. To provide the ability for a multiplicity of users and/or processes to share information in a carefully controllable way. Controls should be associated with information units of arbitrary size and type of usage.

There are also various secondary goals:

3. To make actual storage addresses invisible, and to provide a single-level store (virtual memory). (Virtual memories have been implemented in varying degrees in such systems as ATLAS, Burroughs B5000, Multics, IBM 360/67 TSS and CP/CMS, Michigan MTS, Hitachi HITAC 5020, as well as in System/370.)

4. To furnish allocation of storage space at each memory level only as warranted by use or by special requirements. This action should be invisible within the mechanisms of (1) and (3) above. This is the multi-level memory management problem, and includes the most expensive levels as well as the least expensive levels of storage.

Two more specific goals are included here that have recently been increasing in importance. They deal with the dynamic accessing of information.

5. To permit dynamic run-time symbolic addressing of procedures and data, with knowledge of only the appropriate symbolic names. This is the concept of dynamic linking.

   Various types of sharing are possible, ranging from no sharing, to obtaining a copy of the original, to live use of the original by all sharers. The last of these cases falls into two subtypes, static sharing (one-at-a-time use of the original) and dynamic sharing (multiple simultaneous use of the original). For present purposes, the possibility of dynamic sharing is highly desirable.

6. To require normally only a single copy of a procedure (e.g., a compiler or a system function) or of data being shared. This is facilitated by the use of *pure* procedure, that is, procedure that is unchanged by execution (although associated data and linkage information may of course change). Note that the system itself is typically the biggest customer of shareable pure procedures. (This goal is also desirable within a network, especially with respect to collaboratively maintained data.)

SEGMENTATION.   Each of these goals is aided considerably by the use of segmentation and segments [60], discussed next. A *segment* is a collection of procedures or a collection of data that has a symbolic name (with possibly various synonyms) and various access rights for each user or process independent of any other segment. If it is a data segment, its length (size) may grow or shrink as needed independently of any other data segment.

Segmentation is then the splitting up of procedures and of data into segments, each of which is an independent entity (apart from the avoidance of naming conflicts). There are three levels of segment addressing. At the lowest level is the per-system physical address space, consisting of actual memory addresses. The next level is a per-process virtual address space, with addresses typically consisting of a segment number meaningful to the system and a word number within the segment; these addresses are thus two dimensional. The third level is a per-system virtual address space, with each segment accessible by its symbolic name(s). At this level segments are organized into directories (see Section 2.2.2.1). At the lowest level, a segment may actually be scattered about dynamically at various physical levels of memory.

Some of the advantages of segmentation are mentioned above. These include the ability to partition virtual memory into distinct entities, each of which may be independently named, created, deleted, accessed, protected, used, grown, and shrunk, freeing users and implementers from many of the problems of physical storage management with a single linear address dimension.

Segmentation itself may exist at various levels, each corresponding to successive partitions of the symbolic virtual memory. In addition to the directory structure (organizing collections of segments), it may be useful to consider subsegments, which may be considered separately in some ways, e.g., individually protected on a logical record basis, or interlocked on such a basis. The reader should take care, however, to distinguish such concepts of virtual memory from partitions of physical memory, such as blocks and pages (see Section 2.2.2.2). Care must also be taken in the hardware–software design if it is desirable to have many small segments, a situation that might otherwise cause very inefficient use of the system.

Implicit in the above functional goals are the various motivational goals discussed in Section 2.1.6, most of which are applicable here. In particular, the most relevant ones are simplicity and convenience of use (via machine independence of the human interface and uniformity of access), efficiency (a goal of the virtual memory implementation), and reliability. Capability is of course essential. The basic design presented here includes a wide range of capability. The design of the Multics storage-management system is described in [5], replacing Section 4 of that reference with [61]. Various other relevant aspects of storage management are treated in [37, 62, 63].

There are four basic aspects of storage management discussed here, the first two oriented toward virtual memory, the last two toward real memory. The *directory structure* reflects a logical organization of all segments in the system, with *access control* enforcing the desired protection. The *multilevel storage management* reflects the physical organization of all segments in the hierarchy of storage devices, with the *backup* and *retrieval system* providing the desired reliability and continued availability of all segments.

2.2.2.1 Directories—Virtual Structure. All segments in the system are organized into a single system-wide tree structure of directories maintaining information about the segments and their usage. These directories are the responsibility of the system. The resulting directory structure serves to compartmentalize segment usage, and greatly facilitates system development and use. In particular, each directory contains entries representing segments and other directories. For each segment there is a *branch* in exactly one directory that contains the desired information, including a pointer to the physical whereabouts of the segment. (Note that a directory is a segment, although its behavior is different from nondirectory segments.) The information associated with each branch includes the following.

1. Segment name(s) and a system-wide unique identifier (implicitly network wide).
2. When created, by whom (what user, what process, or whatever is relevant).
3. When last used, by whom.
4. Current length.
5. Maximum length (e.g., if data).
6. Access control attributes (see below).
7. Physical whereabouts; if on line: pointer to device map; if off line: pointer to retrieval information.
8. When copied onto backup.
9. Special information peculiar to the segment, e.g., advice for multilevel storage management (possibly user supplied) and usage information.
10. User-definable information, such as descriptors of formats, data types, substructure within the segment.

A second kind of entry is functionally redundant but highly convenient, providing a pointer not directly to a segment but rather to a branch pointing to the desired segment. Such an entry is called an *indirect branch* (often called a "link," despite confusion with call linkage). By requiring that each segment be pointed to directly from exactly one branch, the directory structure is always a tree rather than a directed graph (ignoring indirect branches, which serve as shortcuts). This structure eliminates the need for various back pointers and for the duplication of branch information.

As noted above, the use of directories, as in this design, can greatly improve system development and system usability. It permits the organization of all segments into directories along functional lines. As a result, the scope of potential naming conflicts can be kept small since names need be unique only within each directory. Similarly, it simplifies various naming conventions required for system sanity. It provides ease of program development, using various versions of identically named segments residing in different directories, and permits dynamic selection of which version is desired. It facilitates the organization of system libraries on various levels.

The concept of a *distributed monitor* is central to the virtual memory design presented here; i.e., all system data and procedure segments appear in the virtual memory for each process, being used just as if they were user segments (apart from issues involving protection and fault handling). The distributed monitor requires dynamic sharing for a reasonable implementation, and is greatly enhanced by segmentation and by the directory structure. As a result, it is easy to provide each user or each process with a virtual system tailored to its own needs, but possibly looking totally dissimilar from any other virtual system. The directory structure also helps in controlling exactly what environment is being used.

ACCESS CONTROL.   In a multiuser system the need for protection arises in several ways. These involve avoiding both externally inflicted and self-inflicted damage caused either maliciously or accidentally (by users, processes, or even equipment); such use may be under false pretenses (e.g., one user masquerading as another) or may be legitimate. All the resulting eight combinations (by whom, how, under what guise) are meaningful cases.

As mentioned in Section 2.2.1.1, the needs for protection exist at various levels and among various resources. Lampson [24] gives the name *object* to any of those resources needing protection. He defines a *capability* as the name of such a protected object. Typical capabilities might represent segments, minisegments, units of physical allocation (e.g., pages), processes, input–output devices such as typewriters and other terminals, event channels, locking locations (such as the Y in STAC Y), interrupt cells, and *domains*. (A domain is a collection of capabilities.) Lampson provides a general mechanism for protecting objects [24], whereas the Multics ring structure [23, 29] is concerned only with segments and processes.

For purposes of segment access control, various approaches exist. The one given here is inherently both simple and powerful [5]. Five basic attributes exist, called READ, WRITE, APPEND, EXECUTE and TRAP. Consider first the significance of these attributes with respect to a nondirectory segment. The READ attribute implies permission to read the contents of the segment. The WRITE attribute implies permission to alter (write over) the existing contents of the segment, including the ability to truncate the segment to a shorter length (e.g., to zero length). The APPEND attribute implies permission to add to the end of the existing contents (append), but by itself does not imply permission to write over the existing contents. The EXECUTE attribute implies permission to execute the segment as a procedure. Thus these four attributes are independently specifiable, resulting in sixteen possible combinations, or modes. For example, the presence of all attributes (the mode RWAE) implies total permission in the use of the segment (but not necessarily the ability to modify the branch pointing to the segment—see below). The presence of just the READ and APPEND attributes but not the WRITE and EXECUTE attributes (RA) is the capability required for transmitting to and appending to an event-channel mailbox (without being able to modify it), but still being able to read it. The mode A is that required for an append-only postal-like mailbox, which cannot be read by the sender. The mode E is that required for proprietary programs that may be executed but not read (and certainly not modified). (The TRAP attribute is discussed below.)

For a nondirectory segment, the mode governing the use of the segment for a given user (person, process, or other entity) is contained in the branch information associated with the segment. This branch in general may contain a list of users and their associated modes. For efficiency reasons the implementation should permit simply definable and simply specifiable classes of users. There should also be a directory-wide default mode or list of users and modes applicable for all segments in the directory unless otherwise specified by the mode (list) associated with a particular segment.

For purposes of directory access control the mode governing the use of each directory for each user is contained in the branch information associated with the directory segment, as above. Exactly the same attributes are used. The READ attribute on a directory branch (that is, a branch pointing to a directory) governs the ability to obtain a summary of all branches (pointing to segments and directories) in the specified directory. The WRITE attribute governs the ability to modify existing branches in the directory. This is the most powerful attribute, for it implies permission to change branch information, such as the access-control information for any branch in the directory, or in fact to delete a branch from the directory (and thus to cause the contents of the segment associated with that branch to disappear). The APPEND attribute governs the ability to add branches to the directory, but by itself does not permit modification of the existing branches. The EXECUTE attribute on a directory branch governs the ability to search through the given directory at execution time, looking for some particular branch.

Note that all access-control information for a given segment (or directory) is on the branch for that segment, with the exception of information common to all branches in the directory. There is no access-control information on an indirect branch. The access control must be adequately supported by the hardware. In Multics there is a set of potentially different hardware-enforced protection bits for each segment in each ring of each process, evaluated in hardware on each instruction.

The remaining attribute (TRAP) is an escape mechanism to add flexibility to that provided by the four standard attributes discussed above. The TRAP attribute permits user-provided and system-provided special-handling procedures to be interposed in the access-evaluation mechanism. The TRAP attribute causes successive invocation of a sequence of trap procedures following the preliminary evaluation of the desired mode for the given access attempt. The trap procedures may be specified interpretively at run time, although great care must be taken not to violate the security of the system in the implementation of the TRAP mechanism (see [29]). Trap procedures may be used to monitor usage of the segment. They may also be used to impose additional access control, e.g., to enforce a special user-supplied locking mechanism (or to provide an additional layer of protection for particular segments, such as a classified-secret clearance protocol with need-to-know validatation) or to control access on a finer mesh than a per-segment basis, such as with per-word or per-data-element control. At some levels a trap procedure may be invoked to transmit a message concerning the use of a particular segment.

2.2.2.2 Multilevel Storage Management—Physical Structure. In a virtual memory implementation, all manipulation of information in the multilevel hierarchy of storage devices is done by the system. For present purposes it is desirable to refer to a multilevel storage hierarchy in terms of a generalized concept of level, rather than in terms of the traditional primary and secondary memory levels. Six level *collections* are identified, with the first two levels normally invisible to the software. They are ranked roughly according to decreasing access time.

(-1) Microprogram control memory.

(0) Very fast execution buffers (cache memories) and associative memories not normally readable or writeable to the software.

(1) Normal primary memories, readable and writeable with random access, executable unless all execution forced through level (0).

(2) Extended primary memories readable and writeable, block-oriented access often random by block, usually not directly executable. Portions of this memory and of the primary memory may be read-only or once-writeable, especially those portions storing stable parts of the system itself.

(3) Normal on-line secondary storage (e.g., drums and disks), readable and normally writeable, block-oriented access, perhaps sequential by block.

(4) Normal off-line (tertiary) storage (e.g., system-managed backup tapes, disk packs), detachable, usually used via the input–output system (see Section 2.2.3).

These level collections are illustrative rather than specific; there may be more than six recognizable levels, and some levels may have considerable variety. By convention, moving "up" the hierarchy is moving information to a faster (lower-level!) memory, moving "down" to a slower memory level.

The multilevel storage-management problem involves allocation of storage to processes as warranted by the needs of the processes and by the cost-effectiveness arguments of system balance. The latter arguments involve the relative costs of storing and accessing information and of moving it as needed, including the costs attributable to the delays due to moving. It is desired to keep all segments or subsegments at just that level justified by such arguments [62]. The moving of information up and down in the hierarchy resembles the multilevel queueing strategies used for scheduling (Section 2.2.1 and Chapter 4). See also Chapter 3.

It should be noted that some of the multilevel management is typically done in hardware, such as the block transfers to level 0, and the use of associative memories [64, 65]. It is clearly desirable that multilevel mechanisms should be in hardware or microware wherever the duty cycle warrants.

It is also noted that a careful distinction is made throughout this chapter between storage transfer mechanisms (within the memory hierarchy) and input–output mechanisms, which concern communication logically outside the system. (Explicitly, secondary storage transfers are never regarded as input–output in this context.) However, as seen in Section 2.2.3, the storage-management system itself uses (tape) input–output for backup and retrieval, whereas the input–output system in some cases uses segments in the virtual memory as if that memory were a virtual input–output device.

UP THE HIERARCHY.   When a word in a segment is required that resides at a level from which direct use is undesirable or impossible, the word must be transferred up the hierarchy to a suitable level. For most procedure segments and many data segments, such transfers can profitably be done in blocks. The usage of a segment itself may dictate whether it is most economical to move the entire segment or just a piece of it. The cost of displacing the contents of other blocks of fast storage as a result of transferring large units must be balanced against the cost of having many transfers of small units.

In the following discussion, a *block* is a unit of physical storage. A *page* is a unit of data or procedure relevant to physical storage allocation; in fact, it is a unit that may be scattered arbitrarily in memory and whose whereabouts can be found by the system. A *hyperpage* is a unit of transfer of information, involved in moving information up and down in the hierarchy.

To be more specific, a segment may be broken up by the system into a sequence of pages, each of which may reside on an arbitrary memory device, with physical addresses not necessarily contiguously mapped from the virtual addresses. *Dynamic relocation* is the activity of mapping the virtual address space onto the physical address space at execution time. In recent hardware implementations of virtual memories, this relocation involves only primary memory (or, in a sense, execution buffers). Significant hardware mapping aids are likely in the future, involving several levels of memory directly.

Moving information up the hierarchy to faster storage is called *placement;* moving to slower storage is called *replacement*. The unit of placement and replacement, the hyperpage, may be a single page, or a sequence of pages with contiguous virtual addresses within a segment, or in fact an entire segment. The size of this unit may vary from segment to segment, level to level, and time to time. There are also various strategies, such as doing placement only when necessary (popularly called *demand paging*) on a fixed hyperpage size equal to the page size. Placement on demand is reasonably effective for small computations, but unwieldy for very large computations unless enriched by other strategies, such as being able to increase the hyperpage size, to do group placement, and to guarantee certain minimal residence rights. At the other end of the spectrum from placement on demand is *swapping* or the placement all at once of everything that may be needed during execution. In between these extremes lies the *working set* [25, 66] concept, by which replacement and placement of a collection of procedures and data are somehow related to usage. A suitably chosen working set should be able to execute for the period of its relevance without encountering many missing pages. By swapping the working set and doing placement on demand in addition, with appropriate hyperpage sizes, extremely effective storage management can be achieved.

DOWN THE HIERARCHY.   Transfers down the hierarchy are required whenever memory space at one level becomes exhausted (or nearly exhausted). Whereas placement is in some way or another related to demand for use, replacement should be related to the lack of demand for use on the basis of recency and frequency of use. Various least- recently used replacement algorithms are seen to be highly effective [67, 68]. Pure procedure and data that have not been modified may not need to be transferred back down the hierarchy if a usable version already exists at a lower level. The storage space they occupy may be simply reallocated. (Here and in general, care must be taken first to clear any such space, since it is possible to breach system security otherwise.) Cache and associative memory words often have this property [64, 65].

If on-line space at all levels of storage is limited, segments in the virtual memory that have not been recently used may have to be moved to off-line devices. If a segment in some directory is so moved, the directory branch is unaffected except for a flag indicating the segment is not on line, along with the pointers necessary to retrieve the segment when it is next accessed. On subsequent access the system automatically retrieves the segment, although the delay to the user may be significant unless he has planned ahead.

As a result of the off-line overflow of on-line storage, the amount of storage available to a user appears to be unlimited. In fact, there need to be quotas for each user on how much storage can be used at each level (although these quotas may be largely invisible to the user). Generally, a segment is handled in its entirety below the secondary storage level, so that it normally resides all on one medium in off-line storage. (Duplicate copies may be desired for reliability reasons.)

BACKUP STORAGE FOR RELIABILITY.   In addition to the downward transfers to off-line storage necessitated by the lack of on-line space, copies of on-line segments are maintained off-line for reliability reasons in such a way that these segments may be retrieved in the event of user errors or of system malfunction. The backup storage system is responsible for duplicating on-line segments onto reliable off-line storage (say, a magnetic tape, or, for even greater reliability, a pair of tapes in duplicate). The backup storage media must be once-writable and often-readable (reliably), but need not be rewritable. (Thus some cheap optical medium could be highly economical.)

Backup exists in various forms. Ideally, every segment could be copied off-line as it is created on-line. This is of course unrealistic, because of the overhead required and because many of these segments are temporary. One approach is to require users to specify that particular segments should be copied. A user may request explicitly that a segment be copied asynchronously (preferably at some time in the near future), or synchronously (with his process waiting for completion of the copy). Such usage should be exceptional, however, with the normal usage being a virtual backup facility that is invisible to the users. Such a facility involves incremental backup and complete backup.

The activity of continually copying segments eligible for backup is *incremental backup*. Some time T after a segment is created it becomes eligible for backup, unless explicitly made eligible, as above. When the copying is done, the directory branch for the segment is modified to indicate when the copy was made. Records are maintained by the backup facility on the contents of each backup medium. The choice of the time T is based on the need for reliability (small T) and the overhead due to the facility (dictating a larger T). A value of T of about one half an hour is desirable, but may be too costly in terms of overhead.

In the event of loss of a segment through user inadvertence, the user may request retrieval of the segment, knowing only its approximate time of creation. In the event of loss through system malfunction which is discovered by the system, it may be possible to recover without retrieval (*salvaging*) by use of redundancy in the system similar to the use of error-correcting codes. Otherwise the system invokes retrieval. In the event of system collapse from which salvaging cannot recover, retrieval from incremental backup is impractical. For this reason, complete backup is also provided. However, complete backup need not be done all at once, and may be distributed in time according to various functional partitions of the directory hierarchy. For example, system directories may be handled separately from library directories and from user directories. The design of the backup and retrieval facility should be carefully integrated with the strategy for system startup, guaranteeing the integrity of the directory structure irrespective of the version of the system being used. Generally the system should facilitate a hierarchy of recovery capabilities, normally very rapid in regaining the viability of the system, but possibly less rapid in recovering for a particular user.

2.2.3 Input–Output Management

Input–output management is concerned with interfacing user programs and input–output (I–O) devices such as typewriters, unit record equipment (card readers, card punches, line printers), tapes, and diverse other media. In many systems I–O processing involves enormous concern for device-dependent detail on the part of casual users as well as system programmers. In addition, I–O implementations are often strongly embedded in the inner levels of system software. The design sketched here (based on the Multics I–O design [67, 69–71]) is conceptually a virtual I–O system, with various explicit levels of invisibility. Specific knowledge of device characteristics is invisible to the casual user, becoming visible only to those few system programmers and system programs explicitly concerned with specific devices in ways which cannot avoid such knowledge.

A goal of this design is that there be a single basic device-independent set of I–O calls, each call more or less applicable to all devices. There should be sufficient uniformity in the use of this interface that input or output or both may be redirected from one device to another without changing any procedures, whenever this is meaningful. A second goal is that high efficiency must be obtainable despite the desire for machine independence. Where sophisticated mechanisms are optionally available, their cost should be paid only when these mechanisms are invoked, and then only by their immediate users. A third goal is flexibility in being able to add new devices to the system, and being able to add the system to a network.

The central concept in this design is that of a symbolic name (an *ioname*) associated with a sequence of data called a *stream*. One ioname, "user-io," is reserved for the process command input–output. This stream may be split into two streams "user-input" and "user-output" if desired, e.g., if input is to come from a typewriter and output is to go to another typewriter as well as simultaneously to a graphical display. Each stream is interpreted as a sequence of *elements*, each element having some specified number (the element size) of binary digits. The association of an ioname with a particular stream of data (e.g., the data being input from a typewriter, or the data on a particular tape—with or without system-supplied formatting) is an *attachment*. An attachment is made by an *attach* call, and removed by a *detach* call. (These calls are similar in purpose to the traditional "open" and "close" calls, and are a form of dynamic linking.) The attachment process includes verification of access privileges for the device and the medium, possibly involving advanced reservations. Involved in the case of tapes, for example, is permission to use tapes at all, to use a particular drive at a particular time, and to use a particular tape. Permission may even include the ability to use a particular portion of the data on the tape. Attachments may also be made to virtual devices instead of real devices. Use of the data on a stream is then made with *read* and *write* calls, with the appropriate symbolic name specified.

Central to an efficient implementation of such a design is the mechanism for associating symbolic ionames with streams during execution. In Multics this is done in software by an I–O *switch* that catches all calls to the I–O system and forwards them appropriately. Dynamic overhead in making the association occurs on the first use of the symbolic name. Dedicated names such as "user-io" do not incur such overhead. The switch is necessary only where dynamic flexibility is desired. In other cases it need not be present. Hardware design can simplify greatly the effort required by such an implementation.

The I–O switch forwards calls to the appropriate module (a procedure or collection of procedures) on the basis of the device type in the *attach* call. An I–O module may control a device directly, or may be a virtual device that has many properties of a device. One example of a virtual device is the *segment interface module*, which makes all segments in the directory system potentially available via I–O streams. (This is of course not the normal usage.) By this means it is possible to have a virtual segment whose length is greater than the maximum segment length, and which is formed (by the I–O system) as a sequence of segments. (Access control is of course respected.)

Another example of a virtual device is the *virtual printer*. Printing on a line printer is normally asynchronous to the process requesting printing for reasons of efficiency. This is accomplished by an independent virtual printer process that accepts queued requests for printing.

A third example of a virtual device is a *broadcaster*, which in receipt of a single *write* call issues comparable *write* calls to each of various different modules as desired. This is useful after an emergency attachment to broadcast an emergency message to all interactive users (iosilver?).

A fourth example involves a tree-structured decomposition of a stream into various levels of logical structure. A symbolic name may be attached to the data at each level. The mechanism for this logical structure involves a virtual device (the logical record formatter) that interprets *read* and *write* calls, in turn invoking appropriate I–O modules.

The modules controlling physical input–output are themselves substructured. At least three levels of software are identifiable. From the lowest level up, these correspond to control of I–O multiplexing in hardware, of the device-dependent details for a given device (e.g., timing, device codes, control signals), and of the strategies for a given device class (e.g., asynchrony of reading, writing, and buffer usage, and error recovery, e.g., for all typewriter terminals). The organizational structure among the various I–O modules may vary dynamically, being dependent on the attachments in effect at any moment for a given process. The per-process structure is tree structured in many cases (ignoring recursion) with respect to the flow of control, but may legitimately become directed graphs.

2.2.4 Command Management

The command system has one overriding motivational goal: to isolate the user from countless idiosyncrasies of the operating system (including the hardware) in a way that permits easy and safe use of the system. It should provide a wide range of capability, from a highly simplified interface for the casual user to a much more complicated interface for the skilled user, that reflects the full range of hardware and software. It should permit flexibility of program use without having to require repeated reassembly or recompilation. For example, there should be no internal program changes required to run an interactively developed program noninteractively or to reroute input–output. The command system should also provide access to arbitrary system and user procedures as commands, as well as to the (presumably) carefully designed system commands. It should rigorously adhere to a set of command standards, uniform from one command to the next. Examples of such standards include the use of a single character set throughout the system, uniform syntax and argument conventions for all commands, standardized linkage and error handling, standardized strategies for searching through the directory hierarchy (although the actual order of search should be dynamically alterable, possibly even interpretively), coordinated documentation available on and off line, command exiting and completion facilities, naming conventions and the use of various intracommand facilities such as argument nesting, iteration, and macro expansion capabilities. (For specific examples, see [1].) In general, any user procedure can be used as a command, although the system commands all adhere to the standard conventions.

In addition to the uniformity provided by such standards, it is desirable that the command interface present as few restrictions as possible. Examples of such restrictions (to be avoided!) include having different (or awkward) segment formats under differing conditions (e.g., under interactive and noninteractive use), having only lower-case characters, having only short segment names, and having to beware of system-wide naming conflicts.

A basic set of commands is outlined here as an illustration of the range of command capability. This set includes directory-manipulating commands, I–O commands, editing, language-processing, debugging, and various other facilities. There are also command-manipulating commands that permit high-level programs to be written using only other commands.

Directory commands include the ability (as permitted by the access control) to create a branch in a directory, to delete a branch, to create an indirect branch in one directory pointing to a branch in another directory (or in the same directory), to remove an indirect branch, to copy a segment in some directory into some other directory (resulting in one copy of the segment in each of the two directories), to move a segment from one directory to another (resulting in just one copy of the segment), to rename a segment, to add synonyms to the existing name(s) of a segment, to remove such a synonym, to list by symbolic name the segments in a given directory (with various options as to how to format the listing, what branch information to include, and what subset of segments to include), to obtain status about the current use of a segment, to read the access-control information, to change the access-control information, and to change from one working directory to another.

The simplest I–O commands are those involving virtual input–output, e.g., using card readers, card punches, and high-speed printers. These commands typically invoke independent processes and interface with segments in the directory structure.

Input from a typewriter is normally handled by means of an editing command that accepts text as typed and also permits the text to be edited as desired. Editors come in many flavors, involving various degrees of symbolic referencing of text. Requests to editor environments (which may be used interactively and/or noninteractively) include the ability to edit existing segments as well as to create new ones. This involves appending or inserting text at arbitrary places in the text, modifying text by context, by symbolic line number, by light-pen or cursor position on a graphic display, by numerical line number and symbolic contextual position, etc.

Input–output commands also include all the I–O calls modified to include the appropriate calling conventions and command-level error returns. In Multics, all these calls are available through a single command "iocall," whose first argument is the call name. In this way attachments, detachments, and changemode calls may be affected from command level, for example.

A wide range of language commands may be found in general-purpose computing facilities, providing languages and interactive computing environments such as FORTRAN IV, PL/I, ALGOL, COBOL, APL, BASIC, and numerous others. The directory structure permits simple use of such language "processors." As an example, suppose that a segment named "prog.pl" consisting of a PL/I source program is to be compiled. In Multics, the command "pl prog" invokes the PL/I compiler, which produces a collection of segments whose names are derived from the segment name "prog" in a standard way, such as the following:

prog	the object code, to be executed
prog.link	the linkage information necessary for static and dynamic linking of "prog"
prog.symbol	a symbol table useful for symbolic debugging
prog.list	a formatted listing of the source and object code for debugging and documentation purposes
prog.gnosis	an abbreviated history of the actions of the compiler, providing error comments, diagnostics, suggestions for optimized compilation, etc.

Various options on the compiler commands enable just a desired subset of these segments to be produced. These segments follow system-wide standards, and thus should permit programs written in one language to call upon programs written in other languages, and permit a common debugging environment.

Debugging commands also come in many flavors. Useful debugging techniques include virtual maps of relevant storage with unscrambled stacks, list structures, and symbolic segment names; interpretive execution; monitoring of particular virtual resources; tracing of flow; and inserting breakpoints. The design of language processors should be integrated with the design of the debugging environments.

Additional commands include logging onto the system with some identification of the user (e.g., based on a password or a unique and nontamperable console identifier), with provisions for a specifiable default directory with which the user normally desires to be associated, and for a specifiable default charge authorization; logging off the system; requesting a change of password or of resource allocations and quotas; negotiating for advance reservations or special handling; sending messages to other users; observing the status of other users or other processes, whether independent or cooperating, whether interactive or noninteractive; requesting retrieval from backup storage; commands for using other systems in the same network (see Section 2.3). (It is highly desirable that the network commands mask highly system-dependent concepts of other systems in the network.)

Command-manipulating commands, or *macrocommands*, permit a sequence of commands and their arguments to be treated as a single command and saved. The sequence is given a segment name, which acts as the name of a new command. Various forms of execution-time modification may be permitted at command level by means of arguments to the macrocommand. Thus arguments to the individual commands that form the macrocommand can be assigned dynamically at command time, or even interpretively at the time of execution of each constituent command.

In an interactive environment it is essential to be able in a controlled way to terminate executing processes, just as this is desirable for certain noninteractive processes. This is normally accomplished by some sort of signaling mechanism, triggered in the interactive case typically by an interrupt signal ("quit") generated from the user's console. Following a quit signal, a user has several options at his disposal. The user may continue the process as if it had not been interrupted. He may also do this after doing something else, e.g., interrogating partial results, modifying a data base, or even saving the entire process. (This may or may not require the creation of a new process in order not to disturb the interrupted process.) Various strategies also exist when a family of processes is associated with a given terminal.

2.3 NETWORK DESIGN FUNDAMENTALS

Given a collection of multiprocessor systems, there are several reasons for wanting to interface them into a network. The basic motivation is to expand the scope of each of the component systems, providing the combined user communities with capabilities and economies otherwise not attainable. Some of the component systems may also be able to offer special-purpose services not otherwise justified.

2.3.1 Network Functions

Network functions fall into three broad overlapping classes: program sharing, data sharing, and load sharing. Message store-and-forward is a form of data sharing. Remote interrogation of another system combines elements of program sharing and data sharing. In general, a network may permit a combination of local and remote execution of local and remote programs, with local and remote data, and with locally and remotely available results. (Suitable transmission facilities discussed elsewhere in this book are assumed to be available as needed for the purposes of this chapter.) Since execution, procedures, and data may all be split up among different systems, there is a wide variety of possible network capabilities. Most combinations are meaningful. For example,

1. Remote execution of local procedures and data, with results returned (e.g., load sharing).
2. Remote execution of remote procedures and data, with results returned (e.g., interrogation, program and data sharing).
3. Local execution of remote procedures together with local procedures, with no results transmitted (e.g., program sharing).
4. Transmission (or retransmission) of data (e.g., message service).

In view of this wide assortment of possible categories of network usage, it is desirable here to concentrate on the most environment-independent system commands not included in the intrasystem functions. A greatly oversimplified minimal set consists of a *transmit* request and a *receive* request. The *transmit* request may convey procedures, data, and signals, specifying the source and destination (possibly by default) of each. It may also convey a sequence of commands that are executed sometime after receipt. The *receive* request is similar. If a transmitted command sequence may itself contain *transmit* requests (e.g., to return results to the original requestor or to another destination) and *receive* requests (e.g., to receive more requests as needed), a wide range of capability can be obtained from such nesting of network requests within a single *transmit* request.

Considerable flexibility can be built into the *transmit* and *receive* requests if the systems are readily compatible. It should be possible, for example, to check progress of network requests asynchronously (via signals or status calls). It should also be possible to have results sent back conditionally, depending upon progress. Thus the requests should contain run-time evaluation of parameters and conditional capabilities based on these parameters.

The ways in which such a network can be used effectively depend largely on the coupling of the systems in the network and the transmission facilities (as well as on the capabilities of the individual systems). Heavy interactive use of the network is unlikely unless the coupling is strong and unless the transmission facilities do not require frequent dynamic switching, with switching times long by comparison with the requested transmissions (see Chapters 5 and 6). Heavy interactive use may or may not be desirable at all (see Chapter 9). However, with only teletype-speed communication, dedicated lines (possibly multiplexed for economy) make it relatively easy to use an I–O system structured along the lines of Section 2.2.3 for network communication. Each other system in the network can easily be made to appear as a typewriter-like I–O device, especially in the symmetric case of identical systems.

The problems in the use of a network of systems are very closely related to the problems of using a multiprocessor system, but are sometimes greatly increased in scale. The problems in providing flexible and reliable transmission facilities for the network communication are quite different from most intersystem communication problems. Other problems are conceptually familiar, including multiresource allocation and scheduling, accounting, event signaling, and locking strategies in the virtual process area; intersystem file linkage and protection in the virtual memory area; and synchronization and buffering in the I–O area. Under the best conditions these problems at the network level can be handled with virtual mechanisms, producing a clean virtual network interface.

Valuable references in addition to the other chapters of this book are [9], pp. 470–476 and 504–512, and [72–79].

2.4   CONCLUSIONS

In summary, the main intent of this chapter is to present fundamental concepts common to individual computer systems and to networks of such systems, more or less independent of the levels at which they appear. A basic tenet of this chapter is that the extensive and careful structuring of both systems and networks can be of enormous benefit.* Such structuring aids

---

*An example of the utility of this tenet is found in [80], with respect to a system's ability to tolerate faults. Other relevant references are [81], [83].

greatly (for both hardware and software) in all of the stages of development mentioned at the beginning of Section 2.1.2, as well as in the use and continued evolution of the systems and their networks.

REFERENCES

The following sources provide fruitful (although occasionally seedy) material for further study. Many additional references may be obtained from the sources cited below, in particular from references [8]–[19].

[1] The Multiplexed Information and Computing Service: Programmers' Manual, MIT Project MAC, Cambridge, Mass., 1973. (Periodically updated.)

[2] F. J. CORBATÓ and V. A. VYSSOTSKY, Introduction and Overview of the Multics System, Fall Joint Computer Conf., *AFIPS Conf. Proc.* (1965), 203–212.

[3] E. L. GLASER, J. F. COULEUR, and G. A. OLIVER, System Design of a Computer Conf., Fall Joint Computer Conference, *AFIPS Conf. Proc.* (1965), 197–202.

[4] V. A. VYSSOTSKY, F. J. CORBATÓ, and R. M. GRAHAM, Structure of the Multics Supervisor, Fall Joint Computer Conf., *AFIPS Conf. Proc.* (1965), 203–212.

[5] R. C. DALEY and P. G. NEUMANN, A General-Purpose File System for Secondary Storage, Fall Joint Computer Conf., *AFIPS Conf. Proc.* (1965), 213–229.

[6] J. F. OSSANNA, L. E. MIKUS, and S. D. DUNTEN, Communications and Input/Output Switching in a Multiplex Computing System, Fall Joint Computer Conf., *AFIPS Conf. Proc.* (1965), 231–241.

[7] E. I. ORGANICK, *A Guide to Multics for Subsystem Writers*, MIT Press, Cambridge, Mass., 1972.

[8] S. ROSEN, Electronic Computers: a Historical Survey, *Computing Surv.*, 1 (March 1969), 7–36.

[9] C. G. BELL and A. NEWELL, *Computer Structures: Readings and Examples*, McGraw-Hill, New York, 1971.

[10] H. HELLERMAN, *Digital Computer System Principles*, McGraw-Hill, New York, 1967.

[11] R. ROSIN, Supervisory and Monitor Systems, *Computing Surv.*, 1 (March 1969), 37–54.

[12] S. ROSEN, *Programming Systems and Languages*, McGraw-Hill, New York, 1967.

[13] M. V. WILKES, *Time-Sharing Computer Systems*, American Elsevier, New York, 1968.

[14] R. W. WATSON, *Timesharing System Design Concepts*, McGraw-Hill, New York, 1970.

[15] The COMTRE Corporation, *Analysis of Major Computing Operating Systems*, Coral Gables, Fla., Aug. 1970. (AD 715 919.)

[16] COSINE Committee, *An Undergraduate Course Description on Operating Systems Principles*, Commission on Education, National Academy of Engineering, Washington, D.C., June 1971. Appears in *IEEE Computer*, 5 (Jan./Feb. 1972), 40–59.

[17] H. KATZAN, JR., Operating Systems Architecture, Spring Joint Computer Conf., *AFIPS Conf. Proc.* (1970), 109–181.

[18] L. C. HOBBS, D. J. THEIS, J. TRIMBLE, H. TITUS, and I. HIGHBERG, *Parallel Processor Systems, Technologies and Applications*, Spartan Books, New York, 1970.

[19] M. V. WILKES, The Growth of Interest in Microprogramming, A Literature Survey, *Computing Surv.*, 1 (Sept. 1969), 139–145.

[20] C. V. RAMAMOORTHY and M. TSUCHIYA, A Study of User Microprogrammable Computers, Spring Joint Computer Conf., *AFIPS Conf. Proc.* (1970), 165–181.

[21] H. A. SIMON, The Architecture of Complexity, *Proc. Am. Phil. Soc.*, **106** (December 1962), 467–82.

[22] E. W. DIJKSTRA, The Structure of the "THE"-Multiprogramming System, *Commun. Assoc. Computing Machinery*, **11** (May 1968), 341–346.

[23] R. M. GRAHAM, Protection in an Information Processing Utility, *Commun. Assoc. Computing Machinery*, **11** (May 1968), 365–369.

[24] B. W. LAMPSON, Dynamic Protection Structures, Fall Joint Computer Conf., *AFIPS Conf. Proc.* (1969), 27–38.

[25] P. J. DENNING, The Working-Set Model for Program Behavior, *Commun. Assoc. Computing Machinery*, **11** (May 1968), 323–333.

[26] Computer Operations, Inc., *A Technical Review of the Gemini Computer System*, Costa Mesa, Calif., Aug. 1970.

[27] T. KILBURN, D. B. G. EDWARDS, M. J. LANIGAN, and F. H. SUMNER, One-Level Storage System, *IRE Trans.*, **EC-11** (April 1962), 233–235. See also Chap. 23 of Ref. 9.

[28] S. MOTOBAYASHI, T. MASADA, and N. TAKAHASHI, The HITAC 5020 Time-Sharing System, *Proc. ACM 24th Natl. Conf.* (Aug. 1969), 419–429.

[29] M. D. SCHROEDER and J. H. SALTZER, A Hardware Architecture for Implementing Protection Rings, *Commun. Assoc. Computing Machinery*, **15** (Mar. 1972), 157–170. Also in ACM Third Symp. Operating Syst. Principles, Palo Alto, Calif. (Oct. 18–20, 1971), 42–54.

[30] Oral communication. References seem legendary.

[31] P. HARTMAN and D. OWENS, How to Write Software Specifications, Fall Joint Computer Conf., *AFIPS Conf. Proc.* (1967), 779–790. See also Spring Joint Computer Conf., *AFIPS Conf. Proc.* 1969 papers by F. M. Trapnell and by R. M. Kay.

[32] G. H. MEALY, The System Design Cycle, ACM Second Symp. Operating Syst. Principles, Princeton, N.J. (Oct. 20–23, 1969), 1–7.

[33] R. M. NEEDHAM and D. E. HARTLEY, Theory and Practice in Operating System Design, ACM Second Symp. Operating Syst. Principles, Princeton, N.J. (Oct. 20–23, 1969), 8–12.

[34] P. G. NEUMANN, The Role of Motherhood in the Pop Art of System Programming, ACM Second Symp. Operating Syst. Principles, Princeton, N.J. (Oct. 20–23, 1969), 13–18.

[35] P. NAUR and B. RANDELL, eds., *Software Engineering*, report on a conference sponsored by the NATO Science Committee, Garmisch, West Germany, Oct. 1968, issued Jan. 1969.

[36] J. N. BUXTON and B. RANDELL, eds., *Software Engineering Techniques*, report on a conference sponsored by the NATO Science Committee, Rome, Italy, Oct. 1969, issued April 1970.

[37] R. C. DALEY and J. B. DENNIS, Virtual Memory Processes and Sharing in Multics, *Commun. Assoc. Computing Machinery*, **11** (May 1968), 306–312.

[38] F. J. CORBATÓ, PL/I as a Tool for System Programming, *Datamation*, **15** (May 1969), 68–76.

[39] R. M. GRAHAM, Use of High-Level Languages for System Programming, *MIT Project MAC Tech. Mem. 13*, Cambridge, Mass., Sept. 1970.

[40] R. A. FREIBURGHOUSE, The Multics PL/I Compiler, Fall Joint Computer Conf., *AFIPS Conf. Proc.* (1969), 187–199.

[41] R. RICE et al., The New Technology: Computer Architecture, a session of four papers on the Symbol system, Spring Joint Computer Conf., *AFIPS Conf. Proc.* (1971), 563–616.

[42] S. C. DARDEN and S. B. HELLER, Streamline Your Software Development, *Computer Decisions* (Oct. 1970), 29–33.

[43] H. SACKMAN, W. J. ERIKSON, and E. E. GRANT, Exploratory Studies Comparing On-Line and Off-Line Programming Performance, *Commun. Assoc. Computing Machinery* (Jan. 1968), 3–11.

[44] D. FERRARI and V. HOFFMEISTER, *Bibliography on Computer Performance Evaluation*, Computer Systems Research Project, Department of Electrical Engineering and Computer Sciences, University of California, Berkeley, March 1971.

[45] J. H. SALTZER and J. W. GINTELL, The Instrumentation of Multics, *Commun. Assoc. Computing Machinery*, **13** (Aug. 1970), 495–500. Also in ACM Second Symp. Operating Syst. Principles, Princeton, N.J. (Oct. 20–22, 1969), 167–174, in slightly different form.

[46] B. ARDEN and D. BOETTNER, Measurement and Performance of a Multiprogramming System, ACM Second Symp. Operating Syst. Principles, Princeton, N.J. (Oct. 20–22, 1969), 130–146.

[47] A. D. KARUSH, Two Approaches for Measuring the Performance of Time-Sharing Systems, ACM Second Symp. Operating Syst. Principles, Princeton, N.J. (Oct. 20–22, 1969), 159–166.

[48] C. C. GOTLIEB and G. H. MACEWEN, System Evaluation tools, in [36], 93–99.

[49] M. J. SPIER and E. I. ORGANICK, The Multics Interprocess Communication Facility, ACM Second Symp. Operating Syst. Principles, Princeton, N.J. (Oct. 20–22, 1969), 83–91.

[50] E. W. DIJKSTRA, Solution of a Problem in Concurrent Programming Control, *Commun. Assoc. Computing Machinery*, **12** (Sept. 1965), 569.

[51] J. B. DENNIS and E. C. VAN HORN, Programming Semantics for Multiprogrammed Computations, *Commun. Assoc. Computing Machinery*, **9** (March 1966), 143–155.

[52] P. B. HANSEN, The Nucleus of a Multiprogramming System, *Commun. Assoc. Computing Machinery*, **13** (April 1970), 238–241, 250.

[53] S. S. PATIL, Limitations and capabilities of Dijkstra's semaphore primitives for coordination among processes, MIT Project MAC Computation Structures Group Memo 57, Cambridge, Mass., Feb. 1971. See also 1972 Carnegie-Mellon memos by D. L. Parnas by A. N. Habermann.

[54] D. E. KNUTH, Additional Comments on a Problem in Concurrent Programming Control, *Commun. Assoc. Computing Machinery*, **9** (May 1966), 321–322.

[55] A. N. HABERMANN, Prevention of System Deadlocks, *Commun. Assoc. Computing Machinery*, **12** (July 1969), 373–385.

[56] E. G. COFFMAN, M. J. ELPHICK, and A. SHOSHANI, System Deadlocks, *Computing Surv.* 3(2) (1971), 67–78.

[57] B. W. LAMPSON, A Scheduling Philosophy for Multiprocessing Systems, *Commun. Assoc. Computing Machinery*, **11** (May 1968), 347–360.

[58] H. HELLERMAN, Time-Sharing Scheduling Strategies, *IBM Syst. J.*, **8** (1969), 94–117.

[59] P. J. DENNING, Thrashing: Its Causes and Prevention, Fall Joint Computer Conf., *AFIPS Conf. Proc.* (1968), 915–922.

[60] J. B. DENNIS, Segmentation and the Design of Multiprogrammed Computer Systems, *J. Assoc. Computing Machinery*, **12** (Oct. 1965), 589–602.

[61] A. BENSOUSSAN, C. T. CLINGEN, and R. C. DALEY, The Multics Virtual Memory, *Commun. Assoc. Computing Machinery*, **15** (May 1972), 308–318. Also in ACM Second Symp. Operating Syst. Principles, Princeton, N.J. (Oct. 20–22, 1969), 30–42.

[62] P. J. DENNING, Virtual Memory, *Computing Surv.*, **2** (Sept. 1970), 153–189.

[63] S. E. MADNICK and J. W. ALSOP II, A Modular Approach to File System Design, Spring Joint Computer Conf., *AFIPS Conf. Proc.* (1969), 1–13.

[64] J. S. LIPTAY, Structural Aspects of the System/360 Model 85: II. The Cache, *IBM Syst. J.*, **7**(1) (1968), 15–21.

[65] M. D. SCHROEDER, Performance of the GE-645 Associative Memory While Multics Is in Operation, ACM Symp. Performance Evaluation, Harvard University, April 1971.

[66] P. J. DENNING and S. C. SCHWARTZ, Properties of the Working Set Model, ACM Third Symp. Operating Syst. Principles, Palo Alto, Calif. (Oct. 18–20, 1971), 130–140.

[67] F. J. CORBATÓ, A Paging Experiment with the Multics System, *Festschrift in Honor of P. M. Morse*, MIT Press, Cambridge, Mass. (1969), 217–228.

[68] R. L. MATTSON, J. GECSEI, D. R. SLUTZ, and I. L. TRAIGER, Evaluation Techniques for Storage Hierarchies, *IBM Syst. J.*, **9**(2) (1970), 78–117.

[69] R. J. Feiertag and E. I. Organick, The Multics Input/Output System, ACM Third Symp. Operating Syst. Principles, Palo Alto, Calif. (Oct. 18–20, 1971), 35–41.

[70] J. H. Saltzer and J. F. Ossanna, Remote Terminal Character Stream Processing in Multics, Spring Joint Computer Conf., *AFIPS Conf. Proc.* (1970), 621–627.

[71] J. F. Ossanna and J. H. Saltzer, Technical and Human Engineering Problems in Connecting Terminals to a Time-Sharing System, Fall Joint Computer Conf., *AFIPS Conf. Proc.* (1970), 355–362.

[72] L. G. Roberts, Multiple Computer Networks and Intercomputer Communication, ACM Symp. Operating Syst. Principles, Gatlinburg, Tenn. (Oct. 1–4, 1967).

[73] J. B. Dennis, A Position Paper on Computing and Communications, *Commun. Assoc. Computing Machinery*, 11 (May 1968), 370–377.

[74] C. G. Bell, A. N. Habermann, J. McCredie, R. Rutledge, and W. Wulf, Computer Networks, *Computer* (Sept./Oct. 1970), 14–32.

[75] T. H. Bonn, A Standard for Computer Networks, *Computer* (May/June 1971), 10–14.

[76] L. G. Roberts et al., Resource Sharing Computer Networks, five papers in the Spring Joint Computer Conf., *AFIPS Conf. Proc.* (1970), 543–597 (references may be found in Chap. 13). See also a session in the 1972 Spring Joint Conf.

[77] R. M. Rutledge, A. L. Vareha, L. C. Varian, et al., An Interactive Network of Time-Sharing Computers, *Proc. ACM* 24th *Natl. Conf.* (Aug. 1969), 431–441.

[78] D. W. Davies, K. A. Bartlett, R. A. Scantlebury, and P. T. Wilkinson, A Digital Communication Network for Computers Giving Rapid Response at Remote Terminals, ACM Symp. Operating Syst. Principles, Gatlinburg, Tenn. (Oct. 1–4, 1967).

[79] D. C. Walden, "A System for Interprocess Communication in a Resource Sharing Computer Network," *Commun. Assoc. Computing Machinery*, 15 (4) (Apr. 1972), 221–230.

[80] P. G. Neumann, "A Hierarchical Framework for Fault-Tolerant Computing Systems, "*Digest of the IEEE COMPCON '72* (Sept. 1972), 337–340.

[81] F. J. Corbató, C. T. Clingen, and J. H. Saltzer, "Multics—the First Seven Years," Spring Joint Computer Conference, *AFIPS Conf. Proc.* (1972), 571–583.

[82] B. Elspas, K. N. Levitt, R. J. Waldinger, and A. Waksman, "An Assessment of Techniques for Proving Correctness," *Computing Surveys*, Vol. 4, No. 2 (June 1972), 97–147.

[83] C. R. Spooner, A Software Architecture for the 70's: Part I—The General Approach, *Software Practice and Experience*, 1 (1971), 5–37.

3

Optimal File Allocation in a Computer Network

WESLEY W. CHU

Computer Science Department
University of California, Los Angeles

INTRODUCTION

In the automation of large information systems, a major portion of the planning is concerned with storing large quantities of information in a computer system. This requires study of information storage, modification, and transmission. Examples of such efforts are found in business, medical, library, and management-information systems. These systems, which may consist of several geographically separated divisions (subsystems), need to process information files in common.

It is apparent that when a given information file is required in common by several computers, it may be stored in at least one of them and accessed by the others via communication links when needed. This shared usage of files via interconnected computers permits many users to economically share data bases and computer software systems. These shared computing facilities can greatly increase our information processing capabilities. Furthermore, the noncoincident busy periods of each computer may allow lower system costs through load sharing. The overall operating cost related to the files is considered to consist of transmission and storage costs. The problem is: Given a number of computers that process common information files, how can we allocate files so that the allocation yields minimum overall operating costs subject to the following constraints: (1) the expected time to access each file is less than a given bound, (2) the amount of storage needed at each computer does not exceed the available storage capacity, and (3) the availability (the portion of the time the system is operating) of each file is greater than a given level.

The above-stated problem with the first two constraints has been treated by this author previously [1]. In this chapter we have also considered the file availability requirement, which is an additional important constraint to the file allocation problem. The main body of this chapter, however, is based on [1].

The file allocation problem can be formulated into a nonlinear integer zero–one programming problem, which may be reduced to a linear zero–one programming problem. A simple example is given to illustrate the model.

3.1 FILE ALLOCATION MODEL

The file allocation problem can be formulated as an integer (0 or 1) programming model.

Let X_{ij} indicate that the jth file is stored in the ith computer:

$$X_{ij} = \begin{cases} 1 & j\text{th file stored in the } i\text{th computer} \\ 0 & \text{otherwise} \end{cases} \tag{3.1}$$

where $i = 1, 2, \ldots, n$
$\quad j = 1, 2, \ldots, m$
$\quad n =$ total number of computers in the computer network
$\quad m =$ total number of distinct files in the computer network

The availability of the jth file, A_j, describes the portion of the time that the system is in operation so that the jth file is available to users. It should be noted that the availability is independent of any queuing delay which may be experienced by the file. For example, $A_j = 0.9985$ means that within a 10,000-hour(h) period, the jth file is available (operating) for 9985 h and unavailable (system down) for 15 h. Clearly, the availability of the file is dependent upon the reliability of the computers, the reliability of the communication channels, average repair time, network-routing algorithm, and the number of redundant copies of the file stored in the interconnected computer network. Thus, given the required availability of a file and the reliability of the system (computer and communication channel), the availability constraint can be satisfied by selecting the required number of redundant copies of the file. For example, if the computers within the network are allowed only to communicate with their immediate neighboring computers, and all the equipment in the system is assumed to have exponential failure distributions, and furthermore if all the computers within the system have identical availability,* a_p, and all the channels have identical availability, a_c, then the availability of the jth file for storing r_j redundant copies in the system is

$$A_j = a_p[1 - (1 - a_c a_p)^{r_j}] \tag{3.2}$$

For example, if $a_p = 0.98$ and $a_c = 0.99$, then $A_j = 0.956$ for $r_j = 1$ and $A_j = 0.979$ for $r_j = 2$. Equation (3.2) states that the availability of the jth file is equal to the product of the availability of the requesting computer, a_p, and the availability of the r_j copies of the jth file, $1 - (1 - a_c a_p)^{r_j}$.

For storing r_j redundant copies of the jth file in the information system, we have

$$\sum_i X_{ij} = r_j \qquad \text{for} \qquad 1 \leq j \leq m \tag{3.3}$$

To assure that the storage capacity of each computer is not exceeded, we have

$$\sum_j X_{ij} L_j \leq b_i \qquad \text{for} \qquad 1 \leq i \leq n \tag{3.4}$$

where L_j = length of the jth file
b_i = available memory size of the ith computer

The expected time for the ith computer to retrieve the jth file from the kth computer (from initiation of request until start of reception) is denoted as a_{ijk}. The maximum allowable retrieval time of the jth file to the ith computer is T_{ij}. We required that a_{ijk} be less than T_{ij}; i.e.,

$$(1 - X_{ij})X_{kj}a_{ijk} \leq T_{ij} \qquad \text{for} \qquad i \neq k, 1 \leq j \leq m \tag{3.5}$$

When $r_j = 1$ for all j, then, from (3.3), we know that $X_{ij}X_{kj} = 0$ for $i \neq k$. Thus (3.5) reduces to

$$X_{kj}a_{ijk} \leq T_{ij} \qquad \text{for} \qquad i \neq k, 1 \leq j \leq m \tag{3.6}$$

Now, a_{ijk} is equal to the sum of the expected queuing delay at the ith computer for the channel to the kth computer,† $w_{ik}^{(1)}$; the expected queuing delay at the kth computer for the channel to the ith computer, $w_{ki}^{(2)}$; and the ex-

---

*The availability a_p or a_c is equal to the ratio of mean time between failures to mean repair time plus mean time between failures of the equipment in question [2]. The availability function for other types of network-routing algorithms and/or other types of equipment-failure distributions will be more complex than (3.2). For recent work on availability, the reader should consult [3].

†The number in the superscripts of $w_{ik}^{(\cdot)}$ and $w_{ki}^{(\cdot)}$ denotes the priority class of the messages transmitted between the ith and kth computers, which will be discussed shortly.

pected computer excess time to the jth file, t_{kj}. In most cases, the quantity t_{kj} is much smaller than $w_{ik} = w_{ik}^{(1)} + w_{ki}^{(2)}$ and can be nelgected. Hence

$$a_{ijk} \doteq w_{ik} \qquad (3.7)$$

Next we shall discuss the mechanism involved in the queuing delay. Each pair of computers is assumed to be able to transmit information in both directions simultaneously. This is known as full-duplex operation. Furthermore, the files can be accessed by the local and remote computers at the same time. One pair of transmission paths links each pair of computers; one of these paths carries *requests* for the files from the ith computer to the kth computer, and *reply* messages (files) from the ith computer to the kth computer, whereas the other path carries *requests* for files from the kth computer to the ith computer, and *reply* messages from kth to the ith computer (Fig. 3.1). In most cases, the request message is much shorter than the reply

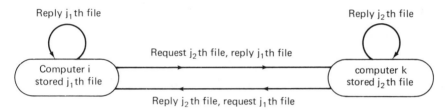

FIGURE 3.1   Transmission paths between each pair of computers.

message. Therefore, we shall assign a higher priority to request messages than to reply messages. Messages of the same priority are served in the order of their arrival. Assume, for example, that a reply message is being transmitted on a particular transmission path at the time a new request is initiated. The request will interrupt the current reply and the computer will transmit the request first. After finishing transmission of that new request, the computer resumes transmitting the previous reply. Such preemptive-resume priority servicing facilitates optimization, since the queuing delay will be minimum if the shortest messages are serviced first [4, 5]. Recalling that the requested message length is much shorter than that of the reply message, the delay due to the request message can be neglected.* Under these conditions, the queuing system can be viewed as a single-server queue with constant service time.

In many cases it is reasonable to model the file accessing process as a Poisson process. Then the rate of requests from the ith computer to the kth

---

*Preemptive priority servicing permits the assumption that $w_{ki} \doteq w_{ki}^{(2)}$. Note that the file-retrieval-time constraint as shown in (3.5) also applies to the nonpreemptive priority case, but a more complex expression would be required for w_{ik}, since $w_{ik}^{(1)}$ can no longer be neglected.

computer (arrival rate), λ_{ik}, is the sum of the requesting rates for those files not stored in the ith computer but stored in the kth computer. The requested file length may be less than the entire storage file length and is defined as the length of each transaction; that is, the length of each transaction of the jth file, l_j, should be less than or equal to the entire jth file length, L_j. The average time required to transmit the reply from the kth computer to the ith computer, $1/\mu_{ik}$ (i.e., service time) is dependent on l_j and λ_{ik}. Clearly, both λ_{ik} and $1/\mu_{ik}$ depend on the file allocation, yet the allocation is unknown in advance. Hence we shall express λ_{ik} and $1/\mu_{ik}$ in terms of the X_{ij}'s:

$$\lambda_{ik} = \sum_j u_{ij}(1 - X_{ij})X_{kj} \qquad (3.8)$$

where u_{ij} is the request rate* of the entire or part of the jth file at the ith computer per unit time.

For example, if the usage rates of the five information files at computer 1 are $u_{11} = 5$ times/s, $u_{12} = u_{14} = 0$, $u_{13} = 3$ times/s, and $u_{15} = 1$ time/s, then the sum of the requesting rates of transaction for those files not stored in computer 1 but stored in computer 3 is

$$\lambda_{13} = 5(1 - x_{11})x_{31} + 3(1 - x_{13})x_{33} + 1(1 - x_{15})x_{35}$$

The average time required to transmit a reply message from the kth to the ith computer via a line with transmission rate, R, is

$$\frac{1}{\mu_{ik}} = \frac{1}{\lambda_{ik}} \sum_j \frac{1}{\mu_j} u_{ij}(1 - X_{ij})X_{kj} \qquad (3.9)$$

where $1/\mu_j = l_j/R = $ required time to transmit the transaction of the jth file.

Equation (3.9) states that $1/\mu_{ik}$ is equal to the time required for the kth computer to reply with all the messages requested from the ith computer divided by the total number of requests initiated from the ith computer to the kth computer. Since the l_j's and R are constants, μ_j and μ_{ik} are also constants.

The traffic intensity from the kth to the ith computer, ρ_{ik}, measures the degree of congestion of the line that provides the transmission path between the kth and ith computer, or the fraction of time that the line is busy. It is defined as

$$\rho_{ik} = \frac{\lambda_{ik}}{\mu_{ik}} = \sum_j \frac{1}{\mu_j} u_{ij}(1 - X_{ij})X_{kj} \qquad (3.10)$$

Since physically it is impossible for the transmission line to be 100 per cent busy, the traffic intensity is less than 1; that is, $\rho_{ik} < 1$.

---

*In general, the request rate may be time dependent. In the analysis here we are concerned with the request rate of the busy period.

When only a single copy of the file is stored in the information system, then $X_{ij}X_{kj} = 0$ for $i \neq k$; hence

$$\lambda_{ik} = \sum_j u_{ij}X_{kj} \qquad \text{for } i \neq k \tag{3.11}$$

and

$$\frac{1}{\mu_{ik}} = \frac{1}{\lambda_{ik}} \sum_j u_{ij}\frac{1}{\mu_j}X_{kj} \qquad \text{for } i \neq k \tag{3.12}$$

when all the $\mu_j = \mu$; then (3.12) reduces to

$$\frac{1}{\mu_{ik}} = \frac{1}{\mu} \tag{3.13}$$

The average waiting time [4, 5] from the initiation of a request at the ith computer to the receipt of the requested message from the kth computer, with the above assumptions (single-server queue with Poisson arrivals and constant service time), is

$$w_{ik} \doteq w_{ki}^{(2)} = \frac{1}{\mu_{ik}} \frac{\rho_{ik}}{2(1 - \rho_{ik})} \qquad \text{for } i \neq k \tag{3.14}$$

where $1/\mu_{ik}$ and ρ_{ik} are functions of X_{ij}'s as given by (3.9) and (3.10). The variance and probability distribution of w_{ik} of a specific allocation can be computed from its ρ_{ik} and μ_{ik} [4, 5].

Substituting (3.14) into (3.7) and (3.5), we have

$$(1 - X_{ij})X_{kj}\frac{1}{\mu_{ik}} \frac{\rho_{ik}}{2(1 - \rho_{ik})} \leq T_{ij}$$

which can be rearranged into the form

$$(1 - X_{ij})X_{kj}\lambda_{ik} - 2\mu_{ik}(\mu_{ik} - \lambda_{ik})T_{ij} \leq 0 \tag{3.15}$$

For the special case that $\mu_{ik}(X) = \mu$, and $r_j = 1$, then (3.15) reduces to

$$\sum_{\substack{j_1 \\ j \neq j_1}} u_{ij}X_{kj_1}X_{kj} + 2T_{ij}\mu \sum_{j_1} u_{ij_1}X_{kj_1} + u_{ij}X_{kj} - 2\mu^2 T_{ij} \leq 0 \tag{3.16}$$

Finally, we shall express the operating cost (objective function) in terms of the allocation (X_{ij}'s). Suppose that we know the storage cost of the jth file per unit length and unit time at the ith computer, C_{ij}; the transmission cost from the kth computer to the ith computer per unit time, C'_{ik}; the request rate for the entire or part of the jth file at the ith computer per unit time, u_{ij}; the frequency of modification of the jth file at the ith computer after each transaction, P_{ij}; the length of each transaction for the jth file, l_j; and the number of redundant copies of the jth file stored in the system, r_j. Then the overall operating cost per unit time, C, for processing m distinct files required in common by n computers is

$$C = C_{\text{storage}} + C_{\text{transmission}}$$

where

$$C_{\text{storage}} = \sum_{i,j} C_{ij} L_j X_{ij}$$

$$C_{\text{transmission}} = \sum_{i,j,k} \frac{1}{r_j} C'_{ik} l_j u_{ij} X_{kj} (1 - X_{ij}) + \sum_{i,j,k} C'_{ik} l_j u_{ij} X_{kj} P_{ij}$$

The storage cost, C_{storage}, can be computed from the total storage space required for storing all the files among the n computers. Since the storage allocation is unknown in advance, the storage cost is expressed in terms of the allocation function. The transmission cost, $C_{\text{transmission}}$, consists of two terms; the first term is the transmission cost due to file transactions, and the second term is the transmission cost due to file updating. The cost can be rearranged into the form

$$C = \sum_{i,j} D_{ij} X_{ij} - \sum_{i,j,k} E_{ijk} X_{kj} X_{ij} \qquad \text{where } D_{ij} > 0, \ E_{ijk} > 0 \quad (3.17)$$

When $r_j = 1$, $1 \leq j \leq m$, then $X_{kj} X_{ij} = 0$ for $k \neq i$, and $C'_{ii} = 0$. Under this case, (3.17) reduces to

$$C = \sum_{i,j} D_{ij} X_{ij} \qquad (3.18)$$

We want to minimize (3.17) subject to storage and access time requirements constraints given in (3.1), (3.2), (3.3), (3.4), and (3.5). As X_{ij}'s take on the value zero or one, the allocation problem becomes one of solving a nonlinear zero–one programming problem. A technique to reduce the nonlinear zero–one equations to the linear zero–one equations is given in the Appendix. With this technique, the allocation problem can then be solved by standard linear zero–one programming techniques [6, 7].

3.2 FILE ALLOCATION IN A MULTIPROCESSOR

Let us consider a multiprocessor with virtual memory system operating in a paging environment. One of the important problems in such a system is how to allocate files to various types of available storage systems, such as cache, cores, disks, drums, data cells, tapes, etc., so that the operating cost is minimum, yet the access time requirements are satisfied for each file, and the storage limitation of each storage system is not exceeded. The model developed in this paper can be directly applied to this problem by letting the distances between computers be equal to zero. Clearly, under this condition, a multiple-computer system becomes a multiprocessor.

3.3 EXAMPLE

Consider a specific computer-communication system consisting of three computers processing five information files in common, as shown in Fig. 3.2.

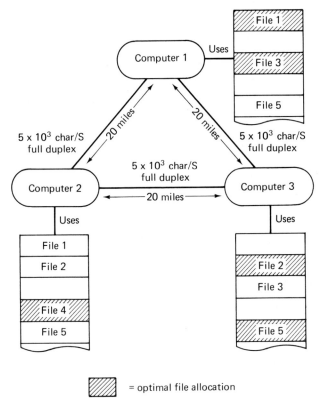

= optimal file allocation

FIGURE 3.2   A specific multiple-computer system.

These computers are located about 20 miles from each other. The transmission facility between each pair of computers has a rate of $R = 5 \times 10^3$ characters/s. The cost of each such facility is \$1050/month or $\$1.4 \times 10^{-7}/$ character (based on 100 h/week and 4.2 weeks/month). The first cost of storage is 35 cents/character or $\$5.8 \times 10^{-7}/$character second.* Table 3.1 gives the lengths of each file, file length per each transaction, the request rate of these files at each computer, the rate of modification of these files at each computer after each transaction, the available storage capacity of each computer, and the maximum allowable retrieval time of each file. Furthermore we assume that the required file availability can be satisfied by storing a single copy of each file. Using the linearized model developed in the Appendix and the Gomory cutting technique [6, 7] for solving the integer linear programming problem, the example was solved on the IBM 360/65.

*The calculation is based on 40 months of machine life, operating at 100 h/week and 4.2 weeks/month.

TABLE 3.1   *Data of Example for File Allocation*

File j	L_j	l_j	P_j	COMPUTER 1		COMPUTER 2		COMPUTER 3	
				u_{1j}	T_{1j}	u_{2j}	T_{2j}	u_{3j}	T_{3j}
1	100×10^3	500	0.5	5	30	2	10	0	0
2	10×10^3	500	0.5	0	0	2	30	5	1
3	10×10^3	500	0.5	3	10	0	0	4	1
4	10×10^3	500	0.5	0	0	4	0.1	0	0
5	100×10^3	500	0.5	1	1	1	1	5	1

P_j = frequency of modification of the jth file after each transaction
L_j = length of the jth file in characters
l_j = file length in characters of each transaction for the jth file
u_{ij} = average hourly request rate of the entire or part of the jth file at the ith computer (the request arrivals are assumed to be Poisson distributed)
T_{ij} = maximum allowable average retrieval time in seconds for the jth file to the ith computer
C_{ij} = (storage cost) = \$0.58 $\times$ 10^{-8}/character second
C'_{ik} = (transmission cost) = \$1.4 $\times$ 10^{-7}/character
b_i = (available storage capacity of the ith computer) = 110×10^3 characters for i = 1, 2, 3
$1/\mu$ = l/R (the time required to transmit the reply message) = 0.1 s

Table 3.2 lists the optimal allocation for the case of no redundant files. The computation time required for this example is about 25 s.

Some characteristics of the optimum allocation are worthy of note. File 4 is stored in computer 2, as it is only used by that computer. File 1 has the highest request rate at computer 1; to minimize the transmission cost, it is stored in computer 1. For the same reason, files 2 and 5 are stored in computer 3. Although file 3 has a high request rate at computer 3, the available storage size of computer 3 (110×10^3 characters) forced file 3 to be stored in computer 1. The overall operation cost under the optimal allocation is \$3620/month. If each file is stored at the computer where it is used, the total

TABLE 3.2   *Optimal File Allocation for Example*

File j	X_{ij}		
	Computer 1	Computer 2	Computer 3
1	1	0	0
2	0	0	1
3	1	0	0
4	0	1	0
5	0	0	1

operating cost under such an arrangement is \$6670/month. The higher operating cost is due to the extra storage cost and the file updating cost.

3.4 CONCLUSION

The file allocation problem can be formulated into a nonlinear zero–one programming problem. By adding additional constraint equations, these nonlinear terms in the objective and constraint equations can be reduced to linear equations. Thus solution of the optimal allocation requires solving a linear zero–one programming problem. The model introduced in this paper provides a common denominator for analysis and comparison of various proposed information system configurations, a tool to study the sensitivity of various parameters and constraints to the operating cost, and a method for evaluating the growth potential of information systems. However, some related problems, such as privacy, file partition, network architecture, etc., still require additional study. All these problems are important considerations for optimal file allocation in a network of interconnected computers.

APPENDIX 3.A   REDUCTION OF ZERO–ONE NONLINEAR PROGRAMMING PROBLEMS TO ZERO–ONE LINEAR PROGRAMMING PROBLEMS*

Because nonlinear programming problems are so complex, we are able to obtain a global optimal solution only for special cases (e.g., convexity). Therefore, it is desirable to reduce the nonlinear zero–one programming problems to the linear zero–one programming problems. We shall now show such a reduction, which is derived from the integer (0 or 1) property.

Suppose that we want to minimize an arbitrary cost function (which need not be convex)

$$C = \min_{x} F(X_1, X_2, \ldots, X_k) \tag{3.A.1}$$

subject to a set of nonconvex constraint equations

$$G_i(X_1, X_2, \ldots, X_k) \leq B_i \qquad i = 1, 2, \ldots, N \tag{3.A.2}$$

where the X_i's are zero–one variables, F and G_i are polynomials of the X_i's with constant coefficients, and B_i is a constant. Clearly, $X_i^q = X_i$ (q = positive integer). Let the coefficient of the product terms in (3.A.1) or (3.A.2), $X_iX_j, \ldots, X_uX_v$, be denoted as $C_{ij\ldots uv}$.

*A similar but less general result has also been obtained independently by Watters [8].

To reduce the above nonlinear zero–one problem to a linear zero–one problem, we first consider the objective function (3.A.1). Let us define

$$X_{ij\ldots uv} = \underbrace{X_i X_j \ldots X_u X_v}_{q} \qquad q = 2, \ldots, Q \qquad (3.A.3)$$

which takes value zero or one, where Q is the highest degree of nonlinearity. We then represent each nonlinear term in (3.A.1) by terms of the form (3.A.3) and then examine its coefficient. If the coefficient of the nonlinear term is positive, we introduce the following constraint equation:

$$\underbrace{X_i + X_j + \cdots + X_u + X_v}_{q} - q + 1 \leq X_{ij\ldots uv} \qquad (3.A.4)$$

If the coefficient of the nonlinear term is negative, we introduce the following constraint equation:

$$\underbrace{X_i + X_j + \cdots + X_u + X_v}_{q} \geq q X_{ij\ldots uv} \qquad (3.A.5)$$

If all the X's in the left side of (3.A.4) have value one, then $X_{ij\ldots uv} = 1$. If one or more of the X's have value zero, then $X_{ij\ldots uv}$ may be either zero or one, but the coefficient of $X_{ij\ldots uv}$ in (3.A.1), $C_{ij\ldots uv}$, is positive. Thus minimizing (3.A.1) under X assures that $X_{ij\ldots uv} = 0$. If we substitute (3.A.3) for each nonlinear term in (3.A.1) that has positive coefficient, and introduce the additional constraint (3.A.4), then the X's in the transformed linear equations take on the same values as the original ones. Similarly, if one or more of the X's in (3.A.3) have value zero, then $X_{ij\ldots uv} = 0$. If all the X's have value one, then $X_{ij\ldots uv}$ may either be zero or one, but the coefficient of $X_{ij\ldots uv}$ in (3.A.1), $C_{ij\ldots uv}$, is negative. Thus minimizing (3.A.1) under X assures that $X_{ijkl\ldots uv} = 1$. If we substitute (3.A.3) for each nonlinear term in (3.A.1) that has negative coefficient, and introduce the additional constraint (3.A.5), then the X's in the transformed linear equations take on the same values as the original ones. Thus we have linearized the objective function (3.A.1).

To linearize the constraint equations, we represent the nonlinear terms in (3.A.2) by (3.A.3) and introduce its corresponding *two* additional constraint equations (3.A.4) and (3.A.5). If one or more of the X's in (3.A.3) have value zero, then $X_{ij\ldots uv} = 0$; this condition is also satisfied by (3.A.4) and (3.A.5). If all the X_{ij}'s have value one in (3.A.3), then $X_{ij\ldots uv}$ is one. Similarly, from (3.A.4), $X_{ij\ldots uv}$ may be either zero or one, but, from (3.A.5), $X_{ij\ldots uv}$ is one. Thus (3.A.4) and (3.A.5) assure that $X_{ij\ldots uv} = 1$. Substituting (3.A.3) and introducing the additional constraint (3.A.4) and (3.A.5) for each nonlinear term in (3.A.2) satisfies all the relationships of X's. Thus we have also linearized the nonlinear constraints equations.

With this reduction technique,* nonlinear zero–one programming problems may be transformed into solution of linear zero–one programming problems. Using available linear integer programming techniques [6, 7], we can obtain the global optimal solutions.

APPENDIX 3.B   LINEARIZATION OF THE OBJECTIVE FUNCTION AND THE ACCESS TIME CONSTANTS

To apply the above technique to linearize the objective function (3.17), we let $X_{ij}X_{kj} = X_{ijkj}$. Since the coefficients of X_{ijkj} in (3.17) are negative, for each X_{ijkj}, we introduce the additional constraint equation

$$X_{ij} + X_{kj} \geq 2X_{ijkj} \tag{3.B.1}$$

Next we shall linearize the constraint equation (3.16). We let $X_{kj_1}X_{kj} = X_{kj_1kj}$. For each X_{kj_1kj}, we introduce two additional constraint equations:

$$\begin{aligned} X_{kj_1} + X_{kj} &\geq 2X_{kj_1kj} \\ X_{kj_1} + X_{kj} - 1 &\leq X_{kj_1kj} \end{aligned} \qquad \text{for } j \neq j_1 \tag{3.B.2}$$

In the same manner, we can linearize (3.15). Hence solution to the optimal file allocation problem is reduced to: minimize (3.17) subject to (3.1)–(3.4), (3.15) or (3.16), (3.A.3), (3.B.1), and (3.B.2), which is a linear zero–one programming problem.

REFERENCES

[1] W. W. CHU, Optimal File Allocation in a Multiple Computer System, *IEEE Trans. Computers*, **C-18**(10) (1969), 885–889.

*This reduction technique can be easily extended to the case when the X_i's in (3.A.1) or (3.A.2) are real numbers. In this case we shall express each X_i in terms of binary variables, X_{ij}'s, as follows:

$$X_i = \sum_{l=1}^{\alpha_i + \beta_i} (X_{il}) 2^{\alpha_i - l}$$

when α_i is chosen large enough for $2^{\alpha_i - 1}$ to be an upper bound on the value of X_i, and β_i is chosen large enough for $2^{-\beta_i}$ to be the maximum allowable accuracy tolerance on the value of X_i. Thus (3.A.1) or (3.A.2) is reduced from a nonlinear equation to a nonlinear zero–one equation.

[2] G. H. SANDLER, *System Reliability Engineering*, Prentice-Hall, Englewood Cliffs, N.J., 1963. pp. 112–144.

[3] Proceedings of the Fifteenth Annual Symposium on Reliability, Session 4, Chicago, Jan. 21–23, 1969.

[4] D. R. COX and W. L. SMITH, *Queues*, Methuen, London, 1961, pp. 50–59.

[5] T. L. SAATY, *Elements of Queuing Theory*, McGraw-Hill, New York, 1961, pp. 153–161.

[6] R. GOMORY, All-Integer Integer Programming Algorithm, in *Industrial Scheduling*, J. F. Muth and G. L. Thompson, eds., Prentice-Hall, Englewood Cliffs, N.J., 1963, pp. 195–206.

[7] J. HALDI and L. M. ISAACSON, *Linear Integer Programming* (Working Paper 45), Graduate School of Business, Stanford University, Dec. 1964.

[8] L. J. WATTERS, Reduction of Integer Polynomial Programming Problems to Zero-One Linear Programming Problems, *Operations Res.*, **15**(6) (1967), 1171–1174.

4

Scheduling, Queueing, and Delays in Time-Shared Systems and Computer Networks

LEONARD KLEINROCK

Computer Science Department
School of Engineering and Applied Science
University of California, Los Angeles

INTRODUCTION

One of the major performance measures for computer networks is the delay experienced by messages. In this chapter we present results of the mathematical analysis of that delay as it pertains to computer systems. We take the point of view that a computer network is a collection of computers (which typically are time-shared computer systems) connected together over a communication network for the purpose of sharing resources and exchanging messages, files, etc. Such a computer network will of necessity introduce delays into the transmission of messages as they are switched in a store-and-forward fashion through the net.

This work was supported by the Advanced Research Projects Agency of the Department of Defense (DAHC-15-69-C-0285).

It is our intention in this chapter to study the kinds of delays that are introduced in this process. We recognize two basic sources of delay: the delay experienced by a message at the external nodes of a network when it requests service of a remote time-shared system; and the delay introduced by the communications network in the transmission of that request for service or of the return transmission from the results of computation. Section 4.1 concerns itself with the former and Section 4.2 with the latter. Each of these two sections is basically self-contained and is presented in the form of a survey of current results. The research taking place is, by and large, separate for these two areas; however, we point out that the methods necessary for solution in both cases are drawn basically from queueing theory, and therefore we present all these results in this single chapter. A rather elaborate list of references is provided from which the interested reader can obtain additional details if he so desires. For further discussion and proofs, the reader is referred to the author's book [41].

4.1 SURVEY OF ANALYTIC RESULTS FOR TIME-SHARED COMPUTER SYSTEMS

4.1.1 Introduction

It is now inexpensive and convenient to gain ready access to computing power. Perhaps in the near future we shall see this power provided to the public through computer utilities. As the computational capacity and data bases grow and as the number of users requesting access to these resources grows, so grows the rate of conflict among these users for access to the system. One means for equitably resolving this competition for simultaneous resources is to incorporate the use of time sharing in such computer systems.

If we are to intelligently design and use time-shared systems, we must be able to predict their performance in a variety of situations. One means for accomplishing this is through the use of mathematical modeling and analysis.

In this chapter we define the problem to be studied, review some of the pertinent mathematical methods, and then present a subset of those results of analysis for time-shared computer systems that have appeared over recent years in the literature. Our purpose is to present the results of these analyses and compare the performance obtained for each. This menu of results of course merely whets one's appetite but does not select the entrées to be ordered. This analogy is not farfetched, since the state of analytical work in this field may be likened to that of creating a menu. In both cases the customer's preference for a particular dish is not known beforehand, and so it is up to the customer to choose from among those offered. We have not yet reached the maturity in this field to be able to optimize over various system alternatives; when we understand the cost of delay well enough, then that optimization can be carried out.

This is not the first work to collect together analytical results for time-shared computer systems, nor it is hoped will it be the last. In 1967 Estrin and Kleinrock [1] described the measures, the models, and the measurements for such systems up to that time. Coffman [2] also summarized some analytical work at around the same time. More recently, in 1969, McKinney [3] surveyed the field; his paper contains an excellent annotated reference list. In this section we express a point of view that represents the author's biased selection of a certain class of results which permits meaningful comparisons and insights into the performance of time-shared computer systems.

We may view a time-shared computer system as a collection of resources and a population of users who compete at various times for the use of these resources. Conflicts arise when simultaneous demands are placed upon the central processing unit (CPU), or upon storage space in memory, or upon the data channels that connect the resources and the users together. To resolve these conflicts, a *scheduling algorithm* is required that allocates resources to users. In this chapter we present results of analysis in which we assume that only one resource (usually assumed to be the CPU) is under demand (most of the successful investigations consider this single-resource case). Clearly, additional work needs to be carried out in the case of multiple resources; certainly, the competition for memory access and for storage capacity, combined with the congestion at the CPU, must be studied.

A very general model to describe the way in which computer systems resolve conflicting requests for attention of the CPU by means of time sharing is shown in Fig. 4.1. This model of a time-sharing system consists of a single resource (*CPU*) and a *system of queues*, which holds those customers awaiting service. In addition, there exists a *scheduling algorithm*, which is a set of decision rules determining which user will next be serviced and for how long. Thus a newly entering request is placed in the system of queues and, when the scheduling algorithm permits, is given a turn in the processing facility. The interval of time during which the customer is permitted to remain in service is referred to as a *quantum*, and the quantum size may vary. The quantum offered may or may not be enough to satisfy the request. If suffi-

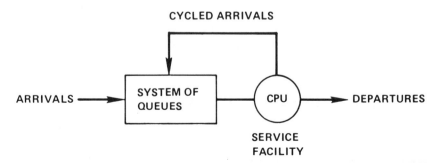

FIGURE 4.1   Feedback queueing model.

cient, the customer departs from the system; if not, he reenters the system of queues as a partially completed task and waits within the system of queues until the scheduling algorithm decides to give him a second quantum, and so on. Eventually, after a sufficient number of visits to the service facility, the customer will have gained enough service and will depart. For obvious reasons we refer to this general model as a feedback queueing system, and the analytical tools required are drawn from queueing theory (see, for example, [4] and [41]).

As mentioned above, we do not know what the cost of delay is, and so we cannot yet optimize the structure of our feedback queueing system. However, it is generally accepted that one of the major advantages of time-shared systems is that they permit interactive use of the computer by many users simultaneously. The goal is to provide to each of these interactive users what he thinks is a computer all to himself. That is, the interactive jobs require rapid response to their frequent requests for short demands. At the same time, those jobs which make large demands on the CPU need not be serviced as quickly, since typically such requests do not expect this interactive type of response. Thus, we wish to give preferential treatment to short jobs at the expense of the longer ones. However, we also take the point of view that we do not know how large a demand each arriving customer places on the CPU. How then can we service the jobs, giving priority in relation to their demands? The solution is an implicit one: we permit each job to demonstrate to us that it is indeed small. We see from the queueing system described above that if a job is small, it will depart after few visits to the CPU, whereas if a job is long, it will require many such visits. Thus by continually "testing" the collection of jobs demanding service, we successfully discover those which are short. By varying the scheduling algorithm, it is possible to effect various degrees of preferential treatment for short jobs. How this is accomplished is described next.

4.1.2 Definitions

Let us now describe the means for specifying the nature of the customer demands as well as the details of the system structure for the model shown in Fig. 4.1. Since we have taken the point of view that customer arrival times and customer demands are unpredictable, we choose to describe these random quantities in terms of probability distribution functions. Accordingly, we define the customer interarrival time distribution as

$$A(\tau) = P[\text{interarrival time} \leq \tau] \tag{4.1}$$

Furthermore, we define the service time distribution as

$$B(t) = P[\text{service time} \leq t] \tag{4.2}$$

The quantum of time offered to a customer may depend upon an externally applied priority as well as upon the number of visits that customer has made to the service facility. Accordingly, we define Q_{pn} as the quantum offered to a customer from priority class p upon his nth entry into service. When a customer's quantum expires, we must remove him from service and insert the next customer; typically, the overhead in time required to perform this operation is a quantity referred to as the *swap time*. Consequently, not all of the assigned quantum may be available to a customer for useful processing. Having specified $A(\tau)$, $B(t)$ and Q_{pn}, it remains to describe the internal structure of the system of queues (which is equivalent to specifying the scheduling algorithm). The nature of some specific scheduling algorithms is discussed in Section 4.1.3.

Once we specify the above quantities, we are then in a position to analyze the feedback queueing system. Typically, one would like to solve for the distribution of time spent in the system. We refer to the total time a customer spends in the system as his *response time*, and it is the distribution of response time that we seek. In some cases we are able to solve for this distribution; however, often we ask only for the average of this quantity, and such is the case in this chapter. If indeed we do solve for the average response time, we certainly should condition it on the amount of service that a customer requires, and this we define as

$$T(t) = \text{average response time for a customer requiring}$$
$$t \text{ seconds of processing} \tag{4.3}$$

Our motivation for conditioning the response time on the service time is, as we discussed in Section 4.1.1, that we wish to give preferential treatment to the short jobs, and the response time is an indication of the preferential treatment. It is generally accepted that the single most important performance measure for these systems is indeed this average response time (sometimes referred to as "response time" in the following).

4.1.3 Results

A variety of models has appeared in the published literature, along with results of many kinds (see, for example, [5–23]). We select here certain of those models and results which we feel will demonstrate and characterize the behavior of many time-shared systems.

Among our assumptions are the following. First we assume that the swap time is some fixed percentage of the quantum offered. In this case the analysis proceeds as if there were no swap time, but with the average service rate decreased by this same percentage; thus, for our purposes, we may omit consideration of swap time. Furthermore, we adopt the point of view that all quanta shrink to zero, resulting in what is commonly known as the *processor-sharing* model for time-shared systems. The justification for this zero quantum limit is merely one of great analytic convenience. The finite quantum studies suffer from the annoying situation that a customer may depart before his current quantum has fully expired; this results in considerable mathematical complexity. When one reduces all quanta to zero, this difficulty disappears and the resulting performance measures are extremely good approximations to the finite quantum results. When we study the round-robin systems (Section 4.1.3.2), it will be clear why we use the name processor sharing. Our selected menu consists only of the processor-sharing results.

One last assumption is that for all the results presented in this chapter we assume that the arrivals form a Poisson process with an average arrival rate of λ customers/sec.; that is,

$$A(\tau) = 1 - e^{-\lambda\tau} \qquad \tau \geq 0 \qquad (4.4)$$

This assumption will be maintained for all our infinite population models, and when we come to the finite input population case, we shall modify that assumption slightly.

4.1.3.1   Batch Processing (First-Come-First-Served).

Before we present results for the time-shared cases, let us describe results for the well-known case of batch processing, which we shall use as a reference system. In this system the structure is as given in Fig. 4.2. Here we see that new arrivals

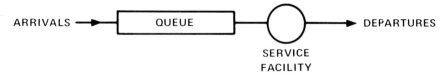

FIGURE 4.2   Batch processing (first come first served.).

join a queue, and that once a customer is allowed into the CPU, he is permitted to run to completion. This is a special case of our general model in Fig. 4.1, where in fact the quantum is infinite (an exception to processor sharing) and therefore no feedback occurs.* For this case the well-known [4, 41] result for average response time is

$$T(t) = \frac{\lambda \overline{t^2}}{2(1 - \rho)} + t \qquad (4.5)$$

where

$$\rho = \lambda \bar{t} \qquad (4.6)$$

$$\bar{t} = \int_0^\infty t \, dB(t) \qquad (4.7)$$

$$\overline{t^2} = \int_0^\infty t^2 \, dB(t) \qquad (4.8)$$

*Alternatively, one may think of it as a processor-sharing model in which a cycled arrival joins the head of the queue, in which case he immediately returns to service.

Here $\bar{t}$ is the average service time for a job and $\overline{t^2}$ is the second moment of the service-time distribution. Similarly, ρ is as usual the utilization factor for the queueing system and represents the fraction of time that the server is busy with customers. In all cases we assume

$$\rho < 1 \tag{4.9}$$

which is the required condition for stable operation of the computing facility. It is convenient to consider the difference between the response time for a job and that job's required service time, i.e., the customer's time in queue (which may properly be described as his *wasted* time due to the fact that he is sharing the system with other customers). Thus let us define

$$W(t) = T(t) - t \tag{4.10}$$

In the case of batch processing we see that the wasted time is independent of the service time and takes the form

$$W(t) = \frac{\lambda \overline{t^2}}{2(1 - \rho)} \tag{4.11}$$

An important special case is that of exponentially distributed service time in which

$$B(t) = 1 - e^{-\mu t} \qquad t \geq 0 \tag{4.12}$$

In this case we have

$$\bar{t} = \frac{1}{\mu} \tag{4.13}$$

$$\overline{t^2} = 2\left(\frac{1}{\mu}\right)^2 \tag{4.14}$$

Thus we arrive at the classical equation for the wasted time in a Poisson-exponential first-come-first-served (FCFS) queueing system:

$$W(t) = \frac{\rho/\mu}{1 - \rho} \tag{4.15}$$

where $\rho = \lambda/\mu$. Thus we see that the waiting time in this system is independent of service time and becomes a very sensitive function of ρ, as ρ approaches unity (this in fact is the case in most queueing systems and indicates the extreme penalty paid when one attempts to run the system near saturation, that is, near $\rho = 1$).

4.1.3.2 Round Robin [5–10]. Perhaps the most well-known and widely used scheduling algorithm for time-shared computer systems is the round-robin (RR) algorithm. The structure of the system here is given in Fig. 4.3. In this case $Q_{pn} = Q \rightarrow 0$; that is, all quanta are the same size and, of course, as we agreed, shrink to zero. Newly arriving customers join the single queue, work their way up to the head of this queue in a first-come-first-served fashion, and then finally receive a quantum of service. When that quantum

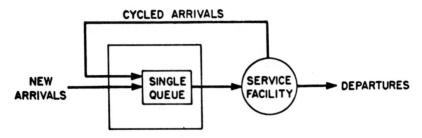

FIGURE 4.3   Round-robin system.

expires and if they need more service, they then return to the tail of that same queue and repeat the cycle. It is clear in this processor-shared system that a customer is required to make an infinite number of cycles each infinitely quickly and each time receiving infinitesimal service, until finally the accumulated service he has received equals that required by him, at which time he departs. Consider for a moment the case in which a customer enters an empty system. In this situation he receives service at the rate of 1 sec./sec. When a new customer arrives and joins him in this frantic cycling, we see that each customer will be receiving service at the rate of $\frac{1}{2}$ sec./sec. since they are leapfrogging with each other in and out of service. When k customers are in the system, each is receiving service at the rate of $1/k$ sec./sec., and hence the name processor sharing, when indeed all customers are sharing the capacity of the processor equally. Thus we may take two points of view, one being that in a time-shared system customers are given the full capacity of the processor on a part-time basis, and the other being that customers are given a part-time processor on a full-time basis; the former is referred to as time sharing and the latter as processor sharing.

This system was first studied by Kleinrock [5] in 1964 as a discrete time model and later studied by him as a processor-sharing case in [6]. Chang [7], Shemer [8], and others have also pursued this model, in all cases assuming exponential service of the form given in (4.12). Sakata et al. [9] were perhaps the first to study the general service time case and found that the solution there for the response time was independent of the service-time distribution! More recently, Coffman, Muntz, and Trotter [10] solved for the waiting-time distribution in the exponential case. The results of some of these analyses are given next.

The round robin is perhaps the simplest system to understand and has some remarkable properties. For the RR system the response time conditioned on the length of service for an arbitrary service distribution is given by

$$T(t) = \frac{t}{1 - \rho} \tag{4.16}$$

Similarly, the waiting time is

$$W(t) = \frac{pt}{1 - \rho} \qquad (4.17)$$

We now list the properties of this solution:

1. The discrimination is *linear*. That is, the response time depends upon service time in a strictly linear fashion, which implies that a job twice as long as some other will spend on the average twice as long in the system.
2. The average response time is independent of the service-time distribution $B(t)$ and depends only upon the mean value of service time through ρ, as shown in (4.6).
3. If we form the ratio of wasted time to service time, we obtain*

$$\frac{W(t)}{t} = \frac{\rho}{1 - \rho} \qquad (4.18)$$

Let us consider Fig. 4.4. In this figure we show the ratio of wasted time to service time as a constant value for the round-robin system with arbitrary service-time distribution. Since this ratio measures how much

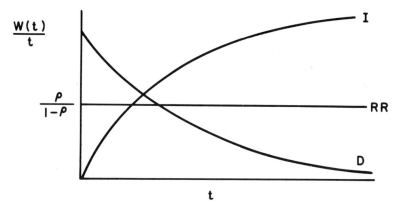

FIGURE 4.4   Wasted time per unit of service time.

*The interpretation here for the case of exponentially distributed service time is that this ratio is equal to the average number of customers found in the system upon arrival [which is given by $\rho/(1 - \rho)$]; thus each time a customer receives an infinitesimal quantum of service, so also does every other customer found in the system upon arrival. The result also implies that the expected number of customers which interfere with a given customer's progress is on the average a constant and equal to the number he finds upon his arrival to the system.

time must be sacrificed in waiting per unit of service time received, we may consider the ratio as some form of penalty function imposed upon a customer for receiving t seconds of service. In the round-robin case we have a very nice property in that the penalty function is independent of a customer's service time and is in that sense "fair." On the other hand, imagine that the penalty function was increasing with service time, such as the curve labeled I. In this case customers with longer service requirements are penalized more heavily *per unit of service time;* in such a case the obvious countermeasure to the scheduling algorithm producing such a function would be for a user to partition his job into a number of smaller jobs, thereby enjoying the preferred treatment (per unit of required service) offered to short jobs! On the other hand, consider the curve labeled D, which shows the results of some scheduling algorithm that produces a decreasing function of service time. Here we see that the longer jobs enjoy the preferred treatment per unit of required service, and so the obvious countermeasure is for many jobs to pool their programs and offer one monstrously long job to the computer. Such tactics on the part of users typically tend to increase the overhead to the system and are generally undesirable; in view of this it appears that the round robin system removes the motivation for any such unusual action on the part of the user.

4. Another very nice property of the round-robin scheduling algorithm for the case of exponential service time is that a job whose service requirement equals the average $(1/\mu)$ will spend on the average as much time in the round-robin system as he would in the batch-processing system [compare (4.15) and (4.17)]. Thus, for exponential service, jobs less than average in length receive better treatment in the round robin as opposed to the batch-processing system; similarly, jobs greater than average receive poorer treatment. Of course, this breakpoint between round robin and batch processing will vary as the second moment of the service-time distribution varies [see (4.11) and (4.17)], and the breakpoint occurs at $t = \overline{t^2}/2\bar{t}$.

4.1.3.3   Last Come First Served.   Another interesting scheduling algorithm to consider is the last-come-first-served (LCFS) system, in which the most recently arrived customer captures the use of the complete processor until he is either preempted by a newly arriving customer or until he receives his total required service. When the customer departs from the service facility, then once again the newest customer in the system is given its complete attention. It is amazing that the average response time here is the same as that for round robin:*

$$T(t) = \frac{t}{1 - \rho} \qquad (4.19)$$

Of course, then, the wasted time will also be given by (4.17), and both these results are independent of the service-time distribution. In this case, therefore, all the average properties shared by the round-robin system are also enjoyed by the last-come-first-served system. One might therefore conclude that the *average* response time is not a very good indicator of system performance, since it is clear that the variance of the response time under LCFS will be greater than that for the round-robin case.

4.1.3.4 Round Robin with Priorities [6]. Here we consider the case in which an external priority assignment is made to the arriving jobs. We assume that there are P priority groups, again with Poisson arrivals, each at an average rate of λ_p/sec. and an exponentially distributed service requirement with a mean of $1/\mu_p$ seconds for the pth priority group ($p = 1, 2 \ldots, P$). We associate a positive number g_p with the pth priority group, with larger values of g_p being given to those groups which are to obtain higher priority. In particular, we assign a customer from the pth priority group a fraction f_p of the processing time when there are n_i customers in the system from the ith group; f_p is given by

$$f_p = \frac{g_p}{\sum_{i=1}^{P} g_i n_i} \qquad (4.20)$$

Thus we have a processor-sharing system for which the share of the processor for a particular customer depends upon his priority group.

The average response time $T_p(t)$ for a customer from the pth priority group who requires t seconds of service is given by

$$T_p(t) = \frac{t}{1 - \rho}\left[1 + \sum_{i=1}^{P} \left(\frac{g_i}{g_p} - 1\right)\rho_i\right] \qquad (4.21)$$

where $\rho_i = \lambda_i/\mu_i$ and $\rho = \sum_{i=1}^{P} \rho_i$. As a consequence the average waiting time for such customers is given by

$$W_p(t) = \frac{\rho t}{1 - \rho}\left[1 + \sum_{i=1}^{P} \left(\frac{g_i}{g_p} - 1\right)\frac{\rho_i}{\rho}\right] \qquad (4.22)$$

Note that we have the same linear dependence upon service time here as in

---

*The proof is simple: the average time spent in the system by a customer requiring t seconds of service equals his service time t plus his waiting time. This last equals the average number (λt) of customers who preempt him from service, times the busy period duration generated by each such interruption. The length of each busy period is, on the average, equal to $\bar{t}/(1 - \rho)$ (see [4], [40], or [41]).

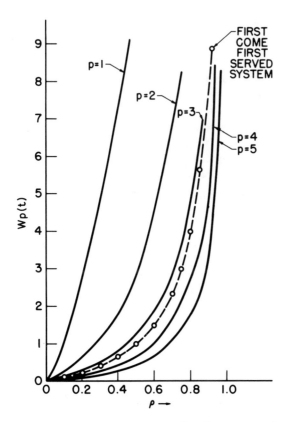

FIGURE 4.5 Priority processor-shared system: performance as a function of ρ for $g_p = p^2$ ($p = (1, 2, 3, 4, 5)$, $\mu_p = \mu$, $\lambda_p = \lambda/P$, $\mu t = 1$.

the round-robin system, and also a dependence upon priority group. Of course, in the case when all $g_p = g$, this system reduces to that of a simple round-robin case. In Fig. 4.5 we show an example of this behavior. Here we have plotted the wasted time for the pth priority group as a function of the system utilization factor ρ. We have chosen $\mu t = 1$ and have taken the case $P = 5$ and $g_p = p^2$. The five curves clearly show the discrimination among priority groups as p varies. In addition, the dashed curve would be the response time in a batch-processing system (first-come-first-served) or in a round-robin system (since we have taken $t = \bar{t}$, and so batch processing and round robin give the same performance). If we change the dependence of g_p on p, we can separate the priority curves shown even more or shrink them down as we please. As the dependence decreases (less discrimination among priority groups), the set of curves will collapse around the dashed curve for the round-robin case.

4.1.3.5 Selfish Round Robin [11]. We now consider a scheduling algorithm that introduces an additional degree of freedom and permits us to define a continuum of algorithms, which range from the batch-processing system all the way to the round-robin system. This we do first for the case of exponential service time.

Let us identify a time-varying value of priority with each customer in this system. This priority value begins at zero upon his entry and, as long as he is not being served, it increases linearly at a rate α; whenever he is "in" the service facility, his priority value increases at a rate β, where $\alpha \geq \beta \geq 0$. The service facility operates as follows: service will be provided to all those customers in the system who currently have the highest value of priority; typically, more than one customer will have this highest value and, in that case, the customers will share the capacity of the processor in a round-robin processor-shared fashion. Note that an entering customer begins to gain priority at a rate greater than the rate of gain for those customers in the service ($\alpha \geq \beta$). Eventually he will catch up with those in service and then join and remain with that group. Since the customers in service are attempting to run away with the processor (at a rate β) and prevent waiting customers from joining them (hopeless as this attempt is), we dub this system the selfish round-robin (SRR) system.

The response time for such a system is

$$T(t) = \frac{1/\mu}{1 - \rho} + \frac{t - (1/\mu)}{1 - \rho[1 - (\beta/\alpha)]} \tag{4.23}$$

and the wasted time is given by

$$W(t) = \frac{\rho/\mu}{1 - \rho} + \frac{[t - (1/\mu)]\rho[1 - (\beta/\alpha)]}{1 - \rho[1 - (\beta/\alpha)]} \tag{4.24}$$

Observe that these functions are once again linear in service time plus an additional constant, as shown in Fig. 4.6 (where $\rho' = \rho[1 - (\beta/\alpha)]$). A number of comments are in order. First, we see from the figure, as well as from the response and waiting-time functions, that a job with average service requirement will receive the same average response in all these SRR systems. Second, we observe in the limit when $\beta/\alpha = 1$ that the response is that of the first-come-first-served system (this is obviously true because that customer which is oldest in the system will capture the processor, run away with it, and no other more recent customer can catch up, since they are both moving at the same rate). Similarly, when $\beta = 0$, we have the round-robin system, since no customer gains priority while being served, and therefore all customers maintain a priority value of zero; thus, all newly entering customers immediately join the service facility, yielding the round-robin case.

The single degree of freedom, β/α, thus permits one to range in a continuous fashion from first-come-first-served to round robin, all the while giving a linear type of response with respect to service time.

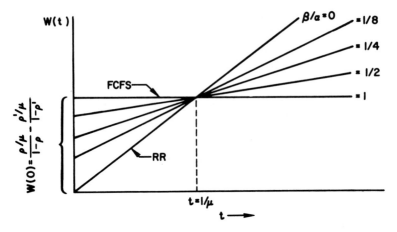

FIGURE 4.6   Waiting time for the SRR system.

It is possible to generalize these results [12] as follows. First, we may consider an arbitrary distribution of service $B(t)$. Second, one can obtain the (Laplace transform of the) distribution of response time in a selfish scheduling system (defined as one in which customers are allowed into the service facility only if they have the same highest value of priority as others in the facility, and once having entered are treated according to *any* defined scheduling algorithm—not necessarily RR) in terms of known quantities and the (Laplace transform of the) distribution of response time for the scheduling algorithm in the service facility. Thus, given *any* time-shared scheduling algorithm, it can be converted to a selfish scheduling algorithm by introducing the parameter β/α; in such cases the average waiting time is given by

$$W(t) = \frac{\lambda \overline{t^2}}{2(1 - \rho)} - \frac{\lambda[1 - \beta/\alpha)]\overline{t^2}}{2\{1 - \rho[1 - (\beta/\alpha)]\}} + V(t) \qquad (4.25)$$

where $V(t)$ is the average waiting time in the original system with λ replaced by $\lambda[1 - (\beta/\alpha)]$.

4.1.3.6   Foreground-Background Models [13, 14].

The systems discussed heretofore give varying degrees of preference to short jobs. As mentioned earlier, this preference comes about by implicit discovery of which are the short jobs. One may inquire as to which scheduling algorithm is capable of discriminating *most* in favor of short jobs. The answer is immediately apparent: it is that scheduling algorithm which next gives service to that job which has so far received the least service of all. This is commonly referred to as a generalized foreground–background (FB) scheduling algorithm.*

---

*The name comes about from a finite quantum algorithm in which there exist two queues. A newly arriving customer joins the first queue and waits in a first-come-first-

The generalized case we consider here is, of course, a processor-sharing model, since the quantum size is effectively zero and certainly more than one job may share the processor, as follows. Consider a new arrival who finds an empty system. The processor gives him its full attention and he receives service at the rate of 1 sec./sec. At some time, say, t_1 later, a new job arrives; the server then ceases to serve the first customer and turns its attention to the second customer, providing 1 sec./sec. of service to this new customer. If no new customers arrive within the next t_1 seconds, the second customer and the first customer will each have received exactly the same amount of service, at which point they share the processor and each receives service at the rate of $\frac{1}{2}$ sec./sec. This will continue until some new customer enters or until one of the two customers has had enough service and departs. And so it goes, with the processor always devoting its complete attention to all those customers who have so far received the least amount of service. The response time in this system for arbitrary service-time distribution is given by

$$T(t) = \frac{W_t + t}{1 - \rho_t} \tag{4.26}$$

where

$$W_t = \frac{\lambda \overline{t_t^2}}{2(1 - \rho_t)} \tag{4.27}$$

$$\overline{t_t^2} = \int_0^t x^2 \, dB(x) + t^2[1 - B(t)] \tag{4.28}$$

$$\bar{t}_t = \int_0^t x \, dB(x) + t[1 - B(t)] \tag{4.29}$$

and

$$\rho_t = \lambda \bar{t}_t \tag{4.30}$$

Note that $\overline{t_t^n}$ is merely the nth moment of the service-time distribution truncated at the point t. Furthermore, $\bar{t}_\infty = \bar{t}$, $\overline{t_\infty^2} = \overline{t^2}$, $\rho_\infty = \rho$, and W_∞ equals the average waiting time in the first-come-first-served system as given in (4.11). Observe that the result for FB depends upon the service-time distribution $B(t)$. The wasted time is given by

$$W(t) = \frac{W_t + \rho_t t}{1 - \rho_t} \tag{4.31}$$

An example of the average response time is given in Fig. 4.7 for the exponential service-time case. Note that the slope of the average response time may

served fashion to receive his first quantum of service; when that quantum expires, he then joins the tail of the second queue, and each time through the system thereafter he will join the tail of the same second queue. The server always gives attention to the first queue as long as anyone there needs service, and only when it is empty does he give attention to the second queue. Thus the first queue may be thought of as the foreground jobs (preferably those requiring one quantum or less) and the second queue may be referred to as the background queue (containing jobs that perhaps require more service and therefore may be considered background operations).

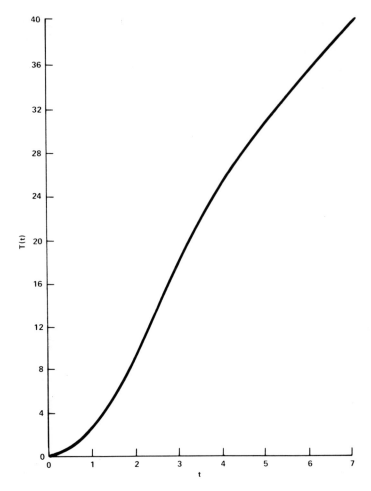

FIGURE 4.7   Response time for FB with $\lambda = 0.75$, $\mu = 1$.

be calculated as

$$\frac{dT(t)}{dt} = \frac{1}{1 - \rho_t} + 2\frac{\lambda t[1 - B(t)]}{(1 - \rho_t)^2} + \lambda^2 \overline{t_t^2}\frac{1 - B(t)}{(1 - \rho_t)^2}$$

We have then

$$\left.\frac{dT(t)}{dt}\right|_{t=0} = 1 \qquad (4.32)$$

$$\left.\frac{dT(t)}{dt}\right|_{t=\infty} = \frac{1}{1 - \rho} \qquad (4.33)$$

The interpretation of these last two equations is the following. Since in this system service is always given to that job with the shortest received service, it is clear that a newly entering job waits not at all, and so a job with extremely short service requirements has a response rate of unity (4.32). Similarly, an extremely long job waits in the system until all the jobs that arrive during its service time have been fully processed; it is clear then that its performance looks like that in either a last-come-first-served system (in which case he gravitates to the position of the oldest customer in the system) or in a round-robin system (since there too he will wait until most other customers have passed through their complete service cycle). In all cases the inverse of the rate at which he gains service is given by (4.33), which is the same as that for round robin and last-come-first-served, as can be seen from (4.16).

4.1.3.7 Multilevel Processor Sharing [15]. Here we describe a mixed scheduling algorithm that allows one to define a very large class of possible algorithms. Again we assume Poisson arrivals, arbitrary service-time distribution, zero quantum size, and the following system of queues. We define a set of attained service times $\{a_i\}$ such that

$$0 = a_0 < a_1 < a_2 < \cdots < a_N < a_{N+1} = \infty \qquad (4.34)$$

At the same time we define $N + 1$ scheduling disciplines, where the discipline followed for a job when it has attained service, τ, in the interval

$$a_{i-1} \le \tau < a_i \qquad i = 1, 2, \ldots, N + 1 \qquad (4.35)$$

will be denoted as D_i. We permit D_i to be either FCFS (batch processing), FB, or RR. In addition, between these intervals the jobs are treated as a set of generalized foreground–background disciplines; that is, the processor will give its complete attention to those jobs in the lowest *level* nonempty queue and will schedule them according to the discipline appropriate for that interval. See Fig. 4.8. For example, when $N = 0$, we have the usual single-level case of either FCFS, RR, or FB. For $N = 1$, we could have any of nine disciplines (FCFS followed by FCFS, ..., RR followed by RR); note that FB followed by FB is just a single FB system (due to the overall FB policy between levels).

Since the discipline between intervals is FB, it turns out that the response time for a job is a function only of the discipline which he is subject to when he departs the system completely serviced. Thus we have three cases to consider:

1. When his last level is level i and is FCFS (batch processing), the result is

$$T(t) = \frac{W_{a_i} + t}{1 - \rho_{a_{i-1}}} \qquad (4.36)$$

   and also

$$W(t) = \frac{W_{a_i} + t\rho_{a_{i-}}}{1 - \rho_{a_{i-1}}} \qquad (4.37)$$

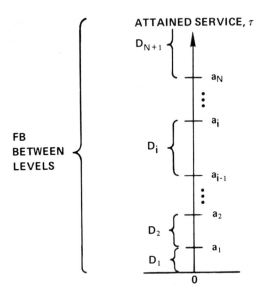

FIGURE 4.8   Intervals of attained service, with disciplines, D_i.

2. When his last level, i, is FB, then the solutions for response and waiting time are the same as if the entire level below him were generalized FB and is given in (4.26) and (4.31).
3. When his ith level is RR, the situation becomes more complex. If he departs during the first level, that is, $0 \le t < a_1$, then the result is

$$T(t) = \frac{t}{1 - \rho_{a_1}} \qquad (4.38)$$

which is like a pure RR system in which service-time distribution is truncated at $t = a_1$. For RR levels beyond the first, solutions have been obtained only when the service-time distribution in the ith level is of the form

$$B(t) = 1 - q(t)e^{-\mu t} \qquad a_{i-1} \le t < a_i \qquad (4.39)$$

where $q(t)$ is a polynomial in t of arbitrary degree. The solution itself is rather complex and we choose not to describe it here. However, examples follow that include this case.

Let us consider some of the behavior possible in this multilevel processor-sharing case. We begin with four examples for the case of exponential service time. As mentioned above, we have nine possible disciplines for the case $N = 1$. Since the behavior of the average conditional response time in any particular level is independent of the discipline in all other levels, we show the behavior of each of the three disciplines in both levels in Fig. 4.9 for the

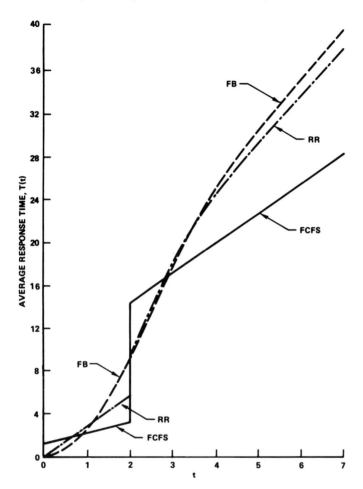

FIGURE 4.9 Response-time possibilities for $N = 1$, M/M/1, $\mu = 1$, $\lambda = 0.75$, $a_1 = 2$.

system $N = 1$.* In Fig. 4.10 we show a case for $N = 3$, where $D_1 =$ RR, $D_2 =$ FB, $D_3 =$ FCFS (batch processing), and $D_4 =$ RR. Also shown is the case of FB over the entire range, which serves as a reference curve for comparison with this more complicated discipline. Figure 4.11 is the case for the iterated structure $D_i =$ FCFS. Again we show the FB case as a reference curve. Our fourth example is given in Fig. 4.12 for the iterated structure $D_i =$ RR. Again the FB curve is shown. It must always be true

*In these figures we use the standard abbreviation in queueing theory, where $M/M/1$ denotes the system with Poisson arrivals with exponential service times; also $M/E_2/1$ denotes the system with Poisson arrivals and Erlangian-2 service times [see (4.40)].

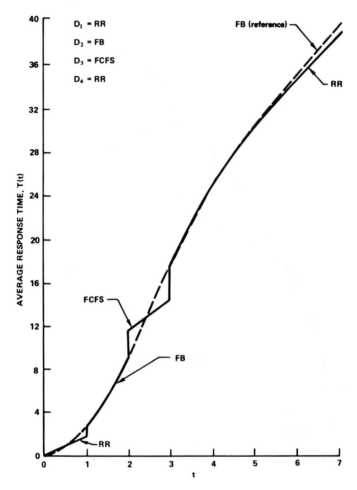

FIGURE 4.10 Response time for an example of $N = 3$, M/M/1, $\mu = 1$, $\lambda = 0.75$, $a_i = i$.

that the FB reference curve never lies above the response function at the beginning of an interval (that is, just beyond a_i), nor may it ever lie below the response curve just before the end of an interval (just before a_i).

For nonexponential service-time distributions we offer two examples. First we assume that

$$\frac{dB(t)}{dt} = (2\mu)^2 t e^{-2\mu t} \qquad t \ge 0 \qquad (4.40)$$

which is known in queueing theory as the Erlangian-2 distribution [4]. The disciplines we consider are $D_1 = \text{RR}$ and $D_2 = \text{FCFS}$. In Fig. 4.13 we show the response time when the breakpoint a_1 is chosen with five different values.

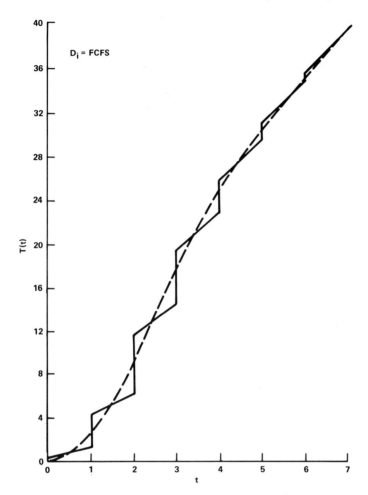

FIGURE 4.11   Response time for example of $N = \infty$, $D_i = $ FCFS, M/M/1, $\mu = 1$, $\lambda = 0.75$, $a_i = i$.

For our second example we choose

$$\frac{dB(t)}{dt} = \begin{cases} 1 & 0 \leq t \leq \frac{1}{2} \\ e^{-2[t-(1/2)]} & \frac{1}{2} \leq t \end{cases} \tag{4.41}$$

The discipline considered is that in which $D_1 = $ FCFS, $D_2 = $ RR, and $D_3 = $ FCFS. The performance of this system is given in Fig. 4.14, where now we show the RR as a reference curve.

4.1.3.8   Attained Service [16].   In all the feedback queueing systems studied so far it is clear that customers within the system have all received various degrees of useful or attained service. For example, in the FB case

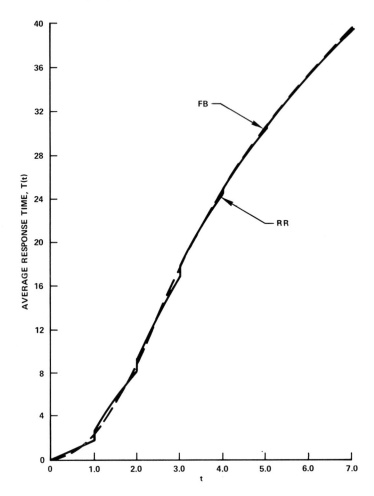

FIGURE 4.12   Response time for example of $N = \infty$, $D_i = RR$, M/M/1, $\mu = 1.0$, $\lambda = 0.75$, $a_i = i$.

we found that customers tend to collect at various points in the system with typically more than one customer having received the same amount of attained service. We may inquire as to what is this distribution of attained service for those customers still in the system for various of our scheduling algorithms. We are able to answer this question for some very general feedback queueing systems, including all of those so far described.

Let us define

$$N_p(t) = \text{average density of customers from the } p\text{th priority} \\ \text{group still in the system who have so far received } t \qquad (4.42) \\ \text{seconds of service}$$

The units of this function are customers per second, and we have defined

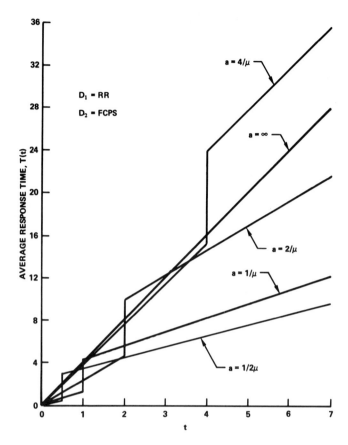

FIGURE 4.13   Response time for RR, FCFS in $M/E_2/1$ with $\mu = 1$, $\lambda = 0.75$, $a = \frac{1}{2}, 1, 2, 4, \infty$.

this density conditioned both on priority group and on attained service, since the results apply for an arbitrary priority discipline. To clarify, let us point out that the integral of this function will give the number of customers with a given degree of service; for example,

$$\int_{T_1}^{T_2} N_p(t)\,dt = \text{average number of customers from the } p\text{th}$$

priority group still in the system who have so   (4.43)
far received between T_1 and T_2 seconds of service

It turns out that this quantity may be expressed very nicely in terms of our performance measure, that is, the average response time conditioned on the service time (and priority group):

$$N_p(t) = \lambda_p[1 - B_p(t)]\frac{dT_p(t)}{dt} \qquad (4.44)$$

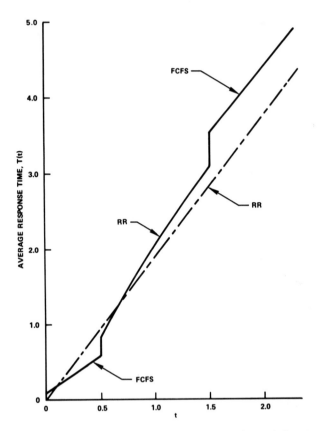

FIGURE 4.14   Response time for an example of $N = 2$, $\lambda = 0.75$, service time density = $b_1(t)$, $a_1 = 0.5$, $a_2 = 1.5$.

where λ_p and $B_p(t)$ refer, respectively, to the arrival rate and service-time distribution for customers from the pth priority group. The result holds for Poisson arrivals. Of course, this function will depend upon the particular priority discipline used, and its dependence upon that discipline is seen through its dependence upon the derivative of the conditional response time. An analogous result also holds for the case of finite quanta [41].

4.1.3.9 Bounds on Performance [17].   For the class of processor-sharing systems studied above, we now wish to consider the function $W(t)$ and inquire as to whether or not this function is confined to any particular region in the $(W(t), t)$ plane. The answer is in the affirmative, and we give the results below.

Some interesting observations are first in order. It can be shown, and it follows directly from physical arguments, that

$$\frac{dW(t)}{dt} \geq 0. \tag{4.45}$$

The interpretation here is that the wasted time in the system must increase as the demand for service time is increased. Moreover, it is possible to show that any feasible $W(t)$ must satisfy the following conservation law:

$$\int_0^\infty W(t)[1 - B(t)]\, dt = \frac{\rho \overline{t^2}}{2(1 - \rho)} \qquad (4.46)$$

This result holds again for arbitrary service-time distribution $B(t)$. It effectively says that the average "work" in the system must remain constant.

Now we come to the more general question as to how large and how small the function $W(t)$ can be. It has been established that the average wasted time in the system has *tight* upper and lower bounds on its value as a function of t. These bounds are

$$\frac{\lambda \overline{t_t^2}}{2(1 - \rho_t)} \le W(t) \le \frac{\lambda \overline{t^2}}{2(1 - \rho_t)(1 - \rho)} + \frac{t\rho_t}{1 - \rho_t} \qquad (4.47)$$

As an example of these bounds, we show in Fig. 4.15 a large collection of some of our previous results for the RR system, the FB system, the ML system (this is the system referred to above as multilevel processor sharing), and the SRR system along with the bounds themselves. The curves shown are for exponential service time with $\rho = 0.75$. We note at $t = 0$ that the upper bound and FCFS curve start at the same point because, under the constraint of the conservation law, no other scheduling algorithm can give longer average waiting time at $t = 0$ than FCFS. The upper bound approaches the FB response asymptotically as t approaches infinity; therefore, a customer with a very long requested service time (as compared to the mean) can never be delayed more than he is with FB. The lower bound starts at zero (as does the FB curve) with zero slope. It approaches the FCFS curve asymptotically as t goes to infinity. Thus we know that the *least* discriminating scheduling algorithm (FCFS) touches the upper bound at $t = 0$ and forms the asymptote for the lower bound as t approaches infinity (that is, it treats tiny jobs in the worst possible way, and enormous jobs in the best possible way); conversely, the *most* discriminating scheduling algorithm (FB) touches the lower bound $t = 0$ and forms the asymptote of the upper bound as t approaches infinity (i.e., best possible treatment of tiny jobs and worst possible for enormous jobs). The above-mentioned behavior of the upper and lower bounds applies not only to the M/M/1 system, but also holds true for any M/G/1 system in general, although the rate of convergence for the bounds to their respective limits varies for different service distributions.

This type of result is especially enlightening and permits one to determine if a proposed system behavior is in fact feasible. For example, if one were asked to design a scheduling algorithm for a time-shared system such that all jobs with less than t_0 seconds of required service must, on the average, have average waiting times of at most W_0 seconds, then one could respond as

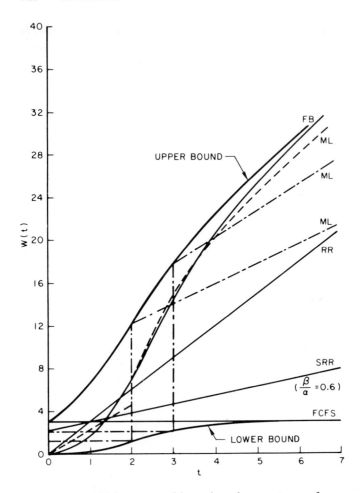

FIGURE 4.15   Tight upper and lower bounds on system performance M/M/1, $\mu = 1.0$, $\lambda = 0.75$.

follows: (1) if the point (W_0, t_0) lies below the lower bound curve, no such
algorithm exists; (2) if (W_0, t_0) lies in the feasible range, it is easy to display
a (multilevel) algorithm to guarantee this behavior.

4.1.3.10   Finite Input Population for Round-Robin System [18–23].   All
the models so far described have assumed that the input population was
infinite and, in fact, the arrival process was Poisson [see assumption in (4.4)].
Of course, we have no infinite populations, and so we may inquire as to
when we may approximate an input population by an infinite one. The
answer is merely that an infinite input population is a good approximation
when the nature of the arrival process depends only in a negligible way upon
the number of customers already in the system. Such is the case certainly for

telephone and telegraph traffic and many other cases of interest. Moreover, when time-shared computing becomes available to the public at large, perhaps that population of users will be able to be considered as infinite; thus what we have described so far in this chapter is the behavior for futuristic systems and provides some insight into the existing and planned systems.

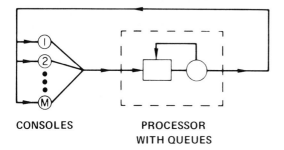

CONSOLES   PROCESSOR
                  WITH QUEUES

FIGURE 4.16   Finite input population.

Nevertheless, we must consider the case of a finite input population. Consider Fig. 4.16. Here we have the case in which there are M users, or consoles, which make demands upon the time-shared computer system. The dashed lines in that figure surround a feedback queueing model similar to that shown in Fig. 4.1. What we are therefore describing is a view of the world external to that of the feedback queueing system, which is itself a larger feedback loop. The finite population model operates as follows: When a console makes a request for service of the computer, it "enters" the dashed box and proceeds to receive service according to the scheduling algorithm for this time-shared processor. When finally that request is complete, the response is fed back to the console, at which point the user at the console "wakes up" and then begins to generate a new request for the computer. The time spent by the user in generating this new request is referred to as the *think time*. Thus alternating periods of thinking and processing take place.

We assume that the thinking time is exponentially distributed as given by

$$P[\text{think time} \leq \tau] = 1 - e^{-\gamma\tau} \qquad \tau \geq 0 \qquad (4.48)$$

If $M \to \infty$ and $\gamma \to 0$ such that $M\gamma = \lambda$, we can create a Poisson arrival process at average rate λ from this finite population case.

Scherr [18] considered this case for which he assumed exponentially distributed service time and a round-robin processor-sharing scheduling algorithm. He solved for the average response time in the system without conditioning that result on the service time required. His result is

$$T = \frac{M/\mu}{1 - p_0} - \frac{1}{\gamma} \qquad (4.49)$$

where p_0 is the probability that no customers are in the dashed box and is given by

$$p_0 = \left[\sum_{m=0}^{M} \frac{M!}{(M-m)!} \left(\frac{\gamma}{\mu} \right)^m \right]^{-1}. \qquad (4.50)$$

Normalizing this average response time with respect to the average service time (that is, forming μT), we may plot this normalized response time as a function of the number of consoles M. See Fig. 4.17. From this figure we note

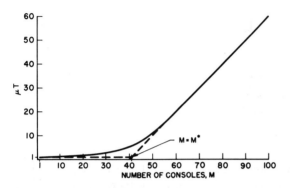

FIGURE 4.17   Finite population performance and saturation.

the very slow rise in the response time as the number of consoles increases from 1; however, after passing through a transition region the normalized response function becomes linear, with a slope of unity. This behavior is readily understandable. In the region where the response time is growing very slowly, it is clear that the number of users is so small that the periods when a customer needs service are often the periods when other customers are thinking and therefore not interfering with him. However, when the number of customers increases, we can see from (4.49) that the normalized response time must go linear (with the slope of unity) if p_0 approaches zero. Clearly p_0, the probability of an empty processor, will go to zero when the number of active consoles increases to a large enough value.

Due to the finite value of M, one questions whether it is possible to saturate the system. Indeed, if we define saturation as that point where the system goes unstable in some sense, such as average response time growing to infinity, we see immediately that our system is never saturated (for $\gamma/\mu < \infty$). Nevertheless, there does exist an appropriate definition for saturation, which we define as M^* and which is given by [19]

$$M^* = \frac{(1/\mu) + (1/\gamma)}{1/\mu} = \frac{\mu + \gamma}{\gamma} \qquad (4.51)$$

We are here defining the saturation number as the sum of the thinking time plus the average service time divided by the average service time. In Fig. 4.17 we see that the extrapolation of the linear portion of the response time back to the position where the normalized response time equals unity occurs at a number of consoles equal to the saturation number, M^*. The behavior of this asymptote shows, for $M \gg M^*$, that the system has "absorbed" M^* users and converted them into one user, and is now experiencing complete interference among the other $M - M^*$ users. This effect and numerous others are described in [19].

Greenberger [20] also considered a system of this sort in which he permitted swap time and finite quanta. He solved for the average response time conditioned on the service time and found a very good approximation to the behavior of this function. Adiri and Avi-Itzhak [21] also considered such a case and also solved for the average conditional response time. If we take the limit of Greenberger's result, where both the swap time and quantum are driven to zero, we find that the conditional response time may be given as

$$T(t) = \mu t T \tag{4.52}$$

where T is given through (4.49) and is the average unconditional response time. This behavior is also apparent from the graphical results presented in [21]. Once again we see that the round-robin scheduling algorithm gives linear behavior with respect to service time.

4.1.4 Measured Performance

It is of interest to compare the theoretical results described in Section 4.1.3 to actual system measurements. Unfortunately, there seems not to be a wealth of published literature on measurements of time-shared system response and behavior, although in the past two years this activity has accelerated somewhat.

In 1967 Estrin and Kleinrock [1] reported upon some results of simulation and, in particular, on certain measurements which had taken place prior to that time, notably the work of Scherr [18], Totschek [24], Sutherland [25], and Cantrell [26]. In that report the measurements described in the four papers were compared with certain simulation results and results from analytical modeling. A number of others have also studied certain user characteristics in a time-sharing environment. In 1968 Campbell and Haefner [27] reported upon the measurements of the GE (General Electric) time-sharing system. More recently, some work has come out of Bell Telephone Laboratories on the study of user and performance measurements, with particular emphasis on computer-communications traffic models. In particular, Jackson and Stubbs [28] presented a paper in 1969 that gave average values for a variety of measurements on a number of time-shared systems. For example, they measured average think time, average idle time, average response time, average number of characters per user burst, average number of bursts in a communications session, etc. Following that work, Fuchs and Jackson [29] estimated the distribution of many of these random variables in the computer-communication process. The most significant finding on their part was that the geometric distribution was capable of describing every discrete process measured; in addition, for all the continuous random variables studied they found that the gamma distribution was an excellent fit. Moreover, the parameter in the gamma distribution was confined to the range between 1.0 and 1.8; the significance of this is that when the parameter equals 1.0 it becomes the exponential distribution, and even at 1.8 certainly the tail of the distribution is exponential. Thus many analytical models studied under the assumption of exponential distribution seem not to be far from the truth. These last two reported papers have made significant contributions to the understanding of time-sharing systems and mark a major milestone in our progress toward understanding system behavior. Recently a paper by Van de Goor, Bell, and Witcraft [30] reported upon the measurement of a PDP-8 based time-sharing system. They present curves of response time versus number of users, which reflect behavior very much like that shown in Fig. 4.17.

It seems pointless to go into great detail as to what each measurement study produced. Such an activity is best carried out by referring back to the original sources. However, we can say that many of these measurement studies lend support to our analytical models in that both the assumptions and the performance predicted tend to correlate with the measurements.

4.1.5 *Open Problems and Conclusions*

It can be seen from the selected set of results as presented in Section 4.1.3 that significant progress has been made in modeling and analyzing a variety of interesting scheduling algorithms. We have demonstrated models and solutions which range from that algorithm (batch processing) which shows no discrimination with regard to job length among customers in a system to that discipline which shows the maximum possible discrimination on this basis (the FB model). In particular, one very natural intermediary discriminating algorithm is that of the RR; its properties were amply discussed in Section 4.1.3.

We took the liberty in this chapter of considering predominately only those scheduling algorithms in which the quantum approached zero. The motivation was one of simplicity both of analysis and in the presentation of results, and we feel it served the purpose well. Clearly, considerably more work could be done in pursuing the finite quantum cases and the cases for more general distributions of both service and interarrival time.

However, it is apparent to this author that two related problems of much greater significance should next be considered before more effort is put into yet bigger and better scheduling studies. The first of these problems is that of incorporating the effects of other points of congestion in a time-shared computer system: the storage capacity, the input-output devices, and the data channels which connect these devices together, as well as to the users. For example, the effect of page faulting in a paged memory system is often a source of delay and congestion as large or larger than is the scheduling algorithm. Little work has been done in attempting to study this effect in its relationship to the scheduling algorithm. However, recent work by Moore [31] and Buzen [32] has applied the general solution of finite Markovian closed queueing systems by Gordon and Newell [33] to the multiple-resource problem in time-shared systems. Their analytical computations compare very favorably with measurements they report upon. The multiple-resource model has been extended in the recent work of Baskett and Muntz [60].

The second significant problem is related to the question of optimization. So far we are capable only of analyzing a given scheduling algorithm and not of optimizing performance over the class of all such algorithms. Clearly, one cannot proceed in the direction of optimization until one has appropriately defined a criterion for optimality. We refer here to the cost of delay. This cost function varies from user to user and from application to application. Nevertheless, one must face up to the need for a definition of such a criterion if one hopes ever to optimize the system design. This question is not a new one and has been raised in a number of different contexts. Sutherland [34] discusses a simple bidding system to allocate time in a small community of users. Coffman and Kleinrock [35] consider countermeasures a user may adopt in order to defeat a given scheduling algorithm. One of the early works to discuss this question is that of Greenberger [20] in which he raised important questions regarding waiting time and cost. Diamond and Selwyn [36] consider a method for charging a user for use in a computer utility. Van den Heever [37] raises similar questions, as does Williams [38]. Recently, Mahl [39] considered pricing and allocation of resources in a time-shared environment.

In spite of these difficulties, it is fair to say that much has been gained through the mathematical modeling and analysis approach. The purpose of this approach is not to provide specific design parameters in exact numerical form for a given system, but rather to provide understanding as to how performance will vary as the system parameters change, and thereby gain insight into the behavior of a time-shared system. In this regard the progress has been good. The challenge now is to consider the coupled effects of other aspects of system behavior, as well as to formulate an appropriate criterion that will permit optimization.

4.2 SURVEY OF ANALYTIC METHODS
FOR COMPUTER NETWORK DESIGN

4.2.1 Introduction

Delay in communication and computer networks has recently become a subject of considerable interest. In this section we address ourselves to the topics of analysis and optimization of such nets. Those we consider are of the store-and-forward type more commonly known as message-switching networks.

The problem confronting the network designer is to create a system that provides suitable network performance at an acceptable system cost. Since in message-switched networks the messages experience queueing delays as they pass from node to node, the performance measure is usually taken to be the speed at which messages can be delivered. The optimization problem is to achieve minimal average delay at a fixed network cost by appropriately choosing the network topology, the channel capacity assignment, and the message routing and flow control procedure. The purpose of this section is to review some of the methods for handling various aspects of this problem.

4.2.2 Analytical Tools

The appropriate analytical methods are those which have developed from queueing theory. The basic tools from this theory are given in [4, 40, 41]. In the following subsections we consider first single-server and then multiple-server queueing systems, and discuss the usefulness of the basic results in each for our computer-network studies.

4.2.2.1 Single-Server Systems Much of queueing theory considers systems in which messages (customers) place demands for transmission (service) upon a single communication channel (the single server). When the average demand for service is less than the capacity of the channel to handle these demands, the system is said to be *stable*. The literature on stable single-server queueing systems is fairly voluminous, as exemplified by the excellent work by Cohen [40]. As in Section 4.1.2, single-server systems are characterized by $A(\tau)$, the distribution of interarrival times, and $B(t)$, the distribution of service times.

In the case when $A(\tau)$ is exponential (that is, Poisson arrivals), the literature contains fairly complete results. For such systems, in the case of first-come-first-served order of service, we know that W, the average waiting time in the queue, is given in (4.11); T, the average time in system (averaged over all service times as well) is given by

$$T = W + \bar{t} = \frac{\lambda \overline{t^2}}{2(1 - \rho)} + \bar{t} \tag{4.53}$$

where λ is the average arrival rate of messages, $\bar{t}$ and $\overline{t^2}$ are the first and second moments of $B(t)$, respectively, and $\rho = \lambda \bar{t} (< 1)$, as in Section 4.1.3.1. In the case when service time is also exponential, we have the well-known result

$$T = \frac{\bar{t}}{1 - \rho}. \tag{4.54}$$

When both $A(\tau)$ and $B(t)$ are arbitrary, the situation becomes much more complex, and only weak results are available. For example, in this case we cannot even give an expression for the average time in system T. Recently attention has been directed to developing *approximate* solution methods. These methods include placing bounds on the behavior of the system, studying the system behavior under light and heavy traffic conditions, and forming diffusion approximations to the physical queueing systems. A central result from this study of approximate solutions is that the average waiting time W in this general system is bounded from above by

$$W \le \frac{\lambda(\sigma_a^2 + \sigma_b^2)}{2(1 - \rho)} \tag{4.55}$$

where σ_a^2 and σ_b^2 are the variance of the arrival-time and service-time distributions, respectively. This upper bound was first shown by Kingman [42], and he also showed [43] in the heavy traffic case ($\rho \to 1$) that the average queueing time (W) in fact approached its upper bound and, moreover, that the distribution of waiting time was given, for $w \ge 0$, by

$$P[\text{waiting time} \le w] \cong 1 - e^{-2(1-\rho)w/[\lambda(\sigma_a^2 + \sigma_b^2)]} \tag{4.56}$$

This quite general result is a remarkably simple one, and shows that in the heavy-traffic case one expects the waiting-time distribution to be exponentially distributed with a mean given as the bound in (4.55). Equations (4.55) and (4.56) are the key results in queueing approximations.

The diffusion approximation to queueing (which is related to the heavy-traffic approximation) involves replacing the discontinuous random processes in queueing systems with continuous random walks (Brownian motion), typically with a reflecting barrier at the origin to prevent queue sizes and waiting times from going negative (see Gaver [44]). The main point here is that the pertinent distribution functions of a queueing system may be said to approximately obey a rather simple partial differential equation (a diffusion equation). From this, one may obtain approximate expressions for the time-dependent behavior (transient behavior). In the limit, as the transient disappears, this diffusion approximation shows that the equilibrium solution for the random process is given, for $w \geq 0$, by

$$P[\text{value of the random process} \leq w] \cong 1 - e^{2mw/\sigma^2} \qquad (4.57)$$

where m and σ^2 are the infinitesimal mean and variance of the diffusion process (Brownian motion). We note that (4.56) and (4.57) are of the same form, which merely points out that the two results are basically the same fundamental approximation to queueing systems under heavy traffic conditions. Numerical results that have been obtained using the diffusion approximation have been startling in terms of their accuracy when compared to the original queueing problem, and so one is encouraged that such an approach may be useful in obtaining approximate results for more difficult queueing problems.

4.2.2.2   Multiple Nodes and Networks.   The case of interest here, however, is that of multiple nodes in a network environment. The queueing problems encountered in networks are far more difficult than single-server problems. The difficulties are both deterministic and stochastic in nature. The deterministic problems come about due to the combinatorial features of networks. As a result, considerations from network flow theory (see, for example, [45]) become important in evaluating the maximum traffic that a given network can support and in providing methods for determining good topological configurations for networks. The topological design problem is at this stage still an unsolved problem, although good suboptimal procedures are available ([46–48]).

Besides new deterministic phenomena, networks give rise to new stochastic phenomena. For example, traffic entering a node in the network is dependent upon traffic elsewhere in the network and on other nodes through which this traffic has passed. A second difficulty is the phenomenon of *blocking*, which occurs when the finite storage capacity of a node becomes filled and the further reception of messages is temporarily prohibited. This then places a burden on neighboring nodes and they too tend to get blocked, causing the effect to propagate in the network. This effect is probably one of the least understood queueing effects in the study of nets and has significant impact upon performance. Another new phenomenon is the effect of the traffic matrix upon performance. In single-node problems, delays come about due to the variability of interarrival and service times. In networks, another source of variability (and therefore congestion) is the choice of source and destination for a message. For example, even with deterministic arrivals and service times, the randomness in the message destination causes bunching of traffic and therefore conflicting demands for service within the net.

The basic approach to solving these stochastic network problems is to find a means by which the network can be *decomposed* into analyzable single-server problems, and then to piece together the solution in a fashion that reproduces the original network structure and traffic flow.

Prior to the study of communication and computer networks, consideration had been given to networks of queues, and it is appropriate to summarize these previous results at this point. The system in which customers are permitted to enter, move among, and leave a collection of *independent* queueing stations in some random fashion was studied by Jackson [49]. His major result was to show, when the system is stable, that each node in the system could indeed be analyzed as a single queueing facility (under Markovian assumptions). This represents perhaps one of the first successful attempts at decomposing a network problem into a series of simpler single-node problems. The effect of the network on the solution was manifested in the calculation of the traffic that each node (looked upon as a node in isolation) was required to handle. Another fundamental result that permits decomposition of queueing networks is due to Burke [50]; he showed that if $A(\tau)$ and $B(t)$ are exponential, the interdeparture times are also exponentially distributed. Thus we preserve the Poisson nature of the traffic flow between network nodes. Using the simple structure of the linear equations of motion governing Markovian queues, Wallace [51] has developed a procedure for solving the system of equations numerically. More recently, Gordon and Newell [33], as mentioned in Section 4.15, have studied a system similar to Jackson's in which no customers are permitted to enter or leave, but rather exist in a closed system with constant circulation according to some transition probabilities; their results also indicate that a near decomposition of the network may be carried out.

The results referred to in the previous paragraph do not carry over trivially into message-oriented communication or computer nets, since messages maintain their lengths as they pass through the net and therefore service times and interarrival times are correlated. Fortunately, in the first comprehensive treatment of communication nets (reported in 1964 [52]) it could be shown for a wide variety of communication nets that it was possible to introduce an assumption which once again permitted a decomposition of the network into a collection of single channels. This "independence" assumption takes advantage of the fact that in networks of reasonable connectivity this correlation essentially disappears. With this assumption then, the decomposition which Jackson obtained applies also to our case, and a channel-by-channel analysis is possible, as follows.

For our networks we define the message delay as the total time that a message spends in the network from the time of its entry until the time it is delivered at its destination. We define T to be the average message delay, averaged over all messages. Furthermore, we let Z_{jk} be the average message delay for those messages whose origin is node j and whose destination is node

k; we assume a Poisson arrival process for such messages with an average of γ_{jk} messages per second and an exponential distribution of message lengths with an average of $1/\mu$ bits per message. Thus the total traffic entering the network (messages per second) has an average given by

$$\gamma = \sum_{j,k} \gamma_{jk} \tag{4.58}$$

With these definitions it is clear that an appropriate expression for the average message delay T is given by

$$T = \sum_{j,k} \frac{\gamma_{jk}}{\gamma} Z_{jk} \tag{4.59}$$

So far we have described a decomposition on the basis of origin-destination traffic. Of course, another decomposition is necessary to take us down to the single-channel level. For this purpose, we focus on each channel in the network. We define the following quantities for the ith channel: C_i as its capacity (bits per second); λ_i as the average message traffic it carries (messages per second); and T_i as the average time a message spends waiting for and using the ith channel. By relating the $\{\lambda_i\}$ to the $\{\gamma_{jk}\}$ via the paths taken by this jk traffic, it is easy to show that the performance measure of our system, T, may also be given as a sum over channels [52], viz.,

$$T = \sum_i \frac{\lambda_i}{\gamma} T_i \tag{4.60}$$

We have successfully decomposed our analysis problem into a set of simple single-channel analysis problems, that is, into the calculation of the set of delays $\{T_i\}$. Our decomposition has also resulted in the simplest stochastic assumptions: Poisson traffic and exponential service times. The solution to each of these single-server problems is already available to us through (4.54). The average service time $\bar{t}$ is related to the average message length $1/\mu$ (bits per message) and the channel capacity C_i (bits per second) as $\bar{t} = 1/\mu C_i$ (seconds per message). Thus this simple model gives us

$$T_i = \frac{1}{\mu C_i - \lambda_i} \tag{4.61}$$

This then provides a solution to the basic analysis problem for networks. A refinement on this decomposition is possible by permitting a nonexponential message-length distribution and making use of (4.53) rather than (4.54) in the calculation of T_i; of course, the result due to Burke will no longer apply, but, as an approximation, we may assume that the Markovian character of the traffic is preserved. Furthermore, in the case of computer networks one must include the effect of propagation time over long paths (approximately the speed of light) and the effect of overhead traffic within the network (e.g., routing information, acknowledgments, error control, etc.). Such models are discussed in [53] and [54] and lead to the following equation for average message delay in a computer network:

$$T = K + \sum_i \frac{\lambda_i}{\gamma} \left[\frac{1}{\mu' C_i} + \frac{\lambda_i/\mu C_i}{\mu C_i - \lambda_i} + PL_i + K \right] \qquad (4.62)$$

Here $1/\mu'$ represents the average message length for text data, whereas $1/\mu$ represents the average message length for text plus acknowledgment messages traveling within the network; PL_i represents the propagation delay over the ith channel; and K represents an assumed constant for nodal processing time. This model has been tested against a simulation of the ARPA Network.* The result of that comparison is given in Fig. 4.18 and shows an excellent fit

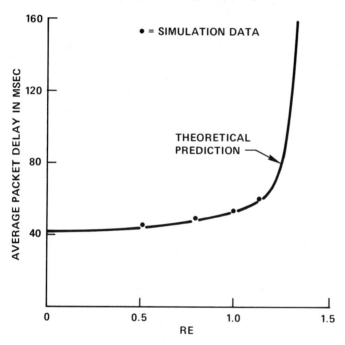

FIGURE 4.18   Single-packet message delay.

to the simulated data. In the ARPA Network short messages are given priority over long messages, and this effect may also be accounted for once again by using a decomposition of the sort described above, but by now introducing a two-priority class structure; theoretical and simulated results for this case are also excellent, as described in [56].

The conclusion one can draw from this section on analysis is that the key to the solution is a decomposition of a network into a collection of single-

*In 1967 Roberts [55] introduced the idea of an experimental computer network, which later developed into the Advanced Research Projects Agency (ARPA) Computer Network—see Chapter 13.

channel problems. The solution of each such problem is simple and contributes to the overall message delay through (4.60).

4.2.3 Optimization Tools

Having discussed some of the analytical techniques available for the study of networks, we now move on to the questions of synthesis and optimization. Perhaps the first communications network optimization problem was posed and solved by Kleinrock [52], in which he assumed that the network topology and the channel traffic were known quantities. Also, he assumed that the traffic was Markovian (Poisson arrivals and exponential message lengths) and justified certain of the above decomposition assumptions. For each channel the *optimal* assignment of capacity C_i was found that minimized the average message delay T, at a fixed total system cost D. The total cost of the network was assumed to be the cost of providing the channel capacities, and it was also assumed that this cost was linear with capacity at a rate of d_i dollars per unit of channel capacity on the ith channel. The simpler form for T_i given in (4.61) is used in this formulation. This problem takes the following form:

> PROBLEM A: Choose the set of channel capacities, C_i, to minimize T at fixed cost D where

$$T = \sum_i \frac{\lambda_i}{\gamma} T_i \qquad (4.63)$$

$$D = \sum_i d_i C_i \qquad (4.64)$$

The solution to this problem assigns a capacity to the ith channel in an amount equal to the average traffic carried plus an excess capacity proportional to the square root of that traffic as follows:*

$$C_i = \frac{\lambda_i}{\mu} + \frac{D_e}{d_i} \frac{\sqrt{\lambda_i d_i}}{\sum_j \sqrt{\lambda_j d_j}} \qquad (4.65)$$

where

$$D_e = D - \sum_i \frac{\lambda_i d_i}{\mu} \qquad (4.66)$$

The expression for D_e that represents the excess dollars is merely the difference between the total number of dollars available to build the network and the amount that must be spent in providing each channel with its minimum

---

*Any efficient channel capacity assignment will clearly provide more than the minimum (λ_i/μ) to the ith channel in order to avoid the infinite delay which that channel would otherwise introduce. When any such assignment is then substituted back into (4.61), the term involving λ_i disappears and all that remains is a term which depends upon the fashion in which the excess dollars are used to assign excess capacity to each of the channels.

capacity, λ_i/μ, which represents the average rate at which bits will enter the ith channel. Any sensible capacity assignment will provide more than this minimal capacity to each channel; this is clear, since we find from (4.61) that T_i will grow to infinity with less than (or equal to) this amount of capacity, thereby rendering the overall performance as given in (4.60) unacceptable. Clearly, D_e must be greater than zero if we are to keep away from the unbounded delay that awaits us at $C_i = \lambda_i/\mu$. The excess dollars are divided in a way that distributes capacity according to the square root of the weighted traffic on a channel. When this assignment is substituted back into the performance function, we obtain

$$T = \frac{\bar{n}}{\mu D_e} \left(\sum_i \sqrt{d_i \frac{\lambda_i}{\lambda}} \right)^2 \tag{4.67}$$

where $\lambda = \sum_i \lambda_i$ and represents the total rate at which messages move around within the net. Moreover,

$$\bar{n} = \frac{\lambda}{\gamma} \tag{4.68}$$

which is easily shown [52] to represent the average path length; note that it equals the ratio of the rate at which messages move around within the network to the rate at which messages enter the network, and so represents the average number of steps a message will take before emerging from the network. In the special case when $d_i = 1$ for all channels (which says that channel capacity costs the same per unit of capacity independent of the location of the channel), we have that the cost function given in (4.64) may be replaced by $D = \sum_i C_i = C$, where we have defined C to represent the total capacity within the network. In this case we have

$$D_e = \mu C(1 - \bar{n}\rho) \tag{4.69}$$

Here $\rho = \gamma/\mu C$ and represents the ratio of the rate at which bits enter the network per second (γ/μ) to the rate at which the network can handle bits (C). Thus ρ represents what we have called the network load. Substituting this special form for D_e into (4.67), we obtain the result

$$T = \frac{\bar{n}}{\mu C(1 - \bar{n}\rho)} \left(\sum_i \sqrt{\frac{\lambda_i}{\lambda}} \right)^2 \tag{4.70}$$

Here we see the effect of the pole at $\bar{n}\rho = 1$: as the network load ρ approaches $1/\bar{n}$, the delay T grows very quickly to infinity, and so the point $\rho = 1/\bar{n}$ represents the maximum load or flow that the network can support. This corresponds in a real sense to the maximum flow calculation that one would make using arguments from network flow theory. Of course, $\bar{n}$ is a design parameter and depends upon the topology and the routing procedure, whereas ρ itself is an input parameter, which depends upon the input rate and the total capacity of the network.

It is possible to obtain insight regarding preferred network topologies and preferred routing procedures from the result given in (4.70). These, and other related results, were published as Kleinrock's Ph.D. thesis (at the Massachusetts Institute of Technology) in 1962 (this work later appeared as [52]). Little was published in this field from then until 1969 [53]. Whatever the reason for this past inactivity, it is clear that current interest is due to the development of computer networks.

In a recent paper by Meister, Mueller, and Rudin [57], it was observed that in minimizing T in Problem A, wide variation was possible among the channel delays T_i. As a result, they posed the following problem, whose solution is closely related to that of Problem A.

PROBLEM B: Same as Problem A except the performance measure T is replaced by $T^{(k)}$ and one wishes to find that set of channel capacities which minimizes $T^{(k)}$:

$$T^{(k)} = \left[\sum_i \frac{\lambda_i}{\gamma} (T_i)^k \right]^{1/k} \tag{4.71}$$

By raising T_i to the kth power, they found that for $k > 1$ a reduction is forced in the variation among the T_i. Their solution for the optimal channel capacity assignment with a given value k, which we denote by $C_i^{(k)}$, may be written as

$$C_i^{(k)} = \frac{\lambda_i}{\mu} + \frac{D_e}{d_i} \frac{(\lambda_i d_i^k)^{1/(k+1)}}{\sum_j (\lambda_j d_j^k)^{1/(k+1)}} \tag{4.72}$$

For $k = 1$, note that $C_i^{(1)}$ is exactly the solution given in (4.65). Furthermore, using this channel capacity assignment in the expression for $T^{(k)}$ given in (4.71) yields

$$T^{(k)} = \frac{(\bar{n})^{1/k}}{\mu D_e} \left[\sum_i \left(\frac{\lambda_i d_i^k}{\lambda} \right)^{1/(1+k)} \right]^{\frac{1+k}{k}} \tag{4.73}$$

which again reduces to the result in (4.67) for $k = 1$. As we mentioned earlier, as k gets large, the variation in the numbers T_i reduces. In particular, let us examine the case $k \rightarrow \infty$. Here we have

$$C_i^{(\infty)} = \frac{\lambda_i}{\mu} + \frac{D_e}{\sum_j d_j} \tag{4.74}$$

Thus we see the channel capacity is assigned so as to give each channel its minimum required amount (λ_i/μ) plus a constant additional amount to each channel. In this case it is clear from (4.61) that each T_i is the same (no variation among them). If we use the assignment $C_i^{(\infty)}$ in our basic performance equation, (4.60), we obtain

$$T = \frac{\bar{n}}{\mu D_e} \sum_j d_j \qquad k = \infty \tag{4.75}$$

We note that in this particular case $T = T^{(\infty)}$. At the other extreme, let us examine the case $k = 0$, which results in

$$C_i^{(0)} = \frac{\lambda_i}{\mu} + \frac{\lambda_i D_e}{\bar{n}\gamma d_i} \qquad (4.76)$$

In the case when all $d_i = 1$, this assignment gives capacity to a channel in proportion to the traffic carried by that channel (commonly known as the proportional capacity assignment). Using this value in (4.60), we obtain

$$T = \frac{\bar{n}}{\mu D_e} \sum_j d_j \qquad k = 0 \qquad (4.77)$$

which is exactly the same expression as when we used the capacity assignment for $k \longrightarrow \infty$. It is quite amazing that at both extremes $(k = 0, \infty)$ we find different channel capacity assignments each of which gives the same performance. Of course, the performance at these extremes (and for values of $k \neq 1$) will be inferior to the performance for $k = 1$ as given in (4.67). The remarkable observation is that T increases very slowly as k varies from unity, as shown, for example, in [57]. Moreover, in that reference it is shown that the variance of message delay is minimized when k is chosen equal to 2.

In applying the above methods to the study of the ARPA Computer Network, Kleinrock [54] introduced the following variation to Problem A, since the cost function as given in (4.64) was found not to represent tariffs for high-speed telephone data channels used in that network.

PROBLEM C: Same as Problem A except D is given by

$$D = \sum d_i C_i^\alpha \qquad (4.78)$$

where $0 \leq \alpha \leq 1$.

The channel capacity assignment that solves Problem C must satisfy the following equation:

$$C_i - \frac{\lambda_i}{\mu} - C_i^{(1-\alpha)/2} g_i = 0 \qquad (4.79)$$

where g_i depends upon λ_i, d_i, and other constants of the problem. This equation is, in general, nonlinear and cannot be solved explicitly. Nevertheless, in applying a numerical solution of this problem for the ARPA net it was found that the message delay T varied insignificantly with α for $0.3 \leq \alpha \leq 1$. This indicates that the closed-form solution to Problem A ($\alpha = 1$) may serve as an approximation to the more difficult Problem C.

It can be shown that most efficient* channel capacity assignments yield behavior of the form $T = K/(1 - \bar{n}\rho)$ in the vicinity $\rho \approx 1/\bar{n}$ (near saturation), where K is a slowly varying function of ρ. This implies that the domi-

---

*That is, assignments which give capacity C_i equal to λ_i/μ plus *some* excess.

nant behavior of T is given by the pole at $\rho = 1/\bar{n}$ and behaves as a simple pole there. This invariant behavior is due to the fact that as ρ approaches $1/\bar{n}$, all T_i remain finite until $\rho = 1/\bar{n}$ (that is, all channels saturate at the *same* external load that corresponds to the point $D_e = 0$). However, with *inefficient* channel capacity assignments, it is typical that as ρ increases, *one* channel saturates before the others and its delay suddenly dominates the sum in (4.60); this causes a very *rapid* increase in T, since below this point the guilty channel contributes only a small fraction to the sum (4.60). Thus we see a sharp threshold effect where delay remains almost constant until ρ reaches this critical value (below $1/\bar{n}$), at which point it grows enormously; this behavior will be typical in networks when the $\{\gamma_{jk}\}$ vary in time. The critical value of ρ may be calculated by considering a new traffic matrix with entries $\beta\gamma_{jk}$. For $\beta \ll 1$, one needs merely to calculate each channel load $\beta\lambda_i/\mu C_i$ and identify the largest such load. Then β is increased until it reaches a maximum value, β^*, at which point the largest channel load equals unity. Then, the critical (maximum) network load is given by $\rho^* = \beta^*\gamma/\mu C$. The (almost) constant message delay experienced for loads below ρ^* is given by the zero-traffic delay ($\rho \to 0$). This two-parameter model is discussed further in [41] and [61].

4.2.4 Additional Considerations

Minimizing cost at fixed average message delay by appropriately choosing the channel capacities is the *dual* for Problems A, B, and C. This was studied in [54] and considered recently by Whitney [58]. Choice of network topology was considered in Kleinrock's original work. Recently, Frank et al. [47] considered this problem for the ARPA net and developed suboptimal topological search procedures. They also addressed the problem of choosing an optimal channel assignment when capacities must be chosen from a finite set; Meister, Mueller, and Rudin [57] also give an approach to this problem, and Whitney [58] and Doll [46] considered this problem for a fixed tree topology. Doll also addressed the important question of multiplexing and concentrating the data traffic. Frank et al. [48] devised an *optimal* procedure for selecting discrete channel capacities for tree networks, making use of the analytical techniques discussed in Section 4.2.2, and much of this work is discussed in Chapter 1 of this volume. Meister et al. [57] further consider the case of nodal costs and capacities.

Message *routing procedures* must also be considered. Of all those so far discussed, this problem lends itself least to analysis. A routing procedure is merely a decision rule that determines the node a message will next visit in its path through the network. A discussion and classification of routing procedures is given in [56]. A related and very important question is that of flow control of messages within the network. Here we refer to methods incorporated at the inputs to the network which control the message traffic that may enter in order to reduce congestion and blocking in the network itself (a recent paper by Kahn and Crowther [59] discusses this issue).

Last, we note that the ultimate standard in these problems is measurement of real systems. This is receiving considerable attention in the ARPA net (see, for example, [62-64]).

4.2.5 Conclusion

The attempt in this section has been to describe and to evaluate various tools for studying delay in communication and computer nets. These tools must be considerably improved. Nevertheless, they have been useful in network studies. Among the most difficult remaining problems, we mention the blocking effect due to finite storage capacity, the analysis and design of routing procedures, the study of network flow control, and the design of network topologies.

4.3 CONCLUSIONS

We have attempted to survey some of the pertinent methods and results that we obtain from a delay analysis of computer systems. As we have shown, the results available for the modeling of time-shared computer systems in Section 4.1 are far more advanced than is the material described in Section 4.2 for the analysis and design of computer networks. This is no surprise, since the latter problem is significantly more difficult than the former. Presently, considerably more effort is being put into the computer network design problem, and some of the progress there has been reported in Section 4.2. Happily, a careful measurement program is now under way (specifically for the ARPA Computer Network) so that we may verify the correctness of our analytical models. Results to date indicate that our models are reasonably accurate, and work with these current models is in progress.

REFERENCES

[1] G. ESTRIN and L. KLEINROCK, Measures, Models, and Measurements for Time-Shared Computer Utilities, *Proc. ACM Natl. Conf.* (1967), 85–96.

[2] E. G. COFFMAN, Studying Multiprogramming Systems with the Queueing Theory, *Datamation*, **13** (June 1967), 47–54.

[3] J. M. MCKINNEY, A Survey of Analytical Time-Sharing Models, *Computing Surv.*, **1** (June 1969), 105–116.

[4] D. R. Cox and W. L. Smith, *Queues*, Methuen, London, 1961.

[5] L. Kleinrock, Analysis of a Time-Shared Processor, *Naval Res. Logistics Quart.*, **11** (1964), 59–73.

[6] L. Kleinrock, Time-Shared Systems: A Theoretical Treatment, *J. Assoc. Computing Machinery*, **14** (April 1967), 242–261.

[7] W. Chang, A Queueing Model for a Simple Case of Time-Sharing, *IBM Syst. J.*, **5** (1966), 115–125.

[8] J. E. Shemer, Some Mathematical Considerations of Time-Sharing Scheduling Algorithms, *J. Assoc. Computing Machinery*, **14** (April 1967), 262–272.

[9] M. Sakata, S. Noguchi, and J. Oizumi, Analysis of a Processor-Shared Queueing Model for Time-Sharing Systems, *Proc. 2nd Hawaii Intern. Conf. Syst. Sci.* (Jan. 1969), 625–628.

[10] E. G. Coffman, R. R. Muntz, and H. Trotter, Waiting Time Distributions for Processor-Sharing Systems, *J. Assoc. Computing Machinery*, **17** (Jan. 1970), 123–130.

[11] L. Kleinrock, A Continuum of Time-Sharing Scheduling Algorithms, Spring Joint Computer Conf., *AFIPS Conf. Proc.* (May 1970), 453–458.

[12] J. Hsu, Analysis of a Continuum of Processor-Sharing Models for Time-Shared Computer Systems, Ph.D. dissertation, School of Engineering and Applied Science, Computer Science Department, University of California, Los Angeles, 1971.

[13] E. G. Coffman and L. Kleinrock, Feedback Queueing Models for Time-Shared Systems, *J. Assoc. Computing Machinery*, **15** (Oct. 1968) 549–576.

[14] L. E. Schrage and L. W. Miller, The Queue M/G/1 with Feedback to Lower Priority Queues, *Management Sci.*, **13** (1967), 466–474.

[15] L. Kleinrock and R. R. Muntz, Multilevel Processor-Sharing Queueing Models for Time-Shared Systems, *Proc. Sixth Intern. Teletraffic Congr.*, Munich, Germany (Aug. 1970), 341/1–341/8.

[16] L. Kleinrock and E. G. Coffman, Distribution of Attained Service in Time-Shared Systems, *J. Computers Syst. Sci.*, **1** (1967), 287–298.

[17] L. Kleinrock, R. R. Muntz, and J. Hsu, Tight Bounds on Average Response Time for Processor-Sharing Models of Time-Shared Computer Systems, *Proc. IFIP Congress* **1971**, Ljubljana, Yugoslavia (Aug. 1971), TA2, 50–58.

[18] A. L. Scherr, *An Analysis of Time-Shared Computer Systems*, MIT Press, Cambridge, Mass., 1967.

[19] L. Kleinrock, Certain Analytic Results for Time-Shared Processors, *Proc. IFIP Congress* **1968**, Edinburgh, Scotland (Aug. 1968), 838–845.

[20] M. Greenberger, The Priority Problem and Computer Time-Sharing, *Management Sci.*, **12** (1966), 888–906.

[21] I. Adiri and B. Avi-Itzhak, A Time-Sharing Queue with a Finite Number of Customers, *J. Assoc. Computing Machinery*, **16** (April 1969), 315–323.

[22] E. G. Coffman, and B. Krishnamoorthi, Preliminary Analyses of Time-Shared Computer Operation, *Doc. SP-1719*, System Development Corp., Santa Monica, Calif., Aug. 1964.

[23] B. KRISHNAMOORTHI and R. C. WOOD, Time-Shared Computer Operations with Both Interarrival and Service Times Exponential, *J. Assoc. Computing Machinery*, **13** (July 1966), 317–338.

[24] R. A. TOTSCHEK, An Empirical Investigation into the Behavior of the SDC Time-Sharing System, *SDC Report SP-2191*, Aug. 1965.

[25] G. G. SUTHERLAND, talk presented at workshop on models for time-shared processing in symposium sponsored by the IEEE Communications Technology Group and the Computer Group.

[26] H. CANTRELL, talk presented at workshop on models for time-shared processing in symposium sponsored by the IEEE Communications Technology Group and the Computer Group.

[27] D. J. CAMPBELL and W. J. HAEFNER, Measurement and Analysis of Large Operating Systems during System Development, Fall Joint Computer Conf., *AFIPS Conf. Proc.*, **33** (1968), 903–914.

[28] P. E. JACKSON and C. D. STUBBS, A Study of Multi-access Computer Communications, Spring Joint Computer Conf., *AFIPS Conf. Proc.*, **34** (1969), 491–504.

[29] E. FUCHS and P. E. JACKSON, Estimates of Distributions of Random Variables for Certain Computer Communications Traffic Models, *Commun. ACM*, **13** (Dec. 1970), 752–757.

[30] A VAN DER GOOR, C. G. BELL, and B. WITCRAFT, A Control Unit for a DEC PDP-8 Computer and a Burroughs Disk, *IEEE Trans. Computers*, **C-18** (Nov. 1969), 1044–1048.

[31] C. G. MOORE, III, Network Models for Large-Scale Time-Sharing Systems, *Tech. Rept.* **71-1**, ISDOS Research Project, Department of Industrial Engineering, University of Michigan, April 30, 1971.

[32] BUZEN, J., Analysis of System Bottlenecks Using a Queueing Network Model, *Proc. ACM SIGOPS Workshop on Syst. Performance Evaluation*, Harvard University, April 5–7, 1971, 82–103.

[33] W. J. GORDON and G. F. NEWELL, Closed Queueing Systems with Exponential Servers, *Operations Res.*, **15** (April 1967), 254–265.

[34] I. E. SUTHERLAND, A Futures Market in Computer Time, *Commun. ACM*, **11** (June 1968), 449–451.

[35] E. G. COFFMAN and L. KLEINROCK, Computer Scheduling Methods and Their Countermeasures, *Proc. SJFF*, **32** (1968), 11–21.

[36] D. S. DIAMOND and L. L. SELWYN, Considerations for Computer Utility Pricing Policies, *Proc. 23rd ACM Natl. Conf.* (1968), 189–200.

[37] R. J. VAN DEN HEEVER, Computer Time-Sharing Priority Systems, *Operations Res. Center Rept. ORC 69-22*, College of Engineering, University of California, Berkeley, Aug. 1969.

[38] J. G. WILLIAMS, A Mathematical Study of Some Pricing and Scheduling Algorithms for a Shared Computer Facility, Ph.D. dissertation, School of Engineering and Applied Science, University of Virginia, Aug. 1969.

[39] R. MAHL, An Analytical Approach to Computer Systems Scheduling, Ph.D. dissertation, Department of Electrical Engineering, University of Utah, June 1970.

[40] J. COHEN, *The Single Server Queue*, Wiley, New York, 1969.

[41] L. KLEINROCK, *Queueing Systems: Theory and Applications*, to be published by Wiley Interscience, New York, 1973.

[42] J. F. C. KINGMAN, Some Inequalities for the Queue GI/G/1, *Biometrica*, **49** (1962), 315–324.

[43] J. F. C. KINGMAN, On Queues in Heavy Traffic, *J. Roy. Statistical Soc.*, **B24** (1962), 383–392.

[44] D. GAVER, Diffusion Approximations and Models for Certain Congestion Problems, *J. Appl. Probability*, **5** (1968), 607–623.

[45] H. FRANK and I. T. FRISCH, *Communication, Transmission and Transportation Networks*, Addison-Wesley, Reading, Mass., 1971.

[46] D. DOLL, Efficient Allocation of Resources in Centralized Computer-Communication Network Design, *SEL Tech. Rept. 36*, University of Michigan, 1969.

[47] H. FRANK, I. T. FRISCH, and W. CHOU, Topological Considerations in the Design of the ARPA Computer Network, Spring Joint Computer Conf., *AFIPS Conf. Proc.* (May 1970), 581–587.

[48] H. FRANK, I. T. FRISCH, R. VAN SLYKE, and W. S. CHOU, Optimal Design of Centralized Computer Networks, *Networks*, **1** (1971), 43–57.

[49] J. JACKSON, Networks of Waiting Lines, *Operations Res.*, **5** (1957), 518–521.

[50] P. BURKE, The Output of a Queueing System, *Operations Res.*, **4** (1956), 699–704.

[51] V. WALLACE, Representation of Markovian Systems by Network Models, *SEL Tech. Rept. 42*, University of Michigan, 1969.

[52] L. KLEINROCK, *Communication Nets: Stochastic Flow and Delay*, McGraw-Hill, New York, 1964. Reprint. New York: Dover Publications, 1972.

[53] L. KLEINROCK, Models for Computer Networks, *Proc. Intern. Conf. Commun.* (1969), 21–9 to 21–16.

[54] L. KLEINROCK, Analytic and Simulation Methods in Computer Network Design, Spring Joint Computer Conf., *AFIPS Conf. Proc.* (May 1970), 569–579.

[55] L. ROBERTS, Multiple Computer Networks and Inter-computer Communications, ACM Symp. Operating Syst. Principles, Gatlinburg, Tenn. (Oct. 1–4, 1967).

[56] G. FULTZ and L. KLEINROCK, Adaptive Routing Techniques for Store-and-Forward Computer-Communication Networks, *Proc. Intern. Conf. Commun.* (1971), 39–1 to 39–8.

[57] B. MEISTER, H. MUELLER, and H. RUDIN, New Optimization Criteria for Message-Switching Networks, *IEEE Trans. Commun. Technol.* **Com-19** (June 1971), 256–260.

[58] V. WHITNEY, A Study of Optimal File Assignment and Communication Network Configuration in Remote-Access Computer Message Processing and Communication Systems, *SEL Tech. Rept. 48*, University of Michigan, 1970.

[59] R. E. KAHN and W. R. CROWTHER, Flow Control in a Resource-Sharing Computer Network, *IEEE Trans. Commun. Com-20* (June 1972), 539–546.

[60] F. BASKETT and R. R. MUNTZ, Queueing Network Models with Different Classes of Customers, *Proc. COMPCON 72* (September 1972), 205–209.

[61] H. FRANK, R. E KAHN, and L. KLEINROCK, Computer Communication Network Design—Experience with Theory and Practice, Spring Joint Computer Conf., *AFIPS Conf. Proc.* (May 1972), 255–270.

[62] G. COLE, Computer Network Measurements: Techniques and Experiments, Ph.D. dissertation, School of Engineering and Applied Science, Computer Science Department, University of California, Los Angeles, 1971.

[63] V. CERF and W. NAYLOR, Storage Considerations in Store-and-Forward Message Switching, *Proc. Wescon* (September 1972), Session 7, Paper 3.

[64] L. KLEINROCK, Performance Models and Measurements of the ARPA Computer Network, *ONLINE 72 Conf. Proc.* (September 1972), to be published.

5

Common-Carrier
Data Communication

ROBERT W. LUCKY

Bell Telephone Laboratories, Inc., Holmdel, New Jersey

INTRODUCTION

For the most part the other chapters in this volume are concerned with the design of communication networks primarily designed for computer communication. There are few such networks in existence today. Virtually all the present demand for man–machine and machine–machine communication is handled by the facilities of the common carriers—the Bell System, Western Union, and General Telephone and the many other independent telephone companies. Although the need for data services has become increasingly evident during the past decade, the bulk of the common-carrier plant has been designed using voice-transmission objectives. In most cases these facilities can be adapted quite well for data transmission using modulators and demodulators (modems) that convert digital information into voice-like, analog signals. The data traffic is then usually handled and switched exactly like voice traffic on the Direct Distance Dialed (DDD) telephone network.

For some communication networks, such as the ARPA Network described elsewhere in this book, or in the example of airline reservation systems, the data transmission links are leased from the common carriers on a private-line basis, while the switching and network control functions are provided by the user. Here again, the transmission characteristics of the network are dependent upon the voice telephone facilities. It is the use of these telephone facilities for data transmission that is the subject of the present chapter. The services of the common carriers for data transmission, the basic techniques and equipment for transmission, and the idiosyncracies and the behavior of the network will be described. Finally, we must note the evolution within the common carriers towards providing transmission techniques specifically engineered for data communication—making use of existing pulse code modulation systems as backbone carriers for time-multiplexed computer-communications systems of the type described elsewhere in this volume.

5.1 DATA TRANSMISSION FACILITIES AND SERVICES

The voice telephone network is perhaps the most remarkable information processing system yet constructed by man. In 1970 it served 100,000,000 telephones in the United States. The number of possible interconnections is clearly enormous. The worth of this plant is approximately 50 billion dollars. Over 1 million people are employed by AT & T alone in the care and feeding of this huge network. Virtually every statistic associated with the telephone network can be phrased in some extraordinary manner. Its ready accessibility and virtual ubiquity make it the obvious first contender for handling data traffic.

The data services obtainable from the telephone companies are quite varied and are completely described only by the tariff documents, which can differ from state to state and from time to time. Here we can only give a brief and incomplete sketch of the categories of service offerings. Turning to the description of the telephone facilities for data, we encounter the great diversity in age and type of equipment that can appear in a telephone link. In this section we shall describe the equipment makeup of a typical telephone connection, stressing those factors that can determine data transmission performance. In Section 5.4 the important question of the error statistics of the end-to-end behavior of a telephone connection for data transmission will be considered.

5.1.1   Data Services

Data service offerings can be divided into *private* (or leased) lines and *switched* (public) lines. In either case a variety of bandwidths and other specifications can be obtained. For voice bandwidth facilities the switched data calls are routed through the ordinary DDD telephone network and a different connection is usually obtained each time a call is dialed. On the other hand, a private line does not traverse the switching equipment and its composition is fixed over long durations. Because switching equipment is not involved in private lines, these facilities are less prone to the chief source of errors on switched connections—impulse noise originating in switching offices. (No quantitative measurements on the magnitude of this advantage appear to be available.)

Since the composition of a private line is fixed, its transmission characteristics can be compensated by fixed equalizing filters to provide greater bandwidth and quality for data transmission than a switched connection. This compensation, arranged by the telephone companies, is known as *conditioning* and is available in several grades for voiceband lines. The top grade of conditioning, type C4, specifies an amplitude variation of -2- to $+3$-dB variation over a bandwidth of from 500 to 3000 Hz, and a -2- to $+6$-dB variation over the 3000- 3200-Hz to bandwidth. By contrast, an "average" switched connection would have only a bandwidth of from about 400 to 2700 Hz. Lesser grades of conditioning available are known as types C1 and C2 conditioning. In each case, complete specifications on leased lines are available from the telephone companies.

Depending on the length of the line and on the usage pattern, the cost of a private line can be more or less than the equivalent usage of the switched network. Typically, if more than several hours of traffic are to be carried each day between two points, the private line is the more economical of the two alternatives.

5.1.2   Bandwidths and Data Rates

Most of this chapter will stress voiceband data communication, in which the available band of something less than 3000 Hz will support data rates of up to about 4800 bps on DDD calls and up to about 10,000 bps on private lines. However, other bandwidth packages, both of a private and switched nature, can be obtained from the common carriers. *Narrowband* facilities are those of less than voice bandwidth. These are commonly employed for telegraph transmission at speeds of less than 300 bps.

There are in existence two fairly extensive switched narrowband networks —the Western Union TWX and TELEX networks. Both of these networks use portions of the AT&T voiceband transmission plant. Long-haul telegraph transmission is generally accomplished by frequency dividing voiceband channels into subparcels of six or eight telegraph channels apiece. Local distribution and some short-haul transmission use loops and other facilities ordinarily associated with voiceband transmission. In these cases the cost of multiplexing narrowband channels into voiceband parcels is greater than the potential bandwidth cost savings. In fact, the cost of telegraph transmission via a narrowband channel is often very little different from that charged for Dataphone transmission at an equivalent speed over the DDD network. This paradox is due to the difficulty in taking real advantage of bandwidth sharing among the narrowband customers because of their relative sparseness.

Wideband facilities are those of greater width than a single voice channel. The next larger unit that naturally occurs in the telephone-transmission hierarchy is the *group* bandwidth equivalent to 12 voice channels. A group-band is 48 kHz in width and, with associated modulation and demodulation devices, has a normal data rate of 50 kbps. Although speeds of over 100 kbps have been demonstrated on groupbands, at this time there does not appear to be sufficient commercial demand for the introduction of such data rates.

Nearly all wideband channels are private-line arrangements. However, there are switched networks available for broadband transmission. Western Union has what it terms Broadband Exchange Service, while AT&T has (still under experimental tariffing) Data-Phone 50, operating between five cities with 50-kbps transmission.

Data speeds in the range of 200 to 500 kbps have been obtained by utilizing greater bandwidths than that of the group. Generally, there is an economy in larger bandwidth offerings; i.e., the cost per bit per second is less per unit bandwidth. The common carriers offer bulk bandwidth packages for private-line usage through their Telpak tariffs. For example, Telpak D has an equivalent capacity of 240 voice channels, which can be subdivided by the customer into whatever combination of bands he desires.

5.1.3 Direction of Transmission

Whether or not a communication facility has the capability of transmitting in both directions simultaneously can be an important consideration in system design. Virtually all lines obtained from common carriers are inherently either *half-duplex*, in which transmission at full capacity can be from A to B *or* from B to A, or *full-duplex*, in which transmission at full capacity can proceed in both directions simultaneously. This distinction is equivalent to describing the facility as two wire or four wire.

All long-haul facilities are four wire, so that separate paths exist for each direction and they are clearly full duplex. However, especially in DDD service, the local connection is a two-wire loop, and the end-to-end service is reduced to half-duplex operation. It is still possible to use a two-wire facility in a full-duplex data mode by frequency dividing the band into forward and reverse channels. This subdivision is normally accomplished by the modem, with a high-speed forward channel and a low-speed reverse channel. The dichotomy between full- and half-duplex service is then blurred. The only real difference is whether or not the *full* channel capacity is available in both directions simultaneously. Where two-wire loops are used, this is generally not the case. In private- line long-haul offerings, full-duplex service can usually be obtained at a slight extra charge by the installation of four-wire local loop connections.

5.1.4 Common-Carrier Facilities

To plan computer-communication systems, it is not usually necessary to know in detail the types and characteristics of equipment present in the common-carrier plant. What is important is rather the behavior from end to end on a given connection. This behavior is determined by the types, ages, and conditions of equipment that a given call encounters, as well as by many factors both internal and external to the telephone plant. At this point it will be helpful to describe briefly the overall transmission and switching plans of the telephone system and some of the individual equipment makeup that can affect data performance.

5.1.5 Switching

The switching plan used to interconnect telephone (or data) customers is a hierarchical system with the important feature of alternative routing. Each subscriber is connected by a loop (copper cable pair) to a *local central office*. In calls intended for other subscribers served by this same office a direct connection is made by switches within the local central office.

Often calls are made to subscribers within the same city, but served by a different central office. In this case the call may be routed directly between central offices via a transmission facility known as a trunk. However, in most cities there are too many central offices for it to be economical to have direct trunk interconnections between each possible pair. Therefore, the local central offices are interconnected via trunks to a *tandem office*, which serves a cluster of local offices.

When calls are placed to points outside a city, they are routed via another kind of office known as a *toll office*, and from here on to intercity trunks. The complete switching hierarchy consists of four levels of toll offices, as shown in Fig. 5.1. When a connection is established through the toll plant, the route is picked automatically by the switches in each center according to a predetermined plan. At any level in the hierarchy there will be a first choice of routing, which will give the shortest (and usually best-quality)

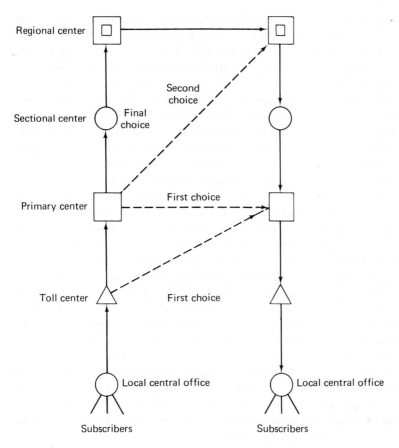

Regional center

Second choice

Sectional center   Final choice

Primary center   First choice

Toll center   First choice

Local central office   Local central office

Subscribers   Subscribers

FIGURE 5.1

connection. However, this route may be filled and an alternative path must be found. Then a second-choice route will be tried, and so on, until only a final choice remains. This final choice routes the call upward to the next level in the hierarchy. Sometimes the final choice is the only choice, but there are many trunks which shortcut through the hierarchy where high traffic concentration exists. The dotted paths in Fig. 5.1 show the choices that might be present for routing a call at the first two centers encountered. Similar kinds of alternatives, not shown on the figure, would also be present at the other centers for the call illustrated.

It is easy to understand from the switching hierarchy how calls between the same two subscribers can differ greatly in transmission characteristics. For example, the call in Fig. 5.1 traverses a minimum of four trunks when traffic permits. At worst, however, on another occasion the same call might pass through nine (the maximum possible number under any circumstances) connection trunks. This latter circumstance would be extremely remote. In a Bell System study made in 1961 in dialing calls between White Plains, New York, and Sacramento, California, the probability of requiring only a single trunk was 0.5, that of requiring two trunks, 0.3, and so on down to a 0.01 probability of requiring the maximum (in this particular route) of five trunks.

In data transmission the switching offices themselves are of importance because of the noise they introduce into data calls. With the constant switching of adjacent circuits, sometimes involving high voltages as in ringing, various transient voltages can be coupled into a given line. In this respect the local central offices are usually the weak points. There is a wide diversity in the types and ages of switching equipment employed, with the older equipment generally resulting in the worst impulse noise contamination. The oldest switches in use are the *step-by-step* switches. Central offices using this type of switching are sometimes unsuitable for data transmission. A data customer who might ordinarily be served for voice calls through such an unsuitable office would be routed to another central office for data service.

The step-by-step switches were the first type of automatic switching gear used by the telephone companies. In the 1920s a significant conceptual innovation was the introduction of common control in switching, which was used in the *panel* switching systems. Electrical noise in switching was later reduced considerably by the use of crossbar switches. A popular type of equipment, the No. 5 Crossbar system, was introduced in the late 1940s. The latest kinds of switching office, using stored program control, are the electronic offices called No. 1 and No. 2 ESS. These types of offices are being installed rapidly, but still constitute a small minority of the total number of switching offices. An approximate breakdown of offices in 1971 showed 8600 step-by-step offices, 500 panel offices, 5700 crossbar offices, and 286 of No. 1 ESS.

5.1.6 Supervisory Signals

To establish and maintain connections through the switched network, the switching machines must exchange information with each other and with the calling and called terminals. There is address information, used to route the call, status information as to whether the call has been answered (on hook and off hook), network control information to seize and disconnect lines, and various types of ringing signals. Many of these signals are internal to the network and of little concern to the data user. However, the need to exchange such signals and the way in which they are exchanged affect the switched network's data-handling capabilities in two important qualities—the call setup time and the permissible energy spectrum that can be transmitted.

The average time required to complete a long-distance DDD call is approximately 9 s after the last digit has been dialed. For some computer-communication-network applications, this seems like an exorbitant figure. The blame in these cases is often pointed at the switching gear in the telephone network; however, the bulk of this call setup duration is taken up by the passage of supervisory information through the switching hierarchy to the called party, and then back again to the calling party. The problem of obtaining faster call setup is not just the problem of designing faster switches (even mechanical crossbar switches can actually make connections relatively quickly), but that of a redesign of the internal signaling methods.

A number of different techniques are used to transmit supervisory signals. The most popular of these is *in-band* signaling using a single frequency (called SF signaling) at 2600 Hz. This signal is not present when data (or voice) is actually being transmitted through the channel, so there is no danger of this kind of interference from supervisory signals. However, there is some risk that a particular segment of the data signal itself will be misinterpreted as a supervisory signal, i.e., a tone at 2600 Hz. In this case some improper action, such as premature disconnect, may be taken by the automatic gear in the network. Therefore, the presence of in-band signaling causes some restriction on the type of data signals that may be transmitted. More specifically, the data signal must not appear to be a 2600-Hz tone of a certain power (while energy is not elsewhere present in the voiceband) for more than a certain duration. This restriction is actually a rather mild one, which only rules out such techniques as that of using a frequency modulation data modem one of whose rest frequencies is near 2600 Hz.

5.1.7 Transmission

Just as the switching plan is a hierarchical structure, so too is the structure of the overall plan for transmission in the telephone system. A data call begins its journey on a pair of wires, the local loop, which are exclusively devoted to that call alone. From the local central office this call may be frequency multiplexed with other calls onto a carrier system. Eventually, the call may find itself on a high-capacity, long-haul carrier system—one often likened to a superhighway for communication. Nearer the destination, the call may once again be separated in layers from its thousands of fellow calls, finally ending on its own pair of wires at the distant receiver.

The intricacies of the transmission plan and the specifics of all the short- and long-haul carrier systems of which it is constituted are not of primary concern to the data user or system planner. However, there are certain characteristics and idiosyncracies that do affect data performance in specific ways which must be described. Generally speaking, the transmission of a signal has three components—the local loop, short-haul transmission, and long-haul transmission. The local loop is, of course, always present. If the call is not destined for another subscriber at that same local office, a short-haul carrier is usually involved in the route to a higher toll center. Long-haul carrier systems are then used in routes between major cities. In what follows we shall point out some of the salient features and weaknesses that affect data transmission in each of these three phases.

5.1.8 Local Loops

The local loop is extremely simple, in essence merely a pair of copper wires twisted in a cable between the subscriber and the central office. It is a constant source of surprise to data network planners that so much of the cost of a network can lie in this simple local distribution system. Here there are no possibilities within the common-carrier constraint of economies to be gained by the sharing of lines. The cost of the connection, including the greatest factor of all—that of *maintaining* the loop and its share of the central office— must be borne by the single subscriber.

Local loops average about 1 to 2 miles in length and are very seldom longer than 5 miles. The resistance of a loop varies with distance and with the gauges of wires employed, but data modems are adjusted so that their power levels at the central offices are a standard -12 dBm. Thus a modem connected to a longer loop is adjusted to a higher power output than one connected to a shorter loop.

The attenuation of a wire pair increases with frequency, but relatively slowly. The loop has none of the sharply bandlimited nature usually associated with a telephone channel. On the other hand, within the voiceband the rising attenuation (and associated nonconstant delay) is less "flat" than the design objectives of short- and long-haul carrier systems. Often the transmission characteristics of a loop are improved by *loading*, which is the serial introduction of inductance at specified intervals. Although loading helps flatten the attenuation characteristic of a loop within the voiceband, it also causes it to be more bandlimited and less suitable for wider-band transmission.

With or without loading, the local loop and its entrance to the carrier system through channelizing filters largely determine the amplitude and delay characteristics of a data call. Because of this, a number of calls placed from a given subscriber to diverse places can all have superficially similar analog transmission characteristics. Data modems usually contain compromise equalization filters, designed to compensate for an average-length loop. When the subscriber is closer to the local office, his characteristics, because of this compromise equalization, may actually be worse than those of a subscriber located farther from the central office.

Local loops have very high signal-to-noise ratios—usually 50 dB or better, depending on loop length. Since they are also essentially non-bandlimited, it would appear that they have a very high data-handling capacity. In fact, speeds of up to 50 kbps have been experimentally transmitted over loops using simple baseband signaling techniques (the task is simplified since loops pass direct current) while conforming to tariff requirements. However, their capacity is not as large as it might seem, because the spectral distribution of energy on a loop must be constrained toward use of essentially only those frequencies below 3 kHz to minimize *crosstalk* into adjacent cable pairs.

Crosstalk is a limiting factor on the engineering of the local plant. Crosstalk increases with frequency, which leads to the reduced power constraint at higher frequencies, even where it would appear that transmission was supported well by the twisted-pair medium itself. (Nevertheless, wideband data is transmitted over the local loop using a broad, baseband spectrum. For this purpose loading coils are removed and crosstalk precautions are individually considered.)

5.1.9 Short-Haul Transmission

Carrier systems designed for short-haul transmission combine a moderate number of voice channels in a manner that is engineered to be economical, rather than efficient in a communication theoretic sense. Thus, for example, the prevalent N-carrier system uses double sideband, amplitude modulation. It is a rugged, cost-effective system. At this point in the transmission hierarchy, the cost of multiplexing and transmission by carrier using modulation and demodulation must compete with the alternative of individual-wire line transmission. Each carrier system has a prove-in distance, beyond which it becomes economical to use. If this prove-in distance is kept small, the system can find a broad use throughout the telephone network. For example, a rough approximation to this distance for the N-carrier system is 25 miles, but there are of course many factors to consider in the actual decision to employ the system in a given instance.

Some of the pertinent characteristics of short-haul carriers are listed in Table 5.1.

Short-haul carriers tend to be much noisier and more sharply bandlimited than the local loop system. In the channelizing filter banks used to frequency multiplex the voice channels, 4 kHz is allotted to each voiceband signal, but due to filter roll-off and guardspace requirements, a nominal 3 kHz remains for good transmission quality. Unlike the local loop system, the carriers do not transmit direct current. Usually the attenuation increases sharply below about 400 Hz.

The N-carrier systems use a technique for noise reduction called *companding*, which can cause difficulties in data transmission. Companding relies

TABLE 5.1   *Short-Haul Carrier Systems*

Carrier Designation	Modulation Technique	Medium	Capacity (Voice Channels)	Amplifier-Repeater Spacing (miles)	Length Restriction (miles)
N	AM	cable	12	8	200
ON	AM	cable	20	8	200
T-1	PCM	cable	24	1	50
O	AM	open wire	16	50	150

on a psycho-acoustic phenomenon that is effective in voice transmission, but has no meaning for data transmission. At the entrance to the system the signal is compressed using a nonlinear transformation, which amplifies low-amplitude levels and attenuates high-amplitude signals. At the exit from the carrier an expandor undoes this nonlinear transformation with its inverse. As a result, noise introduced by the carrier is attenuated for low-level signals, where it would be most noticeable in listening to speech, and amplified for loud signals, where it would not be noticed. The gain of the compandor fluctuates at the normal syllabic rate, so that it follows the speech envelope up and down, neither too quickly nor too slowly.

A data signal has a much more constant power than a speech signal. The envelope of an FM signal is perfectly constant; others are either nearly constant or else change more rapidly than the speech syllabic rate. If the compandors were perfectly adjusted, so that the expandor were the exact inverse of the compressor, then the system would have little or no effect on data signals. (Since bandlimiting filtering intervenes between the compressor and expandor, the nonlinear operation cannot be exactly undone, but this residual effect appears not to be of practical importance.) However, compandors do not track exactly, so that the compressing operation is not, in fact, exactly compensated by expansion. The resulting residual nonlinear operation on the signal serves to distort data signals in a particularly harmful way. (Harmful in the sense that it is not easily undone.) It may be that this nonlinear distortion is the primary, ultimate limiting factor in obtaining high data rates over DDD channels.

This same nonlinear distortion as a result of mistracking compandors is also present in another type of short-haul carrier, called T-1, which has revolutionary importance for data communication. The T-1 system differs from all other present carrier systems in that it is a true digital transmission system using pulse code modulation (PCM). The incoming voiceband signal is sampled 8000 times/s, and each sample is quantized into one of 128 possible levels (7-bit quantization). The analog voiceband signal is thus represented by a 56 kbps digital stream.

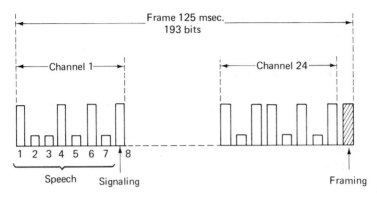

FIGURE 5.2   T-1 frame.

In the T-1 carrier 24 voice channels are time division multiplexed together in an overall frame of 193 bits, as shown in Fig. 5.2. To each 7-bit sample from each of the constituent channels is added an eighth bit, a "one," for timing purposes. The last bit of the frame is used to maintain frame synchronization. With 193 bits and a frame rate of 8000/s, the overall bit rate of the carrier is 1.544 Mbps. These pulses are transmitted in a baseband, three-level format over a twisted pair of wires. Approximately every mile there is a digital repeater, a regenerator, which detects the pulses, and sends out new, noiseless, retimed pulses to the next repeater. The advantage of PCM transmission is that noise and signal distortions are not allowed to be cumulative; at each mile the signal is cleansed. This can obviously only be done when the signal is in a digital form, as in PCM. The disadvantage of PCM is that 56 kbps is required for the transmission of each voice channel. (However the quality of channel used for this purpose need not be high, because of digital regeneration.)

The noise inherent in T-1 carrier transmission is quantizing noise, rather than the additive random noises present in other carrier systems. This noise, together with the troublesome nonlinear distortion resulting from imperfect tracking of quantizers and their counterpart digital-analog converters (in certain types of T-1 systems using "D-1" channel banks-newer models are much improved) make many observers feel that T-1 is one of the poorest carrier systems for the transmission of data signals *in analog form.* However, as will be discussed in a subsequent portion of this chapter, the T-1 carrier represents the wave of the future for all-digital data transmission. Within the T-1 carrier system, 56 kbps of nearly error-free data are transmitted for the cost of a single voice telephone channel. The catch is, of course, being able to multiplex data directly into the T-1 frame without going through analog modems and analog-digital conversion to get there. The range of T-1 carrier is also limited to less than 50 miles. Although a longer-range carrier, T-2, has been developed with a capacity of four T-1 systems and a range of 500 miles, its deployment has only begun in 1971.

5.1.10 Long-Haul Transmission

Long-haul carriers, in contrast to short-haul requirements, are designed to be extremely efficient transmission systems. Here thousands of voice channels are combined in a multiplexing hierarchy for transmission over coaxial cable or microwave channels. The way the voice channels are put together and taken apart is in large chunks of bandwidth known as groups, supergroups, mastergroups, etc., as shown in Table 5.2.

TABLE 5.2 *Multiplexing Hierarchy*

	Designation	*Composition*	*Frequency Range* (kHz)
1.	Group	12 voice channels	60–108
2.	Supergroup	5 groups	312–552
3.	Mastergroup	10 supergroups	564–3084

The principal long-haul carriers are described briefly by the characteristics listed in Table 5.3.

TABLE 5.3 *Long-Haul Carrier Systems*

Carrier Designation	*Modulation*	*Medium*	*Capacity (Voice channels)*	*Repeater Spacing (miles)*
L	single sideband	coaxial cable	1860	8
TD	FM	microwave	1800	30
TH	FM	microwave	1800	30
K	AM	cable	12	17

To carry signals in relatively undistorted form over several thousand miles, these carrier systems must be designed to exacting standards. They do a remarkable job. They usually contribute less noise and distortion, both linear and nonlinear, than do short-haul systems. Naturally, calls over longer distances tend on average to have worse data transmission characteristics than do those over shorter distances. (Of course, all calls over 100 miles or so will probably contain short-haul carrier segments, so their effect is felt on long-distance calls as well as on the shorter-distance calls.) The remarkable observation is that very long calls, e.g., transcontinental calls, are very little worse than calls of several hundred miles.

The L-carrier systems do have one idiosyncracy for data transmission, which does no harm to voice, and that is *phase jitter*. Since single sideband transmission is used, it is necessary to employ reference carrier frequencies to translate up in frequency at the L transmitter and down at the L receiver. Ideally the modulating and demodulating frequencies are identical. In practice they differ slightly, resulting in a *frequency offset* of the signal. More troublesome, however, is the presence of a random phase (of, say, 6° peak-to-peak sway at a rate of something less than 120 Hz) on top of modulating and demodulating carriers. Thus a pure sine wave, $\cos \omega t$, transmitted through such a system comes out as $\cos[(\omega + \omega_o)t + \phi(t)]$, where ω_o is frequency offset, and $\phi(t)$ is the random phase jitter.

Phase jitter comes about from the way in which power is supplied to the L-carrier oscillators. Since speech is relatively unchanged in intelligibility by phase rotations, the phenomenon was almost unnoticed until relatively efficient data modems began appearing in the mid-1960s. A correctional program instituted by the telephone companies has since resulted in much improvement, but phase jitter is still a troublesome factor in high-speed data transmission over long-haul carriers.

5.1.11 Echo Suppressors

As mentioned earlier, carrier systems use four-wire transmission, that is, a pair of wires for transmission in each direction, as shown in Fig. 5.3. The signal from the single pair of wires constituting the local loop is split by a bal-

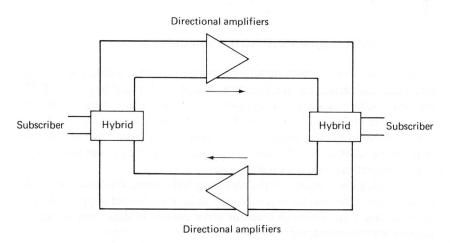

FIGURE 5.3 Two- and four-wire transmission.

anced hybrid network into two separate channels, one for each direction of transmission. Each of these separate legs uses directional amplifiers that amplify only in the direction indicated. This particular plan permits stable signal amplification of hundreds or thousands of decibels, which would otherwise be difficult, if not impossible, to achieve if one pair of wires served for both directions.

Since the hybrids are not exactly balanced to each loop, some portion of an incident signal passes through them and returns to the originator as an echo. In speech transmission this echo is only objectionable in long-distance calls, where the echo is clearly distinguished in arrival time. To counter this bothersome phenomenon, echo suppressors are employed in each leg of the carrier system. When energy is detected flowing in one directional leg, the echo suppressor opens the other leg to prevent the echo from passing. This is permissible in speech transmission, unless both parties want to talk at once, which is rare. However, the echo suppressors prohibit full-duplex data transmission.

To allow energy to flow in both legs, so as to permit full-duplex data transmission, the echo suppressors must be disengaged. It has been arranged that this disengagement can be accomplished by a tone of about 2025 Hz from the data modem. If an echo suppressor detects such a tone for more than 400 ms, while energy is absent in the rest of the voiceband, it disengages until such time as the data signal ceases for more than 400 ms. Thus disengaging echo suppressors and making sure that they stay disengaged for the duration of the call are normal functions of full-duplex modems. For half-duplex operation, in which the channel is used first in one direction and then in the other, the echo suppressors add about 100 ms to the time required to turn around the transmission direction.

5.2   DATA TRANSMISSION PRINCIPLES

In this section the basic signaling techniques used for data communications, their properties, and their fundamental limitations will be described. The methods include baseband, amplitude modulation, phase modulation, and frequency modulation. All modems for data transmission use variations and combinations of these techniques. Some specific applications will be discussed in the subsequent section devoted to modems, but in the present section only simple theoretical principles will be given.

Following descriptions of the signaling techniques, fundamental limitations on data rates and accuracies due to noise and channel impairments will be described. Last, methods used for error control in data communication systems will be considered.

5.2.1 Transmission Techniques

The basic methods of AM, PM, and FM have been used in communication systems for decades. Their application to data transmission is perhaps 15 years old, and throughout this period theoretical investigations of their properties have been continually made. Surprisingly, the evaluation of comparative systems is far from complete. It is still almost impossible to say that one technique is better than another. One only needs to look at the dozens of advertisements for modems in trade journals, all proclaiming revolutionary new and superior modulation techniques, to realize how chaotic the situation is. Each basic modulation technique has its particular strengths and its primary applications. The uninitiated often ask which is best, but perhaps the question is really meaningless—what follows is merely a description of each.

5.2.2 Baseband Signaling

Baseband signals are the most elementary means of conveying digital information in analog form. The baseband signal is merely a train of pulses. No modulating carrier is used, so the energy remains near direct current in frequency content—hence "baseband," as opposed to passband. Mathematically, a baseband signal is represented by

$$s(t) = \sum_{n=-\infty}^{\infty} a_n g(t - nT)$$

where the amplitude level of the nth pulse in the train is a_n, the common shape of all pulses is $g(t)$, and the interval between pulses is T seconds.

Three common forms of baseband signals are shown in Fig. 5.4. The first of these uses a rectangular pulse for $g(t)$ and $a_n = \pm 1$, depending on whether a binary one or zero is to be conveyed. This kind of signal is also termed bipolar, since both positive and negative levels are used. The interfaces to modems and computer-communications controllers require such a signal. In fact, there is an industry standard, RS 232, which specifies the levels and other parameters involved in these interface, baseband signals.

The second baseband signal, in Fig. 5.4b, illustrates *multilevel* operation. In this instance four levels are possible for each pulse; therefore, each interval carries 2 bits of information. Clearly, multilevel signaling permits increasing the data rate over binary signaling. If 2^L levels are used, then the data rate is L/T bits. This increase in rate is accomplished without change in the bandwidth of the signal, which in baseband signaling is determined solely by the shape of the pulse $g(t)$, and the pulse repetition rate $1/T$ (provided successive levels are statistically uncorrelated, which is not always true). However,

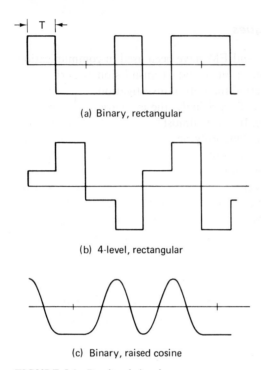

(a) Binary, rectangular

(b) 4-level, rectangular

(c) Binary, raised cosine

FIGURE 5.4   Baseband signals.

there is obviously a signal-to-noise penalty involved in multilevel signaling. The more amplitude levels used, the more susceptible the system is to error due to noise or distortion.

Rectangular pulses are simple to generate for use in interface situations. However, their energy distribution is wasteful of bandwidth in a communications application. The sharp corners at the signal transition points contain high-frequency content that does not pass through bandlimited media. Consequently, the pulse arrives severely distorted. To make for easier passage through band-limited channels, "shaped" pulses are used instead of the rectangular pulses. What this amounts to is that a signal like that in Fig. 5.4a is passed through a low-pass filter to arrive at a more smoothly bandlimited shape, as illustrated in Fig. 5.4c. However, not just any low-pass filter is suitable for this purpose. The filter must be carefully chosen so that the filtered waveform is undistorted at the times it will be sampled by the receiver to determine the symbol amplitudes a_n.

When the receiver samples the baseband signal at time $t = kT$, it should see only the amplitude a_k. In fact, the sample is

$$s(kT) = \sum_{n=-\infty}^{\infty} a_n g[(k - n)T]$$

In order for $s(kT) = a_k$, we must have

$$g(nT) = 0 \quad \text{for} \quad n \neq 0$$

$$g(0) = 1$$

Pulses with this property are called *Nyquist pulses*. An example pulse is shown in Fig. 5.5. Obviously, a pulse of this type will not interfere with neighboring pulses at their sampling times. A train of these pulses can be strung together without mutual interference at times nT.

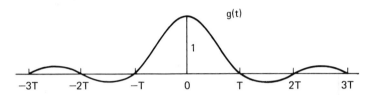

FIGURE 5.5   Nyquist pulse.

The bandwidth and energy distributions of data signals are important, since they determine the ease of passage through bandlimited communications media. Apart from a constant, the spectral density (power density in the signal as a function of frequency) of a baseband signal is $|G(\omega)|^2$, where $G(\omega)$ is the Fourier transform of $g(t)$:

$$G(\omega) = \int_{-\infty}^{+\infty} g(t)e^{-i\omega t}\, dt$$

Since the Fourier transform of the pulse $g(t)$ relates directly to the power density of the baseband signal, it is natural to pick $G(\omega)$ initially to be a smoothly bandlimited function, rather than dealing with the pulse shape $g(t)$ in the time domain. In so doing, it is necessary to be sure that the resulting pulse $g(t)$ is in fact a Nyquist pulse. This imposes a constraint on the selection of $G(\omega)$, which is outlined by a simple and famous test known as the *Nyquist criterion*.

According to the Nyquist criterion, the pulse transform $G(\omega)$ must have a bandwidth of at least $\frac{1}{2}T$ Hz (π/T rad/s). If it has less, the pulse cannot be a Nyquist pulse. If $G(\omega)$ has greater bandwidth, there are an infinite number of possibilities for meeting the Nyquist criterion. They are all characterized by the fact that their sampled data spectrum

$$\sum_{k=-\infty}^{\infty} G\left(\omega - \frac{2k\pi}{T}\right)$$

is a constant.

In the usual case, the bandwidth occupied by $G(\omega)$ is less than twice the minimum of π/T rad/s. Then the Nyquist test reduces to a simple "folding" operation on $G(\omega)$, illustrated in Fig. 5.6. The bandwidth that $G(\omega)$ possesses

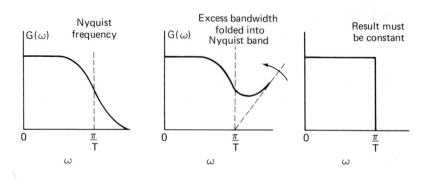

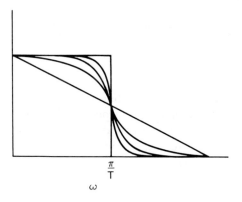

FIGURE 5.6

in excess of π/T rad/s is folded back about the Nyquist point π/T and added in; the result must be a perfect rectangle:

$$G(\omega) + G^*\left(\frac{2\pi}{T} - \omega\right) = \text{constant} \qquad 0 \le \omega \le \frac{\omega}{T}.$$

Obviously the only characteristic $G(\omega)$ that meets the Nyquist test and has exactly the minimum bandwidth of π/T is the rectangular characteristic.

A family of Nyquist characteristics is shown in Fig. 5.6. To simplify pictorial representation, the $G(\omega)$ are shown to be real, but a phase characteristic may be involved, providing the complex addition still yields a constant.

Baseband signals are only useful in communications applications where the medium passes direct current. In telephone uses this is only possible on the local loop. None of the carrier systems leaving the local switching office will pass direct current. Nevertheless, baseband signals are useful on the loop itself. For example, in wideband transmission a baseband signal carries the data from the subscriber to the central office. From that point it is handled by a different modulation technique.

5.2.3 Amplitude Modulation

Since most media for communications cannot accept baseband signals, it becomes necessary to translate the signal to some passband location. For voice telephone transmission the data signal energy should be centered somewhere about 1700 or 1800 Hz, with the band extending from about 600 to 3000 Hz. Any of a number of modulation techniques can take the baseband signal $s(t)$ and move it to this location; perhaps the simplest conceptual method is amplitude modulation, in which $s(t)$ controls the amplitude (or envelope) of a carrier frequency ω_c:

$$v(t) = [s(t) + c] \cos \omega_c t \cdot$$

The constant c can be adjusted so as to ensure that the quantity $[s(t) + c]$ is always positive, so that simple envelope detection suffices to demodulate $s(t)$.

The spectral density of $v(t)$ is shown in Fig. 5.7. The entire baseband spectrum is simply moved, or translated, to a passband location centered about ω_c. Now, however, the bandwidth has been *doubled* over that required for baseband, since the baseband spectrum appears on *both* sides of ω_o. There is also a discrete component of the spectrum at ω_c, corresponding to the value of the added constant c. In *suppressed carrier* transmission this

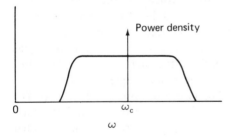

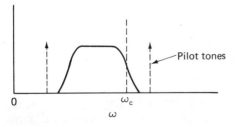

FIGURE 5.7

carrier frequency is removed before transmission, and effectively reinserted during demodulation at the receiver.

Because ordinary AM requires twice the bandwidth of baseband, it is inefficient in restricted bandwidth applications like voiceband data transmission. Amplitude modulation is not especially simple to implement either. Level changes of many decibels can occur during transmission and from call to call. Therefore, a powerful and automatic gain control cirucit must accompany the basic demodulation circuitry. For these reasons AM is seldom used in data transmission.

There is a form of AM, called *vestigial sideband*, that does find important usage. The two sidebands, upper and lower, about the carrier ω_c carry redundant information. If one sideband is eliminated before transmission, the signal $s(t)$ can still be recovered by proper demodulation. The complete elimination of one sideband yields what is called a *single sideband* signal. This form is only possible to implement in those cases where the data spectrum has been designed to have a null at the carrier frequency. In other cases, the filter that removes the unwanted sideband leaves a vestige of this sideband attached, as illustrated in Fig. 5.7b. This vestige enables easier filter design and more dependable demodulation than would otherwise be possible. In practice the vestige is anywhere from 7 to 50 per cent of the original sideband.

Vestigial sideband (VSB) has all the efficiency of baseband, but at a passband location. It is used in many high-speed voiceband data modems. Unfortunately, this efficiency comes at a cost of difficult implementation. To demodulate VSB, the carrier frequency ω_c is needed at the receiver. The carrier cannot easily be transmitted directly, because the data signal has energy at ω_c that would interfere. Therefore, the carrier is generally transmitted as the difference frequency (or some other simple function) of two pilots located outside the data spectrum, as shown dotted in Fig. 5.7b. The detection of $s(t)$ is still tricky in VSB, and the modems for this technique are more complicated and sensitive to channel perturbations than are other modems. Only when high efficiency is required are these drawbacks worth overcoming.

5.2.4 Phase Modulation

In phase modulation the baseband signal is conveyed as the phase of a carrier frequency located near midband; i.e.,

$$v(t) = A \cos[\omega_c t + s(t)]$$

A slightly different form is commonly used for easier signal generation, in which the output signal is a train of passband pulses whose phases are given by the input data:

$$v(t) = \sum_{n=-\infty}^{\infty} g(t - nT) \cos \left[\omega_c t + \phi_n\right].$$

Here $g(t)$ is the desired envelope shaping of the passband pulse and ϕ_n is the phase of the nth pulse. In binary phase modulation $\phi_n = 0$ or π; in four-phase signaling $\phi_n = 0, \pi/2, \pi,$ or $3\pi/2$, etc. Obviously, in this latter form a certain amount of amplitude modulation is incidentally present.

Like AM, phase modulation has a double sideband spectrum shaped by the Fourier transform of $g(t)$. In fact, binary PM is equivalent to binary AM with suppressed carrier. If four or more levels are used for signaling, PM is more efficient than double sideband AM. Their bandwidths are essentially identical, but PM has a greater margin against noise for a given signal power.

Conceptually, the simplest way of detecting phase modulated data is to compare the phases of samples of the received signal at T-second intervals against an ideal reference carrier $\cos \omega_c t$. This is known as coherent demodulation, and it can be shown theoretically to be the best possible method. Like VSB, deriving an ideal reference at the receiver is a costly and sensitive procedure. Since phase modulation is less efficient than VSB, there is little reason to go to all the difficulty associated with coherent demodulation.

Most practical PM modems use *differentially coherent* reception, in which the phase sample ϕ_n is compared with the previous sample ϕ_{n-1}, instead of with an ideal reference. The input phases are correspondingly encoded as phase *changes;* e.g., $(\phi_n - \phi_{n-1}) = 0, \pi/2, \pi,$ or $3\pi/2$ for four-phase transmission. This scheme is simple to implement, requires no pilot tones, and is extremely rugged against channel perturbations. Since the reference phases themselves "ride" with phase jitter and other channel anomalies, the system inherits a kind of immunity against these impairments.

On the debit side against differential detection are two factors. The differentially coherent system has a noise margin of 2 to 3 dB less than coherent detection. Hence under ideal conditions it has a higher error rate. The other factor is its propensity to double up errors. When an error does occur, due to some perturbation of the signal, the following symbol also tends to be in error, due to the use of an incorrect phase as a reference for detection. The presence of double errors can harm data transmission which depends on simple parity check error detection. The double error passes undetected by these codes.

Four- and eight-phase modems using differential detection are extremely popular for moderate-speed data transmission on voiceband channels. They provide reasonable efficiency at a moderate cost. In addition, the phase-comparison technique enables very fast startup. This factor can assume overriding importance in polled systems, where the slower startup associated with the initial aquisition of carrier in VSB would decrease the throughput efficiency of the overall system.

5.2.5 Frequency Modulation

In frequency modulation (FM) the baseband signal $s(t)$ controls the frequency of a carrier:

$$v(t) = A \cos \left[\omega_c t + d \int_0^t s(x) dx \right].$$

In contrast to VSB and PM signaling methods, the operation of an FM modem is usually *asynchronous*. The signal $v(t)$ is demodulated by a discriminator, following limiting, to yield the baseband signal $s(t)$. No sampling is involved in the demodulation procedure, so that analog signals such as facsimile, or start-stop signals as outputted by teletypewriters, can be handled without distortion of the signal transition points.

Frequency modulation is theoretically efficient only in wide-bandwidth applications, where the band is essentially unlimited. Traditionally, FM is used to trade bandwidth for improved signal-to-noise ratio. However, in voiceband applications this is out of the question. In fact, FM is quite inefficient in a theoretical sense—the least efficient of the methods described here. Fortunately, FM is very simple to implement and is extremely rugged in the face of certain signal perturbations and distortions. Therefore, FM finds application in low-cost low-speed transmission. This, of course, is the biggest modem application. Probably 90 per cent of all modems sold have used FM transmission.

The spectral density of FM is quite complicated. Unlike AM and PM, changing the number of levels changes the bandwidth. For exact expressions and example spectra the reader is referred to [1]. Approximately, the FM bandwidth is given by Carson's rule—twice the baseband bandwidth plus twice the peak frequency deviation. The peak frequency deviation is the maximum frequency swing away from the carrier, determined by the constant d and the baseband signal.

Virtually all FM modems are binary. The signal $v(t)$ swings between two frequencies, the mark frequency and the space frequency; therefore, in telegraph transmission binary FM was called frequency shift keying (FSK). This terminology has tended to carry over to data modems. In FSK the peak frequency deviation is half the spread between mark and space frequencies. For optimum results this deviation should be related to the bit signaling rate. Although there is some argument about the exact proportion, about 0.7 times the bit rate is usually considered a good choice.

5.2.6 *Transmission Limitations*

In passage through a voice telephone channel a data signal suffers various distortions that limit the data rates and accuracies which can be attained. These signal impairments can be divided into two categories—deterministic and random, depending on whether or not the effect of the impairment on the signal can be predicted in advance. The kinds of impairments indigenous to voice channels are:

A. Deterministic Impairments
   1. Amplitude and delay distortion.
   2. Nonlinear distortion.
   3. Frequency offset.
B. Random impairments
   1. Gaussian noise.
   2. Impulse noise.
   3. Phase jitter.

Amplitude and delay distortion are used to describe the linear distortion the signal undergoes during transmission. Ideally, the channel has a perfectly flat amplitude characteristic and a linear phase response. In actuality, however, the amplitude response drops sharply at both upper and lower ends of the band, while the delay curve (derivative of the phase response) is parabolic with minimum delay near the center of the band and rising delay toward both ends. This imperfect response distorts the pulse $g(t)$ into a shape $x(t)$ which is not Nyquist; that is, $x(nT) \neq 0$. Therefore, successive pulses interfere with one another at sampling times. This *intersymbol interference* decreases the noise margin and increases the error rate. A later section describes this phenomenon in more detail.

Nonlinear distortion arises primarily from imperfect compandor action, as described earlier. The effect of the channel nonlinearity is usually described in terms of the ratios in decibels of the fundamental to the various harmonics present in the received signal. If the channel were perfectly linear, a sine-wave input would yield a sine-wave output. However, the output usually contains second and third harmonics of the order of 35 dB lower than the fundamental. Such a description implies that the nonlinearity is memoryless; i.e., $x = g(s)$ independent of time or past signal history. Unfortunately, some memory is involved, and the measurement and analysis of such phenomena are extremely complicated. Nonlinear distortion causes intersymbol interference, just like linear distortion, but generally of a much lower magnitude. Only when the linear distortion is virtually eliminated by automatic equalization does the nonlinear distortion appear. Then, however, it can be the fundamental limiting impairment in the quest for attainment of high data rates.

Frequency offset is the shift of all transmitted frequencies by a small amount, typically about 1 Hz, due to the difference in modulating and demodulating frequencies in the carrier systems. This shift is unimportant in any of the modulation techniques described earlier; however, it would prohibit simple baseband transmission of data through carrier systems.

Gaussian noise is an inevitable perturbation in any real communications system. Due to the thermal motion of electrons, it has a fairly uniform power spectrum across the band with a total average power of about 30 dB less than the average signal power. In theory, this low-level noise is the limiting factor in high-speed data transmission. In practice, gaussian noise rarely causes errors in low- and medium-speed data communication. Nevertheless, it is the only useful mathematical model to assume for noise. Gaussian noise is also used for nearly all theoretical evaluations, computer simulations, and laboratory tests.

Impulse noise is characterized by high amplitude peaks of bursts that can obliterate data signals over intervals of anywhere from one to thousands of bits. Ordinarily, impulse noise is thought of as those kinds of short, high-level, additive transients which originate in switching offices, electrical storms, maintenance work, etc. For our purposes here we shall also include any sort of signal disturbance that results in clustered errors in the data stream. For example, multiplicative noise also has this property—line drop-outs in which the connection is opened for several milliseconds (or permanently!), or sudden level changes of the received signal are fairly common. Abrupt phase changes in the data signal are another not unusual cause of clustered errors in the detected output. These types of phenomena are the chief sources of errors in low- and medium-speed data transmission.

Phase jitter, as described earlier in conjunction with long-haul carrier systems, is another signal irritant that is not felt except in high-speed transmission. It can be particularly troublesome in 8- or 16-phase modulation, or in VSB communication. Otherwise, at lower data rates it is rarely felt over amplitude and delay distortion and impulse noise.

All the above effects help to contribute to errors in data transmission. Ultimately, errors are *caused* by what we call noise. The other effects— amplitude and delay distortion, nonlinear distortion, etc.—lower the margin that the data signal has against noise. Most errors in low- and medium-speed data transmission are directly attributable to impulse noise events, many of which are catastrophic and not at all dependent upon the type of modulation technique employed. Balkovic et al. [2], based on an inspection of the data waveforms in the neighborhood of errors, have given the percentage breakdown of error events in medium speed (2000 bps) transmission over the DDD network listed in Table 5.4.

TABLE 5.4 *Breakdown of Error Events*

Cause	Events (%)	Errors (%)
Short additive transients (<4 ms)	79	63
Additive signals (4 ms)	6	25
Amplitude changes	4	5
Phase changes	11	7

The main concern in the design of data modems is maximizing the margin against noise. For this purpose a mathematical model of a channel consisting of a bandlimited filter followed by a gaussian noise source is perfectly acceptable. For high-speed transmission this model is rather close to the actual error mechanism. At lower speeds, even though the real error causes are not gaussian noise, the philosophy is that a modem designed to perform well against gaussian noise will also perform well in the actual telephone environment. In the following sections we discuss the theoretical performance of communication techniques over bandlimited channels in the presence of gaussian noise.

5.2.7 Theoretical Rate Limitations

The bandlimited nature of a channel limits the rate at which pulses can be transmitted without incurring intersymbol interference to less than $2W$ per second, where W is the bandwidth in hertz. This famous relationship, due to Nyquist in 1928, puts an upper bound on the *baud rate* of a data system. (The baud rate is the number of symbols, or signaling elements, per second.) For example, a typical voiceband channel with a bandwidth of about 2400 Hz can only support data transmission at baud rates lower than 4800. This Nyquist constraint is a useful and powerful mathematical result. There is no method of signaling that has the necessary zero crossings (so as not to interfere with neighboring pulses) closer together than $\frac{1}{2}W$ second.

Practically speaking, only the most expensive and efficient modems approach the Nyquist baud-rate limit. Any double sideband modulation technique, AM, PM, or FM, immediately halves the achievable rate. In addition, the problem of filter design to achieve the near-rectangular frequency response required as the Nyquist limit is approached is formidable. The sensitivities to small perturbations from design also become large in this region. Therefore most modems operate in the range of one half to one quarter of the Nyquist limit. In the case of high-speed modems, however, it is extremely important to squeeze all the pulses per second that the channel can sustain. Here the penalties inherent to the Nyquist approach must be paid, for to do otherwise is not to use the full bandwidth of the channel.

It is important to realize that the Nyquist restriction applies only to the system *baud* rate—not to the actual data rate in bits per second. The intrinsic bandwidth of a channel limits the pulse repetition rate, but not the amount of information each pulse carries. The number of bits per pulse, on the other hand, is limited by the noise. In simple modulation and detection techniques, e.g., multilevel AM, only so many levels can be distinguished in the presence of the additive gaussian noise. With a signal-to-noise ratio of 30 dB, a baseband or VSB system could support 8-level transmission with an error rate of about 10^{-5}, at 16 levels (4 bits/pulse) the error rate would be 10^{-3}, and at 32 levels (5 bits/pulse), 10^{-1}. Therefore, it could be said that this amount of noise limits reliable data transmission to about 4 bits/pulse.

The simple pulse-by-pulse transmission systems we have discussed thus far are not the best means of combatting gaussian noise. In theory, the information is better protected by spreading it out over many signaling intervals. Instead of making frequent decisions among a few alternatives (e.g., deciding among 8 alternatives, representing 3 bits, in each T-second interval), decisions should be made infrequently among many alternatives (e.g., deciding among 2^{300} alternatives, representing 300 bits, in each 100 T-second interval). Whereas the amplitude of a noise sample at one instant is unpredictable, certain properties of noise become well known over many samples. By taking advantage of this law of large numbers, data can be received with a probability of error approaching zero in the limit as the time between decisions approaches infinity.

The study of encoding and decoding methods to achieve this noise immunity, called information theory, was originated by C. Shannon in 1948. In his original paper [3] Shannon proved that information could be transmitted through a bandlimited channel with additive white, gaussian noise at any rate up to a capacity C with probability of error zero. At rates higher than C the probability of error cannot be made vanishingly small. Shannon's simple, celebrated capacity equation is

$$C = W \log_2 \left(1 + \frac{S}{N}\right),$$

where S/N is the ratio of signal power to noise power.

For a telephone channel with bandwidth 2400 Hz and a signal-to-noise ratio of 30 dB, Shannon's capacity would be about 24,000 bps. This figure represents the ultimate goal and challenge in modem design. Current high-speed modems attain something less than 14,000 bps on private lines, and only about 5000 on DDD, so channel capacity is a long way off. Nevertheless, there is little effort currently being devoted to pushing toward high fractions of capacity on voice telephone channels. Mostly this is because of the inevitability of diminishing returns in higher bit rates from more and more complex modems. But there are both practical and theoretical reasons why near-capacity rates will not soon, if ever, be attained.

It is sometimes written that Shannon's equation does not apply to actual telephone channels, because the conditions under which it was derived do not include amplitude and delay distortion, or nonlinearities, or impulse noise, or some of the other real impairments. Indeed, the capacity equation may well be the most misused formula in science. There are very few instances of real communications channels in which it applies. However, if there is one place where it *can* actually be applied, it is probably the voice telephone channel. All the impairments mentioned earlier do have some effect on the channel's intrinsic capacity. Sometimes the effect is calculable (see, e.g., Gallager [4]), sometimes not. But in most cases it can be argued that the effect is small. The essence of the argument lies in the *predictability* of all impairments except gaussian noise. The capacity equation probably gives a good estimate, even in its most simple form, of the ultimate capability of a voice telephone channel.

Practically speaking, the sundry other impairments, which can in theory be dismissed—such as nonlinearities—do very much get in the way. Impulse noise is the first to be seen, even at very low data rates. It can only be overcome by digital error control techniques. At moderate data rates intersymbol interference becomes the predominant limiting factor. When this is eliminated at the expense of an automatic equalizer, the phase jitter and nonlinearities show up. If these in turn were eliminated, other, theretofore hidden, impairments might appear.

There are also theoretical difficulties. No one knows theoretically how to achieve data speeds near capacity with vanishingly small error rates. Shannon's proof is only an existence proof, and no constructive methods are known. It is often incorrectly stated that the problem of approaching capacity is that of increasing complexity of requisite equipment. That is true, of course, but the fundamental difficulty lies much deeper, since no *recipe* is known, even given unlimited equipment availability. Clearly, Shannon's challenge will be with us for a long time!

5.2.8 Efficiencies of Modulation Techniques

Turning aside from the question of fundamental rate limitations, one can ask the efficiencies of the techniques, like AM, FM, and PM, that are used for data transmission. Considering only the bandlimited, gaussian noise channel, expressions can be derived in each case for the probability of error. For example, in baseband transmission the probability of error is given by

$$P_e = 2\left(1 - \frac{1}{L}\right)Q\left[\left(\frac{3}{L^2 - 1}\frac{P_s}{P_N}\right)^{1/2}\right].$$

where there are L levels, P_s is the signal power input to the channel, P_N is the noise power in the Nyquist bandwidth $[0, 1/2T]$, and $Q(x)$ is the normal probability integral

$$Q(x) = \frac{1}{\sqrt{2\pi}} \int_x^\infty e^{-t^2/2} \, dt.$$

This expression for P_e assumes that the baseband system has been optimized, which in this case only means that the pulse shape $g(t)$ is "split" between the transmitter and receiver. That is, if $G(\omega)$ is the transform of $g(t)$, then the transmitter shaping filter has characteristic $|G^{1/2}(\omega)|$, and so also does the receiver. Thus the composite characteristic for the pulse passing through both transmitter and receiver is $G(\omega)$. On the other hand, the noise passes only through the receiver filter $|G^{1/2}(\omega)|$.

Consider now an L-level system sending at the maximum baud rate allowed by the Nyquist limit of $2W$ pulses/s. The rate of the system is $2W \log_2 L$ bps. Normalized by the bandwidth, the rate in bits per second per hertz of bandwidth is

$$\frac{R}{W} = 2 \log_2 L.$$

For any desired probability of error we can compute the required signal-to-noise ratio. The normalized rate, R/W, and the required signal-to-noise ratio characterize the performance of the system.

As an example, a four-level baseband system transmits at a normalized rate of 4 bps/Hz. For a probability of error $P_e = 10^{-6}$, it requires a 20-dB signal-to-noise ratio. Similar figures could be obtained for other systems and compared on the basis of signal-to-noise required for a given bit-speed performance.

If a smooth curve is drawn to connect the points indicating the efficiencies of two-level, four-level, eight-level, etc, baseband systems, the result is a graph showing the performance of baseband systems as a class. These types of curves are shown in Fig. 5.8 for the modulation techniques described earlier. (Figure 5.8. is taken from a paper by J. Salz [5].)

For the most part, Fig. 5.8 is self-explanatory. Single sideband is the most efficient modulation technique, though it is seen to be some 7 to 10 dB inferior to the Shannon bound at which zero error rates can be achieved theoretically. Vestigial sideband (not shown) is very close to single sideband (SSB), depending on the amount of vestige transmitted. The least efficient method is FM, which would not be at all useful for high-speed transmission over channels with high signal-to-noise ratios.

There are several modulation techniques which have not been previously mentioned that are capable of very efficient operation. Quadrature carrier modulation, in which two AM systems are combined using the same carrier frequency but at 90° phase angles, is equivalent to single sideband. Another means of achieving the efficiency of single sideband is combining amplitude modulation with phase modulation. Both of these latter systems are sometimes used in modems for high-speed data transmission.

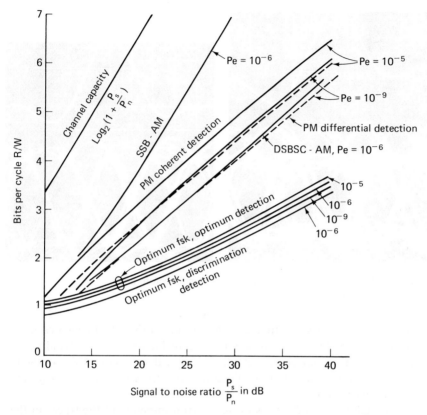

FIGURE 5.8

INTERSYMBOL INTERFERENCE AND EYE PATTERNS. The single most important missing factor in the theoretical efficiencies just discussed is the degradation caused by amplitude and delay distortion in the channel. In the right-hand side of Fig. 5.9 is shown a typical pulse $g(t)$ as used for baseband data transmission. The sampling instants at times nt are seen to coincide with zero crossings of $g(t)$. Because of amplitude and delay distortion, the pulse actually arrives at the receiver in a distorted form, say, $x(t)$, as shown in the left-hand side of Fig. 5.9. Since $x(nt) \neq 0$, the pulses interfere with each other at their respective sampling times. The exact value of this interference at any given sampling time in the signal is a random variable that depends on the sequence of data symbols being transmitted.

To visualize and to gauge the effect of intersymbol interference, a display called an *eye pattern* is used. Eye patterns corresponding to data transmission with each of the pulses in Fig. 5.9 are shown underneath their respective pulses. Eye patterns are probably more easily understood intuitively than they are explained. Clearly, the pattern on the right is well defined and

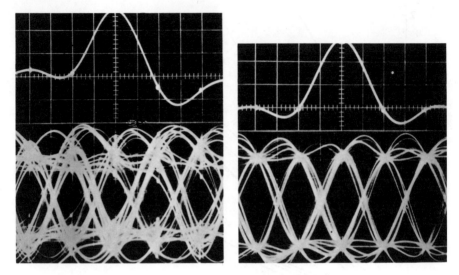

FIGURE 5.9   Oscillograms of received data signals before and
after autoequalization.

relatively distortionless compared with the one on the left. In each case the
pattern is formed by superimposing many possible received baseband waveforms so that their sampling instants are aligned vertically. This is exactly
what is seen on the face of an oscilloscope when the scope sweep is adjusted
to be an integer multiple of T.

If the pulse is distortionless in binary transmission, all the traces in the
eye pattern pass through two points, say, $+1$ and -1, at the sampling times.
If there is distortion present, a range of values about $+1$ and -1 appears,
representing the possible perturbations of the signal due to interference
from symbols other than the one being sampled. The innermost traces are
those most vulnerable to noise; the decrease in noise margin can be seen
immediately as the amount the inside of the eye has been narrowed. When
the interference is large enough that no opening appears in the center (the
eye is closed), then the system will make errors just due to intersymbol interference, even without additive noise.

If the received pulse $x(t)$ is normalized such that $x(0) = 1$, then the maximum excursion from the quiescent values ± 1 is

$$D = \sum_{\substack{n=-\infty \\ n \neq 0}}^{\infty} |x(nT)|.$$

Such an excursion only happens in data transmission when a particular
sample is surrounded by the worst possible sequence of neighboring symbol
values, so that all the interfering tails move the sample in the same direction.

On the other hand, the mean-square value of interference at a sample is given by

$$M = \sum_{\substack{n=-\infty \\ n \neq 0}}^{\infty} [x(nT)]^2.$$

If the intersymbol interference were gaussian, this quantity would add directly to the noise in the channel. However, the intersymbol interference is not normally distributed. Sometimes it is useful to think of it this way, nonetheless. In other cases it leads to better approximations by considering the interference to always decrease the noise margin by the amount D. A probability of error bound derived by Saltzberg [6] takes both effects into consideration.

In low- and medium-speed data transmission the "self-noise" from intersymbol interference is larger in mean-square value than the noise present on a typical channel. For high-speed transmission the pulse $x(t)$ must be passed through some sort of adaptive filter to correct its shape to a distortionless one. Only when the intersymbol interference is virtually removed does the channel noise appear substantial in comparison.

5.2.9   Error Control

Errors are inevitable in any real communication system. No modulation technique can be designed to deliver error-free data in spite of noise bursts, dropouts, and the various other phenomena common to the telephone channel. The average error rate for low- and medium-speed transmission is roughly 1 in 100,000. For some applications, this may be acceptable; others would require greater accuracy. In either case there are two important factors to consider:

1. There is great variation in error rate from call to call.

It is often said that 80 per cent of calls have a better-than-average error rate. This seeming paradox results from the observation that most calls are very good, with error rates of 10^{-5} or better, whereas in any given test almost all the errors occur in a few very bad calls. (Section 5.4 contains error-rate distributions.) Sometimes these bad calls can be identified and redialed. In other cases, whatever form of error control is employed must be able to accommodate to high raw error rate conditions.

2. Errors tend to occur in clusters.

The result of burst noise, dropouts, and longer transient interferences is to cause errors to occur in clumps, rather than as widely scattered, isolated events. For example, if errors were in fact independent occurrences, the probability of an error immediately following another error would be about 10^{-5} (if that were the average error rate). Actually, it is observed that about one-third of the time an error is immediately followed by another error in the next bit position. Not only do short bursts containing small numbers of errors occur, but also very long bursts with thousands of bits.

The error mechanism in a telephone channel is often modeled as a two-state process. In one state, the "good" state, the error rate is very low, say, 10^{-6}. While in this good state, errors are independent, uniformly scattered events. The probability of staying in this good state is very high, nearly unity, but there is a small probability of the channel's changing to a "bad" state. Once the channel gets into a bad state the error rate is high, say, 0.1 to 0.2, while the probability of remaining in the bad state might be about 0.5. This particular phenomenological model is known as the Gilbert model. It is the simplest of a number of attempts to characterize error distributions on telephone data calls. Though it does not accurately predict the frequencies of occurrences of long bursts, it does contain the essential element of scattered errors superimposed onto a burst error structure.

In some applications the burst nature of errors aids in their identification, as when a human interprets the data directly. When errors are machine detected, however, the prevalence of errors in clusters can often defeat the error detection mechanism. Again, whatever form of error control is used must be able to cope with both randomly scattered errors and error bursts.

CODES.   To detect and ultimately correct errors in data transmission, the input data is encoded in such a form as to contain redundant information that can be checked at the receiver. For example, every bit could be repeated twice. This would cut the effective data rate in half, but would enable the receiver to detect the presence of a single error, since in that event the two bits would not agree. (Such simple repetition schemes are quite inefficient and are not really used in data transmission.)

The codes used in data transmission are known as *parity-check* codes. A parity check is a bit that "checks" the parity (the oddness or evenness of the number of ones) in some subset of the information bits. The simplest example is the single parity check used as the eighth bit in the standard ASCII code for data interchange. The first seven bits in the block signify the alpha-numeric character being transmitted; the eighth bit is a one if there are an odd number of ones in the preceding seven, and a zero otherwise. After transmission the receiver can recalculate this check and ascertain whether or not it agrees with the parity check as received.

Most codes have this same structure, in which the data is transmitted in a sequence of blocks and each block contains a number of information bits followed by a number of check bits. These codes are known as *block codes* and are usually described using the notation (n, k) to indicate a code containing n total bits in each block, of which k are information bits.

TABLE 5.5   *Code Words in the (7, 4) Code*

0000 000	0100 111	1000 101	1100 010
0001 011	0101 100	1001 110	1101 001
0010 110	1001 110	1010 011	1110 100
0011 101	0111 010	1011 000	1111 111

An example of a particularly simple block code is the (7, 4) code illustrated in Fig. 5.10. In this code a block of 7 bits contains 3 check bits. Each of the check bits checks the parity of a particular subset of 3 of the 4 information bits in the block. The rules for calculating each of the checks are shown on the figure. (The addition indicated is modulo 2, so that $1 + 1 = 0, 1 + 0 = 1, 0 + 0 = 0$.) A complete listing of the $2^4 = 16$ code words is given in Table 5.5. The 4 information bits are listed first, followed by the 3 check bits.

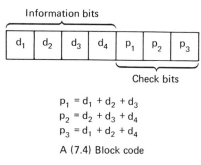

Information bits

d_1	d_2	d_3	d_4	p_1	p_2	p_3

Check bits

$p_1 = d_1 + d_2 + d_3$
$p_2 = d_2 + d_3 + d_4$
$p_3 = d_1 + d_2 + d_4$

A (7.4) Block code

FIGURE 5.10

In this example code, as in all codes used in data transmission, the generation of the parity check bits is implemented with a simple feedback shift register circuit. The rules for generating the check bits are chosen to facilitate this implementation, while at the same time defining a useful code. Basically, the desire is to have code words as *different* as possible (in terms of the number of bit positions in which they disagree), so that additive errors are unlikely to cause one code word to be confused with another.

The subjects of the construction and theory of error-correcting codes are highly mathematical and well beyond the simple, expository scope of this chapter. To understand the theory of codes, the reader is referred to [7, 8]. Here we shall only be concerned with a few of their properties and how they are used in data transmission systems. Of importance to us now is not how the rules for the example code were derived (there are tables of such codes in the references), but how it can be used for either error detection or error correction.

In *error detection* the decoder recomputes the check bits and sees if there is agreement in the checks actually received. Equivalently, the decoder asks whether or not the received word is an allowable word in the code, e.g., one of the 16 words listed in Table 5.5. If not, then one or more errors must have occurred in transmission. In this case the receiver requests, via some feedback channel to the transmitter, that the offending portion of the data be retransmitted. Such systems are known as *detection-retransmission* systems or (an older terminology) *ARQ* systems, from Automatic Request for Retransmission.

In *forward error correction*, when the recomputed check bits do not agree with those actually received, the decoder makes use of the pattern of disagreements to attempt to correct the data itself, without resorting to retransmission. In correcting the received word the decoder changes as few bits as needed to make the checks agree, that is, to make the word an allowable code word. This is equivalent to the receiver attempting to find the *most likely* pattern of errors that could have led to the disagreements in the checks, and then changing the affected bits.

In either error detection or error correction the fundamental property of the code that is relevant is its *minimum distance*. The minimum distance is the minimum number of errors that must be made in a block to change one code word into another. Obviously, the greater the minimum distance is, the more powerful the code is in random error correction and detection.

In the example code the minimum distance is 3. It can be observed from Table 5.5 that at least 3 bits must be changed in any code word to arrive at another allowable code word. Because the code words form a mathematical group, we can take any of the code words and look at the distances (number of differing bits) to all the other words and be assured that these same distances would be found if we had started with any other code word as the reference. In particular, the code word with all zeros can be used as the reference. Notice that all the other code words have at least three 1's; therefore, the minimum distance is 3. If this code were used for error detection, at least three errors would have to occur in a code word before an erroneous word would escape detection.

The particular code we have been using as an example is called a Hamming code, but it is a special case of an important class of codes known as BCH codes (after the discoverers, Bose–Chaudhuri–Hocquenghem). The minimum distances attainable with this class of codes can serve as a guide to what error-detecting power a code can have in terms of its block length n and rate (or efficiency) k/n. In BCH codes, a code of length $n = 2^m - 1$ with a minimum distance $d = 2t + 1 \leq n$ requires at most mt parity checks. A listing of length n, number of information bits k, and minimum distance d for some of the shorter BCH codes is given in Table 5.6.

Not all codes have the block structure discussed thus far. There is another class of codes, called *convolutional codes*, in which the check bits are scattered

TABLE 5.6   *Parameters of Example BCH Codes*

n	k	d	n	k	d	n	k	d
7	4	3	31	26	3	63	57	3
	1	7		21	5		51	5
15	11	3		16	7		45	7
	7	5		11	11		39	9
	5	7		6	15		36	11
	1	15		1	31		30	13

among the information bits but there is no block of bits. The example code illustrated in Fig. 5.11 probably serves to explain the structure of convolutional codes better than a general definition. The code shown has rate 5/6. The basic "block" length of this code is 24, but the check bits within this block check information bits outside the block as well. One check bit follows 5 information bits. Every check bit is calculated using the same algorithm—the summation of a certain subset (illustrated) of the previous 20 information bits. In the figure the leftmost check is being calculated. Subsequently, the data would be shifted 6 bits to the right, with new information bits filling in on the left. The new check bit on the left-hand side would be computed using this same summation rule and the data shifted another 6 bits, and so on.

Code generation

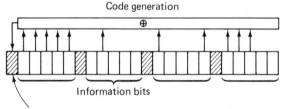

Information bits

Each of the shaded check bits is calculated using the illustrated algorithm when placed in the lefthand position.

FIGURE 5.11

Although much theoretical work has been done on convolutional codes, they have not permeated significantly in forward-acting error control, but for the purposes of this chapter it may be assumed that their properties are similar to those of block codes of the same rate and block length.

DETECTION-RETRANSMISSION SYSTEMS. When used strictly for error detection, a code is guaranteed to be able to detect all patterns of errors, as long as there are fewer errors than its minimum distance d. The example (7, 4) Hamming code will detect all patterns of two errors. On the other hand, if three or more errors occur within the same block, the received word may or may not appear to be a legitimate code word. It may happen that a particular pattern of d errors changes one code word exactly into another, but actually this is quite rare if the code length is large.

In an (n, k) block code there are 2^k possible sequences of the k information bits and 2^n possible words of length n. Thus only the fraction $(1/2)^{n-k}$ of the possible words are actually allowable code words. When the channel is very bad, as in the midst of a long burst, about this fraction of the time the received word will be in the code and the errors will go undetected. Notice that this fraction is exponential in the number of check bits, so generally speaking the number of check bits should be fairly large and, in order to have a high rate (highly efficient) code, the overall length n should be much longer. One typical system for computer communication uses 16 check bits and an overall block length n, which might be of the order of 1000.

A better approximation to the probability of undetected error would be the fraction $(1/2)^{n-k}$ times the probability of d or more errors occurring in a block of n bits. The latter probability is available from several studies of telephone error statistics. One such example was in the Townsend-Watts [9] tests conducted in 1961. These data were collected in conjunction with an experiment in which a (31, 21) code was used for error detection on calls over the switched network. The undetected error rate for this code was approximately 10^{-9}. As a matter of fact, this level of performance is typical. Simple, highly efficient codes are easily implemented to yield very accurate data output in a detection-retransmission mode of operation.

In detection-retransmission operation it is usually assumed that the undetected error rate is negligible, and that the code rate k/n is near unity. The only remaining question is what is the data throughput? Since some time must be wasted in requesting and carrying out retransmissions, the effective data rate, or throughput, to the ultimate user is reduced from the free-running speed of the data modem. There are two systems of retransmission logic that are used; they are *stop-and-wait-* and *continuous-retransmission*-type systems. The systems differ in their throughput characteristics.

In stop-and-wait operation the transmitter sends a block of n bits and then stops to wait for an acknowledgement from the receiver via some reverse channel. If the block is positively acknowledged (no errors), the transmitter proceeds to send the second block; otherwise the first block is transmitted again.

The effective throughput of a stop-and-wait system depends on the round-trip delay D required in transmission to the receiver and back via the acknowledgement channel, as well as on the block length n and the fraction of blocks Pe requiring retransmission.

$$\text{stop-and-wait throughput} = \frac{n(1 - P_e)}{n + D}$$

Obviously, the block length n should be made large relative to the delay, or dead space between blocks, D. However, if the block length is made too large, the probability of a block error P_e becomes significant and the frequency of requiring retransmission cuts down on the effective throughput.

As a guide, for ordinary terrestrial circuits the delay D might be about $\frac{1}{2}$ s, including the turnaround time taken in changing the half-duplex modem from one direction to the other. A good block size n is approximately 5000 bits, and the relative throughput 0.85. If satellites are used in the transmission links in each direction (a future data consideration), the delay D is almost doubled and the efficiency of a stop-and-wait system using optimum block lengths drops by about 10 per cent to 0.75. For additional information the reader might refer to the paper of Balkovic and Muench [10].

Although most error control systems use stop-and-wait operation because of its simplicity, there is another technique, called continuous retransmission, that has a higher throughput efficiency when the round-trip delay is large (as in satellite transmission). In continuous retransmission the transmitter does not wait between blocks for acknowledgements, but continues sending contiguous blocks until a retransmission request is received. At this point the transmitter must go back Q blocks, where the transmission time required for Q blocks is greater than the round-trip delay D. The transmitter must drop back this far since the block in error at the receiver occurred at this earlier point in time.

Suppose for example that the round-trip delay is somewhere between one and two blocks. Then the transmitter and receiver agree to drop back two blocks whenever an erroneous block is detected. If the fifth data block is detected in error, the receiver notifies the transmitter via a reverse channel. The transmitter receives this notification while it is in the process of sending the seventh block. After completing this seventh block the transmitter returns to the fifth block, and then continues in the normal order to the sixth, seventh, etc. In the meantime, the receiver discards the two blocks following the erroneous fifth block, and then resumes reception in the usual manner.

Continuous retransmission requires a full-duplex channel, although only a small capacity is required in the reverse direction. This is in contrast to a stop-and-wait operation in which a half-duplex channel can be turned around at the end of each block. In addition, the continuous system is somewhat more difficult to implement. However, the continuous system is generally more efficient in terms of throughput, since there are no pauses for acknowledgements between blocks. Only when an error is made does the system stop and the round-trip delay become significant. It can easily be shown that the efficiency of a continuous system is given by

$$\text{continuous throughput} = \frac{n(1 - P_e)}{n + P_e \cdot D}$$

where again n is the block length, D the round-trip delay, and P_e the probability of a block error.

Continuous retransmission systems are almost nonexistent at present in practice. The stop-and-wait systems are simple and provide acceptable throughput under most circumstances. Nevertheless, the throughputs of many of these systems will drop when satellite transmission begins to be used in common-carrier facilities. Some of this drop in throughput can be reclaimed by going to longer block lengths, if this is possible in the individual application. In the long run, it may be necessary to change the operation of data systems subject to satellite delays from stop-and-wait to continuous retransmission.

FORWARD ERROR CORRECTION.   The same codes useful for error detection can also be used for forward-acting error correction. For example, the (7, 4) Hamming code listed in Table 5.5 can be used for single-error correction, instead of error detection. Since at least $d = 3$ errors are required to move from one code word to another, if only one error occurs the received word is still "closer" to the correct code word than to any other code word. However, if more than one error occurs, the received word may be closer to an incorrect code word than to the correct one. In this case the process of error correction results in outputting an erroneous code word.

To be specific, suppose that the all-zero code word 0000 000 is transmitted and an error occurs in the first bit to give 1000 000 at the receiver. Notice from the listing in Table 5.5 that only the correct word 0000 000 can be reached by changing any single bit in the received word. Now suppose instead that *two* errors occur in the first two bits to give 1100 000 at the receiver. This time the erroneous code word 1100 010 can be reached by a single bit change. This erroneous word is closer to received sequence than the correct all-zero code word.

The previous example is easily generalized. A code with minimum distance d can be used to correct up to $t = (d - 1)/2$ errors. As long as there are fewer than t errors in the block, they may be corrected. However, if more than t errors occur, the decoder will probably output an erroneous word. Notice that this differs from error detection, wherein the likelihood of errors passing undetected is small, even when there are more errors than the minimum distance d.

Error-correcting codes may also be constructed that are specifically good in correcting bursts of errors. We define a burst length b as the number of bits in a given cluster of errors, including the first bit in error, the last bit in error, and all those (correct and incorrect) in between. A simple rule here is that the burst-correcting ability of a block code is limited to not more than half the number of check bits. For instance, the (31, 21) BCH code has a minimum distance of 5. It can be used to correct any two errors, but since there are 10 check bits we might expect that an alternative decoding algorithm which looks for bursts of errors could correct bursts of up to length $b = 5$. (But it could not correct all double errors at the same time.)

The best-known codes for error correction on telephone channels use some combination of burst correction and random-error correction. Some of the schemes that have been discovered are quite ingenious; e.g., a technique due to Tong [11] (called burst trapping) enables the decoder to use its power in either burst- or random-error correction in an individual block depending on which the decoder believes to be better for that block. Unfortunately, forward error correction is complex compared to detection-retransmission. It is also less efficient, in the sense that more check bits are required in a given block length to give anywhere near the performance of detection codes. In general, the error rates obtained after decoding with even the best of forward-acting systems are considerably worse than even simple detection-retransmission systems.

In spite of the considerable literature on the subject, forward error control systems are virtually never used in practice. The only cases in which they would be preferred would be when the error rate on the channel is so high that the throughput of detection-retransmission is small, or when there is no reverse channel available. Neither of these situations is prevalent, if even existent, in current computer-communication systems.

5.3 DATA MODEMS

A bewildering array of modems (modulator-demodulators) is commercially available for transmitting data over the telephone network. The majority of these modems is supplied by the telephone companies, but there are dozens of independent manufacturers from whom modems can be purchased or leased. The purpose of the present section is to summarize the features, types, and available speeds that can be obtained in modems. The emphasis is unavoidably on those modems supplied by the Bell System through Western Electric and the operating telephone companies. In almost all cases equivalent (and sometimes electrically compatible) modems can be supplied by the independent manufacturers.

5.3.1 Modem Functions

From the overwhelming amount of literature on the subjects of modulation and detection it is natural to assume that these are the sole functions of modems. As a matter of fact, in most low-cost modems these functions are but a small fraction of the overall size and cost of the data set. The chores that consume the largest portion of the set are the auxilliary functions, which include the capability to set up a connection, the "handshaking" and control between transmitter, receiver, and associated terminals, alternate voice capability, and maintenance testing functions.

The establishing of a connection between data modems can be initiated by a manual dialing (or push-button) operation or through what are known as *automatic calling units*, which do the equivalent of automatic dialing under the direction of the business machine. At the called terminal the answering also may be either manual or, perhaps more usual, by an automatic answering option. Following the receiver off-hook indication, the transmitter and receiver collaborate in a sequence of tone transmissions that constitutes the "handshaking" period. During this period the transmitter and receiver establish synchronization, any echo suppressors in the connection are disabled (full-duplex transmission), and the business machines at each end are given "ready" signals.

The interface between the modem and the business machine is in the form of connector whose leads have been fairly well standardized throughout the industry. Usually the voltages at the interface conform to an E.I.A. standard RS-232, which specifies bipolar, baseband signals within a certain voltage range. (In some cases the interface leads are simply actuated by contact closures, rather than by a signal voltage.) In the simplest cases the interface contains leads devoted to outgoing and incoming data signals, and commands such as "clear to send," "data set ready," and "data terminal ready." Through these control leads the terminal informs the modem when it wants to transmit, and the modem in turn informs the terminal when the connection has been prepared for data transmission.

Most data sets have some built-in capacity for performing simple maintenance tests. Some of the tests which can be performed are local tests, initiated and verified at the terminal location. For instance a four-wire terminal can be looped around locally so the transmitter and receiver can be connected "back to back" to check modem operation. Other tests are remote tests. These are interpreted at *Data Test Centers* located at key points in the telephone system throughout the country. The modem attendant pushes test buttons on the data set under the telephone supervision of a tester at the data test center. The modem's signals can be diagnosed for proper operation during the tests at the test center. Often these simple, quick checks can isolate the difficulty and save expensive and time-consuming maintenance visits.

5.3.2 Types of Modems

Modems come in such a great variety that it is almost impossible to categorize them. Most are intended for connection to private-line voice channels, but since the abolition of general prohibitions in tariffs against the interconnection of foreign attachments, there has been a growing number of modems offered for DDD connection through telephone-company-provided couplers. Prior to the Carterfone ruling in 1968, only modems offered by the telephone companies could be electrically connected to the switched network. A way around this tariff restriction was through the use of acoustic coupling, in which a standard telephone handset was inserted into an acoustic interface connected to a data modem.

Acoustic-coupled modems are restricted because of the nonlinearity of the coupling mechanism to speeds of about 1200 bps. Nevertheless, the easy portability of acoustic-coupled modems has made them popular for teletypewriter connection even now that electrical connection to the switched network is permitted.

Most private-line modems are available for four-wire, full-duplex operation. In modems intended for two-wire or DDD operation a reverse channel for slow-speed signaling in the reverse direction is usually present, but there are important exceptions. Full-duplex signaling on two-wire channels is only possible at the low data rates. In half-duplex operation the time required to turn the direction of transmission around becomes important. Also related to this turnaround time is the initial acquisition period, i.e., the delay between a business machine's requesting and receiving permission to transmit. The modem's setup time can vary from about 7 ms to almost 10 s. In polled systems this delay can become quite important.

Synchronous and asynchronous operation have been described earlier. Some modems will accept asynchronous signals whose timing or zero crossings are not rigidly prescribed. Almost all higher-speed modems are synchronous. In this case the timing of the bit stream from the business machine is precisely defined, usually under the control of a timing signal from the modem.

Modems are also described as being either *serial* or *parallel* in operation. In parallel operation all the bits constituting a single data character are transmitted simultaneously over parallel, frequency-multiplexed channels. This usually makes for a simpler interface with the terminal, since it then becomes unnecessary to do the parallel-serial conversion associated with ordinary serial transmission of data characters. However, parallel modems are more specialized, and are usually confined to lower-speed operation.

Modems also differ in the type of line conditioning required (for private lines). The lower grades of conditioning are obviously preferable from an economic standpoint, but these conditioning requirements are only manufacturer's recommendations and no industry standards for modem performance exist.

In many high-speed modems *automatic equalization* is used to combat amplitude and delay distortion and alleviate conditioning requirements. For the most part, automatic (or adaptive) equalizers are implemented using transversal filters, which are delay lines tapped at symbol interval periods

(*T*-second intervals). At each tap along the delay line an adjustable gain feeds a portion of the signal to a summing amplifier. The adjustable gains (usually between 17 and 39 are involved) are set by feedback circuitry, which examines the signal distortion during data transmission and attempts to minimize the average mean-square error at the sampling times. One drawback of automatic equalization is a necessary extension of the modem setup interval required to achieve approximate tap settings using special test signals. However, automatic equalization can double the data rates achievable on telephone channels, and in many cases the extra expense and setup delay are small penalties to pay for this substantial rate increase. (For technical details on adaptive equalization see [1].)

TABLE 5.7 *Representative Western Electric Modems*

SWITCHED, VOICE NETWORK (DDD)

Type Designation	Speed (bps)	Modulation	Directional Capability	Synch./Asynch.
103	≲300	FM	Full duplex	Asynch.
202	≲1200	FM	Reverse channel	Asynch.
201	2000	PM (differential det.)	Half duplex	Synch.
203	3600, 4800	AM-VSB, auto eq.	Reverse channel	Synch.

PRIVATE-LINE VOICE CHANNELS

Type Designation	Speed (bps)	Modulation	Synch./Asynch.
202	≲1800	FM	Asynch.
201	2400	PM (differential det.)	Synch.
203	4800, 7200, 9600, 10,800	AM-VSB, auto eq.	Synch.

WIDEBAND

Type Designation	Band	Speed (bps)	Modulation	Synch./Asynch.
303	Half-group	19.2×10^3	Baseband	Asynch.
301	Group	40.8×10^3	PM	Synch.
303	Group	50×10^3	Baseband	Asynch.
303	Supergroup	$200 \times 10^3, 230 \times 10^3$	Baseband	Asynch.
303	T-1 carrier	$460.8 \times 10^3, 500 \times 10^3$	Baseband	Asynch.
306	T-1 carrier	1.344×10^6	Time-division multiplex	Synch.

Some of the properties of the principal Bell System data modems manufactured by Western Electric are summarized in Table 5.7. The reader would be advised to use this table as an indication of the types of modems available, rather than as a specific recommendation. There are many, many more kinds of modems—available both from the Bell System, the independents, and other manufacturers.

5.4 DATA PERFORMANCE AND TELEPHONE NETWORK CHARACTERISTICS

In planning and evaluating data communication systems for use on the switched telephone network it is necessary to have access to some statistical characterization of the telephone plant. The modem designer needs information concerning the types of analog characteristics encountered on DDD calls—amplitude and delay responses, burst and gaussian noise, nonlinearities and phase jitter. The modem user needs a statistical description of the error patterns that occur—the frequency of errors, the frequency of error bursts, the number of total bits and errors in bursts, etc.

Obviously, the dialed telephone network is too large and diverse to expect any survey of its characteristics to be exhaustive. However, the statistical information gathered in a number of tests and surveys over the last decade has shown a rather remarkable consistency. In any particular location the outgoing calls may be dominated by local conditions and so appear atypical for the network as a whole, but on the average across an ensemble of locations the data-connection parameters and performance may be fairly accurately predicted.

Almost all the present knowledge concerning the performance of the telephone network for data transmission comes from three sources. The Alexander–Gryb–Nast [12] (AGN) survey, conducted in 1958–1959, was the first and until recently the most complete survey of dialed connections available. In the AGN tests a predecessor of the current 202 Western Electric modem was used at speeds of 600 and 1200 bps in approximately 1100 calls of 10- and 30-min durations between points located in the areas of New York, Chicago, Dallas, San Francisco, and Los Angeles. A total of about $1\frac{1}{2}$ billion bits was transmitted, about 70 per cent of which were in the long-haul 1200-bps category. Both analog channel parameters and error-rate statistics were presented in the extensive report published in the *Bell System Technical Journal* in 1960.

The Townsend–Watts [9] (TW) survey was completed in 1962 using a Western Electric 201A data set at a speed of 2000/s. Unlike the AGN survey, in the TW tests the receiving terminal was stationary. All the calls were short- and long-haul toll connections from various points in the continental United States to a New Jersey receiver. Only error-rate statistics were compiled in the TW survey, whose main purpose was the study of error-control effectiveness.

In 1969–1970 the latest and most extensive survey of dialed connections was made at speeds of 1200, 2000, 3600, and 4800 bps using standard Bell System data sets. Both analog and digital characteristics were compiled and published in a 1971 issue of the *Bell System Technical Journal* [13]. The results were based on measurements made on approximately 600 toll connections, dialed from 12 receiving to 92 transmitting sites in the United States and Canada. To give some flavor of the available statistics, a few of the many figures presented in this 1969–1970 connection survey are reproduced in the remainder of this section.

5.4.1 Analog Characteristics

In the 1969–1970 connection survey calls were placed directly between end offices, so that local loops were not involved in the connections. The loops themselves are, of course, much quieter and more predictable than the other components in the makeup of a telephone connection. Furthermore, the loop is a fixed component in connections originating from a given point, and would thus tend to bias averages compiled at that location.

The analog channel characteristics measured in the connection survey included loss (attenuation), envelope delay, C-message noise (a frequency-weighted average noise measurement), impulse noise events, phase jitter, and harmonic distortion. In addition, the received waveforms at the times errors occurred were studied to determine what phenomena were involved in the causes of the errors. Of these extensive measurements, probably the most important modem operation to a first-order approximation are the loss and envelope-delay characteristics. The mean values of loss and envelope delay have been tabulated in Tables 5.8 and 5.9.

5.4.2 Error Statistics

The error rate in data transmission varies greatly from call to call. Most calls are relatively error free, but the mean error rate is dragged down by a few very bad calls. In the 1960–1970 connection survey the distribution of error rates was plotted for each of the modem speeds considered (1200, 2000, 3600, and 4800) and for calls in each of three mileage bands—short haul (0–180 miles), medium (180–725 miles), and long haul (725–3000 miles). As an example, the error rate distribution for calls at 1200 bps is shown in each of the three mileage bands in Fig. 5.12. Naturally, the short calls are the

TABLE 5.8 *Attenuation Distortion Relative to 1000 Hz on Toll Connections*[a]

Frequency (Hz)	ALL		0–180 Miles		180–725 Miles		725–2900 Miles	
	Mean (dB)	S.D. (dB)	Mean (dB)	S.D. (dB)	Mean (dB)	S.D. (dB)	Mean (dB)	S.D. (dB)
200[b]	11.8 ± 1.9	5.1	11.4 ± 2.4	5.1	13.7 ± 1.5	4.5	12.4 ± 2.4	5.0
250	6.6 ± 0.9	3.0	6.4 ± 1.1	2.7	8.0 ± 1.3	3.7	6.8 ± 1.6	3.1
300	4.1 ± 0.6	2.1	4.0 ± 0.7	1.9	4.8 ± 0.9	2.8	4.0 ± 0.9	2.1
400	2.3 ± 0.3	1.6	2.2 ± 0.4	1.4	2.8 ± 0.6	2.2	2.0 ± 0.3	1.4
600	1.1 ± 0.1	1.1	0.9 ± 0.1	0.9	1.6 ± 0.4	1.9	1.2 ± 0.2	0.8
800	0.5 ± 0.1	0.5	0.4 ± 0.0	0.5	0.7 ± 0.2	0.5	0.5 ± 0.1	0.4
1200	−0.1 ± 0.1	0.3	−0.1 ± 0.1	0.3	−0.3 ± 0.1	0.4	−0.3 ± 0.0	0.4
1400	−0.1 ± 0.1	0.6	0.0 ± 0.1	0.6	−0.3 ± 0.1	0.6	−0.3 ± 0.1	0.5
1700	0.3 ± 0.1	0.9	0.3 ± 0.1	0.9	0.1 ± 0.2	0.8	0.2 ± 0.2	0.8
2000	0.8 ± 0.1	1.1	0.8 ± 0.1	1.1	0.8 ± 0.2	1.1	0.7 ± 0.3	1.0
2300	1.4 ± 0.2	1.4	1.4 ± 0.3	1.3	1.4 ± 0.3	1.4	1.7 ± 0.5	1.4
2450	1.9 ± 0.4	1.6	1.8 ± 0.4	1.5	2.0 ± 0.4	1.6	2.4 ± 0.6	1.7
2750	3.7 ± 0.8	2.5	3.5 ± 1.0	2.5	4.1 ± 0.5	2.2	4.7 ± 1.0	2.3
2850	4.7 ± 1.1	3.0	4.4 ± 1.2	3.0	5.4 ± 0.6	2.6	6.1 ± 1.1	2.7
3000	6.9 ± 1.5	4.1	6.4 ± 1.6	4.1	8.1 ± 1.0	3.6	9.2 ± 1.9	4.3
3100	9.5 ± 1.7	5.7	9.0 ± 1.9	5.9	10.6 ± 1.5	4.7	11.6 ± 2.7	5.2
3200[b]	13.4 ± 2.1	7.8	12.9 ± 2.5	8.0	14.7 ± 2.1	6.8	15.2 ± 3.4	6.6
3300[b]	18.2 ± 2.7	9.5	17.6 ± 3.2	10.0	20.0 ± 3.1	8.0	19.8 ± 3.7	7.6
3400[b]	22.1 ± 3.0	9.2	21.2 ± 3.6	9.8	24.4 ± 2.8	6.4	25.1 ± 1.7	6.1

[a]Taken from [13].
[b]Distortion values at these frequencies are at least as great as shown.

TABLE 5.9 *Envelope-Delay Distortion Relative to 1700 Hz on Toll Connections*[a]

Frequency (Hz)	ALL		0–180 MILES		180–725 MILES		725–2900 MILES	
	Mean (μs)	S.D. (μs)	Mean (μs)	S.D. (μs)	Mean (μs)	S.D. (μs)	Mean (μs)	S.D. (μs)
200[b]	5187 ± 566	2672	4580 ± 518	2461	7526 ± 404	1851	7505 ± 473	2422
250[b]	3934 ± 410	2010	3384 ± 326	1727	5866 ± 417	1595	5880 ± 314	1870
300	3290 ± 289	1660	2816 ± 209	1407	4884 ± 384	1375	4901 ± 297	1510
400	2091 ± 221	1220	1695 ± 128	930	3413 ± 341	1215	3163 ± 218	1144
600	843 ± 96	583	656 ± 43	430	1467 ± 183	628	1335 ± 127	592
800	392 ± 50	342	290 ± 20	263	737 ± 114	371	649 ± 88	350
1000	190 ± 28	206	133 ± 15	165	380 ± 73	227	335 ± 53	209
1200	80 ± 16	125	48 ± 10	103	187 ± 45	139	156 ± 32	128
1400	17 ± 5	74	3 ± 8	66	63 ± 16	83	56 ± 15	76
2000	51 ± 20	67	50 ± 18	62	36 ± 26	66	80 ± 51	95
2300	175 ± 47	136	152 ± 43	122	226 ± 54	133	273 ± 76	180
2450	284 ± 65	179	248 ± 64	159	363 ± 48	153	442 ± 89	230
2750	577 ± 120	339	485 ± 102	276	811 ± 99	273	934 ± 189	457
2850	729 ± 144	420	616 ± 120	338	1017 ± 137	348	1166 ± 263	573
3000	1041 ± 183	570	889 ± 164	456	1437 ± 144	468	1614 ± 303	816
3100	1335 ± 241	728	1128 ± 217	578	1903 ± 153	585	2071 ± 329	993
3200	1636 ± 330	956	1319 ± 279	697	2475 ± 191	750	2734 ± 414	1285
3300[b]	1919 ± 461	1227	1526 ± 363	917	3208 ± 343	1095	3333 ± 395	1356
3400[b]	2367 ± 693	1645	1935 ± 556	1277	4040 ± 553	1634	4248 ± 752	2018

[a]Taken from [13].
[b]A significant percentage of connections was not measurable at these frequencies.

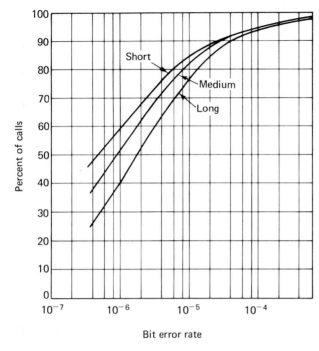

FIGURE 5.12

best and the long-haul connections the worst. A reference point which is often observed in this figure is that some 77 per cent of long-haul connections have an error rate lower than 10^{-5}. In the AGN tests conducted a decade earlier only about 60 percent of the long-haul connections had 10^{-5} perform-ance or better. It is conjectured that the telephone plant has been improving in data performance. There has been a determined program on the part of the telephone companies to eliminate major sources of errors in data transmis-sion.

Figures 5.13–5.15, taken from the connection survey, are useful in deter-mining the performance of error-control systems. Figure 5.13 shows the probabilities of blocks of various lengths being in error, which are needed to evaluate the throughput of retransmission systems. Also shown on this figure is the distribution of burst error events. A burst here is defined as a collection of one or more bits beginning and ending with an error and sepa-rated from neighboring bursts by 50 or more error-free bits.

Some idea of the frequency of occurrence of bursts of various lengths is given in Fig. 5.14. It can be seen that, although most bursts are relatively short, there is a significant fraction of bursts which are quite long. This is an important factor in the design of forward-acting error-control systems.

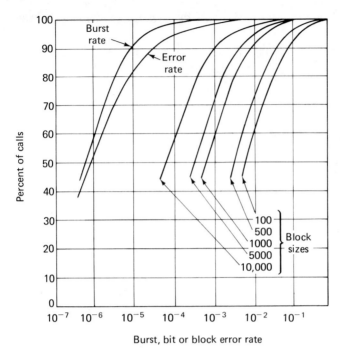

FIGURE 5.13

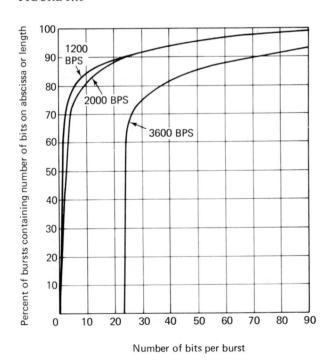

FIGURE 5.14

190

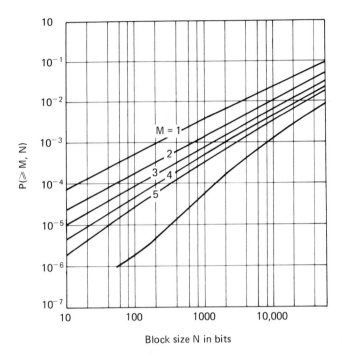

FIGURE 5.15

Such systems must be capable of correcting quite long bursts. Unfortunately, there are theoretical limits to the burst-correcting abilities of codes in terms of their requirements of an error-free "guardspace" for recuperation between bursts. (See H. O. Burton [14] for a discussion.) As the burst-correcting ability of a code becomes large, so does its guardspace requirement, and this latter condition begins to be violated by the channel at the longer lengths.

The final figure in this section, Fig. 5.15, shows the probability of *m* or more errors in a block of *n* bits. This is precisely the information needed to evaluate the performance of random-error detecting or correcting codes. For example, to determine the probability of a block error in using a (63, 51) double-error-correcting BCH code, we need only read the probability of occurrence of 3 or more errors in a block or length 63.

5.5 FUTURE CONSIDERATIONS

In the past decade the emphasis in data communications has been on obtaining greater efficiencies and increased flexibility of usage from existing facilities. In the past several years the climate in telecommunications has undergone a dramatic change. The inevitability of diminishing returns in optimizing a single communications link has led to much increased study of networks connecting many subscribers. At the same time a number of regula-tory and legal issues have come to a head—interconnection, specialized carriers, such as Datran (Data Transmission Co.), MCI (Microwave Com-munications of America, Inc.), etc. Also basic research and development in new transmission systems and techniques are in a particularly fertile period. Whatever the outcome of the present revolution in the handling of the data market, new transmission systems of high capacity and of a kind particularly amenable to data traffic will soon be available. In the remainder of this closing section the new topics and issues in regulation, transmission, and data net-works will be briefly introduced.

5.5.1 Regulation

Regulatory issues in telecommunications are covered in detail in Chapter 9. At this point it suffices to speculate on the impact of these issues on the sub-jects considered earlier in this chapter.

Both Datran and the existing common carriers are implementing separate networks designed specifically for data communication using digital carrier facilities and time-division multiplexing. A separate network, such as the one proposed by Datran, would potentially offer faster setup times, greater speed flexibility, lower error rates, a more relevant pricing structure, and (most important) lower cost. From the descriptions of the telephone plant in the preceding sections it should be clear that, although some of these attributes can be obtained from the present analog facilities, the combination of ad-vantages inherent to a digital system cannot be achieved throughout the existing analog plant. Nevertheless, the extensive coverage of the analog plant dictates that it will handle the majority of data users for many years to come. In addition, there will undoubtedly be large classes of customers for whom the voice dialed network will for reasons of economy or convenience be pre-ferable to service through one of the proposed data networks.

The issue of interconnection is an active one at present. Since the Carter-fone decision in 1968, the tariff structure has permitted the interconnection of user-provided terminal equipment through a special access arrangement provided by the telephone companies. The data access arrangement consists of a coupler that limits the average power delivered by the terminal equip-ment to the central office. The coupler also provides isolation and protection against dangerous voltages, longitudinal balance, and network control signal-ing. These couplers are available in both manual and automatic versions.

The rationale of interconnection must be that the telephone plant and (ultimately) its users are protected against network degradation due to the misuse of the plant by customer attachments. For example, if an intercon-nected attachment puts out too high a power level, amplifiers in carrier sys-tems carrying many other voice channels might overload, causing crosstalk and distortion to the other customers. The present interconnection policy protects the plant in two ways—first through a tariff that contains technical specifications as to allowable signals, and second through the physical interjection of the coupler unit itself.

Recently, couplers have been proposed as a requirement for private-line connection as well as on DDD. This new policy has added fuel to a growing controversy about how interconnection should be implemented—whether through the present protective couplers or through some certification program. Regardless of how the attachment policy is finally implemented, it is clear that interconnection in many forms (PBXs, private networks, specialized carriers, etc.) is here to stay. The equipment available to the data user should proliferate through many sources because of this liberalization of common-carrier tariff restrictions.

5.5.2 Transmission

Research in transmission systems should provide a growing capacity in the common carriers for long-haul data transmission. Presently, almost all long-haul traffic is handled by microwave and coaxial-cable carrier systems. Within a few years satellite transmission may also become common. Although the satellite links will increase the available transmission capacity, the time delay inherent to these systems will affect the throughput of data communication systems using detection-retransmission error control.

Looking beyond satellites towards the high-capacity systems of the future, the millimeter waveguide system is seen. In this system a circular waveguide with a bandwidth of about 80 GHz is used. On a given route the waveguides could carry as many as 250,000 voice channels, which might be compared with the present maximum of about 14,000 on microwave radio.

A great deal of research is also being done on optical transmission systems. The capacity of an optical system would truly be enormous. Such a system might carry an order of magnitude more voice circuits than the wave-guide. Optical techniques are also being investigated for local distribution at rates of the order of 1 to 30 Mbps. In this application noncoherent optical sources, e.g., light-emitting diodes, could provide an inexpensive alternative to wire-pair transmission.

Most important for future data-transmission considerations is the growing hierarchy of digital carrier transmission systems. The first of these systems, T-1, was described in Section 5.1. The T-1 system is already a firmly established short-haul carrier in the common-carrier plant. In this system 24 voice channels are time division multiplexed into a frame, as illustrated previously in Fig. 5.2. Each voice channel is represented by a 7-bit sample. The frame rate is 8000/s, so each voice channel uses 56 kbps. If the T-1 carrier can be used for data transmission directly via time multiplexing into the T-1 frame, then 56 kbps of capacity can be obtained for the equivalent of one voice channel. Furthermore, no modems are required, since the entire system would deal only in digital pulses.

At present there is no equipment that enables a customer to take advantage of the economy of T-carrier transmission other than the Western Electric 306 data subset, which multiplexes a customer data stream of 1.344 mbit/s onto the T-1 system. (The bit rate of T-1 is 1.544 Mbps, but 25 of the 193 bits in each frame are devoted to synchronization and timing.) Thus in this service the customer must use (or at least pay for) the entire capacity of the system. There is no provision for multiplexing many subscribers at various speeds onto the T-1 frame. Obviously, this latter step is the necessary ingredient in the proposals for new data networks.

The T-1 system is usually limited to rather short distances, some 50 miles. To build up a nationwide digital network, long-haul digital carrier systems are required. The first of these is the T-2 system, consisting basically of four T-1 systems, with a range of about 500 miles. The bit rate of T-2, at 6.3 Mbps, is ideal for the digital transmission of Picturephone signals.

The growing presence of Picturephone in the common-carrier system will promote the deployment of T-2 carrier systems; however, it will be years before any digital carrier network spans the United States. Partly for this reason, some of the existing coaxial-cable and microwave system will be used for long-haul digital transmission. This plan is easily implemented using wideband modems at the entry and exit ports of the carrier systems, but it should be realized that these "digits-on-radio" and "digits-on-cable" systems have not the efficiency of true digital systems using frequent regenerative repeaters.

5.5.3 Data Networks

As discussed more fully in Chapter 9, Datran has announced plans for a network designed solely for data-communication subscribers. American Telephone & Telegraph is also in the process of designing and implementing a special service for data customers—the Digital Data System. This service will be a private-line offering at synchronous speeds of 2.4, 4.8, 9.6, and 56 kbps. Subscribers at these various speeds will be multiplexed onto the T-carrier frame to realize the accuracies and economies of digital carrier systems. Both the Datran and AT&T systems should offer the data subscriber substantial advantages over current data transmission over ordinary analog voice circuits.

The proposed AT&T Digital Data System is strictly a private-line, i.e., nonswitched, network, At this time plans have not yet been announced for a separate switched data network. Such a system would of course make use of the backbone digital carrier systems and multiplexers in the private-line serivce. However, there are numerous proposals as to how the switching should be accomplished best. Ordinary line (or space-division) switching as used in the present DDD network is a possibility, although the network signaling arrangements would need to be modified to provide fast setup. In this proposal the digital stream would have to be demultiplexed at each switching point. Another alternative would be the development of a new time-division (or bit-interchange) switch, which would obviate the necessity of demultiplexing at switches.

A buffered data network would offer advantages to data subscribers over the space- and time-division switched systems. Store-and-forward operation in the data network would be used with each message carrying its own address, so that it could be stored and routed individually according to network conditions at the moment. Such a system would be radically different from the present line-switched voice network. A difficulty would be the substantial investment required both in development and hardware for the buffered switch. The large initial cost would be borne in the early stages by a relatively sparse collection of data customers. In other words, there is a difficult "getting started" problem.

A recent proposal by J. R. Pierce [15] outlines still another data network configuration and philosophy. In the Pierce proposal the data subscribers are arranged in a loop topology. Data flows around the loop in the form of synchronous "packets" or blocks of bits, each of which contains an address and other control information. Each terminal on the loop sends information by inserting packets into empty slots in the loop stream and receives information by removing those packets with its own address. Since the control function in the loop is distributed among the terminals themselves, the initial investment may be relatively small and proportional to the number of subscribers. A national network using such a concept would consist of interlocking, hierarchical loops with loop interchange points where those packets not destined for their own loop would be transferred.

REFERENCES

[1] R. W. LUCKY, J. SALZ, and E. J. WELDON, JR., *Principles of Data Communication*, McGraw-Hill, New York, 1968.
[2] M. D. BALKOVIC, H. W. KLANCER, S. W. KLARE, and W. G. McGRUTHER, High Speed Voiceband Data Transmission Performance on the Switched Telecommunications Network, *Bell Syst. Tech. J.*, **50** (April 1971).
[3] C. E. SHANNON, The Mathematical Theory of Communication, *Bell. Syst. Tech. J.*, **27** (July and Oct. 1948).
[4] R. G. GALLAGER, *Information Theory and Reliable Communication*, Wiley, New York, 1968.

[5] J. SALZ, Communications Efficiency of Certain Digital Modulation Systems, *IEEE Trans. Commun. Technol.*, **Com-18** (April 1970).

[6] B. R. SALTZBERG, Intersymbol Inteference Error Bounds with Application to Ideal Band-Limited Signaling, *IEEE Trans. Inform. Theory*, **IT-14** (July 1968).

[7] W. W. PETERSON, *Error-Correcting Codes*, Wiley, New York, 1961.

[8] E. R. BERLEKAMP, *Algebraic Coding Theory*, McGraw-Hill, New York, 1968.

[9] R. W. TOWNSEND and R. N. WATTS, Effectiveness of Error Control in Data Communications Over the Switched Telephone Network, *Bell Syst. Tech. J.*, **43** (Nov. 1964).

[10] M. D. BALKOVIC and P. E. MUENCH, Effect of Propagation Delay, Caused by Satellite Circuits, on Data Communications Systems That Use Block Retransmission for Error Correction, *1969 IEEE Intern. Conf. Commun. Conf. Record 69 C29-COM* (June 1969).

[11] S. Y. TONG, Burst Trapping Techniques for a Compound Channel, *IEEE Trans. Inform. Theory*, **IT-15** (Nov. 1969).

[12] A. A. ALEXANDER, R. M. GRYB, and D. W. NAST, Capabilities of the Telephone Network for Data Transmission, *Bell Syst. Tech. J.*, **39** (May 1960).

[13] M. D. BALKOVIC et al., The 1969–1970 Data Connection Survey, *Bell Syst. Tech. J.* (three companion papers), **50** (April 1971).

[14] H. O. BURTON, A Survey of Error Correcting Techniques for Data on Telephone Facilities, IEEE Intern. Conf. Commun., San Francisco, June 1970.

[15] J. R. PIERCE, Network for Block Switching of Data, *Bell Syst. Tech. J.*, **50** (July 1971).

Additional Reading

[16] W. R. BENNETT and J. R. DAVEY, *Data Transmission*, McGraw-Hill, New York, 1965.

[17] J. MARTIN, *Telecommunications and the Computer*, Prentice-Hall, Englewood Cliffs, N.J., 1969.

[18] Bell Telephone Laboratories, *Transmission Systems for Communications*, 4th ed., Western Electric Corp., Technical Publications, Winston-Salem, N.C., 1970.

6

Interfacing and Data Concentration

DAVID L. PEHRSON

University of California, Livermore

INTRODUCTION

The communications interface is a requirement for any computer-communication network, whether it is a stand-alone minicomputer system with a couple of Teletypes or a large hierarchical system spread over a wide geographical area. Communication usually implies serial transmission, since only this type of channel is available from common carriers. The option of parallel data transmission may be available at individual sites where computer data channels may be directly coupled to each other (multiprocessor systems) or to terminal equipment.

This work was supported by the Lawrence Livermore Laboratory of the University of California under AEC Contract W-7405-eng-48.

197

Remote terminal equipment is usually designed to use serial communications facilities for generalized application. Local installation of these terminals via direct-wired facilities may eliminate the requirement for modems (modulator–demodulators). However, it requires solving the same communications interface problem on the supporting computer systems.

A principal advantage of serial communication is standardization. Multiple standard formats do exist for serial communication, but the format choice tends to be application-dependent rather than vendor-dependent. As an example, remote batch terminals (including card readers and line printers) are offered by dozens of manufacturers, and nearly all use "binary synchronous" serial communication formats. However, differences do exist in the data rate or organization within the data records. The format of the entire transmitted blocks, including synchronization, control characters, and handshaking protocol on the line, is relatively well standardized.

There is little standardization among equipment vendors for parallel data channels. Equipments of different manufacture can be interconnected only by using special channel adapter units or by purchase of peripherals specifically designed for that given system. The parallel data channel is not always compatible between systems from a single vendor, although this situation is gradually disappearing.

The inherent standardization offered by the serial communication formats adds flexibility in two areas. The first, mentioned above, is the ability to organize systems with hardware from different manufacturers. The second is the relative ease of upgrading parts of large hierarchical systems. Replacement of any node (end point of a serial line) usually has little effect on the remainder of the network.

6.1   SERIAL COMMUNICATIONS PROBLEM

6.1.1   Parallel-to-Serial and Serial-to-Parallel Conversion

Almost all computer system data are logically organized in parallel form. Alphanumeric data are encoded as characters; numeric quantities are encoded as defined sets of bits in either fixed or floating point notation. Even arbitrary sets of binary bits are viewed as equivalent to octal or hexadecimal digits. Consequently, computers, storage devices, terminals, and even the standard punched card are organized around sets of bits in parallel.

The interconnection of various computer subsystems over serial transmission facilities therefore requires two conversion processes: (1) serialization at the transmitting end (parallel-to-serial conversion); and (2) deserialization at the receiving end (serial-to-parallel conversion). Both are accomplished via the communications interfaces. Other functions required for serial transmission (adding synchronization characters or bits, error-control data, and line-control information, etc.) are added by the communications interfaces. Such added functions are invisible to the end user who sees the serial link as a mechanism for transmitting logically parallel data.

Virtually all serial computer communications are standardized around character transmission. A character may be of several forms, but the 8-bit byte is most common. Alphanumeric data are transmitted as serialized character sequences that are deserialized at the receiving end. Binary data are also transmitted as characters. A transmitted bit string of arbitrary length will end up as a bit string of the same length at the receiving end. Additional bits or data are added and deleted by the communications interfaces, and sets of binary bits are defined as characters. However, these are unimportant to the user. It is similar to a magnetic tape record that includes gaps, parity bits, synchronization characters, and check characters. The data may or may not be character organized, but they are always recorded as characters.

6.1.2 Asynchronous and Synchronous Character Formats

All approaches to serial data transmission may be classified as either asynchronous or synchronous format. The time dependency relative to preceding characters of the set of serial bits that make up one character is the basic difference.

Each character is transmitted on an independent entity with asynchronous formats. That is, the elapsed time between the last bit of one character to the first bit of the next character is not fixed and can vary over an arbitrary time interval, and it need not be a multiple of the line bit rate (except when clocked or synchronous modems are used; see the next section).

Asynchronous formats require that 1 or more bits be added to the beginning of each transmitted character for synchronization, since the receiving end of a link must be able to detect the beginning of each new character. One or more bits are often also added to the end of each character.

A common example of asynchronous format conventions is provided by the 11-unit (or 11-bit) Start–Stop code used with standard Teletypes, as shown in Fig. 6.1. Each 8-bit character is preceded by a Start bit (logic zero) and followed by two Stop bits (logic one). The Start bit of the next character can occur anytime after the second Stop bit. The static (nontransmitting) state of the line is also logic one. Therefore, the transition of the Start bit to the zero state can be used to detect the beginning of each character.

Asynchronous formats do not efficiently utilize the capability of a serial transmission line of limited bandwidth or data rate. In the example above, three bits were added (one Start and two Stops) to each set of 8 information

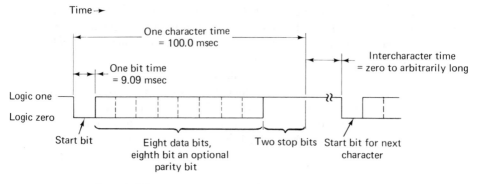

Characteristics:
    Line rate — 110 bit/sec
    Format — asynchronous by character
    Character rate — variable, 10 character/sec max.

FIGURE 6.1

bits so that the line is $\frac{8}{11}$, or about 73 per cent, efficient. Asynchronous formats are widely used, however, for low-speed terminal communications where maximal use of line capability is relatively unimportant. Characters may be sent as they are typed on a keyboard without regard to delays between successive characters. Also, the asynchronous format lends itself to simplified terminal design. Each character is independent of preceding or following characters, and multiple character buffering is not required.

Synchronous formats provide an alternative for more efficient line utilization for block-oriented transmissions. Characters are transmitted in succession with no additional bits. Each block of characters must be preceded by one or more predefined Synchronous Idle, or SYN, characters; see Figs. 6.2 and 6.3. The receiving end achieves synchronization by detecting the bit pattern defining the SYN character. Each set of bits following the SYN detection is interpreted as another character until the control characters that indicate the end of the block are received.

Synchronous formats, although more efficient, place additional requirements on both ends of a serial communications link. The transmitter must supply characters at the rate required by the serial line. Any pause between characters would cause the receiving end to lose synchronization for the remainder of the transmission. Therefore, synchronous formats can be used only for applications in which data buffering provides characters at the required line rate.

Similarly, the receiving end must accept characters at the synchronous rate. Character buffering at an interface level may be required, since no time elapses between characters. Extra SYN characters may be inserted within a transmission to maintain line synchronization during a pause, but these are redundant and must be removed by the receiver.

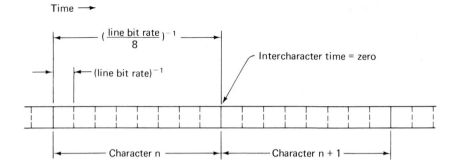

FIGURE 6.2

Transmitting station	Receiving station	Comments
SYN		Two or more synchronous idle
SYN		characters for bit synchronization
ENQ		Enquiry to bid for line
	SYN	Response sequence terminated
	SYN	by acknowledge in response to
	ACKO	line bid
SYN		Beginning of first data
SYN		transmission
STX		Start of text control character
⋮		
text		Transmitted data
ETB		End of block
⋮		
BCC		Binary check character
	SYN	Response sequence indicating
	SYN	a "good" transmission
	ACK 1	ACK 0 and ACK 1 alternate
SYN		Beginning of second data
SYN		block transmission
STX		
⋮		
text		Transmitted data
⋮		
ETX		End of text
BCC·		Binary check character
	SYN	Positive acknowledge sequence
	SYN	for second received block
	ACK 1	

FIGURE 6.3

201

Message formats are rather standardized for synchronous communications. Various control characters permit the transmitter to structure the message and enable positive or negative responses by the receiver. A complete discussion of these formats is provided in [1–4].

Transmission of binary data is possible in "transparent" mode. The DLE (Data Link Escape) character, with other control characters, defines control functions in transparent mode as two-character sequences. Therefore, all single-character bit combinations, including the control characters themselves, may be transmitted as data (a necessary condition for transmitting binary information). The combination equivalent to the DLE character is transmitted as a DLE–DLE pair. Any other DLE–*xyz* combination is interpreted as if the *xyz* character were alone and the transparent mode were not operating.

6.1.3 Clocked and Nonclocked Communication Links

The communication link, with modems (or data sets) at each end, may be either clocked or nonclocked. The modems are sometimes referred to as synchronous or asynchronous modems, respectively. That convention will not be used here to avoid confusion with synchronous and asynchronous formats. A format type does not imply the use of an equivalent modem type, as described in the next section.

A modem includes a modulator–demodulator and its interface to the digital equipment. The modulator converts the binary digital data to a form suitable for transmission over a non-direct-current-coupled communication channel. The demodulator performs the inverse function of converting back to binary digital data, one hopes with form identical to that presented at the transmitting end.

A clocked communication channel is one in which the receiving modem supplies a "clock signal" to the digital interface to specify strobing of each data bit. This strobe occurs near the center of each transmitted bit to minimize error. The basic line rate is controlled by a timing source at the transmitting end, which may originate either in the modem itself or in the attached digital equipment. In either case, binary data are sent to the modem synchronously at the defined rate. The receiving modem recovers the clock from the modulated data via phase-locked-loop techniques, or their equivalent.

Clocked communication channels simplify data recovery at the receiver communications interface. The timing is provided by the modem. They have the additional advantage of greater data rate for a given line bandwidth, compared to nonclocked modems. Modems, such as the Bell System 203 series, provide 3600-bps (possibly 4800-bps) operation over the dial-up voice network through use of dynamic equalization techniques [5]. Even greater rates are possible over dedicated channels. Clocked modems do place minor constraints on the transmitting equipment, since data must be supplied synchronously at the defined line rate. Use of a clocked modem with asynchronous character format therefore requires intercharacter delays that are a multiple of the line bit rate.

Nonclocked communication channels are ideally suited to low-speed asynchronous terminals. The received data are exact duplicates of the transmitted data (within line bandwidth and linearity considerations). No clock is provided to the receiver to specify bit sampling time. This means that a nonclocked modem is equivalent to a direct wire except for reduced bandwidth considerations. Receiver interfaces in both cases must incorporate clock recovery functions. This subject is pursued in Section 6.2.

The primary handicap of nonclocked modems is limited usable data rate for a given communication line bandwidth. A dedicated voice-grade line can support only about 1800 bps using Bell System 202 series modems. By comparison, a dynamically equalized clocked modem could transmit at 7200 bps over the same line. A discussion of various modem types is provided in Chapter 12 of [6].

6.1.4 Format and Link Combinations and Their Application

Four combinations of character-format type and communication-link type are possible, as shown in Fig. 6.4.

ASYNCHRONOUS FORMAT WITH NONCLOCKED LINK. This combination is equivalent to sending characters asynchronously over a direct wire. It is typically used for low-speed communications with individual terminals, such as teleprinters at rates up to 30 characters/s (300 bps). Asynchronous character formats are almost always used with these devices, since the data transmitted to and from the teleprinters is character-oriented, not block oriented. This is a characteristic of the electromechanical terminals, not of the overall system in which sequences of characters (or lines) have logical meaning. Assembling input characters into line messages (and disassembling output messages into individual characters) is performed by the computer or concentrator to which the terminal is attached via the communication link.

ASYNCHRONOUS FORMAT WITH CLOCKED LINK. A clocked communication link with an asynchronous character format retains most of the advantages of character-oriented communications while also making available the improved data rates possible with clocked modems. Any individual character can still be transmitted as an independent item with a synchronization bit (the Start bit) and one or more Stop bits. The Start bit for the next character can follow immediately or be delayed any multiple of the bit time for that clocked link.

Character format

	Asynchronous	Synchronous
Non-clocked	— Low speed terminal communications (usually full-duplex) — To 300 bit/sec — Character oriented	Seldom used
Clocked	— Medium speed — Terminals or buffered concentrators — 1200 to 9600 bit/sec — Character oriented	— Medium speed — Block transmission for maximum efficiency — Buffered terminals and store and forward concentrators — 2400 to 9600 bit/sec

Communication link

FIGURE 6.4

The data equipment must be synchronized to the clock-controlling transmission over the line. This normally precludes using electromechanical terminals with clocked links.

This combination is often used for character-oriented transmission between computer systems, and remote-line concentrators or medium-speed terminals, when insufficient logic and buffering are available for block-oriented synchronous transmission. The effective data rate of the communication line is reduced by the addition of Start and Stop bits. For example, a system transmitting 8-bit characters with one Start bit and one Stop bit per character is 80 per cent efficient.

SYNCHRONOUS FORMAT WITH CLOCKED LINK. This combination is widely used to transmit block-oriented data when the prime consideration is maximum achievable data rate. A clocked or synchronous modem allows maximized rates for a given line quality (to 9600 bps for a dedicated and conditioned voice-grade line). Synchronous character format for transmission also allows more efficient use of the available data rate. A few extra control characters are transmitted with the block of data. However, they reduce the effective data rate by no more than a few per cent for long records. Individual characters are transmitted at exactly the line data rate, since characters are sent in immediate succession.

Theoretically, block transmission with synchronous format has an asymptotic limit of 100 per cent efficiency. This is not achieved because the line has a finite error rate. Check characters appended to the end of each block transmitted are verified by the receiving end, which responds with an ACK (Acknowledge) for a correct check or NAK (Negative Acknowledge) for an incorrect check. The block must be retransmitted when NAK is the response. Therefore, link efficiency degrades in proportion to the number of blocks that must be retransmitted. Line error rates are typically between 10^{-4} and 10^{-5}, and tend to occur in bursts. A few thousand characters is a reasonable maximum record length under these conditions.

SYNCHRONOUS FORMAT WITH NONCLOCKED LINK. A nonclocked communication channel is seldom used with synchronous-format transmission. The receive interface must include logic for clock recovery, which is not required with a clocked link. Also, data rates over a communication line are limited to about one-fourth of those obtainable with a clocked modem.

Buffering and intelligence requirements at both ends of the link are the same as for clocked, synchronous formats. This combination thus has the complexity and cost of the clocked, synchronous format with considerable relative loss in transmission capability.

6.1.5 Half-Duplex and Full-Duplex Communication Channels

Half-duplex and full-duplex are communication terms that mean nonsimultaneous and simultaneous two-way transmission, respectively. The terms two-wire and four-wire are also encountered for communication channels where it is possible to send *and* receive simultaneously over a four-wire system. Note that the term four-wire means logically independent send and receive paths but does not necessarily imply the use of physically separate wire paths, and conversely for two-wire channels.

Full-duplex channels are obviously more flexible since data may be transmitted whether or not other data are being received. But full-duplex operation requires, in effect, two independent communication channels, which become a significant factor over long distances.

Full duplex is commonly used for communications with low-speed terminals, such as teleprinters and CRT/keyboard systems in which the input and output devices are logically separated. Full duplex is less commonly used for long-distance synchronous transmission between computers or from "intelligent" terminals because of line cost. Also, line control is rather complex in the full-duplex mode with synchronous formats. Another way of classifying the application areas is by data format: asynchronous character-oriented data typically use full-duplex, whereas synchronous block-oriented data typically use half-duplex.

6.2 INTERFACE REQUIREMENTS

6.2.1 Character Synchronization by the Receive Interface

The character synchronization requirements are almost entirely dependent on the transmission format used. The differences between use of clocked and nonclocked modems are associated with bit synchronization only, as discussed in the next section.

ASYNCHRONOUS FORMAT.   There is no fixed time relationship between successive characters. The interval between the end of the Stop bit(s) of one character and the beginning of the Start bit of the following character is arbitrary, varying from zero to arbitrarily long (see Fig. 6.1). The sequence of bits in a single character has a very specific relationship, since the N bits defining the character follow the Start bit at the defined transmission rate.

The interface must assemble the N bits (typically 8) following the Start bit of asynchronous format characters into parallel form and forward the character to the attached computer equipment. The interface must be ready to accept the next character Start bit any time after the last Stop bit.

Standard Teletype code with two Stop bits, as shown in Fig. 6.1, allows at least two bit times for the assembled character to be forwarded. When sampling occurs at the middle of each bit, a minimum two and one-half bit times always elapses before the next Start bit transition (22.73 ms at 110 bps). The interface must not begin looking for the Start bit until after the beginning of the first Stop bit, however, to avoid false interpretation of the end of the eighth data bit as a Start bit transition. It is also desirable to incorporate logic to require a Start bit of the width corresponding to the line bit rate (less some tolerance for bit-width distortion). This guards against interpreting a narrow noise pulse as a false Start bit.

SYNCHRONOUS FORMAT.   Sequentially transmitted characters are tightly packed with no gaps. Character synchronization requires determining which set of 8 bits in the continuous bit stream defines the first character. All transmitted blocks are initiated with a sequence of two or more SYN characters (Synchronous Idle), which has the code 026_8 in USASCII.

The receive interface must establish character synchronization by detecting the SYN code at the beginning of each block. This is accomplished by examining the character that is formed as each bit is received along with the previous 7 bits. The SYN character will eventually be found establishing character synchronization. Each subsequent set of 8 bits is another character. To validate character synchronization, the reception of at least one more SYN character is commonly required following initial synchronization.

Another additional level of character buffering is often required by the interface with synchronous formats, since no time elapses between the end of one character and the beginning of the next. With clocked modems in which each bit is sampled at the middle, only one bit time is available for passing the character on; or about 208 μs at a 4800-bps data rate.

6.2.2 Bit Synchronization by the Receive Interface

CLOCKED COMMUNICATION LINK SYNCHRONIZATION.   The use of clocked modems in the communication channel makes the bit synchronization problem straightforward. A clock is derived in the modem from the modulated received data and supplied to the receive interface to define the time at which to strobe, or sample, the received and demodulated digital bit string.

NONCLOCKED COMMUNICATION LINK SYNCHRONIZATION, ASYNCHRONOUS FORMAT.   Bit synchronization is accomplished with asynchronously transmitted characters by sensing the transition of the Start bit for each character. If no distortion is present, the first data bit of the character should be sampled one and one-half times later (that center of the first data bit), and each subsequent bit sampled one bit time thereafter.

In practice, all transmission links introduce some distortion on the transmitted data so that received bit transitions do not occur exactly at multiples of the line rate. Sampling near the center of each bit relative to the Start bit transition allows correct data recovery.

Sampling rates at some multiple of the transmitted data rate are commonly employed to provide bit synchronization. Larger multiples allow a closer approximation to the ideal middle sampling. If phase distortion is defined as the percentage variation of any bit transition from the ideal transition point relative to the Start bit transition, then

$$\text{allowable phase distortion (in per cent)} = \begin{cases} 100\%\left(\dfrac{m-1}{2m}\right), & m \text{ odd} \\[2ex] 100\%\left(\dfrac{m-2}{2m}\right), & m \text{ even} \end{cases}$$

where m is sampling rate/bit rate. Allowable phase distortion for various values of m is shown in Fig. 6.5. Sampling at an add multiple is seen to be desirable for small multiples (small m). Also, data cannot be correctly recovered for any m if the phase distortion exceeds 50 per cent (without use of error correction coding techniques).

Consider an example using Teletype formats (11-bit code at 110 bps) with a sampling multiple of $m = 3$. Detection of the Start bit will occur sometime during the first one-third of the Start bit. The middle third of the Start bit may be examined on the next sample (one-third of a bit time after initial Start-bit

Sampling multiple, m	Allowable phase distortion, in %
1	0
2	0
3	33.3
4	25.0
5	40.0
6	33.3
7	42.9
8	37.5
9	44.4
10	40.0
⋮	⋮
∞	50

FIGURE 6.5

detection) to verify that detection was of a Start bit and not just a momentary noise condition. Similarly, the middle third of each subsequent data bit can be strobed each third sample thereafter.

In general, when m is odd the first strobe occurs at $(m - 1)/2$ samples *after* detection of the Start bit, and subsequent strobes occur every m samples thereafter.

NONCLOCKED COMMUNICATION LINK SYNCHRONIZATION, SYNCHRONOUS FORMAT. This combination is seldom encountered and seldom desirable. Nonreturn to zero (NRZ) data encoding is assumed. Return to zero (RZ) allows simplified clock recovery, but it halves the data rate over a given facility, which is already limited by use of nonclocked modems.

A multiple sampling scheme must again be used to derive the time at which to strobe each data bit. Clock adjustment (digital phase lock) is required for long-term drift between transmit and receive clocks, which are independent. Each bit transition should occur a multiple of m samples after a previous transition. Many bit times may elapse between successive transitions with NRZ data encoding, since a string of binary ones or binary zeros produces no transition.

As an example, consider 1200-bps NRZ-encoded synchronous-format data received from a nonclocked modem. Assume a sampling multiple of 32, which gives a sampling clock rate of 38.40 kHz. The initial transition of a transmitted bit string will cause a phase counter in the receive interface to reset to zero.

Each subsequent transition should occur at a multiple of 32 samples. Data strobing occurs when the phase counter reaches 16. If transitions occur before the phase counter gets to 32, the clock is slow and the phase counter should be adjusted by adding an extra increment. Conversely, if transitions occur after 33 or more counts, modulo 32, the clock is fast and the phase counter should be slowed by inhibiting an increment. To minimize instability from local time variations of the received data, phase-counter adjustments may be made only if two or more transitions show an error of the same sign.

6.2.3 *Character Assembly and Disassembly*

Assembling the received serial data into parallel characters or disassembling characters for serial transmission requires implementation of the shift register function. Various techniques are described in Section 6.3. Control and buffering requirements are considered in this section.

ASYNCHRONOUS FORMAT.   Two counters are required for asynchronous assembly by the receiver: a phase counter to determine the time at which each bit is strobed and shifted into the assembly shift register; and a bit counter to count the number of bits to be assembled as a character.

The bit count may be implemented by the addition of an extra stage to the shift register. Detection of the Start bit would preset all shift register stages to the one state. Then the zero corresponding to the Start bit would appear in the last shift register stage only after all data bits for the character have been strobed and shifted. Permutations of this scheme are of course possible.

The receive interface then has $1\frac{1}{2}$ or $2\frac{1}{2}$ bit times, for 1 and 2 Stop bits, respectively, to pass on the character to the computer equipment and prepare for the next Start bit. This time interval is large enough that additional buffering is seldom required in the communication interface.

The transmit interface is similar except that a multiple phase clock is not required. The bits are shifted out at the required data rate with all data being transmitted after placing the first Stop bit on the line. The next character may be loaded into the Shift Register for transmission any time thereafter providing the bit count logic does not initiate transmission until the time corresponding to the Stop bit(s) of the previous character has elapsed. Alternatively, the next character may not be loaded until completion of the Stop bit(s), but this may reduce effective line rate if transmission is clocked at discrete time periods. A nonmultiple rate clock would introduce a full bit-time delay for any arbitrarily small delay in loading the next character. Note that any delay is allowable with asynchronous format transmission, just not desirable.

SYNCHRONOUS FORMAT.   Only bit counters are required for both transmit and receive interfaces. (The case of synchronous format with nonclocked modems requires that a phase adjusting clock be derived as described above, but this is logically an independent requirement.) Each assembled character must be forwarded before the first bit of the following character is received. Each successive character must be available for transmission within a similar time period. Since data rates are typically higher (2400 bps or greater) and no time elapses between the data of successive characters, a level of character buffering is usually required in the communications interfaces at both the transmitter and receiver. Character synchronization is required by the receive interface as previously described.

Message format interpretation to recognize the various control characters requires considerable capability. This may be implemented in hardware in the communications interfaces, but is more typically done by software or firmware in the attached computer equipment.

VARIABLE LINE SPEED.   Some communication systems allow transmission at more than one rate over a given line, particularly binary synchronous applications. A common situation is one in which the transmission rate is halved occasionally to accommodate temporarily poor line conditions. Throughput can be improved by halving the transmission rate for a while to reduce the number of retransmissions due to error. This case is not difficult to implement, since control responses by the receiver can control the rate switch.

The case in which the line rate is initially unknown to the receiver is more difficult. The received data must be assembled at each of the possible rates with detection of the SYN character at one of the rates used to determine the correct line speed.

6.3 APPROACHES TO INTERFACE IMPLEMENTATION

Communications interfaces for one or more lines can be straightforwardly implemented using logic circuits in the manner just outlined. This is usually the preferred approach for a very small number of lines and is also the interface type most often offered with computer systems that are not particularly communications oriented. Several other approaches are used, particularly for multiple-line interfaces.

6.3.1 A Shift Register Is Not Necessarily a Shift Register

The implication to this point has been that the assembly and disassembly functions are implemented with conventional-hardware shift registers of a length corresponding to the number of bits that form a character. The shift register function (and therefore the communications interface) may be implemented in several other ways.

Words in computer core memory are commonly used as shift registers. Data are shifted by programmed operations referencing the memory location, or directly by the communications interface by read–modify–write operations using *cycle-steal* or *direct-memory-access* facilities on computer systems.

Another implementation commonly used for multiple-line interfaces uses a parallel set of recirculating delay lines (electroacoustic, MOS shift registers, etc). A single delay line is just a special case. The delay lines are recirculated at the scanning rate of m times the bit rate of the communication lines. The shifting function is then accomplished by reinserting the data in the delay line in modified form as required. Assembled characters are passed from the delay line to the computer system via conventional I–0 facilities. Characters are also inserted in the delay line for transmission serialization.

A logical extension of the above ideas is to use the same facilities for the counters controlling the assembly–disassembly process.

6.3.2 Multiple-Line Interface

Communications interfaces for multiple lines tend to fall in three basic categories.

REITERATED SINGLE-LINE INTERFACES. The most common technique available from commercial manufacturers just provides the equivalent of several individual-line interfaces, each containing control logic, counters, and shift registers for the required functions. This has the advantage of convenient modular expansion and flexibility, since each line may be of a different type or data rate.

It is often costly for large interfaces, however, since few economy-through-scale effects are achieved. Little or no logic is used in common, so that costs are about linearly proportional to the number of lines. This type of system is seldom the most cost effective for capacities of 16 or more lines.

SOFTWARE INTERFACES. All algorithms required for sampling may be implemented by real-time program. The hardware interface becomes minimal and requires only a flip–flop to drive each line, a gate to sample each line, and line-selection circuitry to select the desired line under program control.

Each line must be sampled at the multiple rate, m, for receiving, and serviced at an $m = 1$ rate when transmitting. The required scans are programmatically executed after initiation by a real-time clock. Multiple line rates are handled by interleaving multiple scans at the required rates over subsets of the lines operating at the corresponding rates.

This approach is often used with minicomputer-based low-speed line concentrators operating in a dedicated fashion. The required software algorithms are not complex logically, but require considerable bit-testing and shifting and therefore considerable real time. Minicomputers are nearly as efficient as large main frames for this. Therefore, large computers without front-end processors can seldom perform these functions efficiently. Processing rates limit this approach for medium-speed applications above 2400 bps.

Programs for implementing an interface of this form are difficult to write due to the stringent real-time requirements. Large systems of 64 or more communication lines require considerable task-queueing to ensure that all lines are guaranteed a response time which does not result in loss of data.

COMMUNICATIONS PROCESSORS. Communications processors include a rather wide spectrum of techniques that have in common the sharing of special equipment to implement the interface requirements for multiple lines. In a sense, a multiprocessor computer system with a small front-end computer and software-type interface dedicated to the communications task also falls into this category.

Processors for communications handling often incorporate some form of storage other than discrete shift registers per line. One common approach uses the core memory of the computer. Memory locations are assigned for each line to serve as temporary registers for the assembly and disassembly process; other locations serve as counters for the phase and bit count associated with the multiple-scan process.

Consider a hypothetical system of this type servicing 32 full-duplex lines, each operating at a rate of 110 bps (e.g., Teletypes). Assume also that a multiple of three is used for sampling so that each receive line must be sampled 330 times/s, or every 3.03 ms. Each line would have four locations assigned to it in a typical minicomputer. They are

1. Receive counter.
2. Transmit counter.
3. Receive assembly register.
4. Transmit disassembly register.

The 32 locations of each type are conveniently assigned as contiguous 32-word blocks that are easily addressed using the line number as an index into each block relative to the base address defining the block origin. The assembly or disassembly register along with its corresponding counter may be combined into the two halves of a single memory location given sufficient word length.

Each counter serves three functions. The least two significant bits specify phase by counting in a modulo 3 fashion. The sign bit (most significant) can serve as an activity indicator; that is, the receive or transmit line associated with the location is in the process of assembling or disassembling a character. The remaining bits in each counter serve as a bit counter. Judicious planning allows the counter to be incremented (or decremented) to zero at the time at which servicing of a particular character is completed.

The communications processor in this example would access these core memory locations by direct memory access, or cycle stealing for small computers with only a single path to memory. Every 3.03 ms (three times the line data rate), a scan of the counter words would be initiated and the state of each line correspondingly sampled. Each active counter would be incremented (upcounter conventions assumed) and restored in memory. Additional memory cycles would be taken by the communications processor, as necessary, to shift a bit into the Receive Assembly Register (assembling a character) or to shift a bit out of the Transmit Disassembly Register (to serialize a character for transmission). The communications processor executes a well-defined algorithm, dependent only on the states of the referenced counters and the corresponding serial lines, and is easily implemented in firmware or hardware.

Handling of a received character, or setting up a character for transmission, is relatively easy, since only core memory locations are involved, to which the associated programmed processor has direct access. To indicate completion of processing a character, interrupts may be used in conjunction with line identification, or the counters themselves may just be programmatically scanned to determine which has counted out.

The hypothetical system described provides a good balance. Minimal computer processing time is involved since all repetitive and time-consuming tasks are efficiently handled by the communications processor. Correspondingly, all the flexibility available with general-purpose machines remains for scheduling and processing of the characters as they are received or transmitted.

Variants of the above example are frequently encountered. A very similar system is possible wherein the core memory buffer for the various registers and counters is not part of the computer memory but a separate dedicated memory stack in the communications processor. (This may, in fact, just be another minicomputer.) The major advantage is elimination of the communication processor core memory load on the computer system. But flexibility in processing characters may be reduced, since the communications processor and the computer itself are less tightly coupled. A similar system results through replacement of the separate core memory with a set of delay lines. The serial nature of delay lines is not a serious limitation, since the lines scanning process is basically a serially sequential process.

An interesting capability of communications processors of the type described above is the ability to transmit characters of longer than standard length. In the example, bits 2^2 through 2^{14} of a 16-bit computer word serve as the bit count in the Receive or Transmit Count location. Line delays may be inserted of nearly arbitrary length. This is very useful for teleprinter devices whose carriage return time is a function of position and may require several character times to elapse before the next printable character may be given. Delays of many seconds may be inserted for line-control purposes, or for providing delays on line turnaround, without necessitating programmed time delays.

6.4 CONCENTRATOR TYPES

6.4.1 Nonbuffered Concentrators

A class of communications interface equipment exists in which data are multiplexed by bit with minimal delay. Nonbuffered is a slight misnomer, since delays of a fractional bit time are incurred, but this type does not buffer at a character, or more, level. Both time-division and frequency-division techniques are employed in these systems, as described in earlier chapters.

Nonbuffered concentrators are commonly used to mix multiple low-speed communication channels onto one or more higher-speed links for economy of transmission charges. A symmetrical pair of nonbuffered concentrators at each end of a long transmission link provides the equivalent of separate low-speed links at significant tariff reduction. The concentrators are completely transparent in that no data or format modification is possible.

Concentrators of this type are very common within the common-carrier facilities for long-distance data transmission. Equipment for nonbuffered concentrator application tends to be available from communication-systems manufacturers rather than computer-equipment vendors.

6.4.2 Buffered Concentrators

Concentrators that buffer at a character level before forwarding shall be classed as buffered concentrators for this discussion. One or more characters are assembled as they are received, before forwarding at a higher rate. In a sense, concentrators of this type are quite analogous to a "multiplexor data channel" on a computer system where time-multiplexed data at a character level are forwarded to or from several points via a single computer data channel. Communications interfaces on a computer system are a particular case of this type of system.

Character-level buffered concentrators are not transparent, since appreciable transmission delays are inserted. Any application requiring a fast echo of the transmitted character, such as a full-duplex teleprinter, therefore requires that the echoing be done by the first level of concentration that provides character-level buffering. If this is not done, a minimum of two character time delays are additionally inserted at each level of character buffered concentration of a hierarchical network structure.

Buffered concentrators often serve as remote concentrators in commercial time-sharing systems. Concentrators are located in a service area so that connected terminals may dial in on a local basis. The concentrator is typically connected into the network by medium-speed links of 2400 bps or greater. Each character is forwarded as received by the concentrator from the terminal along with an identifier character. Each character thus requires that two or more characters be transmitted over the network. This still is likely more efficient than a nonbuffered-type system, since a nonbuffered system usually requires reservation of a time or frequency slot for the duration of a connection (dynamic, or statistical, assignment is rather costly and economical for only very expensive transmission facilities). Buffered concentrators transmit data only as required, providing a built-in dynamic assignment capability. Activity of teleprinters almost always averages significantly less than 50 per cent, providing more efficient line utilization, even with the identification requirement.

6.4.3 Store-and-Forward Concentrator Systems

Store-and-forward systems are "block-" or "message-"oriented, rather than character oriented as above. A block of data may be a teleprinter line, a card image, an impact printer line, a tape record, a CRT screen load of characters, etc. The store-and-forward concentrator system is therefore often referred to as a message-switching system.

Message-switching systems introduce additional delay if they are cascaded in hierarchical networks, each level delaying for the period required for transmission of the block. But they enable more efficient use of the communication channel, since the entire message need be identified only once (as opposed to every character being identified with character-level buffering). The identification overhead reduces to a few per cent or less.

The store-and-forward concentrator is analogous to the use of a "selector data channel" on a computer where the data channel is dedicated to a specific device or function for the duration of a block-oriented data transfer. It follows that concentrators of this type must have considerably greater data-buffering capability than the above types.

Considerable flexibility is possible with a store-and-forward-type system. The concentrator becomes an ideal point at which to modify or reformat the message. This is particularly attractive when multiple character sets and/or multiple transmission formats exist within a large network. Conversion to a standard format, for forwarding farther up the network hierarchy, is possible at this concentrator level with inverse conversion performed for transmission down the hierarchy toward the end terminal or user. For example, Hollerith data from cards, BCD characters for printing, and data from EBCDIC-oriented devices may all be converted to or from a common character set such as USASCII.

6.5   CONCENTRATOR APPLICATIONS

Various concentrator types exist, consisting of a communications interface supported by varying amounts of buffering and intelligence, or message-processing, capability. Each concentrator type described above may be used at any of the levels of a simple network hierarchy, such as shown in Fig. 6.6. The network hierarchy diagrammed excludes any concentration or multiplexing that may be performed by the common carrier. Each link between the concentrators may, in fact, go through several levels of communications multiplexing and demultiplexing through wideband carrier systems.

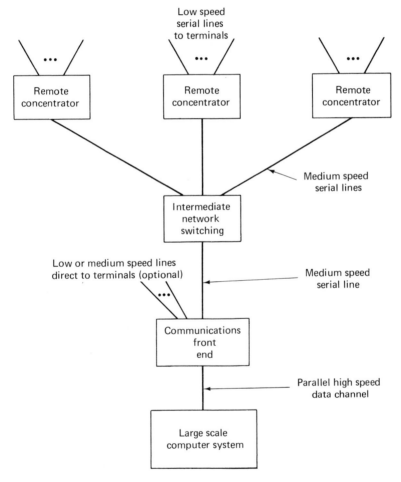

FIGURE 6.6

6.5.1 Communication Front Ends for Computer Systems

Communications systems attached to computer main frames (Fig. 6.7) commonly take the form of a separate subsystem, which is either a character-level, or message-level, buffered concentrator. There is little difference in the organization of a front-end concentrator and a remote concentrator, both performing similar functions.

Virtually all front-end concentrator systems include a character-level interface. When the interface is supported by a small computer with buffered memory, the advantages of a message-buffering system are possible.

Large amounts of character-level input–output are costly, in terms of machine resources, for large multiprogrammed computer systems. Core memory must be reserved for message assembly, or disassembly, as well as for programs to control the process. Frequent interrupts of the main processing tasks to service real-time character-oriented communications reduce processing efficiency. It is therefore desirable to maximize the amount of data transferred and processed via any I–0 transaction by the large system. The largest unit of data that is meaningful in interactive terminal applications is the line message. For data files, it may be a card image, print line, or more.

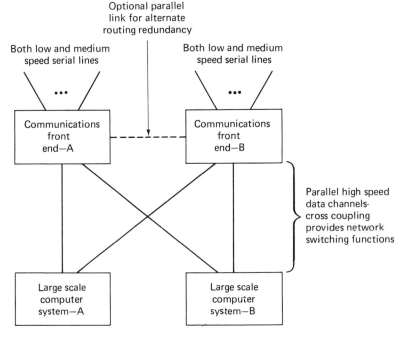

FIGURE 6.7

Message-buffering, or store-and-forward, concentrator systems are achieved with large systems in various ways. A separate and dedicated front-end system certainly is a possible approach. Alternatively, multiprocessor systems in which one or more systems serve as I-0 processors or controllers can perform message-buffering functions in combination with a lower-level communications interface. The distinction between these approaches is in implementation only, not in the logical end result.

The use of a separate and dedicated front-end system adds a degree of flexibility for very large networks. Message-forwarding to multiple main frames is possible, and reduced vulnerability results. Alternative routing of messages becomes reasonable so that network-switching functions may be incorporated in front-end concentrator configurations. Outage of a single main frame need not remove the communications capability for the remaining resources in the network.

6.5.2 Network Switching

Communications switching systems, at intermediate network levels, are often implemented with buffered concentrator systems. The use of buffered concentrators differs as a class from common-carrier switches, since the latter insert no delay in the transmission. Concentrators insert delays of at least a character time.

Some network switching is possible in front-end systems, as suggested above. The prime difference between switching via front-end concentrators and via remote concentrators is the transmission scheme used to forward data up the network hierarchy. Parallel, high-speed data channels are usually used for the direct connection of front-end systems, whereas remote concentrator switches are entirely reliant on serial transmission facilities.

Remote network switches are not frequently implemented as separate systems except in very large structures. Their prime advantage, as a separately distinguishable function, is economic. The use of message-buffering concentrators, or store-and-forward systems, as switches permits statistical use of sets of network links to achieve higher average utilization. Significant improvements can be achieved only if more than a small number of transmission lines are used, however.

6.5.3 Remote Line Concentrators

The use of remote concentrators is almost always motivated by transmission line costs. Long-distance line costs direct from a terminal to a distant computer system can easily exceed the cost of the computer services. A single-voice channel can support a data rate sufficient for two dozen, or more, low-speed terminals through straight time-division or frequency-division multiplexing using nonbuffered concentrators, or through reliance on the statistical nature of terminal activity [7] when using a buffered organization. The remote concentrator provides the necessary multiplexing functions to allow the multiple low-speed lines to share the higher-speed facility. Individual line costs are borne only for the terminal-to-concentrator connection.

All three concentrator types described in Section 6.4 are used for remote-concentrator application. Both nonbuffered and character-buffered types are common; but store-and-forward systems are not often encountered for low-speed line concentration. Minimal buffering and processing minimizes the complexity and sophistication (and therefore cost) of the remote concentrator. Remote-concentrator complexity is an important factor in large networks, since many are required to cover a wide geographic area. Nationwide computer service networks include dozens of remote concentrators.

A special class of remote concentrators is represented by sophisticated remote computer terminals. This terminal type is in fact a satellite computer system dedicated to input–output tasks and typically includes a card reader and line printer, and may include graphics-oriented I–0 facilities. Considerable local processing may be performed, with access to the network being required only for processes that require the power of larger computing facilities. Data transmission rates over voice-grade lines are a serious limitation to these applications today. The satellite computer system may also perform multiplexing functions for a few low-speed terminals. The multiplexing function can be achieved at low incremental cost over the basic satellite system.

6.6 CONCENTRATOR TRADEOFFS

6.1.1 Buffering and Sophistication Requirements

Increased buffering in concentrators has advantages in nearly all applications. As buffering is placed farther from the large computer main frame, the input–output load on the main frame is reduced and preprocessing and/or reformatting are possible. Many of the more routine functions can be remoted, such as the echoing of typed characters for teleprinters. Improved transmission efficiency also results as the routine functions are remoted. Smaller amounts of data are transmitted and that data can use the more efficient synchronous modem links.

Buffering requires more sophisticated concentrator systems. The need for a buffer memory is apparent, but buffering also complicates the control requirements for buffer and communication-line management. Increased buffering also requires that the functions which are highly real-time dependent be included in the concentrator, such as the character echo.

Various approaches to buffer management are possible, the choice being highly application-dependent. The approaches fall into two categories: dedicated buffers and dynamically assigned buffers. Dedicated buffers require the assignment and reservation of buffer storage for every line serviced by the concentrator, whereas dynamic techniques provide a pool of buffers assigned on an as-needed basis. The total buffer capacity provided with dynamic assignment would be less than would be required for dedicated assignment, since advantage is taken of the statistical nature of buffer requirements for each line. Other overhead is incurred to handle the allocation of buffers on a dynamic basis, however.

Dynamic buffering becomes more efficient if each individual buffer in the pool is a fraction of the length of the maximum message. The buffer(s) for a single message are then allocated and chained on a demand basis. Many messages in a typical system are a small fraction of the maximum message length. Fractional-sized buffers are advantageous also for long messages. Each message is accumulated over time and is statistically independent in time from other messages flowing through the concentrator. The several small buffers that may be required for the full message are assigned sequentially as the message is received, and may be released in the same manner as the message is forwarded. Since all messages do not complete simultaneously, this technique can significantly reduce total buffer requirements in a concentrator, compared to that required by dynamically assigned buffer systems in which a maximum-length-message buffer is reserved upon reception of the first character. Buffer capacity requirements using fractional-message-length buffers can approach one-half that required for dynamically assigned full-message-length buffers (providing all messages are statistically independent in time).

Dynamic buffer assignment is practical when dealing with sizable multiple-line systems. Any dynamic scheme that is assumed to have fewer total buffers than the worst case demands must rely on the statistical nature of buffer requirements. The probability of encountering a situation in which the buffer capacity is exceeded decreases rapidly as the set of lines being serviced increases, assuming a fixed buffer-to-line ratio. The overhead for both hardware resources and program to control a dynamic buffer assignment scheme is also progressively less costly when amortized over a larger number of lines. An example of dynamic buffer assignment as implemented for the LLL OCTOPUS system is described in Section 6.8.

6.6.2   Code and Format Conversion

Character-set compatibility is an often encountered problem with any large network. This situation is further compounded when equipment from multiple computer vendors is used. Any large network requires that the multiple possibilities be reduced to a very small number to be manageable. Character-set conversions are reasonably accomplished at the concentrator level, either remotely or at the communications front-end level. As an example, terminals requiring ASCII, BCD, and EBCDIC character sets may all be accom-modated by a single remote concentrator that uses ASCII for network transmission.

Format conversion is even more commonly required. Any scheme that uses remote concentrators for line multiplexing at a buffered level forwards the data with message formats which differ from that received from the terminal. At a minimum, message identification must be added. If binary synchronous message formats are used within the network, all the control characters required by the convention must be added for transmission, and stripped out as they are received.

Alternatively, all varieties of character sets and message formats could be forwarded directly to the large computer main frame via a variety of com-munication interfaces. All character-set conversion then becomes the responsibility of software within the main system. This is usually a more cumbersome and costly approach, since the use of more expensive large computer resources is required.

6.6.3   Message Control

Message control falls into two primary categories: line control and error control, both of which are primarily dependent on message format. The simplest case is asynchronous, full-duplex Teletype communication. Charac-ters are individually transmitted as required with no overall check of message integrity. The only error control is the option of a parity bit on each character. Line control reduces to a decision at the time a message is to be sent to the Teletype to be printed: "is a typed line being currently echoed."

The other extreme is typified by block transmission of data to satellite terminals using a binary synchronous format. Sophisticated error-checking is provided by transmitting one or more check characters along with each mes-sage block. They may take the form of a longitudinal parity check or may use more comprehensive Boolean polynomial techniques. Positive or negative acknowledgments are required after each data block is received. Negative acknowledgment, indicating erroneous received data, requires the retrans-mission of the whole block. A limit should be placed on the number of attempts, since it is possible that incorrect check data have been appended to the data block and retries could then go on indefinitely. A transmission link offering multiple transmission rates can be switched to the lower rate tem-porarily if line conditions deteriorate.

In general, concentrator capability must be increased as the requirements on message control correspondingly increase. Line efficiency and error control also go up. Few definitive rules can be given, though, since requirements are virtually always application dependent.

6.7 PARALLEL COMMUNICATION INTERFACE

6.7.1 Applicable Areas

Most computer systems and peripheral equipments are implemented to handle data in parallel form as bytes (characters) or words. Secondary storage devices are organized around parallel characters or words, as on disk or drum systems, even though the device itself may operate serially. Teleprinter terminals are basically parallel character-oriented devices; the serial interface is only an addition to accommodate serial transmission line requirements.

Parallel interconnections in communications networks are possible only when distances are short enough to allow direct connection via parallel data paths. The several lines implementing the parallel path must have closely matched characteristics to assure comparable transmission delay to minimize deskewing problems at the receiver. This restricts the use of multiple dial-up network lines for long-distance transmission, since no assumptions can be made for the routing obtained and the delay characteristics.

Parallel data paths are commonly used with concentrators in two applications. The first is the use of a front-end concentrator in conjunction with a large host computer system. The front-end system is most often connected to the host system by means of one of its standard data channels, a parallel path. The conventional data channel offers greater data rate and therefore reduced channel loading, since any file can be transferred at rates comparable to high-performance storage devices. Data channel time is a system resource, just as central processor time, core memory, or disk storage. The time during which these other large systems resources are tied up (reserved for transferring the file) is directly related to the time required to forward the message to or from the front-end system. Furthermore, it is usually less costly, since the use of a serial technique requires the addition of serial facilities to the data channels of both the host system and the front-end system.

The second application area in which parallel data paths are used with concentrators is the interconnection of two or more concentrators at a single location. This is a form of network switching. Multiple concentrators may be used to provide sufficient capacity along with, possibly, redundancy in case of subsystem failure.

6.7.2 Design for Dissimilar Computer Communications

One of the major advantages of computer networks is flexibility. Various resources in the network can be modified or upgraded, as required, with minimal impact on the rest of the network. Serial communication facilities provide a common medium for interconnecting geographically separated terminal equipment or dissimilar computer systems. Serial transmission has serious rate limitations for local use, however, as just described.

When multiple systems are coupled at a single site, the same generality is desirable. Dissimilar computer systems may be acquired and tailored to particular applications. New systems may be added to the network (possibly replacing older systems) as an augmentation of existing facilities. The interconnection of nonidentical systems via parallel data paths presents a serious problem. Data channels on systems from different manufacturers are never identical; data channels on succeeding generations from a single manufacturer are often dissimilar; and channel characteristics may often vary even within a single series of systems.

A mechanism analogous to the standard serial formats can be used to achieve generality in parallel data channel interconnection. Implement a standard data channel just for parallel interconnection. This standard may be a type used on one or more of the systems composing the network; or it may have unique specifications to allow for longer-distance transmission to several hundred feet.

Parallel data channel converters, or adapters, are required for each system type to be interconnected if a unique data channel is specified. They connect each system to the common data channel and provide time synchronization, data buffering, and electrical signal compatibility. Assembly and disassembly functions may also be required to accommodate differences in word lengths among the interconnected systems.

This is a more economical approach as well in complex networks consisting of multiple system types. Only one channel converter design is required per system type. For N system types, N converter designs are required for any arbitrary network topology.

Conversely, consider an approach in which one end of each link is adapted to the channel type provided by the other end of the link. This would require C_2^N converter types where all N systems are dissimilar and the network topology interconnects each system to every other. This is certainly a worst-case example, however.

6.8   NETWORK EXAMPLE—THE LLL OCTOPUS SYSTEM

6.8.1   Background

A large network system has been implemented at the Lawrence Livermore Laboratory, Livermore, California. This system is termed OCTOPUS because of its early topological similarity. Initial emphasis was on the connection of several very large computer systems to a centralized data base, whereas directions over the past couple of years have emphasized communications capability to support remote terminal activities.

Lawrence Livermore Laboratory is a major research laboratory run under contract with the U.S. Atomic Energy Commission by the University of California. The OCTOPUS system is local to the Livermore site, which occupies a 1-mile-square facility and offers no off-site access due to security restrictions.

The OCTOPUS network is separated into independent functional networks, each providing a class of I–0 activity to all the major computer systems. A basic motivation for implementing OCTOPUS is the ability for each individual user to view the collection of large computer systems as a computing utility; any terminal type has access to all major computers, and problem programs in any major computer have access to any network I–0 capability.

Two networks were operational in early 1971: the File Transport or centralized data base facility, and the Teletype network, which supports 350 Teletype terminals. A third network supporting binary synchronous communications for remote job entry terminals became operational later in 1971, and implementation of a fourth network to support a large number of graphics CRT terminals has been initiated.

The various I–0 networks are implemented in an overlay fashion, each overlay being a superimposed functional capability. The overlay approach has been employed as the most practicable structure in the face of required network change and evolution. Each functional network is connected to each large worker computer. The overlaid networks may be viewed alternatively as having a crossbar architecture with I–0 concentrators and the File Transport system on one axis and large worker computers on the other axis.

The set of machines comprising the set of worker computers is steadily changing at the rate of about one machine per year. Therefore, one requirement is the ability to quickly integrate a new large computer capability into the network while retaining continuity of capability by the network whole. The OCTOPUS network allows quick connection of a new system to the network, adding additional computer power but not requiring any simultaneous change in network data base or I-0 communication organization.

Similarly, the functions provided by the network evolve, such as display terminal capabilities that will augment the existing Teletype capability. Any additions must be added while maintaining continuous operation of already existing capabilities. The addition of new functions by means of superimposed networks provides independence at both hardware and software levels so that minimal perturbation of already existing operational capability results during the development period.

The large computers currently connected to the OCTOPUS networks include two CDC 6600 systems and two CDC 7600 systems. Another large system, the CDC STAR system, is being added. The network has evolved from a single CDC 6600 and 3600, a UNIVAC LARC, an IBM STRETCH, and a pair of IBM 7094 systems, which composed the set of major computers 5 years ago. The necessity for reacting quickly is apparent and is possible by use of the network approach.

6.8.2 File Transport Network

Interactive multiprogramming of the large CDC machines creates a requirement for on-line storage in vast quantities. Batch operation can rely heavily on the use of magnetic tape, since user interaction is essentially over the counter. Tape is very awkward when interactive remote terminals are introduced, particularly in a large center where 100 or more active users may be logged in. Delays encountered for tape use are at least minutes in duration and can degrade seriously beyond this under heavy load. Reliance on tape does *not* provide interactive operation. Interaction requires the on-line availability of mass storage (of tape capacity) with access times comparable to human response—a few seconds. In a multicomputer network system it is reasonable to centralize and share this storage resource.

CENTRAL DATA BASE. The shared data base concept is not new, but examples of implementation of this concept are uncommon, even today. Currently, LLL's OCTOPUS data base has a hierarchy of a Librascope fixed head disk (billion bit, rapid access, high transfer rate), and an intermediate device, the IBM Data Cell, both of which support the large IBM Photostore (trillion bit, photographic chip store) as the major mass-storage media. This hierarchy is diagrammed in Fig. 6.8 along with the network data channels interconnecting the major computer systems.

The centralized data base organization has two major motivations: economics and flexibility. Economics favor the centralized facility, since the low cost per bit required for mass storage is achievable only in very large

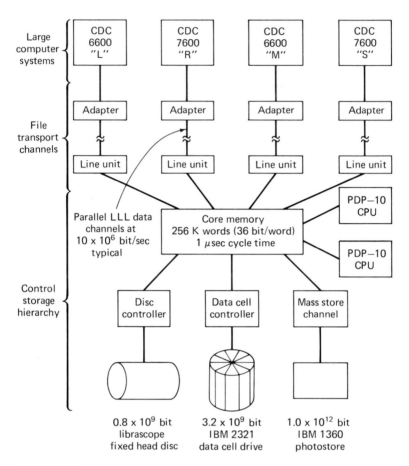

FIGURE 6.8

storage devices with capacities on the order of 10^{11} bits or more. The centralized capability provides flexibility by making the storage facility a utility function associated with the network, not just a resource dedicated to a particular computer system. Files can be created on one major computer, transported to the centralized data base, and accessed subsequently from another major system. The centralized facility is also capable of store-and-forward functions to allow computer-to-computer transactions.

The centralized hierarchy is controlled by dual DEC PDP-10 processors. The 256K words of core memory are part of the hierarchy, being placed above the disk in performance and cost. Core also serves as the intermediate buffer when files are moved up or down the hierarchy, as between disk and Data Cell. Direct transfers between secondary storage devices are not possible due to their synchronous nature (mechanical rotation) and mismatch of data rates.

Although the Photostore is very large, it has several operating constraints. It employs a photographic process in which chips of silver emulsion film are exposed by an electron beam in a vacuum, and then developed with an automatic developing system. When finished, it is read-only storage (the developed emulsion cannot be reexposed). If a file is to be modified, it must be read back onto magnetic storage, modified, and then rewritten in its entirety on a new film chip.

Approximately 5 million data bits (plus redundancy) can be recorded on a single chip in an area approximately 1 by $2\frac{1}{4}$ in. Thirty-two chips are stored in a plastic container termed a cell. Since one cannot expose part of a chip, develop it, and then come back and write some more on it, queueing of files prior to writing a chip is necessary to make efficient utilization of the system.

OCTOPUS FILE TRANSPORT CHANNELS. A basic difficulty faced in implementing the file transport network was the need to connect a dissimilar and changing set of worker computers to the centralized storage hierarchy. A standard parallel data channel has been defined to interconnect the various systems, as suggested in Section 6.7, to accommodate this changing set. This LLL data channel is a first cousin to the CDC 3000 series channel and exists in both 12-bit parallel and 36-bit parallel form.

Each channel consists of a data channel at the central facility termed a line unit and an adapter, or channel converter unit, to adapt the standard LLL data channel to the channel provided by the particular large computer system. Channel data rates between the large computer systems and the PDP-10 are approximately 10×10^6 bps. Long-term rates are reduced by required pauses and setup time. In the CDC 6000 and 7000 series systems, data channels connect to PPUs (Peripheral Processing Units), which are programmed I-0 processors, and forward data either to the computer main frame or to other storage devices over another I-0 channel.

Data transfers to the 6600 systems go directly from PDP-10 core to 6600 disk, bypassing the main frame (or from 6600 disk to PDP-6 core). A pair of PPUs alternate between connection to the 6600 disk and the file transport data channel to stream data continuously, and eliminate the requirement for intermediate-level core buffering in the central processing unit. This reduces overhead on the 6600 system but requires tighter communication between the two systems in scheduling, since a 6600 disk must be allocated and the heads positioned before initiating the transfer.

Direct transfers are possible because (1) each PPU can connect to any data channel on the system via a time-division channel control structure, and (2) LLL channel data rates match (actually exceed) 6600 disk rates. Neither of these factors is true for the 7600 systems. Therefore, data transfers to a 7600 proceed through the adapter unit, to the PPU, to central core, and back out to secondary disk storage via another PPU.

6.8.3 Teletype Network

Teletype terminals are the primary terminal type currently operating on the OCTOPUS system with about 350 installed. All Teletypes are located on site and connected by direct wire. No modems are used, since maximum distance to any terminal is limited to 1 mile. All Teletypes operate full duplex at 10 characters/s.

NETWORK ORGANIZATION.   The Teletype network organization is shown in Fig. 6.9. Three concentrators are employed and serve both communication front-end and switching functions. Each large computer has a parallel data channel link to one of the three PDP-8 based concentrators where the links are the same type as for the File Transport network. That is, all connections

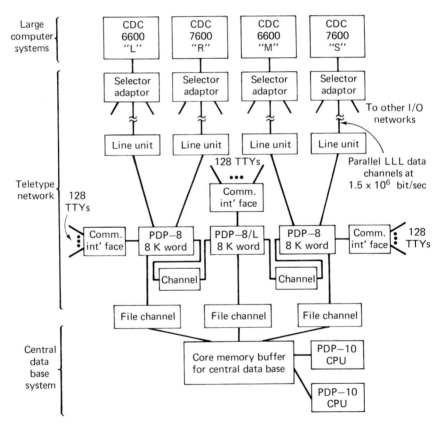

FIGURE 6.9

are based upon the standard LLL data channel with line units at the PDP-8 end and adapters at the large machine end. Each concentrator also has a parallel data channel to the PDP-10 controlled central data base.

The adapters used for Teletype network links are selector type; a connection to one of N LLL channels is established for the duration of the transfer. One port on each selector adapter is used for the Teletype network with the remaining ports available for other I–0 networks.

Two channels are used on each CDC machine for all OCTOPUS network functions: one for File Transport and one for all other OCTOPUS I–0 activities via the selector adapter. A PPU on each machine is dedicated to I–0 activities to ensure real-time response to interactive terminal operation. The PPUs (or PPU pair for the 6600 case) for File Transport are nondedicated and assigned as required by overlaying PPU programs when transfer of files to or from the data base is required.

The File Transport system makes use of the Teletype network links for passing control messages between the large systems and the PDP-10, since this network provides a mechanism for transferring of packet messages within the OCTOPUS system. The Teletype messages are a subset of the class of short messages termed "packets." This is done for two reasons. First, the packet messages are all short and do not mix well in a time statistic sense with the much larger files transported over the file transport links. Second, a dedicated I–0 PPU ensures quick response as compared with the File Transport PPU(s), which is dynamically assigned.

Network switching functions are performed by the Teletype concentrators. Each large machine has connection to only one concentrator. Therefore, communication with a terminal connected to another concentrator requires store-and-forward message transfers through the concentrators to reach the required terminal.

Two levels of alternative routing are possible within this network. The preferred path is direct from concentrator to concentrator. Failure of one of these direct links is backed up by transferring the message by way of the central data base system. A backup path also exists for the concentrator to large machine links. If one of these links fails, the message may be forwarded over the File Transport link between the central data base and the large system by transferring the message first to the central data base system.

The network is not fully redundant but provides fail-safe capability. Alternative routes are used if any parallel link fails. If a concentrator fails, that set of Teletypes is lost. Since full access for the remaining two concentrators exists, failure of a concentrator is not catastrophic. It is only undesirable, since one third of the terminal capability is temporarily lost.

MESSAGE-BUFFERING TELETYPE CONCENTRATOR. Each PDP-8 based concentrator system services up to 128 full-duplex Teletype lines. The communications interface uses core memory locations for both shift registers and counter functions as described in the example of Section 6.3. A scan multiple of $m = 3$ is used so that all 128 input lines and 128 output lines are examined every 3.03 ms by the hardware algorithm in the communications interface. A block diagram of a concentrator is shown in Fig. 6.10.

Software within each concentrator handles received characters that are deserialized by the communications interface and assembles them into line messages. They are forwarded via the network to the designated large system when the line is terminated by one of the action characters (line feed, or one of several control functions). Similarly, output messages are buffered in the concentrator. Software disassembles the line message, forwarding each character to the communications interface for serialization and transmission to the terminal. The logical connection between a terminal and a particular large computer is established at log-in time. When logging in, the user specifies the destination machine within the log-in message. All network mapping is based upon this specification.

Full-duplex operation allows overlapped input and output. An input message may be accepted while a different output message is being printed. The typed line is echoed, in this case, after the output message is complete. The software decision to echo is simply based upon whether an output message is being printed.

All Teletypes in the network are equipped with timers that turn the unit off if no characters are printed for approximately 2 minutes. This minimizes wear on the units when no activity is occurring. The unit is turned back on either by push-button at the Teletype or by sensing a zero on the printer line (a Start bit). A delay of about $\frac{1}{2}$ s is required for the motor to get up to speed. The concentrator performs two functions accociated with these timers. First, it must measure time elapsing between successive print messages (either input echo or system output) for a logged-in Teletype. The 12-bit word length of the PDP-8 allows a maximum count of 4.5 s to be specified by the counter location associated with an output line. Therefore, multiples of 4.5 s can be accumulated (a considerably smaller load than counting 100 ms intervals). Second, only a single action is required for the 500-ms warm-up sequence, if necessary because of time out. A Rub Out character (a Start bit with all ones for data) may be output with a count equivalent to 5 character times, or 500 ms. These functions illustrate the flexibility possible with sophisticated concentrator implementation.

The second 4K words of memory are used for dynamic message buffers. The 4K words are divided into 256 buffers, each 16 words long. Each buffer consists of a chain word followed by 15 data words. Each buffer can therefore store $22\frac{1}{2}$ characters (8 bits/character), since the PDP-8 has a 12-bit word length. Buffers are chained together as required and returned to the pool of available buffers as emptied. Buffer capacity has never been insufficient with a peak load of about 70 per cent of the teletypes logged in. Considerable

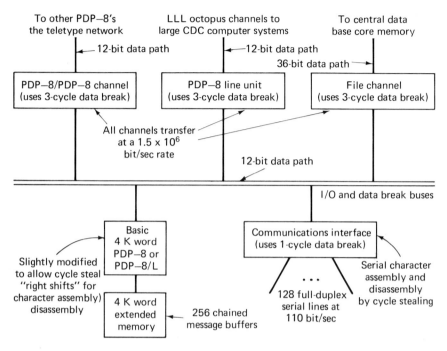

FIGURE 6.10

savings are achieved compared with using dedicated buffers. Eight buffers (four for input and four for output) for 80-character line messages for each of 128 lines, or 16K words, would be required for a dedicated buffer arrangement.

Dynamically assigned buffers imply that a single long message may be assembled in a noncontiguous set of buffers in the 4K word core bank. To accommodate this situation, all parallel data channels linking the concentrator to the network have data-chaining capability. After transferring one block, a pause occurs during which the PDP-8 is interrupted and the next command given to transfer the next buffer to be chained. A single transfer thus consists of 15-word (12-bits/word) bursts with pauses between each burst.

6.8.4   Remote Job Entry Terminal Network

The third OCTOPUS communication network (Fig. 6.11) provides binary synchronous format communications capability to support Remote Job Entry Terminals (RJETs). A minimal RJET terminal consists of a line printer and card reader supported by a minicomputer and synchronous communications interface.

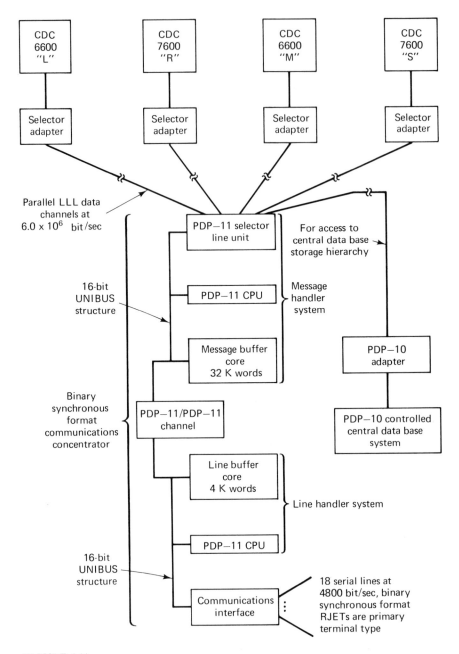

FIGURE 6.11

The RJET network uses a dedicated line concentrator and message buffer (a dual DEC PDP-11 system) to interface each of the serial lines to the set of worker machines. The individual lines use standard binary synchronous communications protocol for compatibility with industry standards at speed multiples of 1200 bps. Standard communication with RJET terminals is at 4800 bps, half-duplex, with a nominal block transmission size of 1024 characters.

The "front-end" Communications Handler PDP-11 provides line interfacing with a capacity of 18 lines at 4800 bps, half-duplex. Expansion beyond this would require another (duplicate) PDP-11. The other PDP-11, the Message Handler, has responsibility for controlling OCTOPUS network communications and buffering of partial messages as they are received from or transmitted to the respective terminals.

Connection to each large machine is via one of the subports on the selector adapter in a similar manner to the Teletype network connections. Translation from the 12-bit LLL data channels to the 16-bit word length of the PDP-11 is performed in the selector line unit. Connection to the centralized data base is via an adapter unit so that the data base appears logically as another large machine.

6.8.5 Keyboard Interactive Display System Network

A fourth network is underway for OCTOPUS. This network will support relatively capable CRT terminals in substantial quantity. Particular emphasis is placed on the ability to present complex graphics images with graphics interaction limited to that attainable with a terminal controlled cursor.

The terminals will be supported by concentrators in a manner similar to the Teletype network. Each concentrator will be expandable to 128 serial lines with display refresh being a local terminal function. It is planned to provide direct parallel data channels to each large system from each concentrator to reduce concentrator switching load. Serial line data rates of 55 kbps are planned so that network loading considerations are much greater with this network as compared with the Teletype network.

The provision of more capable terminals is a needed addition to the present network. The present printer load of 60 million pages/year is costly. The ability to rapidly present pages of alphanumeric data on a CRT from either a large system or the central data base can reduce this print load significantly, as well as reducing the paper storage problem. On-line graphics display will become a common capability rather than a resource limited to a few users with access to sophisticated (and costly) interactive graphics systems as at present.

6.8.6   Other OCTOPUS Capabilities

Several other resources are available on OCTOPUS that have not yet been described, since they are not implemented as separate networks.

TELEVISION MONITOR DISPLAY SYSTEM.   A 16-channel visual display system, based on disk refresh of static images on standard television monitors for low cost, has been implemented on the PDP-10 system controlling the central data base. The disk has 32 tracks and rotates synchronously at 3600 rpm, twice the standard TV frame rate of 30 frames/s. Standard TV is interlaced so that either ODD or EVEN scan lines are refreshed in $\frac{1}{60}$ s on an alternating basis. Therefore, two disk tracks are assigned per channel, one for the ODD line field and one for the EVEN line field.

Information is recorded digitally on the disk, corresponding to black or white picture points on a 512 by 512 display area. A total of 559 scan lines are required to provide 512 visible horizontal lines (allowing for vertical retrace). Display data is recorded once with refresh coming from the disk. A controller connects the disk refresh subsystem to the PDP-10 core as the source of the display data to be stored on the refresh disk. This is the same core buffer used for file-transport applications. The controller incorporates a scan converter for alphanumeric characters, but vector display data must be converted to faster scan format by software prior to writing the disk.

The television monitor is an output-only device and is used in conjunction with a standard Teletype. A 16 by 64 electronic crossbar switch is included in the system to switch the 16 available display channels among a larger number of terminals.

DATA ACQUISITION SYSTEM.   Another I–0 capability that has been implemented on the PDP-10 system is a medium-speed serial line concentrator for 16 lines, asynchronous format, full duplex, at 1200 bps. The system provides a mechanism for data transmission between the computer center (OCTOPUS network) and remote laboratory experimental areas for input of data or output of results. This concentrator has connection only to the PDP-10 central data base at present, and is similar to the PDP-8-based Teletype concentrators with a corresponding tradeoff in line speed versus number of lines.

HIGH-PERFORMANCE GRAPHICS SYSTEM.   A requirement exists, in conjunction with some of LLL's research programs, for a fast and highly interactive graphics system capability. The interaction required here is of the dynamic light pen tracking variety with perspective three-dimensional display. This requirement is partially met by multiple consoles on a Sigma 7/Sigma 3 time-shared system, and a single graphics console on an IBM 7094 used in a dedicated mode. Both capabilities are not part of the OCTOPUS network, so that they are off line from LLL's main computer power.

A two-console graphics processing system is being added to the OCTO-PUS system to augment the existing systems and provide an on-line capability closely coupled to the network. This graphics system will be attached to the central data base to provide direct access to all file-transport capabilities and therefore access to all major computer systems.

OFF-LINE OUTPUT CAPABILITIES.   Various off-line output functions are provided, all driven by magnetic tape generated on each CDC machine. The major device is a high-speed printer capable of 30,000 lines/min. This is a stylitype printer and has been in operation for about 7 years. Current print load is about 3.6 million pages/month.

Graphics hard copy is provided by a DD-80 graphics terminal coupled to a 35-mm film transport, which is driven by one of the 6600s. Processed film produces hard copy by means of an upgraded Xerox Copyflow printer. Current output is about 0.50 million pages/month.

A microfilm–micro fiche system has been acquired to augment the above capabilities. Initial operation is off line via magnetic tape, but it is planned to couple this resource on line to each of the major systems as the start of a hard-copy output functional network.

6.8.7 Overview

The several individual networks, both implemented and planned, making up OCTOPUS are communications networks with various unique emphases or capabilities. The provision of I–0 resources is common to all of them and offers stability and independence of these resources from changes in, and additions to, the large computing resources. The networks allow a degree of dynamism in the makeup of the overall system, and provide longevity through gradual evolution, which may in the end be their greatest strength.

REFERENCES

[1] General Information—Binary Synchronous Communications, *IBM Syst. Ref. Library*, File No. TP-09, Form GA27-3004-1.

[2] J. L. EISENBIES, Conventions for Digital Data Communication Link Design, *IBM Syst. J.*, **6**(4) (1967), 267–302.

[3] E. L. LOHSE, ed., Proposed USA Standard, Data Communications Control Procedures for the USA Standard Code for Information Interchange, *Commun. ACM*, **12**(3) (1969), 166–178.

[4] Publications of the ANSI Standards Committee on Data Processing, Technical Committee X353 on Data Communications, Business Manufacturers Association, New York.

[5] L. N. HOLZMAN and W. J. LAWLESS, Data Set 203, a New High Speed Voice-band Modem, *Computer, IEEE Computer Group Publ.*, 3(5) (1970), 24–30.

[6] J. Z. MILLAR, Data Transmission Equipment, *Communication System Engineering Handbook*, McGraw-Hill, New York, 1967, Chap. 12.

[7] E. FUCHS and P. E. JACKSON, Estimates of Distribution of Random Variables for Certain Computer Communications Traffic Models, *Commun. ACM*, **13**(12) (1970), 752–757.

7

Asynchronous Time-Division Multiplexing Systems

WESLEY W. CHU

Computer Science Department
University of California, Los Angeles

INTRODUCTION

To increase the utilization of a computer facility, we frequently share the computational resources of remotely located computers and/or terminals by using an interconnected computer-communication system. Such integrated systems allow many users to economically share data bases and computer software systems.

In the design and planning of such systems, the communication problems between computers and terminals greatly influence the system performance and the overall system costs. Hence communication becomes an integral part of overall system design considerations. To reduce communication costs in computer-communication systems, multiplexing techniques have been introduced. Frequency-division multiplexing (FDM) and Synchronous time-division multiplexing (STDM) are two commonly used multiplexing techniques in data communication systems. Frequency-division multiplexing divides a channel bandwidth into several subchannels such that the bandwidth of each subchannel is at least as great as that required for a single message channel. Addressing is usually not required since the user is identified by his frequency position. In STDM each user (terminal) is assigned a fixed time duration or time slot on the communication channel for the transmission of messages from terminals to computer. The multiplexing apparatus scans the set of users in a cyclic fashion. After one user's time duration has elapsed, the channel is switched to another user. With appropriately designed synchronous operation, the required buffering for STDM can be limited to one character for each transmission line. Addressing is usually not required, since the user is identified by his time-slot position.

Because of the need to employ *guard bands* to prevent data signals from each of the data channels from feeding into adjacent channels, and because of the relatively poor data-transmission characteristics of the voice-band channel near the edges of its bandwidth, frequency-division multiplexing does not make as efficient use of the voice band as does synchronous time-division multiplexing. The STDM technique also has certain disadvantages. As shown in Fig. 7.1, it is inefficient in channel utilization to permanently assign a segment of bandwidth that is utilized only a portion of the time. Statistical data collected from several typical operating time-sharing systems [1] have shown that during a call (connect to disconnect) the user-to-computer traffic is active only 5 per cent of the time. This indicates that during a call the system is idling for a large amount of time, and only a small fraction of the time is active and actually sending information. Thus the conventional STDM technique would be very inefficient in channel utilization in such an environment, since it would allocate a time slot to each user whether or not the user were active. To increase channel utilization, the asynchronous time-division multiplexing (ATDM) technique for computer communications has been proposed [2, 3]. The basic idea of ATDM is that of message-switching rather than channel switching, since we switch from one user to another whenever the one user is idle and the other is ready to transmit data. The data is asynchronously multiplexed with respect to the users. With such an arrangement each user is granted access to the channel only when he has a message to transmit. A segment of a typical ATDM data stream is shown in Fig. 7.1. The crucial attributes of the ATDM technique are that (1) an address is required for each transmitted message, and (2) buffering is required to handle statistical peaks in random message arrivals.* If the buffer is empty during a transmission interval, the channel will be idle for that interval.

---

*There may be other reasons for providing buffering, such as tolerating momentary loss of signals (e.g., fading), momentary interruptions of data flow, permitting error control on the line, etc. Under these conditions, the buffer should be designed to also satisfy these specific requirements.

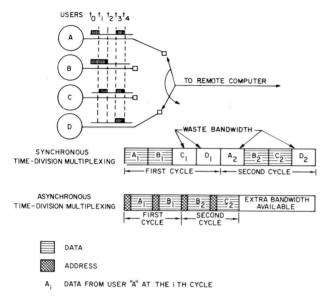

FIGURE 7.1   Time-division multiplexing systems.

An operating example of an ATDM system for analog speech is the time assignment speech interpolation (TASI) system used by the Bell System on the Atlantic Ocean cable [4]. Using TASI, the effective transmission capacity has been doubled, and this system operates with a negligible overflow probability (with respect to voice transmission) of about 0.5 per cent, even without buffering.

Here we propose the ATDM technique for data transmission. Since the data transmitted in computer-communication systems characteristically do not have the quantity of redundant information that exists in speech, the system design considerations are drastically different. A typical ATDM system may consist of a buffer, encoding–decoding circuit, and switching circuit (in the case of multiple multiplexed lines). Since ATDM systems multiplex data according to the data arrival statistics, such systems have also been called statistical multiplexors [5] as shown in Fig. 7.2.

The feasibility of an ATDM system depends on (1) an acceptable low overflow probability—in the same or lower order of magnitude as the line error rate—that can be achieved with moderate buffer size, and (2) an acceptable expected queueing delay due to buffering. To estimate these parameters, the statistical behavior of several types of input data structures is presented in the next section. Since demultiplexing is an integral part of the design of an ATDM system, design considerations of statistical demultiplexing are discussed in the second section. Optimal design of a statistical multiplexor is treated in the third section. An example is given in the last section to illustrate a design of an ATDM system for a time-sharing system.

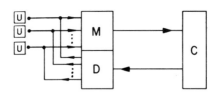

(a) for a time sharing system

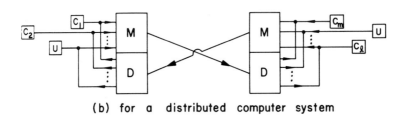

(b) for a distributed computer system

U : user terminal

D : statistical demultiplexor

M : statistical multiplexor

C : computer

C_i : i^{th} computer

FIGURE 7.2   Statistical multiplexing systems.

7.1.1 Analyses of Buffer Behavior

Buffer design is an important consideration in planning an ATDM system. The analysis of buffer behavior is based on queueing models with a finite waiting line.

The parameters of interest in describing buffer behavior are the buffer overflow probability, P_{of}, which is the fraction of total number of characters that overflow from the buffer; traffic intensity, ρ, which gives a measure of the degree of congestion of the multiplexed channel(s); expected queueing delay due to buffering, D; buffer size, N; and average burst (a string of characters) length, $\bar{l}$. To study the statistical relationships among these parameters, queueing models are used to analyze the relationships among these parameters and to analyze the statistical behavior of the buffer. Statistical data collected from several typical operating time-sharing systems [6] revealed that the message interarrival times to the buffer are approximately exponentially distributed. Assuming the transmission line (output) from the buffer transmits data at a constant speed, the time to transmit each fixed-length character (service time), $1/\mu$, is constant. Furthermore for reliability and simplicity in data transmission, synchronous transmission is assumed; that is, each data character is taken out synchronously from the buffer for transmission at each discrete clock time. The data arriving at the buffer during the period between clock times have to wait to begin transmission at the beginning of the next clock time, even if the transmission facility is idle at the time of arrival.

In queueing-theory terminology, the above system implies that there is a gate between the server and waiting room which is opened (and instantaneously closed) at fixed intervals, regardless of whether or not the waiting area is occupied. A customer arriving to find all N waiting positions occupied leaves the system and does not return. When at least one waiting position is vacant, an arriving customer queues up in order of arrival. If a system has C servers and if there are at most C customers in the waiting area when the gate opens, then all C customers are allowed to enter the service area at the same time and their service commences at once. If more than C customers are waiting at a gate opening instant, only the first C customers at the head of the queue are allowed to enter the service area. In all cases service is completed in a unit service time. When service is completed, the served customers leave the system.

The types of input messages to the buffer that are considered in this chapter are (1) constant-length messages, (2) random-length messages, (3) random-length messages segmented into fixed-sized blocks, and (4) mixed messages. The first three types of messages are shown in Fig. 7.3. The mixed message is a combination of the constant-length message and the random-length message.

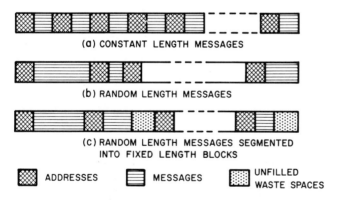

(a) CONSTANT LENGTH MESSAGES

(b) RANDOM LENGTH MESSAGES

(c) RANDOM LENGTH MESSAGES SEGMENTED
INTO FIXED LENGTH BLOCKS

ADDRESSES   MESSAGES   UNFILLED
WASTE SPACES

FIGURE 7.3   Three types of data structures.

7.1.2 Constant-Length Messages

The constant-length message input corresponds to the user-to-computer traffic where users type characters one at a time at the terminals. The computer-to-user traffic is in burst form, which has different statistical properties.

In the analysis of the statistical behavior of the buffer for constant-length messages, the interarrival times of characters at the buffer from each user are assumed to be independent and exponentially distributed; that is, the characters are arriving randomly (Poisson arrivals) at the buffer. The average character arrival rate at the buffer from the m independent users is $\lambda_u = \sum_{i=1}^{m} \lambda_i$, where λ_i is the character arrival rate from the ith user. Since the line is assumed to transmit at a constant speed, the service time for each character, $1/\mu$, is assumed to be constant. The analysis of buffer behavior with constant message length input reduces to the analysis of a queueing model with Poisson arrivals, constant transmission rate (service time), finite buffer size (waiting line), and synchronous multiple transmission channels (servers). Powell and Avi-Itzhak [7] analyzed a similar queueing model with an unlimited waiting room. Birdsall [8] and later Dor [9] analyzed a queueing model with limited waiting room but with a single server. Chu [10] generalized this queueing model into the multiple-server finite-waiting-room case. To analyze the buffer behavior, we can express the state probabilities as a set of linear equations, or as a matrix. For the single-server case, that is, $C = 1$, the set of state equations reduces to an embedded Markov chain, and can be solved iteratively to obtain the state probabilities, as shown [8, 9]. For the multiple-server case, however, the multiple dependence on the various states prevents us from using the iterative technique for solution. Thus the set of state probabilities must be solved from the set of linear equations in which the size of the matrix corresponds to the buffer length. The elements of the matrix are the probabilities of n characters ($n < N$) arriving at the buffer during the unit service interval. It can be shown that the magnitude of these elements ranges from 10^{-1} to less than 10^{-15}. The Gauss elimination method [11] is used to numerically solve for the set of state probabilities. For purposes of accuracy, double precision was used in all phases of the computation. Due to the limitation of computer word size, double precision on IBM 360/65 provides 15-digit accuracy. Therefore, when a coefficient was less than 10^{-15}, it was set equal to zero. The buffer overflow probability and the expected queueing delay due to buffering were then computed from this set of state probabilities [10]. The traffic intensity for m independent identically distributed Poisson arrivals and C transmission lines having a transmission rate of μ of each is $\rho_u = \lambda_u / C \cdot \mu$.

Figure 7.4 portrays the relationships between overflow probabilities and buffer sizes for selected traffic intensities and selected numbers of servers. The curves for two, three, and four servers lie in the region between the single and the five-server curves. For a given buffer size, the difference in overflow probability between single and multiple servers decreases as their traffic intensities increase. For a given traffic intensity, the overflow probability decreases exponentially with buffer size. For a typical traffic intensity of 0.8, a buffer with a single output of 28 characters will achieve an overflow

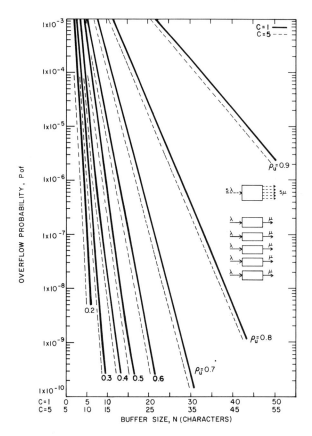

FIGURE 7.4   Overflow probability as a function of buffer size for constant-length message inputs.

probability in the order of 10^{-6}. A larger buffer size is needed for $\rho_u > 0.8$ to achieve the same degree of buffer performance. As shown in Fig. 7.5, for a given ρ, the queueing delay increases as the overflow probability decreases (or the buffer size increases). When the overflow probability is less than 10^{-4} (for $\rho_u = 0.8$, this overflow probability corresponds to a buffer size of about 18 characters), the delay increment with buffer length becomes negligible and can be approximated as a constant.

The expected queueing delay due to buffering is expressed in terms of character-service-times. Figure 7.6 describes the queueing delay for various traffic intensities at overflow probability equal to 10^{-6}. The queueing delay increases exponentially with ρ_u. For a given ρ_u the queueing delay decreases with an increase in the number of servers. Figures 7.4 and 7.6 indicate that for reasonable values of overflow probability and queueing delay, a buffer size in the order of 10 to 100 characters is usually sufficient for ATDM sys-

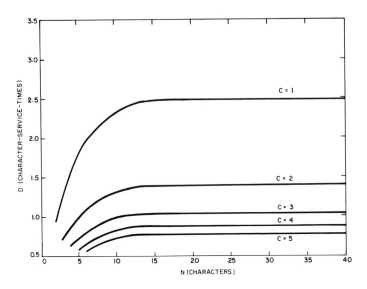

FIGURE 7.5   Expected queueing delay as a function of buffer size for constant-length message inputs and C constant outputs.

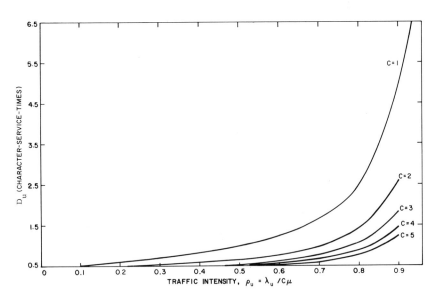

FIGURE 7.6   Expected queueing delay as a function of traffic intensity for constant-length message inputs and C constant outputs at overflow probability $= 10^{-6}$.

tems with constant message length inputs. Whenever multiple servers are used, it is always more advantageous in delay as well as in buffer size to use a common buffer rather than several single transmission lines each with a separate buffer. Furthermore, we note that the queueing delay and overflow probability for Poisson arrivals and constant service time are about half the corresponding values for the exponential service time case [12] even though the average service time is the same.

Buffer behavior for binomial input arrivals has been studied by H. Rudin [13]. Since binomial distribution approaches the Poisson as m gets large (in this case, m is the number of terminals), buffer behavior with binary arrival is similar to that of the Poisson-arrivals case. We should note that the binary arrival is not the only finite-population (in terms of terminals) model. In fact, traffic statistics measured from several time-sharing systems reveal that the message interarrival times can be approximated as exponentially distributed. Thus the traffic generated by the m independent identically distributed terminals is the convolution sum of m Poisson arrivals, which is still a Poisson arrival with an average arrival rate $\lambda_u = \sum_{i=1}^m \lambda_i$, where λ_i is the average arrival rate generated by the ith terminal.

When the input traffic to the buffer is regulated in some fashion at each terminal, then the Poisson arrival changes to an Erlang arrival with parameter K. We can approximate the non-Poisson input as an Erlang arrival by selecting an appropriate value for K. Maritsas and Hartley [14] have analyzed buffer overflow probability with Erlang arrivals and constant output rate. Results of buffer overflow probability versus buffer size for selected traffic intensities for $K = 2, 3, 4$, and 5 are reported in their paper. Tzafestas [15] has also studied the buffer length for Erlang arrivals and multiple synchronous constant outputs. For a given-sized buffer and a given traffic intensity, the buffer overflow probability decreases as the parameter K increases. This is true because the input traffic becomes less random as K increases. In general, the buffer behavior of Erlang arrivals with $1 < K < \infty$ should lie in between that for Poisson arrivals (i.e., when $K = 1$) and that for constant arrivals (i.e., as $K \longrightarrow \infty$).

7.1.3 Random-Length Messages

The random-length-message model provides a good approximation of the computer output traffic that consists of strings of characters (bursts). Buffer behavior for bursty input traffic is very different from that of constant-length message inputs and is discussed in this section.

To describe the bursty input, let us determine the analytical expression for the bursty input arrivals. The time to transmit a character on the multiplexed line is defined as a unit service interval and denoted as $1/\mu$. Hence the unit service time for a line with a transmission rate of μ characters per second is $1/\mu$ seconds.

Measurements of some operating computer systems reveal that interburst arrival times are approximately exponentially distributed, and burst lengths are approximately geometrically distributed [6]. Therefore, we assume the burst length, X, is geometrically distributed with mean $\bar{l} = 1/\theta$, and the number of bursts that arrive during a unit service interval, Y, is Poisson distributed with a rate of λ_r bursts per service time:

$$f_X(l) = \theta(1 - \theta)^{l-1} \qquad l = 1, 2, \ldots \tag{7.1}$$

$$f_Y(n) = \exp(-\lambda_r)\lambda_r^n/n! \qquad n = 0, 1, 2, \ldots \tag{7.2}$$

The total number of characters, S, that arrives during the time to transmit a character on the multiplexed line is a random sum and

$$S = \sum_{i=0}^{Y} X_i \tag{7.3}$$

where X_i is a random variable distributed as in (7.1), which represents the number of characters contained in the ith arriving burst, and Y is a random variable distributed as in (7.2), which represents the total number of bursts arriving during the unit service interval.

It can be shown that $\Pr\{S = j\}$, the probability that exactly j characters will arrive at the buffer during a unit service interval, has compound Poisson form:

$$\Pr\{S = j\} = \begin{cases} \sum_{k=1}^{j} \binom{j-1}{k-1} (\lambda_r\theta)^k (1 - \theta)^{j-k} \dfrac{\exp(-\lambda_r)}{k!} & j = 1, 2, \ldots \\ \exp(-\lambda_r) & j = 0 \end{cases} \tag{7.4}$$

The expected value of S is $E[S] = E[X] \cdot E[Y] = \lambda_r/\theta$ and the variance of S is

$$\mathrm{var}[S] = \frac{\lambda_r(2 - \theta)}{\theta^2} \tag{7.5}$$

Thus the buffer behavior of random-length message inputs can be analyzed as a finite-waiting-room queueing model with compound Poisson arrivals and constant service time.

The time required to compute the probabilities of arrivals at the buffer, $\Pr\{S = j\}$, from (7.4) depends on the size of j. For large j (e.g., $j > 1000$), the computation time could be very large and prohibitive. A convenient and less time-consuming way to compute $\Pr\{S = j\}$ is from the characteristic function of S by using the fast Fourier transform inversion method [16]. $\Pr\{S = j\}$ is computed from the characteristic function of S using double precision on the IBM 360/65, which provides 15-digit accuracy. Because of the word length limitation of this computer, $\Pr\{S = j\}$ is set to zero whenever $\Pr\{S = j\} < 10^{-15}$.

Using the time to transmit each character as the service time, the set of state equations for a buffer size of N characters can be established and solved numerically from $\Pr\{S = j\}, j = 1, 2, \ldots$. The overflow probability can be computed from this set of state probabilities [16].

Relationships among average burst lengths and buffer sizes for selected traffic intensities at $P_{of} = 10^{-6}$ are portrayed in Fig. 7.7. For more detailed information about buffer behavior at other buffer overflow probabilities, the reader should consult [16].

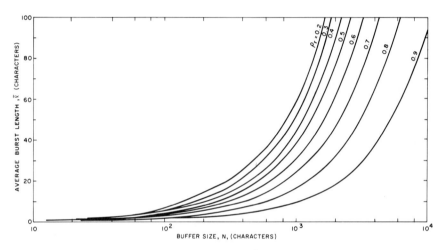

FIGURE 7.7   Buffer size as a function of average message length for random-length message inputs at overflow probability = 10^{-6}.

In computing the expected burst delay, D_r, due to buffering, we should treat each burst as a unit. The service time is now the time required to transmit the entire burst. For a line with constant transmission rate, the service-time distribution is the same as the burst-length distribution, except for a constant transmission-rate factor. Hence the service time is also geometrically distributed. When the overflow probability is very small, a good approximation for the expected delay can be computed from a queueing model with finite-waiting-room Poisson arrivals and single server with geometric service time. The expected burst delay can be expressed in terms of the expected number of bursts in the buffer, L, and the effective burst arrival rate, $\lambda_{eff} = \lambda_r(1 - P_{of})$. When overflow probability is very small, for example, $P_{of} = 10^{-6}$, then $D_r = L/\lambda_{eff} \cong L/\lambda_r$, which implies that D_r can be approximated by the expected burst delay of the infinite-waiting-room M/G/1 model [12]. Hence

$$D_r = \frac{\lambda_r E(X^2)}{2(1 - \rho_r)} = \frac{\lambda_r(2 - \theta)}{2(\theta - \lambda_r)\theta} \text{ character service times} \qquad (7.6)$$

where $E(X^2)$ is equal to the second moment of the burst length, X. The delays are computed from (7.6) for selected traffic intensities and burst lengths. Figure 7.8 portrays the relationship between expected burst queueing delay

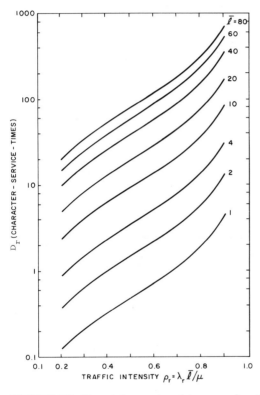

FIGURE 7.8   Expected queueing delay as a function of traffic intensity for random-length message inputs.

and traffic intensity for selected expected burst lengths. For a given expected burst length, the expected queueing delay increases as traffic intensity increases; for a given traffic intensity, the expected queueing delay increases with burst length. These are important factors that affect the delay. A simulation result of the buffer behavior of a specific statistical multiplexor with bursty message inputs is presented in [17].

7.1.4 Random-Length Message Segmented into Fixed-Sized Blocks

In the preceding section we discussed the buffer behavior for random-length message inputs. The random nature of the message length, however, greatly complicates the problem of storage allocation. A way to simplify this problem is to segment messages into fixed-sized blocks. An address, as well as linking information to subsequent blocks, is assigned to each block, as shown in Fig. 7.3. Since each block has an address and is uniform in size, a block can be stored in any vacant position in the buffer. It is not necessary to rearrange the buffer to obtain adequate space for the entire burst. Thus the storage-allocation problem is greatly simplified. The wasted storage space of each message created by segmentation is (1) some number of address characters, b, to identify each block and to link the subsequent blocks, and (2) the unfilled space of the last block.

When the message length is geometrically distributed, the optimal segmented block size, B', that minimized the waste space [18] is

$$B' = \sqrt{2b\bar{l}} - \frac{b}{3} + \frac{31b^{3/2}}{9\sqrt{2\bar{l}}} + o\left(\frac{1}{\bar{l}}\right) \tag{7.7}$$

For reliability reasons [19, 20] error detection and retransmission are used by many data communication systems. The optimal block size when error control is used should also consider the time wasted in acknowledgments, A, and retransmissions due to errors in transmissions. When transmission cost is more dominant than storage cost, the optimal block size for both random-error channels and burst-error channels has been studied [21]. The optimal block size depends on the average message length, $\bar{l}$, the product of the acknowledgment time and transmission rate, $A\mu$, the block overhead for addressing and error control, b, and the channel error characteristics. The optimal fixed message block size B' for selected average message lengths $\bar{l}$ for random-error channels is plotted against the number of acknowledgment characters $A\mu$, as shown in Fig. 7.9. For the detailed mathematical model and the optimal fixed message block size for bursty error channels, the reader should refer to [21].

The actual block size B is equal to the sum of the optimal segmented block size B' and the required address length or block overhead if error control is used. Thus

$$B = B' + b \tag{7.8}$$

We shall now study buffer behavior for the segmented fixed-sized block inputs. It can be shown that when burst lengths are geometrically distributed

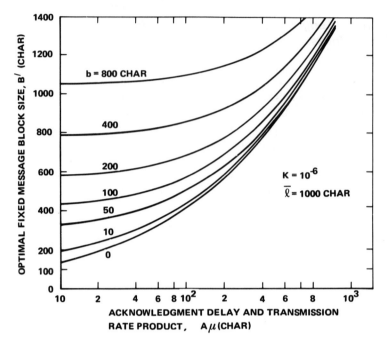

FIGURE 7.9   Optimal fixed message block size, B', as a function of the acknowledgment transmission rate product, $A\mu$, for random-error channel at $K = 10^{-6}$ characters and $\bar{l} = 1000$ characters.

with parameters p and $q = 1 - p$, and when the burst is segmented into fixed-sized blocks B', then the number of blocks per burst is also geometrically distributed [21] with parameters $Q = q^{B'}$ and $P = 1 - Q$. The average number of blocks per burst is $\bar{n}(l) = 1/P$. Although each character is synchronously transmitted, service for the block may be assumed to be asynchronous (i.e., if the channel is idle, the message arriving at the buffer is transmitted immediately) as a good approximation.* For Poisson burst arrivals with geometrically distributed burst lengths, the number of segmented blocks arriving during a unit service interval (the time required to transmit a fixed-sized block of characters) has a compound Poisson distribution. The distribution is similar to (7.4), except that in this case $\theta = 1/\bar{n}(l)$. Using the finite-waiting-room queueing model with compound Poisson arrivals and asynchronous constant service [5], the relationships among block overflow probabilities (the average fraction of the total number of blocks that overflow from the buffer), $\bar{n}(l)$, and buffer sizes are portrayed in Fig.

*When the block is very short, we should assume that the block service is synchronous and buffer behavior is the same as the constant-length-message case (Section 7.12), except characters now should be viewed as blocks.

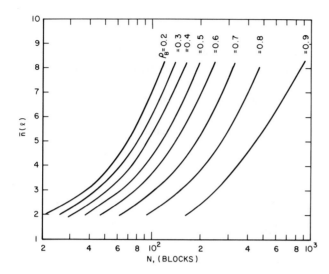

FIGURE 7.10 Buffer size as a function of average number of blocks per burst for fixed-sized message block inputs at overflow probabilities $= 10^{-6}$.

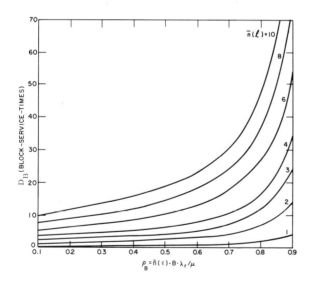

FIGURE 7.11 Expected queueing delay as a function of traffic intensity for fixed-sized message blocks at overflow probability $= 10^{-6}$.

251

7.10. The results show that for a given traffic intensity and average message length, a much larger buffer is needed to achieve the desired level of buffer overflow probability. This extra buffer space is due to the wasted space of the last unfilled block for the blocked messages. The average delays of each block for selected traffic intensities are shown in Fig. 7.11.

7.1.5 Mixed Messages

The user-to-computer traffic discussed in Section 7.1.2 is mainly for type-writer users who type in one character at a time for the computer. However, in many computer-communication systems there may be other types of input terminals, such as paper tapes, cathode-ray tubes (CRT), magnetic tape inputs, etc. Since CRT and tape outputs are in bursts, the inputs no longer can be viewed as constant-length message inputs; rather, we should view the inputs as mixtures of constant-length messages and random-length messages. Assuming the various inputs are statistically independent of each other, the density function of the total number of characters arriving at the buffer during a unit service interval is the convolution sum of all the input arrival density functions. For a system that has m_u terminals that generate constant-length message inputs with a message arrival rate λ_u character/s, and m_r terminals that generate random-length message inputs with a message arrival rate $\lambda_r \bar{l}$ character/s (where $\bar{l}$ is the average message burst length, and λ_r is the average burst arrival rate), the total traffic intensity for a buffer with such mixed message inputs and an output rate of μ characters/s is

$$\rho_m = \frac{m_u \lambda_u + m_r \lambda_r \bar{l}}{\mu} \tag{7.9}$$

Let α be the input traffic mixture rate, which describes the percentage of the traffic (in terms of percentage of characters) that is random-length messages. Clearly, $1 - \alpha$ is the percentage of the traffic that is constant-length messages. Thus

$$\alpha = \frac{m_r \lambda_r \bar{l}}{\rho_m \mu} \tag{7.10}$$

and

$$1 - \alpha = \frac{m_u \lambda_u}{\rho_m \mu}$$

It can be shown that $\Pr\{S_m = n\}$ (the probabilities that exactly n characters will arrive for mixed message inputs during a unit service interval) has the following form [22]:

$$\Pr\{S_m = n\} = \sum_{j=1}^{n} \frac{\lambda_p^{n-j} \exp(-\lambda_p)}{(n-j)!} \sum_{k=1}^{j} \binom{j-1}{k-1} \frac{(\lambda_c \theta)^k (1-\theta)^{j-k} \exp(-\lambda_c)}{k!}$$

$$+ \frac{\lambda_p^n}{n!} \exp[-(\lambda_p + \lambda_c)], \qquad n = 0, 1, 2, \ldots \tag{7.11}$$

where
$$\lambda_p = m_u \lambda_u$$
$$\lambda_c = m_r \lambda_r$$

In the same manner as before, the state probabilities can be solved numerically from the mixed message input statistics and the set of state equations. The traffic intensity of such inputs can be computed from (7.9). The buffer behavior can be studied from the set of state probabilities.

The relationships of buffer lengths versus overflow probabilities are computed for $p_m = 0.8$, $\bar{l} = 20$ characters and selected input traffic mixture rate α as shown in Fig. 7.12. For buffer behavior of other p_m's and $\bar{l}$'s, the interested reader should consult [22].

The overflow probability depends upon buffer size N, p_m, $\bar{l}$, and α. For a given buffer size, the overflow probability increases as p_m, $\bar{l}$, and α increase. For a given overflow probability, the required buffer size increases as p_m, $\bar{l}$,

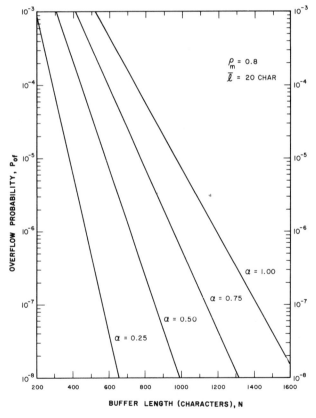

FIGURE 7.12   Overflow probability as a function of buffer size for selected traffic mixture rate at $p_m = 0.8$ and $\bar{l} = 20$ characters.

and α increase. Furthermore, for a given p_m and $\bar{l}$, the buffer size required to achieve a desired level of p_m is not linearly proportional to α. In general, the required buffer size for average burst length $\bar{l}$, N_l, is much greater than that of $\bar{l} \cdot N_1$, where N_1 is the buffer length for $\bar{l} = 1$ or constant-length message inputs.

To compute the expected message delay of mixed message inputs, D_m, due to buffering, we should treat each message as a unit. The service time is the time required to transmit the entire message. When the buffer size N is large, for a line with constant transmission rate, the service-time distribution is the same as the message-length distribution, except by a constant transmission-rate factor. For most systems, the allowable buffer overflow probability is very small, e.g., $P_{of} < 10^{-4}$. D_m can be computed from an M/G/1 queueing system with infinite waiting room. It can be shown [22] that

$$D_m = \frac{p_m}{2(1 - p_m)} + \frac{\alpha(\bar{l} - 1)p_m}{1 - p_m} \text{ character service times}$$

We note that D_m is linearly proportional to α and $\bar{l}$. This agrees with our intuition that for a given traffic intensity the message delay increases as the message length increases and as the number of random-length messages increases.

For a given traffic intensity and an input traffic mixture rate the buffer behavior (in terms of buffer overflow probability and average queueing delay) lies in between that of constant-length message inputs and that of random-length message inputs. When the traffic mixture rate α approaches 0 or $\bar{l} = 1$, the buffer behavior reduces to the constant-length-message case. When α equals 1, buffer behavior corresponds to the random-length-message case.

7.2.1 Demultiplexing Considerations

In the last section we discussed buffer behavior for four types of input to the asychronous time-division multiplexing system. The analyses are based on finite-waiting-room queueing models. In this section we shall study the asychronous time-division demultiplexing system, which is an integral part of the statistical multiplexor design. In the multiplexing case, the outputs from the system go to a single destination—e.g., to a computer—while the outputs from the demultiplexing system go to many destinations, such as to different users and/or computers, as shown in Fig. 7.2.

The demultiplexor may consist of a buffer and a switching circuit. The input traffic to the buffer consists of strings of characters (bursts). The switching circuit distributes the output from the buffer to the appropriate destinations according to the designation in the message address. Thus demultiplexor performance is strongly influenced by buffer behavior, which depends on buffer input traffic and its destination characteristics.

A queueing model with a finite waiting room, batch Poisson arrivals, and multiple *distinct* constant outputs is used to study buffer behavior. The complexity of the demultiplexing buffer makes exact analysis of such a model mathematically intractable. Therefore, computer simulation has been used to study the relationships among message destination function, average traffic level, message burst length, overflow probability (the fraction of the total number of messages rejected by the buffer), and buffer size.

7.2.2 Analysis of the Demultiplexing Buffer

The input messages to the buffer can be represented by three parameters: message arrivals, message lengths, and message destinations. These parameters are intimately related to buffer behavior. To describe the input messages arriving at the buffer, three random number generators are used: α, which corresponds to message interarrival times; β, which corresponds to the number of characters in the message; and γ, which corresponds to the destination of the message. In the simulation model, the message interarrival times α are assumed to be exponentially distributed,* and the message lengths β are assumed to be geometrically distributed. The destination distribution is transformed from the destination function as follows:

The destination function describes traffic intensities for the set of m destinations; that is,

$$f_d(i) = p_i = \frac{\lambda_i \bar{l}_i}{\mu_i} \qquad i = 1, 2, \ldots, m \qquad (7.12)$$

where p_i = traffic intensity for the ith destinations
$\quad \lambda_i$ = message arrival rate for the ith destinations
$\quad \bar{l}_i$ = average message length for the ith destination
$\quad \mu_i$ = transmission rate for the ith destination
$\quad m$ = total number of message destinations

The average traffic level, $\bar{p}$, for the demultiplexing system is the average of the traffic intensities of the m destinations; i.e.,

$$\bar{p} = \frac{1}{m} \sum_{i=1}^{m} p_i \qquad (7.13)$$

*In the distributed computer network shown in Fig. 7.2b the traffic input to the demultiplexor is the output from the multiplexor. In some cases the traffic output from the multiplexor can be approximated as Poisson distributed. Should the multiplexor output become very different from Poisson [23], then the actual message interarrival-time statistics should be used in the simulation.

The message destination function for a given set of users depends on its application and should be derived from measured statistics.

To perform random sampling on traffic destination, we need to transform $f_d(i)$ into a message destination distribution, $f_\gamma(i)$. This transformation can be performed by normalizing (7.12) to a probability destination function; i.e.,

$$f_\gamma(i) = \frac{f_d(i)}{\sum\limits_{j=1}^{m} \rho_j} \qquad i = 1, 2, \ldots, m \qquad (7.14)$$

Thus,
$$\sum_{i=1}^{m} f_\gamma(i) = 1$$

A set of random numbers, $\{\xi_\alpha, \xi_\beta, \xi_\gamma\}$, corresponding to random variables α, β, and γ, is generated to represent a message arriving at the demultiplexing system. When a message arrives at the buffer, two operations take place. First, the status of the designated facility is interrogated. If the facility is busy and the buffer is not full, the burst enters the buffer and is concatenated with the queue of characters. If the facility is idle, and if the buffer is not full, the first character of the burst is sent to the facility, while the remaining characters enter into the buffer and output at each subsequent clock time. Second, the contents of the register that keeps track of the total length of the buffer are updated. Because of distinct destinations, the total volume of output from the buffer varies with α, β, and γ. The output from the demultiplexing buffer depends on both the number of characters in the buffer and their destinations. The simulation program keeps a record of the number of characters in the buffer at the beginning of each message service interval. When the length of an arriving message exceeds the unoccupied storage space of the buffer, a buffer overflow event has occurred. The frequency of occurrence of such an overflow event gives the estimate of buffer overflow probability, P_{of}. Using the above finite-buffer-size model for estimating buffer overflow probability requires simulating buffer behavior at various buffer sizes. As a result, the computation time required for such a model, especially for estimating small overflow probabilities, could be prohibitive. Therefore, we introduce an infinite-buffer-size model, as shown in the flow chart (Fig. 7.13), to estimate buffer overflow probabilities. In this case, we say that an overflow event has occurred if the buffer queue length from simulation exceeds the fictitious buffer size. Thus this provides us with a way to estimate buffer overflow events for various buffer sizes via buffer queue length statistics, which can be obtained from a single simulation pass. This represents a significant reduction in computation time. In the case of small overflow probabilities (e.g., $P_{of} < 10^{-4}$), this model provides a good approximation of the finite-buffer-size model.

To study the effect of destination distributions on buffer behavior, five types of destination functions are used in the simulation model shown in Fig. 7.14. The relationships among P_{of}, buffer sizes, and destination distri-

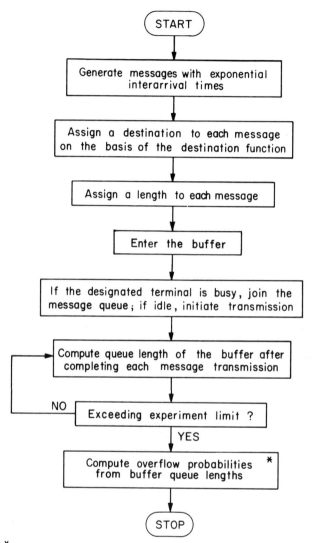

* The buffer overflow probabilities were computed from the buffer queue lengths obtained from the GPSS simulation.

FIGURE 7.13   A flow chart for simulating the demultiplexing buffer.

butions for $\bar{p} = 0.8$ and $\bar{l} = 20$ characters are portrayed in Fig. 7.15. For behavior of other $\bar{p}$'s and $\bar{l}$'s, the interested reader should consult [24].

Simulation results reveal that for a given average message length and desired level of overflow probability, the required buffer size increases as the average traffic level increases. Furthermore, the required buffer size varies

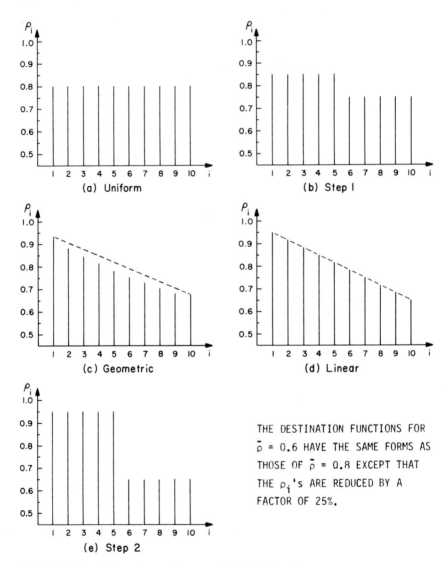

FIGURE 7.14   Various types of message destination functions.

drastically with the message destination functions. Comparing the five types of traffic destination functions used in our simulation, for a given average traffic level, the uniform traffic destination function required the smallest buffer size, and the Step 2 destination function required the largest buffer size. This is because both buffer size and queueing delay increase exponentially with p_i. Thus, for a given average traffic level, different types of

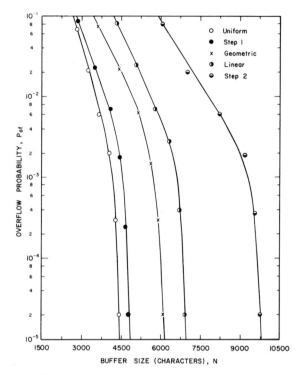

FIGURE 7.15   Overflow probability as a function of buffer size for various types of destination functions at $p = 0.8$ and $\bar{l} = 20$ characters.

destination functions yield different buffer behavior. Furthermore, the effect of destination function on buffer behavior increases as average traffic level increases.

For reliability reasons most practical systems allow a very low overflow probability. Thus the expected waiting time of each burst due to buffering in the demultiplexor can be approximated by the waiting time of an infinite-waiting-room queueing model with Poisson arrivals and geometric service time. The expected waiting time is similar to (7.6), except that the average arrival rate and the average message length for each destination may be different. Thus the expected queueing delay due to demultiplexing for each destination is different and should be computed separately.

Simulation results of buffer behavior shed light on the relationships between the demultiplexor traffic inputs and the demultiplexing system performance. More specifically, the results show that to minimize the size of the demultiplexing buffer and queueing delay due to buffering, we should schedule the inputs to the demultiplexor buffer approximately equally. This can be achieved by controlling the volume of input traffic to the buffer for various destinations, and selecting the proper output transmission rate for the buffer, or both. In a time-sharing system, input traffic to the demultiplexor buffer emanates from the CPU, which in turn is governed by the computer scheduling algorithm, such as the size of the CPU quantum time. If we know the relationship* between the CPU quantum time and the volume of the CPU outputs, then a variable quantum time-scheduling algorithm would be effective to schedule an equal amount of output traffic to various destinations. The buffer output rate can also be changed to adjust the traffic intensity. To achieve a uniform traffic destination distribution, we should assign high transmission rate lines to those destinations that have high volumes of traffic. At present, most scheduling algorithms attempt to maximize the efficiency of the CPU operations [25–27], which might not necessarily yield optimal demultiplexing performance. Therefore, further study of the relationship among scheduling algorithms, message destination functions, and program behavior would be desirable. Results from these studies will enable us to jointly optimize the CPU throughput and the demultiplexor performance.

7.3.1 Optimal Design of a Statistical Multiplexor

The operating cost of a statistical multiplexor consists of two components: communication cost and storage cost. To design such a system we are usually confronted with a set of performance constraints. In practice we would like to design a multiplexing system that minimizes the operating cost, yet satisfies the set of required constraints.

In the following section, we first present a model of how one should select the transmission channel rate of a multiplexor to minimize the operating cost, subject to the required constraints in buffer overflow probability and in queueing delay due to buffering. Next we discuss the relationship between the CPU scheduling algorithm and the performance of the statistical multiplexor. Finally, we present design considerations for data structures.

7.3.2 Optimal Transmission Rate for Statistical Multiplexors

For a given amount of input traffic, σ, (let σ have the same units as the transmission rate μ), a higher transmission rate channel will yield a lower traffic intensity, and thus will require a smaller buffer size. On the other hand, a lower transmission-rate channel will yield a higher traffic intensity and will

---

*This relationship depends on the computer system and program behavior in question, and could be obtained via measurement or simulation.

require a larger buffer size. Thus the transmission rate of the channel is the parameter that provides a tradeoff between communications cost and buffer storage cost. Knowing the input traffic load, the communication distance d, and the buffer behavior, the selection of the optimal transmission rate for a statistical multiplexor is equivalent to the problem of operating the multiplexing system at an optimal traffic intensity [28].

For a given distance, communications cost depends upon the transmission rate of the channel. Hence for a given input traffic load and distance, transmission cost is related to the traffic intensity of the channel. The higher the traffic intensity, i.e., the lower the transmission rate, the lower the communications cost. Thus the communications cost per month, $C_t(\rho)$, is a monotonic decreasing function of ρ. Furthermore $C_t(\rho)$ can be easily generated from σ and the channel costs [29] of the set of available transmission rates. Since there is a practical upper limit on the available transmission rates, ρ can never reach zero. We shall denote the minimum ρ as ρ_{min}.

The required buffer size, to achieve a certain probability of overflow P_{of}, at a certain traffic intensity ρ, $N(\rho, P_{of})$, can be obtained from an analysis of buffer behavior, as discussed in Section 7.1.1.

The storage cost per month is equal to the monthly cost* of a unit of storage, C_b, multiplied by the required buffer size, $N(\rho, P_{of})$; i.e., $C_s(\rho) = C_b \cdot N(\rho, P_{of})$.

For a given input traffic load, required buffer overflow probability, and transmission distance, the operating cost of a statistical multiplexor is

$$C(\rho) = C_s(\rho) + C_t(\rho) \quad \text{for } \rho_{min} \leq \rho < 1 \tag{7.15}$$

We wish to minimize (7.16) with respect to ρ and subject to the delay requirements; i.e.,

$$C(\rho^0) = \min_\rho C(\rho) = \min_\rho [C_s(\rho) + C_t(\rho)]$$

subject to

$$D(\rho) \leq D_a \quad \text{for } \rho_{min} \leq \rho < 1$$

where $D(\rho)$ is the expected queueing delay of each message due to buffering, and D_a is the maximum allowable expected queueing delay of each message. Note that the overflow probability requirement is satisfied if $N(\rho, P_{of})$ is represented by the corresponding overflow probability.

Since in almost all the queueing models $D(\rho)$ is a montonic increasing function of ρ, $D(\rho) \leq D_a$ is equivalent to $\rho \leq \rho_{max}$, where ρ_{max} is the maximum allowable traffic intensity such that the expected queueing delay is less than or equal to the maximum allowable delay. We obtain ρ_{max} either from the buffer delay characteristic curves (Figs. 7.6, 7.8, and 7.11) or by approximating (if $P_{of} < 10^{-4}$) from the analytical expression of expected delay

---

*The monthly cost of a unit of storage can be computed from the life of the system.

function of an infinite-waiting-room model. Thus (7.16) reduces to

$$C(\rho^0) = \min_\rho C(p) = \min_\rho [C_s(p) + C_t(p)] \qquad \text{for } \rho_{\min} \le \rho \le \rho_{\max}$$

(7.16)

To express $C(\rho)$ analytically, a least-square curve-fitting technique [11] may be used to represent $C_t(\rho)$ and $C_s(\rho)$. For most cases, $C_t(\rho)$ and $C_s(\rho)$ can be approximated as convex functions. In this case, $C(\rho)$ is also a convex function, which greatly simplifies the problem for finding the optimal traffic intensity ρ^0.

There are many methods that can be used to numerically solve (7.16) for ρ^0, such as convex nonlinear programming, finding the set of ρ's that satisfies $[dC(\rho)/d\rho] = 0$ and $\rho_{\min} \le \rho \le \rho_{\max}$, or solving ρ^0 geometrically, as shown in Fig. 7.16, where ρ^0 is the optimal traffic intensity that minimized (7.16).

The optimal channel transmission rate for the statistical multiplexor,

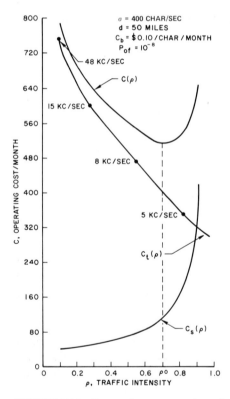

FIGURE 7.16   Geometric representation of optimal traffic intensity, ρ^0.

μ^0, can be computed from ρ^0 and the input traffic load σ; that is,

$$\mu^0 = \frac{\sigma}{\rho^0} \qquad \text{characters/s}$$

Although the above model is mainly for a statistical multiplexor that has a single transmission line output, it can be generalized to the multiple transmission line case. In the multiple transmission line case, $C_t(\rho)$ in (7.16) should be viewed as the total transmission cost of the multiple transmission lines as a function of traffic intensity, and $C_s(\rho)$ is the storage cost for the buffer (with multiple outputs) to achieve a desired level of probability of overflow. For a given system configuration (the number of output transmission lines and their transmission rates), based on the above model, the optimal transmission rates and the corresponding operating cost can be determined. We should consider not only the design tradeoff between storage cost and transmission cost, but also the tradeoffs among various system configurations, such as the tradeoff between using more low-speed transmission lines or fewer high-speed transmission lines. The optimal system configuration is the one that yields minimum operating cost among the set of feasible system configurations.

7.3.3 Scheduling Algorithms and Statistical Multiplexors

From Section 7.1.1 we know that the input traffic to the buffer has strong impact on the buffer behavior. For a computer-to-user demultiplexor, the inputs to the buffer are emanating from the CPU. The scheduling algorithm of the CPU directly affects its output traffic statistics and thus influences buffer behavior. At present, most scheduling algorithms attempt to maximize the efficiency of the CPU operation. This might not yield optimal buffer performance. For example, if the CPU scheduling algorithm is based on buffer status, the scheduler may assign more input to the buffer when buffer occupancy is low and less when buffer occupancy is high; or he may use a variable size quantum time scheduling algorithm, which would enable us to schedule the output volume to various destinations approximately equally [24]. Employing such scheduling algorithms on a given buffer, buffer performance in overflow probability would be greatly improved. The CPU, however, might not be as efficiently utilized as it would be with other scheduling algorithms. Thus the relationships among the computer scheduling algorithms, CPU output traffic characteristics, and buffer behavior are essential in the joint optimization of multiplexing system performance and the throughput of the CPU. Some work in this direction has been reported recently [23, 30].

7.3.4   Design Considerations of Data Structures

When random-length messages are segmented into fixed-sized blocks, due to the extra linking information required as well as the wasted space in the last unfilled block, the storage requirements will be larger than in the case of random-length message inputs. On the other hand, since all the messages are addressed and are uniform in size, it is not necessary to rearrange the buffer to obtain an adequate space for the entire burst. Thus the storage-allocation problem is greatly simplified. The tradeoff between the extra storage cost and the saving in buffer management is the main consideration in deciding whether random-length messages should be segmented into fixed-sized blocks or should be treated as random-length messages.

There are two ways to segment random messages into fixed-sized blocks: instantaneous segmentation and holding segmentation. The former method transmits fixed-sized message blocks immediately after their segmentations regardless of whether or not the block is full. The latter method transmits a message block instantaneously if the block is full, but will hold the block for a period of time before transmission if a block is not full. The holding time not only involves a tradeoff between delay performance and storage costs, but also influences the output traffic statistics, which in turn affect the design of the demultiplexor.

In practice, we would design a system that has minimum operating cost, yet satisfies all the requirements. Since the multiplexing system and the CPU intimately interact with each other, the multiplexing system should be treated as a subsystem of the computer-communication system. The economical and performance optimization should be carried out jointly between the computer and the available communication facilities.

7.4.1   Example

Consider the planning of the transmission facility for a time-shared system that consists of many remote teletypewriter terminals. All the teletypewriters are assumed to transmit at a rate of 10 characters/s. A private-line voice-grade channel can easily support a transmission rate of 2400 bps with a generally acceptable error rate. Thus a rudimentary implementation of a synchronous time-division multiplexor could employ 24 10-bit character terminals. In practice, some of the channels are utilized for word synchronous and error control, so a more common realization is 16 or so terminals per 2400-bps voice-grade line.

Next we shall consider the planning of the same system employing the asynchronous time-division multiplexing (statistical multiplexing) technique.

To carry out such a design, we need to know the user and computer traffic characteristics. Measured traffic characteristics from several in-service time-sharing systems have revealed that the character interarrival time per user can be approximated as exponentially distributed with a mean about 0.5 s. Thus the character arrivals can be treated as Poisson arrivals with a rate of 2 characters/s. A reasonably conservative estimate is that 50 per cent of the source information is sufficient for addressing and framing. The buffer is designed such that the overflow probability is less than about 10^{-6} characters. To operate the multiplexor at traffic intensity $\rho_u = 0.6$, the number of terminals that may be supported is

$$m = \frac{\mu\rho_u}{1.5\lambda_u} = \frac{240 \times 0.6}{1.5 \times 2} = 48 \text{ terminals}$$

From Fig. 7.4 the required buffer is 14 characters; from Fig. 7.6 the expected waiting time due to buffering is 1.24 character-service-times or $1.24/240 = 5.06$ ms. If we operate the multiplexor at $\rho_u = 0.8$, which corresponds to $m = \mu\rho_u/(1.5\lambda_u) = 240 \times 0.8/(1.5 \times 2) = 64$ terminals, the required buffer is 28 characters and the expected queueing time for each character is 9.56 ms. Comparing the number of terminals a voice-grade line can support using the ATDM and STDM techniques, we note that with a small amount of buffer and a generally tolerable delay, a significant improvement in transmission efficiency can be achieved by statistical multiplexing.

Next we shall consider the buffer design problem employing the ATDM technique to transmit data from the central processor to remote terminals. The traffic statistics as well as the message length are different from that of the users. Measured traffic characteristics from several in-service time-sharing systems revealed that the burst interarrival time can be approximated as exponentially distributed with a mean of 2.84s[6]. Thus the bursts can be approximated as Poisson arrivals with a rate of $\lambda_r = 0.35$ burst/s. Furthermore, the burst length can be approximated as geometrically distributed with a mean of $\bar{l} = 20$ characters. Suppose that we use a wideband transmission channel which transmits 960 characters/s to provide communication from the central processor to 48 terminals. Assuming that 20 per cent of the transmitted information is used for addressing and framing, the traffic intensity is $\rho_r = m \cdot 1.2\lambda_r(\bar{l}/\mu) = 48 \times 1.2 \times 0.35 \times 20/960 = 0.42$. To achieve an overflow probability of 10^{-6}, from Fig. 7.7 we find that the required buffer size is 480 characters. From Fig. 7.8 the expected queueing delay for each burst is 15 character-service-times, or $15/960 = 16$ ms.

For the convenience of buffer management, we would like to segment the random-length messages into fixed-sized blocks. The required address message is about 20 per cent of the average burst length; i.e., $b = 0.2 \times 20 = 4$ characters. The segmented block size, B', that minimizes the wasted storage space can be computed from (7.17); thus $B' = 12$ characters. The actual optimal block size $B = 12 + 4 = 16$ characters. The average number of blocks per burst is $\bar{n}(l) = (1 - qB')^{-1} = 2.32$ blocks/burst. For the same wideband channel that transmits 960 characters/s to provide communications from the central processor to 48 terminals, the traffic intensity is $\rho_B = m \cdot \lambda_r \cdot \bar{n}(l) \cdot B/\mu = 48 \cdot 0.35 \cdot 2.32 \cdot 16/960 = 0.65$. To achieve an overflow probability of 10^{-6}, from Fig. 7.10, the required buffer size is 65 blocks or 1040 characters. From Fig. 7.11, the average delay for each block is 4.5 block-service-times or 75 ms. We note that the required buffer size for the fixed-sized blocks is about twice as large as that of the random-length message inputs, and the delay is about four times larger. This is the extra storage cost and queueing delay for segmenting the random messages into fixed-sized blocks. On the other hand, the buffer management is much simpler than that of the random-length messages.

CONCLUSION

In an ATDM system an acceptable buffer overflow probability can be achieved by a reasonable buffer size; the expected queueing delay due to buffering is very small and is acceptable for most applications. Hence ATDM or statistical multiplexing is a feasible technique for data communications. From this study we also learn that statistical multiplexing greatly improves channel efficiency, system organization for error control, and message scheduling. The gain in communication cost, especially in long-distance transmission, by employing ATDM in computer communication could far outweigh the extra costs of overhead in addressing and storage for buffering. Therefore, statistical multiplexing should have high potential for use in future computer-communication systems. In fact, statistical multiplexors were offered on the market in 1971.

We also have demonstrated that there are interactive effects among communication network architectures, memory management, and computer operating system performance. Further study along this direction would be very desirable. Results obtained in this area will be essential to the joint optimization of the overall performance of such computer-communication systems.

Acknowledgment

I would like to thank R. J. Roddy of Bell Telephone Laboratories for carefully reviewing a draft of this chapter.

REFERENCES

[1] P. E. JACKSON and C. D. STUBBS, A Study of Multiaccess Computer Communications, *AFIPS Conf. Proc.*, **34** (1969), 491–504.

[2] W. W. CHU, A Study of the Technique of Asynchronous Time Division Multiplexing for Time-Sharing Computer Communications, *Proc. Second Hawaii Intern. Conf. Syst. Sci.*, (Jan. 1969), 607–710.

[3] W. W. CHU, A Study of Asynchronous Time Division Multiplexing for Time-Sharing Computer System, *AFIPS Conf. Proc.*, **35** (1969), 669–678.

[4] K. BULLINGTON and J. M. FRASER, Engineering Aspects of TASI, *Bell Syst. Tech. J.* (March 1959), 353–364.

[5] W. W. CHU, Design Considerations of Statistical Multiplexors, *Proc. ACM Symp. Problems in the Optimization of Data Commun. Syst.*, Pine Mountain, Ga., (1969), 36–60.

[6] E. FUCHS and P. E. JACKSON, Estimates of Distributions of Random Variables for Certain Computer Communications Traffic Model, *Proc. ACM Symp. Problems in the Optimization of Data Commun. Syst.*, Pine Mountain, Ga., Oct. 13–16, 1969), 202–225.

[7] B. A. POWELL and B. AVI-ITZHAK, Queueing Systems with Enforced Idle Time, *Operations Res.*, **15**(16) (1967), 1145–1156.

[8] T. G. BIRDSALL et al., Analysis of Asynchronous Time Multiplexing of Speech Sources, *IRE Trans. Commun. Syst.* (Dec. 1962), 390–397.

[9] N. M. DOR, Guide to the Length of Buffer Storage Required for Random (Poisson) Input and Constant Output Rates, *IEEE Trans. Electron. Computer*, (Oct. 1967), 683–684.

[10] W. W. CHU, Buffer Behavior for Poisson Arrivals and Multiple Constant Outputs, *IEEE Trans. Computer* **C-19** (June 1970), 530–534.

[11] R. W. Hamming, *Numerical Methods for Scientists and Engineers*, McGraw-Hill, New York, 1962, 363–364.

[12] N. U. PRABHU, *Queues and Inventories*, Wiley, New York, 1965, p. 42.

[13] H. RUDIN, JR., Performance of a Simple Multiplexor-Concentrator for Data Communication, *1970 Intern. Conf. Commun.*, San Francisco, (June 8–10, 1970), 35–32 to 35–38.

[14] D. G. MARITSAS and M. G. HARTLEY, Buffer Length for Erlang Input and Constant Removal Rate, *IEEE Trans. Computers*, **C-19**(9) (1970), 839–843.

[15] S. TZAFESTAS, Buffer Length for Erlang Arrivals and Multiple Synchronous Regular Removals, *Electron. Letter*, **7**(8) (1971).

[16] W. W. CHU, Buffer Behavior for Batched Poisson Arrivals and Single Constant Output, *IEEE Trans. Commun. Technol.* **Com-18**(5) (1970), 613–618.

[17] T. H. GORDON et al., Design and Performance of a Statistical Multiplexor,

Proc. 1970 Intern. Conf. Commun., San Francisco, (June 8–10, 1970), 28-7 to 28-21.

[18] E. WOLMAN, A Fixed Optimum Cell-Size for Records of Various Lengths, *J. Assoc. Computing Machinery*, **12**(1), (1965), 53–70.

[19] R. L. TOWNSENT and R. N. WATTS, Effectiveness of Error Control in Data Communication over the Switched Telephone Network, *Bell Syst. Tech. J.* (Nov. 1964), 2611–2638.

[20] S. Y. TONG, A Survey of Error Control Techniques on Telephone Channels, *Proc. 1970 Natl. Electron. Conf.*, Chicago (Dec. 7–9, 1970), 462–467.

[21] W. W. CHU, Optimal Fixed Message Block Size for Computer Communications, *Proc. IFIP Congress 71*, Ljubljana, Yugoslavai (Aug. 23–28, 1971).

[22] W. W. CHU and L. LIANG, Buffer Behavior for Mixed Input Traffic and Single Constant Output Rate, *IEEE Trans. Commun. Technol.* Com-20(2) (1972), 230–235.

[23] C. D. PACK, The Effects of Multiplexing on Computer-Communication Systems, submitted to *Commun. ACM*.

[24] W. W. CHU, Demultiplexing Considerations for Statistical Multiplexors, *IEEE Trans. Commun. Technol.* Com-20(3) (1972), 603–609.

[25] J. E. SHEMER, Some Mathematical Considerations of Time-Sharing Scheduling Algorithms, *J. ACM*, **14**(2) (April 1967), 262–272.

[26] P. E. DENNING, Effect of Scheduling on File Memory Operations, *AFIPS Conf. Proc.* **30** (1967), 9–21.

[27] L. KLEINROCK, Scheduling, Queuing, and Delays in Time-Shared Systems and Computer Networks, Chap. 4 of this book.

[28] W. W. CHU, Selection of Optimal Transmission Rate for Statistical Multiplexors, *Proc. 1970 Intern. Conf. Commun.*, San Francisco (June 8–10, 1970), 28-22 to 28-25.

[29] R. G. GOULD, Comments on Generalized Cost Expressions for Private-Line Communications Channels, *IEEE Trans. Commun. Technol.* (Sept. 1965), 374–377.

[30] J. H. CHANG, Comparison of Synchronous and Asynchronous Time Division Multiplexing Techniques, *Proc. 1970 Intern. Conf. Commun.*, San Francisco (June 8–10, 1970), 16-10 to 16-17.

8

Multiple-Access Communications for Computer Nets

JAY W. SCHWARTZ

Institute for Defense Analyses

MICHAEL MUNTNER

Defense Communications Agency—System Engineering Facility

INTRODUCTION

Most of the experience with communication networks for achieving remote access to computers has involved point-to-point links characteristic of common-carrier systems. Yet the broadcast multipoint feature of radio transmissions has great apparent utility for netted operations [1, 2]. The purpose of this chapter is to indicate ways in which this feature can be employed efficiently in line-of-sight (LOS) and satellite relay networks.

A principal reason for the preeminence of point-to-point links is the availability of such links through leased common-carrier service, providing an approach that minimizes a user's initial investment. In common-carrier facilities, capacity is usually derived from point-to-point links along paths of high traffic density. These links are provided by wire or point-to-point radio relays. Sharing is achieved through the various multiplexing and switching techniques available at focal points of the network.

A geographically widespread distribution of users may preclude joint usage of such a point-to-point communications facility. Depending upon the particular locations of the users, it can be more economical to provide each with a separate transmission path to the computer. Furthermore, commercially available transmission capability is often ill-suited for the data communications required in some remote computer access applications. Most of today's transmission assets were conceived and implemented to handle voice communications as opposed to digital traffic. The analog facilities often cannot ensure the tolerable error rates, timing, phase jitter, and other parameters that are essential in the high-speed digital world.

Under these conditions, netted operations with multipoint radio links can provide an alternative means of communications. By appropriately choosing the operating frequency and multiple-access technique, multipoint links have the potential of simultaneously connecting many users and providing a reliable broadband digital communications capability. In general, network organizations that arise with netted operations are distinct from conventional modes employed with point-to-point links. In effect, netting provides an alternative to both message and channel switching.

The applications of netted radio communications will be the focal point for this chapter. The multipoint environment raises several unique factors that must be considered if the potential benefits of the media are to be realized. These are discussed in the following sections.

8.1 TRANSMISSION MEDIA CONSIDERATIONS

The nature of radio propagation depends on the frequency of transmission. The high-frequency (HF) radio band, nominally 3 to 30 MHz, enables communications over the horizon and does not require the transmitter and receiver to be within line of sight.

At lower frequencies, large communications complexes are required to generate and transmit radio signals, and the spectrum availability is limited. Frequencies above the HF range use less costly antenna systems to maintain effective communications. In the very high frequency (VHF) range and above (i.e., nominally greater than 30 MHz), radio waves propagate in a straight line with little or no ionospheric reflections. Communications at these frequencies are by line-of-sight links; long-distance connections require relay devices, such as microwave relay towers or communication satellites.

High-frequency radio propagates by reflections off the ionosphere, a constantly changing medium. Prior to the advent of communication satellites, it represented the major means of achieving long-haul multipoint communications. Although historically there has been considerable use of such links, they are ill suited for reliable computer access communications [3]. The general transmission properties of a path differ, depending upon day or night and time of year. Moreover, the detailed characteristics reflect fraction-of-a-second variations, and narrow- and broadband fading associated with these variations complicate the use of HF radio. Error rates are highly variable; limited bandwidth, as well as varying path delay between transmitter and receiver, accompanies use of this medium. Overcrowding within a limited spectrum and the natural beyond-the-horizon propagation often leads to undesirable interference. As a result, HF radio is fraught with problems in providing high-quality digital links.

8.1.1 Satellite Medium

In contrast to HF radio, satellite communications permit reliable wideband communications over long distances. At VHF and higher frequencies, an orbiting satellite repeater can reliably relay the transmitted signal to distant points on the globe; the satellite, of course, must be within line of sight of both the transmitting and receiving stations. Typically, the satellite has a broadband repeater that simply amplifies all received signals and retransmits them earthward. If several terminals use the satellite at the same time, access techniques must be employed to ensure that links are not disabled by mutual interference, that the receiving terminals can identify the desired signals, and that efficient usage is made of the overall capacity of the satellite. Multiple-access techniques, discussed in Section 8.2, permit the simultaneous utilization of the satellite by many terminals. *Multiple access*, which permits the sharing of communications capacity, is distinguished from *multiplexing* in that the latter refers to joint usage by several baseband signals, whereas the former is concerned with joint usage by several radio-frequency (rf) signals.

A communication-satellite channel has many unique characteristics that distinguish it from links derived from other media. The satellite orbit, the frequency, the nature of the ground terminals, and the satellite itself determine the characteristics of the channel. The most interesting orbit for communications applications is the 24-h earth synchronous circular equatorial orbit in which the satellite is at an altitude of some 19,300 nautical miles. This is the geostationary orbit, because a satellite in this orbit moving from west to east will appear motionless relative to any point on the earth. There is then no need for terminal antennas to provide much tracking capability unless they themselves are moving. Doppler frequency shifts are minimized, thereby simplifying design, and continuous view of the satellite ensures availability of communications to all stations within the zone of coverage.

This zone of coverage permits a separation of ground stations of up to 8500 nautical miles on the equator. Coverage from synchronous altitude is illustrated in Fig. 8.1.

The synchronous orbit does introduce a path delay that is significant for highly responsive, interactive computer networks. The one-way path delay (e.g., from the user to computer) is 0.25 s and the round-trip delay time is almost 0.5 s. This factor has an impact on error control and procedures. An

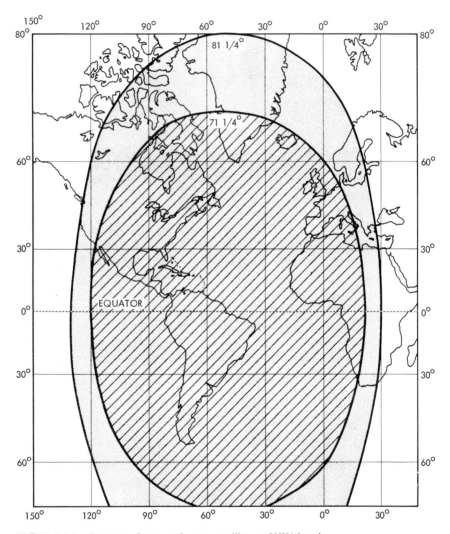

FIGURE 8.1   Coverage from stationary satellite at 50°W longitude. Shaded area = coverage for ground antenna elevation angle, $a_{min} = 0°$; crosshatched area = coverage for $a_{min} = 10°$.

error detection and retransmission system requires the sender to store data, perhaps until the receiver acknowledges its correct reception. The lengthy round-trip transmission time can also delay the processing of large amounts of data received between the original transmission with errors and its subsequent repeat. Hence forward-acting error control is likely to find wide usage with satellite links.

In satellite communications the capacity is typically determined by the *down link*, the effect of *up-link* noise being generally negligible. A key parameter is the quotient of the signal power received from the satellite, P_R, and the noise power spectral density at the ground station receiver, N_{OR}. The ratio of P_R/N_{OR} in Hertz is often called the *capacity quotient*. The capacity quotient determines the maximum permissible data rate, R, in terms of β, the required ratio between the received signal energy per bit and the noise spectral density (E_b/N_o);

$$R = \frac{P_R/N_{OR}}{\beta}$$

Alternatively, β specifies the minimum P_R/N_{OR} for a given data rate.

The power transmitted by a satellite is restricted by international agreement limiting the maximum flux density in any 4-kHz band to -152 dBw/m^2 at the horizon.* A simple receiver with a tunnel diode mixer can provide a system noise temperature of less than 1000°K at frequencies of interest. With this noise temperature the noise power in a 4-kHz band is -163 dBw. Hence an antenna aperture of about 1 m^2 ($\sim$4-ft diameter) is adequate for an rf signal-to-noise ratio of 6 dB (allowing $\sim$5 dB for losses and margin). This signal-to-noise ratio would require threshold extension demodulation techniques for analog signaling, but permits utilization of standard digital signaling techniques: for example, frequency shift keying at a rate of $\frac{1}{2}$ bps/Hz. Good overall system design, however, might include a larger antenna or better receiver.

The satellite effective radiated power (ERP) required to achieve this maximum flux density is given by

$$\frac{\text{ERP}}{4\pi D^2} = -152 \text{ dBw/4 KHz/m}^2$$

where D is the range to the satellite in meters from a point on earth at which the satellite has a 0° elevation angle. For synchronous orbit, the ERP corresponding to this flux density is about 14 dBw/4 kHz. An ERP of 41 dBw spread over a 2-MHz band would permit about 250 digital signals of rate 2.4 kbps. An ERP of 41 dBw might require a satellite weighing approximately 1000 lb, if the satellite beam covers the full solid angle (17°) subtended by the

---

*The allowable flux density increases with higher elevation angles to a value of -148 dBw/m^2/4 kHz at the zenith following the expression $[-152 + (\theta/15)]$ dBw/m^2/4 kHz, where θ is the elevation angle in degrees [4].

earth at synchronous altitude, or perhaps 500 lb, if the satellite employs a higher gain antenna to spotlight a smaller area.

The design of a system to operate with maximum allowable flux density would in effect maximize satellite cost per unit of capacity. However, this cost is not exorbitant if the satellite use factor is high. A rule of thumb often used to estimate the cost of a satellite at synchronous orbit is $20,000/lb in orbit. This includes the cost to build the satellite and place it in synchronous equatorial orbit. Although the initial satellite investment is large, about $20 million for a 1000-lb satellite, the cost is modest if amortized over the lifetime of a satellite, which is designed for at least a 5-year expected lifetime. For example, the $20 million cost for 250 data channels amortized over 5 years yields an average cost of approximately 3 cents/min/channel.

To overcome the effect of noise at the satellite input, a terminal would have to radiate about 100 W/4 kHz of transmitted bandwidth. (A single terminal would not necessarily transmit a signal using the entire satellite bandwidth.) Investment for these modest ground terminals increases with frequency. At about 300 MHz, terminals capable of 1 kW should cost less than $50,000 in large quantities. Such terminals at 5 GHz should cost less than $500,000.* However, spectrum availability permits greater communication capacity at higher frequencies. At UHF (about 300 MHz) terminals tend to be small, because capacity is limited by spectrum availability. At microwave frequencies terminals will tend to be large, because high capacity is required to justify high terminal costs.

Present commercial satellites operate in the microwave region between 4 and 7 GHz. Large terminals are employed with 95-ft antennas and noise temperatures below 100°K. With these terminals, an INTELSAT III satellite with 26-dBw ERP and weighing 334 lb provides a 6-dB rf signal-to-noise ratio (plus margin) over two channels, each with 250-MHz bandwidth. This signal-to-noise ratio is adequate with the threshold extension demodulators employed.

8.1.2 Line-of-Sight Medium

The application of multiple access for computer networks is not restricted to over-the-horizon systems using satellites and high-frequency radio. Multipoint operation can be achieved with line-of-sight (LOS) links between a central computer and a large number of outlying stations. Although any radio frequency can be considered for LOS links, the low end of the UHF band, about 300 MHz, will probably be most appropriate in many applica-

---

*These costs are not documented but are approximations based on experience with military systems.

tions. Spectrum allocation in the VHF range is very difficult to obtain. In LOS operation, frequencies below VHF will yield poorer channel characteristics without compensating benefits. Higher equipment costs at frequencies above the low end of the UHF band will not be justified unless required to obtain spectrum allocation.

The computer terminal can use an omnidirectional (or broad-beam) antenna system that covers all user locations. The area of coverage is determined by antenna heights. In the absence of terrain pecularities, the radio line-of-sight distance is somewhat greater than the geometric line of sight, since the radio waves "bend," or refract, in the atmosphere. If the user and computer station antennas are at heights of h_1 feet and h_2 feet, respectively, the geometric line of sight between the antennas, d, in statute miles is approximately [5]

$$d = \sqrt{2h_1} + \sqrt{2h_2}$$

Thus, if there is a distance of, say, 50 miles between the user and computer, the antenna heights in feet must obey the relation of $35.3 \leq \sqrt{h_1} + \sqrt{h_2}$. Utilizing natural terrain features, such as placing the antenna on a mountaintop, assists in achieving long line-of-sight ranges.

This distance estimate is, of course, a simplification. The presence of irregular intervening terrain features can markedly affect the actual range of coverage as well as operating conditions. Not only would midpath blockage be unacceptable, but energy reflections from midpath objects or ground reflections (multipath) can be received with sufficient delay to interfere with the direct transmission. Although reflections from terrain obstacles and perhaps water surfaces are of prime importance, atmospheric refraction also can be a significant factor, and may occasionally alter transmission characteristics [5]. Changes in the atmospheric dielectric constant can bend, and sometimes trap, the transmitted signal on a side of a sharp gradient. This ducting may enhance the multipath effect or decrease the direct-path transmission so as to degrade the overall performance.

These as well as other phenomena contribute to the signal fading observed in line-of-sight transmission. The stability of the medium is nevertheless far greater than that achieved in beyond-the-horizon high-frequency radio. The options available for dealing with signal fading typically involve diversity reception, in which the signals are received with spatial, frequency, and time differences [6]. Signal modulation formats and multiple-access techniques may be chosen to assist in overcoming these propagation degradations.

The modest cost of line-of-sight radios can make them attractive candidates for short-distance links and networks. As an example, a typical inexpensive system at 300 MHz may have a user terminal with a 10-W transmitter and a cost of about $1000. The user locations might utilize a directional

Yagi antenna with a gain of 10 dB. The central station might have an antenna such as a "blade" or "squirrel cage," which has very little directional capabilities and essentially 0-dB gain. At a somewhat greater expense, a "pancake" pattern covering the users can be fabricated by using several, say, eight, conical sections, resulting in a gain of 10 dB. A typical noise temperature is perhaps 1200°K, but a preamplifier and preselector filter could reduce this to 300°K and might be justified for the central station. Although the cost of the individual-user transceiver is about $1000, the central site, because of the need for the omnidirectional elevated antenna, may cost much more. The capacity of even these modest radios is sufficient that the limiting factor is typically spectrum availability and the antenna heights required for the stations to be in view of one another.

8.2   MULTIPLE-ACCESS TECHNIQUES

8.2.1   Satellite Channels

Consider a communication satellite network in which a terminal is associated with each user and each central computer. In practice a single terminal might serve several users and computers, but generality is not lost in discussion by assuming a terminal associated with each member of the network.

Signal flow for the generalized multiple-access problem is illustrated by Fig. 8.2. Each user transmits a signal into a *channel*. The signal contains address information as well as message information. In Fig. 8.2 this is shown to be accomplished with two distinct modulation processes, but in some techniques this model would seem artificial. In any case, each transmitted signal must have a structure such that (1) it will be possible for a receiver to separate it from the composite channel signal, and (2) it will interfere as little as possible with reception of the other signals. Each signal is transmitted into the channel and each user station receives a composite channel signal. With communication satellites employing a single repeater channel, all users receive the same composite signal, and this case will be assumed here.* By appropriately demodulating the composite channel signal he receives, a user detects desired signals and ignores the others.

An upper bound on the receiving capacity of a given terminal can be determined from the relative powers of signal and noise. If all noise is assumed to be gaussian and distributed uniformly over the total satellite bandwidth W, receiving capacity associated with a desired signal and a given

---

*When all users do not receive the same composite signal from the satellite (e.g., satellites with narrow-beam antennas), more questions akin to networks of point-to-point links arise (e.g., choices between channel switching and message switching among antenna beams).

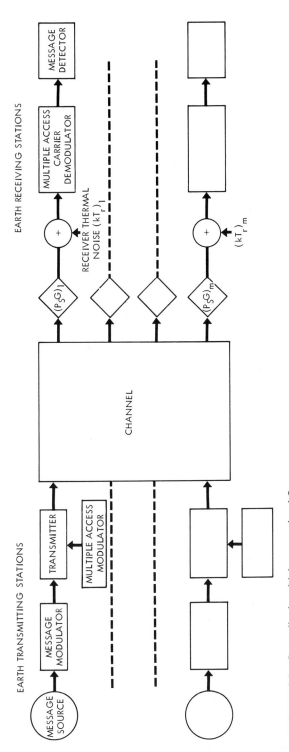

FIGURE 8.2 Generalized multiple-access signal flow.

receiving terminal is given by [7]

$$r \leq \frac{1}{\beta} \frac{P_r}{N_{OR} + \gamma P_R/W} \qquad \text{bps}$$

where

$r \equiv$ receiving capacity, bits per second
$\beta \equiv$ required digital signal-to-noise (E_b/N_o)
$P_r \equiv$ received power of desired signal, watts
$N_{OR} \equiv$ ambient noise spectral density, watts/hertz
$P_R \equiv$ total power received from the satellite, watts
$\gamma \equiv$ fraction of the satellite signal power that contributes clutter

For convenience in discussion, all terminals are assumed to have equal receiving capabilities. This implies equal values of P_R/N_{OR}, β, and γ. Then the total rate of the satellite is bounded by

$$R \leq \frac{1}{\beta} \frac{LP_R}{N_{OR} + \gamma P_R/W} \qquad \text{bps} \qquad (8.1)$$

where $L \equiv$ useful fraction of satellite signal power.

The values of L and γ depend on the linearity of the satellite repeater and the structure of the communication signals. If the satellite acts as a limiting amplifier, intermodulation noise and capture effects can result. In a hard limiter, intermodulation effects result in $\gamma \approx \frac{1}{8}$ and a maximum value of $L = \pi/4$ whenever two or more signals are present in the amplifier [8, 9]. Capture, which results when the power in one signal is greater than the sum of all other signals, can reduce the value of L to $\frac{1}{4}$. Although limiting repeaters are of importance for military satellites, commercial satellites will normally be operated in a quasilinear mode to reduce the effects of intermodulation.

There are four basic categories of multiple-access techniques [8]. Frequency-division multiple access (FDMA) and time-division multiple access (TDMA) are techniques in which signals are orthogonal, and introduce no mutual interference except for intermodulation noise (clutter). Spread-spectrum multiple access (SSMA) and pulse-address multiple access (PAMA) are nonorthogonal schemes in which mutual interference results even without intermodulation noise.

With sufficient guard bands and a quasilinear satellite repeater, the clutter, γP_R, can be made effectively zero for both TDMA and FDMA. However, for FDMA the best design is usually to deviate somewhat from linearity and suffer some effects from intermodulation noise in order to increase L; in such cases $\gamma P_R/W$ is made approximately equal to N_{OR}. An advantage of TDMA is that only one signal is present in the repeater at any one time, so that there is no clutter even if the satellite operates in a hard limiting or saturated mode. The saturated mode provides an additional 20 per cent or more effective radiated power compared to quasilinear operation. The value of L is also reduced by imperfect power coordination in FDMA or imprecise synchronization in TDMA. However, these losses can be minimized with sufficient terminal complexity. INTELSAT terminals operate with power coordination near 0.1 dB, and timing accuracies better than 0.1 μs have been predicted by analysis [8] and demonstrated [10]. The value of L will be close to unity for TDMA and about -1 to -2 dB for FDMA.

The choice between using FDMA and TDMA is based primarily on questions of implementation. The current use of FDMA reflects past investment in analog equipment. The trend is toward TDMA because of its advantages with digital signaling and modern switching technology. The examples of orthogonal systems that are presented in Section 8.4 employ TDMA.

Spread-spectrum multiple access employs full-period, constant-envelope carriers. The spectrum of each covers essentially the entire repeater band W. Implementations of SSMA typically employ *pseudonoise* carriers with wideband phase shift keying, or *frequency-hopped* carriers in which a relatively narrow band signal is hopped periodically to different portions of the channel bandwidth. Spread-spectrum multiple access can be employed to avoid the need to coordinate the signals on the channel. Each unwanted signal appears as clutter at a receiver "tuned" to a particular signal. In frequency-hopped systems, error correction coding is typically employed to provide an acceptable error rate [11]. Pseudonoise signals permit long periods of coherent integration [7, 8, 12], but error correction coding can be used for most efficient operation (reduced values of β). With frequency-hopped signals and coding, or with pseudonoise signals, the clutter can be modeled as an equivalent gaussian source to permit the calculation of capacity from (8.1) with $\gamma = 1$. If $W \gg P_R/N_{OR}$ (power-limited systems), clutter does not materially reduce capacity. But if $W \lesssim P_R/N_{OR}$ (bandwidth-limited systems), as will be true for many commercial applications, SSMA can provide significantly less capacity than either FDMA or TDMA.

Spread-spectrum multiple access has been used for multiple access in power-limited military communication satellites [11, 13]. However, it is unattractive for (nonmilitary) computer nets because of its large multiple-access loss in bandwidth-limited systems. If uncoordinated use is desired for computer access systems, PAMA appears more attractive. Pulse-address multiple access techniques are many and varied, giving rise to systems with diverse properties—a PAMA technique can be devised with almost any single desirable property [8]. A pulse-address carrier waveform is a series of pulses, or packets of digits, within specific frequency bands. The pulses and the intervals between the pulses in a given carrier waveform constitute a distinct pattern. The duty factor of each carrier is small: i.e., the amount of time during which pulse is present is much less than the amount of time no pulse is present. In typical systems of this class, the same pattern is used to carry each sample of a message [14–19].

Each waveform can be specified by dividing the time-frequency plane into a matrix, as shown in Fig. 8.3. The time axis is divided into frames of length T, each of which is divided into N numbered slots of length t_s. The frequency

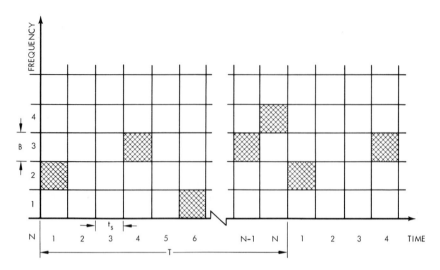

FIGURE 8.3 Time-frequency space in matrix form. The cross-hatched squares illustrate the access channel 2, 0, 0, 3, 0, 1, . . . , 3, 4.

spectrum is divided into numbered bands of width B. One message sample is transmitted in T seconds, the minimum pulse length is t_s, and B must be at least as great as the bandwidth of a pulse. An access channel consists of a distinct pattern of pulses in time and frequency, and is specified by a sequence of numbers. For example, the access channel 2, 0, 0, 3, 0, 1, . . . , 3, 4 is illustrated in Fig. 8.3.* If equipment permits each signal to use the full bandwidth W (i.e., $B = W$), t_s can be reduced to the minimum value for a given data rate, and the maximum allowable number of pulse positions can be obtained along the time access, without frequency changes. The clutter in PAMA is best analyzed with combinatorial statistics, since the gaussian assumption used in (8.1) is not appropriate. In section 8.4 examples of PAMA systems are analyzed.

8.2.2 Line-of-Sight Channels

In general, terrestrial radio networks cannot be analyzed without detailed consideration of power levels, multipath, and path lengths determined by network topology. However, in some network arrangements of interest the access problem is very similar to satellite access. For example, in a network in which a large number of users communicate with a single central computer,

*In some techniques, the pulses themselves contain multiple-access modulation; then an access channel consists of more than a specification of pulse positions in the time-frequency matrix. For instance, spread-spectrum pulses might be used, or address bits can be included in each pulse, or packet.

the problem of links from the users to the computer is akin to that of a large number of users sharing a communication satellite repeater. The examples of Section 8.4 can apply to this situation.

8.3 NETWORK ORGANIZATION

For computer networks the model of each user being able to communicate with any other user, as shown in Fig. 8.2, may be too general. In the simplest network organization a large community of users is linked with a single central computer. This organization suggests dividing the problem into links to and from the central computer, as shown in Fig. 8.4. When this

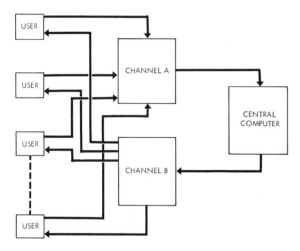

FIGURE 8.4   Signal flow for a large community of users linked with a central computer.

is done, a *channelized* system with two subnetworks or nets is obtained. Signal flow in a more complex network is shown in Fig. 8.5. Here a large community of users is linked with several central computers, and the central computers are interconnected. Three nets are shown, but additional subdivision might be appropriate. Networks combining user-to-computer, computer-to-user, and computer-to-computer links can also be organized along the lines illustrated in Fig. 8.6. Computer-to-computer links are integrated into the user-to-computer and computer-to-user nets. This can be convenient for some use factors and network topologies.

Four categories of nets are illustrated in these figures:

1. *User-to-computer nets* in which many low-rate, low-duty-cycle users vie for access in order to transmit data to a small number of large terminals, perhaps a single central computer.

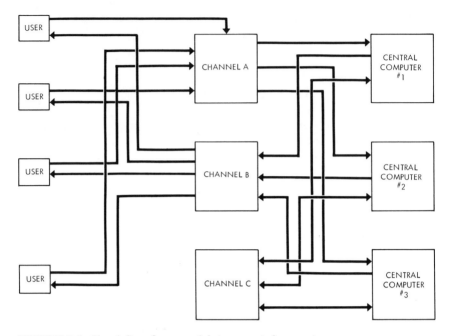

FIGURE 8.5 Signal flow for several interconnected computers
and a large community of users.

2. *Computer-to-user nets* in which a small number of large terminals, perhaps a single computer, transmit to a large number of users.
3. *Computer-to-computer nets* in which several computer terminals are interconnected.
4. *Composite nets* in which more than one of the above functions are performed.

Each of these four categories has distinct characteristics and is likely to lead to a different system design.

First consider the use of terrestrial radio. Links from users to a central terminal present a problem that is amenable to multiple-access techniques typical of satellites. Example systems are discussed in the following section. Links from a central terminal to a large group of users suggest a broadcast mode in which signals to individual users are transmitted in sequence with appropriate addressing. Since efficient operation will require the central terminal to be able to transmit on one net and receive on the other simultaneously, the links to and from that terminal must be on different frequencies.

A link between two large computers may have a higher use factor than a typical user–computer link. Furthermore, the organization of links among computer pairs can introduce problems of dynamic range associated with terrestrial radio nets with many user pairs. Depending on the specific topology

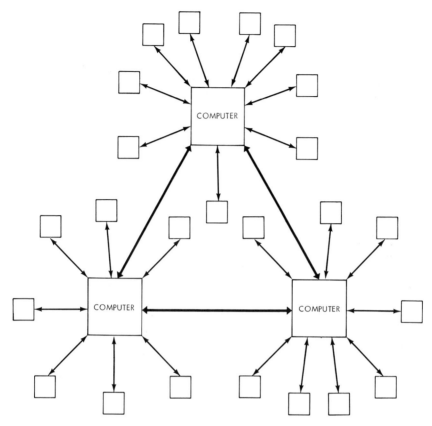

FIGURE 8.6 An alternative signal flow for several interconnected computers and a large community of users.

and traffic patterns, the best solution for this organization is likely to be (1) point-to-point trunks between computer pairs, or (2) links to and from each computer to a central relay or switching center, or (3) a combination of both. The second solution can be amenable to multiple-access techniques, and in fact the central relay could be a communication satellite.

In any case, it appears that multiple access and netted operations can be convenient if central foci are available in the form of central computers or omnidirectional radio relays. A communication satellite can perform the function of a central focus for any network, thereby accommodating any of the four categories of nets. Since the up-link and down-link frequencies are always different for active satellites, a terminal can receive and transmit simultaneously, even when all signals share a common frequency band at the satellite. As a result, a single TDMA format can provide access for all signals in the several nets. Of course, it might be desirable to separate nets in frequency and perhaps employ several amplifiers in the satellite with different passbands. This would serve to avoid excessively complex electronic logic at the terminals or to make efficient use of available satellite power in serving a network of terminals with diverse antenna sizes and receiver capabilities.

8.4   EXAMPLES OF MULTIPLE-ACCESS SYSTEMS

The multiple-access systems discussed here emphasize simplicity in terminal design. Design goals include service to many users and limited delays. The model used for numerical values is a net in which a large number of teletypewriter users transmits to a single computer. It is assumed that computer-to-user links are available from another net for control signals as well as for data. The users share a transmission channel with a capacity $C = 24$ kbps. This capacity is consistent with a 50-kHz bandwidth, a standard allocation at UHF, and is a multiple of 2.4 kbps, which is currently a standard data channel on satellites and other transmission media.

For efficient use of this channel at teletypewriter rates, FDMA would introduce stringent requirements for frequency stability and filtering at both user and computer terminals. Therefore, TDMA or PAMA approaches are preferred. Examples of four classes of systems with variations will be presented: two with orthogonal signaling (TDMA) and two in which mutual interference occurs (PAMA). In all examples, a user transmits bursts of data at the 24-kbps rate. The central terminal uses a single demodulator, relying upon logic operations on baseband signals to identify the sender. The example systems are applicable with either terrestrial radio or satellite media.

8.4.1   Traffic Model

To derive design parameter values and to estimate system performance, data presented by Fuchs and Jackson [20], based on Bell Telephone Laboratories studies, are employed. These data were derived from four multiple-access computer systems said to be representative of the several systems studied.

Table 8.1 presents average parameter values derived from the calculations of Fuchs and Jackson. Communications between a user and computer are typically comprised of a sequence of time periods in which the user transmits, interleaved with periods in which the computer transmits. These time periods are labeled *user burst segments* and *computer burst segments* according to which terminal is transmitting. A user burst segment begins, by definition, at the end of the last character of the previous computer burst segment. Similarly, a computer burst segment begins at the end of the last character in the previous user burst segment. A *burst* is defined as a series of characters

TABLE 8.1   *Traffic Model for Category (1) and (2) Nets [20]*

	Mean	*Standard Deviation*
User burst segment		
Think time (s)	5.0	3.1
Interburst time (s)	1.5	0.83
No. bursts/segment	11.	2.8
No. characters/burst	1.1	0.1
Time per burst (s)	0.10	0.010
User burst segment (s)	21.	10.
Computer burst segment		
Idle time (s)	0.81	0.44
Interburst time (s)	13.	21.
No. bursts/segment	2.9	2.4
No. characters/burst	41.	24.
Time per burst (s)	38.	22.
Computer burst segment (s)	140.	170.

in which the time between characters is never greater than one-half the time
required for transmitting a single character. A burst segment is then made
up of one or more bursts of one or more characters. *Think time* is the time
from the beginning of a user burst segment until the beginning of first burst in
the segment; similarly, *idle time* is the time from the beginning of a computer
burst segment until the beginning of the first burst in that segment.

In the Fuchs and Jackson model, characteristic of most existing multiple-
access systems, a user transmits directly from a teletypewriter console, and
user bursts are usually one character in length (1.1 characters on the average).
In TDMA and PAMA systems, channel efficiency can be increased by transmitting data in fewer numbers of relatively longer bursts. Therefore, in the
example systems, user data is transmitted in bursts of several characters,
typically complete teletypewriter lines, rather than character by character.

The following parameters are basic to the design and evaluation of the
example systems. The values are estimated on the basis of Table 8.1.

AVERAGE USER BIT RATE.   On the average there are 12.1 8-bit characters/
user burst segment, and one user burst segment every 161 s. Therefore, the
average user bit rate is taken as $97/161 \approx 0.6$ bps. Also of interest is the
average user bit rate during user burst segments. This is taken to be $\frac{97}{21} \approx 5$
bps.

AVERAGE RATE OF USER-GENERATED TELETYPEWRITER LINES.   This parameter
is not available directly from Table 8.1. It is estimated by noting that since an
average user burst segment consists of 12.1 characters, the average number
of lines per burst segment is likely to be less than 2. The average rate of

user-generated character lines, defined as λ, is therefore taken conservatively to be

$$\lambda = \tfrac{2}{161} \approx \tfrac{1}{80} \text{ lines/s.}$$

ACCEPTABLE POLLING INTERVAL.   In TDMA systems each user is polled at either a regular or average rate (in periodic or aperiodic schemes, respectively). The polling interval will represent a compromise between the two stated goals: many users and limited delays. Lacking detailed studies of human factors, it appears that the acceptability of a polling interval might be judged relative to any of several criteria: λ ($\tfrac{1}{80}$ lines/s), user burst segment length (21-s average, 10-s standard deviations), computer burst segment length (140-s average, 170-s standard deviation), or idle time (0.81-s average, 0.44-s standard deviation). These possible criteria yield a wide range for choosing an acceptable polling interval. In the examples, a polling interval of 8 s is assumed.

8.4.2   Orthogonal Systems: TDMA

8.4.2.1   Periodic Transmission.   The simplest time-division scheme has each user* transmit a fixed-length burst of data periodically, using a system timing arrangement to prevent transmission overlaps. Such a scheme in practice will be relatively easy to implement and can be quite effective. Rather than require accurate timing at each terminal, it will be convenient to maintain a time reference in the central station only, and have terminals transmit automatically on command.

Several other implementations can be considered, but a user terminal can be assumed to include an electronic buffer that is loaded from the teletypewriter console character by character and is read out in bursts or packets of a fixed number of binary digits (including blank characters). Readout will be on commands received from the computer. In addition and in conjunction with this buffer, certain housekeeping digits must be generated to be transmitted with each packet to provide user and packet identification, as well as parity checks as needed for error detection or correction at the computer terminal. Housekeeping data are assumed conservatively to number 40 binary digits/ packet. Furthermore, the user terminal buffer will have to be able to retransmit, on command or in the absence of acknowledgment, packets received in error at the central computer.

Timing and housekeeping for the network will be maintained at the central station. Each user will be assigned an access, and several accesses can be left vacant (1) to accommodate retransmissions, and (2) for subscribers to call in for access to the computer and the communication channel.

---

*Here *subscribers* are defined as potential users. *Users* are defined as active subscribers with assigned access to the computer and the communication channel.

A polling interval of 8 s for each user would result in few bursts containing more than one line of characters. Packets with 800 data bits (840 binary digits overall) would provide for the maximum teletypewriter rate of 100 bps; packets of 40 data bits would provide for the average rate in a user burst segment, 5 bps. For this example a packet consisting of 40 housekeeping digits and 128 data digits ($\sim$16 bps) is chosen. Such a packet will require 7 ms for transmission at the 4-kbps rate.

Guard times between adjacent bursts need not be greater than 2 ms, and could readily be made smaller. For example, 2 ms would allow for two-way transmission over an 80-mile path as well as a 1 ms delay in the terminal response. For networks with short paths, guard times of this order might be permitted to simplify the task of the computer terminal. However, the guard time could be reduced to a small fraction of 1 ms if the central station measures the delay for each user. This will be possible even with very long paths. (Note also that it is not necessary to allow the same guard time for each user.)

To accommodate packets of 7 ms (168 digits at a 24-kbps rate) and guard times of 2 ms, 9-ms time slots would be needed. Thus

$$M = \frac{8}{0.009} \approx 900 \text{ users}$$

could be accommodated. Reducing the guard time below 1 ms could permit more than 1000 users.

The polling interval need not be fixed and could be adjusted depending on the number of users and percentage of packets requiring retransmission. In fact, with a polling interval of 16 s, and the same provision for 128 data bits/packet, an average data rate of 8 bps/user could be accommodated. (This is above the average user-generated rates, but delays might not be acceptable for interactive systems.) A polling interval of 16 s could permit about 2000 users.

8.4.2.2 Aperiodic Transmission. It is apparent that strict periodicity is not required by either the user or the central station. It is only important that the polling interval for any user does not result in unacceptable delay. With an average user rate of 0.6 bps and an 8-s polling interval, an average packet would contain 5 data bits or a total of 45 digits with housekeeping, compared to the packet length of 168 digits provided with fixed-length packets in the periodic scheme. A 45-digit packet would require $\sim$2 ms to transmit, and if a 2-ms guard time were allowed,

$$M = \frac{8}{0.004} \approx 2000 \text{ users}$$

could be accommodated. In a network with a computer terminal performing this level of housekeeping, it would be reasonable to reduce guard times by computing path delays and compensating for them. Guard times of a small fraction of a bit period can then be achieved. This would permit up to 4000 users. Furthermore, if a 16-s polling interval were acceptable, up to 8000 users could be accommodated.

In a network with long path delays, special provisions would have to be made to give the central station early notice of the packet length. Otherwise, guard times would more than cancel all the savings in packet length. To avoid this inefficiency, the user can transmit two bursts/packet. Both bursts would be transmitted on command. In response to the first command, a user terminal composes the data package and transmits a burst containing a fixed number of housekeeping bits (say, 40), but no data. This would be used to inform the central station of the number of data bits, if any, in the packet. If there are data to be transmitted, then at any time after receiving this first burst the computer terminal can command the transmission of the remainder of the packet with full knowledge of the length of the second burst. The second burst would contain additional housekeeping digits (say, 40), plus data digits. On the average a user generates data (an end-of-line symbol) every 80 s, so that the second burst will be required for about 10 per cent of the packets. On the average a second burst will contain $8 \times 0.6 \approx 5$ bits of data. Therefore, the average packet length will be $40 + (0.10 \times 40) + 5 = 49$ digits. An average packet would thus require about 2 ms of transmission time. Furthermore, fewer than 40 housekeeping digits would probably suffice in the first burst. Therefore, long path delays need not result in fewer users in aperiodic schemes.

8.4.3 Nonorthogonal Systems: PAMA

8.4.3.1 Error Detection and Retransmission. Consider the same community of users as in Section 8.4.2 and a scheme in which a user transmits a data packet at the end of each teletypewriter line, without regard to whether the channel is occupied or not. A transmitted packet can be received in error because of random noise or because of interference from a packet transmitted by another user. When the channel is heavily loaded, almost all errors will be due to interference, so that in calculating the number of users which can share the channel, random noise can be neglected.

In this example, the system will employ error detection and retransmission. It is assumed conservatively that whenever two or more packets overlap in as few as one digit position, both packets are received in error by the computer, and both packets must be retransmitted. When the computer receives a packet with no errors, an acknowledgment is sent. If a user sends a packet and does not receive an acknowledgment within a specified time, the packet is automatically retransmitted.

This scheme has been analyzed for THE ALOHA SYSTEM [21]. In this analysis it is convenient to distinguish between the first transmission of a packet and any retransmissions of the packet. The first transmissions are referred to as *message packets*, and retransmissions as *repetitions*. Let M be the number of users, λ be the average number of message packets transmitted per second per user, and τ be the average packet length. Then $k = M\lambda$ is the average number of message packets transmitted on the channel in 1 s, and $k\tau$ is referred to as the *channel utilization*. We define K as the average number of message packets plus repetitions transmitted per second by the M users. Then $K \ge k$, and $K\tau$ is defined as the *channel traffic*. It can be readily shown [21] that $k\tau$ and $K\tau$ are related by the equation

$$k\tau = K\tau e^{-2K\tau}$$

This relationship is plotted in Fig. 8.7, where it is seen that channel utilization reaches a maximum value of $1/2e = 0.184$. At this operating point, however, retransmissions make up almost two-thirds of the channel traffic and become unbounded with any short-term increase in channel utilization. A more appropriate operating point might be at a channel utilization $k\tau \approx 0.15$. Even here almost two out of three message packets are received in error, but computer simulation indicates that the channel remains stable [22].

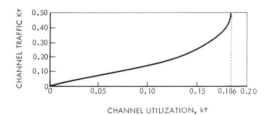

CHANNEL TRAFFIC $K\tau$

CHANNEL UTILIZATION, $k\tau$

FIGURE 8.7   Channel utilization versus channel traffic.

Assume as before that the average rate per user is ~ 0.6 bps, and that a line of characters is generated every 80 s ($\lambda \approx \frac{1}{80}$). Because of the random occurrence of transmissions, somewhat more housekeeping digits are probably appropriate here than for orthogonal systems. A total of 64 digits (32 for identification and control, 32 for parity checks) has been considered for THE ALOHA SYSTEM [21]. With an average user data rate of 0.6 bps, an average packet would contain 48 data bits for a total of 112 binary digits. The average packet length $\tau \approx 4.7$ ms and

$$\lambda\tau \approx 0.06 \times 10^{-3}$$

At the maximum channel utilization of 0.15,

$$k\tau = M\lambda\tau = 0.15$$

so that

$$M \approx 2500 \text{ users}$$

Thus with a scheme of modest complexity, PAMA can permit a large number of users to share a single channel. Note that this figure is considerably greater than that calculated for THE ALOHA SYSTEM because of the use of a variable-length packet feature not yet available in THE ALOHA SYSTEM.

A disadvantage of this uncoordinated usage compared to TDMA schemes is the limitations on positive controls when the network operates near saturation. In TDMA the central terminal can readily adjust the polling interval to provide for short-term fluctuations in channel utilization. In PAMA schemes control over the number of users, M, can be exerted by the central terminal; but positive control over λ and τ, the other components determining channel utilization, are cumbersome.

8.4.3.2   Forward-Acting Error Correction.   It is natural to inquire whether by using error correction coding at each terminal communication efficiency can be improved significantly over that attained with detection and retransmission. With the application of random coding and very powerful sequential decoding, the significant transmission rate parameter is r_{comp}, given by

$$r_{\text{comp}} = 1 - \log_2[1 + 2\sqrt{p(1-p)}]   \text{bits/digit}$$

for binary decisions, where p = probability of incorrect binary digit decision [23]. The quantity r_{comp} can be interpreted as the maximum data rate attainable for a given raw channel error rate. Figure 8.8 is a plot of r_{comp} versus p.

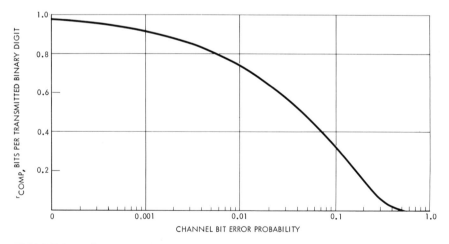

FIGURE 8.8   Bit error probability versus r_{comp} for sequential deciding in a binary symmetric channel with hard decision.

Assume that when two signals overlap, the probability of a digit error is 0.5, and that the probability of error is the same in all digit positions. (At full loading random noise can be ignored.) A possible choice of signaling is a rate one-fourth code (one data digit for every four transmitted digits), which according to Fig. 8.8 can permit operation at a channel error rate of about one-eighth. This error rate would result at the computer terminal if interference occurs for one-fourth of the digits transmitted. Assuming that the number of signals is large, the total number of digit positions occupied at that operating point is approximately one fourth. Since about one out of every four transmitted digits overlaps with a digit transmitted by another user, the channel traffic (i.e., the number of digits transmitted by all users) is given by $\frac{1}{4}(1 + \frac{1}{4} + \frac{1}{16} + \ldots) \approx \frac{1}{3}$. Because four digits are transmitted for each data bit, the channel utilization (that is, the ratio of the number of bits transmitted by all users to the channel capacity) is one-twelfth. This channel utilization compares unfavorably with the value of 0.15 for the case of error detection and retransmission.

The definitions of channel utilization for the two cases are comparable. However, the analysis of the system with error detection and retransmission did not account for capacity required for acknowledgments (from computer to user), which are not required with forward-acting error correction. Furthermore, to account for parity-check digits, the channel utilization for detection and retransmission should be reduced by 20 per cent ($\frac{32}{160}$) to 0.12. This still leaves an advantage for the system with simpler implementation.

Sommer [18] and Cahn [19] have shown that by using on–off coding and making use of information in unoccupied digit positions as well as occupied ones for forward-acting error correction, PAMA can make efficient use of a channel. Assume that M low duty factor signals simultaneously access through a common channel. The modulation on each signal is on–off, and the pulse positions are random. Thus, for any signal,

$$p = \text{probability of "on" for any digit}$$
$$1 - p = \text{probability of "off" for any digit}$$
$$\delta = \text{duty factor of the signal}$$
$$\frac{\delta}{p} = \text{digit rate of each signal (per digit position)}$$

The digit rate given above relates duty factor and probability of a transmitter being "on". An asymmetric source is allowed; i.e., p need not equal 0.5.

The model under discussion assumes that the digits of each signal occupy random positions known a priori to the intended receiver. The transmitter may or may not be turned "on" during one of these allowed positions.* The

---

*This is the system analyzed by Cahn. Sommer's approach is similar, but all digit positions are used by each signal so that δ is the only parameter characterizing each signal. The results are similar for the two systems.

parameter

$$\epsilon = 1 - (1 - \delta)^{M-1}$$

denotes the probability of at least one other signal being turned on during a given digit. Once again, random noise can be ignored at full loading. Assuming that cancellation (i.e., overlap of two signals appearing as "no signal") can never take place, the transition probabilities can be written, in terms of ϵ, as

$$\text{Prob}(0/0) = 1 - \epsilon$$
$$\text{Prob}(1/0) = \epsilon$$
$$\text{Prob}(0/1) = 0$$
$$\text{Prob}(1/1) = 1$$

For any signal, expressed in bits per digit, the significant rate parameter associated with sequential decoding is [23]

$$r_{comp} = -\log_2 \sum_j \left[\sum_i p(i)\sqrt{p(j/i)} \right]^2$$
$$= -\log_2\{(1 - p)^2(1 - \epsilon) + [(1 - p)\sqrt{\epsilon} + p]^2\}$$
$$= -\log_2[1 - 2p(1 - p)(1 - \sqrt{\epsilon})]$$

The total rate parameter for all M signals, expressed in bits per digit position, is

$$R_{comp} = -M \frac{\delta}{p} r_{comp}$$
$$= -M \frac{\delta}{p} \log_2[1 - 2p(1 - p)(1 - \sqrt{\epsilon})]$$

As an approximation for p small and M large,

$$R_{comp} = \frac{-\log(1 - \epsilon)}{\delta} \frac{\delta}{p} \frac{2p(1 - p)(1 - \sqrt{\epsilon})}{0.693}$$
$$= -2.88(1 - p)(1 - \sqrt{\epsilon})\log(1 - \epsilon) \qquad \text{bits/digit position}$$
(8.2)

and (8.2) is maximized at $\epsilon = 0.578$ to give

$$[R_{comp}]_{max} = 0.596(1 - p) \text{ bits/digit position}$$

as $p \rightarrow 0$

$$R_{comp} \longrightarrow 0.596 \text{ bits/digit position}$$

As far as any one signal is concerned, the probability of "on" should be small. Taking $p = 0.1$ degrades performance to 0.9 of the maximum possible $p \rightarrow 0$. Also, the approximation of (8.2) is very accurate at this value of p. For this selection

$$r_{comp} = -\log_2[1 - 2p(1 - p)(1 - \sqrt{\epsilon})]$$
$$= -\log_2[1 - 2(0.1)(0.9)(1 - \sqrt{0.578}]$$
$$= 0.0622 \text{ bit/digit position}$$

which is independent of the number of signals M. The digit rate is then

$$\frac{\delta}{p} = -\frac{\log(1 - \epsilon)}{p(M - 1)} \simeq \frac{8.6}{M} \quad \text{digits/digit position}$$

only 0.1 of which is actually "on," of course:

$$R_{\text{comp}} \sim 8.6(0.0622) \sim 0.53 \text{ bit/digit position}$$

Hence a channel utilization as large as ~ 0.5 can be attained with PAMA, although with terminal complexity. Note that sequential decoding must be performed simultaneously for all M users. This is the lowest multiple-access loss that has been shown for PAMA schemes.

8.5 SUMMARY

This chapter has demonstrated that a large number of users can be accommodated with netted operation in terrestrial radio and communication satellite channels. Line-of-sight and satellite-transmission media were discussed and found amenable to use for this function. With multiple-access systems permitting the use of relatively simple terminals, a 24-kbps channel was found to provide access for from 900 to as many as 8000 teletypewriter users, depending on the particular system. Time-gated systems using TDMA or PAMA are considered to be preferable to full-period systems using FDMA or SSMA for the rates considered.

REFERENCES

[1] H. S. BLACK, *Modulation Theory*, Van Nostrand, New York, 1953.

[2] T. G. BELDEN and J. W. SCHWARTZ, Application of Communication Satellites to the Military Command Structure, *Institute for Defense Analyses Paper P-371* (Jan. 1969).

[3] K. BRAYER, "Error Patterns Measured on Transequatorial HF Communications Links," *IEEE Trans. Commun. Tech.*, **Com-16**(2) (April 1968).

[4] S. H. DURRANI and D. W. LIPKE, Satellite Communications for Manned Spacecraft, *Proc. IEEE*, **59** (Feb. 1971).

[5] H. R. REED and C. M. RUSSELL, *Ultra High Frequency Propagation*, Wiley, New York, 1953.

[6] M. SCHWARTZ, W. R. BENNETT, and S. STEIN, *Communications Systems and Techniques*, McGraw-Hill, New York, 1966.

[7] J. M. AEIN, Multiple Access to a Hard Limiting Communication-Satellite Repeater, *IEEE Trans. Space Electron. Telemetry*, **Set-10** (Dec. 1964), 159–167.

[8] J. W. Schwartz et al., Modulation Techniques for Multiple Access to a Hard Limiting Satellite Repeater, *Proc. IEEE*, **54** (May 1966), 763–777.

[9] W. Doyle, Crosstalk of Frequency-Multiplexed Signal in Saturating Amplifiers, *Rand Corp. Mem. RM-3576-NASA* (April 1963).

[10] T. Sekimoto and J. G. Puente, A Satellite Time Division Multiple Access Experiment, *IEEE Trans. Commun. Technol.*, **Com-16** (Aug. 1968), 581–588.

[11] P. Drouilhet and S. Bernstein, TATS—A Band Spread Modulation-Demodulation System for Multiple Access Tactical Satellite Communication, *EASCON Conv. Record*, (1969), 126–132.

[12] D. R. Anderson and P. A. Wintz, Analysis of a Spread Spectrum Multiple-Access System with a Hard Limiter, *IEEE Trans. Commun. Technol.*, **Com-17** (April 1969), 285–290.

[13] I. L. Lebow et al., Satellite Communications to Mobile Platforms, *Proc. IEEE*, **59** (Feb. 1971), 139–159.

[14] J. E. Taylor, Asynchronous Multiplexing, *AIEE Trans. Commun. Electron.*, **78** Jan. 1960), 1054–1062.

[15] J. R. Pierce and A. L. Hopper, Nonsynchronous Time Division with Holding and with Random Sampling, *Proc. IRE*, **40** (Sept. 1952), 1079–1088.

[16] W. D. White, Theoretical Aspects of Asynchronous Multiplexing, *Proc. IRE*, **38** (March 1950), 270–275.

[17] M. R. Schroeder, U.S. Patent 3160711, Dec. 8, 1964.

[18] R. C. Sommer, High Efficiency Multiple Access Communications Through a Signal Processing Repeater, *IEEE Trans. Commun. Technol.*, **Com-16** (April 1968), 222–232.

[19] C. R. Cahn, Modulation System for TACSAT(X), Magnavox Research Laboratories Report MX-TM-8-671-3046-68, Aug. 23, 1968.

[20] E. Fuchs and P. E. Jackson, Estimates of Distributions of Random Variables for Certain Computer Communication Traffic Models, *Commun. ACM*, **13** (Dec. 1970), 752–757.

[21] N. Abramson, The Aloha System—Another Alternative for Computer Communications, *University of Hawaii Tech. Rept. 870-1* (April 1970).

[22] W. H. Bortels, Simulation of Interference of Packets in the Aloha Time-Sharing System, *University of Hawaii Tech. Rept. B70-2* (March 1970).

[23] J. M. Wozencraft and I. M. Jacobs, *Principles of Communication Engineering*, Wiley, New York, 1965.

9

Regulatory Policy and Future Data Transmission Services

PHILIP M. WALKER

STUART L. MATHISON

Telenet Communications Corp., Waltham, Mass.

INTRODUCTION

The range of communication services available for the transmission of digital data will expand substantially in the 1970s. In part the changes will take the form of additional service offerings provided by today's communication common carriers—the telephone companies and Western Union. These services, however, will be supplemented by the offerings of new common-carrier entities, the subject of this chapter.

The advent of data-oriented common carriers in the United States is taking place within the framework of regulatory policy set down by the Federal Communications Commission.* In a general policy statement issued

*Under the Communications Act of 1934, the construction of common-carrier communications facilities and the provision of common-carrier communications services must be approved by the FCC.

in 1971, the FCC set the stage for the establishment of these new carriers, termed specialized carriers, and the data communicator is likely to be the benefactor.

In this chapter we describe the present and planned data transmission services provided by today's common carriers, the emergence of new data-oriented carriers, the various policy considerations, and the likely effects of new entry from the viewpoint of the user and designer of computer-communication systems.

9.1   USE OF TODAY'S COMMUNICATIONS NETWORK FOR DATA TRANSMISSION

9.1.1   Data Transmission in the United States

Accompanying the recent development and rapid growth of the computer industry, a need has arisen for the efficient transmission of information in digital form. Optimal transmission of digital information requires telecommunication facilities and services quite different from those used today for voice and conventional forms of record transmission. However, due to the relatively limited data traffic volumes of previous years (only a few per cent of total telephone-line holding time), the approach of "making do" with available facilities has been more economic than the construction of separate or discrete digital facilities and the introduction of special data-oriented communication services. Therefore, despite the fact that the national communications network and its philosophy have been geared to the needs of the traditional voice and telegraph users, virtually all data transmission today occurs over ordinary telephone and telegraph channels supplied by the telephone companies and the Western Union Telegraph Company (W.U.). In a few instances user organizations with private microwave or cable facilities transmit digital data over their own facilities rather than over common-carrier channels.

The importance of the need for suitable and efficient data transmission facilities should not be underestimated. Computer systems and data networks are proliferating and assuming ever-increasing importance in virtually all sectors of our economy. Vital industries and government organizations are becoming increasingly dependent upon data transmission facilities—in some cases to the same degree that they have come to depend upon nationwide telephone service for their day-to-day operations. The operations of the stock exchanges, the airlines, and the national air defense system, for example, would be crippled were their data communication links to fail. The growth of data transmission both among these users and throughout the U.S.

economy reflects the fact that data transmission facilities will, in the not-too-distant future, become a part of the nation's infrastructure.

Various trends illustrate the recent rate of data transmission growth. For example, from a negligible population in 1960, the number of modems grew to more than 150,000 in 1970—at an annual growth rate of some 60 per cent during the 1965–1970 period. Several studies conducted for the Data Transmission Company, or Datran (discussed subsequently), furnish estimates of the rate of future data terminal and data traffic growth—assuming the establishment of efficient data transmission facilities [1]. This expected growth is summarized in Fig. 9.1.

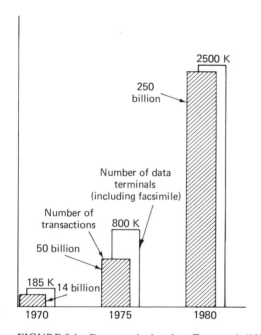

FIGURE 9.1   Data terminal and traffic growth (1970–1980).

Significant progress has been made by the telephone companies in adapting the existing communications network to the requirements of the computer industry (witness line conditioning, automatically equalized modems, reduced impulse noise, etc.), but as data traffic grows, the telephone network shortcomings become more evident and costly. Realizing this, the established carriers have begun to introduce new services designed to meet the specific needs of data communication users (e.g., the Bell System's data line concentrator service). Furthermore, in the long run digital transmission and switching techniques will, in many instances, be more economic for voice, video, and record services, as well as for data transmission, and data users' requirements may thus be served through "fallout" from other services. However, the *primary* thrust of telephone company effort, and necessarily so, is toward the needs of its most numerous subscribers—voice telephone users. And it appears that the Bell System's *secondary* thrust is toward developing and promoting Picturephone® service, rather than data-transmission services, if one measures effort by dollar expenditures for research, development, and physical plant investment. So it remains to be seen whether optimal data transmission services will be forthcoming from the telephone companies within a reasonable time frame.

9.1.2 *Presently Available Data Transmission Services*

Today's common-carrier communications network is built around the voice telephone channel—an analog channel of 4-kHz nominal bandwidth, suitable for transmitting either the human voice or computer data up to several thousand bits per second (using appropriate modem equipment to convert the data to analog form for transmission). Using frequency-division multiplexing (FDM) techniques, this *voice-grade* channel can be subdivided into a number of *telegraph-grade* channels for low-speed teletypewriter transmission. Frequency-division multiplexing techniques are also used to combine multiple voice-grade channels into larger-bandwidth blocks (groups, supergroups, and so on) for transmission over long-distance carrier systems; this standard transmission hierarchy gives us the *broadband* channels, equivalent in size to 12, 60, and 240 voice-grade channels.

Using this menu of telegraph-grade, voice-grade, and broadband channel capabilities, together with conventional telephone-oriented switching facilities, the telephone companies and Western Union offer a variety of circuit-switched and leased-line data transmission services. These are outlined in Table 9.1. The pertinent carrier tariffs are indicated in parentheses following each service title, and the data transfer rates available to users of each service are indicated in the right-hand column.

9.1.3 *Shortcomings of Present Data Transmission Services and Facilities*

The predominant type of traffic over the U.S. communications network has always been speech and—to a much smaller degree—conventional record communications. Therefore, understandably, the network facilities and the tariff regulations, pricing structures, and operating practices regarding their

---

®Registered AT & T service mark.

TABLE 9.1   *Currently Available Common-Carrier Communications*
Offerings Useful for Data Transmission

	Data Transfer Rate (*bps*)
Circuit-switched service offerings	
Telegraph grade	
TWX (W.U. Tariff FCC No. 258)[a]	45–150
Telex (W.U. Tariff FCC No. 240)	50
Voice grade	
Long Distance Message Telecommunications	
(AT&T Tariff FCC No. 263)	1200–3600
WATS (AT&T Tariff FCC No. 259)	1200–3600
Broadband Exchange (W.U. Tariff FCC No. 246)	1200–2400
Dataphone 50 (AT&T Tariff FCC No. 263)[b]	50,000
Private-line (*leased*) ***service offerings***	
(AT&T Tariff FCC No. 260; W.U. Tariff FCC No. 237)	
Telegraph grade	45–180
Voice grade	1200–9600[c]
Broadband	
12 voice channels (Series 8000)	50,000
60 voice channels (Telpak C)	230,400
240 voice channels (Telpak D)[d]	230,400[d]

[a]TWX was transferred from AT&T to W.U. in 1971.

[b]Data-phone 50 is an experimental offering available only in five cities, for a several-year trial period.

[c]One of the factors limiting the data transfer rate on a given communications channel is the performance characteristics of the modems at the end points of the channel. Modems operating above 4800 bps on voice-grade lines are infrequently used today because of their high cost and sensitivity to time-varying channel characteristics.

[d]Although Telpak D service could theoretically be used for data transmission at speeds up to the limits of the full baseband capacity—approximately 1 Mbps—modems operating above 230.4 kbps are not available today from the carriers (and use of customer-supplied modems is not permitted on such broadband channels).

use have evolved with these requirements in mind. But the requirements for data transmission differ in many respects from those of traditional record and voice communications, and thus the conventional carrier network exhibits many shortcomings when used for various data transmission applications [2, 3].

Most intercity data transmission today uses either dedicated or circuit-switched voice-grade or telegraph-grade channels. Figure 9.2 illustrates the most common usage: low-speed or medium-speed (up to perhaps 3600 bps) data transmission over a dial-up long-distance telephone channel. Many of the present network's shortcomings are illustrated in this figure, which is keyed to the discussion in the following paragraphs. Subsequent sections of the chapter then discuss the approaches planned by the telephone companies,

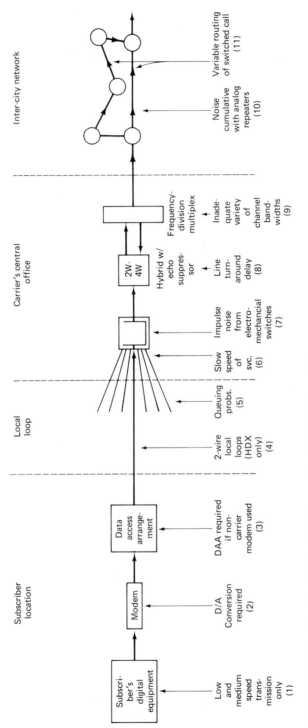

FIGURE 9.2 Shortcomings of today's telephone network for data transmission.

Western Union, and the new specialized carriers, especially Datran, to alleviate these difficulties.

9.1.3.1 Switched Network Limited to Low- and Medium-Speed Transmission.
Today's switched (dial-up) network provides, in most locations, only two types of channels for data transmission—telegraph-grade channels usable up to 150 bps (the TWX–Telex networks) and suited to low-speed data terminal devices such as teletypewriters and paper-tape devices; and voice-grade channels of 4-kHz nominal bandwidth, which can be used for synchronous or asynchronous data transmission at speeds up to 2400 or 3600 bps, depending upon the type of modem selected by the user.*

Data transmission at higher speeds (e.g., from remote batch terminals) can be accomplished only over leased lines, even though the low-frequency, high-volume user's requirements might be more economically satisfied by an available-upon-demand circuit-switched or message-switched channel rather than a full-time leased circuit.

9.1.3.2 Digital-to-Analog Conversion Required.
Since today's transmission plant is predominantly analog rather than digital in nature, digital data signals must be converted to analog form before transmission, through the use of a modulation–demodulation device, or modem. The modem purchase or lease cost is a significant factor in many user applications and may even make certain applications economically infeasible. (The purchase price of a modem typically ranges from several hundred to several thousand dollars. As a rough rule of thumb, presently available modems cost $1.00/bps; i.e., a 300-bps modem costs about $300; a 4800-bps modem costs roughly $4000 to $5000; however, these costs are falling rapidly.)

9.1.3.3 Data Access Arrangement Required.
Under the present interconnection regulations, direct attachment to the telephone network of a customer-provided modem or other equipment or systems requires the use of an appropriate protective connecting device leased from the telephone company. Various types of these devices, known as data access arrangements, are available today for use with different types of modems and user applications. Data access arrangement rental costs (several dollars per month) and operating efficiency vary widely—sometimes imposing unnecessary cost burdens upon the user and/or equipment design limitations upon the modem manufacturer. Effective programs for type acceptance of user equipment and certification of maintenance personnel may permit the future interconnection of data equipment without the use of a data access arrangement.

9.1.3.4 Two-Wire Local Loop.
Both the TWX–Telex and dial telephone networks employ two-wire rather than four-wire local loop channels from the

---

*Switched voice-grade channels may also transmit data at higher speeds, such as 4800 bps, through the use of adaptively equalized modems, but this is seldom done today due to the high error rates associated with such techniques.

carrier's central office to the customer's premises. Even though the long-haul transmission circuits between central offices are four-wire, full-duplex (having simultaneous two-way transmission capability) in nature, the two-wire local loop limits many dial-up medium-speed data transmission applications to a half-duplex (two-way transmission, but in only one direction at a time) mode of operation. (Simultaneous two-way transmission is possible at low speeds.) The availability of four-wire local loops, together with associated four-wire switchgear in the central office—rather than the two-wire circuit-switching equipment in predominant use today—would give the data communications user an unrestricted full-duplex transmission capability, with completely separate "send" and "receive" channels. Four-wire end-to-end designs have been employed in some of the newer switched communications networks (e.g., Western Union's Broadband Exchange service and the Defense Department's AUTOVON telephone network), but this approach has been considered too costly for general use in the voice telephone network.

9.1.3.5 Queueing Problems. The configuration and capacity of telephone exchanges and trunking facilities are based upon the statistical properties (e.g., expected number of calls per *busy hour*, distribution of *call holding times*, etc.) of the traffic such exchanges and trunks are expected to handle and the desired *grade of service*. When some of the subscribers then begin to make data calls, rather than the voice calls for which the exchange was designed, two difficulties may arise.

First, the statistical distribution of call holding times is quite different for various data transmission applications than it is for ordinary voice telephone usage. For some data applications, holding time may be much shorter than the average voice telephone call—perhaps only 10 to 20 s or less—whereas, at the other extreme, data users logged into a conversational time-sharing computer or engaged in bulk data transmission may have holding times ranging from 10 min to 1 h or more. Not only do the mean holding times for a data call fail to approximate those of a voice call, but the unimodal distribution of voice holding times is replaced with a bimodal distribution of data holding times —frequently rather tightly clustered around widely disparate mean values. A single subscriber placing relatively long data calls, such as to a time-sharing computer, may impose a load upon the telephone exchange equivalent to that of several conventional voice telephone subscribers.* It does not take much data traffic of this variety to overload an exchange, tying up its trunk channels and degrading the service to other subscribers.

Second, for some dial-up data communication applications effective operation is dependent upon the availability of a very high grade of service

---

*Several telephone companies, have, in fact, proposed special tariffs for Information Service Access Lines (ISAL) on the theory that such data users impose an added burden upon central offices and should pay accordingly.

from the telephone exchange. For example, users of a remote-access computer system, such as a reservation or credit-authorization system, may be very intolerant of difficulties (e.g., lengthy dial-tone delays and trunk-busy conditions) encountered in getting an open channel to the computer. When the data communications user finds the grade of service in his local exchange inadequate for an application of this nature, he is forced to employ leased rather than switched circuits (perhaps at substantially increased costs) or abandon the application.

9.1.3.6 Slow Speed of Service. The next parameter determining the utility of the switched telephone system to a particular subscriber is its *speed of service*, which may be defined as the total time consumed between calling-party off-hook and start of called-party ringing. This time has three components: dial-tone delay, dialing time (receipt of dial tone to end of dialing), and connect time (end of dialing to start of ringing). Dial-tone delay is directly proportional to traffic load conditions, and with light traffic through the exchange is relatively insignificant (less than 500 ms); however, under abnormally heavy traffic load conditions, this delay may amount to many seconds or even minutes. Dialing time is usually a more significant component of speed of service in the telephone system. For rotary dials (direct current dial pulses), dialing time averages about 10 s for manually dialed calls and takes at least 8.8 s when using an automatic calling unit (ACU). For Touch-Tone service, the corresponding times are 4 s and 0.7 s.*

The third element of speed of service, connect time, is a function of the type of switchgear and the number of stages of switching involved (number of trunk links in tandem). The average number of trunk links required to establish a connection between two points is directly proportional to the distance between those points, and is inversely proportional to normal traffic volumes passing between the points (because direct trunk routes are established between points whenever traffic volumes justify their existence). Table 9.2 shows average connect times experienced on the long-distance telephone network.

Rapid speed of service over the dial telephone network is important to most data users, but particularly to data users either sending very short messages or requiring immediate responses to inquiries (e.g., credit-authorization inquiries, with an impatient customer standing by). In the first case, the call setup delay (dial-tone delay, dialing time, and connect time) may be nearly equal to the length of time required to transmit the entire message. In the second case, when the user may desire a response within 5 s, for example, the call setup delay could well make this infeasible if it is greater than a few seconds, as it is today. Quick response time is not an uncommon

*Bell System Technical Reference, Data Communications Using the Switched Telecommunications Network, *PUB 41005* (Aug. 1970), 9.

TABLE 9.2   *Connect Time for DDD Calls[a]*

	CONNECT TIME (sec)	
AIRLINE DISTANCE (MILES)	Mean	Standard Deviation
0–180	11.1	4.6
180–725	15.6	5.0
725–2900	17.6	6.6

[a]Bell System Technical Reference, Data Communications Using the Switched Telecommunications Network, *PUB 41005* (Aug. 1970), 9.

requirement in computer-communication systems. In the first on-line airline reservations system, American Airlines' SABRE System, International Business Machines (IBM) was under contract to provide a system response time of less than 3 s for more than 90 per cent of the inquiries. The same is true for many computer-based inquiry systems today. In these situations, the user is forced to lease dedicated circuits—the speed of service of the dial telephone network today is unacceptably slow.

9.1.3.7   Impulse Noise from Electromechanical Switches.   One of the most important causes of errors in data transmission is impulse noise, which consists of relatively short (typically less than 4 ms) high-amplitude spikes, frequently occurring in bursts lasting more than 100 ms. There exist many sources of impulse noise both in the outside plant (lightning and line maintenance personnel) and in the central office, but certain types of electromechanical switchgear are a major cause of this noise. The vintage panel switching systems found in some metropolitan areas today create so much impulse noise as to be generally unsatisfactory for data transmission above 300 bps. Step-by-step switchgear (the oldest form of automatic telephone switching equipment, but still in wide use today, especially in the smaller central offices) is also frequently responsible for the generation of unacceptable amounts of impulse noise. Crossbar systems and electronic switching systems, by contrast, are almost always satisfactory in this regard. Sometimes data transmission users served by a panel or step-by-step central office can obtain a remote exchange (RX) line to an adjacent crossbar or ESS office; when this is physically or economically infeasible, considerable user unhappiness may result. The panel systems and many of the older step-by-step systems are being gradually phased out of the telephone network—frequently to be replaced by an electronic switching system—but this process will take several decades for completion.

9.1.3.8 Line Turnaround Delay. The local distribution portion of the switched telephone network consists of two-wire transmission facilities; however, the long-haul transmission portion of the network is composed of multichannel carrier facilities (generally cable or microwave) that are always four-wire in nature. Where the two-wire local loop joins the four-wire long-distance trunk at the central office, a connecting circuit (hybrid coil) is required. For proper operation, the impedance of the local loop must be matched through the use of a balancing network; but the loop impedance is generally not precisely known, and it varies somewhat with ambient temperature and with different equipment attached to the loop, so a precise impedance match is not possible. Any mismatch causes signal reflections and results in echoes on the line. Since echoes with a round-trip delay of more than about 45 ms are very annoying in voice telephone conversation, an echo suppressor is inserted in long trunk channels (virtually all circuits over 1500 miles in length, and often in circuits as short as 300 miles). The echo suppressor operates by sensing the presence of human speech in one direction on a channel and blocking the reverse transmission path for the duration of that speech; full-duplex data transmission on such a channel is therefore impossible with the echo suppressor in operation. Half-duplex data transmission can take place, but a difficulty remains. The echo suppressor requires up to 100 ms to "turn around" (i.e., to permit transmission in the opposite direction). This line turnaround delay significantly reduces data system throughput, especially in those data transmission applications in which the transmitting station is sending short blocks of data and must await receipt of an acknowledgement or request for retransmission from the remote station after each block.

To permit full-duplex transmission on the telephone network, or to avoid the difficulties in half-duplex transmission, the echo suppressor on a data circuit may be disabled by the transmission of an audio tone of proper frequency. The disabling process requires 400 ms, however, and must be repeated if data transmission over a channel is subsequently interrupted for more than 50 to 100 ms. In certain applications this delay may measureably reduce effective channel throughput. A more important difficulty associated with disabling the echo suppressor, however, is that twice-reflected echoes may reach the receiving data terminal as unwanted noise, and may cause substantial data errors if the time delay is significant and the echo is of sufficient amplitude.

9.1.3.9 Inadequate Variety of Channel Bandwidths. To achieve substantial economies in transmission, intercity circuits in the telephone and telegraph networks are derived using multichannel carrier systems (employing microwave, cable, or open wire transmission media) rather than giving each circuit an actual "copper connection," as is done with local loops. As noted earlier, the vast bulk of the carrier systems in operation today uses frequency-division multiplexing (FDM) techniques, "stacking" small-bandwidth channels to form a hierarchy of larger channels for long-haul transmission. Thus we obtain the channel bandwidths available from the common carriers today: telegraph-grade channels of a few hundred hertz bandwidth, voice-grade channels of nominal 4-kHz bandwidth, and broadband channels of 48-, 240-, and 960-kHz bandwidth. Since these are analog channels, modems must be used for data transmission, and the combination of channel bandwidth and modem characteristics determines the available data transmission speed for each channel, as shown in Table 9.1.

Many users may have requirements for data transmission at speeds other than this limited assortment. When this occurs, several alternatives may be open to the user and his equipment supplier, all of them with undesirable economic consequences: (1) If an intermediate-sized channel is needed, the user can obtain the next larger size and use less than its full capacity; the waste here is obvious. (2) If the cost of using only part of a larger channel is excessive, or if a larger channel is not available (as, for example, if data transmission above 230.4 kbps is contemplated), the user can transmit his data at a lower speed matched to the next smaller channel. Anticipating this outcome, the data terminal manufacturer may design his device to operate at the lower speed, although it is technologically capable of operation at a higher speed. The user may thus pay significant opportunity costs in the end, through inefficient use of his data terminal equipment. (3) To a limited degree, a user can press the capacity of a channel toward its theoretical limit through the use of more sophisticated modems, which use multilevel encoding and line-equalizing techniques to achieve more bits per hertz of bandwidth; however, such modems are too costly for many applications, and also suffer from a higher error rate due to their greater sensitivity to noise and to time-varying channel characteristics.

All three difficulties could be alleviated through the provision by the carriers of a greater variety of analog-channel bandwidths or by the use of time-division multiplexing (TDM) to provide digital channels in a variety of transmission speeds. Incorporating greater bandwidth flexibility into the analog telephone plant would be exceedingly cumbersome at best, so for the existing carriers the use of TDM appears to offer the most promise for the future. The new specialized carriers, being unconstrained by an existing plant, plan to utilize both approaches toward meeting user requirements for a variety of data transmission speeds—although in the long run the use of TDM will probably prove to be the most cost-effective alternative, due to its inherent flexibility; Datran will use TDM exclusively in its planned network.

9.1.3.10 Cumulative Buildup of Noise with Analog Repeaters. Today's analog communication facilities tend to cause errors during the transmission of data to a greater degree than would digital transmission facilities. All signals lose power as they pass through a transmission medium, and must be amplified at regular intervals to restore their strength. An *analog* network employs linear (proportional) amplifiers for this purpose; along with the desired signal, all spurious noise is cumulatively amplified and, as a result, the data error rate increases exponentially with distance. On the other hand, a *digital* network uses nonlinear regenerative repeaters that respond only to pulses and thus cannot be used on analog waveforms. Since regenerative repeaters do not pass noise below a given intensity level, noise in such a system is not cumulative; and data errors increase linearly, rather than exponentially, with distance. Therefore, improved data-transmission error performance may be obtained in digital as opposed to analog carrier systems [4].

9.1.3.11   Variable Routing of Switched Call.   To ensure the availability of a through trunk line, even during periods of peak traffic, the long-distance dial telephone network is designed with a hierarchy of switching exchanges providing alternative paths for calls between local exchanges. During normal periods long-distance calls are routed directly through the calling party's local exchange, through two or three toll centers, and then through the local exchange of the called party. However, during periods of heavy network utilization when direct trunk lines are busy, calls may be routed through a series of switching centers, perhaps as many as eight under the busiest conditions. Although this alternative routing capability of the network tends to reduce the amount of total plant required to handle peak traffic loads, it causes certain problems when data are transmitted over the dial network.

First, the error rates tend to increase during periods of high traffic, since calls, during these hours, tend to pass through a larger number of exchanges and trunk circuits and over greater distances than ordinarily. Second, since plant facilities vary widely in terms of age and type of equipment, consecutive calls traversing different paths between the same pair of points encounter channels with substantially different transmission characteristics. Therefore, modems operating above 2000 bps on the DDD network must incorporate costly automatic equalization circuitry to cope with the range of attenuation and delay distortion.

9.2 PLANNED EVOLUTION OF TODAY'S NETWORKS FOR DATA TRANSMISSION

9.2.1 Evolution of the Telephone Network for Data Transmission

As discussed earlier, most present data transmission services are provided over switched analog voice telephone facilities. These channels are less than ideal for data transmission, and considerable effort has been expended in developing modem equipment capable of compensating for those channel parameters (e.g., amplitude and delay distortion, nonlinearities, and frequency offset) which interfere with the transmission of data. The Bell System, however, has recognized that these measures represent only a temporary expedient; and, in the long term, *digital* transmission facilities (using non-linear, regenerative pulse transmission and time-division multiplexing) will more efficiently provide the nation's data transmission services. Digital transmission, which in many instances has advantages for voice as well as data, reduces the effect of circuit noise, substantially increases the bit rate possible on a given transmission medium, and simplifies the mixing of various kinds of services (such as data, voice, and video) to minimize total costs [5].

The first digital carrier system was introduced by Bell in 1962, and is used to provide 24 voice channels over two wire-pairs for short-haul interexchange trunks (less than 50 miles in length), usually located in metropolitan areas. This T-1 carrier uses pulse code modulation (PCM) to convert the analog voice signals into 64-kbps bit streams, and time-division multiplexing (TDM) to combine 24 such signals into a 1.544-Mbps bit stream for transmission over the line. The system offers a cost advantage over a bundle of 24 individual wire pairs for interexchange channels longer than 6 to 7 miles; and it greatly increases the capacity of existing buried cables—thus allowing the expansion of telephone service without digging up the streets to install more cable. At the end of 1971, approximately 15 million channel miles of T-1 were in service (with an average circuit length of 12 miles), making T-1 a small but growing percentage of the overall telephone network.

The T-1 carrier's usefulness is not, of course, restricted to voice communications. Through the use of a data multiplex unit, the T1DM, twenty-three 56-kbps synchronous digital data channels can be derived from the T-1 line. These 56-kbps channels can be used to transmit customer data at that speed, or they can be subdivided to create smaller channels; AT&T plans to develop submultiplex equipment that will provide either five 9.6-kbps, ten 4.8-kbps, or twenty 2.4-kbps channels from each 56-kbps channel [6]. The T-1 line can also be used be used for data transmission at speeds above 56 kbps, although there is less demand at present for higher speeds. Interface equipment has been available for several years to derive a single asynchronous 513-kbps data channel from a T-1 line, or two 256-kbps channels, and equipment will soon be available to enable data transmission at 1.344 Mbps over the T-1 line.

Since T-1 carrier is limited to short-haul applications, nationwide digital transmission capabilities will not be available to the data communications user until suitable long-haul carrier systems are also available. From the telephone company's point of view, there is another—and more compelling—reason for the development of such long-haul, high-capacity digital systems. The Bell System appears to be firmly committed to the future of its fledgling Picturephone service. Picturephone was first introduced on an intracity basis in 1970, and limited intercity service was scheduled to begin in 1971; by 1980,

Bell expects to have 500,000 Picturephone sets in service, interconnected on a nationwide basis.* Although the Picturephone station transmits and receives analog signals (both video and audio), for distortion-free long-distance transmission these signals are encoded into digital form at the local central office, then combined using TDM, and transmitted over a digital carrier system.**

Several types of long-haul, high-capacity digital carrier systems are currently in different stages of development. The T-2 carrier system, which began to be introduced into the telephone network in 1972, operates at 6.3 Mbps on paired-wire cables up to 500 miles in length, and provides 96 voice channels or one Picturephone channel. Three "hybrid" transmission systems are also being developed to derive digital channels from existing analog transmission media: The *digits-on-coax* system will use one master-group on an L-4 or L-5 analog coaxial-cable carrier system to provide a 13.3-Mbps channel capable of carrying two T-2 bit streams over a 4000-mile distance [7]. Similarly, the *digits-on-radio* system will use one radio channel of a conventional TD-2 microwave system to provide a 20.2-Mbps digital channel capable of carrying three T-2 bit streams [8]. Finally, the Data Under Voice (DUV) system will use the lower baseband of a microwave radio channel to carry a 1.5-Mbps (T-1) bit stream [6]. Since each such radio channel can accommodate a 1.5-Mbps stream, a fully developed TD/TH microwave system can carry up to 18 Data Under Voice channels for a total of 27 Mbps. The DUV

---

*Intercity service was to have begun in 1971 with the interconnection of three cities—New York, Chicago, and Pittsburgh. Expansion of the service would take place first by creating a regional network interconnecting cities along the Boston–Washington corridor, then—toward the mid-1970s—by forming additional regional networks interconnecting "communities of interest," such as Los Angeles–San Francisco and Dallas–Houston. Nationwide Picturephone service would subsequently be provided by interconnecting the several regional networks via AT&T's planned domestic communications satellite.

At this time, the implemementation plan for Picturephone service is behind schedule due to several factors. Generally poor telephone service in Manhattan led the New York State Public Service Commission to deny AT&T's application to offer the service in New York City, the nation's key Picturephone market, until plain old telephone service was up to par. This, plus the economic slump at the time the service was being introduced in Pittsburgh and Chicago, reduced the rate of Picturephone installation well below AT&T's initial estimates. There is, in fact, the possibility that Picturephone service may be too large a quantum jump in communications technology and cost for the business consumer —and thus the "by-product" data services, which are dependent upon the success of Picturephone, may be jeopardized.

**Although analog in nature, Picturephone signals are ill-suited for long-haul transmission through the use of FDM carrier systems. Unlike voice signals, which are highly random and thus create an evenly distributed energy spectrum when combined together using FDM, video Picturephone signals are highly repetitive (at the scan rate) and concentrate their energy at discrete frequencies. Use of FDM carrier to transmit such signals —without creating excessive intermodulation distortion—would require highly linear modulation and amplification of the multiplexed signals, and would thus be costly and inefficient.

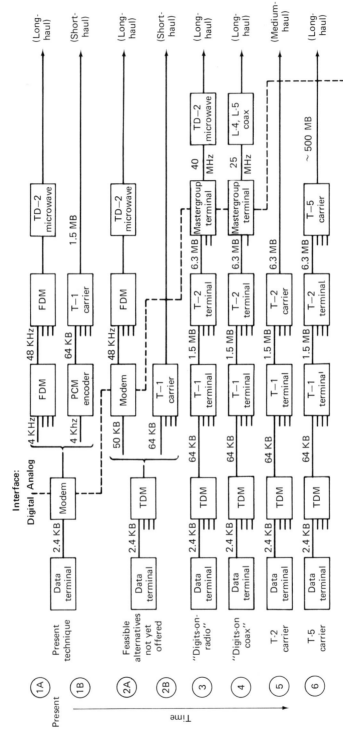

FIGURE 9.3 Expected evolution of digital data transmission in the telephone network.

310

channels will be the primary intercity digital data transmission facility for the foreseeable future. These systems will begin service in 1974. In addition, during the late 1970s, all-digital coaxial cable and waveguide systems (T-5 and WT-4) with several hundred megabits per second capacity are expected to be introduced into the network.

Figure 9.3 shows the expected evolution of digital data transmission as these all-digital and hybrid digital–analog transmission systems are gradually introduced into the telephone network. It can be seen that, over time, the locus of the digital–analog interface shifts away from the user and toward the backbone transmission plant, until finally end-to-end all-digital transmission is available—first, for short-haul links, then for medium- and long-haul circuits. Both systems 1A and 1B, in use today, are equivalent from the user's standpoint; with either he needs a modem at his data terminal location, and suffers all the shortcomings of the present analog telephone network. Both systems 2A and 2B are feasible with today's technology, but neither is presently offered by the telephone companies. With each, the modem (2400 bps in this example) on the user's premises would be eliminated, error rates would be reduced, and transmission costs (excluding the cost of the TDM unit itself) could be lower by a factor of approximately 2 to 20 times (due to greater bandwidth efficiency), for 2A and 2B, respectively. System 2B could only be used for short-haul circuits where T-1 carrier is presently installed, but for many user applications, this would pose no handicap. Systems 3, 4, 5, and 6 are planned for future implementation, and are discussed above.

These various digital transmission systems, together with digital end links (local loops) to the users and appropriate switching equipment as required, will enable the telephone company to offer a variety of end-to-end digital data channels. No such channel offerings are available today; but in 1970 AT&T announced its plans to construct a digital data network serving most major cities [9]. This network would initially, in early 1974, provide *private-line* channels operating at four different data speeds (2.4, 4.8, 9.6, and 56 kbps) with a 10^{-7}-bit error rate; at the outset AT&T plans to provide this service in and between New York City, Philadelphia, Boston, Chicago, and Washington, D.C. By the end of 1974 it is expected that 24 cities will be served, and by 1976 the number of cities will have grown to approximately 96. "Soon after that" (probably several years later) a *switched* digital service is planned, with features such as a variety of data speeds, full-duplex transmission, fast call setup time, and short charging intervals [9, 10]. During the same time frame, Bell also plans to offer high-speed switched digital data transmission over its Picturephone channels as this latter network is gradually implemented. In the early years of the service, a data rate of 460.8 kbps will be possible on Picturephone channels.

Bell appears to be more firmly committed to Picturephone than to the provision of new data communication services. Although we may debate the socioeconomic merits of Picturephone,* nonetheless it seems clear that this service will have a beneficial fallout for data communications. It appears unlikely that in the absence of Picturephone the digital transmission facilities discussed above would have been developed or planned for installation as rapidly as has occurred. Also, the spector of competition from new specialized data-oriented common carriers cannot be discounted as a factor motivating Bell's current planning.

In any event, as digital facilities are introduced into the telephone network, efforts will continue toward improving the characteristics of the conventional analog voice network for the handling of data transmission. This will remain quite important even after the major metropolitan areas on the U.S. mainland are interconnected with digital transmission facilities, since data communications users in other countries and in the smaller cities and towns of the United States will, for decades, rely upon ordinary voice channels—the only circuits available to them.

9.2.2 Evolution of the Western Union Network for Data Transmission

The Western Union Telegraph Company presently provides a variety of message–data transmission services largely over its own transcontinental microwave network and a series of circuit- and message-switching centers. Building upon this network, the telegraph company plans to become "the nation's number one source of electronic data communications."

Western Union's present circuit-switched services include the telegraph-grade teletypewriter exchange services—Telex and TWX (acquired from AT&T in 1971)—and Broadband Exchange, which is a circuit-switched four-wire service designed for medium-speed data transmission. The telegraph company also offers several store-and-forward message-switching services—Infocom (Information Communications) and Sicom (Securities Industry Communications)—that, at the time of this writing, are used solely to provide corporate users with *private* message systems over shared facilities. In addition, the company operates a store-and-forward service called TCCS (Telex Computer Communications Service) that enables Telex teletypewriter terminals to transmit "broadcast" messages to multiple addressees, and to send messages from Telex to TWX terminals (and ultimately vice versa). Finally, Western Union leases telegraph-grade, voice-grade, and wideband channels similar to those offered by the telephone companies.

Despite the fact that most of the signals carried over Western Union's network are digital in nature (record message information rather than voice

---

*Considering the huge investment required for this service and the limited sector of the population that will be able to benefit from it, Picturephone has been referred to by pundits as "the SST of the communications industry."

or video signals), the network itself is analog (linear repeaters and frequency-division multiplexing). To more efficiently handle the digital signals generated by message data traffic, Western Union plans to gradually introduce digital transmission/multiplexing and other data-oriented features into the network.

In the long term, Western Union's network is expected to include a variety of facilities—both digital and analog microwave radio relay routes, both time-division and frequency-division multiplexing equipment, low-speed data concentrators, computer-controlled circuit-switching equipment, and message-switching computer centers. These transmission and switching facilities will enable the telegraph company to provide public circuit-switched and message-switched data communication services, and private switching networks for business and government users, as well as private-line data channels; furthermore, Western Union can interconnect its public and private switched data networks to enhance the utility of them all. This is shown schematically in Fig. 9.4.

The Western Union network will ultimately provide circuit-switched end-to-end digital channels ranging in speed from 75 bps to 50 kbps, various store-and forward message-switching services, and private-line digital data services operating asynchronously at 0 to 1200 bps, and synchronously at 2400, 4800, 9600, and 50,000 bps.

9.2.2.1 Western Union Transmission Plans. Either digital or analog carrier systems (modulation–multiplexing) may be used, with varying degrees of efficiency, to transmit signals that originated in either analog or digital form.* Table 9.3 compares the efficiencies of the two approaches for both analog and digital input signals [11]. From the table it can be seen that 1800 voice channels can be provided with analog (FDM) multiplexing over a 6-GHz microwave radio beam, whereas only 288 voice channels (digitized using pulse code modulation) can be transmitted using digital multiplexing over the same radio beam using a 20-Mbit total data rate.

On the other hand, it is evident from the table that for the transmission of digital input signals ranging from 75 bps to 50 kbps a larger number of channels can be obtained using digital rather than analog carrier systems. Where cable transmission media are available, substantially higher-speed bit streams may be transmitted (because coaxial cable has more usable

---

*Digital microwave carrier systems consist of time-division multiplexing equipment, digital modulation equipment, and microwave radio transmitters and receivers. The TDM equipment combines the data signals from a number of low-speed channels by interleaving these digital pulse streams to form a single high-speed pulse stream. The modulator then impresses the high-speed digital bit stream upon a super-high frequency (SHF, commonly known as microwave) carrier signal, which is transmitted over line-of-sight path to the next microwave repeater station. Conventional analog microwave systems require that data traffic be converted into analog form (e.g., audible tones), which is then combined using frequency-division multiplexing equipment, impressed upon the microwave carrier, and transmitted.

TABLE 9.3   *Comparison of the Number of Channels Provided Over*
a 6-GHz Microwave Radio Link with Analog
and Digital Multiplexing[a]

Type of Channel	*Analog Multiplex*	*Digital (20 Mbps) (operational)*	*Digital (40 Mbps) (operational)*	*Digital (120 Mbps) (experimental)*
Voice (4-kHz)	1,800	288	576	1,728
data:				
50 kbps	150	288	576	1,728
2400 bps	1,800[b]	4,608	9,216	27,648
110 bps	36,000	92,160	184,320	552,960
75 bps	54,000	138,240	276,480	729,340

[a]Source: Western Union Telegraph Company.
[b]Signal loading considerations actually limit the number of data channels to well under 1800.

bandwidth), and the tradeoff swings even more in favor of the digital multiplexor; in fact, in most cases where coaxial cable is available, it will be more economic to transmit *all* traffic, including voice and video, in digital form.

To handle both digital and analog traffic, Western Union plans to add digital carrier systems to its present facilities. (The company's present intercity transmission plant consists of its own transcontinental microwave system and wideband channels leased from AT&T. At present all microwave radios are operating with FDM baseband channels.) Two basic approaches will be used. The first approach, used over routes with light traffic loads, will employ hybrid transmission (see Fig. 9.5a). The same 6-GHz band microwave FM radio formerly used to transmit 1200 FDM-FM voice channels will be modified to carry a 6.3-Mbps digital signal in the lower half of the baseband and a 600 voice-channel FDM mastergroup in the upper half of the band. At the time of writing, the first Western Union hybrid radio route was under construction between Atlanta and Cincinnati.

As additional route capacity is needed beyond that of a single hybrid radio, a second radio channel sharing the same facilities and antennas will be added to existing microwave routes. Western Union has termed this phase of the system expansion *digital overbuild* (see Fig. 9.5b). This digital radio will initially have a capacity of 20 Mbps, although expansion to as high as 40 Mbps may be possible using sophisticated modulation and detection schemes. The initial sections of Western Union's digital overbuild will interconnect New York City, Washington, D.C., and Chicago.

9.2.2.2   Western Union Switching Plans.   To make possible the future provision of more efficient and flexible switched data transmission services,

315

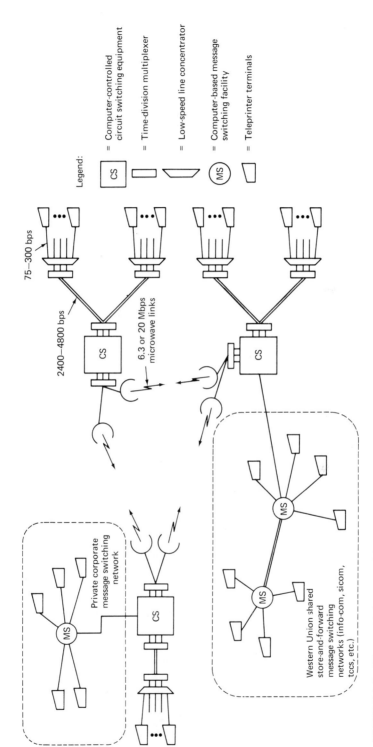

Legend:

CS = Computer-controlled circuit switching equipment

= Time-division multiplexer

= Low-speed line concentrator

MS = Computer-based message switching facility

= Teleprinter terminals

75–300 bps

2400–4800 bps

6.3 or 20 Mbps microwave links

Private corporate message switching network

Western Union shared store-and-forward message switching networks (info-com, sicom, tccs, etc.)

FIGURE 9.4   Western Union record/data network.

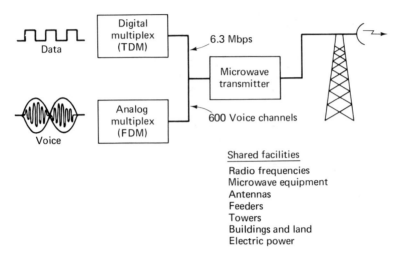

FIGURE 9.5a   Hybrid microwave system.

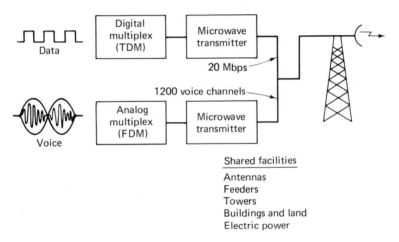

FIGURE 9.5b   Digital overbuild microwave system.

the telegraph company has begun the installation of new electronic circuit-switching equipment—the Electronic Data Switching system (EDS) developed by Siemens. This equipment will have two important features that will enhance the utility of the Western Union network for handling digital data. First, the switches will operate under stored program control, similar to the electronic switching systems (ESS) of the telephone companies.* Features

*Since the Western Union Network incorporates only a few hundred switching centers, whereas the telephone network (both Bell and independent) incorporates more than

to be provided through program control include the following:

1. *Camp-on and ringback.* A calling subscriber can hold (*camp-on*) a busy called-party line until the called line becomes idle, or the caller can be rung back at that time.
2. *Quick line.* A subscriber can be connected to a single terminal of his choice simply by initiating a service request.
3. *Abbreviated dialing.* Abbreviated dialing will be provided on either a one- or two-digit basis.
4. *Call forwarding.* Incoming calls to a terminal may be rerouted to another terminal (e.g., if the primary terminal is temporarily out of service).
5. *Scheduled calling.* Preprogrammed connections may be set up automatically, e.g., for periodic polling of terminals.
6. *Restricted address.* Subscribers in a particular group may be restricted to access only other subscribers in their group. *Escape codes* would be required for accessing subscribers outside of the group.

The second significant feature of the Western Union circuit-switching equipment is the use of two switching matrices, one for digital data traffic, and the other for analog signals. The digital switching network will use solid-state time-division switching; for analog signals, space-division switching is more economical and will be employed.

To connect subscriber terminals with the circuit-switching centers, versatile line concentrators will be employed. These concentrators, operating under the control of the stored-program control unit located at the switching center, will provide terminations for analog and digital signals from a variety of terminal types.

9.2.3 Network Trends

As we have discussed, both AT&T and Western Union are gradually introducing digitally oriented facilities into their respective networks, and are in the process of introducing new data transmission service offerings built around these facilities. The principal motivation for AT&T's introduction of digital facilities is to reduce voice transmission costs, in the case of local interexchange channels (where T-1 digital carrier is widely used), and to obtain satisfactory long-haul transmission of Picturephone signals at reasonable cost. The transmission of computer data has not played an important

---

20,000 switching centers, Western Union will complete conversion of its network to stored-program control well before the telephone companies (conversion of telephone company exchanges is not scheduled for completion before the year 2000).

role in shaping the telephone company's physical plant—despite all the ballyhoo about the growth of data transmission, in the past data has been a relatively small element in total traffic and telephone company revenues. Customer requirements must reach significant proportions before the telephone company responds. Data traffic is only beginning to reach those proportions, and thus the long lead times common in the telephone industry place data-oriented transmission services several years into the future.

Western Union has a greater motivation than AT&T to employ digital facilities—most of the company's traffic is digital in nature. Thus the company may be expected to move more quickly than AT&T in introducing data-oriented services. The limited resources of the telegraph company may, however, limit its ability to provide data services as widely and as dependably as Bell.

Since telecommunications common carriage is generally considered to be a natural monopoly, over the years few new firms have proposed to offer services complementing or competing with those of the established carriers in the United States. Thus when the Federal Communications Commission authorized a new "specialized common carrier" to compete with Bell and Western Union in providing intercity communications service, and subsequently made a general policy decision in favor of the entry of additional specialized carriers, the action was considered unprecedented. In the following sections we discuss these new carriers, their planned service offerings, and the short- and long-term effects of their entrance onto the U.S. communications scene.

9.3   ENTRY OF NEW SPECIALIZED CARRIERS

9.3.1   Introduction

In 1969 the Federal Communications Commission approved the application of a small new company to lease microwave communications channels to the public between Chicago and St. Louis. This sounds like an innocuous enough proposal, but the FCC's decision startled the communications industry; within a year the Commission was flooded with more than 1700 new microwave station applications by dozens of firms proposing to construct some 40,000 route miles of new common-carrier communication facilities throughout the country.

Many of the applicants are affiliated with the company that started it all, Microwave Communications, Inc. (MCI), and propose to offer similar services to the public in different areas of the country. Dedicated point-to-point communication channels of various types and bandwidths will be leased to subscribers, "customized" for use in transmitting voice, data, teletype, facsimile, remote metering, or other types of electrical signals between business offices, industrial and educational facilities, and government agencies.

Many of the remaining applicants propose MCI-like "private line" services, but two other types of specialized carrier systems, of perhaps greater interest to the data communications user, have also been proposed. First, the Data Transmission Company (Datran), a subsidiary of University Computing Company, proposes to construct and operate a coast-to-coast all-digital microwave system with computer-controlled switching centers along the route, which will be dedicated to providing both dial-up and private line circuits exclusively for data transmission. Second, several companies are, at this writing, planning to file applications with the FCC for authorization to provide data transmission services using existing private line facilities and a store-and-forward switching technique developed under the auspices of the Advanced Research Projects Agency (ARPA) of the Defense Department. The feasibility of this technology, called "packet switching," has been clearly demonstrated in an experimental nationwide network, which has been in operation since 1970 and today serves more than thirty universities and other ARPA contractors. (The ARPA network and packet switching technology are explained in greater detail in Chapter 13.)

Having approved the first small specialized carrier in 1969, and having subsequently been inundated with applications for similar but larger and overlapping systems, the FCC recognized the need for further examination of the board policy and procedural issues involved. Therefore, in 1970 the Commission initiated a public inquiry concerning the desirability of authorizing specialized carriers and the development of guidelines for the establishment and operation of such carriers. The outcome of the Commission's policy-making effort (discussed in more detail later in this chapter) was to permit virtually free entry of competing specialized common carriers, with only limited checks on the financial and technical competence of each applicant. As will be seen shortly, the new specialized carriers plan to offer a variety of data-oriented communication services (and certain other types of communication services as well), which promise to be more cost effective than the common-carrier services available today; this new competition will also likely stimulate the telephone companies and Western Union to give greater attention to their data communication customers and to upgrade and expand their data service offerings.

The specialized carrier networks, other than the packet switching networks, are largely based on the construction and use of microwave transmission facilities. The following section explains how this technology led to the emergence of the specialized-carrier concept.

9.3.2 Use and Regulation of Microwave

Microwave radio is one of several different intercity transmission media used by the telephone companies and Western Union (the other principal transmission media being multipair and coaxial cable). Developed during World War II for antiaircraft radar purposes, it quickly became a vital component of the backbone long-distance telephone network.* In addition, the use of microwave transmission makes it possible for organizations other than the telephone company to install and operate intercity communications systems— for example, "miscellaneous microwave carriers" now transmit one-way video signals to distant television broadcast stations and CATV systems. Use of buried or aerial cable, the only alternatives before the advent of microwave, was (and still is) usually a practical impossibility for such organizations —and for private users—due to the high investment costs and the need to obtain rights-of-way along the entire intercity route. It was the availability of microwave transmission technology that enabled both MCI and Datran to consider the construction of specialized common-carrier microwave systems and to submit proposals to the FCC.

The FCC, which supervises the use of microwave radio in the United States,** initially limited the use of this medium to the established communications common carriers. In 1959, in what has become known as the *Above 890* decision, the FCC concluded that any communications user could also construct and operate its own private microwave system, and that certain restricted classes of user organizations (state and municipal agencies, regulated public utilities, and right-of-way companies such as railroads and pipelines) could share the use of a single system. Shortly thereafter numerous private microwave systems were constructed—largely by those organizations with sharing privileges—for purposes of voice, data, and telegraph communications, remote metering, supervisory control, and signaling.

The major prerequisites for the construction of a private microwave system are heavy demand for point-to-point communications capacity over

*Microwave frequencies (roughly 10^9 to 30×10^9 Hz, or 1 to 30 GHz) are particularly suitable for high reliability point-to-point communications for two reasons: microwave signals can be focused into narrow beams that require little transmitter power, so the same frequencies can be used by adjacent systems without causing mutual interference; and such frequencies offer substantial usable bandwidth—enough for the transmission of several thousand multiplexed voice-bandwidth signals over a single microwave radio link.

A typical microwave system involves a series of relay towers, spaced some 20 to 30 miles apart, each within line of sight of the next. Installation costs are low compared with the costs of laying coaxial cables underground or stringing cable from pole to pole, and the construction time is measured in months rather than years. Microwave is today the workhorse of long-haul communications, providing some 70 per cent of all interstate voice-channel mileage.

**The FCC, under the Communications Act of 1934, regulates the use of the electromagnetic spectrum and licenses all nongovernment radio transmitters in the United States.

a given route, plus the financial and technical resources necessary for the system's construction and operation. The size of the capital investment alone would preclude most corporations from using private microwave systems for their communication needs. However, if a number of different users can share the same system, it may then become financially feasible. To provide the flexibility of a private microwave system, without burdening the user with heavy capital investment requirements and operating responsibilities, the specialized microwave common-carrier concept was proposed a decade ago.

9.3.3 Emergence of the Specialized-Carrier Concept

An application was filed with the FCC in 1963 for authorization to construct and operate a common-carrier microwave system between Chicago and St. Louis. The applicant, Microwave Communications, Inc.—a small new firm founded in Joliet, Illinois for this purpose—proposed to operate as a *specialized*, or alternatively, *customized* common carrier, offering a wide range of dedicated point-to-point or private-line channels for business communications, with more flexible service features and lower prices than those available from the existing carriers. (Table 9.4 traces the evolution of this specialized-carrier concept.)

In 1969, after an unusually long series of hearings and protracted deliberation and over the strong opposition of the established carriers, the Commission voted four to three in favor of MCI. Construction permits for the MCI microwave system were then issued, and later modified at MCI request (to permit the system to be reengineered and its capacity expanded beyond that contemplated in MCI's original 1963 application). MCI engaged Raytheon Company to provide the system on a turn-key basis, using 1800-channel

TABLE 9.4 *History of the Specialized-Carrier Concept*

Early	1940s	Microwave technology developed.
	1945	Microwave first used by communications common carriers.
	1959	FCC issues *Above 890* decision authorizing private microwave systems.
	1961	AT&T introduces bulk-discount private-line service (Telpak) to counter competition of private microwave.
December	1963	MCI files with FCC for authorization to construct Chicago–St. Louis common-carrier microwave system.
February	1966	FCC sets MCI application for hearing.
Spring	1967	FCC hearings on MCI application.
October	1967	FCC hearing examiner issues Initial Decision

TABLE 9.4   (Continued)

		approving MCI's application; established carriers appeal to the full Commission.
April	1968	Oral argument before the full Commission.
December	1968	Interdata Communications, Inc. files with FCC for authorization to construct MCI-like microwave system between New York City and Washington, D.C.
December	1968	President's Task Force on Communications Policy submits report endorsing specialized common-carrier concept.
February	1969	AT&T permits sharing of its voice-grade and telegraph-grade private-line services (sharing was a service feature previously proposed by MCI).
March	1969	AT&T announces Series 11,000 wideband private-line service largely designed to compete with MCI.
August	1969	FCC issues landmark decision granting MCI construction permits (6 years after MCI's original application).
September	1969	Established carriers petition FCC to reconsider its MCI decision.
September–December	1969	Four MCI affiliates file applications for various routes, and one non-MCI firm (New York-Penn Microwave Corp.) files for one of the same routes.
November	1969	Data Transmission Company (Datran), a subsidiary of University Computing Company, files application for nationwide common-carrier system using digital microwave and computer switching, designed exclusively for data transmission.
January	1970	FCC denies established carriers' petitions for reconsideration of its MCI decision.
February–March	1970	Nine more firms (one MCI affiliate, eight independent firms) file specialized-carrier applications.
March	1970	AT&T appeals FCC's MCI decision to the U.S. Court of Appeals (Washington, D.C., Circuit).
March	1970	MCI files with FCC to modify its construction permits for the Chicago–St. Louis system (largely to increase capacity).
April–June	1970	Twenty-one more firms (seven MCI affiliates, fourteen independent firms) file specialized carrier applications.
July	1970	FCC issues notice of inquiry and tentative rule making regarding specialized carriers (Docket No. 18920).
October	1970	FCC receives comments from over 150 interested parties in Docket 18920. Another MCI affiliate files specialized-carrier application.
December	1970	FCC receives reply comments in Docket 18920.
January	1971	FCC hears oral argument in Docket 18920.

TABLE 9.4   (Continued)

March	1971	Another MCI affiliate files specialized-carrier application.
March	1971	MCI and its affiliates, in a joint venture with Lockheed Aircraft Corporation, file FCC application for a domestic communication satellite system to complement MCI's proposed terrestrial microwave network.
May	1971	FCC issues First Report and Order in Docket 18920, giving overall policy approval of the specialized-carrier concept.
June	1971	FCC issues further notice of inquiry regarding allocation of frequencies for local distribution and quality and reliability of service.
July	1971	AT&T and Western Union withdraw their court appeals of the FCC's 1969 MCI decision.
July–August	1971	Three more specialized-carrier-route applications are filed.
August	1971	FCC receives comments from interested parties regarding local distribution and quality of service.
August	1971	Construction and system acceptance testing of MCI Chicago–St. Louis microwave system completed.
October	1971	FCC grants construction permits to Interdata Communications, Inc. for specialized carrier service between New York City and Washington, D.C.—the first grant under the Commission's new open-entry policy.
December	1971	The National Association of Regulatory Utility Commissioners (NARUC) and the Washington State Public Utility Commission appeal the FCC's June 1971 policy decision to the U.S. Court of Appeals.
January	1972	MCI files its first tariff and begins commercial specialized carrier service between Chicago and St. Louis.
April	1972	FCC grants construction permits to Datran for the western half (from Palo Alto, California, to Houston, Texas) of its network.
May–December	1972	FCC grants construction permits to all or portions of the following specialized carrier systems: Nebraska Consolidated Communications Corp. (Minneapolis to Houston); Western Telecommunications, Inc. (San Francisco to Seattle and Los Angeles to El Paso, Texas); Southern Pacific Communications Co. (Los Angeles to San Francisco); West Texas Microwave Co. (Ft. Worth to El Paso); MCI New York West, Inc.; MCI Michigan, Inc.; MCI New England, Inc.; MCI St. Louis-Texas, Inc.; MCI North Central States, Inc.; MCI Mid-Continent, Inc.; and MCI Texas East, Inc.

microwave equipment initially equipped with multiplex for 300 voice-grade channels or the equivalent in total bandwidth. Construction of the system was completed in 1971, and the first paying subscribers went on-line in January 1972.

During the two years following the authorization of the Chicago–St. Louis system, MCI and several dozen other companies filed applications for more than 40 intercity routes involving some 1900 microwave relay stations. (Table 9.5 details these applications, and Fig. 9.6 shows the five most extensive net-

TABLE 9.5   *Specialized-Carrier Applicants (As of January 1973)*

Company and Proposed Route	Date Filed	Number of Microwave Stations
MCI Affiliates		
Microwave Communications, Inc. (Chicago to St. Louis)	Approved	11
MCI (Extension of original system)	June 1970	20
MCI (Extension of original system)	July 1970	13
Interdata Communications, Inc. (New York City to Washington, D.C.)	Approved	13
MCI New York West, Inc.	Approved	73
MCI Pacific Coast, Inc.	November 1969	56
MCI North Central States, Inc.	Approved	18
MCI New England, Inc.	Approved	20
MCI Michigan, Inc.	Approved	27
MCI St. Louis-Texas, Inc.	Approved	42
MCI Texas East Microwave, Inc.	Approved	42
MCI Mid-Atlantic Communications, Inc.	April 1970	37
MCI Kentucky Central, Inc.	April 1970	34
MCI Texas-Pacific, Inc.	April 1970	64
MCI Mid-Continent Communications, Inc.	Portion approved	62
MCI Mid-South, Inc.	June 1970	48
MCI Indiana-Ohio, Inc.	July 1970	31
MCI Pacific Mountain States, Inc.	October, 1970	20
MCI Southeast Communications, Inc.	March 1971	72
	Total	703
Data Transmission Co. (Datran)		
35 major metropolitan areas, Boston to San Francisco	Western half approved	259
United Video, Inc.		
Chicago to Fort Worth–Dallas	Portion approved	104
Fort Worth–Dallas to Houston (East Texas Transmission Co.)	April 1970	5
Houston to New Orleans (KHC Microwave Corp.)	April 1970	24
New Orleans to Chicago	April 1970	69
	Total	202

TABLE 9.5   (Continued)

Company and Proposed Route	Date Filed	Number of Microwave Stations
Western Tele-Communications, Inc.		
San Diego to Seattle	Portion approved	26
Los Angeles to El Paso	Approved	18
Minneapolis–St. Paul to Sioux Falls, S.D.	June 1970	8
Sioux Falls, S.D., to Denver	June 1970	27
Denver to Kansas City	June 1970	32
Cedar Point N.M., to Albuquerque	July 1970	6
Sandia Crest, N.M., to Colorado Springs	July 1970	8
Denver to San Francisco	August 1970	25
Salt Lake City to Spokane and Portland	July 1971	22
Chicago to Omaha	August 1971	24
	Total	196
Southern Pacific Communications Co.		
San Diego to Seattle	Portion approved	55
St. Louis to Los Angeles	April 1970	95
	Total	150
Nebraska Consolidated Communications Corp.		
Minneapolis to Houston, Chicago,		
St. Louis, Atlanta, and Phoenix	Portion approved	149
New York-Penn Microwave Corp.		
New York to Chicago and Detroit	November 1969	67
Washington, D.C., to Boston	February 1970	22
	Total	89
CPI Telecommunications, Inc.		
Dallas to El Paso and Amarillo, Texas	Approved	31
Dallas to Houston, Beaumont, and		
San Antonio, Texas	Approved	26
Beaumont, Texas,to New Orleans	August 1971	21
	Total	78
Telephone Utilities Service Corp.		
Central Texas Region	June 1970	36
Associated Independent Telephone Microwave, Inc.		
Houston to New Orleans	June 1970	17
Microwave Transmission Corp. (Affiliated with Datran)		
Los Angeles to San Francisco	February 1970	15
	Grand Total*	1894

*Due to continuing changes in and expansion of the detailed system plans of many of the specialized carrier applicants, the exact total number of microwave stations is difficult to ascertain. Several route applications which were filed with the FCC and later withdrawn are omitted from this tabulation.

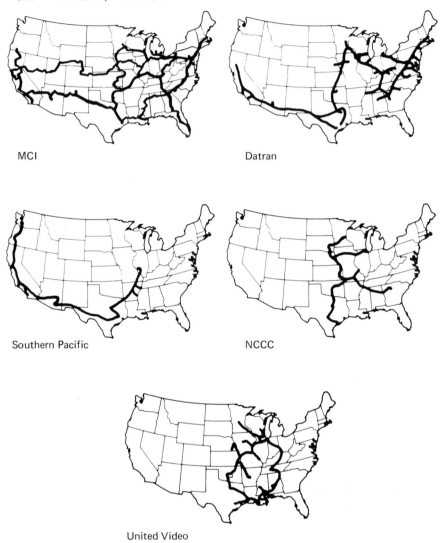

MCI

Datran

Southern Pacific

NCCC

United Video

FIGURE 9.6 Five most extensive specialized carrier proposals.

work proposals.) Several of the new applicants presently operate extensive microwave systems for their own private use or for carrying video signals to distant television broadcast stations or cable TV operators. Western Tele-Communications, Inc., for example, operates approximately 14,000 route miles of video relay microwave in 16 western states. The Southern Pacific Communications Co., another applicant, operates private microwave systems along the rail rights-of-way of its parent company, Southern Pacific Railway. Both applicants propose to use their existing facilities to offer common-carrier voice and data channels, thereby achieving economies for present and future subscribers.

Most of these specialized carriers, as previously mentioned, plan to offer a broad range of dedicated point-to-point channels for various communication requirements, including data transmission. However, their forte may well become the transmission of digital data (Datran, of course, will offer only data services), partly because of the shortcomings in the present telephone network when used for nonvoice communications. Let us now examine the specific nature of the common-carrier systems proposed by MCI (representative of the other private-line specialized carriers as well) and by Datran.

9.3.4 The MCI System

The MCI-affiliated companies are each proposing to build and operate separate but compatible regional microwave systems owned and operated locally. The MCI carriers plan to interconnect their systems and cooperate with each other to provide a nationwide private-line communications network. To plan and coordinate the development of this national network, a common-carrier service company called MCI Communications Corporation (formerly known as Microwave Communications of America, Inc.) was formed. This firm has an equity interest in each of the MCI carriers and provides them with a variety of services on a contractual basis: Microwave route engineering and frequency interference analysis, securing of lease options for microwave repeater sites, preparation of FCC license applications and supporting data, such as market studies, selection of and negotiation with equipment suppliers, supervision of system construction, and various advisory and information services. After the MCI carriers are in operation, MCI Communications Corporation will also provide them with national marketing and intercarrier technical coordination services—thus giving the customer a single point of contact wherever his communications requirements may be, and assuring that the overall network is operated in a compatible and integrated manner.

The MCI-carrier applicants intend to offer the following services and service features using their future nationwide network:

1. Dedicated (nonswitched, private-line) channels will be provided for the transmission of voice, data, facsimile, Teletype, telemetry, control, and video signals.
2. Digital and analog signal inputs will be accepted.
3. Data-transmission channels derived using time-division multiplexing (TDM) will be offered, with an error-rate objective two orders of magnitude better than that experienced on today's telephone network. Prices for such channels will be based upon actual data-transmission speed rather than channel bandwidth.

4. Multifunctional analog channels will be available in a wide variety of bandwidths (e.g., 200, 400, 600, . . . , 1000 Hz; 2, 4, 6, . . . , 16 kHz; 20, 24, 28, . . . , 48 kHz; 64, 80, 96, . . . , 240 kHz; and 288, 336, 384, . . . , 960 kHz).
5. A variety of channel arrangements will be offered: Simplex (one-way transmission), full duplex (two-way), and asymmetrical (two-way with different bandwidths in each direction of transmission).
6. Channels will be available on either a part-time (day or night) or full-time (24 h/day, 7 days/week) basis.
7. Customers will be permitted to share channels (e.g., resell unused portions of their channels).
8. Customers will be permitted to interconnect their own equipment or communication systems to MCI channels, using MCI tower and shelter space for their equipment if desired.
9. Rates will, in many cases, be substantially lower than those charged by the existing carriers for functionally equivalent service.

Although many of these features are entirely new, MCI emphasizes that the basic distinction between its proposed services and the ones available from the present carriers "is not the facility itself but the manner in which a customer may utilize it in order to provide a customized intracompany point-to-point communications system of his own design and capability." For example, free to choose among the above-listed features, a customer may lease channels of the exact bandwidth required, transmit any form of signal (voice, data, facsimile, etc.), arrange two-way channels with different bandwidths in each direction, use his own multiplex and terminal equipment, resell the unused portion of his channel to another organization, and so forth.

Since the MCI network is intended to serve a broad range of point-to-point business communication requirements and is not exclusively dedicated to data transmission, a variety of system design concepts and hardware configurations will be employed. The backbone microwave system will be primarily analog in nature with frequency-division multiplexing, because the largest share of the MCI-carriers' traffic is expected to be analog, at least in the early years of system operation. These analog FDM channels can, of course, be used for data transmission in the same way that today's telephone network is employed, through the customer's use of modems to convert his digital data into analog form. The microwave systems have been engineered by MCI to exceed the international CCIR transmission performance standards, which in turn equal or exceed those contained in the Bell System Practices and used as design objectives by AT&T.* Thus the transmission

*It is also interesting to note that the overall bandwidth efficiency of MCI's micro-microwave system will exceed that of many Bell System microwave routes in service today; MCI plans to use microwave equipment with a capacity of 1800 voice-grade channels per

parameters of MCI analog channels, such as faded and unfaded noise levels, envelope-delay distortion, and frequency response (attenuation distortion), should equal or exceed those of corresponding Bell channels. The reliability of MCI's microwave system (its freedom from outages due to equipment failures, microwave path fading, etc.) should also rival that of the established carriers,* since the MCI carriers are taking extensive precautions in this regard: all solid-state microwave and multiplex equipment, with high MTBF and low MTTR; redundant "hot standby" transmitters and receivers; one-for-one (one protection channel for each working channel) space diversity, or in a few cases frequency diversity, on all microwave hops to protect against fading; automatic fault alarm systems to notify maintenance personnel of system difficulties; and regional network control facilities to monitor circuit performance and reroute circuits affected by system outages.

In implementing the digital portion of its systems, MCI has several options available. Each would provide high-quality digital data circuits with error performance substantially better than that of the telephone network today, and the choice will primarily depend upon the volume of data traffic anticipated over a particular route within a given time frame. The first MCI system, from Chicago to St. Louis, may initially provide low- and medium-speed digital data channels through the use of 50-kbps-capacity TDM equipment, which would in turn employ a 50-kbit modem to transmit over a 48-kHz analog "group" channel. This relatively low-capacity "piggyback" approach, using TDM to subdivide a broadband FDM channel, corresponds to system 2A of Fig. 9.3, discussed previously, and offers several advantages in the early stages of the development of the MCI network: Initial TDM investment costs are low; only a modest amount of the microwave system's total bandwidth is "locked in" to data transmission exclusively; installation is straightforward, using off-the-shelf equipment; and flexible modular expansion is possible as data traffic grows (multiple 50-kbps TDM systems can be installed on separate group channels, or a higher-capacity TDM system can be installed using one or more supergroup channels).

The volume of data traffic in a few years along some of the MCI routes (especially the high-density routes such as between New York and Chicago)

---

radio beam (e.g., Raytheon KTR-3A equipment with this capacity has been installed on the initial Chicago–St. Louis route), whereas more than half of Bell's microwave routes use the older TD-2 systems with only 1200-channel capacity per radio beam.

*However, the reliability of end-to-end MCI service will be a function of several important variables in addition to the reliability of the backbone microwave system itself, such as the type and quality of local loops used (discussed subsequently) and the MCI-carriers' maintenance personnel and procedures. There is no reason why MCI could not equal or exceed the performance of the established carriers in these areas—certainly it has every incentive to try to do so—but at this point in time one can only speculate as to overall reliability.

may be sufficient to warrant the installation of a hybrid digital–analog microwave system, such as planned by Western Union and shown in Fig. 9.5a. In such a system a high-speed digital bit stream (6.3 Mbps in the Western Union case) from a hierarchy of TDM equipment would directly modulate a portion of the microwave baseband, with one or two FDM mastergroups in the remainder of the baseband. This approach would be more efficient and economical than the "piggyback" concept discussed above, if and when MCI had a need for the much greater digital capacity that it would offer— some 2500 data channels at 2400 bps, or some 40,000 channels at 150 bps. Finally, if MCI's data-channel requirements were ever to exceed the capacity of a hybrid microwave system, the company could employ the *digital-overbuild* concept shown in Fig. 9.5b. In a manner similar to that planned for installation at some point in time by all three of the other carriers— Bell, Western Union, and Datran—MCI would dedicate an entire microwave radio beam along one or more routes to digital transmission (i.e., MCI would then have two parallel but separate radio beams, one multiplexed using FDM and the other using TDM, sharing the same towers and antennas). This would provide a digital transmission capacity of 20 Mbps or more, which exceeds data traffic projections for the early years of the MCI network's operation, but may be required in the more distant future.

An important distinction between the specialized-common-carrier concept and the traditional telephone service philosophy is in the provision of local channels (called *local loops*) between the customer's premises and the carrier's microwave terminal. Whereas the telephone companies always provide complete end-to-end service, MCI originally proposed to build and operate only an intercity microwave system, leaving the tower-to-subscriber local loops to be filled in by the individual subscriber. Perhaps realizing the limited marketability of such an approach, MCI now proposes three options for local loops:

1. The needed channels (normally, ordinary telephone wire pairs) could be obtained by MCI from the local telephone company, on a contractual basis, and thus MCI could offer and take responsibility for complete end-to-end service. Alternatively, the customer might obtain such channels directly from the telephone company, but he would then have to deal with two organizations rather than one, and would encounter problems of divided maintenance responsibility and possibly increased costs. The former approach therefore appears preferable, and MCI has negotiated a contract with AT&T—patterned after the AT&T–Western Union contracts whereby Bell provides circuits for lease to Western Union customers—that makes local telephone channels available for use by MCI in providing end-to-end service. (It might appear that Bell would have little incentive to cooperate in providing local

distribution for a competing carrier, but the FCC has stated that it would require the telephone companies to furnish such service on a reasonable basis if requested; refusal to provide service would also raise antitrust questions.)

2. As a tariffed common-carrier service, MCI could furnish local loop channels itself. Radiated line-of-sight transmission would most likely be used, employing equipment such as short-range microwave, millimeter-wave, or infrared transceiver units that could be mounted on the subscriber's rooftop.* Additionally, where feasible—such as within a large office building or industrial park—cable transmission could be used, in lieu of or as an extension to the line-of-sight facilities.

3. The customer could provide his own local loops, using line-of-sight or cable transmission media, when his volume of traffic and other factors would make this economically attractive.

The flexibility inherent in this approach and the opportunity to take advantage of advanced means of short-haul transmission offer potentially important benefits for specialized carriers and their customers; however, at least in the short run, ensuring the availability of adequate and economical local loops poses a challenge for the new carrier applicants. This is discussed in more detail in Section 9.5.1.

The numerous specialized private-line carriers which are not affiliated with MCI are planning to construct systems basically similar to, and compatible with, MCI's. It takes little imagination to envision a future national network of interconnected carriers such as these, which will both complement and compete with the existing telephone network in providing a variety of communication services for data transmission and other purposes.

9.3.5 The Datran System

Datran's thinking is perhaps best understood in terms of the new communications technology it plans to use (whereas MCI, as we have seen, would employ more conventional hardware in an innovative way). Datran proposes to build and operate a nationwide, all-digital switched network that will

---

*Considerable interest has been expressed by MCI in the potential of millimeter-wave transmission for intracity carrier distribution; MCI has askêd the FCC to allocate the heretofore-unused 38.6- to 40-GHz frequency band for this purpose. Use of either millimeter-wave or infrared transmission (the latter requiring no FCC frequency assignment) would avoid the growing frequency congestion in the lower microwave portion of the spectrum. However, reliable operation at these frequencies is limited to very short per-hop distances (less than one-half mile for infrared, several miles for millimeter wave) due to the occurrence of atmospheric conditions such as precipitation and smog, which cause severe signal attenuation over long transmission paths.

initially interconnect subscriber data terminals in 35 cities.* The network, specifically designed and engineered for data transmission, was initially planned to consist of three distinct elements: a nationwide, high-capacity digital micro-wave trunking system laid out across the United States in the shape of a "lazy W" (see Fig. 9.6); computer-controlled switching centers initially arranged for circuit switching, but capable of message switching if the market requires it; and local distribution systems engineered in each of the 35 metropolitan service areas according to the special topographic, climatic, and subscriber characteristics of that area (as in the MCI network, combinations of short-haul microwave, cable, and infrared light would be used for local distribution) [5, 12].

9.3.5.1   System Features and Services.   Datran plans to phase in various data-oriented services and system features, as the market demand develops and within the constraints imposed by capital requirements and construction schedules. Initially the company plans to provide only private-line data transmission services, prior to completion of its switching system. As soon as practicable, circuit-switched service with the following characteristics would be introduced:

1. The capability of establishing, within 3 s, a switched point-to-point connection between two compatible terminals (terminals arranged to operate at the same data transmission speed—see below).
2. End-to-end digital channels, eliminating the need for a modem.
3. Full-duplex data transmission at speeds of 150, 4800, 9600, and 14,400 bps on a switched basis, and 19,200 and 48,000 bps on a private-line basis.
4. Likelihood of a subscriber encountering a "trunk busy" condition during the peak hour guaranteed less than 1 in 100 call attempts.
5. A mean error rate less than 1 bit in error per 10 million bits transmitted.
6. Manual or automatic addressing by the sender.
7. Abbreviated dialing (e.g., one- or two-digit "telephone" numbers).
8. Broadcast transmission of a message to up to six subscribers (with compatible terminals) simultaneously.

*University Computing Company, Datran's parent firm, first attempted to gain a foothold in the common-carrier data-transmission field in 1968, when the diversified computer company made a tender offer for 750,000 shares of the Western Union Telegraph Company's common stock. This move for potential control by UCC was successfully opposed by Western Union management; however, UCC was not deterred in its long-term aim of operating a common-carrier data-transmission system in the United States. University Computing Company formed a subsidiary, the Data Transmission Company (Datran), to apply for FCC authorization to become the nation's first common carrier devoted exclusively to data transmission.

9. Camp-on: when the called party is busy the call is held and the connection automatically established as soon as the line becomes free.
10. A separate flat charging rate for "local" and "regional" (long-distance) calls; i.e., charges are proportional to the length of a call, but other than the distinction between local- and regional-type calls, rates are *independent of distance.*
11. Minimum charge time of 6 s for dial-up calls [as opposed to the minimum of 3 min (1 min during late evening hours) on the telephone network].

Additional service features, using store-and-forward message-switching techniques, may be offered if the market demand is sufficiently large:

1. Code conversion between any two permissible formats.
2. Speed conversion between specified rates.
3. Expedited Information Transfer Service (EXIT), a store-and-forward message-switching service enabling the sender to specify the desired transit time for a message.
4. Other transmission speeds as required.

9.3.5.2 Backbone Transmission Trunking.   Datran's traffic and engineering studies indicate that the minimum-cost routing of its microwave links would consist of 259 microwave stations extending across the United States from San Francisco to Boston in the form of a "lazy W." Traffic studies also indicate that a trunking capacity of 20 Mbps, or 4000 channels each operating at 4800 bps, would suffice to meet anticipated requirements. Using off-the-shelf microwave equipment, with specially developed digital modulators, Datran has engineered a single radio beam (in each direction) microwave system with the required transmission capacity.

System specifications call for a high level of performance in terms of error rate and reliability. Whereas today's telephone plant, when functioning properly, provides an error rate on the order of 10^{-5}, Datran has designed its facilities to achieve an end-to-end bit error rate of 10^{-7}. An additional objective is to reduce system interruption (due to microwave path fading, equipment failure, maintenance procedures, etc.) to negligible levels.

To achieve a satisfactory error rate over long distances, the signal will be demodulated into a 20-Mbps baseband signal at each microwave repeater station, regenerated into a distortion-free and retimed bit stream, and remodulated for transmission to the next repeater. Through regeneration, the error rate can be improved by a factor of 100 over today's long-haul analog transmission systems.

Through the use of one-for-one space diversity* and "proven" microwave equipment, Datran expects to provide uninterrupted service 99.99 per cent of the time. Intuitively, one might consider it unlikely that a transcontinental microwave system, consisting of a single backbone trunk (without provision for alternative routing in case of catastrophic failure), could provide such a high level of reliability. However, experience suggests that Datran should be able to achieve its goal. Western Union has, for some years, operated a transcontinental microwave system, consisting of a single backbone trunk, without serious incident. Similarly, the Canadian telephone system, for a period of 7 years, operated with a single transcontinental microwave trunk (along the southern border of Canada), also without incident, Although guarantees against natural disasters cannot be made, experience with long-haul microwave systems and Datran's intention to use reliable solid-state equipment provide some assurance that catastrophic trunk system failure is unlikely, despite the absence of alternative routing facilities.

9.3.5.3 Multiplexing. Time-division multiplexing (TDM) will be used throughout the Datran network, rather than conventional frequency-division multiplexing (FDM), permitting the maximum quantity of data to be transmitted over the microwave links. In an all-digital network, TDM is used to interleave the lower-speed bit streams to form a single high-speed bit stream (e.g., 20 Mbits in the Datran system) that is synchronized so that the low-speed bit streams can be separated out at the receiving end. This 20-Mbit digital signal is regenerated at each microwave repeater station to minimize data errors *without demultiplexing of the signal.* With an FDM system, in contrast, multiple voice or data channels are each assigned different but adjacent (stacked) frequency bands, which are then raised to a higher frequency and transmitted over a single carrier channel. Regeneration of data signals at each microwave repeater would be prohibitively expensive with FDM, due to the need for demultiplexing of the radio beam, demodulation and regeneration of each individual data signal, and remodulation and remultiplexing for transmission to the next repeater.

Time-division multiplexing offers the additional advantages of flexibility in the mix of data speeds provided, greater utilization of low-cost and reliable digital integrated circuits—including medium- and large-scale integration

*Microwave path fading, which occurs when a portion of a microwave signal is reflected off some surface (e.g., the ground or a lake) and arrives at the receiving antenna 180° out of phase with the primary radio beam, is a statistical phenomenon caused primarily by weather changes. Since a severe fade will interrupt satisfactory signal transmission, most microwave systems employ either frequency or space diversity, in which a second channel is constantly available in the event that the working channel experiences a fade. Frequency diversity uses a second radio channel operating at a different frequency, since fading normally occurs at only one frequency at any given moment. Space diversity uses one transmitting antenna and two spatially separated receiving antennas. Fading will not occur at both receiving antennas simultaneously.

(MSI and LSI)—and simpler automated test and repair procedures (typically replacement of channel circuit cards). Also, as shown earlier in Table 9.3, use of TDM in an all-digital microwave system permits substantially more data channels to be carried on a single microwave radio beam.

Datran will offer three families of data channel speeds: a basic data rate of 4800 bps; multiples of the basic rate, such as 9600 and 14,400 bps, achieved by strapping together several 4800-bps ports; and subdivisions of the basic rate, such as 150 bps, derived through another level of time-division multiplexing. The speed of a subscriber's terminal will be determined by a plug-in oscillator in his digital control console and his local loop connection. A change from one speed to another will require only a minor wiring change.

9.3.5.4 Switching. Datran plans to ultimately use two levels of switching, termed a district exchange and a regional exchange. Subscribers will be connected, through a multiplexing hierarchy, to the nearest district exchange office; the regional exchange will provide network control through the assignment of interoffice trunks. Initially, only one switching center will handle the total traffic for all 35 cities served. At the next stage of development 10 district offices and 1 regional office will handle the total traffic load. Finally, each city served (ultimately, around 50) will have its own district office, interconnected through 5 regional centers (each serving 10 district offices). Briefly, the functions of the two switching levels are as follows:

District Office
1. Provides subscriber terminations.
2. Responds to all requests for service.
3. Verifies subscriber-to-subscriber speed compatibility.
4. Determines and establishes intraoffice connections.
5. Coordinates interoffice trunk assignments with the Regional Office.
6. Maintains records of subscriber calls for billing purposes.
7. Maintains statistical information for subsequent analysis.
8. Provides maintenance status and diagnostic information.

Regional Office
1. Maintains a dynamic record of network status.
2. Assigns trunks within its regional area.
3. Determines and establishes interoffice connections.
4. Establishes alternative connections as required.
5. Periodically collects network utilization information from the district offices.
6. Records statistical, maintenance, and diagnostic information for maintaining and improving network performance.

Designed to handle different usage patterns and a different type of signal, the Datran switching equipment differs from that used in the telephone system in a number of ways:

1. Whereas the telephone system uses electromechanical space-division switching matrices, even in most of the electronic switching systems planned for installation over the remainder of this century, Datran plans to employ solid-state time-division switching. In a TDM network, such as Datran's, time-division switching is lower in cost than space-division (fewer crosspoints are required), and small switching matrices may be readily dispersed throughout the network (as concentrators). Moreover, the solid-state nature of the switching matrix permits very short switching times and ultrahigh reliability.

2. Datran plans to use four-wire switching, rather than two-wire (as used in the telephone system), thus simplifying the provision of full-duplex channels.

3. The Datran switching system does not transmit direct current (dc) over customer loops, whereas the telephone system must do so to provide current to the carbon microphone in the telephone handset and to signal an off-hook condition (by the flow of current). Thus error-producing noise caused by the switching of dc current-carrying circuits is avoided in the Datran network.

4. Telephone switching systems use certain setup and check-out procedures, prior to turning a connection over to subscriber traffic, to verify that a good connection for a voice telephone conversation has been established. The attributes that need to be checked before turning a link over to data traffic are different. Datran thus plans to use more sophisticated methods of determining the actual condition of the link prior to transmission of data traffic.

5. Telephone switching systems use separate circuits at various voltage levels within the exchange for tone and ringing signals. Special care has to be taken to ensure that these signals get properly distributed without getting onto the talking pairs. In the planned Datran system the functions performed by tone and ringing signals are handled by digital messages that have ths same characteristics as the data traffic handled by the exchange, and thus no special separation procedures are required.

The numbering plan used in the Datran network will not be too dissimilar from the telephone-network numbering plan. The first three digits will indicate the city, and the last four digits will indicate a specific subscriber within that city. (A maximum of 9999 subscribers can be accommodated in any one city.)

Abbreviated dialing, using either one, two, three, or no digits, will also be provided. No-digit dialing would be a feature used by specialized network subscribers (such as users of credit-checking terminals) who would, upon keying a *service-request* button, be automatically connected to a predetermined distant station.

9.3.5.5 Local Distribution.   To maintain the proposed grade of service, Datran must provide local distribution facilities with a quality as high as that of the long-haul trunking facilities. Datran claims that use of today's local loops, in many instances, would substantially degrade the end-to-end performance of its system, and therefore the company plans to ultimately construct its own local distribution facilities rather than lease loops from the telephone companies. Initially, however, economics dictate use of telephone company local loops.

An additional factor, which certainly contributed to Datran's decision to ultimately install its own local distribution plant, is the desire to have full control over the availability, installation, and maintenance of loop facilities. Dependence upon a competitor—in this case the local telephone company—for a critical component of one's service offering was felt to be unwise. Datran believes that it might be subject to high charges for loop facilities, delays in obtaining facilities (both before regulatory agencies and in terms of actual requests for service), and less than satisfactory maintenance service.

Today's wire-pair local loop facilities have been installed slowly, over a period of many years. Strict design and installation practices have been followed, resulting in widely accepted standards for local facilities; however, these same standards have somewhat retarded technological progress and innovation in the local plant. Not being constrained by telephone company practices and installed plant, Datran—like the MCI carriers discussed previously—has taken a fresh look at the technological alternatives available to meet various urban and suburban local distribution requirements.

The geographic distribution of data transmission users will influence the local loop design. Subscribers will, for the next decade at least, be largely business rather than residential in nature. Clearly, these subscribers will only be located in those areas zoned for business or industrial use, generally within metropolitan regions, and in suburban shopping centers or industrial parks. Subscribers thus will tend to cluster together, a pattern quite different from the widely dispersed locations of residential telephone and CATV customers. Naturally, the loop engineering will seek to take advantage of the clustered locations of data users.

Another factor influencing the Datran local loop design is the present high level of established demand. Datran will not be afforded the luxury of constructing its local facilities over a several-decade time frame, as has occurred with telephone local loops. Furthermore, although it is clear that local facilities must be installed quickly, the *exact* locations of future subscribers will probably remain, to a large degree, unknown until after system cutover. Therefore, loop facilities that can be installed quickly, while maintaining a high degree of flexibility (and even portability), are preferred over alternative approaches involving long construction times and a high degree of permanence.

An open-minded approach to loop design has led Datran to consider the alternatives of multipair cable, coaxial cable, microwave radio operating at 11, 18, and 39 GHz, and infrared optical links. Because of the customer location pattern—clustering—and the requirement for quick and flexible loop installation, the "mix" of local facilities is likely to include a high proportion of microwave radio. Frequency congestion in metropolitan areas permits usage of only the higher frequencies, which are satisfactory for the short distances involved, but would be unreliable at per-hop distances greater then several miles. The exact "mix" of facilities in a particular city will be determined by the topography.

A local distribution scheme, based upon high-frequency microwave and TDM, has been developed by Raytheon Data Systems Company for Datran. Up to six radio channels, called supergroups, would radiate outward from a district office, each carrying up to 1000 channels operating at 4800 bps. These radio beams would be relayed through various branching points (group multiplexors), each of which could drop and/or insert up to 100 channels operating at 4800 bps. Wherever in the distribution plan radio links are not economic, or are not possible because line-of-sight paths are absent, multiplexed cable would be used.

Radio and group multiplex equipment would generally be located on a building rooftop near the "center of gravity" of a cluster of subscribers. Metallic wire pairs, perhaps multiplexed, would be used for transmission between the group multiplexor and the individual subscribers, perhaps located several miles distant. Because of the relatively short distances involved, wire line drivers using diphase modulation, rather than the order of magnitude more expensive voice-channel modems, would suffice for signal transmission over these links. The line drivers would be incorporated into both the group multiplex equipment and the subscriber's digital communications console. Range capability of the drivers varies from 1 to 7 miles for data rates up to 14,400 bps. Special drivers can extend the bit rate up to 50 kbps.

Available options for obtaining cable runs between subscribers and collection points include (1) laying buried cable, (2) pulling cable through leased duct space, (3) installing aerial cable on leased pole space (telephone or utility poles), and (4) leasing existing telephone company cables or wire pairs. All these options must be compared on a case-by-case basis, considering initial and recurring costs, system expandability, compatibility with local ordinances, and installation time.

Another option for distribution that is becoming increasingly attractive is multiplexed repeatered cable lines, such as the T-1 carrier system used by the telephone companies. T-1 carrier greatly expands the capacity of wire pairs, especially for the transmission of digital data, and is ideally suited to the requirements of local distribution of data signals. A single T-1 system could handle more than 200 channels, each operating at 4800 bps. Of course, additional terminal equipment is required for multiplexing and demultiplexing purposes, and economic tradeoffs are involved.

By not being bound to an existing network and by designing distribution facilities according to the location patterns of data users and the characteristics of data signals, Datran may be able to achieve economies that overcome the inherent high costs of providing its own local distribution facilities.

9.3.6 Packet Switching Data Carriers

As mentioned earlier, several companies, at the time of writing, were planning to file applications with the FCC for authorization to offer public data communications services using circuits leased from the established carriers and their own store-and-forward switching facilities. The technology to be employed in these networks is based upon that of the ARPA network, a research-oriented computer network created under the auspices of the Advanced Research Projects Agency (ARPA) of the Defense Department. Since the detailed plans of the several prospective packet-switching carriers are unclear at this writing, we describe here only the technology of the ARPANET. For a more detailed discussion and additional references, see Chapter 13.

In 1968 the Advanced Research Projects Agency began the implementation of the ARPANET. The network, which has been operating continuously since early 1970, provides the capability for geographically separated computers, called "hosts," and terminals, to communicate with each other via common-carrier circuits. A wide variety of host computers are connected to the ARPANET, differing from one another in make, model, type of operating system, programming languages, and applications software available, etc. Each host is connected into the network through a small local computer called an Interface Message Processor (IMP); each IMP is connected to several other distant IMPs via wideband communication lines. The terminals may either be connected directly to a host computer or, alternatively, to a Terminal IMP (TIP) which is, in turn, connected to several other IMPs and/or TIPs via wideband channels. The IMPs, all of which are virtually identical, and the TIPs are programmed to rapidly store and forward messages (broken down into 1000-bit packets) to their neighbor IMPs based on address information contained in each message.

In a typical network operation a host computer or terminal passes a message, including a destination address, to its local IMP or TIP. The message is split into one or more packets, each with an address appended, which are rapidly passed from IMP to IMP (much like a "hot potato") through the network until they arrive at the destination IMP, which in turn reassembles the message and passes it along to the destination host.

A distributed store-and-forward packet-switching approach was chosen over the more conventional circuit-switching concept for several reasons.

First, packet switching permits simultaneous sharing of wideband transmission facilities by a number of users, creating a high-capacity and quite economical communications medium. Also, it eliminates the long "connect time" delay inherent in circuit switching (see Section 9.1.3.6), thus providing greater responsiveness. A powerful cyclic check sum can be used to detect errors and cause retransmission when such errors occur; this technique has virtually eliminated errors in the ARPANET (estimated bit error rate of 10^{-12}). Also, the path a message follows in the ARPANET is not determined in advance, as is the case with conventional circuit switching. Instead, the optimum routing is determined for each packet as it passes from node to node, taking into account computer and circuit loading and outages. High overall network reliability and utilization is thus achieved.

Design and implementation of the network hardware and software was performed by Bolt Beranek and Newman Inc. (BBN). BBN began work on the design and development of the ARPANET in January 1969; the early experimental phase of the system's operation began in 1970. By 1972, the ARPANET had grown to include over thirty sites across the United States and was continuing to expand at the rate of about one node (IMP or TIP) per month, with continually increasing traffic levels. To meet the need for a higher-capacity and more cost-effective nodal processor, at the time of writing BBN was developing a high-speed modular IMP (the HSMIMP) which will operate with 1.5 Mbps digital transmission lines, such as T-1 and DUV, currently being installed by the telephone company. In addition, IMPs capable of using satellite transmission links have been developed and, at the time of writing, the network was being extended to Hawaii and Europe via INTELSAT satellite. Successful operation of this satellite transmission concept will have important economic implications for domestic U.S. packet-switching networks as well as permitting the implementation of such networks on an international basis.

Clearly the ARPANET represents one of the most significant and valuable advances in computer-communications technology in recent years, and the challenge is to utilize the full potential of this technology in the commercial marketplace. Many uncertainties confront the firms that are attempting to achieve this goal, including a subsidiary of BBN, Telenet Communications Corporation, but the long-term outlook for commercial packet-switched communication services appears bright.

9.4   POLICY CONSIDERATIONS AND THE SPECIALIZED CARRIERS

The proposals of the various proposed specialized carriers have raised numerous questions, both for the FCC and for the data communicator. Consider first the following major policy issues:

1. What is the extent of public need for each of the proposed services?
2. If the services were available, what cost savings would accrue to users? Could the same services be provided more efficiently and thus presumably at lower cost by the established carriers?
3. Would the costs of providing present services by today's carriers be increased because of diversion of traffic and lost economies of scale?
4. How would the establishment of new carriers affect the pricing policies of present carriers? In particular, would uniform nationwide pricing of interstate services be abandoned, and if so, to what degree? How would the overall price levels for individual services be affected?
5. How would the performance of today's carriers be affected by new competitors, in terms of their use of new technology, introduction of new services and improvement of old ones, responsiveness to customer requests for the installation of new services and equipment, system maintenance, assistance in system planning and design, etc.?
6. How would the regulatory process be affected by the entry of specialized common carriers? Would they provide a useful benchmark for evaluating the performance of the existing carriers?
7. Would the entry of new microwave carriers compound the frequency congestion problem beyond tolerable limits?

In the following section we discuss these broad policy issues; Section 9.5 then considers questions relating to the practical effects of specialized carriers from the user's point of view.

9.4.1 Public Need

Before authorizing a new interestate common carrier, the FCC must, according to the Communications Act of 1934, determine that the applicant's proposed service offerings will serve "the public interest, convenience, and necessity." One element in this determination is an assessment of "public need." To what extent does the public require the availability of the proposed services? To what extent are the proposed services already available, at reasonable rates and upon reasonable demand?

The measurement of public need is, at best, an art rather than a science. This is particularly true in estimating future need for untried services. The proposals of the new specialized carriers are, to a large degree, fresh concepts not yet tested in the marketplace; estimates of future usage of these services are thus highly speculative.

One approach to measuring the extent of unsatisfied public need is to consider the expressed requirements of communication subscribers. In the course of the specialized-carrier proceedings, several opportunities for "expressions of need" were provided. In MCI's first hearing before an FCC hearing examiner, various potential users in the Chicago–St. Louis area testified under oath and/or submitted affidavits stating that they would lease MCI channels, if available, because of either the flexibility afforded, the rates charged, or some particular feature of the proposed service (e.g., sharing or half-time usage).

In an FCC public inquiry on computers and communications, initiated in 1966 and extending into 1971, specific attention was focused upon the adequacy of available data transmission services [2, 3]. Comments were received from approximately 60 organizations—common carriers, computer and terminal manufacturers, computer-communication users, government agencies, and assorted industry associations. By and large, these respondents —with the exception of the common carriers—were critical of the limited data transmission service offerings then being provided, and suggested specific service offerings and features as necessary or desirable.

For example, IBM in its comments to the FCC noted that:

The present communications system evolved primarily in response to requirements for voice communications. Since voice constituted a major traffic load, the design of the system centered around providing telephone channels. Data communications requirements have been met to date by adaptations of facilities designed primarily for voice services. While there are important advantages in using a single network, there are fundamental differences in the requirements of voice and data communications.

Booz, Allen, and Hamilton, Inc., in a study prepared for the Business Equipment Manufacturers Association, pointed out that:

Common carriers do not now offer a switching service providing more than 2400 bits per second, nor do they provide leased channels in the range between 2400 bits per second and 50,000 bits per second. The computer user must, therefore, choose between paying for a considerably higher speed transmission line than is required, or operating his terminal or peripheral devices well below their most efficient speeds.

The expected continued growth in data communication, and the basic differences between data and voice transmission requirements, raise the questions of whether, and when, the National Switching Network and the tariffs associated therewith, will need to be modified significantly in the future to accommodate optimum data transmission or even whether a second national network designed specifically for data transmission might become economically feasible.

The Bunker-Ramo Corporation, which operates the Telequote stock quotation service for the securities brokerage industry, one of the largest computer-communication systems in the world, stated:

The existing costs of communication channels and facilities within the present tariff structure are an inhibiting factor to the widespread use of computer services.

Smaller users cannot now afford the huge economic burden of leasing their own private lines at present private-line rates in order to obtain necessary computer services.

In the 1970–71 FCC inquiry on specialized carriers, a wide variety of organizations submitted comments regarding the need for new data transmission services. Excerpts from these comments are included in the following paragraphs.

Sanders Associates, Inc., a defense contractor and manufacturer of computer display terminals, noted that there is "an urgent need for low cost, high speed digital communication facilities. . . . We need them because our existing colossally complex telephone network, while manifestly indispensable for voice transmission, cannot economically be transformed into an efficient data transmission medium."

Tel-Tech Corporation, a manufacturer of data communications hardware, observed:

The need for an independent communications network designed specifically for data has existed for years . . . . Costs of facilities are too high; it takes too long to implement a system; services offered are too limited; interface devices required by the carrier are too expensive and not readily available
. . . .

Joseph T. Ryerson and Son, Inc., a major steel supply company, stated:

The following services . . . are not adequately provided by the existing common carriers: voice and data transmission private line circuits on a twelve hour, five day per week basis; high reliability digital transmission circuits . . . low-cost voice and data circuits between high-density routes . . . ; data transmission circuits of various speeds; prompt delivery of facilities (30 days or less).

Martin Marietta Corporation, a diversified aerospace manufacturer, commented:

. . . requirements of data communications must ultimately . . . be accommodated by specialized all-digital systems which . . . shall: (1) offer improved quality of data transmission; (2) provide faster access time; (3) provide higher bit rates . . . .

These comments reflect the general feeling of industry regarding the need for additional and improved data transmission services. Certainly, some of the organizations expressing their views did not fully appreciate and consider the economics of establishing separate data-oriented transmission facilities. Nevertheless, the tone of their comments clearly suggests the existence of an unfulfilled public need.

After considering comments such as the above, and various market studies, the FCC and its staff concluded that there was, in fact, public need for the proposed services and facilities [13]. The staff specifically concluded:

> There appears to be an increasing public need and demand for the availability of diverse and flexible means for meeting heterogeneous communication requirements . . . . The information before us affords grounds for reasonable belief that there is a substantial public need for the proposed services which is not now being adequately met by the established carriers. The computer inquiry showed that there was dissatisfaction on the part of the computer industry and by many data users who had been attempting to adapt their requirements to existing services. Datran has persuasively stated the public need for rapid, accurate and low-cost data transmission, the drawbacks in using existing facilities engineered for voice and record transmission, and the advantages of a switched, all-digital network with end-to-end compatibility. Moreover, the showings in the MCI applications . . . support the view that there is widespread interest in the types of specialized, private line service proposed by it and other applicants.

The Commission added:

> There is abundant support for the staff's conclusion that the specialized communications market, particularly for data communications, is growing at a rapid rate, and that there is a very large potential market yet to be developed . . . . The market studies of the applicants are generally consistent with forecasts made in independent reports to the Commission . . . other published forecasts . . . the record in the computer inquiry . . . and our own findings in that proceeding.

In the final analysis, the only conclusive determinant of public need is the marketplace. Communication users—just as other consumers—may express an interest in a new service or product offering, but may be reluctant to lay their money on the line when the service or product actually becomes available. On the other hand, many applications of new and highly flexible communications services are not yet conceived. Users are unlikely even to recognize these applications until services are actually available; thus *a priori* market estimates for such services will necessarily be imprecise, and actual experience is the only reliable indicator. Unfortunately, the cost of field trials and test marketing in the communications industry, for all but the established carriers, is prohibitive. Therefore, the FCC's conclusions regarding the need for specialized carrier services appear to be based upon the best information reasonably available today, and the Commission's authorization of these new carriers to go into operation provides the only meaningful way to measure the actual public need more precisely.

9.4.2 Economies of Scale and Duplication of Facilities

An important policy objection to the entry of new competitors (with the exception of packet-switching and other "value added" carriers that would lease transmission facilities from the established carriers) advanced by the established carriers is the fact that the communications industry, as other public utility industries, is characterized by economies of scale, especially with respect to transmission facilities. Therefore, it is argued, the overall cost to the public is lowest with an exclusive common-carrier monopoly. Economies of scale clearly exist in long-haul transmission systems, as shown in Fig. 9.7, although charges to all users may not reflect these economies unless competitive pressure forces rate reductions (e.g., Bell introduced its experimental Series 11,000 service, offering drastically reduced prices for "packages" of leased voice channels, when competition in the form of specialized microwave carriers appeared on the horizon). In fact, despite the

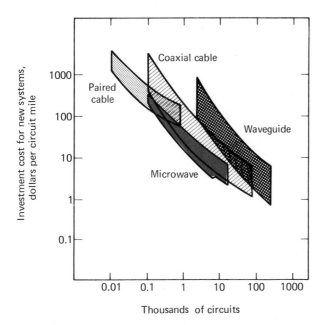

FIGURE 9.7   Economies of scale using different communications technologies.

present downward trend in the cost of long-haul transmission, the telephone company is currently *increasing* its rates for toll (long-distance) calls. The often-claimed reason for this is that the excessive earnings derived from toll calls are used to subsidize the costs of local facilities, which have increased over the years.

Illustrations of the economies of scale associated with transmission facilities, including Fig. 9.7, tend to exaggerate the extent of these economies. The costs of carrier and multiplexing equipment, for example, which do not exhibit noticeable economies of scale (i.e., the cost of multiplexing equipment for 240 voice channels is approximately 20 times the cost for 12 channels), are excluded from these figures. This is done to permit comparisons on a "per mile" basis. However, the costs of carrier and multiplexing equipment represent the largest portion of total transmission costs and therefore tend to dilute the significance of the apparent economies of scale to a substantial degree.

Furthermore, the potentially lower cost per channel of high-capacity transmission systems is diluted by long periods of low utilization and by the industry practice of averaging the costs of new systems with the costs of older and more expensive equipment still in use.

Nevertheless, scale economies do exist, and construction of parallel transmission facilities—e.g., by new specialized carriers—tends to negate these economies to the extent that traffic is diverted to the new facilities. Consider for a moment the possible effect of the MCI-type private-line carriers upon the economies of scale of the telephone network. Private-line services presently account for approximately 25 per cent of the Bell System's total interstate channel mileage. Assuming that MCI-type carriers achieve a 20 per cent penetration of this market, entirely through diversion of traffic from the telephone company, Bell's total interstate channel mileage would be reduced by only 5 per cent. On the other hand, if the new facilities generate additional traffic—through the offering of different services, through lower prices due to specialization, or through greater flexibility or innovation— then the economies of scale of the established carriers will be little affected. It therefore appears quite unlikely that a division of the private-line market between the established carriers and the new specialized carriers (whose penetration would tend to be small and who would also generate new demand by providing new services) would have any significant effect upon whatever scale economies exist in the present network. This is even more apparent when the projected 12 to 15 per cent annual growth of the national network is considered—AT&T estimates that its physical plant will be four times as large in 1980 as it is today!

One problem associated with the attempt to achieve maximum economies of scale is the fact that this requires the consolidation of all services in order to use common facilities. A carrier is then motivated to limit its service offerings to a small set of "least common denominator" services, such as analog channels of voice bandwidth and a few multiples thereof, all derived from the common telephone-oriented plant. In effect, the carrier must forego potential economies of facility specialization. When virtually all users require standard voice services, the single-supplier and common-plant approach is clearly the most economic and sensible; however, when a significant fraction of subscribers seeks an assortment of services—in terms of bandwidth, error rates, reliability, switching times, etc.—the attempt to employ a single carrier system to satisfy all requirements may degrade service to all classes of subscribers and offset the scale economies of a single system.

An analogy may illustrate the point more clearly. In the CATV industry, the economies of using separate facilities (broadband coaxial cable) to provide one-way distribution for broadcast video signals outweigh the economies of scale that would flow from use of common facilities for both telephone and CATV service.

Quantitatively, what is the likely impact of specialized carriers upon the economies of scale in telephone-company transmission facilities? First, the substantial size and capacity of present and future telephone-company transmission facilities must be appreciated. Commonly used long-haul microwave facilities, including TD-2, TD-3, and TH-3, each have a capacity of approximately 10,000 to 12,000 voice channels. In heavily trafficked communications corridors (e.g., along the East Coast, New York to Chicago, etc.), L-4 coaxial cable is being installed, with a capacity of approximately 32,000 voice channels. L-5 coaxial cable, scheduled for installation in the late 1970s, has a capacity of approximately 90,000 voice channels. In contrast, most MCI-type specialized-carrier applicants plan to initially build facilities with capacities of only 1800 voice channels. Moreover, because of the variety of channel bandwidths they propose to offer and their intention to provide service on a one-way and part-time basis, combined with the need for spare capacity to accommodate growth and statistical fluctuation in usage, MCI-type carriers will probably not achieve a system fill of more than 50 to 60 per cent—roughly, 1000 voice channels. Similarly, the Datran network is designed for a maximum channel capacity of 4000 switched 4800-bps channels; but actual utilization, also for statistical reasons, will probably be considerably less.

Comparing the size of the specialized-carrier systems with that of the telephone network reinforces one's notion that the effect of these systems upon telephone-company economies of scale will be negligible.

Implicit in discussion of the impact of new carriers upon the economies of scale in communications is the assumption that such new carriers would offer services identical to presently available services, thereby duplicating existing facilities. When this is in fact true, lost economies of scale must be weighed against the benefits of competition. But when proposed services differ from available services—either in terms of the physical characteristics of the channel offerings, the tariff regulations regarding their use, the pricing structure, the service reliability, or other important characteristics—the degree of duplication is reduced considerably, and any lost economies of scale must then be compared with the value of introducing a previously unavailable service, in addition to the competitive benefits of introducing a new carrier.

After considering these factors the FCC concluded [13]:

> We find no reason to anticipate that new entry in the specialized carrier field would result in any substantial diversion of AT&T's revenues or have any significant adverse impact on telephone users, the installation of large capacity systems to meet growing communication requirements of all kinds, or the realization of declining unit costs. At best, any impact that new entry might have on declining unit costs or economies of scale would be more than offset by the other advantages inuring to the public from such new entry.

9.4.3 Competitive Benefits

Experience and economic theory demonstrate that significant direct and indirect benefits accrue to society when an industry is organized along competitive lines. Only when overriding economies of scale are present (e.g., with electric utilities) or other special factors exist (e.g., national security requirements that dictate government control of uranium production) is a departure from competitive practice warranted. As suggested in the previous section, the economy-of-scale rationale in the case of the long-haul communications industry appears insufficient to offset the benefits of competitive enterprises. These benefits may be summarized as follows:

1. Provide users with a wider range of communication services than presently available from existing carriers.
2. Disperse the burdens and initiatives associated with supplying the rapidly growing and diversifying communications markets.
3. Expand the capability of the communications industry to respond quickly and fully to the rapidly increasing volume and variety of user demands.
4. Enlarge the communications equipment market for manufacturers other than Western Electric.
5. Stimulate technological innovation and the application of new techniques.
6. Reduce costs and tariff rates by more closely applying communications technology to the special requirements of data transmission.
7. Exert pressure on new carriers, from lack of a captive market, to be innovative in offering types of services that would attract and satisfy heterogeneous subscribers.

8. Serve as a useful regulatory tool that would assist the FCC in achieving its objective of adequate and efficient services at reasonable rates by affording a comparative standard for measuring carrier performance.
9. Stimulate the telephone companies and Western Union to counter-innovate and to introduce available technology more rapidly.

The General Services Administration of the Federal Government, in support of increased competition in the communications industry, has concluded in comments submitted during the FCC computer inquiry:

> As customers, the Executive agencies have expressed, in prior proceedings before the Commission, the view that unregulated competition and the encouragement and stimulation of competition in the regulated sector of the communications industry would be productive of the greatest benefits to customers, to industry, and the Commission. We remain convinced of the soundness of this view.

Security Pacific National Bank, a leading bank with several hundred branches throughout the state of California, also submitted comments in the FCC computer inquiry that reflect the sentiments of business communications users:

> Because the common carriers have virtually no competition, they fail consistently in the areas of experience and professional communications advice to customers . . . conditional charges, high data channel charges, high data set charges, little or no technical assistance, long due dates, poor transmission quality and ever changing tariff "interpretations" are a plague to the general public. [It] would be a decided boon to be able to order data services from a data communications oriented company.

The FCC has generally expressed agreement with these views, although with somewhat less emotion than most users. In its specialized carrier inquiry [13] the Commission concluded that "based on our cumulative knowledge of the industry and the entire record in this proceeding—including our staff's analysis. . . there is sufficient ground for a reasonable expectation that new entry here will have some beneficial effects."

9.4.4 Average Cost Pricing and Cream Skimming

Another major policy consideration related to the entry of new carriers is their potential effect upon the telephone companies' current practice of averaging the costs of their facilities across the nation and charging uniform rates for interstate services, irrespective of the actual costs of providing service in a particular locality or along a particular route.

The established carriers contend that such geographic rate averaging is in the public interest, since it permits them to offer reasonably priced service in localities where costs are high; the widespread availability of telephone service is thus assured, to the benefit of all subscribers. They also contend that by building transmission facilities to serve only selected high-traffic, low-cost intercity routes the new carriers would be "skimming the cream" from the communications market—to the detriment of the general public—by pricing their channels below the "average" prices charged by the larger carriers. Ultimately, it is argued, the large carriers would serve only the high-cost areas and would be forced to increase the rates charged to subscribers in those areas. The existing carriers refer to activity of this sort by small firms as "cream skimming," and oppose it, claiming that the new firms' actual costs may be higher than those of the larger carriers in the same localities, whereas the diversion of traffic would adversely affect the scale economies of the larger carriers.

It has been suggested that the FCC encourages and supports the carriers' traditional practice of averaging costs and charging uniform rates. Although this may be true, departures from uniform rates do occur (e.g., Bell's Series 11,000 service). In fact, the FCC hearing examiner who first considered the MCI proposal commented in his decision, "the averaging method is embodied neither in the Decalogue nor in the Constitution."

Rate averaging is, in effect, a mechanism by which those parts of the nation whose communication costs are low on a per-channel basis (e.g., the industrial Northeast) subsidize other regions (e.g., the rural countryside) where costs are higher. To a limited extent, this subsidization is in the overall public interest, since it brings telephone service within economic reach of the rural population and thus increases the utility of the telephone for everyone (by increasing the number of persons whom any subscriber can call). The uniform rates charged as a consequence of averaging also simplify the tariff pricing structure, and thereby facilitate the user's understanding of telephone charges and also the telephone company's task of toll accounting and billing.

Assuming the merits of average-cost pricing and the threat to this practice posed by the potential entry of new competitive carriers, the cream-skimming argument against entry acquires a certain intuitive appeal. Several critical assumptions underlying the argument may be questioned, however. First, the cream-skimming argument assumes that the established carriers are fully and adequately serving the potential market, and that the new entrants would merely provide comparable competing services; but the facts suggest otherwise. We have seen that users with specialized communications requirements, especially for data transmission, have found the standard telephone network facilities and services less than adequate. And the recent deterioration of telephone service in several metropolitan areas has introduced an additional dimension into the comparison between user needs and services provided. Indeed, the existence of unfulfilled needs for certain types of communications service was perhaps the prime motivation for the proposal of new specialized carriers, who would offer new and improved services tailored to meet these needs.

A second reason for questioning the cream-skimming argument is that it assumes the new entrants will operate only over high-density routes. In fact, the initial plans of many of the applicants include the offering of service in areas with low population density, since such areas happen to be where certain of those applicants have existing microwave facilities. Also, it can be expected that other systems which would initially be urban-oriented would in time grow to include outlying areas as well. Although the proposed new carrier networks appear sparse when compared with the gargantuan telephone network, the scope of these proposals is impressive; for example, MCI's planned network will serve 165 cities having an estimated 81 per cent of the U.S. population and 85 per cent of the business community within a 25-mile radius. According to the U.S. Independent Telephone Association, AT&T itself—while serving most of the U.S. population—serves slightly less than 50 per cent of the nation's geographic area in which telephone service is provided.*

It is difficult to say that proposals of this magnitude are merely attempts to "skim the cream" from a few dense routes. But in any event, those new carriers who propose to operate initially over the more heavily trafficked routes are only exercising good business judgment; the established carriers do likewise when introducing any new service. For example, when AT&T developed its television program transmission service during the 1948–1958 period, it chose to serve only the larger population centers and not outlying areas. As a result, the FCC approved the operation of additional intercity microwave relay facilities by the broadcasters themselves and by "miscellaneous" common carriers. Most recently, AT&T has claimed that the costs of high-capacity microwave and cable facilities used between major cities justified its experimental low-cost Series 11,000 broadband service (offered from 1969 to 1973), which was available only between certain large Northeastern and Midwestern cities.

Third, the cream-skimming argument assumes that not only will the introduction of competition have a serious impact upon the continued use of average-cost pricing for common-carrier communications services, but that such average-cost pricing is worthy of continued protection. In this regard, we note first that new carriers under consideration here would be limited to the provision of private-line channels and switched data transmission service, and would offer no switched voice telephone service. Therefore,

---

*Thus it has been said that "AT&T is the biggest cream-skimmer of them all!"

although their entry might cause the existing carriers to modify their rate structure somewhat for private-line service, it would not affect the rate averaging for the dial telephone network. However, the rationale for rate averaging is primarily applicable to switched voice telephone service and loses much of its appeal when applied to private-line and other specialized communications services used chiefly by business organizations. Many would argue that there is no public-interest reason why companies located in areas where communications traffic is heavy should indirectly subsidize the private-line communications costs of companies less favorably located. On the contrary, economic theory suggests that a more optimal allocation of resources occurs when goods and services are priced according to actual costs. But even if an argument could be made for subsidizing the communications expenses of companies located in rural areas, the decision to do so should be made by the people, through the legislative process, rather than by the common carrier; and any such action decided upon could be most effectively accomplished and controlled through direct government subsidies, rather than through subsidies hidden within communications tariffs. Subsidies built into the communications tariff structure are also inconsistent with the FCC's regulatory policy favoring cost-based pricing.

Considering these factors, it does not appear that the specialized carrier proposals at issue here in fact satisfy the criteria implicit in the cream-skimming argument against them: (1) that they propose to only offer service comparable to, and competitive with, existing adequate service; (2) that they would provide such service only on dense routes where the existing carriers' average-cost rates far exceed actual costs; (3) that they would have a substantial effect upon the existing carriers' ability to continue their rate-averaging practices; and (4) that the rate averaging thus imperiled can be shown to be important to the public interest. On the contrary, specialized carriers could offer new and improved communications services—especially for data transmission—to a high percentage of the users needing such services with little attendant jeopardy to socially desirable rate-averaging practices for switched telephone service. In agreement with the above conclusions, the FCC stated [13]:

> Nor do we find grounds for excluding new entry in the miscellaneous arguments advanced by the carriers relating to "cream skimming" . . . We are not persuaded that the charge of "cream skimming" is well founded or would justify a bar against new entry of the type proposed here . . . .

The Commission went on to say, regarding the abandonment of average-cost pricing by AT&T:

> AT&T alleges that new entry might require it to depart from cost averaging and uniform nationwide interstate rates. This approach to the pricing of

AT&T's services in the past has generally been regarded as consistent with the public interest in the context of the predominantly monopoly structure which heretofore has characterized the common carrier communication industry. There is no reason to believe that this approach to pricing of the interstate message service offerings of the Bell System and Western Union (such as dial telephone and public telegraph) need be altered by new entry into the developing specialized communications market. Clearly, none of the uniform rate structures of the existing carriers for such services would appear to be in jeopardy since those services are not being challenged competitively to any substantial degree by the services proposed to be offered by the aspiring new entrants. *Where services may be in direct competition departure from uniform nationwide pricing practices may be in order, and in such circumstances will not be opposed by the Commission.* [Emphasis added.]

Since AT&T's private line services between major cities will, in fact, be in direct competition with similar services offered by specialized carriers, AT&T indicated its intention to depart from uniform nationwide price averaging. In its proposed "high density, low density" rate plan, AT&T distinguishes major intercity routes from minor ones, and provides for lower rates over the major routes. Thus, as a result of competition, private line rates are likely, in the future, to more accurately reflect true costs than they have in the past.

9.4.5 Frequency Congestion

It has been argued by the established carriers that some of the proposed microwave stations of specialized carriers would cause frequency interference to their existing systems and block or impede economical expansion on existing microwave routes; and that the specialized carriers would use the scarce frequency spectrum less efficiently than the telephone companies, since they will carry fewer equivalent channels per radio beam and in some cases originally proposed to use one-for-one frequency diversity (one backup radio channel for each working channel). With more radio channels on most of its routes Bell is able to achieve a higher ratio of working to protection channels and thus ties up proportionately fewer frequencies for backup purposes.

On the other hand, it has been argued that frequency congestion only occurs in and around certain major metropolitan areas; and here congestion may be dealt with through coordination among carriers, use of higher frequencies (e.g., 11 GHz) and, as a last resort, coaxial cable "tails" into that city. It is also argued that these solutions are preferable to the total exclusion of new carriers, which may offer benefits to the public outweighing the cost of dealing with increased frequency congestion. Also, it should be noted that much of Bell's future plant expansion on dense intercity routes will utilize high-capacity coaxial cable rather than microwave, due to the lower costs of the new coaxial systems, thus substantially reducing the number of new microwave frequencies needed on these routes.

After consideration of this question the Commission stated [13]: "Based upon past experience, we believe that most, if not all, of the claimed conflicts can be resolved through coordination and that new entry can be technically accommodated despite the growing frequency congestion." The Commission then issued several technical rules restricting the use of frequency diversity on common-carrier microwave systems, prohibiting certain types of microwave antennas, and improving coordination procedures among carriers with potentially interfering microwave systems.

9.4.6 Other Regulatory Issues

Yet another factor under consideration by the FCC has been the potential value of specialized carriers as a regulatory tool. The regulation of public utilities is an imperfect surrogate for competition, necessary in those industries in which free competition is impractical. No one seriously disputes the need for such regulation in the communications common-carrier industry. However, if competition among communications carriers can also be encouraged, we are no longer dependent solely upon government regulation. The existence of competitive carriers also gives the regulatory agency comparative yardsticks by which to evaluate carrier performance in regard to operating costs, prices charged to the public, responsiveness to users' requirements, efficient use of new technology, and so on.

9.5   IMPLICATIONS FOR THE FUTURE

With the broad policy issues concerning the entry of new specialized carriers largely resolved, and the FCC's go-ahead given for the development of this new industry, a number of questions of direct concern to the designer and user of computer-communication systems are raised. Some of the more important questions, grouped into four general categories, include:

EVOLUTION OF THE INDUSTRY

1. How quickly will specialized-common-carrier facilities be constructed and placed into operation?
2. Will the new carriers be able to obtain adequate financing, local distribution facilities, and necessary approvals from state regulatory bodies for intrastate service?
3. What other problems are likely to be encountered by these carriers in getting their industry off the ground?

COMPETITION
1. Will established carriers provide similar services?
2. What pricing structures and levels will be established by the specialized carriers and by present carriers for similar service offerings?
3. Will there be more than one or two specialized carriers over a given route?

USER BENEFITS AND OPERATING CONSIDERATIONS
1. To what degree will specialized-carrier services alleviate the shortcomings of the present telephone network for data transmission?
2. Will these new services provide significant cost savings for the user?
3. What degree of flexibility and customizing will be provided by the specialized carriers?
4. In an area where specialized services are available, how quickly will arrangement for service be accomplished?
5. How will local distribution be provided and how will lead times be affected?
6. How reliable will be the services provided by the specialized carriers?
7. Will interconnection between one or more specialized carriers, and between a specialized carrier and the present carriers, be possible?
8. What difficulties will result from carrier interconnection?

COMPUTER-COMMUNICATION NETWORK DESIGN
1. What effects will the availability of specialized communication services have upon the design of computer-communication networks?
2. What will be the effects of (a) a greater variety of transmission speeds, (b) faster connect times on dial-up data calls, (c) lower error rates, and (d) asymmetric channels?
3. How will system configurations be altered by lower overall communication costs, and by changing leased-switched channel tradeoffs?
4. What changes in terminal equipment will be required, or desirable, as a result of new data service offerings?

9.5.1 Evolution of the Specialized-Carrier Industry

Although a microwave system can be constructed relatively quickly, it will take several years for the specialized carriers to establish themselves widely as operating organizations. A number of factors will tend to slow the early growth of the industry.

First, FCC approval must be obtained for all microwave transmitting stations, both for initial operation, and for subsequent modifications and extensions. With *policy* questions resolved, this stage of FCC action involves only a check on *technical* aspects of each proposed station—e.g., that use of

the radio frequencies proposed by the applicant will not cause harmful interference to other microwave systems or to communications satellites and their
earth stations, that proper antennas and type-accepted transmitter equipment will be used, etc. At the time of writing, FCC construction permits
had been issued for over a dozen specialized-carrier systems in various parts of
the country (see Table 9.5), and Commission action on other pending route
applications is expected to follow. However, given the limited FCC staff, the
large number of microwave applicants, the time-consuming process of checking and resolving frequency interference questions, and the likelihood of a
continuing flow of new applications, it is probable that the rate of granting
construction permits will be slow; indeed, processing of applications presently
on file may well extend into late 1973 or early 1974.

Second, once construction permits have been granted, financing for actual
construction, staffing, and operation must be obtained. In the case of the
large systems, especially the Datran system, financing will be difficult. Datran,
and the MCI-type carriers, too, must be considered venture capital investments. The MCI systems, however, are each relatively small (usually on the
order of $10 million capitalization) and well within the normal range of
venture capital investments. In fact, at the time of writing the financing for
many of the MCI companies had already been arranged; the parent firm,
MCI Communications Corporation, raised $30 million in a public stock of-
fering in 1972 and obtained substantial additional financing commitments
from several equipment suppliers.

The Datran system, on the other hand, as originally designed would have
required over $350 million of capital for construction alone, these funds be-
ing committed before actual system operation and economic viability could
be established. The underwriting of such a venture is without precedent. (The
only reasonable analogy is the financing of the Communications Satellite
Corporation [Comsat], which involved a $200 million stock issue. In that
unique case the very substantial participation of major prospective Comsat
customers—such as American Telephone & Telegraph, International Telephone & Telegraph, General Telephone & Electronics, and Radio Corporation of America—virtually assured the success of the financing.) Datran
not unexpectedly, therefore, encountered difficulty in financing its proposed
network and was forced to take steps to reduce its capital requirements. By
abandoning (at least for the time being) its goal of constructing its own local
distribution facilities, and by making other changes in the nature and time-
phasing of its system plans, Datran was able to cut its initial capital requirements to the $150 million level. This still represents a very substantial
high-risk investment, and to raise the necessary funds, Datran is likely to require the wholesale support of its suppliers. The banks, insurance companies,
and mutual funds—which represent the principal sources of funds for large

ventures—require the commitment and participation of investors who have a vested interest in the success of the venture. Datran's suppliers will have such an interest; no one customer does. At the time of writing, Datran had received a financial commitment from only one supplier—Nippon Electric Co.—and was continuing to encounter difficulties in obtaining the remainder of its financing.

A third factor likely to retard the development of the specialized-carrier industry is the very critical problem of local distribution. As discussed earlier, the alternative means include leasing facilities from local telephone operating companies or constructing short-haul microwave or cable links. Drawbacks to the construction of local distribution facilities by the specialized carriers include the substantial costs of such a program, the difficulty of forecasting where to build facilities, and the delays involved for their completion. Although it has been suggested that construction of new local plant is necessary for high-quality data transmission, due (according to Datran) to the unavoidably poor error performance of existing telephone company local loops, it is questionable whether the specialized carriers will find this approach economically attractive for general use. Also, even with the use of portable short-haul microwave equipment, route engineering would be required, FCC licenses must be obtained, and so forth. Provision of service would require many months' lead time.

Probably the use of telephone-company facilities will prove most efficient for the majority of the specialized carriers' local distribution requirements, but this will not be without its difficulties. As the FCC has said it must, upon reasonable demand, AT&T has expressed its willingness to provide local circuits to specialized carriers, but the telephone operating companies have little incentive to do their utmost in aiding their new competitors.

In negotiating leasing agreements with the telephone operating companies for local distribution circuits, the specialized carriers will have little bargaining power, and this will undoubtedly be reflected in the terms of these agreements. The circuit needs of the new carriers are certain to be given lower priority than those of the telephone companies themselves; in other words, telephone facilities will be provided on an "as-available" basis, and the new carriers may encounter delays in obtaining circuits in certain areas. Questions that remain unresolved at present include the prices to be charged by the telephone companies, the size of the local area within which service will be provided, the interconnection of customer equipment and communications systems, and so on. Also, and of critical importance, the local transmission plant in use today is designed for voice and certain other services, requiring generally only a 4-kHz channel bandwidth, whereas the specialized carriers will need local circuits with broadband analog capability and with dc transmission capability for digital pulse transmission; to what degree can and should the telephone plant be adapted to meet these requirements?

The FCC has already determined that the public interest requires the provision of local distribution circuits to the specialized carriers by the telephone companies. We agree with this conclusion, and feel that the availability of such circuits on a reasonable basis will be essential to the success of the specialized-carrier industry. To achieve this result, it may be necessary for the FCC to assume regulatory jurisdiction over the relations between the specialized carriers and the telephone companies, although the Commission has been reluctant to assume jurisdiction over intercarrier agreements in the past. Next, the specialized carriers must more fully define the types and quantities of local distribution facilities that they will require, and it must be determined to what degree these requirements will be met using telephone plants. Finally, agreements covering such usage must be drawn up, with recourse to the FCC for resolution of disputed issues.*

A fourth delaying factor facing the new carriers is the necessity of filing tariffs for interstate service offerings with the FCC, and similarly filing tariffs for intrastate services with each state public utility commission in whose state such service is to be rendered. Although lengthy delays in receiving approvals for these tariffs are not expected, the fact that the service offerings and the basis for pricing are new and the possibility that the present carriers will find aspects of the tariffs to object to suggest that delays in receiving tariff approvals will, in fact, occur. This is especially likely with the state commissions, many of which have been hostile to the specialized-carrier concept from the beginning (due largely to their acceptance of the existing carriers' cream-skimming argument, and fear that this will cause local telephone rates to rise). It is probable that some of the specialized carriers (especially the first several operating systems) will be in operation for some time, providing interstate service, before they receive intrastate operating authority.

A fifth delaying factor is the need on the part of most specialized carriers to build an organization capable of marketing, operating, and maintaining the services and facilities that have been authorized.

A sixth factor is the time required to actually construct the microwave systems, which will vary from 6 months for a small MCI-type system, up to several years for the Datran system.

Figure 9.8 illustrates the probable stages of development of the industry, taking into account the above-mentioned delaying factors. Construction of

---

*The FCC should exercise control as necessary to ensure equitable prices and other contract terms, and to require that specialized circuit requirements (e.g., for nonloaded wire pairs for high-speed digital transmission) be met by the telephone companies wherever reasonably feasible, with reimbursement by the specialized carrier for any extra costs incurred. At this writing AT&T and the specialized carriers were negotiating contractual arrangements.

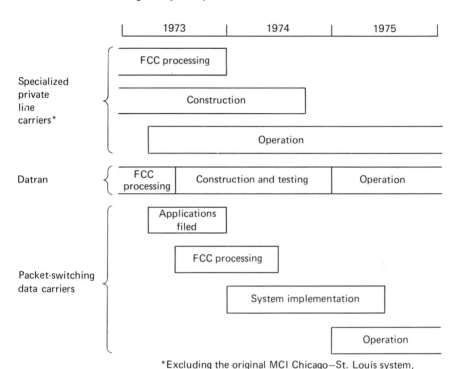

*Excluding the original MCI Chicago—St. Louis system, which became operational in January 1972.

FIGURE 9.8   Expected time table for specialized-carrier operation.

the backbone microwave system on MCI's initial Chicago–St. Louis route, for which the FCC granted amended construction permits in January 1971, was completed and MCI's first tariff went into effect in January 1972. Most of the remaining private-line specialized carriers, whose applications were pending during the FCC's inquiry, saw their applications processed (unless modifications were required to eliminate frequency interference or to improve the system routing) beginning in late 1971 and continuing into 1973. Construction and operation of most of these systems will probably occur in 1973 and 1974. Datran and the "value added" packet-switching carriers are not likely to begin providing service until late 1974 or early 1975.

9.5.2 Competition Among Carriers

Earlier in this chapter, in the context of the policy considerations related to the entry of new common carriers, we discussed the general benefits of competition. Here we consider some of the specific results likely to flow from competition between the present and the specialized carriers.

One of the most frequently predicted results of introducing this sort of competition is a shift on the part of the established carriers away from the average-cost pricing concept. As discussed in Section 9.4.4, communications carriers have traditionally established rates for their services based upon the average cost of providing such services throughout a wide geographic area (an entire state for intrastate services; or the United States as a whole for interstate services). Actual costs vary widely from route to route, however, so that on a dense route there may be a considerable margin between the actual costs of providing communication service and the "average cost" charged for that service. The gist of the established carriers' cream-skimming argument, as discussed above, is that new entrants would select just such routes to serve and would be able to easily undercut the umbrella rates created by the established carriers' average-cost pricing scheme.

For the established carriers to effectively meet new competition of this sort, it is argued, they must be permitted to selectively replace their average-cost pricing with new tariff rates based upon the actual costs of providing service. The comments of William M. Ellinghaus, President of New York Telephone Company (the largest AT&T operating company) illustrate this view: "If the FCC approves enough of these high-volume route applications and these companies begin consistently underpricing us along these routes, we will give very serious thought to our whole system of average pricing. If the result is that in order for us to maintain our fair share of the market we have to move away from average pricing to so-called route pricing, then we will do so." Of course, rate reductions on dense routes where there is competition must be offset by rate increases on less dense monopoly routes, or by subsidies from other classes of service, if the carrier's return on plant investment (*rate base*) is to remain unchanged. How valid are these contentions, and what impact might this have upon the data user?

Although AT&T and other members of the telephone industry have issued warnings suggesting that considerable harm may befall the average telephone user, through inevitable rate increases for dial telephone service, it appears highly unlikely that the establishment of specialized carriers will have this result. This is due both to the nature of the competition presented by specialized carriers and the very small probable dollar impact of such competition. Only about 30 per cent of the Bell System's total revenues are derived from interstate services; and of the interstate revenues some 87 per cent are from Message Toll Telephone (the DDD long distance network) and Wide Area Telephone Service (WATS), which are growing at the rate of about 15 per cent annually [13]. As outlined earlier, the MCI-type carriers plan to offer only interstate private line channels, not exchange telephone service; and although Datran does propose both switched and private line services, its offerings will be limited to data transmission, excluding voice and other types of communications. As a result, the FCC Common Carrier Bureau has estimated that "the proportion of AT&T services that is vulnerable to competitive inroads [by specialized carriers] would be in the order of 2–4% of its existing total business." "Thus," the Bureau concludes, "it is difficult to see how a diversion (if, indeed, there is any diversion) of some portion of that comparatively small percentage of total business represented by interstate specialized services would have any substantial effect on telephone rates and service. . ." [13].

Specifically, it appears quite unlikely that the licensing of new specialized carriers will cause the telephone companies to modify their uniform average cost rate structure for long distance telephone service (switched service using the DDD network). This is, in part, due to the small competitive impact of specialized carriers on this type of service, the administrative and other headaches associated with a nonuniform rate structure, the difficulty in obtaining the necessary approval for rate increases (to compensate for other rate reductions), and also the possibility that such a move would actually *decrease* telephone company revenues. Likewise, local exchange telephone rates should remain unaffected by competitive pressures, and business oriented switched network services such as WATS and TWX–Telex are also unlikely candidates for rate revision.

On the other hand, the established common carriers might reasonably conclude that some sort of pricing response to new competition would be desirable for their interstate *private line* services. Depending upon the degree of market penetration by new specialized carriers, the established carriers may wish to price leased line services more in accordance with the actual circuit costs. As noted earlier, the FCC has approved this practice if it should become desirable, saying [13] "Where services may be in direct competition [as would be the case particularly with respect to private line services], departure from uniform nationwide pricing practices may be in order, and in such circumstances will not be opposed by the Commission." In early 1973 Bell took a first step in this direction, proposing a two-level nationwide rate restructuring which would make available voice-grade leased circuits between any of approximately 370 larger cities ("high density rate centers") in the country at rates one-third those to be charged between all other points ("low density rate centers"). As discussed below, this proposed tariff change must be justified on a cost basis, so the specific rate levels involved are subject to change, but the concept appears to be valid. Depending upon reaction at the FCC and in the marketplace, it is possible that Bell may subsequently revise its rates for other private-line services (Telpak, Series 8000, etc.) in a similar fashion.

In addition to repricing of existing services, the established carriers may also introduce new service offerings designed to compete with the specialized carriers. Bell first tried this approach several years ago, when it introduced an experimental service called Series 11,000. This was a wideband (equivalent of up to 60 voice channels) private-line service, which was introduced about the time of the FCC's initial authorization of the MCI Chicago-St. Louis carrier system. (See Table 9.4.) It was provided over discrete high-capacity facilities, thereby achieving a low per-voice-channel cost, and was available only between major metropolitan areas in the densely-populated industrial Northeast and Midwest. It was significantly lower in price than its historic equivalent—the Telpak C channels that are available throughout the country. Moreover, the Series 11,000 subscriber was offered the opportunity of sharing the channel with other subscribers, a service feature initially proposed by MCI. Because of certain restrictions associated with the service and also its temporary "experimental" nature, Series 11,000 was not widely used; AT&T withdrew it in May 1973.

Bell's planned Digital Data Service represents a much more significant move of this kind. DDS, which is expected to serve approximately 96 cities by 1976, will provide all-digital data channels on a leased—and later also on a switched—basis. It will be directly competitive with the data transmission services of both Datran and the MCI-type carriers, containing many of the same attractive features planned by those organizations.

Western Union's Datacom, a private-line data service introduced after the first MCI system was authorized, is also available only in selected cities and further illustrates the established carriers' tendency to develop new service offerings where dictated by competitive pressures.*

The established carriers are not completely free, however, to make whatever pricing changes or to introduce whatever new or revised services they may choose in order to meet the threat of new competition. All such moves must be approved by the FCC, which has a duty to ensure that common-carrier services are offered to the public on a nondiscriminatory basis (which requires, *inter alia*, preventing undue "cross subsidization" of one carrier service by another) and to prevent carriers under its jurisdiction from engaging in unfair business practices forbidden by the antitrust laws. As a result, the FCC can be expected to reject tariffs submitted by the established carriers

---

*The competitive pressures are, of course, only one of the factors contributing to the decisions of the telephone companies and Western Union to introduce new services or to adjust pricing levels. The growth of demand and the availability of particular technologies, such as time-division multiplexing, are also factors that are motivating the carriers to provide new digital private-line data services among selected metropolitan areas.

that would attempt to drive out their new competitors through predatory (noncompensatory) pricing techniques—probably based upon cross-subsidization of a competitive service by a sheltered monopoly service.

Since all common-carrier rates and tariffs must be able to withstand regulatory scrutiny, the established carriers must be prepared to demonstrate the cost basis for any "competitive response" actions they might propose. Unfortunately, the telephone network is very complex and everchanging from a cost-accounting viewpoint; and both AT&T and the FCC lack adequate data regarding the average and marginal costs actually experienced with each individual route and class of communications service. Therefore, whenever a shift away from average-cost pricing to route pricing is attempted for certain classes of service (e.g., AT&T's proposed high-density/low-density rates for interstate voice-grade leased lines) it will be difficult to establish that the new competitive rates were fully compensatory on either a fully distributed or long-run incremental cost basis (whichever the FCC should permit), and that no covert cross-subsidization was present. This difficulty may, as a practical matter, result in lengthy hearings that could delay significant pricing shifts by the established carriers in response to the entry of new competitors.

In addition to its effect upon the existing carriers' pricing practices and rate structures, the introduction of competition is also likely to affect the amount and type of communications-oriented research conducted by industry, both technological and market research. Independent equipment suppliers, now presented with possible customers in the form of the new specialized carriers, are beginning to investigate new communication products and techniques. Collins Radio has been developing digital microwave equipment for Datran; Stromberg Carlson has been developing rapid-connect time-division switching equipment; Raytheon, and a number of other microwave radio manufacturers, are developing millimeter-wave radio equipment for possible use in local distribution systems.

In addition to the technical research stimulated by the new marketplace, the established carriers themselves have been motivated to begin various market-research programs to determine exactly what types of data services they should offer, in what locations, and at what pricing levels. For example, a month after the FCC staff recommended approval of the specialized carriers, AT&T announced the undertaking of what it termed "the largest data communications-oriented market study ever conducted." One may therefore reasonably expect that new data-oriented service offerings will be forthcoming and will "fit" the requirements of users better than past service offerings have.

Competition will also occur between the specialized carriers themselves. Although there will be a tendency for these carriers to avoid direct competition with each other, indirect competition is almost inevitable. Transcontinental channels may be routed, for example, via a northern carrier or perhaps via a different southern carrier. The situation is somewhat analogous to competition in the trucking field, in which there are local carriers, regional carriers, and national carriers overlapping and competing with one another. Users, therefore, may be faced with choices among several competing specialized private-line carriers in some cases.

9.5.3 User Benefits and Operating Considerations

Once the specialized carriers construct their systems and go into operation they will offer several important benefits to the data communications user: new and improved data transmission services and reduced costs. Section 9.1.3 discussed the shortcomings of the present common carrier network for data transmission; Table 9.6 lists these shortcomings and shows the degree to which they are eliminated in the data transmission facilities planned by MCI and Datran. The future digital services, both private line and switched, planned by AT&T and Western Union are also included in the table for comparison purposes. Although this table provides only a rough insight into the relative merits of the different carrier proposals, it can be seen that the specialized carriers offer more rapid availability of new data transmission services, and that their systems would incorporate features equal to—or in some cases superior to—those planned by the established carriers.

Second, the specialized carriers are expected to offer their services at tariff rates substantially lower than those charged today by the telephone companies and Western Union. Figure 9.9 compares Bell's present monthly tariff rates for commonly used leased lines with those proposed by MCI for channels of equal bandwidth. Similarly, Fig. 9.10 shows the cost of a 3 min daytime station to station call on the DDD network (which can transmit data at up to 3600 bps) versus the proposed costs of 3 min calls at 150 and 4800 bps on the Datran network. These graphs are based upon proposed charges submitted to the FCC by MCI and Datran, but the actual tariff rates that will be filed when the systems go into operation may differ somewhat. If the final tariff rates approximate those proposed by the applicants, data communication users will achieve significant cost savings in most cases.

While considering the above service and cost advantages, the prospective user should keep in mind certain practical aspects of specialized carrier operations. First, although specialized carriers will provide a wide range of service offerings, they will not be entirely free to custom design a service for a given customer, since all services provided must be properly tariffed and approved by regulatory bodies. However, if users make their needs known to the specialized carriers, this will influence the decision to file a tariff and make the desired service generally available—and the specialized carriers

TABLE 9.6 *Shortcomings Inherent in Present and Future Data Transmission Services*

Data Transmission Shortcomings[a]	AT&T AND WESTERN UNION				MCI	DATRAN
			FUTURE DIGITAL SERVICES			
	Present Switched Service	*Present Private Line*	*Private Line*	*Switched*	*Private Line Only*	*Switched and Private Line*
(Time frame for service availability)	Now	Now	1974	?	Now	1974–75
Low and medium speed only	Yes[b]	No	No	?	No	No
Digital–analog conversion required	Yes	Yes	No	No	No[d]	No
Data access arrangement required	Yes	Yes	?	?	No[e]	No[e]
Two-wire local loops	Yes[c]	No	No	?	No	No
Queueing problems at central office	Yes	n/a	n/a	?	n/a	No
Slow speed of service	Yes	n/a	n/a	?	n/a	No
Impulse noise	Yes	No	No	No	No	No
Line turnaround delay	Yes[c]	No	No	No	No	No
Limited variety of channel bandwidths	Yes	Yes	Yes	Yes	No	Yes
Noise cumulative with analog repeaters	Yes	Yes	No	No	?	No
Variable circuit routing (unpredictable quality)	Yes	n/a	n/a	No	n/a	No
High error rates	Yes	Yes	No	No	No	No
Excessive minimum-charge time on switched telephone network	Yes	n/a	n/a	?	n/a	No
No short-period private-line service available	n/a	Yes	?	n/a	No	Yes

[a]See Section 9.1.3 for a description of these problems. "Yes," "no," or "n/a" indicates that the problem is or is not present, or is not applicable, in the particular network. "?" indicates an unresolved question.

[b]Not counting Dataphone 50, a five-city experimental service.

[c]Not true for W.U. Broadband Exchange.

[d]Using MCI's planned digital data channels; not true for MCI analog channels.

[e]May be required if telephone company local loops are used.

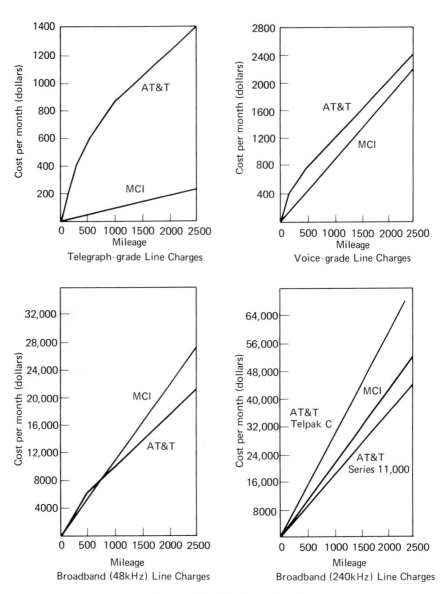

FIGURE 9.9   Comparison of MCI and AT&T charges for private-
line circuits.

will in all probability be much more receptive to such inputs from their
customers than the established carriers have been in the past.

As a practical matter, wide differences in the availability of specialized
carrier services will probably exist from carrier to carrier and from one city

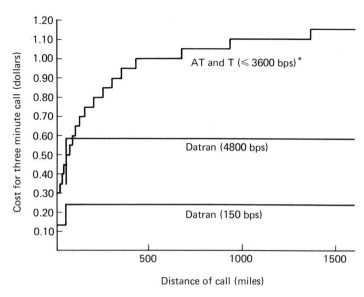

FIGURE 9.10 Comparison of Datran and AT&T charges for switched circuits.

to another for some years. The availability and cost of local distribution facilities may be the most important factor in determining a new specialized carrier's ability to effectively serve the cities along its route. At least initially, the specialized carriers will be largely dependent upon telephone company loop facilities for their local distribution, as discussed above, and delays may occur. However, most of the specialized carriers will probably view the use of telephone company facilities as only a temporary and partial solution to their local distribution requirements, and will install their own facilities as soon as practicable. By way of analogy, in the past Western Union has used telephone company facilities for over 70 per cent of its local distribution requirements, but the undesirability of depending upon its competitor (the telephone company) for local distribution has encouraged W.U. to continuously increase the channel mileage of its own local facilities over the past decade. The evolutionary pattern for specialized carriers may well be similar —initially, leased telephone company local loops, but ultimately owned facilities where distance considerations and subscriber density warrant.

The reliability of the services provided by specialized carriers is difficult to forecast. Technically, the services should be at least as reliable as presently available services, with slight differences; e.g., Datran will not be able to employ alternative routing should a catastrophic failure occur over the back- bone microwave trunk. In practice, however, most circuit difficulties and the time required to remedy them are more a result of people problems and carrier operating procedures than directly attributable to the equipment employed. In the case of the specialized carriers, then, the competitive necessity that they face of "demonstrating the reliability of their services" to hesitant corporate communications managers may perhaps induce them to establish maintenance procedures and standards exceeding those of the present carriers. It is clear that higher-than-telephone-network reliability can be achieved with a customized microwave system if desired. For example, a number of petroleum pipeline companies and electric utilities—needing critical communication circuits to monitor and control the flow of fuel and electricity—have installed private microwave systems to obtain higher levels of reliability than available from the telephone companies. The specialized carriers can engineer and operate their systems to provide similar high reliability if there is a need that would justify any added costs involved.

The specialized carriers will surely interconnect with one another. The terms and conditions of these future agreements are, of course, unknown at present, but the additional traffic to be obtained through interconnection and the likely encouragement by the regulatory bodies leave no doubt as to the outcome. Since the charges of the interconnected carriers may differ, computing through rates may be difficult, and optimizing a corporate tie-line network or the communications portion of a computer communication system is likely to become exceedingly complex. Datran's switched data transmission services are quite different from the services of the other specialized carriers, however, and use of the Datran network is not expected to ordinarily involve interconnection with another long-haul carrier.

9.5.4 Computer-Communication Network Design

As a general matter, the entry of specialized carriers and their data-oriented service offerings will reduce the overall communication costs of data networks. Line charges for services similar in function to those traditionally available will be lower. A wider variety of offerings will permit better matching of user requirements and carrier services. The elimination of modems in some cases, reduced error rates and therefore improved information throughput, faster connect times and therefore reduced calling overhead, and shorter minimum charge times for dial-up data calls will also contribute to reducing the communications costs of future data networks. Additionally, of course, any improvements in the service offerings and responsiveness of the telephone companies and Western Union, sparked by their new competition, will be a boon to the data communicator.

One obvious result of reduced communication costs will be the ability to cost-justify computer communication systems that previously had been marginal and therefore had not been implemented. Another result will be to swing the centralization–decentralization tradeoff somewhat more toward centralization. Datran's proposed tariff rates—which are the same for all calls outside one's local area irrespective of the distance of the call—strongly encourage centralization.

Lowered charges for switched and leased data services will shift the cross-over point (in terms of number of hours of use per day) at which the user is indifferent between switched or leased connections. Whether the balance is toward greater or lesser use of switched circuits will depend upon the distances of the calls and the exact prices established in the tariffs.

The full duplex capability of Datran's switched medium-speed service will encourage full-duplex transmission, which is generally more efficient. The user's software protocols, however, will become more complicated.

In sum, the entry of specialized carriers will be of considerable benefit to the data communicator, although the greater choices among services offered and carrier organizations will greatly complicate the process of designing a data network.

REFERENCES

[1] Comments of Data Transmission Company, *FCC Docket No. 18920* (Specialized Carrier Inquiry), Oct. 1, 1970.

[2] S. L. MATHISON and P. M. WALKER, *Computers and Telecommunications: Issues in Public Policy*, Prentice-Hall, Englewood Cliffs, N.J., 1970.

[3] Stanford Research Institute, *Report to the FCC in Docket No. 16979*, Feb. 1969 (National Technical Information Service, document numbers PB 183 612, PB 183 613).

[4] Bell Telephone Laboratories, *Transmission Systems for Communications*, 4th ed., Murray Hill, N.J., 1970, Chap. 24, 27.

[5] J. MARTIN, *Future Developments in Telecommunications*, Prentice-Hall, Englewood Cliffs, N.J., 1971.

[6] P. E. MUENCH, Bell System Private Line Digital Data Service, *Proc. 1971 IEEE Intern. Conv.*; also AT&T, "Application for authorization to supplement existing facilities by establishing Digital Channel Groups between Boston, Chicago, New York City, Philadelphia, and Washington, D.C.," filed with the FCC October 30, 1972.

[7] J. F. GUNN et al., Mastergroup Digital Transmission on Modern Coaxial Systems, *Bell Syst. Tech. J.*, **50**(2) (1971).

[8] C. W. BRODERICK, A Digital Transmission System for TD-2 Radio, *Bell Syst. Tech. J.*, **50**(2) (1971).

[9] W. M. ELLINGHAUS (President, New York Telephone Company), Meeting Future Communications Requirements, *Conf. Revolution in Business Commun.* New York (Aug. 31, 1970).

[10] Comments of AT&T, *FCC Docket No. 18920* (Specialized Carrier Inquiry), Oct. 1, 1970, App. B.

[11] J. E. Cox, System Objectives of a Switched Digital Data System, *Proc. Natl. Electron. Conf.* Chicago (Dec. 1970).

[12] *Proceedings of International Conference on Communications* (ICC), June 1971, Section 23, "Datran Data Transmission Network."

[13] First Report and Order, *FCC, Docket No. 18920* (Specialized Carrier Inquiry), 1971, 29 FCC 2d 870.

10

Economic Considerations in Computer-Communication Systems

D. A. DUNN

Engineering-Economic Systems Dept., Stanford University

A. J. LIPINSKI

Institute for the Future, Menlo Park, California

INTRODUCTION

In describing the economic considerations in computer-communication systems, it is useful to adopt the point of view of a particular decision maker and to describe those economic considerations that will play a part in his decision. Several levels of analysis are suggested by this viewpoint, corresponding to three different types of decision maker:

1. The system user, concerned with cost–performance comparisons between competing system alternatives.
2. The system provider, concerned not only with cost–performance relationships but also with the market for various classes of services as a function of price and performance.

3. The government as regulator, system planner and user, concerned with the degree of competition in the provider industry, pricing behavior in the industry, relationships between unregulated and regulated firms, cross subsidization of services by regulated firms, and a variety of other questions that concern the economic behavior of firms in the computer and communications industries.

In this chapter our principal emphasis is on economic considerations of concern to users and system providers. Chapter 9 adopts the viewpoint of the government as decision maker and presents the economic and other considerations of greatest concern at that level of decision making.

10.1   COST–PERFORMANCE ANALYSIS

The user's decision to adopt a particular technology in a computer-communication system or the decision to select one form of computer system over another is usually based on a comparison of the cost and performance of several competing alternatives. The ultimate test, as between two systems with the same performance, is of course the cost. However, systems normally do not have identical performance characteristics, so the user is confronted with a choice between competing systems or technologies with different performance characteristics at different costs.

In this section it is our purpose to present a general philosophy of cost–performance analysis and to show how it may be applied to computer communications. We shall illustrate ways of analyzing computer-communication systems in terms of their subsystems or components, such as terminals, software, computers, and communication lines. As will be explained, the allocation of functions and the associated costs to particular parts of the system is often somewhat arbitrary. Therefore, a valid comparison can only take place at the complete system level.

Normally, we must be concerned with cost–performance comparisons over an extended period of time into the future. We must therefore be able to compare competing system costs that are incurred over different periods of time to a common base. The simplest way of doing this is to convert all costs to their present worth, but other approaches may be appropriate [1]. Similarly, we must be concerned with the performance characteristics of competing systems over some period of time into the future. Such a performance comparison requires that we project the development of the technology of each of the various subsystems into the future, and in this process we become directly concerned with the evaluation and comparison of uncertain outcomes. The next section of this chapter provides an introduction to the analysis of decisions of this type.

Changes in technology normally occur stepwise in time, and any estimate of technological change involves us in questions of industrial and governmental organizational behavior. The rate of technological change is strongly dependent on the competitive strategy of the major firms in the computer and communications industries and on the regulatory environment in which they operate. For example, IBM's strategy of competition with peripheral computer equipment manufacturers can strongly influence the rate of change of the technology of peripheral equipment and of the very definition of what is a piece of peripheral equipment. Similarly, changes in AT&T's competitive strategy with respect to potential competitors in the provision of data communication services can cause major revisions of estimates of the rate of change of the technology and service offerings available to AT&T data customers. The FCC can also strongly affect the behavior of these industries through its decisions concerning the interface between the telephone network and data terminals connected to it, as it did in the Carterfone [2] decision discussed in Chapter 9. Federal sponsorship of research and patterns of federal purchases can also have important influences on the development of the industry. Because most of these influences are difficult to predict over very long time periods, the degree of uncertainty associated with any technology projection rapidly increases with increasing time. Time horizons greater than 5 years in the computer-communications field are subject to question from this standpoint, particularly with respect to terminals and computers. Time horizons of 10 or more years are, however, quite reasonable with respect to costs and performance of the telephone network or of competing data networks, because of the much greater time period required to make changes in these networks. In considering cost-trend comparisons in this field, it is important to compare costs over time for doing the same kinds of jobs. Thus it may be quite inappropriate to compare cost reductions in computer hardware with cost reductions in the provision of data transmission and to infer from these trends that computation costs are falling much more rapidly than communication costs. Although meaningful cost analysis may be difficult, it is very important to attempt some sort of comparison of the cost trends of various system components in order to gain an understanding of the way complete systems are likely to evolve. For example, recent design trends in data processing systems are in directions away from master–slave types of systems with minimum-cost terminals toward systems with greater terminal complexity with terminals performing such functions as buffering, as discussed in Chapter 3. Such trends are a result of lower terminal hardware cost in comparison with data transmission cost, such that total system cost is lower with more costly terminals.

10.1.1   Decision Framework

A framework for system planning and decision making that is useful in the present context is illustrated by the block diagram in Fig. 10.1. This model of the decision process allows us to separate any decision problem into a

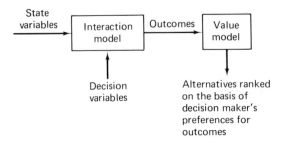

FIGURE 10.1

number of clearly defined elements. We may or may not be able to give a precise form to each element of Fig. 10.1, but by attempting to do so we can become aware of the precise nature of any information lacking and decide whether or not to attempt to acquire the missing information.

In Fig. 10.1 there are two types of variables: (1) decision variables, which are variables under the control of the decision maker, such as system performance specifications; and (2) state variables, which are variables not under the control of the decision maker. For a data communication user as a decision maker an example of a state variable might be the regulatory policy adopted by the FCC with respect to interconnection of private networks with the public message network. For the FCC as decision maker this variable would be a decision variable. A decision maker is normally confronted with a limited set of alternatives. An alternative consists of a complete set of decision variable "settings" in a particular decision problem. For example, in the present context an alternative might be a specific complete system design.

Outcomes are the results associated with each particular choice of a system alternative in the context in which the alternative is to be implemented. The interaction model is whatever model we may have to predict outcomes, and it may be only a very simple verbal model or it may be a mathematical or computer model. Outcomes can be specified in various degrees of detail and at various levels. For example, we shall almost certainly be interested in the outcome that the system performs according to its specifications and is delivered and in operation on time. The cost and technical performance can be viewed as outcomes; in most cases these dimensions of the outcome will be predictable with a high degree of certainty. We would normally also be interested in outcomes related to the use of the system after it is installed. For example, the extent of system usage, by whom the system is used, the time cycle of system usage, and the opinions of users would all be important outcomes.

Finally, the decision maker must be able to provide some kind of value model in order for him to decide among competing alternatives with different outcomes. The decision maker will normally be required to choose among alternatives with different costs and different technical performance characteristics. He will have to be able to specify his tradeoffs between performance characteristics and cost in order to state which alternative he prefers. If he considers probable behavioral outcomes such as usage, he will have to consider tradeoffs at this level as well.

10.1.2 Cost Components

In a computer-communication system it is usually convenient to think of total system cost as the sum of the costs of the four cost components of the total system:

$$\text{total cost} = \begin{bmatrix} \text{cost of} \\ \text{computers} \end{bmatrix} + \begin{bmatrix} \text{cost of user} \\ \text{terminals} \end{bmatrix} + \begin{bmatrix} \text{cost of} \\ \text{software} \end{bmatrix} + \begin{bmatrix} \text{cost of data} \\ \text{transmission} \end{bmatrix}$$

It can be deceptive to look just at the cost of performing a computation or the cost of storing a unit of information. One must, instead, look at the cost of a complete system for providing a particular service. The combined cost of computers, terminals, and software in a large number of system applications is, and will continue to be, a larger fraction of the total cost than the cost of data transmission. In others, the communications costs are dominant.

10.1.3 Performance Dimensions

Computer-communication system performance has many dimensions, some of which are

1. Data rate of transmission of data from user (typical: 100 bps).
2. Data rate of transmission of data to user (typical: 1000 bps).
3. Mode of display of data to user (typical: CRT display).
4. Total amount of data displayed to user at one time and duration of display (typical: one page of text displayed for as long as user wishes).
5. Capability of system to provide a hard copy to user.
6. Degree of privacy offered to users.
7. Total amount of data in central file.
8. Classification system used to access data.
9. Access time for various amounts of data.
10. Time-sharing capability of central file; buffering.
11. Computation speed of central computer.
12. Short-term storage capabilities of central computer; core and disk.
13. Pattern of usage; hours per day per user, number of users, probability of more than n users seeking to use the system simultaneously, etc.

The last performance dimension listed above is an example of a dimension or set of dimensions that seeks to measure user behavior with respect to the system. Ultimately, any system must be measured along some such set of dimensions.

In the next section we consider a decision problem that illustrates cost–performance analysis for the case of a hypothetical computer-communication system designed to provide access to a library of stored data.

10.2 HYPOTHETICAL DECISION PROBLEM

As an example of the type of choice that might be offered to a decision maker, a specific set of alternatives is presented in this section that emphasizes the tradeoff in system design between communication line data rate and terminal complexity for a hypothetical computer-communication system that has the sole function of transmitting stored data to users on demand.

Let us consider a system with a central data file subsystem that stores only written text in the form of standardized characters and is capable of transmitting characters in the form of a standard code with, say, 6 bits/character. With an average of 5 characters/word at a rate of 2000 words/min, such a system can transmit faster than a human can normally read and at a rate sufficient to allow quick scans of the material without much waiting time. The corresponding data rate is $2000 \times 5 \times 6 \times \frac{1}{60}$, or 1000 bps. The average telephone line can transmit at 2000 bps, so this system easily falls into the category that can use such a line.

If the central data system stores ordinary text in the form of microfilmed pages, this system requires a high-speed character recognition and scan system to encode this data, character by character, and convert it to electrical impulses. Such an encoding system is feasible, although costly, and an alternative is a much simpler TV-raster type of scan system that would, however, require a much greater data rate to transmit the signal to the user. A typical value might be of the order of 1000 times the value obtained with efficient coding or 1 Mbps rather than 1 kbps. Consequently, the line costs would be much greater for such a raster-type system.

A related tradeoff in this system occurs at the user terminal, where a raster-type display is also a very simple and low-cost approach. Television sets already are available in almost every home, so if the system were for home use this fact would be very important, and would favor the use of a raster display. The length of time the information needs to be displayed to the user is a critical performance dimension here. Normally a user wishes to be able to look at the information as long as he wishes, up to minutes at a time. If this capability is to be provided, either the information must be stored locally or it must be continually retransmitted from the central data file until the user is through viewing it. A full TV bandwidth is required for the raster display, simply in order to retransmit old information. The basic alternative is a user terminal with sufficient local storage to remember the contents of one page.

One solution is, of course, to make a hard copy. This solution provides both long- and short-term storage and frees the central data file for other tasks as soon as the information is sent once. However, it is difficult, noisy, and costly to produce hard copy at the speed suggested at the beginning of this discussion using present technology, such as line printers. There are two other major alternatives for the user terminal with storage. The first involves conventional digital storage to store the received information for each character using an ordinary computer memory. The present cost of this type of storage for a full page of text (about 10 kbits in the form of characters) is of the order of $1000 or more. Another alternative is to use a magnetic disk or videotape machine to record the information in one TV frame (about 1 to 10 Mbits in the form of an arbitrary pattern)[3]. Either of these techniques allows the use of a TV-raster system, but requires that the signal be sent only once. Such a system could equally well be used to store pictures or other noncharacter information. It would allow a burst of information to be sent using the full TV bandwidth for $\frac{1}{30}$ s (the time of one full frame), and it would retain this information locally until the user asked for a new frame. Obviously, such a system would have the advantage of freeing both the central data file and the wideband channel used to send the information to serve other users on a time-shared basis. Such a system can be imagined as a service offered to homes via cable television during the next few years [4].

We are now in a position to formulate several basically different system alternatives that, if this were a real problem, could be costed out in detail. Here we shall assign some hypothetical cost figures to each alternative in order to pose the problem for analysis in a specific form. In all cases we shall assume that the central data file is the same, except for the presence of the character reader and encoder that we shall use for one system in place of the TV camera that will be used for the two raster-type system alternatives. A list of the components available for this hypothetical system is given in Table 10.1. In addition, we must specify the number of users in order to determine total system costs. We shall consider two cases, a system with 1000 users, which has a cost per user of C_{1000}, and a system with 10,000 users with a cost per user of $C_{10,000}$. It is convenient to express all costs on a per user year basis, which requires that hardware costs be converted from initial total values to annual values. The maintenance costs, life, and interest rate are assumed to be such that the initial costs in Table 10.1 are four times the annual costs.

TABLE 10.1   *Components and Costs for Hypothetical Systems*

	Component	*Hypothetical Cost* ($)
A	Central data file	1,000,000
B	Character reader and encoder	100,000
C	TV camera setup	10,000
D	5-Mhz line for TV-raster transmission	600[a]
E	200-bps line for character transmission	60[a]
F	5-MHz line on time-shared basis	200[a]
G	TV-raster user terminal without storage	300
H	User terminal with local character storage using magnetic core	1,500
I	User terminal with local storage of raster using magnetic disc	Uncertain. Probability 0.2 that it can be produced for $600. Probability 0.8 that cost will be $1000.

[a]These are hypothetical costs expressed on a per user per year basis, assuming an average user to central data file distance and an average usage that is independent of the number of users.

The simplest way to think of annual cost is that this is the price that the decision maker would have to pay to lease rather than buy, because it includes all the factors of cost, including maintenance and capital costs. We can calculate annual cost as follows [5]:

Let
$$\text{life} = N \text{ years}$$
$$\text{interest rate} = i\% \text{ per annum}$$
$$\text{maintenance cost} = m\% \text{ per annum}$$

$$\text{annual cost} = [\text{first cost}]\left[\frac{m}{100} + \frac{i/100}{1 - 1/[1 + (i/100)]^N}\right] \qquad (10.1)$$

For example, if
$$N = 10$$
$$i = 8$$
$$m = 10$$
$$\text{annual cost} = [\text{first cost}][0.25]$$

which is the ratio used in the examples here.

Three system alternatives that can be constructed from the components of Table 10.1 are listed on the following page.

ALTERNATIVE SYSTEM 1

Character coding, transmission using 2-kbps line.
Components A, B, E, H.

C_{1000} = \$710 per user (including \$60 line costs)
$C_{10,000}$ = \$462 per user (including \$60 line costs)

ALTERNATIVE SYSTEM 2

TV-raster transmission using 5-MHz line.
Components A, C, D, G.

C_{1000} = \$928 per user (including \$600 line costs)
$C_{10,000}$ = \$700 per user (including \$600 line costs)

ALTERNATIVE SYSTEM 3

TV-raster transmission using 5-MHz line and local storage.
Components A, C, F, I.

C_{1000} = \$602 per user, with probability 0.2
(including \$200 line costs)
= \$700 per user, with probability 0.8
(including \$200 line costs)
$C_{10,000}$ = \$375 per user, with probability 0.2
(including \$200 line costs)
= \$475 per user, with probability 0.8
(including \$200 line costs)

Note that the terminal costs for system 2 are much less than those for system 1, but the total cost for system 1 is lower. If we regard both systems as having the same performance, the choice is clear as between these two systems. However, system 2 has a potential performance that could be more useful than system 1 if it were later desired to convert the central data file to one that stored diagrams and photographs or pages of printed text with different type sizes and styles.

System 3 is the lowest-cost system for 1000 users, without regard to which terminal design ultimately is developed. If the decision maker does not have to share in the development costs and can delay purchase of his system until system 3 is available, it is a clear choice for a 1000-user system. If the system must serve 10,000 users, the problem is more complex. Only if the lowest-cost terminal is the result of the development program will this system be lower cost than system 1. If the higher-cost terminal is the one that proves feasible, system 1 is lower cost than system 3. How should the decision maker choose between systems 1 and 3, assuming that he must make up his mind before the terminal development program is complete?

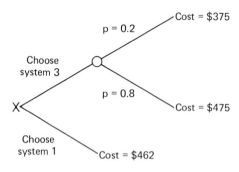

FIGURE 10.2

It is helpful in visualizing problems involving probabilistic outcomes to make use of a *decision tree*, as illustrated in Fig. 10.2. The cross is a *decision node* at which the decision between systems 1 and 3 is made. The circle is a *chance node* at which the outcome can be either of the costs shown, $375 or $475 per user, each with the probability indicated. These probability estimates are those of the decision maker in the light of all the information that he has available. The solution of such problems is the purpose of decision analysis [6–10].

There are two basic steps necessary to the solution of such a problem. First, the decision maker must make probability assessments like those expressed in Fig. 10.2. Second, he must provide a fairly precise indication of how he values the various possible outcomes. The way this is most conveniently done in general is in the form of a utility function. If there were many dimensions to the outcome, he would have to give us his utility when confronted with tradeoffs among all these dimensions. In the present problem all that is involved is the single dimension of dollars of cost. But there is still an issue as to how highly the decision maker values dollars in various quantities. What is needed is a curve of utility (in arbitrary units) as a function of dollars.

Figure 10.3 shows two such curves. The meaning of these curves can be made more clear if we interpret them in terms of "lotteries." A lottery is a situation like that in which the decision maker selects system 3. He then obtains the lottery: with probability 0.2 his cost will be $375; with probability 0.8 his cost will be $475. An important thing about a lottery is its certain equivalent, i.e., the amount that the decision maker would be willing to pay and then be indifferent as to whether he paid this amount or the amount determined from the lottery. If this certain equivalent in our example turns out to be less than $462, the decision maker should choose system 3. If it is greater than $462, he should choose system 1.

In the curves of Fig. 10.3 the interpretation that may be made in terms of lotteries is as follows. We can assign an arbitrary value of utility to a cost of

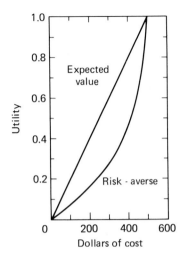

FIGURE 10.3

$500, such as 1.0. Now we ask what is the maximum amount that the decision maker would pay to avoid a lottery in which a fair coin would be flipped and he would pay $500 if it came up heads and $0 if it came up tails. The expected value of an uncertain reward is defined as the probability of receiving the reward times the amount of the reward, summed over all possible rewards. The expected value in this case is $250, so the expected-value decision maker would pay exactly $250 to avoid this lottery, whereas the risk-averse decision maker in Fig. 10.3 would pay more than this amount. The expected-value decision maker is indifferent to risk. The risk-averse decision maker is less inclined to take fair gambles as the stakes become large in comparison with his total resources. Thus we all might be willing to match pennies, but only a few of us enjoy matching $100 bills, even though the game is fair. The risk-averse decision maker in Fig. 10.3 is pictured as a person or organization that is quite sensitive to cost in the vicinity of $400 per user. He is not willing to gamble very much in the hope of getting the cost per user down to $375, as long as there is a risk that he may have to pay $475 if things turn out badly.

Once we know the decision maker's utility curve, we can insert his utility for each outcome and the probability of this outcome occurring in the following equation [7]:

$$u(c) = p(a)u(a) + p(b)u(b) \qquad (10.2)$$

where $u(c) =$ utility of the certain equivalent of the lottery in which a is received with probability $p(a)$ and b is received with probability $p(b)$: $p(b) = 1 - p(a)$
$u(a) =$ utility of receiving a with certainty
$u(b) =$ utility of receiving b with certainty

In our problem, for the expected-value decision maker in Fig. 10.3,

$$u(a) = 0.95$$
$$p(a) = 0.8$$
$$u(b) = 0.75$$
$$p(b) = 0.2$$
$$u(c) = 0.91$$
$$c = \$455$$

so he would prefer system 3. The risk-averse decision maker, on the other hand, has

$$u(a) = 0.77$$
$$p(a) = 0.8$$
$$u(b) = 0.4$$
$$p(b) = 0.2$$
$$u(c) = 0.70$$
$$c = \$462$$

This certain equivalent is just equal to the cost of system 1, so he would be indifferent between systems 1 and 3. Thus the risk-averse decision maker would pay slightly more than the expected-value decision maker to avoid the lottery associated with system 3, but in this case he would be unable to decide between the two systems on this basis alone. In such a case he might reexamine his probability assessments and also reexamine the assumption that the two systems would have identical performance. As noted previously, system 3 seems to have more potential for the future, if there were any likelihood that the system might be used for diagrams and photographs at a later date. Another variable in this decision problem was the number of user terminals, assumed here to be known with certainty. In an actual problem the number of user terminals would be a function of predicted demand. It would be known only probabilistically, and, as we have seen, it clearly affects the decision.

In this, and in almost every decision problem, there is at least one variable that can only be known within broad limits. In such cases the issue arises as to whether or not more information should be gathered. More information always comes with a price tag, and so we must have some measure of the value of information if we are to make a logical choice as to whether or not to gather it. Decision analysis can give a very precise answer to such questions by tracing through the effect that having more information would have on the decision [11, 12]. This process can be carried out by assuming that perfect information is available and examining the cost savings that might result in the best possible case, thus establishing an upper bound on how much it would make sense to pay for perfect information. Of course, we cannot normally get perfect information, so we also may need to know the value of imperfect information. A typical example is the kind of information obtained by sampling opinion or testing quality by random sampling of some manufactured good.

10.3 COSTS OF COMPUTER COMMUNICATIONS

It is extremely difficult to discuss system costs without specifying what system is being discussed. If the system is well defined, as in the hypothetical example of the preceding section, a detailed cost–performance comparison of system alternatives can be carried out. If not, only very general statements can be made. In this section some of these general statements will be attempted, but it should be understood that the purpose of this section is to indicate trends rather than to accurately calculate the cost of any particular system.

The basic system configuration being considered in this book involves one or more computers connected to user terminals through communication lines. Switching between users is normally done at the computer, but there may also be additional switching in the establishment of the communication connection between the user and the computer if the public message telephone network is used (see Chapter 5). There may also be switching in the vicinity of a group of users if line concentration is employed, as in a PBX system.

At the present time substantially all the world's data traffic is carried over the analog voice network. Chapter 5 describes this network and its limitations. In the future several alternatives to the use of this network are likely to become available. One is the data network based on the use of the T-1 (PCM) carrier that is expected to be put into operation in the United States by the Bell System (see Chapter 5). Another is the competing Datran data network or equivalent. Both of these alternatives will seek to take advantage of an all-digital network design to provide data transmission characteristics of special value to data users, including shorter connect (or call setup) time, lower minimum charge per call (for shorter calls), and lower noise. All these improved characteristics are expected to lead to lower-cost data transmission, especially for users with a demand for higher data rates than can presently be handled by a voice-grade line in the analog telephone network and for users wishing to send messages of short duration, such as 1 s.

Although these specialized data networks will be of great importance in the long term, an extremely significant and important fact about data transmission today is that it is possible to successfully make use of the analog voice network in a very wide range of computer-communication system designs at a cost that is small in comparison with the costs of computers, terminals, and software. In essence, this statement is possible because there are many important computer-communication systems in which human users are involved, and humans usually send messages at data rates that can easily be accommodated by a voiceband line, and they usually wish to occupy the line for times of the order of minutes or longer. Thus standard telephone lines and the associated charges are often acceptable for these classes of service. It is in systems such as those in which computers communicate with computers or in which machines such as meter readers or credit-card readers communicate with computers that the new data networks will be able to offer the greatest cost savings.

Another competing network that is likely to become of importance in a somewhat different part of the data market (the video information market) is the cable television network, now being built primarily with an entertainment market in mind [13]. The cable television network has a configuration that is natural for computer communications, with a central origination point linked to, typically, 10,000 terminals in homes and offices within a few miles of the central origination point. Most existing cable TV networks are one-way systems, but many new cable systems being installed today offer limited two-way operation in which data messages can be sent from subscribers to the central computer [14]. Thus subscribers can interact with the computer or can request information stored in the central files and accessed through the computer. Like the telephone network, this network will be built primarily for nondata purposes, but will provide the opportunity for low marginal cost usage by data users. Especially significant is the opportunity to use this system for applications in which rather high data rates are desired from the central origination point to the user, but only low data rates are needed from users back to the origination point. Interconnection of these systems to form a national network is possible, but the costs of long-haul communication are likely to be about the same in this type of system as in the telephone system.

In the following parts of this section we attempt to identify cost trends in the major components of computer-communication systems: data transmission, computers, terminals, and software.

10.3.1   Data Transmission Costs

Here we limit our specific cost estimates to costs of data transmission in the public message (telephone) network. As remarked above, new networks specifically designed for data and also the cable TV network are likely to be available to data users within 5 years. However, during the next 5 years most data transmission is likely to continue to be via the telephone network.

10.3.1.1 Reduction in Connect Time. As described in Chapter 5, the minimum connect time, or call setup time, in the public message network today is about 9 s, and 10 to 30 s is typical. Common channel signaling and the use of ESS switches can reduce connect times to around 1 to 3 s. For data users with very short messages this change could reduce costs by more than a factor of 3, if charges are reduced commensurably for the minimum-length call.

10.3.1.2 Use of Data Concentrators and Line Sharing. For situations in which several data users have terminals in the same building or general area the opportunity exists to share communication lines. The relative cost of data concentrator hardware and line cost savings obviously need to be compared in any practical case, but again major cost savings for some users can be obtained in this way. The replacement of the usual modems with dc data sets in local loop systems, in combination with data concentrators, can reduce costs both by line sharing and by reduction in modem costs. A Bell System private-line offering takes advantage of this combination of factors to reduce costs for some users by around 50 per cent.

10.3.1.3 Modem Costs. Three factors combine to allow us to project a continuing reduction in the price of modems over the next 5 years: increased competition, increased sales volume, and improvements in technology. In 1970 about two-thirds of the data sets (modems) were supplied by the common carriers. This proportion is likely to be reduced as competition increases, and a price reduction of 50 per cent due to increased competition has been projected [15].

Apart from the effect of increased competition, a reduction in the terminal prices will come as a consequence of the growing volume. If the number of data sets reaches even 1 per cent of the number of telephones (a figure likely to be exceeded by 1975), there would be 1 million data sets. Economies of scale at Western Electric would probably come into play at an annual volume of 50,000 or more of a particular data set. Thus we expect that the price of data sets supplied by the Bell System, in the categories in which Western Electric can take advantage of common requirements of many users, will be substantially reduced.

The third encouraging factor in price reduction is a forthcoming change of technology probable within the next 5 years, which is an introduction of LSI (large-scale integrated circuits) into modem design. Even though some features of modems may not lend themselves to LSI circuit design, it is expected that the cost reduction in areas benefiting from LSI may be as high as 50 per cent of the electronics cost, or approximately 15 per cent of the overall cost.

Reviewing the above three factors (competition, volume, and technology), it is estimated that the customer may experience a price reduction that may in some specific categories of usage amount to 75 per cent within the next decade [16]. The greatest benefits would be received by the users of "standard" offerings, because they will profit from all these factors.

The data set cost contributes a proportion of the total cost of a connection that varies with the length of the connection and the connect time. Naturally, the proportion rises as distances grow shorter. To estimate the effect that a data set price reduction might have on the users' costs, the comparison given in Table 10.2 has been made. Consider a type 103A data set (300 bps—a very popular data set) connecting a remote console and a computer. A short-haul system has been chosen because the cost of a data set contributes most to the overall cost when the distances are short. For example, assume that the console is in San Mateo, California, and the computer is 15, 30, or 45 miles away. Table 10.2 gives a comparison of the costs of rental and operation of a data set, a loop connection, and a teletypewriter, with the line costs based on actual usage.

Consider the impact of a reduction in data set costs of 50 per cent, that is, to $15 a month. For the first case (computer 15 miles away) the new total is $76 (instead of $91), a reduction of 16.5 per cent. For longer distances the effect of the price reduction of a data set is even smaller.

10.3.1.4 Voiceband Data Transmission Cost Trends in Short-Haul Systems. The above factors indicate that some users, favorably situated (that is, clustered) near a computer or using a popular large-volume modem, in the next 5 years may enjoy cost reductions amounting to as much as 50 per cent of the current data transmission cost. In most cases we would expect some cost reduction, say, 30 per cent. Few users' needs will be so specialized that they would be unable to gain advantage of the reduced equipment costs that are likely to result from LSI circuit technology and from increased competition.

10.3.1.5 Long-Haul Data Transmission Costs. There has been a steady reduction in the cost of long-haul data transmission over the past several decades, and recent developments discussed in Chapter 5 allow us to reasonably project a continuing cost reduction over the coming decade. An estimate by the AT&T Long-Lines Department [17] given in Table 10.3 shows their projection of relative book cost per circuit mile over the next decade, yielding approximately a 40 per cent reduction in cost over that time period. This estimate is much more useful than the estimated cost of, say, a millimeter waveguide system, because this cost estimate includes the fact that the total plant will consist of a mixture of microwave, coaxial line, waveguide, and other long-haul systems, and the 40 per cent reduction is an overall cost reduction for the system as a whole.

10.3.1.6 Wideband Data Transmission Cost Trends. Wideband data includes all data transmission over bands wider than voiceband. As discussed

TABLE 10.2 Example Showing the Effect of Modem Cost as Seen by the Data Set User
(Users' Monthly Costs in Dollars)
San Francisco Area

	Distance Between Computers and Consoles (miles)		
	15	30	45
Before modem cost reduction			
Approx. service charges for a teletypewriter	$ 60.00	$ 60.00	$ 60.00
Approx. service charges for a single modem[a]	30.00	30.00	30.00
Approx. service charges for a business line	10.00	10.00	10.00
Operating expense (1 h/day, 5 days/week)			
2 calls at 30 min each			
Message units (initial 3 min)	6	10	16
Message units (additional 27 min)	54	108	162
Total message units	60	118	178
Daily operating expense ($)	$ 2.43	$ 4.78	$ 7.20
Monthly operating expense (21 days)	51.00	100.40	151.00
Total expense (rental and operating)	151.00	200.40	251.00
Total communication cost[b] (I)	91.00	140.40	191.00
Per cent modem operating cost to total operating cost	19.9%	15.0%	12.0%
Per cent modem operating cost to total communication cost	33.0	21.4	15.7
After modem cost reduction			
Total communication cost[b] (II)	$ 76.00	$125.40	$176.00
Total operating cost	136.00	185.40	236.00
Per cent modem operating cost to total operating cost	15.3%	11.1%	8.65%
Per cent modem operating cost to total communication cost	28.2	16.6	11.7
Per cent communication cost II/communication cost I	83.5	89.5	92.0
Per cent overall communication cost reduction	16.5	10.5	8.0

[a] A connection could not be made with only one set of terminal equipment and one business line; however, we are showing the charges as they appear to a typical user of computational services.

[b] Excluding a teletypewriter, a sum of modem, business line, and monthly operating expense.

TABLE 10.3 *Trend of Relative Book Cost per Circuit Mile (Special Long Lines Estimate)*[a]

	1969	1970	1971	1972	1973	1974	1975	1976	1977	1978	1979	1980
Relative book cost addns.												
Radio	—	—	1.3	1.3	1.7	2.2	1.5	1.8	1.5	1.5	2.1	2.0
Cable	—	—	2.7	2.1	0.5	1.2	2.1	2.2	2.5	3.4	5.0	5.2
LMX and other terminal equipment	—	—	2.7	3.0	3.0	3.7	3.6	4.1	4.7	4.9	4.8	5.5
Other (less ret.)	—	—	0.3	0.6	0.8	0.9	0.8	0.9	1.3	1.2	1.1	1.3
			7.0	7.0	6.0	8.0	8.0	9.0	10.0	11.0	13.0	14.0
Relative circuit mile addns.												
New routes	—	—	1.2	1.9	3.5	1.6	6.4	4.0	2.2	4.3	2.3	2.9
Existing routes	—	—	13.8	14.1	15.5	18.4	17.6	22.0	26.8	28.7	35.7	39.1
			15.0	16.0	19.0	20.0	24.0	26.0	29.0	33.0	38.0	42.0
Relative book costs	100	107	114	121	127	135	143	152	162	173	186	200
Relative circuit miles	100	110	125	141	160	180	204	230	259	292	330	372
Relative book cost/circuit mile	1.00	0.97	0.92	0.86	0.80	0.75	0.70	0.66	0.63	0.59	0.56	0.54

[a]Source: AT&T.

in Chapter 5, a 50-kbps service using a "group" of twelve voice channels is a natural next step for the common-carrier network. Still wider bands, such as that to be used for Picturephone®, which will provide 6.3 Mbps, can be composed from larger bundles of voice channels. Experimental 50-kbps switched data offerings in the large cities have not found many customers. Some wideband private-line data service is in operation, but the number of wideband data sets was less than 1 per cent of the total number of data sets in 1968 [18]. Although present trends suggest that 50-kbps systems are likely to be the highest data rate systems in general use exclusively for data, the use of Picturephone lines for data, where they are installed for both Picture-phone and data service, could turn out to be an important new factor in this situation. If the number of Picturephones were to become large, say, of the order of 2 million, the possibility of using this 6.3-Mbps system for large networks becomes possible, and high-volume cost reductions in high data rate systems could become important in this case. However, because of the relatively smaller size of this market, it is much less likely that cost reductions will be experienced in short-haul service due to economies of scale in modem production or due to competition than is the case in narrowband service. On the other hand, cost reductions in long-haul wideband transmission are likely to be as great for narrowband service, that is, about 40 per cent over the next decade.

10.3.1.7 Summary of Estimated Cost Reductions in Data Transmission. Our estimate, based on discussions with AT&T personnel, is that by 1976 the percentage distribution of data conversations by distance is likely to be as tabulated below.

Data Speed	Less Than 50 Miles (%)	More Than 50 Miles (%)
Low	75	25
Medium	25	75
High	30	70

For the shorter distances the cost reductions due to the cost reduction of the modem, the use of concentrators, and the improved T-1 transmission plant are of consequence. Let us assign a total cost reduction of 30 per cent by 1976 to a sum of the three factors as the average decrease in the cost of voiceband data. For the longer distances, let us assume a 10 per cent reduction in the overall transmission costs (based on the assumption that long-distance transmission costs are only one-third of the overall transmission costs and that the cost of long-distance transmission has diminished by 30 per cent). Let us assume also that in the short- and long-distance connections switching costs account for 55 and 50 per cent, respectively, of the overall costs. Bearing in mind the extreme roughness of these assumptions, we

TABLE 10.4   *Distribution of the Normalized Cost by Distance*

Data Speed	Data Users (%)	(A) Less Than 50 Miles	(B) More Than 50 Miles
Low	77	$0.77 \times 0.75 \times 0.45 = 0.260$	$0.77 \times 0.25 \times 0.5 = 0.097$
Medium	22	$0.22 \times 0.25 \times 0.45 = 0.025$	$0.22 \times 0.75 \times 0.5 = 0.082$
High	1	$0.01 \times 0.30 \times 0.45 = 0.001$	$0.01 \times 0.70 \times 0.5 = 0.004$
		0.286	0.183

Total cost $= 0.286 + 0.348 + 0.183 + 0.183 = 1.00$, where 0.348 and 0.183 are the switching cost components.

TABLE 10.5   *Distribution of Total Cost by Distance*

Data Speed	Less Than 50 Miles	More Than 50 Miles
Low	$0.260 \times 0.7 = 0.1820$	$0.097 \times 0.9 = 0.0872$
Medium	$0.025 \times 0.7 = 0.0175$	$0.082 \times 0.9 = 0.0738$
High	$0.001 \times 0.7 = 0.007$	$0.004 \times 0.9 = 0.0036$
	0.1965	0.1646

The switching components of the cost are, as before, 0.348 and 0.183. Thus total cost $= 0.1965 + 0.1646 + 0.348 + 0.183 = 0.8921$ for an average reduction of 10.5 per cent for the system as a whole.

nevertheless can construct Tables 10.4 and 10.5, which develop weighted cost reductions according to the percentage of data users in each category (obtained from Section 10.4).

For distances less than 50 miles, the normalized cost of transmission, loop connection, and data set was assumed to be 0.45, with switching cost contributing 0.55, thus making a total cost of 1.0. Similarly, for distances longer than 50 miles, the normalized cost of loop connections, transmission, and data set was assumed to be 0.5, and the cost of switching 0.5, making a total of 1.0.

The first factor in the above calculation (0.77 in column A) corresponds to the percentage of data users in the given category; the second factor corresponds to the percentage of users in that category whose communications extend over the given range of distance; the third factor represents a fraction of the total cost contributed by cost elements other than switching. The switching cost component for distances less than 50 miles bears a ratio of 0.55/0.45 to the transmission cost component; i.e., the switching cost component is $(0.55/0.45) \times 0.286 = 0.348$. Similarly, the switching cost component for distances longer than 50 miles is equal to the transmission

TABLE 10.6 *Intrastate and Interstate Rates for Low-, Medium-, and High-Speed Data Transmission*

Classification	Facility	Bit Rate (bps)	Channel Terminal[a]	Station Arrangement[a]	Modem[a]	Line Charge ($/mile/month)	C-2 Conditioning	California Tariff
Intrastate								
Low-speed data (narrowband)	3A	150	$12.50 to 25 mi $25.00 > 25 mi	$25.00 (each end)	Incl.	0–50 mi, 2.81 > 50 mi, 1.87	None	PUC 46-T
Medium-speed (voiceband)	4B	2,400	$10.00 to 25 mi $20.00 > 25 mi		$75.00 (each end)	3.65	$38.00 (each end)	PUC 50-T
High-speed (wideband)	A1	19,200	$125.00 (each end)		Incl.	22.00	Incl.	PUC 122-T
Interstate								
Low-speed data (narrowband)	1006	150	$31.25 (each end)	$13.75 (each end)	Incl.	0–100 mi, 1.40 101–250 mi, 0.98 251–500 mi, 0.56 501–1000 mi, 0.42 > 1000 mi, 0.28	None	260
Medium-speed (voiceband)	4000	2,400	$25.00 (each end)	No charge	$72.00 (each end)	> 250 mi, 4.00 251–500 mi, 3.00 501–1000 mi, 2.35 next 500 mi, 1.65 > 1500 mi, 1.40	$19.00 (each end)	260
High-speed (wideband)	8001	19,200	$425.00 (each end)	No charge	Incl.	> 250 mi, 15.00 next 250 mi, 10.50 > 500 mi, 7.50	Incl.	260

[a]Intrastate rates for California only.

TABLE 10.7 *Intrastate and Interstate Charges for Low-, Medium-, and High-Speed Data Transmission,*[a] *by Miles (Private-Line Service)*

Speeds and Line Cost	Intrastate ($)			Interstate ($)				
	20	100	500	20	100	500	1000	3000
Low speed (150 bps)								
Per month	131.00	334.00	1,082.00	125.00	265.00	624.00	796.00	1,496.00
Per month per mile	6.56	3.34	2.16	6.25	2.65	1.25	0.80	0.50
Medium speed (2400 bps)								
Per month	319.00	631.00	2,091.00	312.00	632.00	1982.00	3,157.00	6,082.00
Per month per mile	15.95	6.31	4.18	15.60	6.32	3.96	3.16	2.03
High speed (19,200 bps)								
Per month	690.00	2,450.00	11,250.00	1150.00	2350.00	7225.00	10,975.00	25,975.00
Per month per mile	34.50	24.50	22.50	57.50	23.50	14.45	10.98	8.66

[a]Line charges include modem or channel terminal, as appropriate. Charges shown are for interexchange, two-point, nonswitched single service. Installation charges are not included.

cost component, i.e., 0.183. Table 10.5 introduces the additional factor of cost reduction: 30 per cent cost reduction for shorter distances and 10 per cent for longer distances.

Our example serves to indicate a rough estimate of a possible cost reduction. Since even the approximate cost reduction of 10 per cent should be realized only by 1976, it is possible that inflationary tendencies will mask it. However, for some classes of users, as we have noted, the prospect for much greater cost reductions, such as 50 per cent, is very good.

10.3.1.8   Interstate and Intrastate Charges for Data Transmission.   All the preceding cost estimates have been in the form of cost reductions over the next 5 or 10 years relative to present 1971 costs. This section is intended

TABLE 10.8   *Data Transmission Charges per Mile per Month per 10^6 Bits Transmitted (Private-Line Service)*

	CHARGES/MILE/MONTH (\$)		CHARGES/MILE/10^6 BITS (¢)[a]	
	Intrastate	*Interstate*	*Intrastate*	*Interstate*
Low speed (150 bps)				
20 miles	6.56	6.25	1.68	1.60
100 miles	3.34	2.65	0.86	0.68
500 miles	2.16	1.25	0.55	0.32
1000 miles	–	0.80	–	0.21
Medium speed (2400 bps)				
20 miles	15.95	15.60	0.26	0.25
100 miles	6.31	6.32	0.10	0.10
500 miles	4.18	3.96	0.07	0.06
1000 miles	–	3.16	–	0.05
High speed (19.2 kbps)				
20 miles	34.50	57.50	0.07	0.12
100 miles	24.50	23.50	0.05	0.05
500 miles	22.50	14.45	0.04	0.03
1000 miles	–	10.98	–	0.02
WATS[b] (voice/data—1200 bps)				
20 miles	n.a.[c]	67.50[d]	n.a.	2.16
100 miles	n.a.	13.50[d]	n.a.	0.43
500 miles	n.a.	2.70[d]	n.a.	0.08
1000 miles	–	1.95[e]	–	0.06

[a]Based on monthly charges; includes modems, conditioning, loop, and terminal charges where applicable. See Table 10.6 for tariffs.
[b]Full-time service (data).
[c]n.a., not available for full-time service.
[d]Service area 1, maximum mileage about 700 miles.
[e]Service area 3, maximum mileage about 1350 miles.

to provide a general idea of what the charges to a data user might be for typical services. The figures and descriptions of service given are for 1968 in California and were compiled by W. A. Kent [19]. They are believed to be representative of U.S. costs and not very different from 1971 charges.

PRIVATE-LINE SERVICE.   Examples of AT&T narrowband (low speed, 150 bps), voiceband (medium speed, 2400 bps), and wideband (high speed, 19,200 bps) data transmission rates for intrastate (California) and interstate facilities are shown in Table 10.6. The modem and terminal charges, line charges, and line conditioning charges, when applicable, as shown in Table 10.6, were used to compute the intrastate and interstate data rates for various transmission distances, as shown in Table 10.7. These monthly charges are shown for 20, 100, and 500 miles intrastate and 20, 100, 500, 1000, and 3000 miles interstate. Also shown in Table 10.7 are the line charges per mile per month for the above transmission distances.

Table 10.8 shows the transmission charges/mile/month/10^6 bits transmitted for the low-, medium-, and high-speed data rates and for WATS (Wide Area Telephone Service) in the switched network at the 1200-bps data rate.

SWITCHED NETWORK DATA TRANSMISSION

Low- and Medium-Speed Data Transmission   The line rates for intrastate facilities vary from state to state. Table 10.9 shows examples of charges for various distances from San Francisco for the use of the switched network facilities.

TABLE 10.9   *Intrastate and Interstate Charges for Low- and Medium-Speed Data Transmission on the Switched Network[a] (California)*

	MILES							
	INTRASTATE			INTERSTATE				
	20	*100*	*500*	*20*	*100*	*500*	*1000*	*3000*
Line charge first 3 min, less tax ($)	0.28[b]	0.60	1.30	0.70[c]	0.60[d]	1.20	1.40	1.70
Line charge per mile per min (¢)	1.40	0.60	0.26	3.50	0.60	0.24	0.14	0.06

[a]Day, Monday through Friday, station-to-station rates; terminal charges, telephone, teletype Data-Phone, or other modems are not included.
[b]Message unit area: two-message units for each additional minute. Each message unit is 4.05 cents.
[c]Truckee, Calif., to Reno, Nev.
[d]Sacramento, Calif. to Reno, Nev.

TABLE 10.10 *Intrastate and Interstate High-Speed Data Transmission on the Switched Network*

Classification	Bit Rate (bps)	Service Terminal Charges/Month[a]	Station Terminal Charges/Month/Terminal ($)	Installation Charge ($)	Message Service Usage Charges/Minute[b] (miles)	($)	Tariffs
Data-Phone 50[c]	50,000		275, nonsynchronous 300, alternate synchronous and nonsynchronous	125	< 50 51–150 151–300 301–600 601–1200 1200–2000 > 2000	0.50 0.80 1.25 1.75 2.25 2.75 3.25	FCC-260 and FCC-263 PUC-133T
Intrastate Foreign Exchange Service[d]	50,000	$150 Plus voice line[e]		100	.22 per mile 6.50 per mile plus 0.20 per min. per call		FCC-260
Interstate Foreign Exchange Service	50,000	$12.50 half duplex $13.75 full duplex		10	< 25 mi 26–100 101–250 251–500 > 500	3.00/mi[f] 2.10/mi 1.50/mi 1.05/mi 0.75/mi	FCC-260

[a] Type 5708 or 8802.
[b] Or fraction thereof.
[c] Data-Phone 50 service available among four cities: New York, Chicago, Washington, D.C., and Los Angeles.
[d] Service needed to interconnect to Data-Phone 50 switching centers, located in the four cities listed above.
[e] Voice coordinating line required for Data-Phone 50 service.
[f] Rates for half duplex; full duplex 10 per cent additional.

High-Speed Data Transmission American Telephone & Telegraph and associated companies offer a switched high-speed data service (Data-Phone 50) up to 50,000 bps. The intent of this service is to provide wideband service to users that do not have the volume to justify wideband private-line service. The service is offered experimentally on a two-point station-to-station basis within and between New York, Chicago, Los Angeles, and Washington, D.C. Table 10.10 shows the rate information for the Data-Phone 50 service and the Intrastate and Interstate Foreign Exchange Services, which provide connection to the Data-Phone 50 switching centers located in the above-mentioned four cities.

10.3.2   Central Processing Unit Costs

The cost per thousand processing operations has been consistently dropping over the past decade, as illustrated by Fig. 10.4, which is a plot of data from a study of 310 computers by Knight [20]. Economies of scale in large computers are evident in Fig. 10.4 and, in fact, form the economic basis for one class of computer-communication systems in which many remote users share

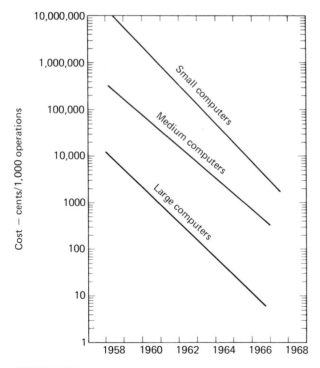

FIGURE 10.4

a single CPU. In such cases the costs of communication must be balanced against the cost savings obtained from using a large computer.

Cost trends in CPU operations since Knight's study have continued at essentially the same rate, but are not readily connected with the curves of Fig. 10.4. Projections over the next 5 years suggest a continuation of the cost trends suggested by this figure [21].

10.3.3 Memory Costs

MEMORIES.   Ideally, a computer would have (1) unlimited capacity for storage of data, and (2) instantaneous delivery (or storage) of the data specified by the program. However, any practical operating system must achieve a reasonable compromise between economics and technology in striving toward these ideals. In searching for such compromises the computer industry has developed a number of classes of memory, each directed toward maximizing (insofar as possible) the performance–cost ratio for a certain type of function.

TABLE 10.11   *Major Types of Computer Memory Available in 1968*
          (*In order of increasing access time requirements*)

Type	*Access Time*[a] (*order of magnitude*)	*Size* (*characters*)
Scratch-pad memory (thin film and integrated circuits)	tenths of microseconds	hundreds to few thousands
Main memory	1 μs	tens to hundreds of thousands
Auxiliary memory		
"Mass" core	few microseconds	few million
Drum/disk	tens to hundreds milliseconds[b]	tens to hundreds of millions
Magnetic strips	$\frac{1}{2}$ s[b]	hundreds of millions
Optical[c]	seconds[b]	thousands of millions
Magnetic tapes	many seconds[b] (average)	hundreds of millions

[a]Magnetic memories are unique in that the data stored are generally destroyed when read —a rewriting operation is therefore required. The time specified above is actually that for a read–write cycle, data being accessed in about half the cycle time.

[b]For these types of memory units, blocks of characters can be processed with *average* access times that are orders of magnitude shorter than the (initial) access times tabulated above.

[c]In general, optical memories are "fixed" after data are once stored and serve as a read-only memory thereafter. Some types are prerecorded with basic information before installation in the computer.

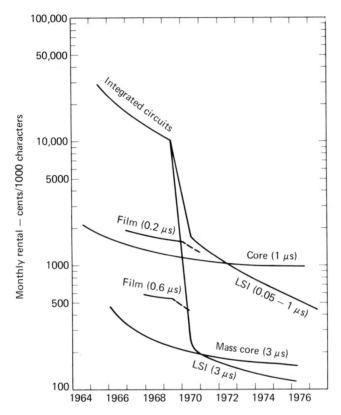

FIGURE 10.5

Zeidler [22] has described the major classes of memory and his results are summarized in Table 10.11 in order of increasing time required for (initial) acquisition of the data (access time). The remainder of this section follows his analysis.

The costs of a number of types of memory systems are plotted in Figs. 10.5 and 10.6 and projected to 1976 [23]. In both cases, costs are normalized on the basis of monthly rental in cents per 1000 characters (50-month amortization assumed).

Data for core, thin-film, integrated-circuit,* and LSI memory units are plotted in Fig. 10.5. Core memories have been under intensive development for many years, and no substantial cost reductions in such units are antici-

---

*It must be stressed that all cost curves such as those in Figs. 10.5 and 10.6 must be considered as representative of average rather than precise costs, because of the large variables related to different manufacturers' sales prices, and in particular due to the variables associated with 5- to 10- year projections into the future.

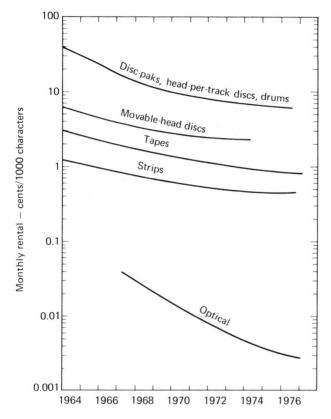

FIGURE 10.6

pated over the next few years. The cost curves for these core units are there-fore relatively "flat" for the period corresponding to the early 1970s. The use of film memories has been much less extensive than that of core memories. Thin-film units have not had the benefit of true mass production, so it is possible that costs can be decreased significantly as proponents are fore-casting.

The first computer use of integrated-circuit memories was in "scratch-pad" units. As noted in Fig. 10.5, it was anticipated in 1968 by Zeidler that the transition to LSI for main memory uses would be realized by about 1970. As it has turned out, this estimate was correct, but, in a 1971 paper, G. E. Moore [24] states that semiconductor memories have become lower cost than core, not only for low-capacity short-access-time memory, but also for high capacities out to 1 million bits or more. On the basis of Moore's data, the graph showing LSI with 3-μs access time in mass core has been added to Zeidler's graphs in Fig. 10.5 to indicate that it is likely that semiconductor memories will be the minimum-cost form of memory even for mass core.

The cost data for various types of memory with electromechanical access mechanisms are plotted in Fig. 10.6. These costs are significantly lower than those of Fig. 10.5 because, in contradistinction to memories in which discrete storage elements are used for each bit of information, these latter techniques use large areas of storage media, each bit of information being designated for a corresponding minute portion of the storage area. The tradeoff for this cost saving is the increased mechanical complexity of the storage units required to locate specific desired areas of storage, which in turn incurs a corresponding increase in data access time. The magnetic tape units are the worst offenders in terms of access time requirements, many seconds or even minutes being required in some cases to access the desired data. However, as noted in Fig. 10.6, the corresponding costs are relatively low.

As noted in Fig. 10.6, another order of magnitude or two in unit rental cost is realized with memories based on optical techniques. However, as noted earlier, the major price paid for this low storage cost is the inability of the (typical) optical system to accommodate any storage operation beyond the initial one for a given area of storage material. Optical systems are therefore "permanent" memory systems.

Nevertheless, it appears that there will be an increasing market for optical memory equipments, and one manufacturer estimates that, relative to the cost of currently available systems, an order of magnitude decrease in cost will be realized by 1975.

10.3.4 User Terminal Costs

As is the case with other types of products, a wide variety of data terminals are produced by a number of manufacturers, and sales and rental prices vary accordingly. Representative price levels are indicated in Fig. 10.7 to establish a general frame of reference for the costs of various categories of data terminals.* This figure and the analysis in this section follow the work of Zeidler [25].

CATHODE-RAY-TUBE (CRT) TERMINALS.   Cost data are shown in Fig. 10.7 for four classes of CRT units. Sophisticated, high-definition equipments must be used for those applications in which a large amount of detail is required for textual or graphical data and display functions are relatively complex. Typically, resolution in both the vertical and horizontal directions is of the order of 1000 elements. In general, units of this type are most often used for on-site operations and therefore do not have as much significance to data communications as do the other less sophisticated KB(keyboard)/CRT

---

*Rental rates for data terminals are specified on the basis of an assumed 40-month amortization. Service is included at the rates specified.

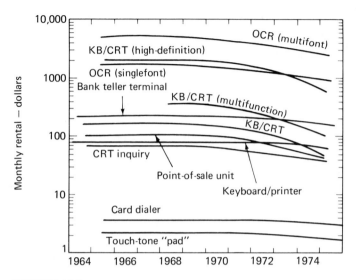

FIGURE 10.7

units.* As indicated in the figure, significant decreases in costs of such units are anticipated over the next few years because of the advances in LSI and display-tube technologies that have been forecast.

OPTICAL-CHARACTER-RECOGNITION (OCR) UNITS. Optical character recognition equipments are thus far used primarily for data entry directly into the computer at the computer site. When operating in this type of mode, they really do not qualify as a user data terminal. However, as data processing operations extending over large geographical areas increase and as the technology for optical reading of both machine and handprinted characters advances, it is probable that OCR operations will extend directly into data communication systems. The reading accuracy of current OCR equipments has increased substantially over that achieved in early equipments to the point where rejects of less than 1 per cent and substitution errors of less than 0.1 per cent can be anticipated for operations in which the scanned text is of reasonably high quality. A sales level of $180 million is projected for 1975, compared with a level of only $14.5 million in 1965. Representative cost data are provided for both multi-font and single-font OCR units in Fig. 10.7. Advancing technology is expected to provide significant decreases in costs by 1975. However, the percentage decreases in cost will probably be somewhat

---

*The KB–CRT (multifunction) type of terminal is designated as one that incorporates an extensive function keyboard, as well as a regular alphanumeric keyboard. The Univac "Uniscope 300" that is incorporated into the "Unimatic" system of United Airlines is representative of this class of terminal.

less than those of the KB–CRT terminals, because the OCR units require a larger proportion of mechanical components for which most probably there will not be corresponding cost decreases.

KEYBOARD–PRINTER UNITS. Keyboard–printer units are almost completely mechanical and have been carried to a fine degree of development over many years of manufacture. Therefore, it is not anticipated that there will be very great reductions in costs of these units, particularly if it develops that production quantities cannot be increased substantially because of increasing competition from KB–CRT terminals.

TOUCH-TONE UNITS. Touch-Tone telephone, Touch-Tone pads, and associated card dialers have proved to be effective, simple units for entry of small amounts of numerical data into communication systems.

There were 2.8 million Touch-Tone telephones in service in 1968, and the Bell System projects that there will be 8.4 million in service by 1972. By 1972, 60 per cent of the system's telephones are expected to be served by offices that are equipped to offer Touch-Tone service. About 75 per cent of the system is expected to be converted by 1977. All new offices are built with Touch-Tone capability.

10.3.5 Software Costs

As data processing systems become increasingly complex, the cost of programming becomes an increasingly significant factor in system planning and implementation. New software techniques now being developed (e.g., higher-level languages) will help to reduce programming costs, and continuing decreases in hardware costs will also help by permitting transfer of some of the load from software to hardware. However (at least for the near future), programming costs must be considered as a major factor in any economic analysis of computer communication systems.

In determining measures for programming costs, it is necessary to define units whereby a program can be measured. A commonly used measure of the size of a programming task is the number of instructions required to carry out the task.

The drawback of such measures is that they ignore the facts that (a) the cost per instruction is lower using high-level languages* than assembly or machine language,† and (2) the cost per instruction is greater for large

---

*By high-level language we mean a computer programming language that possesses a set of properties intended to increase the productivity of a programmer in preparation and checking of a program. Among these properties, the following are common: (1) notation similar to natural (e.g., English) language and/or mathematics; (2) appropriateness for the problem field; (3) independence from the particular computer being used.

†Such languages maintain a simple correspondence between the program statements written by the programmer and the instructions as they are represented in the compu-

jobs than for small ones. Wensley [26] suggests that a more meaningful measure can be developed in which a "phrase" is the unit of a program, and this section follows his analysis of the problem.

In a machine language program, a phrase would typically be a single instruction (although in some cases it would be two, as, for example, when a reject instruction option is available for input–output instructions). In a language such as FORTRAN or COBOL, in which only simple statements are allowed, a phrase would be synonymous with a statement. In higher-level languages, such as ALGOL, LISP, or PL1, each of the various clauses of each statement would be regarded as a phrase.

Under normal circumstances, it is found that the cost of writing a phrase increases as the size of the program is increased. A typical situation is shown in Fig. 10.8. The spread in cost of writing a phrase is large at any one size of program, but a clearly discernable trend is seen. Programs of about 1000 phrases cost about $5 a phrase, a figure that doubles with programs of 10,000

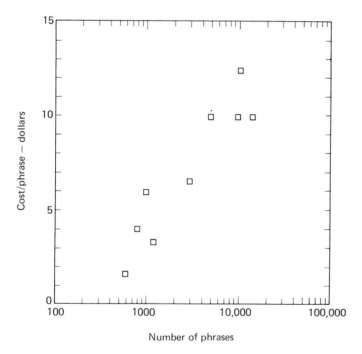

Number of phrases

FIGURE 10.8

---

ter. In machine language, this correspondence is usually on a 1 : 1 basis. In assembly language, a simple programmer-written statement may generate many computer instructions. A characteristic of such languages is that the conversion to computer instructions is independent of context, within the program.

phrases. The major factor in this increase in cost per phrase is the increasing cost of communication among the many writers of a program in the case of large programs. This communication cost is brought to a minimum in the case of smaller programs written by a single programmer. In addition to communication problems, it is far more difficult to isolate and correct faults in a large program than in a small program.

The cost of writing a phrase in a high-level language is approximately the same as in a machine language, but the power of such a phrase is far greater. As a first approximation, high-level language requires three times the storage for machine language, produces a speed of execution three times slower than machine language, and has a programming cost three times less than machine language.

As the computer industry develops, the cost of writing a program for a specific task is reduced. In certain cases the cost of a program has been reduced by 100 to 1 over the space of 10 years. This has been accomplished by the use of more advanced techniques that assisted the programmer in the execution of these tasks. The most significant of such techniques are shown in Table 10.12.

TABLE 10.12   *Advances in Programming Techniques*

Technique	Approximate Date of General Commercial Availability[a]
Assembly languages	1954
Monitor systems	1956
Compilers	1960
Multiprogramming	1966
Time sharing	1968

[a]The approximate date of general commercial availability is not intended to be the first date of availability from a few manufacturers, but the date when most manufacturers offered this facility.

The other significant factor in the reduction of cost of a program is that the computer itself, particularly the central processing unit (CPU), has become more efficient, and therefore the same efficiency of coding is not required to make a particular job economic. This trend will continue and the industry will continue to trade off the increasing power of computers to reduce programming cost. The advent of more efficient computers, on the other hand, will tend to make it economic to carry out certain computations that were not justified previously. Such new applications will tend to be those that are the most difficult to program. The picture of the future is therefore that the

cost of doing a specific job will decrease, but the total expenditure on programming will increase as more sophisticated tasks are undertaken. The
simple tasks of today, e.g., a matrix inversion, were at one time difficult
programming jobs when the computers were more limited in storage space,
speed, lack of floating point facilities, and so forth.

The following statements provide a close approximation in estimating
the cost of programming:

1. The cost per phrase of programming is very close to being constant
   over time.
2. The cost per phrase of programming increases with the size of the
   program, as shown in Fig. 10.8.
3. The cost of writing a program *to carry out a specific task* decreases by
   25 per cent per year (illustrated in Fig. 10.9).

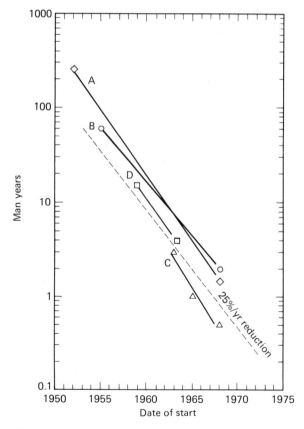

FIGURE 10.9

The implication of the above statements is that, as time passes, the newer programs that carry out a task contain many fewer phrases, thereby reducing the cost of writing the code. The fewer phrases are possible because of the availability of better software, hardware, and libraries of programs and techniques.

10.4   DEMAND FOR COMPUTER COMMUNICATIONS

The preceding section has provided some general estimates of the costs of the necessary components of a computer-communication system. In this section we attempt to estimate the future demand for systems of this type in the United States. We take two approaches. In the first approach we examine the number of data sets that have been connected to the network and other measures of network usage as a function of time over the past few years, and then make some simple projections of these curves into the future. In the second approach we consider the demand for a variety of classes of service separately, project the growth of these segments of the market individually, and then add them together to obtain an estimate of total demand. Underlying both approaches is the assumption that the U.S. economy continues to grow at a modest rate, that there are no drastic changes in the world's economy, that there are no major wars involving mass destruction, that the business and regulatory climate in the United States does not change drastically, and that the U.S. government does not enter this market in a way that would suddenly create new demand on a large scale. In other words, these demand estimates assume no unusual disasters and no unusual windfalls.

10.4.1   Projections of Network Usage

In this section we examine the number of data sets of various types that have been leased from the Bell System during recent years and base projections of future demand on this data. In this section data rates will be referred to as low, medium, and high. Low- and medium-speed data rates are defined as rates that can be carried on a voiceband line. High data rates require wideband lines (see Chapter 5). According to our definitions, low speed refers to 300 bps or less, medium speed is 300 to 10,000 bps (typically 1200 to 9600 bps), and high speed is above 10,000 bps.

Table 10.13 and Fig. 10.10 give the number of data sets leased by the Bell System in the 1963–1969 period [27]. The 1963–1968 average annual growth rate for low-speed data sets (100 series) is 70 per cent; for medium speed (200 series), 42 per cent; the annual rate of growth of the high-speed sets is declining and was 60 per cent in the 1966–1968 period. Continuation of the

TABLE 10.13 Number of Data Sets in the Bell System as of Jan. 1 of Each Year in the Switched Network (DDD) and in the Leased Private-Line Network (PL) by Type (Series Number)[a]

Series	100			200			300			400			600		
Date	DDD	PL	Total	DDD	PL	Total	DDD	PL	Total	DDD	PL	Total	DDD	PL	Total
1963	2,100	50	2,150	1150	750	1,900	—	—	—	2,375	25	2,400	175	—	175
1964	3,400	200	3,600	1775	1025	2,800	—	15	15	3,860	40	3,900	320	5	325
1965	5,300	700	6,000	2300	1600	3,900	—	85	85	6,135	65	6,200	545	5	550
1966	8,150	1550	9,700	3150	2550	5,700	—	250	250	8,710	90	8,800	840	10	850
1967	13,525	2775	16,300	4420	4080	8,500	—	400	400	11,085	115	11,200	1260	15	1275
1968	25,070	5130	30,200	5580	6420	12,000	—	650	650	12,770	130	12,900	1735	15	1750
1969[b]	40,300	9500	49,800	7895	9405	17,300	—	900	900	15,245	155	15,400	2275	25	2300

[a]Source: AT&T.
[b]Estimated.
Note: 100 series are low-speed sets, less than 300 bps currently.
200 series are medium speed, voice bandwidth, 1200 to 2400 bps.
300 series are high speed, currently 19.2 to 230.4 kbps.
400 series are low-speed, multifrequency sets, in the range of 20 to 75 characters/s.
600 series are specialized analog sets for services such as facsimile or electrocardiograms.

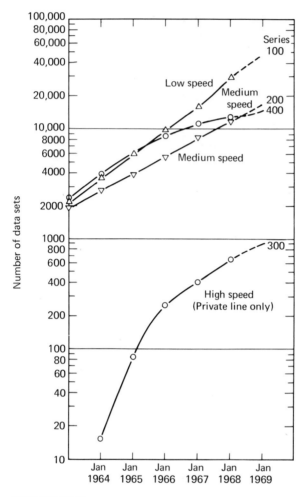

FIGURE 10.10

decreasing trend results in a projected growth rate for high-speed data sets of about 38 per cent per year after 1971. Extrapolation of these growth rates results in the highest rate for low-speed data sets (70 per cent) and the lowest rate (33 per cent) for high-speed sets. We have found that there are several factors indicating a continuous high level of demand for low-speed data sets and other factors that imply a sustained high level of demand for medium-speed sets.

Several applications that currently are below an economic threshold, but that seem likely to generate a large demand in the future, are utility remote meter reading, end of the day accounts transfer from small businesses to the computer, and reporting transactions in the "checkless society." These systems will require a large number of low-speed data sets. It is estimated that the economic threshold in many such applications will be crossed within the next decade and more specifically in the 1975–1980 time frame. The capacity of the voice channel to transmit data in the public message network may reach 4800 bps by 1975 or even earlier. This is about double the current capacity and could stimulate the use of voiceband at the expense of wider bandwidths. The projected annual growth rate of 33 per cent is recognition of a healthy growth in wideband data. However, there are indications that the rate of growth of wideband data may not match the rates of growth of the lower-speed applications. The reasons for this view are

1. Reductions in computation costs will allow smaller computers to preprocess the input information before it is transmitted to a central computer.
2. Improvements in management control systems will reduce the amount of output information required, because only the information significant to a decision will be transmitted.
3. Modest decreases in communication costs (as opposed to order of magnitude decreases in the computation costs per generation of computers) will tend to restrict the information transmitted to the minimum necessary and force the system builder to concentrate his traffic.
4. Projected improvements in the data handling capacity of voice grade channels will allow some transfer of requirements to medium data rate sets.

Table 10.14 and Fig. 10.11 project rates of growth of data sets,* both Bell and non-Bell, that may be connected directly to the public message network by 1980. Note that the 1975 percentage of voiceband sets is 99.4 per cent of the total number of sets in use [27].

Table 10.15 projects the percentage of switched network, wideband switched network, and leased network plant used by data sets, whether Bell or non-Bell. The percentage of data sets (that is, the ratio of data sets to all sets, whether data or telephone) rises from about 0.1 per cent to 12 per cent in the 10-year period. The projections assume that the speed used by the typical wideband data set would be 50 kbps and that the typical set at the most would use about 12 times more "lines" than a typical voice grade data set. Because the rate of growth of high-speed data is much lower than that of voice-grade data, a correction for their wider bandwidths does not change significantly the percentage of switched network plant occupied by data.

---

*The word "data set" is more general than "modem," because modem implies a process of modulation–demodulation of data signals. Some data sets may not contain a modem.

TABLE 10.14 Stanford Research Institute Projection of Data Sets Connected to the Bell System Private and Switched Network[a]

Series	APRIL 1, 1968		JANUARY 1, 1971		JANUARY 1, 1975		JANUARY 1, 1980	
	Sets	%	Sets	%	Sets	%	Sets	%
100	34,300	53.99	114,500	65.09	661,110	76.89	5,917,180	86.91
200	13,200	20.77	34,700	19.73	141,540	16.47	820,490	11.90
400	13,500	21.26	21,600	12.28	42,790	4.97	100,570	1.45
600	1,875	2.96	3,600	2.05	9,230	1.08	30,440	0.44
300	725	1.02	1,600	0.85	5,100	0.59	21,500	0.30
	63,600	100.00	176,000	100.00	859,770	100.00	6,890,190	100.00

[a]The seeming accuracy of these projections is merely a consequence of using a computer program to generate the numbers. Rounding of the projections to a nearest per cent would eliminate some of the information conveyed by Table 10.6, such as the decreasing percentage of the series 300. The *uncertainty* of the projections is indicated elsewhere (Fig. 10.11).

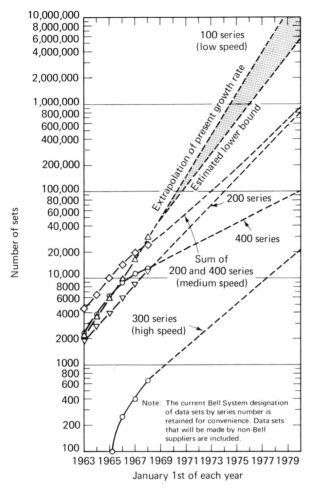

FIGURE 10.11

Table 10.15 shows that about 5 per cent of the total sets used in the Bell System in 1980 may be data sets. However, if data users were to maintain their current holding time per call and have call rates comparable to telephone customers, the occupancy of the switched network plant by data will be much higher than 5 per cent. Currently, the average holding time of a telephone conversation is about 6 min: some data users have holding times of 25 to 30 min, longer by a factor of 5. On the average, 4.25 calls/day were made from each telephone in the United States in 1966, a daily total time of less than $\frac{1}{2}$-h [28]. Statistics describing the use of data sets are as yet unavailable. However, if data users were to make 4.25 calls of a composite total of $\frac{1}{2}$-h

TABLE 10.15 *Percentage of Switched Network, Wideband Network, and Leased Network Plant Used by Data Sets, 1970–1980*[a]

(*millions of data sets and telephones*)

Data Sets	1970		1975		1980	
	Sets	"Lines"	Sets	"Lines"	Sets	"Lines"
Low speed (100 series)	0.0760	0.076	0.6610	0.661	5.917	5.917
Medium speed (200 and 400 series)	0.0420	0.042	0.1840	0.184	0.921	0.921
High speed (300 series)	0.0012	0.014	0.0051	0.061	0.021	0.250
Total data sets or "lines"	0.1192	0.132	0.8501	0.906	6.859	7.088
Total telephone sets or "lines"	98.0000[b]	70.000	116.0000[b]	83.000	138.000[b]	98.500
Total	98.1192	70.132	116.8501	83.906	144.859	105.588
Per cent data/total	0.12	0.18	0.73	1.07	4.75	6.68

[a]Source: Stanford Research Institute.
[b]Assuming that one "line" serves 1.4 telephones (*The World's Telephones*—1967).

TABLE 10.16 *Percentage of Telephone Line Use by Data Sets, 1970–1980*[a]

	(1) $\dfrac{Data\ Sets}{Data\ Sets + Telephone\ Main\ Stations} \times 100$	(2) Calling Rate (calls/day)	(3) Holding Time (min/call)	(4) Total Time/Day (min)	(5) $(1) \times (4)$
Data					
Lower bound	6	4	6	24	1.44
Upper bound	12	4	30	120	14.40
Telephone main stations					
Lower bound	94	4	6	24	22.60
Upper bound	88	4	6	24	21.12
Fraction of network used	$\dfrac{\text{data (lower bound)}}{\text{total (lower bound)}} = \dfrac{1.44}{24.04} = 0.06,$		$\dfrac{\text{data (upper bound)}}{\text{total (upper bound)}} = \dfrac{14.40}{35.52} = 0.406$		

[a]The units in column (5) of this table are per cent of sets × terminal min/day, and the percentage of the switched network is calculated by dividing number of the above units contributed by data sets by the number of units contributed by all sets. The number of telephones used only in private-line service is not included.

413

duration, on the average, about a quarter of the subscriber lines connected to the Bell System's three networks, that is, switched, wideband data, and private, would be occupied with data transmission by 1980. This forecast is based on the assumptions (1) that the very high annual growth rate of low-speed data will continue through the next decade, which assumes in turn that there will be an economic breakthrough in at least one of the areas mentioned above, such as "checkless society" transactions, and (2) that the holding time of 30 min/day is representative of an average data user. However, the majority of data sets in the low-speed range, such as those to be used for "checkless society" transactions, will have short holding times. Because of the uncertainties involved in the percentage of data sets and in the holding time, a calculation is made to develop a range of projected use of subscriber lines. Table 10.16 gives a range of projections of terminal hours, depending on the percentage of data sets, holding time, and frequency of calls. The range in percentages is between 6 and 40 per cent with the lower figure being our present best estimate, since it assumes an average holding time of 6 min/call rather than 30 min/call, which seems more realistic to us in the long term.

10.4.2 Picturephone and Cable Television Data Services

There is a potential for very extensive development of both Picturephone and limited two-way cable television service in the United States for nondata purposes. If this development does occur as projected, it will be possible for data services of many types to be provided over these networks at relatively low marginal cost. The potential size of these two networks is very large, in terms of numbers of terminals, and the critical step in estimating their future use for data services is to estimate what fraction of the total size of each network will be used for these services in preference to the telephone network or new specialized data networks.

Bell System and other estimates of the future size of the Picturephone network are that the number of Picturephone terminals is likely to reach 1 per cent of the number of telephones by 1980, for a total of about 2 million terminals of this type [29].

An estimate of the number of cable television households in the United States can be made by projecting recent data, as shown in Fig. 10.12. In this figure the crosses are actual data [30] and the dashed lines are our projections. We have estimated that some saturation of the number of cable households should begin in 1976, resulting in a total number of households of about 35 million by 1980. A large fraction of the new terminals installed after about 1972 is likely to have limited two-way capability and thus to have the potential for interactive data services of various types. An upper bound on the number of two-way cable TV terminals in 1980 is around 20 million, assum-

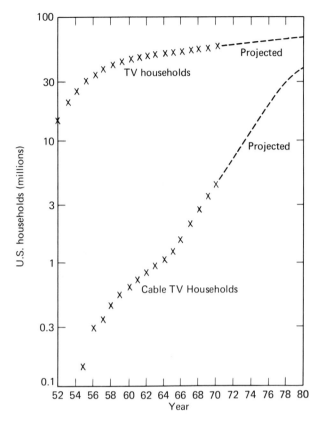

FIGURE 10.12

ing two thirds of the new terminals installed by 1980 are two way. It is obvious that if only one third of these are used for data, there will be more data sets of this type than our lower-bound estimate of 6 million low data rate sets in Fig. 10.11. The potential for competition in providing data services thus will exist between the telephone network, the cable TV network, and specialized data networks. Each is likely to find services it is best suited to. Cable TV seems best suited to the provision of various types of video information services to the home; for potential new services likely to be provided to the home, as discussed next, it seems reasonable to imagine that many will be provided by means of the cable TV or Picturephone networks.

10.4.3 Projection of Submarkets

In this section we consider the market for computer-communication systems in terms of specific uses. In a recent study of this field by Baran and Lipinski [29], 200 experts in the computer-communication field were ques-

TABLE 10.17   *Characteristics of New Nationwide Networks That May Have an Impact on the Public Network*

Network	Median Date of Emergence	MEDIAN SIZE 5 YEARS AFTER EMERGENCE (THOUSANDS)		USE OF PUBLIC NETWORK (% PROBABILITY)		
		Terminals	Locations	10	50	90
1. Banking system for cashless society transactions	1980	20	10			×
2. Stock certificate clearing	1978	5	2			×
3. Biomedical network	1980	10	5			×
4. Motel and hotel reservations	1975	20	10			×
5. Police and crime prevention	1975	10	5			×
6. Educational	1976	50	5		×	
7. Post office	1985	40	10	×	×	
8. Credit-card verification	1976	80	20			×

tioned as to their projections of various segments of the market. Each expert was asked to identify the year in which each class of service considered was likely to start, at what starting level, and what the size of this part of the market would be 5 years after start.

Table 10.17 lists eight services utilizing nationwide networks that these experts believed were likely to have a large impact on the public message network, the median data suggested by the experts for emergence of each network, its median size after 5 years, and the probability that the service will use the public network [29]. It can be argued that some of these services, such as the motel and hotel reservation service, have already emerged, although not in fully automated form. The "cashless" or "checkless" society would be heavily based on the first and eighth of these networks because reliable automated credit-card verification at points of sale would have to be available rather universally for such a society to function. The banking network would presumably be connected to the point-of-sale network to allow charges to be recorded as they are made.

In addition, these experts were asked to consider a list of potential new services, primarily services that might be delivered to the home, and to make

TABLE 10.18 *Potential Revenues for New Home Information Services*
(millions of dollars)

YEAR Service	1980	1981	1982	1983	1984	1985	1986	1987	1988	1989
Cashless society transactions	12.	29.	73.	182.	457.	1,146.	1,438.	1,621.	1,724.	1,810.
Dedicated newspaper	5.	14.	34.	85.	214.	537.	674.	760.	808.	849.
Computer-aided school instructions	0.	14.	34.	86.	216.	542.	1,361.	1,708.	1,925.	2,047.
Shopping transactions	0.	0.	0.	5.	12.	29.	74.	186.	466.	584.
Person to person—paid work at home	0.	0.	0.	0.	0.	43.	108.	272.	683.	1,713.
Plays, movies (video library)	18.	45.	113.	284.	714.	1,791.	2,247.	2,533.	2,694.	2,829.
Computer tutor	9.	23.	57.	14.2	357.	895.	1,123.	1,266.	1,347.	1,414.
Message recording	1.	2.	4.	11.	27.	67.	84.	95.	101.	106.
Secretarial assistance	5.	11.	28.	71.	178.	448.	562.	633.	674.	707.
Household mail and messages	5.	11.	28.	71.	178.	448.	562.	633.	674.	707.
Mass mail and advertising	0.	0.	0.	0.	0.	0.	0.	0.	0.	0.
Answering services	5.	12.	30.	75.	187.	470.	590.	665.	707.	743.
Grocery ordering	4.	9.	23.	57.	143.	358.	449.	507.	539.	566.
File system	0.	0.	0.	0.	0.	1.	3.	7.	18.	46.
Fares and ticket reservation	1.	2.	5.	12.	31.	78.	98.	111.	118.	124.

TABLE 10.18 (continued)

YEAR	1980	1981	1982	1983	1984	1985	1986	1987	1988	1989
Service										
Events calendar	0.	0.	1.	2.	6.	15.	37.	92.	115.	130.
Correspondence school	0.	0.	0.	0.	9.	24.	60.	150.	376.	943.
Appointment reminder	0.	0.	0.	2.	6.	15.	37.	93.	233.	292.
Computer-assisted meetings	5.	11.	28.	71.	178.	448.	562.	633.	674.	707.
General electronic newspaper	0.	0.	0.	0.	0.	5.	13.	32.	80.	200.
Adult evening TV courses	7.	18.	45.	114.	285.	716.	899.	1,013.	1,078.	1,131.
Banking services	4.	9.	23.	57.	143.	358.	449.	507.	539.	566.
Legal information	0.	0.	0.	0.	0.	7.	18.	45.	114.	285.
Special sales information	2.	6.	14.	36.	89.	224.	281.	317.	337.	354.
Consumers' advisory service	2.	6.	14.	36.	89.	224.	281.	317.	337.	354.
Weather bureau	8.	21.	52.	131.	164.	185.	197.	206.	217.	228.
Bus, train, air scheduling	7.	17.	43.	54.	61.	65.	68.	71.	75.	79.
Restaurants	0.	1.	1.	4.	9.	22.	28.	32.	34.	35.
Library access	0.	0.	0.	0.	0.	2.	6.	15.	38.	95.
Index of services	1.	2.	4.	11.	27.	67.	84.	95.	101.	106.
Total market	99.	261.	656.	1,598.	3,781.	9,231.	12,391.	14,613.	16,822.	19,749.

the same set of estimates about these, that is, date of emergence and size after 5 years. From these numbers and an assumed growth curve, a rough estimate of the size of each service over time was computed. The assumed growth curve was exponential for the first 5 years at a rate corresponding to doubling every year. After the first 5 years the rate of growth is halved in each succeeding year. The results of this part of the survey are given in Table 10.18 in the form of revenues in millions of dollars per year for the years 1980–1989 [29]. Most of the services considered did not have a substantial size prior to 1980. The total market shown is only the market for new consumer services and does not include established services or new industrial or governmental services, such as those listed in Table 10.17. Definitions of each of the submarkets considered in Table 10.18 are given in Table 10.19.

It is perhaps surprising to see how large these experts believe the market will become by 1989 for computer-aided instruction, video libraries, computer tutoring, and adult evening classes. These have become four out of six of the largest services on the list, including the cashless society system.

TABLE 10.19 *New Communications Services*

---

1. Cashless Society Transactions: Recording of financial transactions, with a hard-copy output for buyer and seller, a permanent record, and updating of balance in computer memory.
2. Dedicated Newspaper: A set of pages with printed and graphic information, possibly including photographs, the organization of which has been predetermined by the user to suit his preferences.
3. Computer-aided School Instruction: At the very minimum, computer determination of the day's assignment for each pupil, and, at the end of the day, recording of the day's progress report. At its most complex, such a service would use a real-time, interactive video color display with voice input and output and an appropriate program suited to each pupil's progress and temperament.
4. Shopping Transactions (store catalogs): Interactive programs, perhaps video assisted, which describe or show goods at request of the buyer, advise him of the price, location, delivery time, etc.
5. Person-to-Person (paid work at home): Switched video and facsimile service substituting for normal day's contacts of middle-class managerial personnel where daily contact are mostly of a routine nature. May also apply to contacts with the public by receptionist, doctor, or his assistant, etc.
6. Plays and Movies from a Video Library: Selection of all plays and movies. Color and good sound are required.
7. Computer Tutor: From a library of self-help programs available, a computer in an interactive mode coaching the pupil (typically adult) in the chosen subject.
8. Message Recording: Probably of currently available type, but may include video memory (a patient showing doctor the rash he has developed).
9. Secretarial Assistance: Written or dictated letters typed by a remotely situated secretary.
10. Household Mail and Messages: Letters and notes transmitted directly to or from the house by means of home facsimile machines.

TABLE 10.19 (*Continued*)

11. Mass Mail and Direct Advertising Mail: Higher output, larger-size pages, color output may be necessary to attract the attention of the recipient—otherwise similar to item 10 above.

12. Answering Services: Storage of incoming messages or noting whom to call, possibly with computer logic recognizing emergency situation and diverting the call.

13. Grocery Price List, Information, and Ordering: Grocery price list providing up-to-the-minute, undated information about perishable foodstuffs. Video color display may be needed to allow examination of selected merchandise. Ordering follows.

14. Access to Company Files: Information in files coded for security; regularly updated files are available with cross references indicating the code where more detailed information is stored. Synthesis also may be available.

15. Fares and Ticket Reservation: As provided by travel agencies now but more comprehensive and faster. Cheapest rates, information regarding the differences between carriers with respect to service, menus, etc., may be available.

16. Past and Forthcoming Events: Events, dates of events, and their brief description; short previews of future theater plays; and recordings of past events.

17. Correspondence School: Taped or live high school, university, and vocational courses available on request with an option either to audit or take for credit. Course would be on TV, paper support on facsimile.

18. Daily Calendar and Reminder About Appointments: Prerecorded special appointments and regularly occurring appointments stored as a programmed reminder.

19. Computer-Assisted Meetings: Participation of computer as a partner in a meeting, answering questions of fact, deriving correlations, and extrapolating trends.

20. General Electronic Newspaper: Daily newspaper, possibly printed during the night, available in time for breakfast. Special editions following major news breaks.

21. Adult Evening Courses on TV: Noninteractive broadcast mode, live courses on TV—wider choice of subjects than at present.

22. Banking Services: Money orders, transfers, advice.

23. Legal Information: Directory of lawyers, computerized legal counseling giving precedents, rulings in similar cases, describing jurisdiction of various courts and chances of successful suits in a particular area of litigation.

24. Special Sales Information: Any sales within the distance specified by the user and for items specified by him will be "flashed" onto the home display unit.

25. Consumers' Advisory Service: Equivalent of *Consumer Reports*, giving best buy, products rated "acceptable," etc.

26. Weather Bureau: Countrywide, regional forecasts or special forecasts (for farmers, fishermen), hurricane and tornado warnings similar to current AAU special forecast service.

27. Bus, Train, and Air Scheduling: Centrally available information with one number to call.

28. Restaurants: Following a query for a type of restaurant (Japanese, for instance), reservations, menu, prices are shown. Displays of dishes, location of tables, may be included.

29. Library Access: After an interactive "browsing" with a "librarian computer" and a quotation for the cost of hard-copy facsimile or a slow-scan video transmission, a book or magazine is transmitted to the home.

30. Index, All Services Served by the Home Terminal: Includes prices or charges of the above, or available, communications services.

REFERENCES

[1] J. HIRSHLEIFER, On the Theory of Optimal Investment Decision, *J. Political Economy*, **66** (Oct. 1958), 329–352.

[2] In the Matter of the Use of the Carterfone Device in Message Toll Telephone Service, 13 FCC 2d 420 (June 26, 1968).

[3] K. J. STETTEN, R. P. MORTON, and R. P. MAYER, The Design and Testing of a Cost Effective Computer System for CAI/CMI Application, *Mitre Corp. Rept. M69-39 Rev. 1* (April 1970).

[4] Communications Technology for Urban Improvement, Report to the Department of Housing and Urban Development, National Academy of Engineering Committee on Telecommunications (June 1971).

[5] E. L. GRANT and W. G. IRESON, *Principles of Engineering Economy*, 5th ed., Ronald Press, New York, 1970.

[6] R. A. HOWARD, The Foundations of Decision Analysis, *IEEE Trans. Syst. Sci. Cybernetics*, **SSC-4** (Sept. 1968), 211–219.

[7] W. NORTH, A Tutorial Introduction to Decision Theory, *IEEE Trans. Syst. Sci. Cybernetics*, **SSC-4** (Sept 1968), 200–210.

[8] H. RAIFFA, *Decision Analysis*, Addison-Wesley, Reading, Mass., 1968.

[9] M. TRIBUS, *Rational Descriptions, Decisions, and Designs*, Pergamon Press, Elmsford, New York, 1969.

[10] H. RAIFFA and R. SCHLAIFER, *Applied Statistical Decision Theory*, Harvard University Press, Cambridge, Mass., 1961.

[11] R. A. HOWARD, Information Value Theory, *IEEE Trans. Syst. Sci. Cybernetics*, **SSC-2** (Aug. 1966), 22–26.

[12] R. A. HOWARD, Value of Information Lotteries, *IEEE Trans. Syst. Sci. Cybernetics*, **SSC-3** (June 1967), 54–60.

[13] E. B. PARKER, Technological Change and the Mass Media, *Handbook of Communication*, W. Schramm et al., eds., Rand McNally, Skokie, Ill., 1973.

[14] H. J. SCHLAFLY, The Real World of Technological Evolution in Broadband Communications, Report to the Sloan Commission on Cable Communications (Sept. 1970).

[15] Business Equipment Manufacturers Association, *Filing in FCC Docket No. 16979*, Regulatory and Policy Problems Presented by the Interdependence of Computer and Communication Services and Facilities (1968), 121–125.

[16] H. M. ZEIDLER, A. J. LIPINSKI, L. J. MOLL, E. B. SHAPIRO, W. A. KENT, and J. H. WENSLEY, Patterns of Technology in Data Processing and Data Communications, *Rept. 7379B-4*, p. 74, in D. A. Dunn et al., Stanford Research Institute Report to the Federal Communications Commission (FCC Docket No. 16979), Vol. I (1969).

[17] *Ibid.*, p. 89.

[18] *Ibid.*, p. 62.

[19] *Ibid.*, p. A-1.

[20] K. C. KNIGHT, Evolving Computer Performance, *Datamation*, **14** (Jan. 1968), 31–35. Also Changes in Computer Performance, *Datamation*, **12** (Sept. 1966), 40–54.

[21] J. K. WINEKE and M. SPEIGEL, Generation IV, the Shape of Systems to Come, *Computer Decisions*, (Oct. 1970), 18–23.

[22] H. M. ZEIDLER et al., *ibid.*, p. 40.

[23] *Ibid.*, p. 44.

[24] G. E. MOORE, Semiconductor Rams, a Status Report, *Computer*, **4** (March 1971), 6–10.

[25] H. M. ZEIDLER et al., *ibid.*, p. 54.

[26] *Ibid.*, p. 26.

[27] *Ibid.*, p. 62.

[28] *Statistics of Communications Common Carriers*, Federal Communications Commission, 1966.

[29] P. BARAN and A. J. LIPINSKI, The Future of the Telephone Industry 1970–1985, *Institute for the Future*, *Rept. R-20*, Middletown, Conn., and Menlo Park, Calif. (1971).

[30] *Television Fact Book No. 40* (1971).

11

The Dartmouth Time Sharing Network

ROBERT F. HARGRAVES, JR.

THOMAS E. KURTZ

Dartmouth College

INTRODUCTION

Although the communications network may be an interesting feature of a computer network, a totally successful network must combine a good communications system with reliable hardware and software, a wide spectrum of user services, and operating procedures that reflect the utility concept. In this chapter the authors therefore direct some attention to the hardware, software, and user services before discussing the communications network in detail. We begin with a brief historical account showing how the network has evolved along with several major time-sharing computer systems, starting in 1964 with a three-user system and becoming in 1971 the largest educational time-sharing system in actual operation, serving up to 160 simultaneous users at Dartmouth and around New England.

423

11.1 HISTORY

The history of the Dartmouth network involves two different configurations of hardware and three totally different software operating systems since its inception in early 1964. During that time there was a continuous growing and expanding of the communications equipment used to bring Dartmouth Time Sharing System (henceforth abbreviated DTSS) service to the schools and colleges in the network. Although several of the changes in the hardware and software systems were quite noticeable and abrupt, the development of the communications was more continuous; only a few users might be affected by a change and most changes could be planned for summers or other school vacations.

The first system operated on a hardware system consisting of a GE-235 and Datanet-30 as processors and a dual-access disk unit as a storage device. From the beginning, standard communications equipment and Model 35 teletypewriters were used. The software operating system was designed and programmed largely by a small group of Dartmouth undergraduate students. Later General Electric marketed the combination hardware–software unit as a GE-265; GE used the same system as the basis for its commercial time-sharing service Mark I.

A hardware configuration centering around a GE-635 became available in the late fall of 1966. The first time-sharing system on this equipment was actually a crude systems programming and debugging tool called MOLDS, designed and constructed mainly by Dartmouth undergraduate students. A team of GE programmers then designed and built a full-scale time-sharing system for the GE-635, with assistance from Dartmouth students and from MOLDS. This second system served as the primary provider of time-sharing service to the network during the period October 1967–March 1969. It was also the prototype for the General Electric Mark II commercial time-sharing service. During part of this period the system served GE commercial customers in the New York and Boston areas through a simple computer–computer network.

Retaining the same hardware system, the Dartmouth-designed and constructed time-sharing system for the GE-635 (called DTSS for short) went into regularly scheduled operation on April 1, 1969, having begun part-time operation on January 1, 1969. Although the appearance to the users was very similar to that provided by the earlier GE-designed system, the new system was designed around a general file structure that permitted a wide variety of data-base applications and at last allowed debugging of time-sharing systems modules within the time-sharing system itself.

Thus as the network grew during this period, the complexity and sophistication of services grew concomitantly. Behind the scenes a large-scale technological development continued, involving two different hardware systems and three major software operating systems.

11.1.1 First System

In the early 1960s several persons at Dartmouth College recognized that familiarity with computing—what it could do and what it could not do—ought to be a part of the education received by all college students, not only those choosing courses in engineering and science. It was also recognized that decisions affecting the use of computers would be made primarily by businessmen and government officials, most of whom receive no technical training whatever. Yet extremely adverse effects could result from poorly informed decision making about computers. It was therefore decided that exposure to computing and free availability of computing should become a standard part of the liberal arts education at Dartmouth, an undergraduate college where only 25 per cent of the students elect majors in the sciences and engineering.

It was clearly recognized that even sophisticated liberal arts students would not voluntarily accept computing as it was generally available in the early 1960s. The mode of computer operation in the late 1950s was open shop, wherein each user had to deal directly with the machine itself, doing his work when the schedule allowed. The alternative of providing a large number of small individual computers, while easing the scheduling restrictions, still required a certain technical knowledge at the button-pushing level. Nor did it make economic sense to obtain a large number of small and independent machines, no one of which could take on a large problem.

The advent of closed-shop batch processing under the control of a monitor or operating system greatly improved the cost–performance ratio and the efficient use of the equipment, but introduced long delays between the time a user submitted a job and obtained the results, even if the results were only error messages. These batch-operating systems required the user to know about many layers of the computing onion, even when most of them were of no interest whatsoever.

Against this background, it was recognized that the user–computer interface had to be simplified and harmonized with the educational environment if liberal arts students were to ingest a reasonable dose of sensible knowledge about computing. Two important consequences of this recognition were the decisions to bring the computer to the student via remote individual terminals (Teletypes) and to devise an extremely simple user interface.

As important as the user interface is the programming language that most of the students will use. Many institutions elected to teach credit courses in programming, since students could not reasonably be expected to learn even a language such as FORTRAN without considerable effort. Such courses were typically fleshed out with topics from elementary numerical methods and ranged from undesirable to unacceptable for nonscience students. It was therefore concluded that what was needed was a language so simple and self-evident that most students could be expected to learn it either on their own or with the aid of several introductory lectures. The result was the computer language BASIC.

The development of the first system was really a two-pronged affair for which planning began in the summer of 1962. On the one hand, an entire system had to be designed and constructed to bring time-sharing services to large numbers of students. At this point an important decision was made: to use standard computer hardware, communications equipment, and terminals. This left the design and construction of a large-scale software system as the only major technical development that had to take place. Another important decision was now made: to use the only source of programming talent available in any numbers—undergraduate students. They were tried, and found not wanting.

Advancing along with the technical activity devoted to building a time-sharing system was the other prong of the attack. This activity sought to develop ways and means to infuse computing into the course offerings and into the general campus way of life. From this came the decision to place large numbers of terminals in areas available to students. Prior permission procedures or other red tape were never instituted. Before any faculty member had a terminal in his office or department at least a dozen were installed in student-accessible areas.

Using standard communications to connect the terminals to the computer made it trivial to install terminals not only on the campus but also at distant points. One was installed at the local high school in the fall of 1964, and another in a nearby private school early in 1965. As on-campus use grew, so did the number of schools and colleges tied into the Dartmouth system over telephone lines. By 1967 several colleges and half-a-dozen secondary schools had made a connection to the system.

On the technical side, the time-sharing system ran its first program on May 1, 1964, about 2 months after the hardware equipment was installed and made operational. Service to the three terminals was quite poor, but improved enough by June 1964 to justify installing eight more terminals, bringing the total to eleven. A public demonstration and introductory lecture were then offered to more than one-third of the entire faculty and administrative staff of the institution.

By the fall of 1964 the number of terminals was increased to 20, and a formal instructional program for freshmen was devised. It consisted of four 1-hour lectures offered as an adjunct to the advanced placement section of freshman mathematics. Based on that experience the number of lectures was reduced to three during the winter term and two subsequently in the spring as the program developed.

The instructional program provided (and still provides) just enough formal lecture material to allow the student to prepare a simple break-the-ice program. Later in the mathematics course the student is assigned three additional programming problems based on the subject matter of the particular course. Only a relatively low level of programming expertise is required of the students, but in fact most of them receive additional exposure or training in subsequent courses or through self-teaching.

One problem with having even a small number of required programming problems is checking them. In a large group of students there will be a large number of different approaches, and it would be rare to see two programs exactly alike. Human reading and checking of these assignments would require more than the usual amount of homework-reading effort. More to the point, a human reader might not recognize a correct program if the student used an unusual approach. Deciding that the program should be judged correct if it gives the right answers, we devised a simple checking system called TEACH, which runs the student's program with special data and checks the resulting answers. A well-constructed TEACH test program can spot a number of the more commonly made mistakes by employing ingeniously selected test data that would yield known and different incorrect answers for several different standard mistakes.

Hundreds of student programming exercises are TEACH checked each term. The students have come to depend heavily on the TEACH messages to spot and correct errors in their own programs, and thereby become better programmers. TEACH is widely used in areas other than the freshman training program; it works well whenever it is desirable to judge the quality of a program by the answers it produces.

The first system reached its maturity about the summer of 1966. At that time it supported up to 40 simultaneous terminals, although the system did not perform well above about 35 terminals. It worked reliably enough so that it could be left running at night unattended. Except for certain hardware failures that required manual intervention, the software system could recover from many common error situations, reloading itself if necessary, and continuing to run. The system continued to provide service to the Dartmouth community and the network through August 1967, when the equipment was sold and removed.

11.1.2 Second System

The development of a time-sharing system for GE-600 series hardware began in the Spring of 1966. The first of three phases was a simple debugging system called MOLDS. Its purposes were to ease the debugging of the subsequent production system and to learn which programming techniques would match the hardware. This work was completed by early September 1966, with all debugging taking place on machines located away from Dartmouth. Again, it was Dartmouth undergraduate students who designed and programmed MOLDS and who traveled around the country debugging it.

During the Fall of 1966 development activity on the second phase was carried out, partly on the MOLDS system through long-distance communications. This phase of the activity called for the major share of the programming and all the design work to be carried out by a team from GE, though several Dartmouth undergraduates participated as members of this team. This is the systems work that eventually became the GE MARK II Time Sharing Service.

The hardware equipment finally arrived on the Dartmouth campus in the Fall of 1966 and was made operational early in 1967. The GE version went into scheduled operation in October 1967, offering service not only to the Dartmouth community but also to commercial customers of GE in Boston and New York. This remote commercial use continued through 1968, when GE established other sites to provide this service.

The method of transmitting the computing power to the Boston and New York areas is worthy of special mention. The communications end of the time-sharing hardware consists of two Datanet-30 communications processors connected directly to the hardware system. These processors service a large number of low-speed ports called bit buffers. They also service higher speed character buffers connected through standard data sets to telephone lines; 1800 baud was selected for intercomputer communication. The particular configuration is seen in Fig. 11.1.

The operating program for each of the Datanet-30s was identical except for a small number of table entries that served to define the identity of the Datanet-30 and the configuration of lines attached to it. Provision was made for messages from either remote Datanet-30 to pass through either local Datanet-30 on their way to the central computer, thus providing for some continuation of service even when one local processor was out of service.

By April 1967 work on the GE phase of the project had reached a point where the Dartmouth students had largely completed their contributions. Work then began in earnest on the third phase of the project, that of designing and constructing the version of the time-sharing system now in use at Dartmouth and known as DTSS.

The design and construction work continued through the period when the Dartmouth community and network were using the GE-constructed system. In January 1969 DTSS was operational, offering service in the evening while GE service was continued during the day. By April 1969 DTSS took over full time.

Some of the details of the hardware, software, and communications are given in later sections. Here it is sufficient to note that in 1971 DTSS operated with 160 low-speed ports into the communications network, that approximately 50 terminals were in use in schools and colleges away from Dartmouth, and that there were on campus approximately 120 terminals of various types. By actual count, the observed peak load was 122 simultaneous users.

11.1.3 Regional Network

The use of DTSS by schools and colleges outside Dartmouth developed sporadically until the period 1967–1968. Spurred by two grants from the National Science Foundation (NSF), networking for schools and colleges proceeded in an organized way; staff support was sufficient to ensure a full program of activities in the participating schools. One grant was made at the secondary school level for the purpose of developing adjunctive curricular materials for use in the sciences and related subjects in the seventh through the twelfth grades. Eight topic outlines from an original batch of 36 were selected for refinement and attractive publication. Another grant supported the writing of a full-length book on elementary function theory, using the computer as a concomitant part of the course.

At the college level a grant was made to study the usefulness of a regional network for bringing computing power to smaller colleges from a central larger university; the purpose was to improve the curricula at these colleges without the necessity to install local computing centers. Here the emphasis

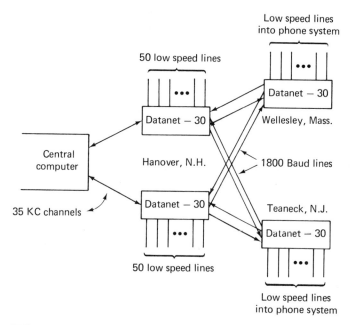

FIGURE 11.1   Interconnections between remote and local communications computers (1968).

was on demonstrating the idea, on accumulating experience, and on exploring what administrative and support mechanisms were attractive. Many of the participating colleges made heavy use of the computer and continued paying for use with their own funds after the grant was over.

Summarizing the experience of both the projects, we may draw these conclusions.

1. The economics of distributed computer service through time sharing over communications networks is acceptable to schools and colleges operating on modest budgets.
2. There are no serious technical problems, though the agonies of startup are discouraging to some.
3. The current state of communications technology and pricing do not pose major problems for networks of this geographical size; communications and terminals account for only about 25 per cent of the total cost of the Dartmouth system.
4. The outstanding remaining problem is the nonavailability of a large and varied menu of curricular materials that would allow a majority of teachers to introduce computing ideas into their teaching without extensive personal effort.

Acting on the idea that curricular materials are more likely to be used if they mesh with existing course outlines and standard textbooks, a response to point 4 was planned. A group of mathematicians, physicists, and engineers at Dartmouth formed Project COEXIST with NSF support to prepare curricular materials in those subjects. Their materials correlate well with existing texts, allowing a teacher to move easily into the computer approach and later to return to the conventional textbook approach. A parallel effort in the environmental sciences called Project COMPUTe was also formed with NSF support.

11.2 APPLICATIONS AND SERVICES OF THE NETWORK

Once installed, a network can be defined according to the kind and quality of services available on it. In this regard a network is a utility. Because it is, reliability is extremely important. Even a low failure rate will discourage users and cause them to refrain from depending on computing for their teaching.

Unlike electrical and similar utilities, which offer a very simple service, computer utilities offer an enormous selection of services. These services take many forms: computer services, program libraries, data-base services. A much wider variety of services is normally found on time-sharing systems than on batch-processing systems; the latter serve a more restricted purpose to a more restricted user community. One fortuitous implication of a time-sharing network is that whatever services are available locally are also available remotely.

11.2.1 Computer Services

One important service is the conventional one: that of providing a way to prepare and run computer programs. These programs can range in size from small ones done as homework exercises by students to large ones connected with major research activities. A network should provide for the complete range of these programs.

STUDENT SERVICES. The primary requirement for student programming is the ability to process extremely small programs with extremely rapid responses for such jobs, particularly if there are any errors. Although many students quickly progress to writing and debugging major programs, the vast majority of the load on a network consists of very small programs executing in a fraction of a second.

As an example, DTSS on one particularly heavy day processed over 19,000 jobs. More than half of these were programs written in the BASIC language, and a good share of these ended after a very short time because of errors. Still, the system carried out the job setup routine over 19,000 times on that particular 17-h day—roughly once every 3 s on the average.

A related requirement is that the languages most widely used must have good, fast compilers that provide concise, informative error messages. In DTSS the BASIC system compiles typical programs at a rate of more than 20,000 statements/min on a machine having a 1 μs memory cycle time.

If the student services are to be widely used by students, the terminals must be available on an open-shop basis to them. The financial support and accounting for student use should encourage, not discourage, such use. Ideally, institutions should treat student computer use as student library use is treated. If any limiting control is required to meter student use, it should be carried out by controlling the number and speed of the terminal devices, and not by imposing budgetary restrictions on the students themselves. Although this may sound financially irresponsible, a few years' experience and the law of averages allow computer-center directors to make fairly accurate budget estimates of student computer use for the year.

RESEARCH SERVICES. Realizing that student services are often useful for research, and that research services are even more useful to some students, we may catalog some of the features a network ought to have if it is to play an important role in college and university research projects.

First, a network should offer language processors for a major subset of BASIC, FORTRAN, COBOL, PL/1, and ALGOL. Other languages, selected according to the interests of the network community, should also be provided —these might include LISP, ALGOL-68, SNOBOL, and machine language, for instance. Dartmouth Time Sharing Service includes BASIC, FORTRAN, ALGOL, COBOL, and ALGOL-68; APL is planned, and compilers or interpreters for fragments of several other languages are available. In addition a wide variety of editing services should be available. Dartmouth Time Sharing Service includes three editors: one specially suited for editing by line or lines, one for string editing within a line or lines, and a third general-purpose string editor. Debuggers, tracers, and other services could also be included when warranted by the tastes of the community.

Second, a network should provide data-base services; these cannot conveniently be carried out on small individual computers. Large data bases not only need a large central storage device, but they require considerable staff and effort to maintain and update them. Providing access to large-scale data bases is an important ability of a time-sharing network, one that is not readily supplied by small individual computers or by large batch-oriented systems.

We have listed two types of service for which a network time-sharing system is admirably suited. There is a third class of service that has been performed in the past on conventional batch-processing systems, and which can usually be provided on networks. Many problems are long running, are production runs, are of a type that does not benefit from quick turnaround, or are not capable of being scheduled. These include the larger research computations and many administrative applications, such as payroll. Many time-sharing systems provide for running such programs during periods of low usage without requiring the attachment of an individual terminal. In DTSS this service is called *background*. In background the system can run jobs for which answers are not needed immediately, jobs that would tie up a terminal for a long time, and jobs that need an unusually large share of the total system resources. All these types of jobs can be initiated and the answers interpreted through the network. An additional kind of job requiring use of the expensive peripheral devices at the computer center cannot be as easily managed over the network.

A fourth type of service that might occasionally be useful on a network is to execute batch-processing software provided by the computer manufacturer. In the GE-635 the operating system GECOS provides a means to access a large collection of applications software provided by the manufacturer. A network time-sharing system should not automatically preclude the operation of this software. In DTSS a special software interface allows any GECOS-compatible program to operate in the background. Users thus have available the manufacturer's version of FORTRAN and COBOL, to name the most important examples.

Certain additional services can be provided by a network time-sharing system. On-line data acquisition in DTSS is trivial to establish if the user works at data rates associated with low-speed terminals. Clearly, if the on-line data are Teletype-compatible ASCII, no problems will be encountered processing the data with DTSS. If they are not, there is an input mode that is transparent to all bit patterns. Thus non-ASCII data can be translated and interpreted later by a special program. A research worker need not contract for the construction of special laboratory machinery to convert his on-line data to exact Teletype format.

Related to on-line acquisition of data is the ability of a time-sharing network to transmit an output stream of data having arbitrary bit patterns through the communications network. These arbitrary patterns can be used to drive special devices, such as plotters and experimental control units. A time-sharing network with these abilities can provide on-line data input and arbitrary control output for a wide variety of laboratory devices, provided the user employs standard bit rates and communications interfaces. Similar services can be provided by small, individual minicomputers at the expense of extensive, special-purpose programming in machine language.

ADMINISTRATIVE SERVICES.   One very important category of services is the wide variety of those needed in the administration of business or educational institutions. Many services that have long been provided on medium-scale, closed-shop, batch-processing systems can be better provided by a time-sharing network. Some small institutions find time-sharing service suitable for payroll accounting and check writing. The amount of printing is actually small, the amount of calculation is small, and the amount of required data is also small. Modern time-sharing networks provide both a sufficiently reliable service and a reasonable level of security to now allow administrators to trust such systems for their payroll accounting.

Both small businesses and small colleges can benefit from distributed data processing services through time-sharing networks. If low-speed terminals are not adequate, medium-speed line printers can be used. It is extremely important to work with standard communications services and to avoid expensive special hookups. A careful analysis will often reveal that very high speed data transmission is not really needed and that 1200- or even 300-bps service will be adequate.

OTHER SERVICES.   In a time-sharing network computing becomes a much more flexible mechanism, capable of being of service in areas not previously invaded by computers. One important such area is text editing and printing. More and more time-sharing networks are being used to receive and store texts of reports, papers, and even books. As later drafts are prepared, the text in the computer storage is modified by suitable editing programs, and the new draft run off on a terminal or line printer in a format suitable for photo-offset reproduction. Many technical books are typeset and run off in this way, eliminating several stages in the printing process. This approach is used on DTSS for preparation of manuals, the output being camera-ready copy.

It is almost mandatory for the collection of documentation and manuals associated with a time-sharing network to be available from the network. In most cases people prefer to use a conventional book or manual, but at the very least these manuals are produced using computer editing systems. The final version that produces the hard copy for photo-offsetting can easily be left in the computer to be accessed through the network terminals.

Naturally, a time-sharing network automatically is self-managing, producing bills for services and keeping statistical summaries of system usage.

11.2.2 Canned Programmed Services

It is generally accepted that a good library of canned programs is an essential part of a computer system serving a community having broad interests. In certain fields such as statistics, well-known collections of programs are widely used and understood.

Despite the notable success of some such special collections of library programs, experience has shown that program libraries have not lived up to all the expectations we held for them. Even assuming that all programs are well debugged and supplied with supporting memoranda, there are other fundamental reasons why program libraries have not achieved more importance. Some of the possible reasons are

1. Often the program does not work properly. Even perfectly debugged mathematically correct programs can give meaningless results because the algorithm chosen is oversensitive to round-off error.
2. The program may not do exactly what the user wants.
3. The program may be in a form less suitable for his use; for instance, it may be in the form of a program when he needs a subprogram.
4. The user may not know that certain programs exist.
5. The user may prefer to prepare his own program, even though suitable library programs exist.

We guess that there are as many as 100,000 programs of all types in computer program libraries. Clearly, many of these do almost the same task. How many different library programs are there, do you suppose, that calculate the mean and variance of a set of data?

Some of these problems can be met by attacking them specifically. For instance, certain programs are published and subsequently reviewed and evaluated by experts in the Algorithms section of the *Communications of the ACM*. Extra efforts can be put into clear and concise instructions for use.

Several versions of the same program can be provided to cater to the tastes of different users.

Networks can mitigate some of the difficulties associated with making high-quality program libraries available, the reasons being that they are able to bring more resources to bear on achieving and maintaining quality, have a much larger user base that can assist in improving the programs, and are able to establish more elaborate schemes for making information about the programs more generally available. The existence of a network does not guarantee better program libraries, but it can contribute in that direction. Network users have available better library programs than computer users working with smaller and more isolated machines.

Although the program library in DTSS is extensive, it is far from comprehensive; it contains only about 500 primary programs, not counting subprograms and essential data files. All these *official* programs are listed in the on-line catalog called DARTCAT***. Their titles and brief descriptions appear in a technical memorandum reissued yearly.

Any official program must include comment or remark statements giving the name of the program, a brief description of one or two lines, the name of the originator or maintainer, and complete instructions for use. Since virtually all programs are stored in source form (usually in BASIC), listing them on any terminal will reveal this information. Occasionally, the instructions are printed when the program is executed; of course, the relevant print statements will also be revealed when the program is listed.

Much more difficult to control is programming and commenting style. With a large and diverse group of contributors, enforcing style conventions is practically impossible. We therefore accept a wide range of formats, dealing individually with those contributors whose styles and commenting inclinations fall short.

An outside reviewing system to approve new programs before they enter the library would be highly desirable. Some large portions of the DTSS library are the responsibility of certain departments, which take on the review and quality-control functions. The Amos Tuck School of Business Administration at Dartmouth is responsible for about 120 programs. In other areas faculty members are asked to review the correctness of programs in their areas of competence.

A *sublibrary* feature of DTSS allows individuals or groups to maintain unofficial programs. Such programs can be obtained by any user who knows of their existence. They need not adhere to the standards for official programs, and they can be maintained or modified by their owners without working through the center staff.

Another feature allows an individual to specify any of his private programs as available either publicly or within his user number group. Students, especially, find this a convenient way to share special programs of their own design with other users of DTSS but without involving either the public program library or any sublibrary.

Perhaps the most important observation about program libraries and networks is that the primary source for library programs is the user community itself. The network provides a large user base with an effective means for *inter-user* communication. Information in a network flows in all directions, greatly facilitating the feedback loop between program providers and program users. Although this structure does not guarantee high quality, it does improve the relevance of what goes into program libraries. Even if a certain collection of programs originates with a computer vendor or some nationally recognized group, a network can play a crucial role in bringing these to the ultimate consumer. In this sense, the network plays a role similar to that of a retail merchant in bringing to the user community the products that are available.

11.2.3 Data-Base Services

Some of the computer services usually found in a network can be provided just as well by local and small free-standing computers. Debugging and running small problem-solving student jobs requires a level of computer service easily found in most small computers. Other types of service can be just as well provided by conventional batch-processing computers. Large, number-crunching scientific calculations do not often require the facilities of a network unless a computer having such power is not readily available. There is one kind of service that cannot be well provided in any system other than a network system—the provision of data-base services.

Data-base service is expensive of machine and people resources for two reasons: the cost of holding the data on the system and the cost of maintaining it in a current state. Thus it is of paramount interest to hold and maintain data bases of general interest in as few locations as possible. Networks provide an ideal mechanism for distributing the services of the data bases to users over a wide geographical area or even within a single institution.

Once a decision is made to maintain a collection of data bases on-line, an investment in on-line storage is needed. If the cost of this storage can be spread over large numbers of applications and users, the cost per use can become small enough to be justified. Furthermore, a large network computer system automatically provides backup in case the data is damaged through fault of hardware, software, or humans.

Another aspect is the cost of maintaining any nonstagnant data base. Such functions as transforming the data, correcting errors, and adding to the data can usually be performed easily through the services of a network. In addition to the advantages for updating data, network systems often provide editing systems and other facilities for handling and modifying data.

IMPRESS—AN EXAMPLE. In the Dartmouth network there exists a social-scientific data-base system called IMPRESS. The system offers its users access to a large number of data bases through a series of interactive responses. Designed primarily for student use, the system can quickly provide a series of standard analyses for whatever subset of the variables the student selects. The more sophisticated user can override the default options and order complicated *transgenerations* of the data, or can even choose to work with the raw data itself.

The system is almost self-teaching. By typing a question mark (?) the user can evoke detailed descriptions and directions on how to use the system at that stage.

IMPRESS is constructed so as to minimize the load on the network computer—both by careful programming of the interactive modules (written entirely in BASIC) and by using *inverted* data carefully packed. It is a tribute to this packing that over 40 data bases, many of them standard and well known, occupy about 10,000,000 characters in the on-line file system. More than 700 complete analysis runs are recorded in a busy week.

IMPRESS can interactively provide some information about each data base. A written code book is available for each data base; it gives a more complete description of the individual variables, the background of the survey, and the standard groupings and dichotomies used as the default options.

The system also contains local opinion surveys of interest; several deal with coeducation, an issue of concern at the time of this writing. No longer do the students have to rely on the expert interpretation of the results of the surveys. Now *any* student can go to *any* terminal and test his own pet hypothesis and reach his own conclusions.

ADMINISTRATIVE DATA PROCESSING. Although the promise of management information systems has been slow to be realized, a careful study of most management operations will reveal certain applications that can be better carried out using on-line data-base services through a network. Institutional planning can be more readily carried out if the primary data (personnel, plant, etc.) can be fed into a network system for analysis directly by administrative officials. Often such analyses lose their value if they have to wait for the monthly report cycle. Administrative data are of interest primarily within the organization; intra-institutional networks are therefore indicated.

Some inter-institutional program sharing has occurred; WICHE* distributes programs to its members in standard languages. Most of the programs

*Western Interstate Commission on Higher Education.

are designed to be run on local computer systems. The network activity thus takes place at the program-sharing level rather than at the operational level.

Computer networks can play a positive role if two or more institutions are willing to employ some of the same programs and data structures. The network can provide routine program maintenance and file backup services for the participating institutions, saving cost and effort. Through a network, smaller institutions can employ whatever sophisticated services are available, services that might not exist on small local computers. Even though the data bases are separate for the separate institutions, the network allows the common usage of the maintenance and analysis programs.

Although administrative use of networks among universities is not yet an important component of use, experience with the Dartmouth network suggests that sophisticated data processing services for small institutions can be provided economically, and a certain small amount of development is being directed to this area.

11.3   TECHNICAL DESCRIPTION OF THE SYSTEM

11.3.1 Hardware

The hardware components around which the DTSS is constructed are conventional and are configured conventionally. Specifically, the components are largely those of the HIS-G635 (formerly GE-635) system with the file storage taking place on IBM-2314 systems. A detailed list follows:

1. *Memory*: 163,840 words of 36 bits (160K words), approximately 1-μs cycle time; two controllers, permitting some overlap (no hardware paging, one base and memory protection register).
2. *Processors*: dual standard 635 processors, one of them switch-set to be the *master* and receive all traps and interrupts.
3. *I/O control*: IOC-C, an input–output controller that stands between the high-speed memory and all peripheral devices. Contains approximately 12 channels, all of which can operate simultaneously. Contends with the processors for memory cycles.
4. *Standard I/O*: dual channel, eight-handler tape-controller, six handlers installed. Low-speed handlers, seven-track, NRZI type. One each of card reader, card punch, and 1200-lines/min printer. Operator's console.
5. *Auxiliary memory*: a standard drum is used as a swapping device, and may thus be thought of as an extension of main memory. About 0.75 million word capacity, with a transfer rate of about 60,000 words/s (which is slow by modern standards).

6. *File storage*: two IBM-2314 systems, eight packs apiece, operated through a single interface unit into the IOC-C. Provide file storage of about 72,000,000 words.
7. *Communications*: dual Datanet-30s operating a total of about 160 low-speed (110, 135, 150, and 300 bps) lines and 3 high-speed (1200 to 2400 bps) lines.

The Datanet-30s collect the incoming teletyped characters and batch transmissions to the main memory, thus minimizing interrupts. This batching takes place about once each half-second. The Datanet-30s also perform the line delete and character delete editing functions, and hold the character translation tables for the several non-ASCII terminals (such as IBM-2741s) that can access the system. On output, the information is batched to the Datanet-30s, which then separate it into characters and distribute them to the terminals, again performing character translation if necessary.

11.3.2 Software

Although the hardware is conventional, the software is not. Designed and constructed entirely at the college, largely by undergraduate students, it can be described as a general-purpose, file-oriented system, but one that falls just short of providing the illusion of infinite resources (as is done with MULTICS or the IBM-360/67-TSS).

The memory and processor hardware has two modes of operation: master mode and slave mode. In slave mode memory references are relocated and bounded by the base-address-register, which completely isolates jobs running in slave mode from one another. All the I/O commands and interrupt and fault processing take place in master mode.

Building on this base, the DTSS executive is a master-mode program that (1) provides fault and interrupt processing, (2) initiates and controls all I/O processing, (3) allocates the use of memory for slave jobs and for I/O buffers, and (4) performs scheduling. In addition, a number of commands are defined and implemented by the executive to provide complete file system services to running jobs. These include searching catalogs, opening files, reading files, writing and appending to files, executing files, scratching files, and a number of other important file services. To a running job such as a monitor, a BASIC compiler, or an editing package, the executive looks like a file system. The matters of memory allocation and scheduling are transparent to running jobs. Furthermore, the file system seen by running jobs is device and record transparent, these details being taken care of by the executive. The file system is word oriented and content independent. The executive also provides miscellaneous services, such as providing the wall-clock time and the date.

Not only are the user's data files and programs part of the file system, but so also are the I/O devices. Tapes, card devices, and the printer are files, although specially marked as serial rather than random-access files. Output to tape is processed by writing into a file, the special device file *tape*, for instance.

The most important idea in DTSS is that interjob communication is also by files—special files called *communications files*. Once the file is established, job A, for instance, sends a message to job B by *writing* into the connecting communications files. Job B receives the message by *reading* from its end of the file, after having been alerted to. the transmission by a *special interrupt*. Since a running job can have any number of files open to it, it can have any number of communications files as well. Normally only one communications file is attached to a simple BASIC job—the file that eventually threads its way to the physical Teletype or other terminal. But several such files may connect to a single running job, so a single job may have multiple terminals connected to it in a very simple and user-initiated way. This permits computer-controlled competitive situations, such as football simulations and business games. In the same way the job which is the monitor (command scanner) connects through communications files to all active users that are not connected to some other running job.

One end of each communications file that represents a terminal is connected to some running job, be it a monitor, a compiler, or an editor. The other end is connected to the top job in the system—the interface to the external communications, called the D-30face, since it interfaces with Datanet-30 communications processors. The D-30face packages outgoing messages from the communications files and pulses them to the D-30s; it performs the reverse process for incoming messages. It thus deals with both communications files and device files—the D-30s themselves. The pulsing takes place on demand, but no more frequently than twice a second for each device and each direction, thus keeping down the frequency of interruptions from these devices.

The file system is tree structured. The top node is the Master File Directory (MFD). From it hang other nodes, which are either other directories or files. One of these directories contains the official system services, such as compilers and editors. Another contains the files that are the monitors and other high-level jobs. The system starts up by invoking an *execute* command on the D-30face file. While in execution, the D-30face file locates other files, such as validation modules and monitors, and issues execute commands on them. A job knows only about jobs that are under it, jobs that it has executed. Lower ends of communications files may be passed along with the execute command, but only to jobs that are under it. The integrity of the tree structure is thus preserved.

Although cross-links in the file system are not permitted, a job can search the file system tree to find a particular file and, if permissions are satisfied, obtain a copy of it. This provision is widely invoked by students as a way of trading programs, while at the same time maintaining the integrity of each other's user numbers, and the billing as well.

11.4 COMMUNICATIONS

11.4.1 Historical Overview

Although communications technology is one of the best developed and integrated technologies of all those that bear upon computing, new developments in modems and multiplexors suggest giving special treatment to them. We shall therefore first discuss standard communications services as they were and are applied to the DTSS, and then discuss some aspects of the modems and multiplexors that are available.

The DTSS was a star-type system, with many small users located at the points of a multipointed star with the central computer at the center. The users at the points had single terminals, or small numbers of terminals, all operating at low speeds. The bulk of the use did not involve heavy point-to-point transmission, nor was there any need for store-and-forward transmission. It was therefore the case that standard communications as provided by the common carriers were adequate for the needs of the network.

As of this writing there are about 60 low-speed terminals in about 35 different locations remote from Dartmouth, most terminals connected full time to the DTSS. These locations are distributed fairly evenly throughout northern New England, with little opportunity to take advantage of clustering.

In the early days outside users had to lease a terminal and a business telephone from a common carrier. From these they would dial another business telephone number located at the computer site, which connected through a 103A DATA-PHONE data set with handset to the computer. Although the handset was in no way required at the computer end, its presence was dictated by franchise agreements with competing common carriers. This service was expensive for users outside the local dialing area because of toll charges; it was more expensive than it should have been for local users because of the necessity to feed through the regular switching system and the consequent requirement for a business telephone.

One very serious problem that arose early and caused major concern with the common carrier was that computer use implied very long holding times. Thus switching circuits and trunk lines were being occupied for much longer periods of time than predicted for ordinary voice service by the statistical models. The specter of a very small number of area schools and colleges tying up the entire long-distance trunk capabilities between Boston and Montreal led the common carrier to install greater trunk capacity for the local region.

It was quickly learned that the cut-over point in cost between using standard dial-up long-distance toll service by the minute and leasing a full-service line was about 2 h/day of steady use. Schools that anticipated more than a very casual use of the network found it to their advantage to arrange for full-service lines. Initially, these were established as foreign exchange lines to the local exchange. This arrangement still implies long holding times for circuits in the local switching center, but at least allows the common carrier to plan more sensibly for the installation of additional trunk lines, of which a certain known number would be leased for full-time service over long periods of time.

A curious situation arose because of the discrepancy between interstate and intrastate rates. At the time intrastate rates were more expensive. A New Hampshire school established a foreign exchange line to a Vermont exchange with local dialing access to the computer, thus taking advantage of the lower interstate rates for line rental.

Very shortly after the advent of the DTSS, Dartmouth College obtained a Centrex internal telephone system. Several advantages accrue from this type of arrangement, although technically speaking there is little difference between a Centrex exchange and a local public exchange. First, the switching mechanisms of the local exchange were no longer subject to long holding times; rather the college was able to order and pay for exactly the switching circuits needed. Second, a full-service line to a remote location could now be classified an off-premises extension rather than a foreign-exchange business telephone. The rates that applied for the telephone connections at either end were determined by the contracted rate for extensions, rather than by the commercial business telephone rates—a large savings. Of course, the long-line rental rate was the same, still being computed according to the airline distance between the points.

Another virtue provided by the Centrex arrangement was that single-digit dialing could be established as the mode of operation for most terminals. It thus became possible to pool together rather large numbers of terminals, and to study the effects of various ways to structure the pooling. Such pooling using mechanical switching does not allow all terminals to access all computer ports, but good statistical performance can still be achieved by careful study and design of the pooling arrangements.

Regular users found it desirable to adopt the off-premises-extension approach rather than the foreign-exchange approach, because the termination charges were much less. They are calculated at the inside rate of about $3.50 per telephone rather than at the outside rate of about $16.00 for a business telephone. Although regular users adopted the off-premises-extension approach, irregular users still needed local telephone numbers to dial; a small number of computer ports and DATA-PHONE data sets accessible to the outside world through the normal switched network were therefore retained.

The common carriers allow subchannels to be derived from a leased line by frequency-division multiplexing. The number of subchannels is determined by the data rates and also by the quality of the line itself. We found it convenient to use standard voice-grade channels rather than those with a higher level of conditioning. The relatively sparse location of the terminal consoles spread over a wide geographical region suggested the use of multi-drop frequency-division multiplexing; the most inexpensive grade of line was employed, since the outer reaches of a given line would certainly carry fewer than the maximum number of subchannels. Also, we felt that telephone company personnel unfamiliar with data communications could more reliably provide voice-grade service.

Some minor inconvenience was caused by the testing and verification that the channel met the specifications of the tariff. Checking a line from central station to central station is fairly easy, but we found it necessary to ask the carrier to check the quality from terminal point to terminal point before we would accept it. Even with this insistence, 90 per cent of new installations failed to meet the specified signal quality when tested by our own personnel prior to making the multiplexing equipment operational. We found that it was important to insist that leased lines be corrected to meet the specifications rather than to adjust the frequency-division multiplexing equipment to work with the channel provided. This avoided marginal operation and made the total system insensitive to subsequent improvements in signal quality due to rerouting of a channel.

11.4.2 Dial-Up Access to the Dartmouth Time Sharing System

CENTREX PRIVATE BUSINESS EXCHANGE (PBX). Voice communications services for Dartmouth College are provided by the common carrier utilizing a Centrex Private Business Exchange (PBX) of the step-by-step type. This system has also worked out well technically and economically for both the telephone company and the college.

Most terminals on the campus are Model 33 Teletypes operating at 110 bps. There is a telephone associated with every terminal from which a computer port may be reached by dialing the single digit 7. This provides maximum convenience for the user at a terminal, yet requires minimal use of the telephone company switching equipment, which can be tied up for long periods of time. The telephone company is informed of all extensions on the campus that intend to use the telephone system for accessing the computer. All such extensions are assigned an individual first-selector 100-position stepping relay. The seventh level of this nonshared first selector can provide hunting over 10 access paths to the computer ports. Standard telephone company techniques may be used to assign access paths to computer ports and to group users to reduce the probability of blocking—a situation in which the user may receive a busy signal even though some port of the system is idle. The advantage of this technique is that the only switching equipment which is in use for the entire duration of the call is the dedicated first selector.

One difficulty with this procedure is brought about by a lack of coordination between persons responsible for data communications and voice communications. For example, although the digit 7 is used to access a computer port, on some telephones the digit 7 is used to access the WATS, which the college purchases from the telephone company. Consequently, telephones equipped with WATS capability cannot alternatively access the computer in the manner described. Additionally, calls coming into the Centrex exchange from other exchanges cannot dial the single digit 7 instead of a four-digit extension number. For these reasons some normal four-digit numbers are assigned to data sets connecting to 110-baud computer ports. There is also the possibility that a user who dials 7 may encounter a busy signal, either because all 7 ports are in use or because the switching network has blocked. On the DTSS, 15 ports are available to the normal switched network in this way.

PORT SPEED SELECTION SERVICES.   The Dartmouth Time Sharing System and many other systems rely upon telephone company switching to separate terminals that operate at different speeds and connect them to the proper ports of the computer system. This is done by assigning different telephone numbers for each class of device that the DTSS is prepared to accept. Thus, for example, different ports have been made available for Model 33/35 Teletypes, Model 37 Teletypes, GE Terminet-300s, Friden Flexowriters, IBM 2741 EBCDIC terminals, IBM 2741 Correspondence terminals, Inktronic terminals, etc. A user at a terminal must know the characteristics of the terminal he is using and must dial the proper telephone number.

11.4.3 Multiplexed Access to the Dartmouth Time Sharing System

MULTIPOINT MULTIPLEXING.   Approximately 35 schools, colleges, and universities in the New England region make use of the DTSS by means of a communication network operated by the Kiewit Computation Center of Dartmouth College. These users are so dispersed throughout the area that it is not feasible to treat these customers as clustered together. If they were collected in groups geographically near each other, communication to the computing facility in Hanover, New Hampshire, could be accomplished by providing simple two-point leased lines from the center of the cluster to the computing center. Multiplexing the use of the channel could then be accomplished by any of a number of techniques, such as fixed time-division multiplexing, variable time-division multiplexing (see Chapters 5 and 6), as well as by frequency-division multiplexing.

The Dartmouth network utilized five multipoint voice-grade leased lines and frequency-division multiplexing to provide up to 70 subchannels. It is important to understand the character of a duplex multipoint layout obtainable from the telephone company. There may be up to approximately 15 nodes on one duplex multinode channel. One of these nodes is designated as the master station; this would be expected to be the station at the central computer facility. The remaining nodes are designated as remote stations; typically, each remote station will service from one to four time-sharing terminals. In a duplex network, two independent communications facilities are employed; one is a *broadcasting facility* and the other a *listening facility*, as seen from the point of view of the master station. Consider the broadcasting facility shown in Fig. 11.2.

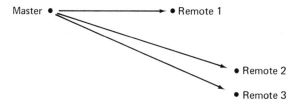

FIGURE 11.2   Broadcasting facility example.

All signals transmitted by the master station are available to each remote station; how these remote stations respond to signals is a function of the multiplexing technique to be employed. The listening facility might be schematically indicated as in Fig. 11.3. All signals transmitted by all remote stations are always received by the master station. The multiplexing technique chosen will separate the signals at the master station.

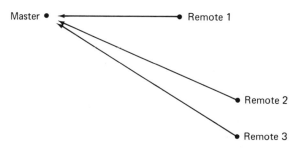

FIGURE 11.3   Listening facility example.

It is important to realize that the broadcasting and listening facilities are completely independent. Thus in this example there is no communication path provided that would allow remote station 1 to send signals to remote station 2.

There are two other diagrams of the layout that are important to the operator of a communications network. One of these is the layout in which the customer indicates to the telephone company how the master and remote stations are to be connected. Figure 11.4 denotes a layout that a customer

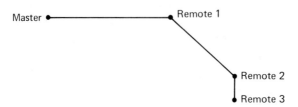

FIGURE 11.4   Optimum interconnection layout example.

might specify. From this layout the telephone company will compute the total mileage requirement of the multipoint layout for the purposes of determining the rental rate for the facility. Thus the network operator should endeavor to see that the total mileage is as short as possible. Figure 11.5 illustrates a layout that would certainly be less desirable from the point of view of the charges incurred. Computer programs can be used to lay out a more complicated network. The NETSET* program is an example of such a program invoking the exact tariff structures filed with the Federal Communications Commission. This program was used to design the original Dartmouth network employing five multipoint duplex leased voice-grade channels.

The other diagram of the layout that is useful for the network operator to know is the manner in which the telephone company actually utilized its facilities to provide the requested service. The manner in which this is done

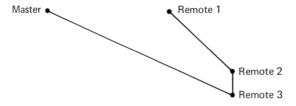

FIGURE 11.5   Undesirable interconnection layout example.

*A service mark of Digital Systems Corporation, Hanover, N. H.

depends upon availability of channel facilities, trained personnel, and many other factors. The layouts employed are often surprising to the network operator. An actual layout for our example might be similar to that in Fig. 11.6. Knowledge of this layout is very useful in diagnosing failures in the communications network. For example, if signals are not being received from both remote station 2 and remote station 3, the trouble might be found in the link between central office B and central office C.

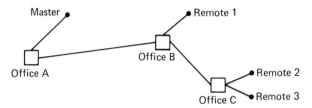

FIGURE 11.6   Actual interconnection layout example.

Loop-back keys can be a useful tool for the diagnosis of a problem of communication with a remote station, but they can be very troublesome if thrown at the wrong time. Suppose that the time-sharing terminal at remote station 1 is not working properly. The trouble may be with the communications service provided by the telephone company, or it may be with the terminal itself. Without actually going to the remote station itself, it is desirable to determine whether the trouble is a telephone company problem or not. Figure 11.7 illustrates how a loop-back key located at remote station 1 might be thrown to cause the broadcast signal received at the remote station to be sent back through the listening facility. If the transmitted signal is properly returned to the central office B, it can safely be assumed that the telephone

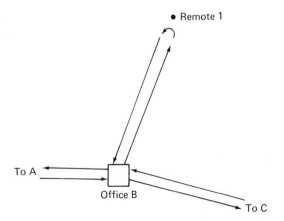

FIGURE 11.7   Loop-back function example for Remote 1.

facilities are not at fault and that the problem lies elsewhere. The loop-back key can be arranged to be remotely controlled from the central office using a phantom circuit or similar arrangement standard with the telephone company.

FREQUENCY-DIVISION MULTIPLEXING.   Where multipoint duplex leased channels are employed for communication between a computer (master station) and terminals (remote stations), the most economical method of separating communications for the various terminals is frequency-division multiplexing. The available bandwidth for an unconditioned type 3002 voice-grade channel ranges approximately from 300 to 3000 Hz. The variations of attenuation of signal power and envelope delay with frequency limit the information that can be transmitted with an inexpensive modulation scheme; on the Dartmouth network the bandwidth from 340 to 2720 Hz has been used successfully. The entire Dartmouth network operates with standard Model 33 Teletypes so that standard 110-baud subchannels with standard spacing may be used throughout the system. For signaling at a rate of 110 baud, subchannels with 170-Hz separation are used. Subchannels are usually denoted by their center frequency. The mark signal is 42.5 Hz above the center frequency, and the space signal is 42.5 Hz below the center frequency.

MODEMS.   At the master station—the Dartmouth Kiewit Computation Center—the communications equipment consists of frequency-division multiplexing apparatus that contains a modulator and demodulator for each 170-Hz subchannel in use on the multipoint duplex leased channel. The modulation technique is frequency-shift keying, and the demodulators are simply filters that detect whether the mark frequency or space frequency is being received in each subchannel band. At a remote station a single modem associated with each terminal performs the same function. Since the broadcasting facility and the listening facility are totally separate, the same frequency assignments for subchannels are used both for transmitting data from the computer to the terminal and for receiving data at the computer from the terminal. Often there is more than one terminal at a remote station of the leased telephone channel, and there is of course one modem for each terminal, although multiple modems are occasionally housed in the same cabinet.

SUBCHANNEL SHARING.   The connection from the modem associated with a particular subchannel at the master station is usually plugged directly into a port of the computer. Thus the computer port is dedicated to the terminal assigned to the appropriate subchannel. Port selecting equipment is not used because the cost of such concentrating equipment has been found to exceed the cost of the additional unused ports on the communications computers. To reduce the costs of computer service and to spread the costs of communications even farther, some geographically distant groups of users opt to split the use of a subchannel and a computer port. They agree to use the computer at mutually exclusive times. When not in use, the modem must be turned off to prevent the transmission of any signals in the shared subchannel so that no interference with the other user is generated.

A few problems have arisen from this technique of subchannel sharing. One is that occasionally one of the partners forgets to turn off his modem when he is not scheduled to have access to the computer port. A trained technician can detect this by observing the beat frequency caused by the two interfering carriers. The other problem is that the lack of a received carrier at the master station may be due either to the fact that all users have turned off their modems or that telephone equipment has failed. This increases the difficulty of maintenance both for the technicians at the computer center and for the telephone repairmen in the central offices. In spite of these difficulties, subchannel sharing has been generally satisfactory to all concerned.

11.4.4 A Snapshot of the Dartmouth Time Sharing System Network

The communications network associated with the DTSS is not a static thing, but changes every week in response to many factors. Some old users discontinue service, some increase the number of terminals, some new users request service. The staff of the computing center must also respond to the demand for different types of ports required for new terminals available commercially. The information that follows is meant to give a snapshot of the port utilization of the system in June 1971.

SWITCHED NETWORK DDD ACCESSIBLE, 110 BPS. These 15 ports are accessible to users who access the DTSS using 110 bps Teletypes. They may be located in exchanges other than the Dartmouth Centrex exchange and they use the normal Bell System DDD switched network, accessing the computer port by direct inward dialing into the Centrex exchange. In addition, these ports are available to on-campus users as four-digit extensions of the internal telephone system.

DIAL 7 ACCESSIBLE, 110 BPS. These 62 ports are accessible only from Teletypes on Centrex extensions for which the telephone company has made special provision. This convenience of single-digit dialing is primarily used for on-campus Teletypes, but it is also used from off-premises extensions where customers have requested this.

DIRECT DEDICATED, 110 BPS. There are 8 ports connected directly to 8 Model 35 Teletypes in the Public Room at the Kiewit Computation Center; these terminals are used so heavily that it makes sense to connect them via short private lines to full-time dedicated ports to the computer system, which is a few rooms away. There is also value in having some terminals from which access to the computer is guaranteed—busy signals will not occur.

450 HARGRAVES / KURTZ

SYSTEM CONTROL, 110 BPS. These 2 ports of the computer system are provided with 103A DATA-PHONE data sets, which are physically controlled by the operator in the computer room. The automatic-answer feature is disabled and all calls to these 2 ports are placed through the machine operator. In fact, he may place a call from the computer port to a Teletype. This provides positive control over the access to the DTSS through these 2 ports. These are designated as control ports; the system will accept commands that modify or control the system only from a Teletype connected to one of these control ports.

DIALCOMM, 110 BPS. There are 2 ports accessible from Telephones of the General Electric Company DialComm network. By arrangement with GE their employees may use the DTSS for such things as system development for their commercial time-sharing service.

FREQUENCY-DIVISION MULTIPLEXOR NETWORKS, 110 BPS. These 56 ports are used to connect remote users to the DTSS. There are five, leased, voice-grade, duplex, private-line data channels in the network; each is divided by frequency-division multiplexing into up to 14 subchannels. The modem for each subchannel is directly connected to a port on the computer; since no switching equipment is employed, such a user has a dedicated port into the system.

IBM EBCDIC 2741 TERMINAL, 134.5 BPS. These 4 ports are Centrex extensions accessible from the Bell DDD network and from on the campus. The ports are for use with the popular IBM terminal, which is based upon the Selectric typewriter. Since the terminal uses a code which is not ASCII, a translation table is employed in the communications computer.

IBM CORRESPONDENCE 2741 TERMINAL, 134.5 BPS. There are 4 ports available for this version of the IBM 2741 terminal. Unfortunately, there are several versions of the IBM 2741 available, differing only in the code translation table used. The computer must know the type of 2741 terminal before any communications can take place; consequently, separate telephone numbers are employed for Correspondence and EBCDIC versions.

SWITCHED NETWORK DDD ACCESSIBLE, 150 BPS. These 7 ports are provided for users who have terminals such as the Model 37 Teletype, which are capable of operating at 15 characters/s. They are accessible from any telephone on the DDD network from on-campus extensions. One of these ports has a secret telephone number which the President of Dartmouth College uses for operating the DTSS from his office or from his home.

SWITCHED NETWORK DDD ACCESSIBLE, 300 BPS. This single port is used for development of service for 30-character/s terminals such as the General Electric Terminet-300, which is a full ASCII, 94 graphic, chain-type, impact-printing terminal.

INKTRONIC PRINTER, 1200 BPS. This single port is used by the receive-only Inktronic ink-squirting printer, which operates at 120 characters/s. This port is available to the DDD switched network and is accessible to any receive-only Dataspeed printer such as the Inktronic.

GRAPHIC 2, 2000 BPS. This single port is primarily utilized by the PDP-9/Graphic 2 system used for development of interactive graphics for the DTSS. This port expects a synchronous, half-duplex transmission scheme and utilizes a Bell 201A DATA-PHONE data-set.

TOTAL PORTS. The 163 total ports substantiate the claim that the DTSS provides more ports which can be simultaneously utilized than any other general-purpose single time-sharing system in the world. Not all ports are ever observed in operation at the same time, although all ports of a given type are occasionally fully utilized. As a part of the snapshot of the state of the Dartmouth network, the dedicated circuits to remote users are shown in Fig. 11.8. There are five separate, duplex, voice-grade, multipoint, leased channels

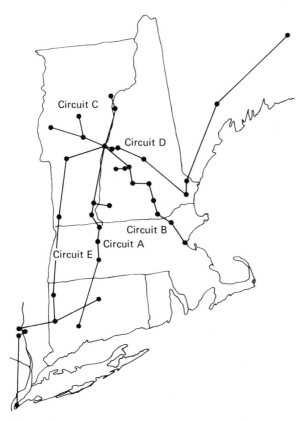

FIGURE 11.8   Frequency-division multiplexed circuits.

Subchannel Frequency (Hz)	User Identification
425	
595	Cheshire National Bank, Conn.
765	Windham College, Vt.
935	Deerfield Academy, Mass.
1105	Mount Holyoke College, Mass.
1275	
1445	Brattleboro High School, Vt.
1615	Mount Holyoke College, Mass.
1785	Mount Holyoke College, Mass.
1955	Mount Holyoke College, Mass.
2125	Northfield School, Mass.
2295	Mount Hermon School, Mass.
2465	Mount Hermon School, Mass.
2635	Keene High School, N.H.

FIGURE 11.9   Subchannel allocations for Circuit A.

Subchannel Frequency (Hz)	User Identification
425	St. Anselm's College, N.H.
595	
765	Concord High School, N.H.
935	New England Regional Computing, Mass.
1105	Andover Academy, Mass.
1275	Andover Academy, Mass.
1445	Andover Academy, Mass.
1615	Andover Academy, Mass.
1785	Sunapee High School, N.H. Newport High School, N.H.
1955	New England Regional Computing, Mass.
2125	New England College, N.H.
2295	St. Paul's School, N.H.
2465	Mt. St. Mary College, N.H. Notre Dame College, N.H. Rivier College, N.H.
2635	New England Regional Computing, Mass.

FIGURE 11.10   Subchannel allocations for Circuit B. Multiple users indicate a shared subchannel and computer port.

Subchannel Frequency (Hz)	User Identification
425	
595	
765	Vermont Technical College, Vt.
935	Vermont Technical College, Vt.
1105	
1275	
1445	Middlebury College, Vt.
1615	Middlebury College, Vt.
1785	Middlebury College, Vt.
	St. Johnsbury Academy, Vt.
1955	
2125	
2295	
2465	Woodsville High School, N.H.
2635	

FIGURE 11.11   Subchannel allocations for Circuit C.

Subchannel Frequency (Hz)	User Identification
425	Exeter Academy, N.H.
595	Exeter Academy, N.H.
	University of New Hampshire, N.H.
765	University of New Hampshire, N.H.
935	Exeter Academy, N.H.
1105	Mascoma Valley Regional High School, N.H.
	Husson Business College, Me.
1275	University of New Hampshire, N.H.
1445	Bates College, Me.
1615	Bates College, Me.
1785	Bates College, Me.
1955	Bates College, Me.
2125	University of New Hampshire, N.H.
2295	Cardigan Mountain School, N.H.
	Tilton School, N.H.
2465	University of New Hampshire, N.H.
2635	

FIGURE 11.12   Subchannel allocations for Circuit D.

Subchannel Frequency (Hz)	User Identification
425	
595	
765	Jersey City, N.J.
935	Jersey City, N.J.
1105	Kent Girls School, Conn. Kent Boys School, Conn.
1275	Kent School, Conn. Salisbury School, Conn.
1445	Dartmouth Club, N.Y.
1615	Dartmouth Club, N.Y.
1785	Loomis School, Conn. Trinity College, Conn.
1955	Loomis School, Conn.
2125	Storm King Mountain School, N.Y. Lady Cliff School, N.Y. Orange County School, N.Y.
2295	Bennington College, Vt.
2465	Rutland High School Vt.
2635	

FIGURE 11.13   Subchannel allocations for Circuit E.

used for this network. Figures 11.9–11.13 give the subchannel assignments and identifications of the users on each of the five circuits.

11.5 BENEFITS OF STANDARDS IN NETWORK OPERATION

In the operation of a time-sharing computer network it is important to develop procedures for technical personnel to install, diagnose, and maintain the network and its associated equipment. In the management of the network a variety of standards are employed to reduce the number of decisions and supporting documentation that must be completed by the technical staff. These standards range from official industry standards approved by such bodies as the American National Standards Institute, to Bell system plant practices, to local in-house procedures. Some of the standards that have been beneficial to the operation of the DTSS are treated below.

CHARACTER CODE.   The American Standard Code for Information Interchange (ASCII) is supported by the DTSS. Any terminal that supports the

ASCII code and conforms to the transmission protocols in use can operate with the DTSS. This code structure provides for 94 printing graphics including the lowercase characters. Nearly all terminals on the network are Model 33 Teletypes, which operate using a 64-character subset of this ASCII character set.

CODE TRANSMISSION. All terminals on the multiplexed networks use bit-serial, asynchronous, 11-unit code for transmission of the ASCII codes. The sequencing of the bits is defined by an American National Standard: a single start bit, seven information bits, a parity-check bit, and two stop bits. One problem is that there is not widespread acceptance of the use of even-parity checking. As a consequence the computer ignores the parity bit on information received from a terminal, and thus no error checking is performed. Most of these terminals operate over full-duplex circuits with the computer in echoplex mode; what is printed is what the computer has received and retransmitted. Thus if a user sees what he has typed, he may feel confident that the computer received the proper characters.

Ports are available at the standard rates of 110, 150, 300, 1200, and 2000 bps. As an accommodation, a rate of 134.5 bps is provided with appropriate code conversion for the IBM 2741 terminal in view of the popularity of this nonstandard device. Even for this terminal, however, there is no standard character code in use; the DTSS supports two of the three codes of which we are aware.

COMMUNICATIONS INTERFACE. The standard interface between terminals or computers and modems is the Electronic Industries Association standard RS-232-C. This interface defines the signals that are exchanged, the pin assignments on the connector, and the signaling circuits characteristics. The signal quality is defined in a companion standard EIA RS-334. Although the physical characteristics of the connector are not defined, there is informal agreement as to the use of a 2-row, 25-pin connector. These standards have made a market for compatible terminals for communicating with computer systems. The wide number of manufacturers participating in this market have relieved the network operator from the responsibility for supporting and tailoring terminals to fit his particular computing system. This standard is also employed at the computer port interface, allowing ports to be assigned to different communications systems such as Centrex, Datrex, etc., without the need for changing hardware or software. A notable exception to this standard is provided by the Model 33/35 Teletype manufactured by Teletype Corporation. As a result the network operator must be able to stock and maintain two kinds of modems, or employ a modem with both interfaces available.

The EIA RS-232-C interface standard is often employed at a point in the system where the responsibility for proper system performance changes hands. For example, the common carrier may supply a 103E5 DATA-PHONE data set, which the computer center connects to a port of the computer. Very often it is not clear whether a malfunction is the responsibility of the common carrier or the computer-center operator. An advantage of the standard EIA RS-232-C interface is that equipment may be swapped quickly to determine the source of the error. Also, because of the standard interface, standard diagnostic equipment may be inserted at the interface point to aid in determining the exact nature of the malfunction.

SUBCHANNEL ALLOCATION.   Standard practices of the telephone companies have been copied by the manufacturers of frequency-division multiplexing equipment. The standard 170-Hz subchannel spacing has made it possible to intermix the equipment of two independent suppliers of these modems, and it has facilitated swapping equipment from one circuit to another.

SIGNALING LEVELS.   Standard Bell system practices for multipoint, leased, voice-grade circuits fix the levels at which signals are exchanged with the telephone company. The nominal level at which signals are transmitted to the telephone company is 0 dB; the received level is -26 dB. This standard facilitates setting up equipment and is useful in placing responsibility in the event of improper operation.

SIGNAL QUANTITY.   The allowable distortions in signals transmitted through a type 3002 leased voice-grade circuit are fixed by tariff and published by the Bell system as PUB41004, "Transmission Specifications for Voice Grade Private Line Data Channels." These allow the designers of the modems to adapt their equipment to predictable distortions. The network operator may also ensure that the supplied circuits meet these specifications on amplitude variations with frequency, envelope delay with frequency, frequency shift, impulse noise, etc. Again this facilitates setting up equipment, and eases placing responsibility for improper performance.

STANDARD COMPUTER LANGUAGES.   The existence of standard languages for the description of algorithms for computers reduces the difficulty of informing the user on how to operate the computer from a remote location. Thus the DTSS supplies ALGOL, FORTRAN, and COBOL without providing complete manuals for these languages. It is assumed that the user can purchase a description of these standard languages, and that he need only be told of variations from the standard in the implementation on the DTSS. In the case of BASIC, for example, the lack of a standard for this language places the responsibility for publication of a complete BASIC manual with Dartmouth College, the network operator.

12

Exploratory Research on Netting at IBM

DOUGLAS B. MCKAY

DONALD P. KARP

JAMES W. MEYER

ROBERT S. NACHBAR

IBM Research Center

INTRODUCTION

The networking together of physically remote computers offers a variety of new ways of enhancing data processing capability. By means of such interconnections, resources can be shared between participating processors, load can be distributed, and operating reliability of each can be increased.

Resource sharing has been the prime motivation so far in the development of computer networks. Network designers have had in mind the idea of accessing from any one of the participating installations resources available only at some other installation. Such resources might be the data bases, the specially developed software, or special peripheral or CPU hardware. Programming talent constitutes still another resource to be shared; often a soft-

457

ware development can be effectively undertaken as a joint effort by programmers thousands of miles apart through network facilities.

All these factors have played a role in motivating the two projects to be described briefly in this chapter. The first of these, the TSS network, involves a *homogeneous* structure, one in which almost identical systems exist at the various nodes. In this interactive network of time-sharing computers, all participating nodes are IBM 360 Model 67s operating under TSS. The net was formed out of the desire of a group of TSS/360 installations to explore both the benefits to be gained and the problems to be encountered from the implementation of a general-purpose network of large-scale computers. Implementing a network in which all participating nodes are identical, with respect to computers and their operating systems, lends itself also to addressing the problem of load sharing. Earlier, the exchange of programs and system modifications between the participating installations had been normally accomplished through the postal system, using magnetic tape or data processing cards. With a network connecting the computers at all installations, programs and system modifications can be transmitted over the common carrier throughout the network in their natural form, that is, the form in which they naturally reside on a system.

The second system to be described here, Network/440, was undertaken with a somewhat different set of objectives. First, the network is highly *inhomogeneous*, since the machines used in it are of disparate hardware model and run under different operating systems. Furthermore, the various processors in the network are viewed as actually comprising one large multiprocessor, so that the different steps of a single job can be executed on different participating systems. Control of the network is centralized in a dedicated *grid node* rather than being equally distributed among the nodes.

12.1   THE TSS NETWORK

A homogeneous network does not share the large set of problems arising from data and hardware incompatibilities within a heterogeneous network. The problems expected to be encountered during the implementation were reduced considerably at the outset as a result of the decision to restrict all nodes to IBM 360 Model 67s operating under TSS. This reduced the implementation problems involved in modifying a system to accomplish a network function for which it was probably neither designed nor intended to be used.

The TSS system appeared to be general and modular enough with well-defined system software interfaces to permit the easy addition of modules to accomplish practically any function the system was capable of performing. This was a necessary requirement, as the network was to be implemented and maintained at many geographically separated locations. Restrictions were also placed on the amount and location of modifications to be made to the existing system to minimize the impact of future system releases.

12.1.1 Design Principles

The network design is a direct propagation of the basic characteristics of the TSS system across all the participating nodes of the network. A user communicates from a remote terminal with the TSS system in an interactive, time-shared manner. In the TSS Network, this idea is extended to include interactive, time-shared communication between the TSS systems on participating nodes. The TSS Network is accessed by a user first initiating a task from a remote terminal on some network member (primary processor), and then, through use of the appropriate network commands, connecting to and initiating a task on some other network member (secondary processor). The network user then, from his terminal, simultaneously obtains full use of both primary and secondary processors for the duration of all work initiated within the network (see Fig. 12.1).

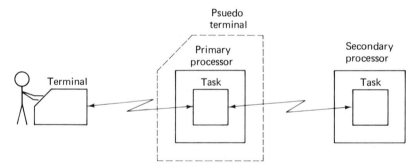

FIGURE 12.1   Basic organization of the TSS net.

Network tasks of network members communicate and request services of each other in an interactive, time-shared manner by making primary processors appear as terminals to secondary processors. This idea was exploited throughout the network design, as the TSS system is basically designed to perform services in an interactive, time-shared manner as requested by terminal users. To communicate with TSS through a terminal, whether real or pseudo (primary processor), is to call upon it to perform services in the manner for which it was designed, through the use of its command language. Given the capability to do this, directing TSS to perform additional desired network functions is then accomplished simply through the addition to the system of the appropriate network commands and their associated processing modules.

Primary processors appear as terminals to secondary processors as the result of network command processing system modules, which essentially duplicate a minimal number of the basic system functions performed by existing TSS modules for real terminal users. Even though they appear as terminals to secondary processors, the primary processors require some special considerations from the very fact that they are processors, and not terminals with users close at hand to react to any abnormal occurrence. These special considerations arise from requirements for methods of network communication, as well as interpretation and reaction to commands peculiar to network-related functions; hence the addition of system modules that duplicate (for network users) minimal required basic system functions normally performed for terminal users. Modifications are also required within a small number of TSS system modules for which the distinction between primary processors and terminals must be made to invoke network command processing system modules.

In TSS the first asynchronous interrupt received from a terminal-type device results in a task being created. Associated with, and labeled as, that particular task's SYSIN and SYSOUT is the device on which the asynchronous interrupt occurred. Each network member has a group of terminal-type devices that are reserved by the system and uniquely identified as those which will be used for task creation for network users. Therefore, receiving an asynchronous interrupt on any of these devices results in a task being created on a TSS system, which is thereafter identified as a secondary processor with respect to that task, for some network user on a primary processor. At the outset the task is marked as one created for a network user, and one which will receive special network-required considerations for its duration on the system.

The TSS system of each participating network member may simultaneously accommodate as many network users as it has network terminal-type devices. However, the manner in which each device is used and its associated task created determines whether that particular network member assumes the role of primary or secondary processor with respect to that task. Each network member may simultaneously assume the roles of either primary or secondary processor with respect to each of the tasks associated with any one of its network devices.

The TSS Network teleprocessing hardware consists of 2701 or 2703 control units using binary synchronous communication over voice-grade switched lines.

12.1.2 Software System Modules

We now discuss the different software modules making up the overall system, as shown in Fig. 12.2.

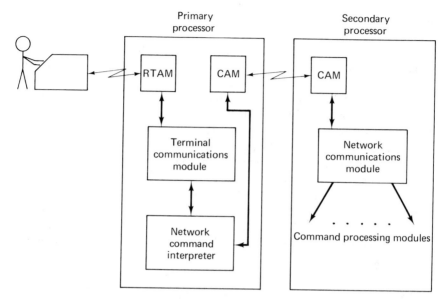

FIGURE 12.2   Software modules of the TSS net.

The Computer Access Method (CAM) is the access method that interfaces with the network teleprocessing hardware and accomplishes all communications between primary and secondary processors. In addition to satisfying communications requirements peculiar to the network, CAM essentially duplicates for network users all functions performed for TSS real terminal users by RTAM (Resident Terminal Access Method). It was created out of a need for network communications that would enable transmission of large quantities of data between participating network members. The hardware and software normally used for real terminal communications would not suffice for this. One of the primary functional objectives of the TSS Network is to provide a facility whereby the network user may transmit and receive complete data sets between network members.

In addition, CAM also accomplishes all communications of the interactive type that normally occur between a terminal user and the TSS system. Recall that the primary processor assumes the role of a terminal in network communications. This requires CAM to maintain synchronization and continuity between the communicating primary and secondary processors. When one processor is reading, the other must be writing. System modules that normally use RTAM for terminal communications are not concerned with the correct sequence of reading and writing, as the terminal simply acts as a remote device attached to and controlled by the processor. This is not true when the terminal is, in fact, the primary processor. Hence a line discipline was defined and integrated into CAM that would permit any of its users to read and write in any sequence and still maintain synchronization and continuity between the communicating processors.

One central terminal communication module is used by all TSS system modules that perform user-requested functions. These modules are invoked and directed with commands entered by the user from the SYSIN terminal-type device, and may in turn convey responses and request additional user direction through the same terminal-type device assuming the role of SYSOUT. Transparent to all normal TSS real terminal users, this central terminal communication module is replaced for network-user tasks with one that essentially duplicates its function, but in addition, provides a system interface to CAM. All network-user tasks are marked at their creation; hence the question does not arise as to whether or not the normal central terminal communication module, or the one replaced for network users, should be used. This module, used by tasks whose network member is assuming the role of secondary processor with respect to the task, enables them to communicate with the primary processor through the SYSIN, SYSOUT terminal-type device. Since the primary processor appears as a terminal to the secondary processor, the TSS command language and thus all system facilities, in addition to network facilities, become available to the user.

A network command interpreter is the facility used by a task on the primary processor to convey user requests to the primary and secondary processors for network services. It is invoked by the user with a command recived from his terminal by the central terminal communication module on the primary processor. After being invoked, the network command interpreter then interacts directly with the user at his terminal. It has the function of providing a means by which the terminal user may achieve simultaneous full use of both primary and secondary processors for the duration of all work initiated within the network. This is accomplished by the network command interpreter through routing of the normal TSS commands, as they are received from the user's terminal, directly to the TSS system of the network member for which they are intended. In addition to routing normal TSS commands, the network command interpreter recognizes all network commands entered by the user from his terminal, and subsequently invokes their associated processing module(s) on the primary or secondary processors, or on both processors in combination with each other if required by the command.

12.1.3   Sample Transaction

A general representation of the network command interpreter, network-user central terminal communications module, and the processors on which they are invoked is depicted in Fig. 12.2. The terminal user is interacting with the primary processor through the terminal-user central communications module.

He enters a command that results in the network command interpreter being invoked on the primary processor. It in turn requests direction from the user at his terminal with regard to the identification of a secondary processor within the network with which he desires to communicate. A network-reserved device is then selected and a connection is established through CAM over a voice-grade switched line to a network-reserved device on the identified secondary processor. The resulting asynchronous interrupt causes the creation of a task on the secondary processor, which is marked as one that will require special network considerations. The network-user central terminal communications module within that task then begins to interact through CAM with the network command interpreter on the primary processor, and subsequently with the user at his terminal, soliciting commands for which the appropriate secondary processor command processing module may be invoked. A particular network command (QCOM), if entered by the user, will be recognized by the network command interpreter on the primary processor, and will result in the temporary suspension of communications with the secondary processor. The network command interpreter will than return control to the TSS command system on the primary processor, which will solicit from the user at his terminal commands for primary processor command processing modules. Hence the terminal user receives full use of both primary and secondary processors for all command-initiated work within the network.

An example reflecting the hard-copy of a terminal session in which facilities of the TSS Network were utilized is given in Fig. 12.3. Figure 12.4 is an abbreviated form of Fig. 12.3, and indicates which processor reacted to and processed each particular command entered by the network user during the terminal session. Facilities of the TSS Network are invoked by entering the appropriate commands, which are subsequently routed to some processor, primary or secondary, within the network. Each of the available network commands and which particular function it achieves are illustrated and explained within the example.

The network user first logs on to the TSS system at installation A using the normal TSS command verb LOGON with user identification USERA and password PASSA. Having acknowledged the correct logon procedure, the TSS system at installation A then responds and assumes the role of primary processor with respect to the newly created task. USERA next enters the network command verb ITASK, which is received on the primary processor and subsequently results in the invoking of the network command interpreter. The network command interpreter then selects a network-reserved device, and requests the user at his terminal to enter, in digit format, the telephone number of an existing data set attached to a network-reserved device at some network installation. USERA responds to the network command interpreter with a telephone number, which is used to establish a network connection through CAM to installation B.

TSS NETWORK TERMINAL SESSION

?

LOGON USERA, PASSA

LOGON TSS/360 TASKID=003C 05/21/71 12:04

_ITASK

ENTER DIGITS OF TELEPHONE NUMBER.

8165493520

+LOGON TSS NETWORK

LOGON NETA,A

+LOGON TSS/360 AT 12:06 ON 05/21/71 TASKID=0018

+_SDS MPSDECK, MPSJOB

MPSDECK TRANSMITTED TO SECONDARY AS MPSJOB.

+_NETOS MPSJOB

+NSN 5783 ASSIGNED.

+_ QCOM

_ (USER CONTINUES NORMAL TSS TERMINAL SESSION)

_SCOM

+RJE91 IS TALKING TO YOU.

+ OUTPUT RECEIVED FROM OS. DSNAME=

NETA****.MPSTEST.SYSPRINT.J6057.T1411218.

+_CATALOG MPSTEST.SYSPRINT.J6057.T1411218,U,U,MPS.OUTPUT

+_RDS MPS.OUTPUT.MPS.RESULTS

MPS'OUTPUT RECEIVED FROM SECONDARY AS MPS.RESULTS

+_QCOM

_PRINT MPS.RESULTS,,,EDIT

PRINT BSN=0368

_CLOGOFF

+LOGOFF AT 13:00 ON 05/21/71

FIGURE 12.3   Typical TSS net terminal session.

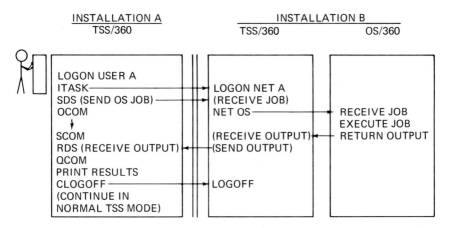

| INSTALLATION A | INSTALLATION B | |
| TSS/360 | TSS/360 | OS/360 |

FIGURE 12.4   Message flow in terminal session illustrated in Fig. 12.3.

A task is created at installation B with its SYSIN and SYSOUT marked as the network link connecting the two processors. The new task now prompts its SYSIN device for the normal TSS logon verb with associated parameters. All such data originating from the secondary processor and destined for the user's terminal are received by the network command interpreter, which prefixes each line of terminal output with the character "+." The use of the + provides a clear distinction between terminal output originating from the secondary and primary processors. The user logs on to the installation-B TSS system with user identification NETA and passwork A.

In this example the TSS Network is being used to allow the user at installation A to access a separate OS/360 system available at installation B. USERA has previously prepared a data set named MPSDECK which contains an entire OS job, including all necessary JCL, in card image format. He will transmit this data set to installation B for subsequent transmission to and execution on the OS system. He also wishes to retrieve the output produced by his OS job for on-line printing at his own machine. Should the results be unsatisfactory, he may wish to modify his data and rerun the job.

The network command SDS (Send Data Set) is used to transmit a data set from a primary processor to a secondary processor. Blocks of 4096 bytes are compressed to eliminate duplicate character strings and then transmitted to the receiving processor. USERA is sending his OS job to installation B, where it will be named MPSJOB. He next invokes the NETOS command, which will transmit the data set MPSJOB to the OS system for execution. Software exists within the installation-B system to allow TSS to function as a remote job entry station to an OS/MVT system utilizing LASP.

QCOM is a network command that temporarily suspends to interaction between primary and secondary processors and returns the terminal user to

TSS command mode on the primary processor. SCOM resumes the suspended interaction and may only be issued subsequent to a QCOM command. These commands allow USERA to utilize his terminal on his own system while waiting for his OS job to complete.

When the OS job completes execution, one of its output data sets is returned by LASP to the TSS system. (This is accomplished by the use of optional LASP control statements contained within the user's JCL.) The command RDS (Receive Data Set) causes the transmission of an entire data set from a secondary processor to a primary processor. Here it is used to retrieve the results of the OS job whose output data set resides on the TSS system at installation B. The output data set is now printed on line at the installation-A TSS system. The user decides that his job has completed successfully and thus issues the network command CLOGOFF to terminate his use of the TSS Network. CLOGOFF is a command recognized by the network command interpreter and results in termination of the TSS task on the secondary processor and the severing of the communications link between the two processors. USERA now returns to normal TSS command mode on the installation-A system.

12.1.4 Operating Experience

An integral part of the TSS Network is a network statistics collection package. Hooks have been inserted into the network software to record events such as the creation and termination of network tasks and the transmission of data sets between processors. The data thus generated is reduced into report format by two PL/I data-reduction programs. Perhaps the greatest inducement for using the TSS Network is its capability of quickly and economically transmitting large amounts of data between processors. Examination of the network statistics for a recent 30-day period at the IBM Research Center shows a total of 9,200,000 8-bit bytes of data transmitted by SDS and RDS commands. When divided by the total amount of time required, the mean data transfer rate was approximately 14,500 bytes/min. This was achieved using voice-grade 2000-baud telephone lines. This efficient line utilization can be attributed primarily to the compression of all data transferred to eliminate the repetition of any character that occurs three or more times in succession. Additionally, it has proved feasible to transfer large blocks of data (4096 bytes/transmission maximum), thereby reducing the number of interrupts that must be serviced.

As mentioned previously, the TSS Network consists entirely of IBM 360 Model 67 computers operating under the control of TSS/360. The network was originally designed and implemented through the joint efforts of Carnegie-Mellon University, Princeton University, and the Research Division of IBM. Current network members include Bell Telephone Laboratory, Napierville, Illinois; Carnegie-Mellon University, Pittsburgh, Pennsylvania;

IBM Research Center, Yorktown Heights, New York; IBM SDD Programming Center, Kingston, New York; NASA Ames Research Center, Moffett Field, California; NASA Lewis Research Center, Cleveland, Ohio; and Princeton University, Princeton, New Jersey.

12.2 NETWORK/440

The basic premise in the Network/440 project* is the concept of a logical network machine.† This concept treats all systems involved in the network as a part of a single (large) multiprocessor system. Although many of the ideas have been based completely on hypothetical concepts, an equal number of ideas were derived from our network implementation and operating experience.

There are basically two physical configurations one could have utilized—central or distributed. A centralized or star network is a network in which all participating systems are connected to a central system. Any two systems sending messages to one another must send them through the central system.

In a distributed network any participating system may be tied to any number of other systems directly. In the extreme case it is possible for one system to have as many communication lines tied to it as there are other systems in the network.

The present implementation of Network/440 is centralized. The central system is called the grid node (GN), and the other systems, the user nodes (UN). This centralized approach was taken for several reasons. First, it provides a dedicated system from which the full impact of our software on existing operating systems can be learned. Second, it provides a central point of control and allows ease of modification. Third, there is a store-and-forward (with buffering) capability provided for all messages. Finally, it provides a central measurement point to record all transactions.

N/440 was operated with the following systems: 360 Model 44, 360/67 (CP), and 360/91 (OS/MVT), all located at the IBM Research Center, Yorktown Heights. In addition there was a Model 50 in Boulder, Colorado, that routed files between itself and the Yorktown 91. The grid-node functions were being operated at Yorktown on a dedicated Model 50 but were then shifted to a dedicated region on the 91.

The problems Network/440 is dealing with are not concerned with the physical configuration (centralized or distributed) of the network. The logical concepts derived by the netting experiment are independent of hardware configuration.

One of the project's major goals is to provide a facility for network job

*The name is taken from the number of the department conducting the project.
†*Intent*—Report 2, Feb. 1, 1970, Computer Science Dept., IBM Research Center, Yorktown Heights, N.Y.

control. The issues are not whether the network is centralized or distributed, but rather what is the best way to control a network and provide maximum utilization of its resources.

If computer networks are to be useful and are to become economically viable, they must be able to provide the following services. The ability must exist to move programs and data through the network in an effortless, intelligent manner and to provide users with the capability of sharing these items. Networks must be able to provide more extensive use of existing facilities, both software and hardware. To make this potential as far-reaching as possible, the network should allow interaction of heterogeneous systems.

The network should achieve the goal of providing all functions of the systems in the network to a user with maximum transparency. It should also be a general-purpose network with specific user applications applied to the general framework. To make the facilities of the network more accessible to the user, there must be a convenient method of allowing the user to convey his needs. Since the network is considered to be a single entity, a language should be provided that can be thought of as a programming language for a network machine.

12.2.1 Network Control Language (ACL)

A unique network control language has been developed for Network/440. To understand the capabilities of our network, it is necessary at this time to define the language developed.

A CONTROL LANGUAGE (ACL)   ACL is the initial language for programming the network machine. This language will be very explicit in that every field must contain a value or a symbolic identifier that references an actual value. At this time there will be no attempt to include any implicit or automatic processing. Table 12.1 gives the ACL Syntax.

TABLE 12.1   *ACL Syntax*

A.   ROUTE (reference name) rn FROM (user node name) unn1 TO unn2
B.   OUTPUT rn FROM unn1 AT unn2
C.   EXECUTE rn FROM unn1 AT unn2
D.   READ dsn, var
E.   WRITE dsn, var
F.   IFXX var1, var2, label XX={EQ,NE,LT,LE, GT, GE}
G.   GOTO label
H.   ASSIGN var1, var2
I.   END
J.   rn:DM message
K.   rn:DV value

Any one of these statements can be labeled by preceding the operation by an identifier. In the case of a DM or DV message, the label field must contain an identifier, which will be used as a message name or variable name.

The semantics of the ACL statements are as follows:

A. ROUTE rn FROM unn1 TO unn2   This statement causes the data set referenced by rn (the actual data set name is given in the message denoted by rn) and located at the user node designated by unn1 to be transmitted to the UN designated by unn2. When the data set has arrived at unn2, it is stored on some peripheral device for future reference. A copy of the data set remains at unn2 as long as the network job containing this statement is active.

B. OUTPUT rn FROM unn1 TO unn2   This statement causes the same operations to be performed as in A, with one exception: when the data set arrives at unn2, it is placed in the output stream at unn2. In the first implementation, the output will always be printed. Other output media will be considered later.

C. EXECUTE rn FROM unn1 AT unn2   This statement also causes the operations in A to be performed with one exception: when the data set arrives at unn2, it is placed in the input stream at unn2 for eventual execution.

D. READ rn, var   This statement causes the variable var to receive a new value from a logical message which originates from a WRITE statement in an executing UN program, referenced by rn. When the WRITE message is received at the grid node, the text of the message becomes the "new" value of var.

E. WRITE rn, var   This statement is the reverse counterpart of D. The value of the variable, var, is placed in a logical message and transmitted to the UN that is executing the data set referenced by rn. This logical message must be interpreted by a READ statement in the executing UN program.

F. IFXX var1, var2, label XX={EQ,NE,LT,GT,GR,LB}   This statement causes the value of var1 to be compared to the value of var2. If the relation defined by XX yields a true value, control is transferred to the statement designated by the label. If not, control continues in the normal order.

G. GOTO Label   This statement causes control to be transferred to the statement designated by the label.

H. ASSIGN var1, var2   This statement causes the value of var2 to be replaced by the current value of var1.

I. END   This statement causes both the end of translation and the end of execution. In its function as the signal for the end of translation, it causes the current program to be placed in execution and provides the appropriate tables for execution. In its role as the signal for the end of execution, it causes the ACL executer to release the current program and transmit an end message to all involved systems.

J. rn:DM Message   As stated earlier, this statement must contain an identifier in the label field. The identifier will be the name of the message contained in the DM statement. In the first implementation, the message will consist of actual names and attributes of data sets referenced in the executable ACL statements.

K. rn:DV value   This statement must also contain an identifier in the label field, which will be the name of a variable whose value is given in the operand field. It is used for initializing variables.

12.2.2 *Sample Network-Type Problem*

Let us suppose that, as shown in Fig. 12.5, location A needs a report requiring data from locations B and C but has a machine of limited capability and is

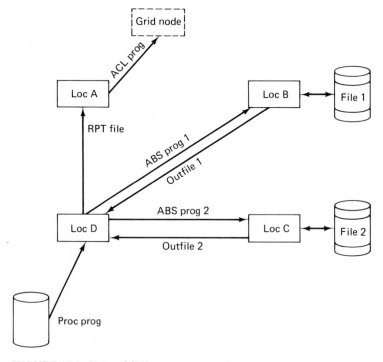

FIGURE 12.5   Network/440 program example.

unable to process the data from B and C. In addition, the data needed from B and C are a subset of the data sets at each location.

Location B has file 1 containing data of interest. Location C has file 2 containing data of interest. Location D has the programs to abstract data from file 1 and file 2 and also has the program to process the two data files and generate an output report file. Location D has the capabilities of running the processing program.

The user at location A would like to extract data moved to D and have

EXAMPLE OF NETWORK SOLUTION PROGRAMMED ON N/440's NETWORK MACHINE

```
                         LOCA:   DV  UN1;
                         LOCB:   DV  UN2;
  DEFINITION             LOCC:   DV  UN3;
  STATEMENTS             LOCD:   DV  UN4;
                         OUTFILE  : DM  SEND  (LIST1);   REC(LIST2);
                         ABSPROG1 : DM  SEND  (LIST3);   REC(LIST4);
                         ABSPROG2 : DM  SEND  (LIST1);   REC(LIST2);
                         OUTFILE2 : DM  SEND  (LIST3);   REC(LIST4);
                         PROCPROG : DM  SEND  (LIST5);   REC(LIST5);
                         RPTFILE  : DM  SEND  (LIST6);   REC(LIST7);

              EXEC    ABSPROG1 FROM LOCD TO LOCB;
              ROUTE   OUTFILE 1 FROM LOCB TO LOCD;
  COMMAND     EXEC    ABSPROG2 FROM LOCD TO LOCC;
  STATEMENTS  ROUTE   OUTFILE2 FROM LOCC TO LOCD;
              EXEC    PROCPROG FROM LOCD TO LOCD;
              ROUTE   RPTFILE FROM LOCD TO LOCA;
              END:
```

SEND(LISTn) — reference to a list of physical attributes necessary to locate and describe files on the system where they reside

REC(LISTn) — Specifies the storage requirements for file coming into a system.

FIGURE 12.6 Example of network solution programmed on N/440's network machine.

the processed results sent back to him for printing. Figure 12.6 shows the actual transaction.

The data definition statements provide two functions. They define the user's symbolic location names he uses in his network job and transforms them into network line addresses. They also define symbolic program names like OUTFILEI in terms of attributes that can be understood by the sending and receiving systems.

The command statement specifies the action to be taken on the file being transferred and the two locations involved in the transfer. Execute implies the file being transferred is loaded into the job stream and executed. Route implies the file is transferred and stored at the receiving system for future reference.

12.2.3 Logical Structure of the Network

There was a necessity to delineate many network functions in setting up an operating protocol. These functions included switching control, buffer control, message control, and operating control. The operating control function becomes further complicated as the user is able to program the network as if it were a single operating system.

The protocol had to be further broken down into more detailed functions, such as error recovery and handling techniques.

The initial method of handling these functions was to provide two control functions. The Network Controller (NC) is a higher-level function that recognizes and controls all aspects of net jobs and the execution of job steps in the network machine. In addition, a communication control facility, referred to as the Communication Subsystem (CS), was incorporated to provide fast service to all messages that are to be moved to a user system without intervention by the NC.

The center of Fig. 12.7 illustrates the major functions of the network. Messages travel in both directions through the CS, except in the case of messages that require action by the NC. These messages will be explained in detail later. These two functions can exist on any system and operate in any physical configuration, provided the control information reflects the configuration in such a way that proper operation is maintained.

Figure 12.7 also shows the logical structure of Network/440 in more detail. The network consists of three basic functions. The NC and the CS are resident at a central system called the grid node. Presently these two modules are running in a user region on a 360/91 under OS/MVT. The third subsystem, the user node interface, is resident on the remote user system participating in the network.

The network will accept a user's network command-language program that states explicitly what he wishes to do. The NC then interprets this pro-

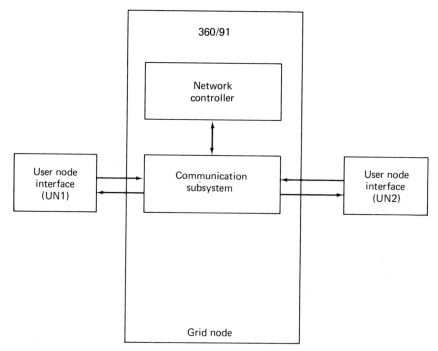

FIGURE 12.7   Basic organization of Network /440.

gram and issues the appropriate commands to manage the transfer of jobs and data through the network. It allows asynchronous execution of each user's network job. It also traces the status of all user nodes in the network (i.e., are nodes up, available for work, down temporarily, or down permanently?).

In addition, Network/440 will manage network job queues to facilitate the simultaneous execution of batch jobs at user nodes. Executing jobs may also be network jobs started to transfer a file or program. Finally, the network will provide and manage storage facilities for messages destined for unavailable user nodes and deliver these messages when the nodes become available.

USER NODE INTERFACE (UNI)   The function the user node interface performs is defined by the commands and protocol of the grid node. First, it provides the communication ability between the user system and the grid node. This is done by the line-handling portion of the UNI and follows the protocol of the CS. Second, it will excute the basic instructions that are sent to it from the NC to realize the execution of a network job.

The UNI can be requested to perform two basic functions—load jobs into the job stream and send receive files. It must send appropriate status information to the NC as each job step in a network job is completed. Accounting information will be sent to provide on-line accounting for network operation.

In addition, the UNI must have the capability to allow users to enter network command-language programs and have them sent to the NC.

COMMUNICATION SUBSYSTEM (CS)   The CS is a store-and-forward digital switch that acts as a central for all messages traversing the network (see Fig. 12.8). It manages all messages in the network queue and transmits them to the proper destination. It treats the NC as a user node and follows the same basic protocol, even though they are both resident in the same machine.

The CS also acts as a concentrator-multiplexor and traffic director for the network. In other words, it takes incoming traffic from the communication

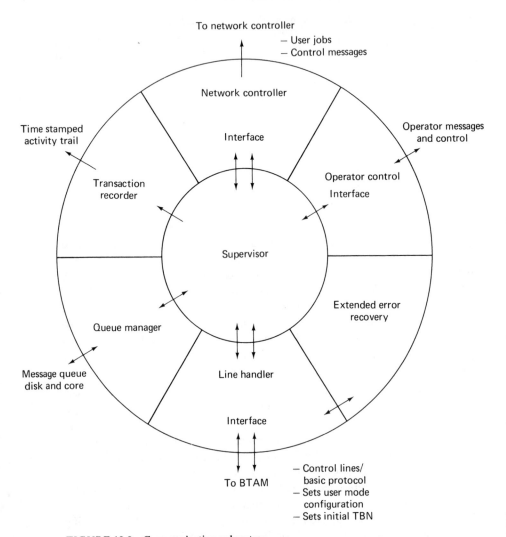

FIGURE 12.8   Communication subsystem.

line(s) and directs it to the proper output line(s), buffering the messages where necessary and establishing the output sequence. An example of this is shown in Fig. 12.9. There may be many blocks of several logical messages all going to the same system; these will be physically multiplexed on the outgoing line. The CS tracks the status of all lines in the network and records this status on line at the operator's console and notifies the NC of any changes. A time-stamped audit trail of every message entering and leaving the grid node is created by the CS.

The CS provides extended error recovery beyond IBM's BTAM error recovery. When the BTAM error recovery procedures are exhausted, the CS

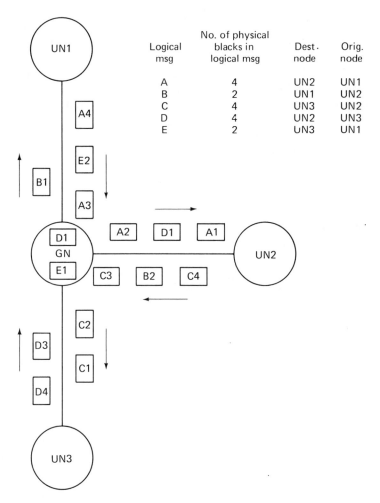

Logical msg	No. of physical blacks in logical msg	Dest. node	Orig. node
A	4	UN2	UN1
B	2	UN1	UN2
C	4	UN3	UN2
D	4	UN2	UN3
E	2	UN3	UN1

FIGURE 12.9   Line multiplexing.

will invoke its own error recovery routines. If an error persists, the CS will notify the operator and will retry the line after an arbitrary length of time.

Both the CS and the NC, which will be discussed next, contain checkpoint restart capability. To ensure the integrity of the grid node, the system has the capability to detect GN software errors and system failures. If either of these conditions occur, the capability exists to warm start the network operation.

The CS is presently operating using synchronous transparent communication in a contention mode over leased half-duplex lines with bandwidths of 2.4 to 40.8 db auds.

NETWORK CONTROLLER (NC)   The NC will accept users network jobs and interpret and assemble them in the ASMBLER (see Fig. 12.10). A listing of the assembled netjob is returned to the originating user node, denoting the state of the job (accepted for execution or rejected due to input errors). When a job is assembled correctly, entries are made into the translated table area and the execution of the job begins.

The translated table for each user net program is copied on to disk and brought into core as each job step is carried out by the executor. As each network job step is completed, a change is recorded in the program tables. The program tables are an instrumental part of the checkpoint restart procedure. The executor transmits the appropriate commands to each user node,

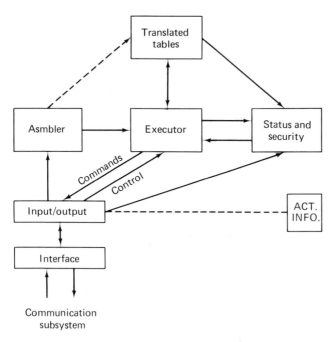

FIGURE 12.10   Network controller.

which starts up a specified function and returns status information to the executor. A more detailed discussion of the NC protocol is treated in another section, but the basic commands sent out have the following logical meanings:

1. Do you have the data set?
2. Can you receive the data set?
3. Send the data set!
4. File the data set!
5. Load the job into the job stream!

The statue messages are returned on these commands to allow proper synchronization of all users' jobs and to make it possible for any number of users' network jobs to be active at any given time.

Status and security information are maintained and constantly referred to by the executor when carrying out steps in a network job. If for any reason a user or user node is not allowed to access another user node, the user job will be ended with an explanation. The executor will also check whether systems are up or down before sending commands. There are system status messages that come directly to the NC that are not generated in response to NC commands; these messages update status tables directly.

One important problem in networks is the definition of accounting procedures. These procedures and associated routines are planned to be added in the near future. The information will be returned to the NC status messages from the appropriate UNs.

12.2.4 Definitions of Header Functions

Before proceeding with the discussion of protocol and control, the basic message content and concepts must be defined.

A transmission block is a physical entity that consists of header and text. A message (logical) consists of many transmission blocks.

The primary purpose of the network is to deliver messages from one user system to another in an orderly, controlled manner. To provide all the information necessary to maintain control, the header contains a set of operational fields. These functions are listed next with the rationals for each.

ACTION CODE (AC). This code selects the immediate destination of the transmitted blocks; the data may be transmitted directly to the user described in the destination system ID field, sent to the NC, or used by the CS. Any conflict in information between this field and any other field in the header will cause an error message to be returned to the originating station. The AC serves a similar function at the user system, indicating to the UNI whether the data block is destined for a user routine or contains control information for the UNI.

TRANSMISSION–BLOCK NUMBER (TBN).   Each block transmitted within the network will contain a sequential number inserted by the transmitting station. As the block flows through the network, every station will insert its own number into the block, overlaying the previous station's number. The purpose of this sequential number is to guarantee that no messages are lost in the physical communications.

NETWORK JOB IDENTIFIER (NJID).   The function of this field is to associate a transmission block with the network job to which it belongs. The identifier is assigned to the network job and to each associated transmission block by the user system or by the NC. In order to establish a unique name for each job within the network, the user node identifier (i.e., the name of the user system originating the net job) will be concatenated with a number generated by each user's system.

JOB STEP (MARKER).   The purpose here is to uniquely identify a job step within a network job. The NC will assign this name, since it maintains control of all network jobs.

ORIGINATING SYSTEM IDENTIFIER.   To route a block of data from one user system to another, a unique name must be associated with each user system. This name will be assigned by the network control group at the time the user system is accepted as a network participant. The station originating a block of data will place its assigned identification in this field in every block of data originating at that system.

MESSAGE PRIORITY.   This field indicates transmission priority (not to be confused with processing priority) by block within the queue for a particular user system.

DESTINATION SYSTEM IDENTIFIER.   This is similar to the originating system identifier except that the identification inserted is that of the system for which the block is destined.

LOGICAL MESSAGE FLAGS.   The message flags denote the first and last blocks of a message; all intermediate blocks are noted by their absence. The flag field in conjunction with the logical message sequence number will enable the user to determine if any blocks are missing from a message and will also provide an identifier that can be used to recover missing blocks. When the first and last indicators are turned on in a single block, the message is contained within that block.

LOGICAL MESSAGE SEQUENCE NUMBER (LMSN).   This field is used to number sequentially that blocks within a message. The first block (denoted by the LMID) will contain the lowest number assigned (not necessarily 1) within a message, while the last block will contain the highest number. Unlike the TBN, this number will remain intact throughout the journey of the block through the network. It is used for error detection and recovery along with the logical message flag.

LOGICAL MESSAGE IDENTIFIER (LMID). Since all communications lines in the network can be multiplexed (blocks within a message will be interleaved with blocks from other messages), a messsge identifier becomes necessary in order to reassemble the message at the user destination. Therefore, each block within a message will contain an identifier unique to the message. In the simple case when the message is contained in one block, the identifier performs no function.

When multiple blocks comprise a message, LMID will enable the user to reassemble the message. There can be any number of physical message blocks associated with any logical message. It is important that the NC assign numbers to this field for all messages it augments, and that this LMID is used in the messages generated in response to NC commands.

LENGTH OF TEXT. This field contains a binary number that equals the number of characters in the text portion of the transmission block. Although there are other means available to obtain this number, it is included in the header for redundancy check purposes.

In the NC association is maintained by NJID for every user job submitted. The illustrated hierarchical structure is set up for a message configuration. Any message pertaining to any step in a network job can be tracked and restarted if necessary. It provides a mapping of the logical structure of any network job into its appropriate message configuration.

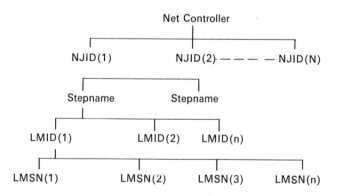

The CS is a combination of functions. It is basically a communication handler and store-and-forward switch. The CS has the ability to keep track of all messages in the network by TBN (defined earlier).

It is therefore possible to record and reflect the entire status of the network down to any detail desired. These concepts are instrumental in our present system checkpoint restart procedures.

12.2.5 System Protocol

The protocol for operating Network/440 has different levels of control. The CS exercises control of the communication link between the GN and the UNI. The NC maintains control at a net job level. However, the functions that each unit performs are combined to handle special control cases. These complementary functions will be discussed in detail as they arise in the protocol discussion.

First, there must be an initialization message sent from one station to another before any actual message transmission takes place. This message is sent between each pair, and a positive acknowledgement must be received in order to complete the initial station hand-shaking.

At any point during the transmission of messages an error can occur, which will be detected and indicated by a negative acknowledgement to the message. The message in error will be retransmitted several times. If the error persists, the CS will time the line out and retry later. The assumption here is that the line may be noisy and may recover if given time to quiesce.

When a station receives an initialization message, it is possible to respond in several ways, depending on the status of the user system. The station receiving the initialization message can acknowledge that it

1. Is ready to receive and transmit.
2. Temporarily cannot receive certain logical messages (actual data transmissions) but can receive special control messages. This option allows a user system to selectively process net jobs as facilities on his system become available.
3. Is unable to receive any traffic (in other words, the user system is logically or physically disconnected from the network).
4. Is unable to receive new network job requests but is able to handle traffic for jobs in progress. The user system may have several jobs in progress that are transmitting and receiving messages. This acknowledgement gives the user system the ability to allow these jobs to continue normal processing.

The last alternative gives the UNI at each user system the mechanism to selectively demultiplex itself to handling one logical message. The UNI also can suspend the message transmission for any task that is temporarily deactivated. Thus all user systems can selectively halt messages throughout the entire network pertinent to their UNI. The destination system can selectively halt all messages for a given NJID or selectively halt logical messages within a net job. The GN will keep accepting messages until its buffer is filled to some operational threshold limit that must be maintained to keep the network from coming to a complete standstill, and then will issue selective halts to systems sending to it.

The same selective halt mechanism can be applied in reverse through a resume message. The resume message can apply to an entire set of messages for a net job or selective logical messages within a job. The reinitiation of a transmission takes place between the GN and a UNI that wants to allow more message blocks to be transmitted. The destination (receiving) station must resume on a particular logical message to allow the message to reach its final destination and complete transmission through the network. The LMID of the message header enables the CS and NC to cooperate in controlling and cleaning up network operation. Not only does this cooperation between logical levels reduce a duplication of effort; it enables the control to become realistic and practical. Complete separation of communication and NC control functions would cause a loss of useful information that must be obtained by some other means.

For example, if a file transmission consisted of many blocks and a transmission error occurred that the network was unable to recover, the CS would notify the NC of the error occurrence on this file transmission, and then the NC would issue purge messages to the CS for those particular logical message blocks. This mechanism allows a general cleanup and management of all file transmissions.

There is also the condition of having a receiving system go down. When this occurs, there may be a number of network jobs involved with that user system. If the user system remains down for an extended period of time and the buffer resources of the CS are filled to threshold limit, it may be necessary to purge pending message blocks. The CS will notify the NC of the user system being down, and the NC will issue purge commands to the CS for all pending messages of those netjobs involved with the down user system.

However, in our present implementation the CS uses disk storage as a logical extension of core for message buffering. In this operation the freeing of real core buffers becomes a simple matter of moving the messages onto disk for later retrieval. In some instances of transmission a file may be stored in segments at the GN until the receiving system is able to come up and receive it.

When the user system comes back on line, the involved user network job will be restarted by issuing resume transmit commands to the CS. If the user is an interactive user controlling the network, he would be notified of the problem and status of his file transmissions. He could then reinstate his command at a later time. The batch network job would be restarted at a point where no unnecessary retransmission would occur.

It has not been determined how long files should reside in a store-and-forward mode before being purged from the network. If a backing storage device is available to network operation, the file can remain for a longer time, but still not indefinitely.

12.2.6 Network Controller Protocol

The file transmission protocol of the NC is primarily concerned with the control and transfer of user files for storage, temporary use at a remote system, and execution. The commands and status messages that pertain to the second-level logic of the NC will be sent and interpreted by the sending and receiving systems. All initiation of file transfers results from direct user commands to the NC.

The sending system is first interrogated to determine if the file is resident at that system. The user must provide the necessary information to locate the file if it is not catalogued at that system. This information would be physical attributes such as volume and serial number. A negative acknowledgement to this message would result in the termination of a net job step with the reason for failure returned to the originator.

When a positive acknowledgment is received by the NC it has two options available. It must first determine the amount of unused buffer space in the CS and, based on the size of the file to be transferred, decide whether to have the data sent immediately or wait for an acknowledgement to the receive message. Our network incorporates a "store-and-forward" philosophy that allows any system to interact with another, even though they need not be up concurrently. If the NC decides to move the file regardless of the state of the receiving system, the NC will issue a send or receive message to both systems simultaneously. If the file was transmitted from the originating system and is resident at the GN, the user will be notified so that it may be moved when required. If the NC chose the second option, the file would still be resident on its original system.

A positive acknowledgement will allow the file to continue its normal flow through the network. The receive message will specify what is to be done with the file. These possibilities include loading the file directly into the job stream (this step assumes the appropriate JCL is included in the text of the file), cataloguing the file at the remote system, or storing it for temporary immediate use. All network files are catalogued with a unique name that includes user ID (unique at his home node), home node ID (unique in the network), and his own data name, which is unique in his own work. The receive message may also contain some special instructions to print or punch a file.

When the sending and receiving stations have completed the file transfer, they send status messages back to the NC indicating they have finished this step. These status messages enable the NC to keep a record of user network job steps and their progress through the network. These status messages play an important part in ensuring proper checkpoint restart of all network jobs.

Files routed specifically for execution require a third status message from the receiving user system. The system must indicate when and how the job completed execution. This status message will also contain the appropriate accounting information to allow dynamic updating of network user and system accounting information. It is not clear at this time what should be accounted for in the network, but it is certain to be an area of prime concern to production networks.

An error in the second logic level can occur during the file transmission. There may be an error moving files from devices into the line buffers or reading from the line buffers. When this occurs, the operating system is aware and must pass this information to the NC. When the NC receives the file error message, it will immediately send a release message to all the network tasks associated with this net job step. In addition, a purge message for that job step will be sent to the CS to purge the message from its buffers. This is another example of the CS and NC combining functional capability and providing effective management of network traffic. The mapping of messages into the job step allows the NC to selectively choose all messages it wishes to purge.

The protocol for interactive use of the network is somewhat different. There are some standard message types that are provided for interactive use to ensure the proper message recognition from one system to another. Terminal-type traffic will be sent across the network through the normal netting interface, and the control information that a terminal sends to its local operating system must be incorporated into the network protocol. The interactive user can request a direct connection to the remote system through the NC. The NC will notify the remote system of the user request and establish the user's direct link. The NC becomes a monitor of the conversation, but no longer becomes involved with the messages. Other conversational messages are sent back and forth through the CS with no interaction by the NC. In the event one of the systems breaks the logical link, the CS will notify the NC, which in turn must notify the other system to terminate.

Once the user's connection is established, three types of messages may be generated. These messages are identified by the action code field in the header. The three basic transmission types covered by the protocol are a response requested, with or without text included in the message; a text message, which is simply a response to the first or just data to be printed out at the user's terminal; and, finally, an interrupt message, which indicates the user wishes to stop a task or talk directly to the operating system.

12.2.7 Conclusions from the N/440 Project

Two areas of prime importance in the operation of networks are efficient utilization of communication facilities and overall network data management.

To make better use of communication facilities, we are investigating concepts that should realize this goal. Full-duplex operation and front-end processors with extensive error-recovery software should help improve the overall effective data rate.

Network data management must provide the ease of transfer for any file or any portion of the file in the network with a minimum effort on the user's part. Ease of data accessibility will probably be the most important facility a network can provide.

The following is a brief description of how we are attacking these problems in terms of the function described here. We are developing an overall architecture to incorporate these new user facilities. Some of the new concepts may or may not contain our present functional identities.

First, the present command language is a low-level explicitly defined user language. The language must provide more implicit function for the user. For example, he should not have to designate the executing system for a job unless he wants to. The NC should have the capability to select the optimum system for execution of the user job.

The NC must have an extensive network catalogue scheme for the entire network. This is important if true data sharing is to become a reality. There has to be an extensive user profile to allow a complete security check for all systems and users.

Data definition statements must be defined and incorporated to allow conversion of data transferred between heterogeneous machines. There must also be proper definition given to the records in files so the network data management will be able to retrieve only the records of interest.

We are presently working on these problems and will have results to report in the near future.

Acknowledgment

The authors wish to acknowledge the design and implementation effort of the contributing members of the Computer Sciences and Computing Systems Departments of the IBM Research Center. The first two authors have been associated with the Network/440 project and the last two with the TSS Network.

13

The ARPA Network

LAWRENCE G. ROBERTS

Advanced Research Projects Agency

BARRY D. WESSLER

University of Utah

INTRODUCTION

One of the most successful aspects of the experiments in the use of time-shared computer systems conducted during the past decade was the ability to share computing resources among all the users of the system. Controlled sharing of data and software, as well as the sharing of the time-sharing system hardware, has led to much higher programmer productivity and better overall utilization of the computing and users resources. One prime reason for the success of resource sharing is the on-line dialogue capability between the man and the machine, which has permitted the user to experiment more easily with new systems. This experimentation with existing resources has fostered greater acceptance and use of these resources. In addition, in more advanced systems, where interprocess communications are permitted, existing programs were often incorporated directly into larger software systems.

These techniques have been especially productive in the systems programming area. One reason for its limited success in the applications are has been the lack of a large enough community (critical mass phenomenon) in a single application area using the same time-sharing system. Resource sharing for large communities has been attempted by transferring the programs or data physically from one machine to another. This can be done only by imposing restrictive language standards and using identical hardware systems. Maintenance and updating problems and small variations of hardware and operating systems have dampened the success of program transferability experiments.

A viable alternative to program transferability, while permitting full resource sharing, is to provide a communications system that will permit users to access remote programs or data as if they were local users to that system. In addition, it should be possible for a user to create a program on his local machine that could make use of existing programs in the network as if they were available on his local machine. Rather than trying to move the programs from machine to machine, the network would allow the user or his program to communicate with a machine on which the program already executes. If enough machines can be connected into such a network, the total community in any particular application area may be sufficiently large enough to reach critical mass. We believe the computer would then become a more powerful tool for its users because of the resource-sharing capability.

This chapter describes the design criteria and implementation of a communications system capable of satisfying resource-sharing communication requirements. The communication system interconnects autonomous, independent computer systems nationwide into a computer network so as to permit interactive resource sharing between any pair of systems.

13.1 DESIGN OF A NETWORK COMMUNICATIONS SERVICE

After initial network experiments conducted in 1966 between The Massachusetts Institute of Technology's Lincoln Laboratory and the System Development Corporation [1], it was clear that a completely new communications service was required to make an effective, useful resource-sharing computer network.

The goal at that time was to interconnect research centers supported by the Information Processing Techniques Office of the Advanced Research Projects Agency (ARPA) in order to (1) develop and test computer-communications techniques, and (2) obtain the benefits of resource sharing for the ARPA community. There were about 20 candidate centers, each with one or more large computing systems of different manufacturers (IBM, GE, XDS, DEC, UNIVAC), different models (360's/65, 67, 75, 91, Sigma 7, PDP10, 1108, etc.), and different operating systems (OS, TSS/360, MULTICS, TENEX, EXEC 8). Many of the centers had operational time-sharing systems and most intended to have one running before the planned network became operational. The goal of this section is to describe the properties of a communications system for interconnecting large computers.

The communication pipelines offered by the carriers would probably have to be a component of the new communications service, but were clearly inadequate by themselves. What was needed was a message service into which any computer could submit a message destined for another computer and be sure it would be delivered promptly and correctly. Each interactive conversation or link between two computers would have messages flowing back and forth similar to the type of traffic between a user console and a computer. Message sizes of from 1 to 1000 characters are characteristic of man–machine interactions, and this should also be true for that network traffic when a man is the end consumer of the information being exchanged. Besides having a heavy bias toward short messages, network traffic will also be diverse. With 20 computers, each with dozens of time-shared users, there might be at peak times one or more conversations between all 190 pairs of computers.

13.1.1 Reliability

Communications systems, being designed to carry very redundant information for direct human consumption, have, for computers, unacceptably high downtime and excessively high error rates. The line errors can easily be fixed through error detection and retransmission; however, this does require the use of some computation and storage at both ends of each communication line. To protect against total line failure, there should be at least two physically separate paths to route each message. Otherwise, the service will appear to be far too unreliable to count on and users will continue to duplicate remote resources rather than access them through the net.

13.1.2 Responsiveness

In those cases in which a user is making more or less direct use of a complete remote software system, the network must not cause the total round-trip delay to exceed the human short-term memory span of 1 to 2 s. Since the time-sharing systems probably introduce at least a 1s delay, the network's end-to-end delay should be less than $\frac{1}{2}$ s. The network response should also be comparable, if possible, to using a remote display console over a private voice-grade line where a 50-character line of text (400 bits) can be sent in

200 ms. Furthermore, if interactive graphics are to be available, the network should be able to send a complete new display page requiring about 20 kbits of information within 1 s and permit interrupts (10 to 100 bits) to get through very quickly, preferably within 30 to 90 ms. When two programs are interacting without a human user being directly involved, the job will obviously get through sooner, the shorter the message delay. There is no clear critical point here, but if the communications system substantially slows up the job, the user will probably choose to duplicate the remote process or data at his site. For such cases, a reasonable measure by which to compare communications systems is the *effective bandwidth* (data block length for the job per end-to-end transmission delay).

13.1.3 Capacity

The capacity required is proportional to the number and variety of services available from the network. As the number of nodes increases, the traffic is expected to increase more than linearly, until new nodes merely duplicate available network resources. The number of nodes in the experimental network was chosen to (1) involve as many computer researchers as possible to develop network protocol and operating procedures, (2) involve special facilities, such as the ILLIAC, to distribute its resources to a wider community, (3) involve as many disciplines of science as possible to measure the effect of the network on those disciplines, and (4) involve many different kinds of computers and systems to prove the generality of the techniques developed. The nodes of the network were generally limited to (1) those centers for which the network would truly provide a cost benefit, (2) government-funded projects because of the use of special-rate government-furnished communications, and (3) ARPA-funded projects in which the problems of intercomputer accounting could be deferred until the network was in stable operation. The size of the experimental network was chosen to be approximately 15 nodes nationwide. It was felt that this would be large and diverse enough to be a useful utility and to provide enough traffic to adequately test the network communication system.

Although it is extremely difficult to estimate the potential traffic levels in a resource-sharing environment, one approach is to examine the traffic created by hardware service sharing, probably the first activity within the network. Hardware service sharing occurs when each node obtains a portion of its computer capability from each of several large service centers instead of operating its own less efficient general-purpose system. The traffic generated by this type of activity can be estimated by examining the total input–output bandwidth to a user of a computer center, the traffic that would have to be transmitted via the network to remote users. This includes traffic to line printers, user consoles, user tape units, and input from card readers, consoles, etc. Since line printers alone usually require 2 to 30 kbauds the total I–0 traffic is likely to be 2 to 50 kbauds.

13.1.4 Cost

To be a useful utility, it was felt that communications costs for the network should be less than 20 per cent of the computing costs of the systems connected through the network. This is in contrast to the rising costs of remote access communications, which often costs as much as the computing equipment.

If we examine why communications usually cost so much, we find that it is not the communications channel per se, but our inefficient use of them, the switching costs, or the operations cost. To obtain a perspective on the price we commonly pay for communications, let us evaluate a few methods. As an example, let us use a distance of 1400 miles, since that is the average distance between pairs of nodes in the projected ARPA Network. A useful measure of communications cost is the cost to move 1 million bits of information in cents per megabit. In Table 13.1 this is computed for each medium. It is assumed for leased equipment and data set rental that the usage is 8 h/working day.

Special care has also been taken to minimize the cost of the multiplexor or switch. Previous store-and-forward systems, like DoD's AUTODIN system, have had such complex, expensive switches that over 95 per cent

TABLE 13.1 *Cost per Megabit for Various Communication Media*
(1400-mile distance)

Media		
Telegram	$3300.00	For 100 words at 30 bits/word, daytime
Night letter	565.00	For 100 words at 30 bits/word overnight delivery
Computer console	374.00	18-baud average use [2], 300-baud DDD service line and data sets only
TELEX	204.00	50-baud teletype service
DDD (103A)	22.50	300-baud data sets, DDD daytime service
AUTODIN	8.20	2400-baud message service, full use during working hours
DDD(202)	3.45	2000-baud data sets
Letter	3.30	Airmail, 4 pages, 250 words/page, 30 bits/word
W.U. Broadband	2.03	2400-baud service, full duplex
WATS	1.54	2000 bauds, used 8 h/working day
Leased line (201)	0.57	2000 bauds, commercial, full duplex
Data 50	0.47	50-Kbaud dial service, utilized full duplex
Leased line (303)	0.23	50 Kbauds, commercial, full duplex
Mail DEC tape	0.20	2.5-Mbit tape, airmail
Mail IBM tape	0.034	100-Mbit tape, airmail

of the total communications service cost was for the switches. Other switch services adding to the system's cost, deemed superfluous in a computer network, were long-term message storage, multiaddress messages, and individual message accounting.

The final cost criterion was to minimize the communications software development cost required at each node site. If the network software could be generated centrally, not only would the cost be significantly reduced, but also the reliability would be significantly enhanced.

13.2 THE ARPA NETWORK

Three classes of communications systems were investigated as candidates for the ARPA Network: fully interconnected point-to-point leased lines, line-switched (dial-up) service, and message-switched (store-and-forward) service. For the kind of service required, it was decided and later verified that the message-switched service provided the greater flexibility, higher effective bandwidth, and lower cost than the other two systems.

The standard message-switched service uses a large central switch with all the nodes connected to the switch via communication lines; this configuration is generally referred to as a star (see Section 13.3). Star systems perform satisfactorily for large blocks of traffic (greater than 100 kbits/message), but the central switch saturates very quickly for small message sizes. This phenomenon adds significant delay to the delivery of the message. Also, a star design has inherently poor reliability, since a single line failure can isolate a node and the failure of the central switch is catastrophic.

An alternative to the star, suggested by the Rand study "On Distributed Communications" [3], is a fully distributed message-switched system. Such a system has a switch or store-and-forward center at every node in the network. Each node has a few transmission lines to other nodes; messages are therefore routed from node to node until reaching their destination. Each transmission line thereby multiplexes messages from a large number of source–destination pairs of nodes. The distributed store-and-forward system was chosen, after careful study, as the ARPA Network communications system. The properties of such a communication system are described below and compared with other systems.

A more complete description of the implementation, optimization, and initial use of the network can be found in a series of five papers presented at the 1970 Spring Joint Computer Conference. The first paper, by Roberts and Wessler [4], from which this chapter was extracted in part, presents an overview of the need for a computer network, communication system requirements, properties of the ARPA Network, and the overall cost factors. The second paper, by Heart et al. [5], describes the design, implementation, and performance characteristics of the message switch. The third paper, by Kleinrock [6], derives procedures for optimizing the capacity of the transmission facility to minimize cost and average message delay. The fourth paper, by Frank et al. [7], describes the procedure for finding optimized network topologies under various constraints. The last paper, by Carr et al. [8], is concerned with the system software required to allow the network computers to talk to one another. This final paper describes a first attempt at intercomputer protocol, which is expected to grow and mature as we gain experience in computer networking.

13.2.1   Network Properties

The switching centers use small general-purpose computers called Interface Message Processors (IMPs) to route messages, to error check the transmission lines, and to provide asynchronous digital interfaces to the main (HOST) computer. The IMPs are connected together via 50-kbps data-transmission facilities using common-carrier (AT&T) point-to-point leased lines. The topology of the network transmission lines was selected to minimize cost, maximize growth potential, and yet satisfy all the design criteria.

RELIABILITY. The network specification requires that the delivered message error rates be matched with computer characteristics, and that the downtime of the communications system be extremely small. Three steps have been taken to ensure these reliability characteristics: (1) at least two transmission paths exist between any two nodes, (2) a 24-bit cyclic check sum is provided for each 1000-bit block of data, and (3) the IMP is ruggedized against external environmental conditions, and its operation is independent of any electromechanical devices (except fans). So far, the downtime of the transmission facility has averaged 2.3 per cent outage for each line; however, the duplication of paths reduces the average downtime between any pair of nodes, due to transmission failure, to approximately 0.4 per cent. The cyclic check sum was chosen based on the performance characteristics of the transmission facility; it is designed to detect long burst errors. The code is used for error detection only, with retransmission on an error. This check reduces the undetected bit error rate to 1 in 10^{12} or about 1 undetected error per year in the entire network.

The ruggedized IMP was chosen to provide as high a reliability as possible; however, solid reliability data are not available yet. The elimination of mass storage devices from the IMP results in lower cost, less downtime, and greater throughput performance of the IMP, but implies no long-term message storage and no message accounting by the IMP. If these functions are later needed they can be added by establishing a special node in the network. This node would accept accounting information from all the IMPs and also could reroute all the traffic destined for HOSTs which are down. We do not believe these functions are necessary, but the network design is capable of providing them.

RESPONSIVENESS. The target goal for responsiveness was 0.5s transit time from any node to any other for a 1000-bit (or less) block of information. Actual response average 0.1 s for 1000-bit blocks and 0.3 s for 8000-bit messages for all traffic levels less than saturation. After saturation the transit time rises quickly because of excessive queueing delays. However, saturation is avoided by the net acting to choke off the inputs for short periods of time, reducing the buffer queues while not significantly increasing the delay.

CAPACITY. The capacity of the network is the throughput rate at which saturation occurs. The saturation level is a function of the topology and capacity of the transmission lines and the average size of the blocks sent over the transmission lines. The analysis of capacity was performed by Network Analysis Corporation during the optimization of the network topology. As that analysis shows, the network has the ability to flexibly increase its capacity by adding additional transmission lines. The use of 230.4-kbaud communication services, where appropriate, considerably improves the cost–performance of the network.

13.2.2 Configuration

The flexibility in topology of communication lines permitted in the ARPA Network (see Table 13.2) allows controlled growth in capacity as the nodes increase their use of the Net. The topology can vary from a simple loop connecting all nodes once to a densely connected system, such as the network shown in Fig. 13.1. The topological flexibility suggests that network users can be charged on the basis of use, since a heavy user will cause the Network manager to put in more lines, increasing the overall cost of the Network. An equitable basis for charging has been found for the currently planned 20-node net. Although current users are not yet being charged, the charging policy is useful for planning purposes and will be implemented later, as the network size and use expands. The basis of the charging scheme is shown in Fig. 13.2 ,where the cost per node is plotted against the average capacity per node. Data for this graph were obtained from H. Frank [7]. Network Analysis Corporation, and are based on dozens of possible optimal network topologies produced by computer analysis. The slope of the ARPANET line represents the incremental cost for increasing the Net's capacity. Frank also determined that the traffic need not be uniformly distributed among the nodes in order to achieve the total traffic capacity capability. Large variations in the distribution of average traffic among the nodes would result in saturation occurring at approximately the same total traffic for the same topology as if the traffic were uniformly distributed. The effect of one node reducing or increasing

TABLE 13.2   *ARPANET Nodes Planned for March 1972*

UCLA	University of California, Los Angeles	XDS Sigma 7
		IBM 360/91
SRI	Stanford Research Institute	PDP10/TENEX
		PDP15-PDP10
UCSB	University of California, Santa Barbara	360/75
UTAH	University of Utah	PDP10-PDP10-Univac 1108
BBN	Bolt Beranek Newman	PDP10/TENEX
MIT	Massachusetts Institute of Technology	Honeywell (GE)
		645/MULTICS
		PDP6/10
RAND	Rand Corporation	IBM 1800-360/65
		PDP10
SDC	Systems Development Corporation	Honeywell 516-360/67
HARVARD	Harvard University	PDP10
		PDP1
		PDP11
LINCOLN	Lincoln Laboratory, MIT	360/67
		TX2
STANFORD	Artificial Intelligence Project, Stanford University	PDP6/10
ILLINOIS	University of Illinois	PDP11
		Burroughs 6500
CASE	Case Western Reserve	PDP10
CMU	Carnegie-Mellon University	PDP10
PAOLI	Burroughs Corporation	PDP11-B6500-ILLIAC
AMES	Ames Research Center, NASA	TIP[a]
		360/67
RADC	Rome Air Development Center	TIP[a]
		Honeywell (GE) 635
MITRE	Mitre Corporation	TIP[a]
NBS	National Bureau of Standards	TIP[a]
		PDP11
ETAC	Environmental Technical Applications Air Weather Service	TIP[a]
DOCB	Department of Commerce, Boulder	TIP[a]
AFGWC	AF Global Weather Central, Air Weather Service	TIP[a]
SAAMA	Sacramento Air Material Area	Univac 418
OCAMA	Oklahoma Air Material Area	Univac 418

[a]Honeywell 316 Terminal Concentrator.

its traffic can therefore be found by reducing or increasing the total network traffic by that amount.

From Fig. 13.2 it can be seen that the cost of increasing the capacity results in an equivalent transmission cost of 11 cents/Mbit. However, since the Network cannot be expected to be always fully loaded to peak capacity,

Arpanet
March 1972

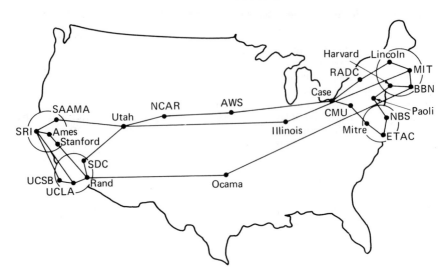

FIGURE 13.1

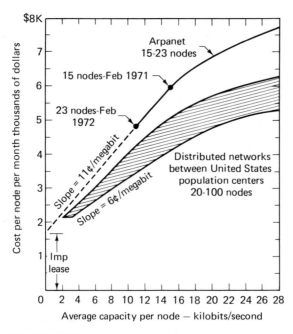

FIGURE 13.2

494

day and night, it is likely the actual rate will be 30 cents/Mbit based on an estimated 36 per cent average loading. The total cost per node would then be $1.7K/month plus 30 cents/Mbit.

13.3 COMPARISON WITH ALTERNATIVE NETWORK COMMUNICATIONS SYSTEMS DESIGNS

For the purpose of this comparison the capacity required was set at 10 to 20 kbauds per node. A minimal buffer for error checking and retransmission at every node is included in the cost of the systems.

Two comparisons are made between the systems: the cost per megabit as a function of the delay, and the effective bandwidth as a function of the block size of the data. Several other functions were plotted and compared; the two chosen were deemed the most informative. The latter graph is particularly informative in showing the effect of using the network for short, interactive message traffic.

The systems chosen for the comparison were fully interconnected 2.4 and 19-kbaud leased-line systems; Data-50, the dial-up 50-kbaud service; DDD, the standard 2-kbaud voice-grade dial-up system; star networks, using 19 and 50-kbaud leased lines into a central switch; and the ARPA Network, using 50-kbaud leased lines.

The graph in Fig. 13.3 shows the cost per megabit versus delay. The rectangles outline the variation caused by a block-size variation of 1 to 10

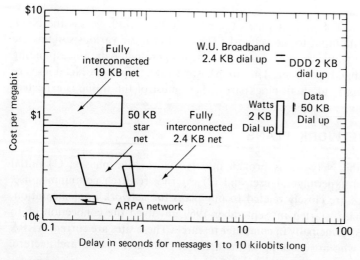

FIGURE 13.3

kbits and capacity requirement variation of 10 to 20 kbauds per node. The dial-up systems were used in a way to minimize the line charges while keeping the delay as low as possible. The technique is to dial a system, then transmit the data accumulated during the dial-up (20 s for DDD, 30 s for Data-50). The dial-up systems are still very expensive and slow compared with other alternatives. The costs of the ARPA Network are for optimally designed topologies. For the 50-kbaud star network, the switch is assumed to be an average distance of 1300 miles from every node.

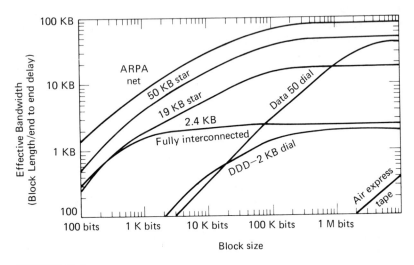

FIGURE 13.4

The graph in Fig. 13.4 shows the effective bandwidth versus the block size of the data input to the network. The curves for the various systems are estimated for traffic rates of 500 to 1000 bauds per node pair, corresponding to 10 to 20 kbauds per node. The comparison shows the ARPA Net does very well, particularly at small block sizes where most of the traffic is expected.

13.4 NETWORK PLANS

Use of the Network is broken into two successive phases: (1) initial research and experimental use, and (2) external research community use. These phases are closely related to our plans for network implementation. The first phase, started in September 1969, involved the connection of 15 sites involved principally in computer research. These sites are current ARPA contractors who are working in the areas of computer system architecture, information system design, information handling, computer-augmented problem solving, intelligent systems, as well as computer networks. This phase was completed by February 1971. The second phase involves the extension of the number of sites to include other applications and research centers. By March 1973 the network had grown to 35 nodes.

13.4.1 Initial Research and Experimental Use

During phase 1, the community of users numbered approximately 2000 people. This community is involved primarily in computer-science research and all have ARPA-funded ongoing research. The major use they are making of the Network is the sharing of software resources and the educational experience of using a wider variety of systems than previously possible. The software resources available to the Network include advanced user programs, such as MATHLAB at MIT, Theorem Provers at Stanford Research Institute (SRI), Natural Language Processors at Bolt Beranek and Newman (BBN), etc.; and new system software and languages, such as LEAP, a graphic language at Lincoln Laboratory LC^2, an interactive ALGOL system at Carnegie-Mellon University, etc.

Another major use of the Network is for accessing the Network Information Center (NIC). The NIC was established at SRI as the repository of information about all systems connected into the Network. The NIC will maintain, update, and distribute hard-copy information to all users. It will also provide file space and a system for accessing and updating (through the net) dynamic information about the systems, such as system modifications, new resources available, etc.

The final major use of the Net during phase 1 was for measurement and experimentation on the Network itself. The primary sites involved in this are BBN, which has responsibility for system development and system maintenance, and UCLA, which has responsibility for the Net measurement and modeling. All the sites were also involved in the generation of inter-computer protocol, the language the systems use to talk to one another.

13.4.2 External Research Community Use

During the time period after August 1971 additional nodes were installed to take advantage of the Network in other ARPA-funded research disciplines: behavioral science, climate dynamics, and seismology. The use of the Network at these nodes will be oriented more toward the distribution and sharing of stored data, and in the latter two fields will make use of the ILLIAC IV.

The data sharing between data management systems or data retrieval systems will begin an important phase in the use of the Network. The concept of distributed data bases and distributed access to the data is one of the most powerful and useful applications of the network for the general data-processing community. As described above, if the Network is responsive in the human time frame, data bases can be stored and maintained at a remote location rather than duplicated at each site where the data is needed. Not only can the data be accessed as if the user were local, but also a Network user can write programs on his own machine to collect data from a number of locations for comparison, merging, or further analysis.

Because of widespread use of the ILLIAC IV, it will undoubtedly be the single most demanding node in the Network. Users will not only be sending requests for service, but will also send very large quantities of input and output data, e.g., a 10^6-bit weather map, over the Net. Projected uses of the ILLIAC include weather and climate modeling, picture processing, linear programming, matrix manipulations, and extensive work in other areas of simulation and modeling.

The ILLIAC installation will also include a trillion-bit mass store. An experiment is being planned to use 10 per cent of the storage (100 billion bits) as archival storage for all the nodes on the Net. This kind of capability may help reduce the number of tape drives and/or data cells in the Network.

13.5 FUTURE

There are many applications of computers for which current communications technology is not adequate. One such application is the specialized customer service computer systems in existence or envisioned for the future; these services provide the customer with information or computational capability. If no commercial computer network service is developed, the future may be as follows: One can envision a corporate officer in the future having many different consoles in his office: one to the stock exchange to monitor his own company's and competitor's activities, one to the commodities market to monitor the demand for his product or raw materials, one to his own company's data management system to monitor inventory, sales, payroll, cash flow, etc., and one to a scientific computer used for modeling and simulation to help plan for the future. There are probably many people within that same organization who need some of the same services and potentially many other services. Also, although the data exists in digital form on other computers, it will probably have to be keypunched into the company's modeling and simulation system in order to perform analyses. Although these services are desirable, the executive would be faced with learning to use several different consoles and protocols.

The organization providing the service has a hard time, too. In addition to collecting and maintaining the data, the service must have field offices to maintain the consoles and the communications multiplexors, adding significantly to their cost. A large fraction of that cost is for communications and consoles, rather than the service itself. Thus the services that can be justified are very limited.

Let us now paint another picture, given a nationwide network for computer-to-computer communication. The service organization need only connect its computer into the net. It probably would not have any consoles other than for data input, maintenance, and system development. In fact, some of the service's data input may come from another service over the net. Users could choose the service they desired based on reliability, cleanliness of data, and ease of use, rather than proximity or sole source.

Large companies would connect their computers into the net and contract with service organizations for the use of those services they desired. The executive would then have one console, connected to his company's machine. He would have one standard way of requesting the service he desires with a far greater number of services available to him.

For the small company, a master service organization might develop, similar to today's time-sharing service, to offer console service to people who cannot afford their own computer. The master service organization would be wholesalers of the services and might even be used by the large companies to avoid contracting with all the individual service organizations.

The kinds of services that will be available and the cost and ultimate capacity required for such service are difficult to predict. It is clear, however, that if the network philosophy is adopted and if it is made widely available through a common carrier, the communications system will not be the limiting factor in the development of these services as it is now.

REFERENCES

[1] T. MARILL and L. ROBERTS, Toward a Cooperative Network of Time-Shared Computers, *AFIPS Conf. Proc.* (Nov. 1966).

[2] P. E. JACKSON and C. D. STUBBS, A Study of Multi-access Computer Communications, *AFIPS Conf. Proc.*, **34** (1969), 491.

[3] PAUL BARAN et al., On Distributed Communications, *RAND Series Reports* (Aug. 1964).

[4] L. G. ROBERTS and B. D. WESSLER, Computer Network Development to Achieve Resource Sharing, *AFIPS Conf. Proc.* (May 1970).

[5] F. E. HEART, R. E. KAHN, S. M. ORNSTEIN, W. R. CROWTHER, and D. C. WALDEN, The Interface Message Processor for the ARPA Network, *AFIPS Conf. Proc.* (May 1970).

[6] L. KLEINROCK, Analytic and Simulation Methods in Computer Network Design, *AFIPS Conf. Proc.* (May 1970).

[7] H. FRANK, I. T. FRISCH, and W. CHOU, Topological Considerations in the Design of the ARPA Computer Network, *AFIPS Conf. Proc.* (May 1970).

[8] S. CARR, S. CROCKER, and V. CERF, HOST-HOST Communication Protocol in the ARPA Network, *AFIPS Conf. Proc.* (May 1970).

14

The Aloha System[*]

NORMAN ABRAMSON

University of Hawaii, Honolulu

INTRODUCTION

In September 1968, the University of Hawaii began work on a research program to investigate alternatives to the use of conventional wire communications for computer–computer and console–computer links. In this chapter we describe an experimental UHF-radio computer-communication network— THE ALOHA SYSTEM—under development as part of that research program.

When the designer of a computer-communication system is freed from the constraints imposed by the use of common-carrier communications, a number

*THE ALOHA SYSTEM is a research project at the University of Hawaii, supported by the Advanced Research Projects Agency under NASA Contract No. NAS2-6700 and by the U.S. Air Force Office of Aerospace Research under Contract No. F44620-69-C-0030.

of new possibilities present themselves. The starting point in the design of
THE ALOHA SYSTEM was the question, "Given the availability of a fixed
amount of communications capacity, how does one employ this capacity to
provide effective communication from remote users to a central machine?".
Stated in these terms it became clear that the simple replacement of the wire
communication channels of the common carriers by equivalent radio channels
was not the answer. Indeed it would have been most surprising had the form
of communication network evolved at the end of the nineteenth century for
purposes of voice communication been the form of communication network
chosen at the end of the twentieth century for communication in computer
networks.

The University of Hawaii is composed of a main campus in Manoa Valley
near Honolulu, a 4-year college in Hilo, Hawaii, and five 2-year community
colleges on the islands of Oahu, Kauai, Maui, and Hawaii. In addition, the
University operates a number of research institutes with operating units
distributed throughout the state within a radius of 200 miles from Honolulu.
The computing center on the main campus operates an IBM 360/65 with
500K bytes of IBM core memory and 2M bytes of Ampex extended core
memory. Several other University units operate smaller machines for research
in computer science, for remote job entry, and for monitoring of a variety of
scientific experiments.

Remote terminals and Remote Job Entry (RJE) devices were introduced
into the University of Hawaii system in 1969. By the end of 1971 approximately 50 terminals and RJE stations were connected using conventional
dial-up and conventional leased-line communications. The cost of this communications system including telephone and leased-line charges, modems,
and communication controllers had become a substantial portion of the
University's computing budget. In June 1971 the central UHF station of
THE ALOHA SYSTEM had been built and tested by the first radio-linked
remote terminal. By the end of 1971, four remote terminals had been connected
to the 360 through THE ALOHA SYSTEM central station, and the design
and construction of new forms of UHF links for intelligent terminals, minicomputers, and RJE stations was in progress. Present plans are to continue
adding new forms of remote links and to continue a program of upgrading
the capabilities of the existing central station through the summer of 1973.
At that time the existing design will be frozen, and a period of experimental
operational use of a statewide radio-linked computer-communication network will begin.

The existing ALOHA SYSTEM computer-communication network uses
two 24,000-bauds channels in the UHF band. The system employs message-
switching techniques similar to those of the ARPANET, in conjunction with
a novel form of random-access radio channel multiplexing, explained in
Section 14.2. By means of these techniques the system has the capacity to

accommodate several hundred active users of alphanumeric consoles on the two channels available. Each user can transmit and receive at a peak data rate of 24,000 bauds, although the average data rate of the users must of course be considerably less.

14.1 WIRE COMMUNICATIONS FOR COMPUTER NETS

At the present time conventional methods of remote access to a large information-processing system are limited to wire communications—either leased lines or dial-up telephone connections. In some situations these alternatives provide adequate capabilities for the designer of a computer-communication system. In other situations, however, the limitations imposed by wire communications restrict the usefulness of remote access computing [1]. The goal of THE ALOHA SYSTEM is to provide another alternative for the system designer and to determine those situations in which radio communications are preferable to conventional wire communications.

We should emphasize that some of the points we make in this section do not apply or apply only in part to unconventional methods of wire communications that have been proposed [2, 3, 16] or that are in the first stages of development [e.g., Datran, MCI (Chapter 9), and the ARPA net (Chapter 13)]. These alternatives were in fact proposed in response to some of the difficulties of conventional wire systems mentioned in this section.

The reasons for widespread use of wire communications in present-day computer-communication systems are not hard to see. Where dial-up telephones and leased lines are available, they can provide inexpensive and moderately reliable communications using an existing and well-developed technology [4]. For short distances the expense of wire communications for most applications is not great.

Nevertheless, there are a number of characteristics of wire communications that can serve as drawbacks in the transmission of binary data. The connect time for dial-up lines may be too long for some applications; data rates on such lines are fixed and limited. Leased lines may sometimes be obtained at a variety of data rates, but at a premium cost. For communication links over large distances (say, 100 miles) the cost of communication for an interactive user on an alphanumeric console can easily exceed the cost of computation [5]. Finally, we note that in many parts of the world a reliable high-quality wire communication network is not available, and the use of radio communications for data transmission is the only alternative.

There are of course some fundamental differences between the data transmitted in an interactive time-shared computer system and the voice signals for which the telephone system is designed [6]. First among these differences is the burst nature of the communication from a user console to the computer and back. The typical 110-baud console may be used at an average data rate of from 1 to 10 bauds over a dial-up or leased line capable of transmitting at a rate of from 2400 to 9600 bauds. Data transmitted in a time-shared computer system comes in a sequence of bursts with extremely long periods of silence between the bursts. If several interactive consoles can be placed in close proximity to each other, multiplexing and data concentration may alleviate this difficulty to some extent. When efficient data concentration is not feasible, however, the user of an alphanumeric console connected by a leased line may find his major costs arising from communication rather than computation, while the communication system used is operated at less than 1 per cent of its capacity.

Another fundamental difference between the requirements of data communications for time-shared systems and voice communications is the asymmetric nature of the communications required for the user of interactive alphanumeric consoles. Statistical analyses of existing systems indicate that the average amount of data transmitted from the central system to the user may be as much as an order of magnitude greater than the amount transmitted from the user to the central system [6]. For wire communications it is usually not possible to arrange for different-capacity channels in the two directions, so this asymmetry is an additional factor in the inefficient use of the wire communication channel.

The reliability requirements of data communications constitute another difference between data communication for computers and voice communication. In addition to errors in binary data caused by random and burst noise, the dial-up channel can produce connection problems, e.g., busy signals, wrong numbers, and disconnects. Meaningful statistics on both of these problems are difficult to obtain and vary from location to location, but there is little doubt that in many locations the reliability of wire communications is well below that of the remainder of the computer-communication system. Furthermore, since wire communications are usually obtained from the common carriers, this portion of the overall computer-communication system is the only portion not under direct control of the system designer.

14.2 THE ALOHA SYSTEM

The central computer of THE ALOHA SYSTEM (an IBM 360/65) is linked to the radio communication channel via a small interface computer (Fig. 14.1). Much of the design of this multiplexor is based on the design of the Interface Message Processors (IMPs) used in the ARPA net [7]. The result is a Hawaiian version of the IMP (taking into account the use of radio communications and other differences), which has been dubbed the MENE-

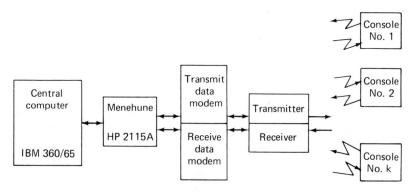

FIGURE 14.1 THE ALOHA SYSTEM.

HUNE (a legendary Hawaiian elf). The Hewlett-Packard 2115A computer has been selected for use as the MENEHUNE. It has a 16-bit word size, a cycle time of 2 μs, and an 8K-word core storage capacity.

THE ALOHA SYSTEM has been assigned two 100-kHz channels, at 407.350 MHz and 413.475zMHz. One of these channels has been assigned for data from the MENEHUNE to the remote stations and the other for data from the stations to the MENEHUNE. Each channel operates at a rate of 24,000 bauds. The communication channel from the MENEHUNE to the consoles provides no problems. Since the transmitter can be controlled and buffering performed by the MENEHUNE at the computer center, messages from the different stations can be ordered in a queue according to any given priority scheme and transmitted sequentially. At the present time a first-in, first-out priority scheme is used, but consideration will be given to other procedures as the capacity of the channel is approached.

Messages from the remote stations to the MENEHUNE are not capable of being multiplexed in such a direct manner. If standard orthogonal multiplexing techniques (such as frequency or time multiplexing) were employed, we would have to divide the channel from the remote stations to the MENEHUNE into a large number of low-speed channels and assign one to each station, whether it is active or not. Because of the fact that at any given time only a fraction of the total number of stations in the system will be active and because of the burst nature of the data from each station, such a scheme would lead to the same sort of inefficiencies found in a wire communication system. This problem may be partly alleviated by a system of central control and channel assignment (such as in a telephone switching net) or by a variety of polling techniques. Any of these methods will tend to make the communication equipment at the consoles more complex and will not solve the most important problem of the communication inefficiency caused by the burst nature of the data from an active remote station. Since we expect to have many such stations, it is important to minimize the complexity of the communication equipment at each station.

We have therefore designed a random-access communication method particularly well suited to the transmission of data packets, allowing each remote station in THE ALOHA SYSTEM to use a common high-speed data channel without the necessity of central control or synchronization. Information to and from the MENEHUNE in THE ALOHA SYSTEM is transmitted in the form of "packets" or "half-packets," corresponding to a single message in the system [8]. Each packet has a fixed maximum length of eighty 8-bit characters plus 32 identification and control bits and 32 parity bits (Fig. 14.2); thus each packet consists of 704 bits and lasts for 29 ms at a data rate of 24,000 bps. Half-packets are identical in structure to packets, except that they contain 40 rather than 80 characters, and thus take up only 16 ms.

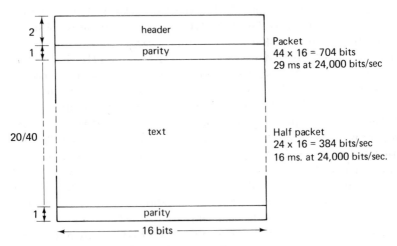

FIGURE 14.2   ALOHA SYSTEM message format.

The parity bits in each packet will be used for a cyclic error-detecting code [9]. Thus if we assume all error patterns are equally likely, the probability that a given error pattern will not be detected by the code is [10]

$$2^{-32} \approx 10^{-9}$$

Since error *detection* is a trivial operation to implement [10], the use of such a code is consistent with the requirement for simple communication equipment at the consoles. The possibility of using the same code for error *correction* at the MENEHUNE will be considered for a later version of THE ALOHA SYSTEM.

Note that 16 parity bits are used to check only the identification and control bits in the 32-bit header, while the last 16 bits are used as a validity check on the entire packet. This configuration provides extra protection for the important identification and control information contained in the header; in addition, it allows the MENEHUNE to discard invalid information after reception of only the first three words of the packet.

The random-access method employed by THE ALOHA SYSTEM is based on the use of this error-detecting code. Each user at a console transmits packets to the MENEHUNE over the same high-data-rate channel in a completely unsynchronized (from one user to another) manner. If and only if a packet is received without error it is acknowledged by the MENEHUNE. After transmitting a packet the transmitting station waits a given amount of time for an acknowledgement; if none is received, the packet is automatically retransmitted. This process is repeated until a successful transmission and acknowledgement occur or until three unsuccessful transmissions have been attempted.

A transmitted packet can be received incorrectly because of two different types of errors: (1) random noise errors, and (2) errors caused by interference with a packet transmitted by another console. The first type of error has not been a serious problem on the UHF channels employed. The second type of error, that caused by interference, will be of importance only when a large number of users are trying to use the channel at the same time. Interference errors will limit the number of users and the amount of data that can be transmitted over this random-access channel as more remote stations are added to THE ALOHA SYSTEM.

14.3 ALOHA INTERFACE*

To connect a remote station into the ALOHA channel, it is necessary to provide buffering up to a full packet of data together with automatic generation of certain identification, control, and parity information. This information is generated in a hardware buffer-control interface unit from each user console to a modem. The buffer-control unit also provides for reception of messages and acknowledgements into its remote station, rejection of unwanted packets, and automatic retransmission of packets not receiving an acknowledgement [8]. In the case of buffered terminals, intelligent terminals, and minicomputers, some of the buffer-control functions may be handled by software packages in the remote station.

A multiplexor program in the MENEHUNE provides the interface between the ALOHA radio channel and the IBM 360 computer [8, 15]. In addition, up to 16 user terminals may be accommodated by hard wire connection or incoherent light channels to the HP computer. Both the radio and the

*Portions of this section were obtained from [15].

other users can utilize the 360 at the same time via the HP multiplexor program and the TSO time-sharing system in the 360.

The multiplexor program utilizes the hardware interrupt structure of the HP, and all processing is initiated by a hardware interrupt from user terminals or the 360. Data are received from the radio link in either 20 or 40 word bursts, each 16-bit word consisting of 2 data characters. Hardware circuits convert the serial bit stream from the radio link to 16-bit words, which are transferred in parallel to a 16-bit buffer register in the MENEHUNE. Upon receipt of each word an interrupt signal is also sent to the MENEHUNE, causing the word to be read in and stored by the program. When the last word of a burst has been read in, the program initiates transfer of the packet to the 360. Similarly, packets are received from the 360 on a word-by-word interrupt basis and then routed to the appropriate user.

To transmit a packet using the radio link, the MENEHUNE places each word of the message in an output buffer register located in the MENEHUNE and sends a flag signal to a hardware device connecting it to the radio transmit modem. The hardware device stores the word in a second buffer and converts it to a serial bit stream, which is then passed to the modem. Whenever a word is read from the MENEHUNE output buffer, an interrupt signal is sent to the MENEHUNE, which causes the program to output the next word of the packet.

In addition to the message words, control words are transferred between the MENEHUNE and the radio link and between the MENEHUNE and the 360. Each packet in the radio link is preceded by two control words (the packet "header") and a header parity word, and each packet's text is followed by a text parity word (Fig. 14.2). At this time the hardware circuits between the radio modems and the MENEHUNE perform the tasks of both parity and syndrome generation. The parity words are inserted into the packet by the hardware prior to entering the transmit modem, and the syndrome words are inserted in place of the received parity words of the packet prior to being placed in the MENEHUNE input buffer register. Consideration is being given to incorporating parity and syndrome generation in the MENEHUNE multiplexor program. A word with all bits set to "one" is also sent to the MENEHUNE by the hardware units preceding the start of each packet, providing synchronization for the MENEHUNE program.

A control word is sent between the MENEHUNE and the 360 prior to a packet transfer in either direction. This word contains the terminal ID number and a packet-length indicator (now restricted to 20 or 40 words). The length information allows the block size to be specified so that direct-memory-access transfers can be made by both the 360 and the MENEHUNE.

The program is modular in design, allowing the processing functions for a particular user channel to be easily changed. Editing functions are localized within each user channel module, allowing the editing characters used by a particular terminal to be changed without affecting the other modules in the program. Fixed buffer areas are assigned for each system user in the program. Because of the relative data transmission rates of the user–MENE-HUNE and MENEHUNE–360 links, it is necessary to store only one packet for each user within the MENEHUNE at any particular time (although the most recent packet sent to a remote station will be kept in storage for user retransmission requests). This fact and the small number of users anticipated for the initial system led to the choice of fixed storage allocation in the current implementation, allowing a later implementation of dynamic storage allocation to be made on the basis of a more detailed study, which can include actual operating characteristics of the system.

To facilitate coding, debugging, and future modifications, the MENE-HUNE program was written in a high-level language, XPL. A compiler was written for this purpose, which produced HP machine code from an XPL source program. The compiler runs on the IBM 360, providing that system's I–O facilities as an aid in debugging syntax errors and in producing program documentation.

The MENEHUNE compiler (HPCOM) was written for use on an IBM 360 to take in a program written in a subset of XPL (called HPL) and emit the proper machine language for a HP 2115A computer. The compiler had two main design considerations, efficiency of the machine language and versatility, so that most operations could be done in the higher-level language.

Since the programs written in HPCOM are to be loaded into the HP 2115A via the IBM 360, the compiler has no input–output in the higher-level language. However, many features and conventions have been implemented in the compiler such that it is easy for the programmer to write his own I–O routines exactly as he wants them, and to utilize the interrupt system of the HP. To do this, the programmer needs a basic knowledge of the HP input–output system, and how to use some of the built-in functions of the compiler.

The output of the compiler is the raw machine code for the HP ready to be loaded into the machine, a printed output of the source program, the machine code resulting from each statement with explanation in assembly code for readability, and error statements.

14.4 CAPACITY OF THE RANDOM-ACCESS ALOHA CHANNEL

In Fig. 14.3 we indicate a sequence of packets as transmitted by k active consoles in the ALOHA random-access communication system.

We define τ as the duration of a packet. In THE ALOHA SYSTEM τ is equal to about 34 ms; of this total, 29 ms is needed for transmission of the

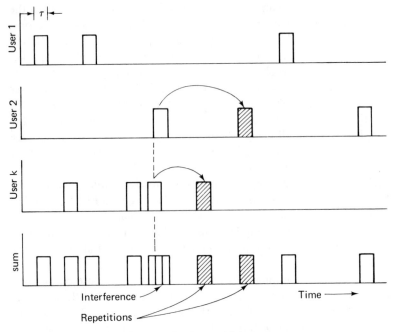

FIGURE 14.3   ALOHA communication multiplexing.

704 bits and the remainder for receiver synchronization. Note the overlap of two packets from different stations in Fig. 14.3. For analysis purposes we make the pessimistic assumption that when an overlap occurs neither packet is received without error, and both packets are therefore retransmitted.* We also assume only full packets are transmitted. Clearly, as the number of active stations increases, the number of interferences and hence the number of retransmissions increases until the channel clogs up with repeated packets [11]. We must therefore compute the average number of active stations that may be supported by the ALOHA random-access channel.

We may define a random point process for each of the k active users by focusing our attention on the starting times of the packets sent by each user. We shall find it useful to make a distinction between those packets transmitting a given message from a station for the first time and those packets transmitted as repetitions of a message. We shall refer to packets of the first type as *message packets* and to the second type as *repetitions*. Let λ be the average rate of occurrence of message packets from a single active user and assume that this rate is identical from user to user. Then the random point process

---

*In order that the retransmitted packets not continue to interfere with each other, we must make sure the retransmission delays in the two consoles are different.

consisting of the starting times of message packets from all the active users has an average rate of occurrence of

$$r = k\lambda \tag{14.1}$$

where r is the average number of message packets per unit time from the k active users. Let τ be the duration of each packet. Then if we were able to pack the messages into the available channel space perfectly with absolutely no space between messages, we would have

$$r\tau \doteq 1 \tag{14.2}$$

Accordingly, we refer to $r\tau$ as the *channel utilization*. Note that the channel utilization is proportional to k, the number of active users. Our objective in this section is to determine the maximum value of the channel utilization, and thus the maximum value of k, that this random-access data communication channel can support.

Define R as the average number of message packets plus retransmissions per unit time from the k active users. Then if there are any retransmissions, we must have $R > r$. We define $R\tau$ as the *channel traffic*, since this quantity represents the average number of message packets plus retransmissions per unit time multiplied by the duration of each packet or retransmission. In this section we calculate $R\tau$ as a function of the channel utilization, $r\tau$.

Now assume that the interarrival times of the point process defined by the start times of all the message packets plus retransmissions are independent and exponential. This assumption, of course, is only an approximation to the true arrival-time distribution. Indeed, because of the retransmissions, it is strictly speaking not even mathematically consistent.* If the retransmission delay is large compared to τ, however, and the number of retransmissions is not too large, this assumption will be reasonably close to the true distribution. Moreover, computer simulations of this channel indicate that the final results are not sensitive to this distribution. Under the exponential assumption the probability that there will be no events (starts of message packets or retransmissions) in a time interval T is $\exp(-RT)$.

Using this assumption, we can calculate the probability that a given message packet or retransmission will need to be retransmitted because of interference with another message packet or retransmission. The first packet will overlap with another packet if there exists at least one other start point τ or less seconds before or τ or less seconds after the start of the given packet. Hence the probability that a given message packet or retransmission will be repeated is

$$[1 - \exp(-2R\tau)] \tag{14.3}$$

---

*Another approach at modeling a channel closely related to the ALOHA random-access channel is provided in reference [12].

Finally, we use (14.3) to relate R, the average number of message packets plus retransmissions per unit time, to r, the average number of message packets per unit time. Using (14.3), the average number of retransmissions per unit time is given by

$$R[1 - \exp(-2R\tau)] \tag{14.4}$$

so that we have

$$R = r + R[1 - \exp(-2R\tau)] \tag{14.5}$$

or

$$\boxed{r\tau = R\tau e^{-2R\tau}} \tag{14.6}$$

Equation (14.6) is the relationship we seek between the channel utilization $r\tau$ and the channel traffic $R\tau$. In Fig. 14.4 we plot $R\tau$ versus $r\tau$.

Note from Fig. 14.4 that the channel utilization reaches a maximum value of $1/2e = 0.184$. For this value of $r\tau$ the channel traffic is equal to 0.5. The traffic on the channel becomes unstable at $r\tau = 1/2e$ and the average number of retransmissions becomes unbounded. Thus we may speak of this value of the channel utilization as the *capacity* of this random-access data channel. Because of the random-access feature, the channel capacity is reduced to roughly one-sixth of its value if we were able to fill the channel with a continuous stream of uninterrupted data.

For THE ALOHA SYSTEM we may use this result to calculate the maximum number of interactive users the system can support.

Setting

$$r\tau = k\lambda\tau = \frac{1}{2e} \tag{14.7}$$

we solve for the maximum number of active users:

$$k_{max} = (2e\lambda\tau)^{-1} \tag{14.8}$$

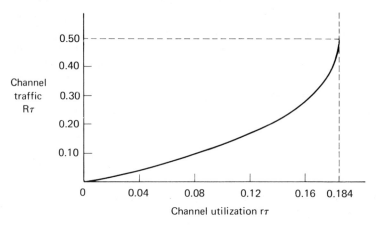

FIGURE 14.4   Channel utilization versus channel traffic.

A conservative estimate of λ would be $1/60(s)^{-1}$, corresponding to each active user sending a message packet at an average rate of 1 every 60 s. With τ equal to 34 ms, we get

$$k_{max} = 324 \tag{14.9}$$

Note that this value includes only the number of active users who can use the communication channel simultaneously. In contrast to usual frequency- or time-multiplexing methods, while a user is not active he consumes no channel capacity, so the total number of users of the system can be considerably greater than indicated by (14.9).

The analysis of the operation of THE ALOHA SYSTEM random-access scheme provided above has been checked by two separate simulations of the system [13, 14]. Agreement with the analysis is excellent for values of the channel utilization less than 0.15. For larger values the system tends to become unstable, as one would expect from Fig. 14.4.

14.5 OPERATION OF THE ALOHA
RANDOM-ACCESS CHANNEL

The calculations of the previous section show that we may expect the ALOHA 24,000-baud channel to support over 300 simultaneous active users. In fact, the real-world operation of THE ALOHA SYSTEM is expected to differ from the model analyzed in several important respects.

First, we note it is clearly wasteful of channel capacity to insist that each packet transmitted on the channel use eighty 8-bit characters. Especially for the case of interactive users of an alphanumeric console, most lines transmitted will contain much less than 80 characters of information. In the present version of THE ALOHA SYSTEM we have provided the capability of transmitting either a full packet of 80 characters or a half-packet of 40 characters. The header of each packet now employs a single bit as an indicator, and the received message is decoded accordingly. A half-packet transmitted with the same number of header and parity bits will consist of a total of 384 rather than 704 bits. Using this figure to obtain a value of τ for (14.8), we obtain a larger value for the maximum number of active users supported by the channel:

$$k_{max} = 594 \tag{14.10}$$

Consideration is now being given to allowing a greater set of packet lengths, ranging down to a single character and up to multiples of 80 characters.

Still another factor that will tend to make the real capacity of the ALOHA channel greater than the calculated capacity is the assumption that a packet overlap will result in errors in both packets. In fact, because of the use of

FM to transmit data in the ALOHA channel, if two packets are involved in an overlap, the packet with the stronger of the two signal strengths will capture the MENEHUNE receiver and may be received without error. Furthermore, this phenomenon can be put to use to provide a simple form of priority scheme on the remote stations of THE ALOHA SYSTEM. By adjusting the received power from different remote stations at the MENE-HUNE receiver, we may cause a station with higher power to override a station with lower power in the MENEHUNE.

The radio nature of the ALOHA channel suggests the use of a broadcast feature to send messages to all users or to a selected subset of users with a single packet. By use of special identification bits the central station can broadcast system status information or special instructions to all users.

Most important of all considerations in trying to anticipate the real-world performance of the ALOHA channel as opposed to the model we have analyzed is that the model is formulated only in terms of a large number of interactive users of alphanumeric terminals. THE ALOHA SYSTEM will be composed of large numbers of such terminals; we also plan to incorporate high-data-rate graphics terminals, remote-job-entry systems, minicomputers, and terminal clusters transmitting into the ALOHA channel by means of a simple form of random-access radio channel multiplexor now under design. Reliable statistics on the number of packets generated by such remote stations is not available, but it seems clear that the average data rate from these stations will be higher than the average data rate from a console of the sort used in our model. The average number of active users of the ALOHA channel will therefore not be as large as the calculations based upon only interactive alphanumeric consoles would indicate. According to (14.7), the 24,000-baud channel into the MENEHUNE is capable of transmitting at an average rate of 24,000 divided by $2e$, or about 4000 bps. (The burst data rate of course is still 24,000 bps.) The average data rate of the channel will always be greater than the sum of the average data rates of all stations feeding into the channel. Therefore, the data communication resources of the total system are most effectively employed by users having a high ratio of peak data rate to average data rate.

It is of considerable interest to determine how user characteristics will be influenced by the resource allocation properties of the ALOHA channel. Each user draws resources from such a channel in direct proportion to the number of bits he transmits over the channel. This is in marked contrast to the usual case of wire communications where a user ordinarily must assume a fixed cost corresponding to the minimum communication channel available (e.g., a single Teletype on a dial-up connection), or a fixed cost corresponding to a required burst data rate (e.g., remote graphics with communications limited response). In THE ALOHA SYSTEM it will be possible to allocate charges for channel use in proportion to the number of bits transmitted. Such a pricing algorithm can be expected to encourage use of the channel by users having the high ratio of peak to average data rate mentioned above. In addition to the interactive users of alphanumeric consoles covered in our analysis, such a policy would make the system attractive to remotely telemetered experiments and to minicomputers requiring intermittent use of peripheral equipment.

As an example of the latter use, we mention that one project now in progress in THE ALOHA SYSTEM plans to link an HP 2114 minicomputer into the ALOHA channel via a simplified communications module consisting of a small interface, a modem, and transceiver. The hardware buffer-control unit will be almost completely absorbed by a software module within the HP 2114 remote station. Once this connection is established it will be possible to load programs into the 2114 from the ALOHA channel rather than from a Teletype paper-tape reader—the only present alternative. Thus assemblers and other programs for the 2114 will be stored on a disk at the central computing center and will be called and loaded into the 2114 by a single command on the 2114's teletype input. This should reduce the time necessary to load the 2114 from 20 min to less than 10s. It will also be possible to write HPL programs on the 2114 Teletype, transmit these programs to the central computer for compilation, and transmit HP machine code back to the remote HP 2114.

In general, it is difficult to predict user characteristics of a channel with the properties of the ALOHA channel. Studies of user characteristics up to now [6] have started with existing wire communication facilities and provided profiles of users on these channels. Our analysis has shown that the ALOHA channel can be of value for users with those characteristics, but we cannot now tell what new characteristics will develop when users are charged by the bit transmitted for the use of communication facilities.

THE ALOHA SYSTEM communications module is used as the sole piece of equipment necessary to connect any console or RJE device into the ALOHA channel. As such it takes the place of two modems, a dial-up connection, and related switching equipment or leased lines usually used for computer networks. The module is composed of a UHF antenna, transceiver, modem, and buffer-control unit. Both the transceivers and modems employed so far have been modified versions of standard equipment designed for purposes different from the rather unconventional use to which they are put in THE ALOHA SYSTEM. This has been done to provide an operating system in a minimum amount of time and to provide us with valuable experience in this new form of data communications. The buffer-control unit, however, was designed and fabricated completely in THE ALOHA SYSTEM laboratories, since no equivalent equipment was available. New versions of the

ALOHA transceiver and modem matched to the characteristics of the UHF random-access channel have now been designed and are in operation.

The development of the first version of the communication module in the present ALOHA SYSTEM Project was accomplished at an equipment cost of around $8000/console. This is the total one-time equipment cost necessary to connect a single user into the system. As with conventional wire communication systems, this figure can be reduced by data concentration at the remote station. This cost is achieved in spite of the use of standard transceivers and modems ill-suited to the special unconventional tasks in which they are employed in THE ALOHA SYSTEM. The improvements already achieved in the design of the second version of THE ALOHA SYS-TEM buffer-control unit have shown that the cost of the ALOHA communication module can be reduced drastically. A communication module cost of $3000 by 1973 is projected. Furthermore, the size and power requirements of the module can be decreased considerably with further development work to the point where the communications module becomes a mobile unit allowing portable and instant access to a central computer system. It is not easy to project how far this miniaturization and cost reduction can proceed. But the vision of a user holding a portable terminal with a built-in communication module and a small protruding antenna is a tempting prospect.

Acknowledgment

THE ALOHA SYSTEM Project is the joint effort of a group of faculty and students of the Information Sciences Department and the Electrical Engineering Department at the University of Hawaii. It is not possible to acknowledge everyone who has contributed to the work reported in this chapter. Four students, however, who should be singled out for having provided effort well above the call of doctoral dissertations and other degree requirements are Richard Binder, John Davidson, Alan Okinaka, and David Wax.

REFERENCES

[1] M. M. GOLD and L. L. SELWYN, Real Time Computer Communications and the Public Interest, Fall Joint Computer Conf., *AFIPS Conf. Proc.* (1968), 1473–1478.
[2] D. W. DAVIES, K. A. BARTLETT, R. A. SCANTLEBURY, and P. T. WILKINSON, A Digital Communication Network for Computers Giving Rapid Response at Remote Terminals, ACM Symp. Operating Syst. Principles, Gatlinburg, Tenn. (Oct. 1–4, 1967).

[3] PAUL BARAN, On Distributed Communications: XI. Summary Overview, *Mem. RM-3767-PR*, The Rand Corporation (Aug. 1964).

[4] R. M. FANO, The MAC System: The Computer Utility Approach, *IEEE Spectrum*, **2**(1) (Jan. 1965).

[5] J. G. KEMENY and T. E. KURTZ, Dartmouth Time-Sharing, *Science*, **162**(3850) (1968), 223.

[6] P. E. JACKSON and C. D. STUBBS, A Study of Multi-access Computer Communications, Spring Joint Computer Conf., *AFIPS Conf. Proc.* (1969), 491–504.

[7] Bolt, Beranek and Newman, Inc., Initial Design for Interface Message Processors for the ARPA Computer Network, *Rept. 1763* (Jan. 1969).

[8] RICHARD BINDER, Multiplexing in THE ALOHA SYSTEM: MENEHUNE-KEIKI Design Considerations, *ALOHA SYSTEM Tech. Rept. B69-3* (Nov. 1969).

[9] W. W. PETERSON and E. J. WELDON, JR., *Error-Correcting Codes*, 2nd ed., MIT Press., New York, 1971.

[10] D. T. BROWN and W. W. PETERSON, Cyclic Codes for Error Detection, *Proc. IRE*, **49** (1961), 228–235.

[11] H. H. J. LIAO, Random Access Discrete Address Multiplexing Communications for THE ALOHA SYSTEM, *ALOHA SYSTEM Tech. Note 69-8* (Aug. 1969).

[12] C. C. LOVELL, Signal Detection in a Multi-user Random Access Channel, *R-771-PR*, The Rand Corporation (July 1971).

[13] W. H. BORTELS, Simulation of Interference of Packets in THE ALOHA SYSTEM, *ALOHA SYSTEM Tech. Rept. B70-2* (March 1970).

[14] P. TRIPATHI, Simulation of a Random Access Discrete Address Communication System, *ALOHA SYSTEM Tech. Note 70-1* (April 1970).

[15] RICHARD BINDER, ALOHA SYSTEM Multiplexor Program Description, *ALOHA SYSTEM Tech. Rept. B71-3* (June 1971).

[16] PAUL BARAN, On Distributed Communications: V. History, Alternative Approaches, and Comparisons, *Mem. RM-3097-PR*, The Rand Corporation (Aug. 1964).

Index